COUNTRY LIVING MAGAZINE

GUIDE TO RURAL ENGLAND

THE SOUTH OF ENGLAND

By David Gerrard

Published by:
Travel Publishing Ltd
7a Apollo House, Calleva Park
Aldermaston, Berks, RG7 8TN

ISBN 1-904-43413-4

First Published: *2001* *Second Edition:* *2004*

Country Living Guides:

East Anglia
Heart of England
Ireland
The North East of England
The North West of England
Scotland
The South of England
The South East of England
The West Country
Wales

Please Note:

All advertisements in this publication have been accepted in good faith by Travel Publishing and they have not necessarily been endorsed by *Country Living* Magazine.

All information is included by the publishers in good faith and is believed to be correct at the time of going to press. No responsibility can be accepted for errors.

Editor: David Gerrard

Printing by: Scotprint, Haddington

Location Maps: © Maps in Minutes ™ (2004) © Crown Copyright, Ordnance Survey 2004

Walks: Walks have been reproduced with kind permission of the internet walking site www.walkingworld.com

Walk Maps: Reproduced from Ordnance Survey mapping on behalf of the Controller of Her Majesty's Stationery Office, © Crown Copyright. Licence Number MC 100035812

Cover Design: Lines & Words, Aldermaston

Cover Photo: River Windrush, Lower Slaughter, Gloucestershire © www.britainonview.com

Text Photos: Text photos have been kindly supplied by the Britain on View photo library © www.britainonview.com

Foreword

From a bracing walk across the hills and tarns of The Lake District to a relaxing weekend spent discovering the unspoilt hamlets of East Anglia, nothing quite matches getting off the beaten track and exploring Britain's areas of outstanding beauty.

Each month, *Country Living Magazine* celebrates the richness and diversity of our countryside with features on rural Britain and the traditions that have their roots there. So it is with great pleasure that I introduce you to the *Country Living Magazine Guide to Rural England* series. Packed with information about unusual and unique aspects of our countryside, the guides will point both fair-weather and intrepid travellers in the right direction.

Each chapter provides a fascinating tour of the South of England area, with insights into local heritage and history and easy-to-read facts on a wealth of places to visit, stay, eat, drink and shop.

I hope that this guide will help make your visit a rewarding and stimulating experience and that you will return inspired, refreshed and ready to head off on your next countryside adventure.

Susy Smith

Susy Smith
Editor, Country Living magazine

PS To subscribe to *Country Living Magazine* each month, call 01858 438844

Introduction

This is the second edition of the *Country Living Guide to Rural England - The South of England* and it is full of information on the traditional English countryside in Bedfordshire, Berkshire, Buckinghamshire, Hampshire, Hertfordshire, Isle of Wight, Oxfordshire and Wiltshire. It is over 2 years since the publication of the very popular first edition and we hope that you enjoy this thoroughly updated version just as much.

David Gerrard, the editor, was a full-time television documentary director and scriptwriter before becoming a travel writer and he has now published more than 30 titles covering many areas of the British Isles. As with the other *Country Living Rural Guides* David has ensured that this edition is packed with vivid descriptions, historical stories, amusing anecdotes and interesting facts on hundreds of places in the South of England.

The coloured advertising panels within each chapter provide further information on places to see, stay, eat, drink, shop and even exercise! We have also selected a number of walks from walkingworld.com (full details of this website may be found to the rear of this guide) which we highly recommend if you wish to appreciate fully the beauty and charm of the varied rural landscapes and coastlines of the South of England.

The guide however is not simply an "armchair tour". Its prime aim is to encourage the reader to visit the places described and discover much more about the wonderful towns, villages and countryside of the South of England. In this respect we would like to thank all the Tourist Information Centres who helped us to provide you with up-to-date information. Whether you decide to explore this region by wheeled transport or on foot we are sure you will find it a very uplifting experience.

We are always interested in receiving comments on places covered (or not covered) in our guides so please do not hesitate to use the reader reaction form provided at the rear of this guide to give us your considered comments. This will help us refine and improve the content of the next edition. We also welcome any general comments which will help improve the overall presentation of the guides themselves.

Finally, for more information on the full range of travel guides published by Travel Publishing please refer to the details and order form at the rear of this guide or log on to our website at www.travelpublishing.co.uk

Travel Publishing

Locator Map

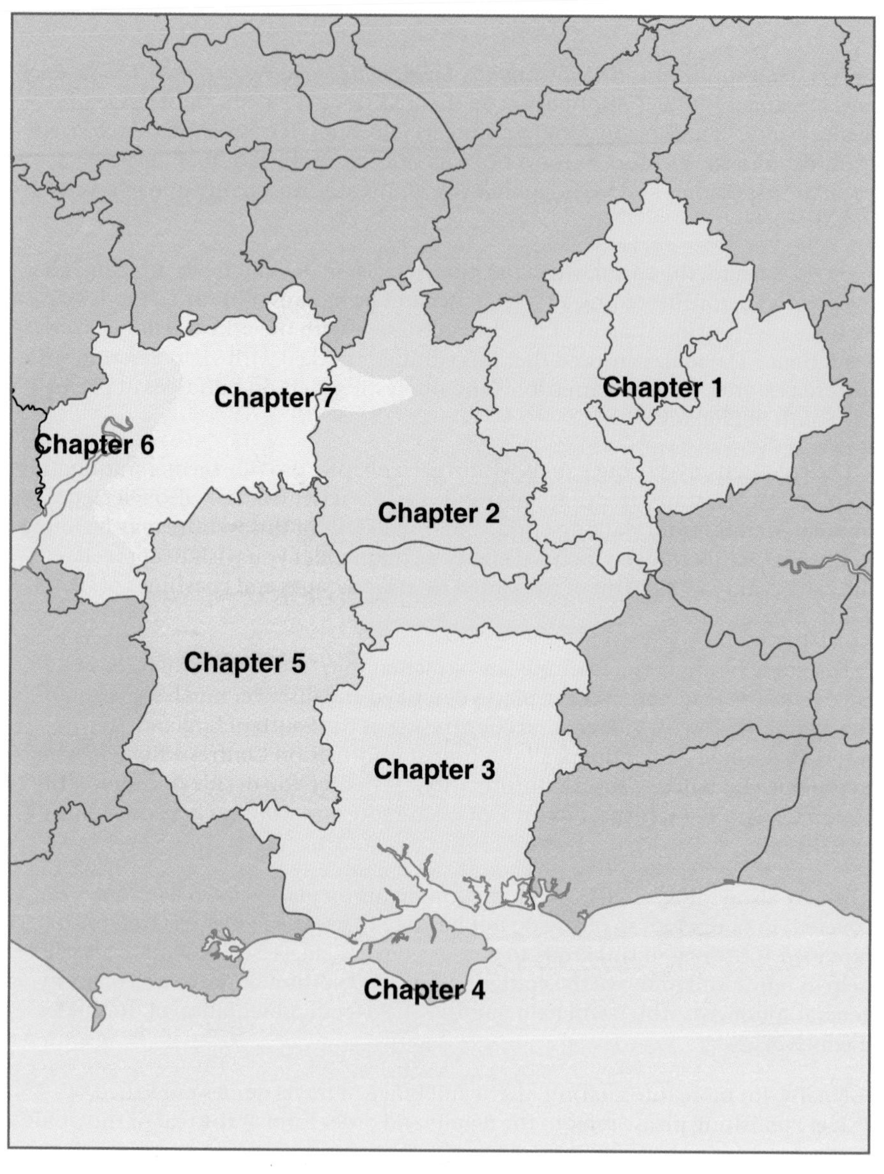
Chapter 7
Chapter 1
Chapter 6
Chapter 2
Chapter 5
Chapter 3
Chapter 4

Contents

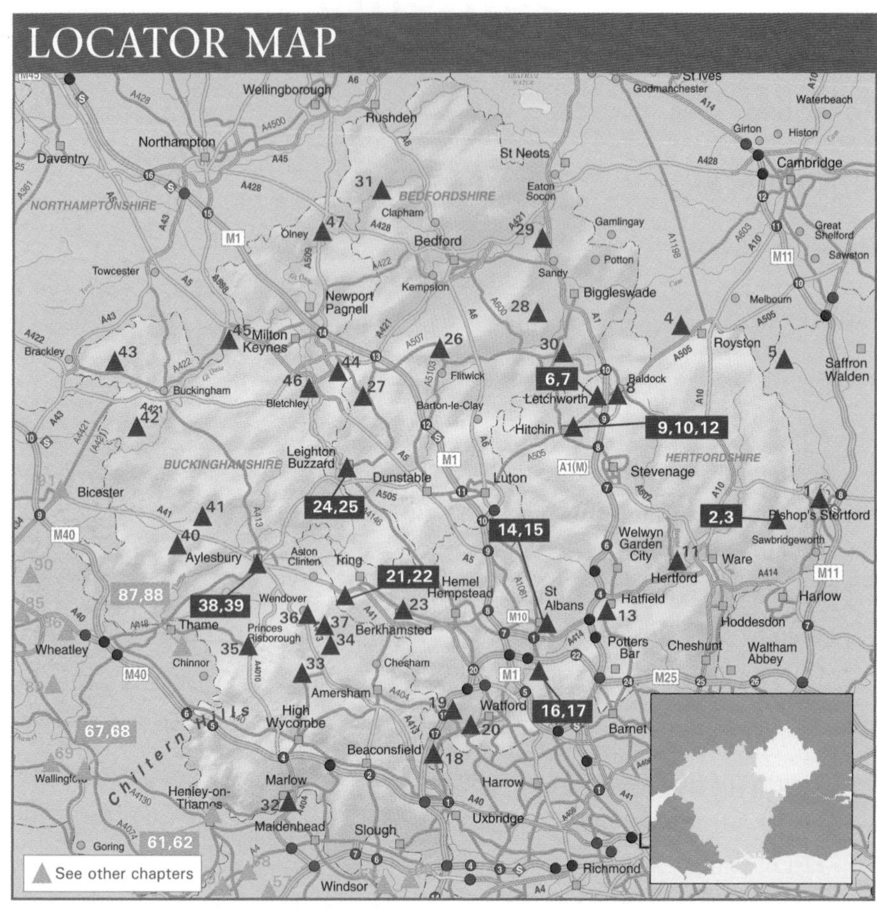

ADVERTISERS AND PLACES OF INTEREST

THE CHILTERNS 1

Running in a wide arc to the northwest of London, the Chilterns are a range of mostly low-lying chalk hills extending from Goring-on-Thames to a point near Hitchin, and are set mainly in the counties of Hertfordshire, Bedfordshire and Buckinghamshire. In an area that is part of the commuter belt around London, the Chilterns nonetheless offer the visitor plenty of unspoilt countryside and much of the range is designated as an Area of Outstanding Natural Beauty.

The highest points in the Chilterns are at Wendover Woods and Coombe Hill, both over 800 feet above sea level and both offering superb views. The woodland in the Chilterns is less extensive than formerly but is still noted chiefly for beech trees that were instrumental in the growth in the 18th century of chairmaking, one of the most important of the Chilterns crafts.

St Mary's Square, Aylesbury

Hatfield House & Gardens

The centre of the industry was High Wycombe, where the Windsor chair was the most famous product.

Because of the area's proximity to the capital, it was favoured by the rich and powerful as a convenient retreat and the three counties possess a wealth of grand houses, most notably the spectacular Hatfield House, childhood home of Elizabeth I. Almost as grand are Woburn Abbey, Cliveden House and Waddesdon Manor.

The Chilterns also appealed to many literary figures. John Milton's cottage at Chalfont St Giles still stands; John Bunyan knew Bedford – and its gaol – intimately; it was at Stoke Poges that Thomas Gray wrote his *Elegy in a Country Churchyard;* the statesman and novelist Benjamin Disraeli had a grand house at Hughenden; George Bernard Shaw lived for more than 40 years at Ayot St Lawrence and, more recently, Roald Dahl spent 30 years in the village of Great Missenden and is buried in the hillside churchyard opposite his home.

Woburn Abbey

HERTFORDSHIRE

The novelist EM Forster, who lived in the county, described Hertfordshire as "England at its quietest; England meditative". When he wrote that in the 1950s the county's population was just over 600,000; as the new millennium opened, it had just topped one million. The more southerly towns expanded as residential areas for London commuters, and after World War II, with an acute housing shortage in the blitzed capital, New Towns such as Stevenage were created to cater for the thousands of Londoners who had lost their homes.

But the centre of the county is still largely agricultural and the southern edge lies within the precarious protection of the Metropolitan Green Belt. There is still some excellent walking and splendid scenery, most notably within the National Trust's Ashridge Estate, where the woodlands and downlands are home to a wide variety of wildlife, and the views from the highest points are magnificent.

The strongest historical ties in the county are to be found in the ancient city of St Albans, while Hatfield combines old and new elements: it was designated a New Town after World War II, but the old town survives, along with the magnificent Hatfield House and part of the medieval Royal Palace, which was the childhood home of the future Elizabeth I.

Close to Hatfield lies Welwyn Garden City, conceived by Ebenezer Howard and built in the 1920s with the aim of providing working people with a pleasant and attractive place to live, with easy access to the countryside. One of the best known monuments in Hertfordshire is the Eleanor Cross at Waltham Cross, one of 13 such crosses erected by Edward I to commemorate the resting places of the funeral cortege of his Queen, Eleanor of Castile.

We begin our tour of the county at Bishop's Stortford and travel westwards, ending up at Berkhamsted.

BISHOP'S STORTFORD

The old Roman road from St Albans to Colchester forded the river here and some nine centuries later the Saxon king Edward the Elder built a castle to protect the crossing. His fortress has disappeared but the great mound on which it was built survives in the town's spacious Castle Gardens. In about 1060 the whole town was sold to the Bishops of London, hence its name. In medieval times Bishop's Stortford was a stopping place on the route between London and both Newmarket and Cambridge and became famous for its many hostelries. Even today, the town still boasts three inns dating back to the 15th and 16th centuries. In the 20th century, the building of Stansted Airport, just seven miles away, has brought the town within easy reach of Europe and beyond.

In the compact town centre markets are still held twice a week, on Thursdays and Saturdays, as they have been for centuries and, standing high on a hill, **St Michael's Church** dominates the surrounding countryside. Inside, a memorial commemorates the life of Cecil Rhodes, son of a former Rector. The great imperialist's exploits are also documented in his former home, Nettlewell House, now the **Rhodes Museum and Commonwealth Centre**. The centre is currently undergoing a major redevelopment programme but is scheduled to re-open in late 2004.

The Rhodes Museum forms part of the **Bishop's Stortford Museum** which

Le Donne

2 Bridge Street, Bishops Stortford,
Hertfordshire CM23 2JY
Tel/Fax: 01279 758388

Ladies shoes to die for are the main attraction at **Le Donne** – Italian for 'The Ladies'. Yorkshire-born Margaret Schofield opened her town centre shop in 1998 and specialises in shoes from some of Italy's leading designers, including Rodo, Baldinini and Martino Osvaldo.

Their exquisite creations are stylishly displayed in the elegant open plan shop, with its profusion of mirrors and down lighting – fashion footwear of a quality not often seen outside the upmarket boutiques of Milan. Le Donne also stocks a dazzling range of accessories such as handbags for every occasion, belts and jewellery.

Andrew Banks

Tel: 01279 842232 Fax: 01279 843014
e-mail: mail@andrewbanks.co.uk
website: www.andrewbanks.co.uk

Based in the attractive village of Much Hadham **Andrew Banks** is a specialist in wood in all its many forms. Wood Floors, made of solid hardwood. Worktops, made to order in wide staves and single lengths. Decking, in both hard and soft wood and garden furniture in traditional, contemporary and bespoke designs that are made to last a lifetime and featuring manufacturers who have been associated with quality for generations. You can expect quality products, expert advice and a personal service from this timber specialist. Contact Andrew for brochures, more information or a home consultation.

contains an exhibit celebrating another famous son – Sir Walter Gilbey who founded the famous gin firm when he was living at nearby Elsenham Hall in the 1860s.

AROUND BISHOP'S STORTFORD

Much Hadham

4 miles W of Bishop's Stortford on B1004

A large and largely unspoilt village, which still retains many old timber-framed houses and cottages, the oldest of which dates back to the 15th century. The **Forge Museum and Victorian Cottage Garden** not only tells the story of the work of the blacksmith over the years but is also home to a delightful cottage garden. As well as displaying and growing plants that would have been familiar to a 19th century country gardener, the garden contains an unusual 19th century bee shelter.

Nearby **Perry Green** became the home of Henry Moore. Following bomb damage to his Hampstead studio in 1941, the famous sculptor moved with his wife Irina to the peace and tranquillity of the village and he remained there for the rest of his life. The Henry Moore Foundation, which operates from Dane Tree House, Perry Green, and from the Henry Moore Institute in Leeds, was established in 1977 "to advance the education of the public by the promotion of their appreciation of the fine arts and in particular the works of Henry Moore". The Perry Green site comprises several studios and two converted barns containing the Foundation's collection of Moore's work, as well as tapestries based on his drawings which were woven at West Dean College in Sussex. On the far side of the village green is a visitor centre selling books, posters, postcards and other Moore-themed merchandise along with a limited number of original prints. The estate contains many fine trees and hedgerows, much loved by Moore and to be seen in many of his works, and it was Irina who over the years created the garden areas in which the studios and sculptures are sited. The Foundation is open to the public from April to September by appointment (call: 01279 843333). Moore, who died in 1986, is buried in the village churchyard.

Standon

6 miles W of Bishop's Stortford on A120

This old village, which once had a weekly market and two annual fairs, derived its importance from the families who held the manor and also from the Order of St John of Jerusalem. Though there is little evidence of it today, the order established a commandery, a hospice and a school which is believed to be the building now known as Knights' Court.

In a field to the west of the village lies the **Balloon Stone**, a giant sandstone boulder which marks the spot where, in 1784, Vincenzo Lunardi completed the first balloon flight in England. He began his flight in Finsbury, north London, and landed here some two hours later having first touched down briefly in a field at North Mimms.

STEVENAGE

Designated the first of Britain's New Towns in 1946, the town grew up along the Great North Road, and as traffic increased from the 13th century it developed round its parish church, the main road becoming its High Street. The idea of New Towns grew from the severe shortage of housing following the World War II air raids on London, and the first new houses in Stevenage were occupied in 1951; the new town centre was completed in 1958. Within the new town area, by a roundabout near the railway station, lie **Six Hills**, reputed to be Roman burial mounds. The history of the town, from the earliest days to the development of the new town and the present day, is told in the **Stevenage Museum** in the undercroft of St George's Church.

AROUND STEVENAGE

Knebworth

3 miles S of Stevenage off A602

The town is best known today for the open-air rock concerts held in the grounds of **Knebworth House**. The home of the Lytton family since 1490, the present magnificent Gothic mansion house was built in 1843 to the design of the Victorian statesman and novelist, Edward Bulwer-Lytton, who wrote *The Last Days of Pompeii*. However, fragments of the original Tudor house remain, including parts of the Great Hall, and there is also some superb 17th century panelling. Other members of the Lytton family of note include Constance, a leading figure in the suffragette movement, and Robert, Viceroy of India. The Raj Exhibition at the house brings to life the story of Lord Lytton's viceroyship and the Great Delhi Durbar of 1877. The house has also played host to such notable visitors as Elizabeth I, Benjamin Disraeli, Sir Winston Churchill and Charles Dickens, who is said to have taken part in amateur theatrical performances here. Dickens christened his tenth child Edward Bulwer Lytton Dickens in honour of their great friendship. The grounds of Knebworth

House are also well worth visiting and, as well as the beautiful formal gardens laid out by Lutyens, there is a wonderful herb garden established by Gertrude Jekyll, a lovely Victorian wilderness area, a maze that was replanted in 1995 and acres of grassland that are home to herds of red and sika deer. Children will enjoy the adventure playground, where they will find Fort Knebworth, a Dinosaur Trail, a monorail suspension slide and a bouncy castle among the amusements.

Knebworth House & Grounds

Also within the grounds is the **Church of St Mary and St Thomas** which contains some spectacular 17th and 18th century monuments to members of the Lytton family. Especially striking is the memorial to Sir William Lytton who died in 1705. A well-fed figure with a marked double chin and dressed in the height of early-18th century fashion, Sir William reclines gracefully atop his tomb, his expression one of impermeable self-satisfaction.

Jousting at the Sealed Knot, Knebworth

Benington

4 miles E of Stevenage off the B1037

One of the county's most attractive villages, Benington has a lovely green fringed by 16th century timber-and-plaster cottages. The village church dates from the 13th century, and next to it, on the site of a largely disappeared castle, is a large Georgian house known as **Benington Lordship**. The house is private but the superb grounds are open at restricted times. The hilltop gardens include lakes, a Norman keep and moat (the remains of the castle), kitchen, rose and water gardens, a charming rockery, magnificent herbaceous borders and a splendid folly dating from 1832.

The Crown

Church Street, Litlington, nr Royston,
Hertfordshire SG8 0QB
Tel: 01763 853859
website: www.thecrownpub.me.uk

Behind a smart white-painted exterior adorned with hanging baskets, **The Crown** is bright, cheerful, traditional and very welcoming, with a strong following from the local villages and towns. Open all day, it's a popular spot to meet for a drink, with several cask ales on tap, and offers an impressive choice of home-cooked food served every lunchtime and Monday to Saturday evenings. The options run from sandwiches, ploughman's platters, pies and steaks to fresh fish specials, Sunday roasts and a mouthwatering list of desserts. Thursday is theme night, with cuisines from around the world adding to the choice, and Saturday night brings a traditional English menu.

The Crown once served as the favourite 'local' for two American Air Force bases - the Fighter squadron at Steeple Morden and the Bomber base at Bassingbourne – and part of the bar is a remembrance corner hung with photographs. This most convivial of country pubs has a games room with pool, darts and big-screen TV, and fields teams for activities ranging from darts and pétanque to football, amateur dramatics and quizzes. It also hosts regular fund-raising events for local charities and for the Great Ormond Street Children's Hospital.

Leys Barn

Bilden End, Chrisall, Nr Royston,
Hertfordshire SG8 8RF
Tel: 01763 838364 e-mail: janbatesleysbarn@yahoo.co.uk

Quietly situated on a working arable farm on the borders of Cambridgeshire, Essex and Hertfordshire, **Leys Barn** has been lovingly converted by its owners to provide comfortable self-catering accommodation for up to five people. There are three bedrooms (one double, one twin, one single), two bathrooms and an open plan double-height lounge/dining area with colour TV. The kitchen is equipped with electric cooker, microwave and fridge. There is a washing machine, freezer and payphone in the utility room. Linen and duvets are included, heating is by electricity, payable by meter reading.

Smokers are accepted; children are welcome – a cot is available if required – and dogs can be accommodated. Locally there are several footpaths to explore, including the Icknield Way. Nearby Cambridge offers its colleges, museums, botanical gardens and even punting on the river. Ely's superb cathedral and the fens are within easy reach, as is Newmarket, the centre of the horse racing industry. Another attraction not far away is Duxford Air Museum or, if you have the energy, London is only an hour away by train.

Cromer

4 miles NE of Stevenage on the B1037

Half a mile east of the village, on the B1037 towards Hare Street, stands Hertfordshire's sole surviving post mill. **Cromer Windmill** was built on an artificial mound where windmills have stood for over 600 years. The present mill dates back at least to 1720, possibly as early as 1681. Blown over in a storm around 1860 and subsequently rebuilt, it was in use until the 1920s, by which time milling by wind had become uneconomic. The mill was basically left to deteriorate until an appeal by local people in 1967 saved its life. On completion of the first phase of restoration work the mill was presented to the current owners the Hertfordshire Building Preservation Trust. The first open days were held in 1991 and the mill was restored to full working order in 1998 with the help of grants from the Heritage Lottery Fund and English Heritage. The mill can be visited on Sundays, Bank Holiday Mondays and the second and fourth Saturdays from the second Sunday in May until the end of August.

Royston

12 miles NE of Stevenage on A10

This light industrial town grew up at the intersection of the Icknield Way and Ermine Street and is named after a wayside cross erected by Lady Roysia. A favourite hunting base for royalty, **James I's Hunting Lodge** can still be seen, though the only original features which remain are the two large chimneys.

Discovered in 1742 below the junction of the two ancient thoroughfares is the man-made **Royston Cave**. Bottle-shaped and cut out of the chalk, the cave is 28 feet deep and 17 feet across. Inside the chamber is a series of crude carvings on the walls, including St Christopher and the Crucifixion; the purpose of the cave and the date of the carvings have never been determined.

The **Royston Museum**, in the former Congregational Schoolroom building, houses the Royston and District Local History Society collections, which relate to the history of this late medieval town and the surrounding area. Also here is a substantial collection of late-19th century ceramics and glass.

Letchworth

6 miles N of Stevenage on A505

This attractive country town is proud to be the first Garden City, where the ideals of Ebenezer Howard were put into practice (see Welwyn Garden City). The site for Letchworth was purchased in 1903 and Barry Parker and Raymond Unwin were appointed architects. The residential cottages were designed and built by different architects for the 1905 Cheap Cottages Exhibition and, with none costing more than £150, they each demonstrated new techniques and styles of building and living accommodation.

Housed in a beautiful thatched Arts and Crafts building of 1907 is the **First Garden City Heritage Museum**, a unique place which traces the history and development of this special town; among the many displays are the original plans and drawings of Letchworth. **Letchworth Museum and Art Gallery** (free) is home to displays of local natural history and archaeology including finds of late Iron Age and Roman origin that were unearthed at Baldock.

On the outskirts of the town, **Standalone Farm** is a working farm which welcomes anyone who wants to

Caffeine

37 Station Road, Letchworth, Hertfordshire SG6 3BQ
Tel: 01462 680893 Fax: 01462 682893
e-mail: caffeineuk@aol.com
website: www.caffeinecoffeeco.com

To enjoy coffee in style, the place to make for is the light and airy **Caffeine** coffee shop at the entrance to the shopping arcade on Letchworth's Station Road. In these stylish surroundings with lots of Art Deco influences and elegant potted plants, you'll find coffee of all styles – Italian, Spanish, French and American – all freshly prepared and courteously served. Caffeine was established in 1999 by Kevin Hunter who hails from Yorkshire, and his wife Kristin from Chicago, whom he met while managing tours in the USA. As well as serving excellent coffees, they also offer an enticing range of appetising light meals that includes bagels, paninis and generously filled sandwiches such as the Veggie Club and the Arcadian – "a double-decker of sour dough bread smothered with our special mushrooms, layered with Cheddar cheese, roast turkey and crispy bacon, then grilled to perfection". A reassuring message on the blackboard menu asks customers to note "This is a microwave-free Zone!" Caffeine is open every day from 8am to 8pm; roadside parking is available.

Bickerdikes Garden Centre

Norton Road, Norton, Letchworth,
Hertfordshire SG6 1AG
Tel: 01462 673333 Fax: 01462 681660
e-mail: info@bickerdikes.co.uk

When **Bickerdikes Garden Centre** moved to its present site in Norton in 1999 there was nothing on the site. But owner Mark Bickerdike is very experienced in the business – as his father was before him – and has created a thriving business. Customers are attracted by the knowledge that whatever their gardening requirements they can be confident of finding them on this three-acre site. In addition to the huge choice of healthy plants, shrubs and trees, Bickerdikes also stocks a comprehensive range of garden furniture and furnishings, barbecue equipment, pots of every shape, size and variety, tools, chemicals, fertilisers, ceramics, giftware, childrens play equipment, climbing frames and much, much more.

Helpful and knowledgeable staff are always at hand to offer advice and information. Another major attraction at Bickerdikes is the excellent Nortons coffee shop which serves a superb selection of meals and light refreshments throughout the day. Parking isn't a problem – there's plenty of space within the grounds.

learn more about farming and raising animals. A wide range of farm animals, including Shire horses, occupy the 170-acre site which also has a recently-planted arboretum containing more than 1,000 trees of 35 species, hides to view wildfowl, a natural history exhibition, a picnic area and café.

Baldock

7 miles N of Stevenage on the A6141

A settlement of some size during the Iron Age and Roman times, the Baldock of today dates from the 13th century; it was founded by the Knights Templar and takes its name from the Old French for Baghdad. The Church of St Mary has an impressive 14th century tower and spike steeple, and the town boasts many handsome Georgian houses, both in the tree-lined main street and in the side streets.

Ashwell

9 miles N of Stevenage off the A505

An appealing village with a wealth of attractive old houses, Ashwell was one of the five boroughs of Hertfordshire in medieval times and took its name from the ash trees around the source of the River Rhee. The village later prospered through a malting industry that only ceased in the 1950s. The 14th century **Church of St Mary** has the highest tower in the county, at 176 feet, and inside there are several inscriptions referring to the Black Death of 1349 and the plague and great storm of 1361. **Ashwell Museum**, in the restored Town House, affords a insight into the natural history, social history and archaeology of the town. It began in 1927 as the private collection of two schoolboys who displayed their treasures in a garden shed.

Truly Scrumptious

24a High Street, Baldock, Hertfordshire SG7 6AX
Tel: 01462 893197
e-mail: john.aitken9@ntlworld.com
website: www.truly-scrumptious-gifts.co.uk

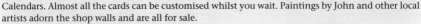

Quality greeting cards, old-fashioned sweets in jars, paintings, gifts and jewellery is the unusual mix you will find at **Truly Scrumptious**, John and Chris Aitken's high street emporium in Baldock. One of John's brilliant ideas is the 'personalised card'. If you've ever had difficulty finding an appropriate card for your 80-year-old uncle who is into vintage malt whisky and bungee-jumping, simply contact Truly Scrumptious and one will be created for you. Amongst the ready-printed cards is the popular 'Greetings from Baldock' range, illustrated with paintings Shirley Smith has done for the Baldock Calendars. Almost all the cards can be customised whilst you wait. Paintings by John and other local artists adorn the shop walls and are all for sale.

Another major attraction here is the sweet shop with its wonderful old-fashioned varieties – humbugs and rhubarb and custard amongst them, including **sugar free** products, not forgetting the scrummy Belgian Chocs, all of which can be gift wrapped to customers' requirements for special occasions. Then there's the interesting and unusual range of gifts and jewellery from around the world, with something to suit everyone. During summer months, Truly Scrumptious also offers Marcello's range of ice creams with 10 mouth-watering flavours including Banana Toffee Swirl, Cappuccino Choc and Mint Choc Chip.

A truly personalised and friendly service waits for all who visit 'Truly Scrumptious'.

Worx of Art Gallery

15c Sun Street, Hitchin, Hertfordshire SG5 1AH
Tel: 01462 423390 Fax: 01462 441600
e-mail: info@worx-of-art.com
website: www.worx-of-art.com

It was in 1998 that Jane Waters and Mandy Sullivan, both of who had a keen interest in Art and Design teamed up and began selling work with an art gallery in Letchworth, Hertfordshire. The business quickly grew and in January 2000 they opened their Worx of Art Gallery in Hitchin's town centre. It provides a showcase for a dazzling range of contemporary art works.

There are paintings by Rory Browne, Ian Flack, Karen Griffiths, Jackie Grisley and Richard Phillips; sculptures by Carol Peace, Melanie Adkins and Christine Cummings; a striking glass studio with pieces by Martin Andrews, Jane Hunt and Julie Langan; and jewellery by Sally Ratcliffe and Sonya Bennett.

The gallery specialises in design led commissioned jewellery- a wedding ring, perhaps, or a piece for some other special event. The gallery also has an excellent hand-made gift shop where you'll find an impressive selection of imaginative and usual gifts.

Worx of Art is open from 9.30am to 5pm, Monday to Saturday, but if you can't get to the gallery during those hours, Jane and Mandy are always happy to arrange a viewing in the evening or on Sundays.

Hitchin

4 miles NW of Stevenage on A600

Pevsner considered that, after St Albans, Hitchin was "the most visually satisfying town in Hertfordshire". Situated on the banks of the River Hiz, this old town was, during medieval times, a vast market area where straw was purchased for the local cottage industry of straw plaiting and where the completed plaits were sold. As the trade in straw declined so the market at Hitchin reduced in size but there is still a small market place today, west of the parish church. Many of the town's older buildings have survived, if now surrounded by newer developments. The oldest parts of **St Mary's Church** date from the 12th century, though there was a minster church here at the time of the Domesday Survey. The low tower is the only part of the original building to have survived an earthquake of 1298. Rebuilt in the 14th century, the grandeur of the church reflects the prosperity which Hitchin once enjoyed. Standing on the site of a Gilbertine Priory is **The Biggin**, constructed in the early 17th century. For a while it was a private residence, then a school, before becoming, in 1723, an almshouse for 'poore, auncient or middle aged women', a function which it still performs today. Another building worthy of mention is **The Priory**, which takes in fragments of a Carmelite Priory founded in the 14th century. Built in 1770 by Robert Adams as the private residence of the Radcliffe family, it was extensively renovated in the 1980s after being disused for many years.

Finally, **Hitchin Museum** (free), home to the county's largest collection of period costumes, is an excellent place to visit. It shares a building with the **Museum of the Hertfordshire Imperial Yeomanry** - a band of men mustered to repel Napoleon's threatened invasion. As

Objets D'art

11 Hermitage Road, Hitchin, Hertfordshire SG5 1BS
Tel/Fax: 01462 422073
website: www.objets-dart.com

Close to the main A505 that circles Hitchin, and just off the B656, **Objets d'Art** specialises in interiors, with a range that runs from major pieces of furniture to small household accessories. Owner Sherri Tomlinson established the business in the early 1990s, wanting to set up a shop that sold something different from the average high street outlet while offering value for money and a constantly changing stock.

Everything on display in the bright modern interior is cutting edge and absolutely up to the minute, including bespoke tables, chairs and stools, sofas, and dining, office and bedroom furniture. Accessories, including mirrors, pictures, clocks and lighting, are equally distinctive, and smaller items such as executive toys for the boys make out-of-the-ordinary gifts. All the stock in this unique shop is sourced from around the world by Sherri, and everything is guaranteed to add style and character to any modern home.

Wiggintons

2 St Andrew Street, Hertford SG14 1JA
Tel/Fax: 01992 551530/505695
website: www.wiggintons.co.uk

It is well worth visiting **Wiggintons** in Hertford because they have four shops and they're all close to each other in the more historic part of town. People come from afar to see the huge selection of beautiful gifts, decorative items, traditional lighting, womens clothes, nostalgic toys and furniture.

The Gift Shop at 2 St Andrew Street is crammed full with interesting gift ideas and the extensive range of lighting will add an extra dimension to your home. The backdrop is ranges of popular painted furniture.

Directly opposite at 1 St Andrew Street is the womens clothes shop which carries collections from Fenn Wright Manson, Sandwich, Sahara and East, together with lots of attractive accessories.

Diagonally opposite you'll discover the Nostalgic Toy Shop. All the leading makes of collectors' teddies are here together with Dolls' Houses with all the accessories – lighting, furniture, miniatures and carpets etc. The playthings include rocking horses, and pedal cars.

In this same building at 6/8 Old Cross there are also eight showrooms of Victorian-style pine furniture. The popular ranges are quality hand-waxed and it's all sensibly priced. The shops are open from 9.30am to 5.30pm, every day except Sunday. There's easy parking in St Andrew Street car park.

The Ginger Jar

6/7 West Alley, Hitchin, Hertfordshire SG5 1EG
Tel: 01462 438333
e-mail: jude@thegingerjar.co.uk
website: www.thegingerjar.co.uk

Distinctive red wooden shutters frame the enticing window display at **The Ginger Jar**, Judy McDonnell's shop selling speciality foods and as many genuine products as can be sourced. The history of ginger goes back at least 5,000 years when it was regarded by the Chinese and Indians as the "universal medicine" – a remedy for many conditions including sea-sickness, indigestion and fever, as well as being effective in helping to prevent coronary artery disease, migraines and rheumatoid and arthritic conditions.

The long list includes Chinese Globe Ginger in Syrup, Dragon's Breath ginger and chilli chutney, and Lyme Bay Ginger Wine & Cream Liqueur. As well as the ginger products Judy also stocks speciality foods from small, individual companies who care about the products they make. "They must also taste good, look good and use natural ingredients," Judy adds, " with a reassuring lack of E-numbers!" Kitchen accessories such as ceramic jugs, bowls, pots, casseroles and dishes are also on sale, and Judy can provide gift boxes and hampers made up to your requirements. The Ginger Jar has an off licence so it can also supply wines, champagnes and spirits. Please write or e-mail for a mail order brochure.

well as the numerous displays of local social history, part of the museum includes the **Victorian Chemist Shop** and **Physic Garden**. This re-creation of a chemist's shop uses much of the stock and fittings from Perks and Llewellyn, who ceased trading as a pharmacy in 1961; the original cabinets still contain the lavender toiletries for which the firm was world famous. To carry the connection further between the town and pharmacy, the medical pioneer Lord Lister had family ties with Hitchin and began his education here. The Physic Garden reflects the historical and modern importance of plants as a source of medicine.

HERTFORD

Dating back to Saxon times, the town was founded at a ford across the River Lea, at that time the boundary between Saxon and Viking England. A once important waterway linking Hertford with London, the River Lea, which became the Lea (Lee) Navigation at Hertford, was used to transport flour and grain but today its traffic is leisure cruisers. The **Hertford Nature Walk** is situated in the meadows between the Rivers Lea and Beane, and takes in the canal basin, known as **The Folly**.

Hertford is very much a mix of the old and new, and among the interesting buildings are the particularly beautiful Norman **Church of St Leonard**, in the area known as Bengeo, and the **Quaker Meeting House**. Said to be the oldest purpose-built meeting house in the world that has been in constant use as a place of worship, the meeting house dates from 1669 and stands behind a walled courtyard; it has a unique four-tiered platform for the ministers that is screened from the entrance. The collections at **Hertford Museum** were started in the 1890s and cover a wide variety of subjects relating to the town and the surrounding area. The Museum is located in a 17th century town house that is complemented by a reconstructed Jacobean garden.

Little remains of the original **Hertford Castle**, which was built by King Alfred's son Prince Edward to protect London from the Danes. However, the 15th century gatehouse is still standing and, now modernised, is used as administrative offices for the town council. The site of the castle is now a public park and evidence of the castle's original motte and bailey can still be seen in the lie of the land. A short length of the massive Norman flint wall, complete with a 14th century postern gate, is also preserved in the park.

To the south of the town lies **Cole Green Way**, a delightful nature trail that follows the route of the now disused Hertford and Welwyn Junction Railway. Passing through attractive meadowland, the trail runs from Hertford to Cole Green, where the former station provides a pleasant picnic spot.

AROUND HERTFORD

Hoddesdon

2 miles S of Hertford on the A1010

The town grew up around the road along the Lea Valley that replaced the Roman Ermine Street in Saxon times. In Lea Valley Park stands the 15th century **Rye House Gatehouse**, a fascinating historic attraction which includes an exhibition where visitors can eavesdrop on the conspirators in the Rye House Plot. In 1683, Rye House was the scene of a plot to assassinate Charles II as he passed through the town on his way back from Newmarket to London. The plot failed and the conspirators, including Richard Rumbold, the then tenant of Rye House, were executed.

Cheshunt

8 miles S of Hertford off the A10

In 1564 Lord Burghley, Chief Minister to Elizabeth I, built his great house Theobalds here. Later, James I was so taken with the house that he persuaded Burghley's son Robert to exchange the house for his palace at Hatfield. Theobalds was all but destroyed in the aftermath of the Civil War, and what remains of the building stands in the public **Cedars Park**. Also in the park is **Temple Bar**, designed by Wren and originally erected at the Fleet Street entrance to the City of London after the Great Fire of 1666. By the 1870s London's traffic had increased to the extent that the gateway was causing an obstruction, so it was removed and rebuilt in the park.

Waltham Cross

9 miles S of Hertford on the A1010

The town takes its name from the cross built in the centre in 1291. It is an **Eleanor Cross**, one of three survivors of the 12 which Edward I erected to commemorate the resting places of the funeral cortege of his Queen, Eleanor of Castile. Eleanor died in Lincolnshire and the cortege took 13 days to travel to Westminster Abbey where she is buried. The building materials in the cross include Caen stone, Sussex and Purbeck marble and precious stones, and it is recorded that the total cost was £95.

The other surviving crosses are at Northampton and Geddington, and a Victorian replica stands in the forecourt of Charing Cross Station. In 1859 Anthony Trollope came to live in

Waltham Cross. He kept pigs, tended his garden and wrote some of his best works while living here.

Ware

3 miles E of Hertford on the A1170

Situated at the point where Ermine Street crosses the River Lea, Ware was the scene of a famous encounter between King Alfred and the Danes in 895 and, during the Middle Ages, it became a trading rival to Hertford. The construction of a viaduct in the 1970s to carry the A10 across the valley has removed much of the traffic from the town and, despite development over the years, Ware still retains many of its original buildings. Behind the east end of the High Street, there is access to Blue Coat Yard where, on the right, stands **Place House**, possibly one of Ware's two Domesday manor houses, which was rebuilt during the 13th century as a splendid aisled hall and in the 1680s was purchased by the governors of Christ's Hospital for use as a school for boys being fostered in Ware. Most of this building still remains and on the opposite side of the yard stand the cottages which were built in 1698 and provided accommodation for a foster mother and up to 14 boys.

The High Street crosses the River Lea at Bridgefoot, and here can still be seen some unique 18th century gazebos, many of which has been restored to their former glory. The riverside path leads on into an attractive public garden behind what was once a Franciscan Priory, of which only a few traces remain. Founded in 1338 as a friary, the priory became a private house in 1568 and remained so for several centuries. In 1920, the owner, Mrs Page-Croft, gave the house and gardens to the town and, fully restored in 1994, the building stands pristine surrounded by seven acres of parkland.

No trip to Ware would be complete without a visit to **Scott's Grotto**, built by the poet John Scott in the late 18th century and located off the A119 Hertford Road. The son of a wealthy Quaker family, Scott devised this elaborate series of six chambers linked by passageways and air tunnels during the 1760s; they are lined with flints, fossils, minerals and thousands of shells. On a hill above the grotto is an octagonal summerhouse approached by horseshoe-shaped steps. The grotto was described by Scott's friend Dr Johnson as "a fairy hall", adding that "none but a poet could have made such a garden". The grotto was extensively restored in 1990, and the replacement shells came from local donors and from as far afield as Japan. It is open every Saturday and Bank Holiday Monday from April to the end of September.

The history of Ware and its major role in the malting industry is explained in **Ware Museum** at Priory Lodge.

Great Amwell

2 miles SE of Ware off the A10

Between 1609 and 1613 the **New River** was created to carry fresh water from local springs by way of Hoddesdon and Cheshunt to the New River Head reservoir at Clerkenwell in London. Wooden pipes then carried the water to the houses and businesses of North London. This enterprise was the brainchild of Sir Hugh Myddelton, whose achievement is commemorated at Great Amwell by an island laid out by the architect of the New River Company in 1800. Just south of the village church lie the imposing buildings of Haileybury College, which was established in 1809 as a training school for the East India Company. The architect was William Wilkins, whose best-known work is the National Gallery in Trafalgar Square.

HATFIELD

This historic town grew up around the gateway to the palace of the abbots and Bishop of Ely. Beside the palace gatehouse stands the **Church of St Etheldreda**, the East Anglian princess and first abbess of Ely in the 7th century. The church is notable for its magnificent memorials to the Cecil family of nearby Hatfield House, the Brocket family chapel from the Tudor era, and dazzling stained glass by Burne-Jones. Also buried here are the novelist Lady Caroline Lamb and her husband Henry William Lamb, 2nd Viscount Melbourne. The viscount, who was Prime Minister in 1834 and from 1835 to 1841, has a memorial in the church, but there is no mention of Lady Caroline, whose public infatuation with Lord Byron had brought about their separation in 1825.

Elizabeth I spent her early life in the Royal Palace of Hatfield, of which only the Banqueting Hall remains. This can be seen in the delightful gardens of the spectacular Jacobean mansion, **Hatfield House**, which now stands on the site. It was built in the early 1600s for Robert Cecil, (later 1st Earl of Salisbury), Chief Minister to both Elizabeth and James I. Designed with entertaining royalty in mind, no expense was spared to make Hatfield the most striking house of its time. The most impressive room is the superb Marble Hall, a richly-decorated version of the medieval Great Hall with a sumptuously carved Screen and Minstrel's Gallery, a specially made 30ft long refectory table and a black and white marble floor. Here hang the two most famous paintings of Elizabeth I – Nicholas Hilliard's *Ermine Portrait* and Isaac Oliver's deeply allegorical *Rainbow Portrait*. The Cecil family still live here, in the East Wing, and the present Marchioness has taken a special interest in restoring the superb gardens to their 17th century appearance, complete with herb and knot gardens, and a foot maze typical of the period. Visitors to the Park can also enjoy the national collection of model soldiers, five miles of marked park trails, a picnic site, children's play area, gift shop, licensed restaurant and tea room.

Back in the centre of town lies the Eight Bells pub, which was frequented by Charles Dickens when, as a newspaper reporter for the *Morning Chronicle*, he visited Hatfield to report on the fire, which not only destroyed a substantial part of Hatfield House but also resulted in the death of the Dowager Lady Salisbury. The pub also features in Dickens' *Oliver Twist*, as following the murder of Nancy, Bill Sikes 'shaped his course' for Hatfield and, in the tap room of the Eight Bells, a fellow drinker saw the blood on Sikes' hat.

The idea of Hatfield New Town was nothing new in post World War II Britain as in 1848 proposals for a new town were advertised to coincide with the completion of the railway line in 1850. Though some development did take place, it was not until the 1950s that the rapid expansion began. However, the two areas remain separate, on either side of the railway line and, fortunately, much of the older part of the town has survived.

AROUND HATFIELD

Brookmans Park

3 miles S of Hatfield on the A1000

A quiet residential area with a large commuting population. To the east lies **Northaw Great Wood**, the remains of the forest that once covered a large part of Hertfordshire. It is now preserved with conservation in mind, and visitors can wander through the woodland and perhaps spot muntjac deer, badgers, foxes and some of the 60 or so species of birds that have been sighted here.

Welwyn

1 mile N of Hatfield on the A1(M)

This historic town has grown up along the route of the Great North Road, which became the High Street, but, since the construction of the A1(M) took the route away from the town centre, Welwyn is now relatively traffic-free. During the excavations for the new motorway, the famous **Welwyn Roman Baths** were uncovered. Part of a 3rd century villa or farm, the bath house is preserved in a steel vault within the motorway embankment.

Welwyn Garden City

2 miles N of Hatfield on the A1000

As the name of this town would suggest, Welwyn is indeed a Garden City, one of two in Hertfordshire that followed the ideas and plans of Ebenezer Howard. After seeing the squalor in which people lived in the cities, particularly London, Howard conceived the idea of providing working people with an opportunity to live in well- spaced housing with access to the clean air of the countryside and to the industrial areas close by. The land for Welwyn Garden City was first acquired in 1919 and the building began a year later, with the present station completed in 1926. Howard's ideas are still perhaps best seen here, as the railway line also acts as the demarcation line for the two areas of the town: industry to the east; the shopping and commercial areas to the west; and the residential areas, with extensive planting and many open spaces beyond.

WALK NUMBER 1

Ayot St Lawrence

Distance:	6.5 miles (10.4 kilometres)
Typical time:	180 mins
Height gain:	80 metres
Map:	Explorer 182
Walk:	www.walkingworld.com ID:353
Contributor:	Les Weeks

Access Information:

Difficult to access by public transport. Car parking is in the sports ground car park just north of the church off the B651 in Kimpton. Follow the unmade track signposted 'Parkfield Sports Ground'. Please close the gate behind you.

Additional Information:

At Ayot St Lawrence a very short detour allows a visit to Shaw's Corner (NT), the home of G. B. Shaw (summer months only).

Description:

Mainly on footpaths and farm tracks with a little road walking. There are some fine views across the Chilterns. Many farmland birds can be seen and sometimes kingfishers can be spotted along the Mimram. In the winter months and after a period of heavy rain, some of the paths can become muddy and boots would be recommended.

Pub food and snacks are available in Kimpton (White Horse and Boot pubs) and Ayot St Lawrence (The Brocket Arms); a phone call beforehand is recommended.

Features:

Hills or Fells, River, Pub, Museum, Church, National Trust/NTS, Wildlife, Birds, Great Views.

Walk Directions:

1 Opposite the track to the car park there is a private drive which is also a footpath. Walk along the drive until you reach a farmhouse. To your right is a stile.

2 Cross the stile and follow the obvious track across the field (E) until it meets the NE corner of a small wood where there is a stile and field-gate. Cross the stile. Keep to the right of the trees close to the fence. If the stinging nettles and brambles are high and your trousers short, it is possible to walk to the left of the trees on the edge of the pasture. At the end of the wood is another stile. Cross this stile and remain on the path along the field edge with the fence/hedge now on your left. Pass through the field boundary and carry straight on to the end of the next field, where there is another stile. Cross this stile and follow the trodden track diagonally left, down past an old sweet chestnut to another stile which meets a made-up drive.

3 Cross this stile and join the drive towards and over a folly bridge now in a state of disrepair. Do not take the footpath marked off to the right before the bridge. Follow the drive until it meets the main road.

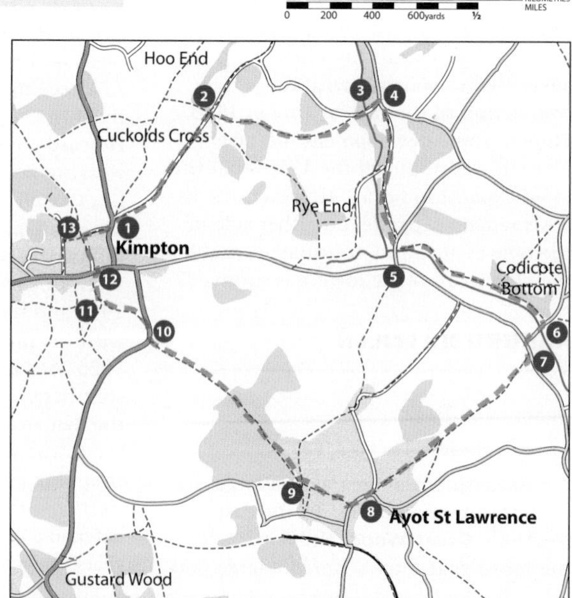

4 Where the drive meets the road, turn sharply to the right along a farm track signposted as a bridleway and part of the Hertfordshire Way. Continue along this track until you reach a farmhouse. At the farmhouse keep left (straight on). Continue until the track meets a minor road joining from the left. Join the road and keep right towards Kimpton Mill. Approx 60m before the mill is a track to the left marked as the Hertfordshire Way. This is our path. However a look at the mill might be of interest. Although now converted, the mill sits over the little River Mimram and is attractive.

5 Take the signposted path. The path runs parallel to the Mimram. A short detour can be taken when a stile is reached down to the shaded riverbank - an ideal place for a short break, especially when the sun is shining. Keep your eyes open for kingfishers. Follow the path for some distance, until it forks. Where the path divides (signpost) we take the right-hand option and follow the brideway. Continue to the road.

6 When you reach the road turn right and walk 100m to the junction at Codicote Bottom Farm. Take care as this road can be busy - it is probably safest to walk on the left. At the junction take the road off to the left signposted Ayot St Lawrence. 50m along this road is a farm track leading off and up to the right.

7 Pass through the gate and make way up the steepish track. Continue until the track makes a turn to the right. At this point a marker on a gate-post opposite you shows that the footpath continues straight ahead alongside a field fence. Keep this fence to your right and follow it until you reach a metal kissing-gate. Once again take the time to stop occasionally and look behind you at the views. Pass through the kissing gate and turn left onto the drive and then right along the quiet road towards Ayot St Lawrence, passing the Brocket Arms pub on your left. Walk past the derelict church until you reach a white house on your right.

8 By the side of the white house there is a footpath that leads towards the Palladian church (built by order to replace the previous one). This is our path. However a small detour is possible here for the literati. Continue along the road a further 50m to Shaw's Corner, home of GBS and now run by the National Trust. Back on our path we follow through wooden kissing-gates and across a field, past the church and through a small metal kissing-gate.

9 After passing through the gate cross the stile to your right and follow the trodden track towards the trees to your left. Pass to the left of the second pine tree. The path eventually comes against the fence under some oaks. The OS map wrongly shows the path inside the wood to your left. Approach a stile in the corner formed by the fencing. Cross this stile into Priors Wood and follow the obvious, signed, track. This track crosses other stiles into a more open area which has been cleared and replanted. The track goes down and then sharply up, to a gap in the wood leading to an open field. A path leads across this open field directly in front of you. This path is well-maintained by the farmer but if newly ploughed and indistinct, the path takes you to a footpath sign just to right of the solitary tree on the horizon. On reaching the post continue left along the farm track until you emerge onto the main road (B651). This road can be busy - take care!

10 Carefully cross the road to the steep and sometimes slippery step through the hedge opposite, onto a path along the edge of the field. Turn right and follow the path beyond where it passes either side of a large oak, to where the field boundary bends to the right. Continue on until just before a sharp turn to the left, there is a break in the hedge leading onto the top of the recreation ground. (if you miss the gap, don't worry, there's another in 50m or so).

11 Pass through the break with the bowling green to your right and chestnuts to the left. Go under the latter and move left along the top of the sports field until you join the track which leads down to a gate onto the High Street. Turn right along the road, cross and turn L into Church Lane.

12 Walk along the lane until, just before a wall starts on the left, there is a gap leading onto an open green area - Garden Fields. The OS map does not show this as open ground. Pass through the gap and keep close along the wall to your right. The right of way stays hard against this wall and the back of the houses, through some apple trees and through an arch cut in some leylandii bushes. It may feel like someone's back garden, but it isn't! You can wander anywhere over the open green.

13 Through and beyond the 'arch' pass through the first of two wooden gates. The car park is on your left.

Just to the south of the town lies **Mill Green Museum**, in the tiny hamlet of Mill Green. Housed in the workers' cottages for the adjoining watermill, this was, between 1911 and 1973, a private residence. There are two permanent galleries here where local items from Roman times to the present day are on display, including pottery, craft tools, underwear and school certificates. A further gallery is used for temporary exhibitions. The adjoining **Mill Green Mill** is a wonderful watermill restored to full working order. Standing on the site of one of the four such mills in Hertfordshire that featured in the Domesday Book, Mill Green Mill was originally owned by the Bishops of Ely. Reconstructed and altered many times, the mill finally ceased to grind corn at the beginning of the 20th century when the incumbent miller emigrated to Australia. Milling recommenced in 1986, after much careful restoration work by the Mill Green Water Mill Restoration Trust, and not only can it be seen working but freshly ground flour is on sale.

Ayot St Lawrence

3 miles NW of Hatfield off the B653

The most famous resident of the village was the playwright George Bernard Shaw, who lived here from 1906 until his death in 1950. It seems that while on a visit to the area looking for a country home he saw a headstone in the churchyard with the inscription 'Her time was short'. The lady in question had in fact died at the age of 70, and Shaw thought that if 70 was considered a short span of years, this was the place for him. The house in which he lived, Shaw's Corner, has been preserved by the National Trust as it was in his lifetime and contains many literary and personal mementos of the great Irish writer. In the lovely garden is the revolving writing hut where he did much of his writing and which could be turned to catch the sunlight. His ashes and those of his wife Charlotte Payne-Townshend were scattered in the garden. Close by, just south of Ayot St Peter, runs **Ayot Greenway**, an attractive footpath, rich in flora, that follows part of the route of the old Luton, Dunstable and Welwyn Junction Railway which hit the buffers under the Beeching axe in 1966.

ST ALBANS

This historic cathedral city, whose skyline is dominated by the magnificent Norman abbey, is a wonderful blend of the old and new. One of the major Roman cities in Britain, the remains of **Verulamium** were excavated only quite recently, but there was already a settlement here before Julius Caesar's invasion in 54 BC. Attacked and ruined by Boadicea in the 1st century, the city was rebuilt and today the remains of the walls, Britain's only Roman theatre (as distinct from an amphitheatre) and a hypocaust can still be seen in Verulamium Park. Also in the park is the **Verulamium Museum**, where the story of everyday life in a Roman city is told; among the displays are ceramics, mosaic floors, personal possessions and room re-creations.

Designated as a cathedral in 1887, **St Albans Abbey** was built on the site where Alban, the first British martyr, was beheaded in 303 for sheltering a Christian priest. Dating from the 11th century and built from flint and bricks taken from the Roman remains, the cathedral has been added to and altered in every century since. Among its many notable features, the medieval paintings, said to be unique in Britain, are the most interesting. In the nearby Church of St

Michael are the tomb and life-size monument of Lord Chancellor Francis Bacon (1561-1626), 1st Baron Verulam and Viscount St Albans, who lived in St Albans for the last five years of his life.

In the town's central market place stands the **Clock Tower**, the only medieval town belfry in England, built between 1403 and 1412. Originally constructed as a political statement by the town, it asserted the citizens' freedom and wealth in the face of the powerful abbey as the town was allowed to sound its own hours and ring the curfew bell. The original 15th century bell, Gabriel, is still in place.

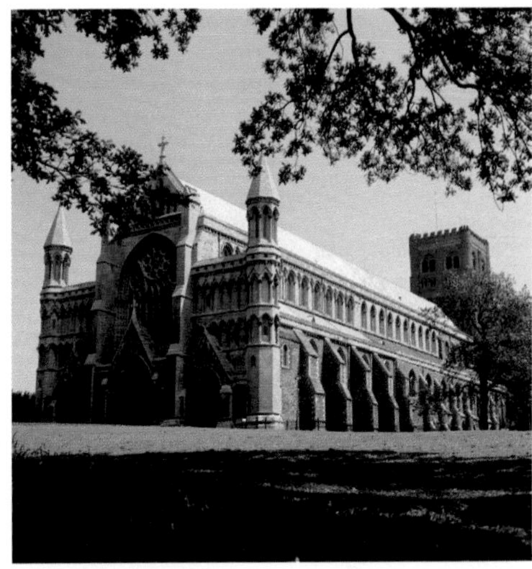

St Albans Cathedral

Close to the peaceful and tranquil Verulamium Park, on the banks of the River Ver, is **Kingsbury Watermill**, a wonderful 16th century mill that is built on the site of an earlier mill that was mentioned in the Domesday Book. Beautifully restored, the waterwheel is still turned by the river and visitors can

St Albans Museums

Hatfield Road, St Albans, Hertfordshire AL1 3RR
Tel: 01727 819340 Fax: 01727 837472
e-mail: museum@stalbans.gov.uk
website: www.stalbansmuseums.org.uk

The fascinating story of historic St Albans, from the departure of the Romans to the present day, is told at the **Museum of St Albans**. The range of lively displays covers the rise of the market town that grew up around its abbey through to its development as a modern commuter city. The museum is also home to the famous Salaman Collection of trade and craft tools that was put together by Raphael Salaman, author of the *Dictionary of Woodworking Tools*.

Just outside St Albans, at Verulamium, is the Museum of everyday life in Roman Britain, set in attractive parkland. Home to some of the best Roman mosaics and wall plasters outside the Mediterranean, the museum houses re-created Roman rooms and there is also an Iron Age gallery.

Finally there is the town's ancient Clock Tower that was erected in the early 15th century by the townsfolk of St Albans so they could sound their own hours and so assert their freedom from the town's abbey.

not only enjoy this idyllic setting but also see the working milling machinery and a collection of agricultural implements.

Two other museums in the town are very well worth a visit. The **Museum of St Albans** relates the fascinating history of the town from Roman times through to the present day and among the exhibits on show is the famous Salaman collection of trade and craft tools that is considered to be the finest in the country. In **St Albans Organ Museum** (open on Sundays) visitors can enjoy the stirring sounds of an amazing collection of working mechanical musical instruments, which include two theatre organs, musical boxes, and reproducing pianos, all of which have been lovingly restored. All the most famous manufacturers are represented, including Mortier, Decap, Bursens, Wurlitzer and Steinway.

Just to the north, in the tiny hamlet of Redbournbury, lies **Redbournbury Mill**, an 18th century watermill that stands on the site of a mill that was mentioned in the Domesday Book. Once owned by the abbey at St Albans, the mill was seized by the crown following the Dissolution of the Monasteries. In 1652 it was sold to an ancestor of the present Earl of Verulam and stayed in his family until 1931 when it once again became Crown property. Now back in private hands, this splendid mill, on the banks of the River Ver, has been restored to its former glory and is now in full working order, powered by a large 1935 Crossley oil

George Street, St Albans

engine. Open to the public on Sundays from March to October, and on other days for special events, the mill also sells its own stone-ground flour and bread.

AROUND ST ALBANS

Chiswell Green

2 miles SW of St Albans on A414

This village is home to probably one of the biggest attractions in Hertfordshire, the **Gardens of the Rose**, a site, (at present closed for renovation), that contains one of the most important rose collections in the world. The Royal National Rose Gardens can boast some 30,000 rose trees and upwards of 1,700 varieties. It isn't necessary to be a horticultural enthusiast to appreciate the sheer natural beauty of gorgeous displays such as the President's Walk or the Queen Mother Rose Garden, named after the garden's patron, which contains some of the oldest varieties of rose, including Damask, Gallicas, Albas and Portland. With the model gardens, the miniature roses, and the breathtaking pergola, it would be difficult to exaggerate the beauty of this place, which really has to be visited to be appreciated.

London Colney

3 miles SE of St Albans off the A414

Among the interesting old buildings in this pleasant village on the River Colne is the late-Victorian All Saints Convent, which stands within the former Colney Park. Begun in 1899 as an Anglican establishment, with a church added in the 1920s, it was bought by the Roman Catholic Church in 1973 as a pastoral centre. A mile south of London Colney, aircraft enthusiasts will be in their element at the **Mosquito Aircraft Museum**, which is run by the de Havilland Aircraft

Derek Howarth ARBS

Colney Park House, Harper Lane, Radlett,
Hertfordshire WD7 9HG
Tel: 01727 822845 Fax: 01727 823087
e-mail: howarthcolneyprk@aol.com
website: www.derekhowarth.co.uk

Elected Associate of the Royal Society of British Sculptors in 1997, **Derek Howarth ARBS** gained an honours degree at Manchester College of Art and Design and then went on to post-graduate work in sculpture. Working as assistant to sculptor Henry Moore increased his knowledge of work on large sculptural pieces. During the ensuing years he returned from time to time to execute large projects for Henry Moore in polystyrene. Derek taught for some time at Norwich School of Art before becoming a freelance sculptor.

Since then he has run his own professional studio/ workshop together with his son Gideon, creating three-dimensional work for films, theatre, TV, industry, shopping centre, public buildings and exhibitions. He is also a visiting tutor in sculpture at various colleges of art and his work is held in private collections in both the UK and the United States.

Derek's varied commissions have included a coat-of-arms for the Prince of Wales' Investiture and the fleur-de-lys placed over the royal canopy; a 12ft x 8ft stylised elephant for a pop group tour; the construction of figures for the Posidonia Exhibition, Athens, Greece – and a 16ft Trojan horse for a gaming establishment.

Derek also created a rock set landscape for the African Aviary in London Zoo; sculpture details for the Malta Exhibition at the National Maritime Museum in Greenwich; and an underground ride for Piper-Heidsieck champagne at Rheims, France.

His versatility extends to work for films where his credits include all the Indiana Jones films, five James Bond films, the *Star Wars* films, *Tomb Raider, Alien/Aliens, Dragonslayer* and more.

Museum Trust. It was here in 1940 that the first Mosquito aircraft was built and taken by road to the de Havilland airfield at Hatfield. In addition to the prototype Mosquito there is a collection of other de Havilland planes, plus various engines and displays of all kinds of aeronautical memorabilia. The museum is located within the grounds of moated Salisbury Hall (private). Built in the mid-1500s, the house was modernised a century later in order to provide a secluded but not too distant refuge for Charles II's mistress, Nell Gwynne.

Shenley

5 miles SE of St Albans on B5378

A traditional country village with, at its centre, two inns, a pond, the site of a former pound for stray animals, and the village lock-up. One of several in Hertfordshire, this **Lock-up** is a brick beehive-shaped construction where the village's drunks and petty criminals were locked up overnight before being put before the magistrate the next day. On either side of the door is the warning sign: 'Be sober, do well, fear not, be vigilant'.

The architect Nicholas Hawksmoor lived near Shenley and is buried in the churchyard of the neighbouring village of Shenleybury. Here, too, is the grave of the dashing racing driver Graham Hill, who was killed in a flying accident at Arkley, three miles from Shenley.

Aldenham

6 miles S of St Albans on the B462

The greatest feature of **Aldenham Country Park**, established in 1971 on what was formerly Aldenham Common, is a large reservoir that was dug by hand by French prisoners of war in the 1790s. Designed to maintain the levels of local rivers following the building of the Grand Union Canal, it is now used for recreational purposes and also supports a wealth of wildfowl and plant life. Coarse fishing is available by permit. The park has a lakeside nature trail and woodland walks and is home to several rare breeds of domestic animals, including Longhorn cattle. Families can have fun in Winnie the Pooh's '100 Aker Wood', where the homes of Pooh Bear, Christopher Robin, Piglet, Eyeore and Owl have been recreated in association with the Disney Corporation.

Markyate

7 miles NW of St Albans off the A5

Markyate's narrow main street is part of the great Roman road, Watling Street, the route between London and Holyhead. A mansion in the village, built on the site of a medieval nunnery known as Markyate Cell, became famous as the home of Lady Katherine Ferrers, the notorious highwaywoman of Nomansland Common near Sandridge, just north of St Albans. Married as a teenager to a man she did not like, Katherine found escape and adventure by disguising herself as a highwayman and holding up the coaches that plied the busy Watling Street. She kept both her disguise and her booty in a secret room above the kitchen in the house. Famed and feared for her audacity, the 'Wicked Lady' always rode a jet black horse. In her last hold-up she was mortally wounded but managed to escape and reach her house, dying at the door of her room. She was buried quietly by her husband, who had her room sealed in the hope that her secret would die with her. It did not.

Harpenden

5 miles N of St Albans on A1081

The whole of the town centre is now a conservation area and, in particular, the High Street is lined with many

C & P Better Homes Garden Centre

West Hyde Nurseries, Old Uxbridge Road, West Hyde, Rickmansworth, Hertfordshire WD3 9XY
Tel: 01895 824787

Well-established as builders and landscapers, the Manger family have recently taken over an existing garden centre which now trades as **C & P Better Homes Garden Centre.** Within the one-acre site gardeners will find just about everything they need. The centre stocks a profusion of healthy and vigorous plants of every kind including roses, perennials, bedding plants and herbs, all well-displayed with plenty of space. You'll also find an extensive range of products for ornamental ponds and other water features. Ready-made hanging baskets are another popular line.

A speciality of the centre is its wide selection of terracotta pots of all sizes and shapes, plain or decorated. Garden furniture, ornaments and sheds are also well-represented. A comprehensive stock of various fertiliser products are available along with garden hoses and tools of every kind. The small shop has seeds and potting products and the friendly, knowledgeable staff are always happy to provide advice and information.

Foodism Delicatessen & Coffee Bar

Unit F, Sheraton House, Lower Road, Chorleywood, Hertfordshire WD3 5LH
Tel/Fax: 01923 285609
e-mail: maisim@foodism.co.uk
website: www.foodism.co.uk

After many years experience in the catering business, sisters Mai Sim and Hunx delighted all the foodies in the region when they teamed up to open their delicatessen and coffee bar **Foodism** in the spring of 2003. Instant success has been richly deserved, as the range and quality of the produce on offer is outstanding. They sell just about everything a gourmet could wish for, from caviar to the finest chocolates by way of pâtés and cheeses, smoked goods, cooked meats, Scotch eggs, hand-made cakes and variety of teas and coffees; there's always a range of goods taking care of special dietary needs, and an interesting selection of Oriental delicacies that reflect the sisters' Chinese origins.

In the coffee bar, sandwiches are made to order on a variety of breads, baps, ciabattas, bagels and baguettes; the gourmet range is well-named indeed, with delectable fillings such as goat's cheese with roasted vegetables and red onions, or hot roast pork with stuffing and apple sauce. Plattered 'Working Lunches' comprise deep-filled sandwiches and hand-cooked chips, with extras such as mini-spring rolls, quiches and cakes adding the final touch. Other offerings at this exceptional place include made-to-order celebration cakes, gift hampers and a gift wrapping service.

listed 17th and 18th century buildings. The **Harpenden Local History Centre** is an ideal place to find out more about this charming old agricultural community and, as well as the small permanent collection there are regularly changing themed exhibitions. The **Harpenden Railway Museum**, a small private collection that was begun in 1963, contains several thousand items of railway memorabilia, many of which originate from the county. The ashes of the comedian Eric Morecambe were scattered in the garden of remembrance next to the Church of St Nicholas.

HEMEL HEMPSTEAD

This is a place with two distinct identities: the charming old town centred around the ancient Church of St Mary and tranquil Gadebridge Park; and the new town, one of the first to be built following World War II, planned as an integrated series of communities, each with its own individual centre.

Gadebridge Park is an extensive expanse of open parkland through which runs the River Gade. The park's attractive walled garden adjoins the High Street of the old town alongside the grounds of **St Mary's** which is an outstanding example of a large Norman parish church. Its interior has remained essentially unchanged since it was completed in 1180. St Mary's 200ft-high spire, made of oak and lead and added in 1340, is believed to be the loftiest in Europe.

Evidence of a settlement here long before the Norman Conquest can be found surprisingly close to the town's industrial area. Protected by a fenced enclosure and visible from the road lies the mound of a Bronze Age barrow.

The **Charter Tower**, just inside one of Gadebridge Park's entrances, is reputed to be the tower from whose upper window Henry VIII handed down Hemel Hempstead's royal charter, but the tower was in fact built long after the charter was given. On the road close to the railway station is a curious stone tablet known as **Snook's Grave**, marking the spot where James Snook, a notorious highwayman, was hanged and buried. Thought to be the last person in England to be taken back to the scene of his crime for the ultimate punishment, Snook was found guilty in 1802 of robbing a postboy and killing him in the process.

The village of **Bedmond**, three miles southeast of Hemel Hempstead, was the birthplace of Nicholas Breakspear, the only British Pope, who was crowned in office as Adrian IV in 1154.

AROUND HEMEL HEMPSTEAD

King's Langley

2 miles S of Hemel Hempstead on the A4251

The home of Ovaltine. A Swiss doctor called George Wander invented the drink in 1865 and his son Albert later took over the business. The King's Langley canal-side factory was built in 1912 and greatly expanded subsequently. Local farms produced eggs, barley, milk and malt for the popular drink, and the factory even had its own narrow boats on the Grand Union Canal. One of these boats has been renovated and bears the name *Albert*.

Watford

5 miles S of Hemel Hempstead on the A411

Originally a country market town, Watford was transformed in the 19th century by the arrival of the railway, which brought new industry and new

LK Interiors

The Studio, 75 Copthorne Road, Croxley Green,
Hertfordshire WD3 4AH
Tel: 01923 711030 Fax: 01923 711040
e-mail: lkinteriors@btconnect.com

LK Interiors is a unique top end Interior Design Showroom situated in the heart of Croxley Green.

The company is owned by Amanda Kaye and Lisa McCartney, designers with 20 years joint experience, and specialises in all aspects of interior design. The showroom has a full range of fabric, wallpaper and trim books from leading names such as: Mulberry, Zoffany, Osborne and Little and Andrew Martin to name but a few.

The designers pride themselves on offering a very personal service, tailored completely to the needs of the individual, and includes specifying and supplying curtains, lighting, furniture, flooring, artwork and accessories.They have a full team of specialist decorators, and general tradesmen, and can also recommend kitchen and bathroom suppliers. Amanda and Lisa are happy to undertake projects nationwide, and insist that no job is too big.....or too small!

Visits and enquiries by prospective clients are welcome by arrangement, and they very much look forward to hearing from you.

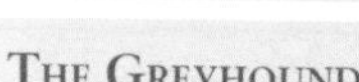

The Greyhound

Chesham Road, Wigginton, Tring,
Hertfordshire HP23 6EH
Tel: 01442 824631

Popular with walkers along the Ridgeway, which passes by the front door, **The Greyhound** is an independently owned, family run gastro pub in the village of Wigginton which is set in picturesque countryside near Tring. When the family arrived here in 2003 they carried out a comprehensive refurbishment while taking care to retain the traditional atmosphere. It is now attractively furnished, has a traditional bar, a relaxing lounge area with sofas and easy chairs, and a stylish dining room which seats 30. Outside there's a shady garden with tables and parasols, and a large car park.

Good food is a priority at The Greyhound – select from the chef's menu or from the blackboard which lists an enticing selection of dishes such as Parma Ham with a celeriac remoulade amongst the starters, and Duck with potato fondant, green beans, and red wine jus as a main dish. If you are planning to stay in the area, The Greyhound has three en suite bedrooms, either double or twin, which have their own separate area. Well-behaved dogs are welcome. Golfers will be pleased to find a choice of three nearby courses – Ashridge, Berkhamsted and Mentmore.

building. Among the few earlier buildings to survive the rapid development are the five-gabled **Bedford Almshouses**, which date back to 1580, and the early-18th century Fuller and Chilcott school. On the high street stands the splendid Mansion House, once the offices of the Benskin Brewery and now home to **Watford Museum**, where visitors can learn about the industrial and social history of the town. The local brewing and printing industries feature prominently, along with a tribute to Watford Football Club.

In the north of the town, off the A411 Hemel Hempstead road, Watford Council manages the gardens at **Cheslyn House.** The 3½-acre garden has woodland, lawns, a bog garden, rock garden, splendid herbaceous borders and an aviary and is open from dawn to dusk every day except Christmas.

TRING

Situated on the edge of the Chiltern Hills and on the banks of the Grand Union Canal, Tring is a bustling little market town whose character has been greatly influenced by the Rothschild family. However, the members of this rich and famous family are not the only people of note to be associated with the town. In **St Mary's Church** can be found the grave of the grandfather of the first US president, George Washington, while the 17th century **Mansion House**, designed by Sir Christopher Wren, was reputedly used by Nell Gwynne.

The town's narrow winding High Street, off which lead little alleyways and courtyards, contains many late-Victorian buildings, all designed by local architect William Huckvale. Of particular note is the **Market House**, built by public

Moored Narrow Boat on Grand Union Canal, Tring

subscription in 1900 to commemorate, albeit a little late, Queen Victoria's Diamond Jubilee. A fine example of the Arts and Crafts style, so popular at the turn of the century, the building was later converted into a fire station and today it serves as the town council chamber.

The old **Silk Mill**, first opened in 1824, once employed over 600 people, but towards the end of the 19th century the silk trade fell into decline and Lord Rothschild ran the mill at a loss to protect his employees rather than see them destitute. Unable to carry on in this fashion, the mill closed to the silk trade and, after losing some its height, the building was converted into a generating station. From 1872 to the 1940s, the Rothschild family lived at Tring Park and from here they exercised their influence over the town. Perhaps their greatest lasting feature is the **Walter Rothschild Zoological Museum**, which first opened in 1892 and, on Walter's death in 1937, became part of the British Museum (Natural History). An eccentric man with a great interest in natural history, Walter collected over 4,000 rare and extinct species of animals, birds and reptiles.

Tring's focal point is **The Square**, remodelled in 1991 and featuring an ingenious **Pavement Maze** in the form of a zebra's head - a tribute to Walter's work. The town's war memorial, unveiled in 1919, stands in The Square, as does the flint and Totternhoe stone Church of St Peter and St Paul. Dating chiefly from the 15th century, this parish church contains some fine medieval carvings as well as 18th century memorials.

AROUND TRING

Marsworth

2 miles N of Tring off B489

Mentioned in the Domesday Book and situated on the banks of the Grand Union Canal, Marsworth was known as Mavvers to the canal people. The village is home to the **Tring Reservoirs National Nature Reserve**. The four reservoirs were built between 1802 and 1839 to store water for the then Grand Junction (now Grand Union) Canal, which reached its summit close by. Declared a nature reserve in 1955, this is a popular place for birdwatchers, and there is also a nature trail and a variety of trees and marshland flora.

Aldbury

2 miles E of Tring off A4251

This picturesque village, with its green, pond, stocks, village shop, timber-framed houses and parish church, dates back to Saxon times and is often used as a film location. There was once a castle in the village that is said to have disappeared in a flash of light sometime during the 14th century. The story goes that the castle's owner Sir Guy de Gravade, in league with the Devil, raised the dead from their graves and from them learned the secret of turning base metals into pure gold. One night a servant, having seen his master at work, decided to experiment on his own; the results were disastrous, for the castle and all the residents within were engulfed in a flash of lightning.

The village lies on the western boundary of the **Ashridge Estate**, formerly part of the estate of Lord Brownlow and now owned by the National Trust. With grounds and woodland extending to some 4,000 acres on the Hertfordshire-Buckinghamshire border, this is a lovely place for walking and spotting the wealth of local flora and fauna. The focal point of the area is the **Bridgewater Monument**, an impressive tower that was erected in memory of the Duke of Bridgewater, who was famous for his pioneering work in the development of canals. Open on afternoons between April and October, the tower offers magnificent views across the countryside.

To the east of Aldbury, a mile south of Little Gaddesdon off the A4146, lie the 150 acres of **Ashridge Management College**, 90 acres of gardens and the rest woodland. Designed by Humphry Repton (he presented his Red Book to the 7th Earl of Bridgewater in 1813), the gardens were actually laid out by Sir Jeffrey Wyatville. Among the highlights are an Italian garden and fountain, a circular rosarie, a large oak planted by Princess (later Queen) Victoria, an avenue of Wellingtonias, a Bible garden, a sunken garden once used as a skating pond and a grotto constructed from Hertfordshire pudding-stone.

The Manor House & village pond, Aldbury

Northchurch

3 miles SE of Tring on A4251

On the south wall of the Church of St Mary is a memorial plaque to Peter the Wild Boy, who is buried close to the porch. Found living wild in a wood near Hanover, Germany, in 1725, he was brought to this country by the royal family and entrusted to the care of a farmer in this parish. He died in 1785 at an estimated age of 75.

Though the full length of the **Grand Union Canal** towpath in Hertfordshire can be walked, the section of canal from Northchurch to Tring has been developed with recreational use particularly in mind. As well as the attractive canal-side walk there are numerous maintenance and conservation projects to preserve this magnificent waterway and the wealth of wildlife and plant life found along its banks.

Berkhamsted

4 miles SE of Tring on the A4251

It was in this historic town - one of Hertfordshire's five boroughs at the time

Cook's Delight Ltd

360-364 High Street, Berkhamsted,
Hertfordshire HP4 1HU
Tel: 01442 863584 Fax: 01442 863702
e-mail: rex@cooksdelight.co.uk
website: www.organiccooksdelight.co.uk

The old market town of Berkhamsted in the foot hills of the Chilterns boasts a unique organic and bio-dynamic food shop, **Cook's Delight**. It has its origins in a food shop and cookery school established in 1981 by Rex Tyler and his wife. The school and shop then developed into a restaurant business based on Malaysian and whole food dishes. Following 15 years of catering, The Tylers decided to concentrate on the retail side of the business.

Cook's Delight is committed to organic foods, fair trade and a greener, healthier environment. "Ethical and compassionate philosophies guide and influence the way we run our business," says Rex. "We sincerely believe that organically grown foods are beneficial for both the external and internal environments."

The Tylers keep themselves abreast of new information about food and its effects on the well-being of their bodies and about the environmental consequences of food production and processing. They are dedicated to buying as much as they can from ethical suppliers and to operate a business based on true compassion, integrity and care for the inhabitants of this planet and for the local and global environment.

A strict buying policy vets all potential suppliers. Rex even refuses to stock products in polystyrene/Aluminum containers and actively campaigns against unnecessary use of packaging that uses materials such as cellophane and plastics that he believes only end up in landfill. The two floors of the Cook's Delight store offer what must be the most comprehensive selection of organic food, drink and clothing to be found anywhere in the country – anything from champagne, wines and beers to fresh pasta and Fair Trade Chocolate.

A subsidiary attraction here is the rural garden at the rear which is left uncultivated so that herbs and wildflowers can flourish. And look out for Rex's poems, either displayed on a blackboard outside the shop or on the Cook's Delight website. They cover whatever topic takes Rex's fancy but here's one about additives:

Ben Feingold told us years ago
About these dreadful things
Flavours, and what's worse these really
Awful colourings
That make our children jumpy.
We knew it, so did they
The great big manufacturers
Who use them anyway.

Cook's Delight is open from 10am to 7pm, Tuesday to Saturday.

of the Domesday Survey - that William of Normandy, William the Conqueror, two months after the Battle of Hastings, accepted the British throne from the defeated Saxons. Shortly afterwards, William's half-brother Robert, Count of Mortain, commenced work on **Berkhamsted Castle**, which as a precaution against the low lie of the land was surrounded by a double moat. The castle entertained many distinguished visitors down the years: the Black Prince on honeymoon with his bride Joan, the Fair Maid of Kent; King John's wife Isabel, besieged in 1216 by the Barons; Thomas à Becket when he was Lord Chancellor; Geoffrey Chaucer as Clerk of the Works. The castle was a place of considerable importance until at least the 15th century, but is now all but ruined.

One of the most interesting of the town's surviving ancient buildings is **Dean John Incent's House**, an impressive black-and-white timbered and jettied building in the main street opposite the 13th century Church of St Peter. A notable feature of this church is a window dedicated to the poet William Cowper, who was born at the local rectory in 1731. The town's cultural connections reach modern times through Graham Greene, son of Berkhamsted School's headmaster, and frequent visitor JM Barrie, creator of Peter Pan.

BEDFORDSHIRE

Bedfordshire is a county of multifarious delights, all within easy reach of London and major road and rail networks. In the Bedfordshire heartlands are to be found two of England's leading animal attractions, Woburn Safari Park and Whipsnade Wildlife Park. There are picturesque villages and historic houses, transport and heritage museums, mills and farms, woodland and nature reserves, great views from the Chilterns escarpment and well-established walking and cycle routes.

The Great Ouse and the Grand Union Canal, once commercial arteries, are finding a new role as leisure attractions, with miles of scenic walks or leisurely cruises to be enjoyed. The south of the county is dominated by the towns of Luton and Dunstable, while the central region of Bedfordshire is an area of ancient settlements and a rich diversity of places to see. Here is perhaps the most impressive dovecote in the country, with nests for 1,500 birds, while just outside Sandy are the headquarters of the Royal Society for the Protection of Birds. At nearby Cardington the skyline is dominated by the huge hangars where the R100 and R101 airships were built. Houghton House at Houghton Conquest is widely believed to have been the inspiration for the House Beautiful in John Bunyan's *Pilgrim's Progress*. Bunyan was born in the village of Elstow, a little way south of Bedford, and many of the places most closely associated with the writer can be visited, in both the town and the village. Bedford, the county capital, offers a blend of history and modern amenity, all set against the backdrop of the River Great Ouse, which passes through the town and many pleasant villages on its journey across the county.

LUTON

The largest town in Bedfordshire and perhaps best known for Luton Airport, Vauxhall cars – and the Luton Girls Choir! Although the town has expanded rapidly from a market town in the early 19th century to a major industrial centre by the mid-20th century, it still boasts more than 100 listed buildings and three Conservation Areas.

Luton first began to prosper in the 17th century on the strength of its straw plaiting and straw hat making industries. These activities are amongst those featured at the **Luton Museum and Art Gallery**, housed within a delightful Victorian mansion in **Wardown Park**, a traditional town park with tennis and bowls. The park was opened to the public in the early years of the reign of Edward VII, but not the house, which was first a restaurant and then, during World War I, a military hospital. It was not until 1931 that the town's museum and art gallery, originally housed in the library, moved here. As well as featuring a re-creation of a Victorian shop and pub, the museum is also home to a range of collections covering the hat trade, costume, local history, archaeology and childhood. As lace making was one of the two main cottage industries in Bedfordshire, visitors will not be surprised to learn that the museum also has the largest collection of lace anywhere in the country outside London.

Visitors can also take a step back in time by seeking out **Stockwood Craft Museum and Gardens**. Occupying a Georgian stable block, the museum has a collection of Bedfordshire craft and rural items enhanced by frequent craft demonstrations. The walled garden is equally impressive and the Period Garden includes knot, medieval, Victorian, cottage, Dutch and Italian sections. The Hamilton Finlay Sculpture Garden showcases six pieces of sculpture by the internationally renowned artist Ian Hamilton Finlay in a lovely natural setting. Also here can be found the **Mossman Collection** of over 60 horse drawn vehicles, the largest of its kind on public display in Britain. The story of transport comes into the 20th century in the Transport Gallery, whose exhibits include bicycles, vintage cars and a model of the Luton tram system. Replicas of some of the vehicles on display here have found their way into such films as *Ben Hur* and *Out of Africa*.

Just to the south of the town is the magnificent house **Luton Hoo**, originally designed by Robert Adams and set in 1500 acres of parkland landscaped by Capability Brown. Construction of the house began in 1767, though it was extensively remodelled in 1827 and again in 1903, when the interior was given a French style for Sir Julius Wernher, who installed his fabulous art collection in the house. Luton Hoo is now a private hotel and no longer open to the public.

Just southeast of Luton is **Someries Castle**, the remains of a fortified medieval manor house dating from the middle to late 15th century. The earliest surviving brick building in the county

Luton Hoo

both the gatehouse and chapel have survived and are still a very impressive sight. The original castle on this site belonged first to the de Someries family and then to the Wenlocks, and the house, of which only a romantic ruin remains, may have been built for the Lord Wenlock who died at the Battle of Tewkesbury in 1471, when the Yorkist victory ended the Wars of the Roses.

AROUND LUTON

Slip End

1 mile S of Luton on the B4540

Woodside Animal Farm is home to more than 200 different breeds and there are hundreds of animals and birds to see and feed. The farm's many attractions include a walk-through monkey house, red squirrel enclosure, alpaca family and hand-reared racoons. There are indoor and outdoor picnic and play areas, pony and tractor rides, a bouncy castle, farm shop, craft shop and coffee shop.

Whipsnade

5 miles SW of Luton off B489

This small village with a charming, simple church is surrounded by common land on which stands **Whipsnade Tree Cathedral** (National Trust). After World War I, a local landowner, Edmund Kell Blyth, planted a variety of trees which have grown into the shape of a cathedral, with a nave, chancel, transepts and cloisters. Designed as a memorial to friends of Blyth killed in the war, it's a curiously moving place. During the summer, services are held here.

To the south of the village can be seen the white silhouette of a lion cut into the green hillside, which is reminiscent of the much older White Horse at Uffington. A magnificent landmark, the lion also advertises the whereabouts of **Whipsnade Wild Animal Park**, the country home of the Zoological Society of London. Whipsnade first opened its doors in 1931, attracting over 26,000 visitors on the first Monday, and in the 70 years since it has grown and developed and continues to provide fun and education for thousands of visitors each year. There are 2,500 animals on show in the park's 600 acres, and behind the scenes Whipsnade is at the forefront of wild animal welfare and conservation, specialising in the breeding of endangered species such as cheetahs, rhinos and the scimitar-horned oryx. There are daily demonstrations - penguin feeding, sea lions, free-flying birds - and other attractions include a railway safari, Discovery Centre, Children's Farm and Adventure Playground. Feeding time for the animals is always a popular occasion, while humans who feel peckish can make tracks for the Café on the Lake or (in summer) the Lookout Café, or graze on ice cream and snacks from the many refreshment kiosks in the park.

Dunstable

2 miles W of Luton on the A505

Dunstable is a bustling town that grew up at the junction of two ancient roads, Icknield Way and Watling Street, and was an important centre in Roman Britain, when it was known as Durocobrivae. The town's finest building is undoubtedly the **Priory Church of St Peter**, all that remains of a Priory founded by Henry I in 1131; only the nave actually dates from that time. It was at the Priory that Archbishop Cranmer's court sat in 1533 to annul the marriage of Henry VIII and Catherine of Aragon. On the B4541 Dunstable-Whipsnade road, **Dunstable Downs** commands some of the finest views over the Vale of Aylesbury. Designated a Site of Special Scientific Interest and a Scheduled

Ancient Monument, it has much to attract the visitor, including a Countryside Centre with interpretive displays and gifts, circular walks and a picnic area; it's a popular spot with hang gliders and kite flyers, and a refreshment kiosk is open all year round. South of Dunstable Downs at the junction of the B4541 and B4540, Whipsnade Heath is a small area of woodland containing some unusual plants and fungi.

Totternhoe

6 miles W of Luton off the A505

This attractive village is situated below **Totternhoe Knolls**, a steeply sloped spur of chalk that is now a nature reserve known nationally for its orchids and its butterflies. On the top of the spur are the remains of a motte and bailey castle dating from Norman times.

Billington

8 miles W of Luton on the A4146

Mead Open Farm is home to a variety of established farm animals and offers a particularly wide range of attractions for children, including an indoor play barn, activity house, sandpit, indoor pets corner and ride-on toys. There's also a tea room and shop and a number of daily activities and weekly events.

Leighton Buzzard

9 miles W of Luton on A505

The town's interesting name tells a lot about its history: Leighton is Old English and refers to a centre for market gardening whilst the Buzzard is a reference not to the bird of prey but to a local clergyman, Theobald de Busar, the town's first Prebendary. The town's past

prosperity as a market centre is reflected in the grandeur of its fine Market Cross, a 15th century pentagonal structure with an open base and statues under vaulted openings all topped off by pinnacles. The market is still held here every Tuesday and Saturday. The spire of **All Saints' Church** is over 190 feet high and is a local landmark. This big ironstone church dates from 1277 and inside there are a number of endearing features in the form of graffiti left by the medieval stonemasons: one shows a man and woman quarrelling over whether to boil or bake a simnel cake. Seriously damaged by fire in 1985, the church has been carefully restored to its medieval glory; the painstaking work included re-gilding the roof, which is particularly fine, with carved figures of angels.

Leighton Buzzard and its neighbour Linslade are on the Grand Union Canal and visitors can now take leisurely boat trips along this once busy commercial waterway on the *Leighton Lady*. Historic forms of transport seem to be the town's speciality as visitors can also take a steam train journey on the **Leighton Buzzard Railway**, one of England's premier narrow gauge operations. It has the largest collection of narrow gauge locomotives in Britain, 50 of them at the last count of which 12 are steam driven. The return journey takes just over an hour and the railway operates on Sundays and Bank Holiday weekends between March and October.

For life at a more leisurely pace than steam trains, the town lies at one end of the **Greensand Ridge Walk** which extends across Bedfordshire to finish some 40 miles away at Gamlingay, Cambridgeshire. The name Greensand comes from the geology of the area, a belt of greensand which stretches from Leighton Buzzard up to Sandy and beyond.

PUTTERIDGE

2 miles NE of Luton on the A505

The University of Luton and the Hertfordshire Garden Trust have restored the gardens at **Putteridge Bury** to the original designs of Sir Edwin Lutyens and Gertrude Jekyll; one of the highlights is a superb rose garden.

AMPTHILL

This historic town, situated on a rise and with fine views over the surrounding countryside, was a great favourite with Henry VIII. It was here that Katherine of Aragon stayed during the divorce proceedings conducted by Henry's court at Dunstable. At that time there was also a castle here, built by Sir John Cornwall for his bride, the sister of Henry IV. On the site now stands Katherine's Cross, erected in 1773, which bears the arms of Castile and Aragon. On land given to his family by Charles II, the 1st Lord Ashburnham built the castle's replacement, **Ampthill Park**, in 1694. The house was enlarged a century later and the 300-acre park was landscaped by the ubiquitous 'Capability' Brown. Ampthill Park is famous for its old oak trees and visitors can also enjoy the views from the Greensand Ridge Walk, which runs through the grounds.

An attractive feature of the town is the **Alameda** (Spanish for a public walk), an avenue of lime trees 700 yards long, presented to the town in 1827 by Lord and Lady Holland.

Ampthill also boasts some fine Georgian and early-19th century buildings, especially in Church Street, Tudor almshouses and the large Church of St Andrew, which has a noble west tower. Inside can be found some 15th century brasses and a 17th century monument to Colonel Richard Nicholls that includes the cannon ball that killed him during the Battle of Sole Bay in 1672. Nicholls, who was born and lived most of his life in Ampthill, served the Stuart kings and was commander of the force that defeated the Dutch at New Amsterdam. He re-named it New York in honour of the Duke of York, later James II.

AROUND AMPTHILL

Flitton

2 miles SE of Ampthill off the A507

Next to the 15th century church is the **de Grey Mausoleum**, a series of rooms containing a remarkable collection of sculpted tombs and monuments to the de Grey family of Wrest Park.

Silsoe

3 miles SE of Ampthill off A6

Although the manor of Wrest has been held by the de Grey family since the late 13th century, the house standing today dates from the 1830s. Built for the 1st Earl de Grey from the designs of a French architect, it follows faithfully the style of a French chateau of the previous century. Parts of the house at **Wrest Park** are open to the public but the real glory is the gardens. They are a living history of English gardening from 1700 to 1850 and are the work of Charles Bridgeman, with later adaptations by Capability Brown. The layout remains basically formal, with a full range of garden appointments in the grand manner - there

Wrest Park, Silsoe

Toddington Manor Gardens

Park Road, Toddington, Bedfordshire LU5 6HJ
Tel: 01525 872576 Fax: 01525 874555
website: toddingtonmanor.co.uk

Toddington Manor Gardens have been developed by the owners Sir Neville and Lady Bowman-Shaw into one of the most attractive in the county. Amid the six acres of gardens and 20 acres of woods are a lovely lime avenue leading into a cherry walk, a walled garden with beds of delphiniums and peonies, a fine herb garden, old-fashioned roses and a very impressive double herbaceous border. There's also a wild garden and three small ponds with nets and buckets available for children to go dipping. Other attractions include rare breeds of livestock, plants for sale, a picnic area and a magnificent collection of over 100 vintage tractors. Open noon to 5pm 1 May to 31 August; closed Sunday.

is a Chinese bridge, an artificial lake, a classical temple, and a rustic ruin.

Two buildings of particular interest are the Baroque Banqueting House, designed by Thomas Archer, which forms a focus of the view from the house across the lake, and the Bowling Green House, dating from about 1740 and said to have been designed by Batty Langley, who was best known as a writer of architectural books for country builders and built little himself. Immediately beside the house is an intricate French-style garden, with an orangery by the French architect Cléphane, flower beds, statues, and fountains. The village of Silsoe itself boasts more than 130 listed buildings.

Toddington

5 miles S of Ampthill on A5120

Situated on a hill above the River Flitt, this village is often overlooked, particularly by those travelling the nearby M1 who think only of the service station of the same name. However, the village is an attractive place, with cottages and elegant houses grouped around the village green. Unfortunately all that remains of **Toddington Manor** is a small oblong building with a hipped roof which is believed to be the Elizabethan kitchen of the large quadrangular house that was built here in around 1570. Toddington is a place which makes much of its folklore and is host to Morris dancers in the summer and mummers who tour the village providing traditional entertainment at Christmas. Local legend also has it that a witch lives under Conger Hill - which is actually a motte that would, at one time, have had a castle on top - and, on Shrove Tuesday, the children put their ears to the ground to listen to her frying pancakes.

Ridgmont

4 miles W of Ampthill on the A507

Part of the Woburn Estate, this is a typical estate village where the owners of the land (in this case the Bedford family) provided the houses and other buildings. Here the workers lived in gabled, redbrick houses. The church, designed by George Gilbert Scott, was also built at the expense of the estate.

Woburn

6 miles W of Ampthill on the A4012

First recorded as a Saxon hamlet in the 10th century, and again mentioned in the Domesday Book, Woburn grew into a small market town after the founding of

WALK NUMBER 2

Around Woburn

Distance:	5.5 miles (8.8 kilometres)
Typical time:	150 mins
Height gain:	37 metres
Map:	Explorer 192
Walk:	www.walkingworld.com ID:1122
Contributor:	Tony Brotherton

Access Information:

Park in free village car park in (where else?) Park Street.

Additional Information:

The deer-park boasts nine species of deer, including the rare Pere David's.

Description:

A gentle walk from the attractive village of Woburn, traversing the 3,000-acre Bedford Estate and deer-park and visiting the Abbey.

Features:

Hills or Fells, Lake/Loch, Pub, Toilets, Play Area, Church, Stately Home, Wildlife, Birds, Flowers, Great Views, Butterflies, Food Shop

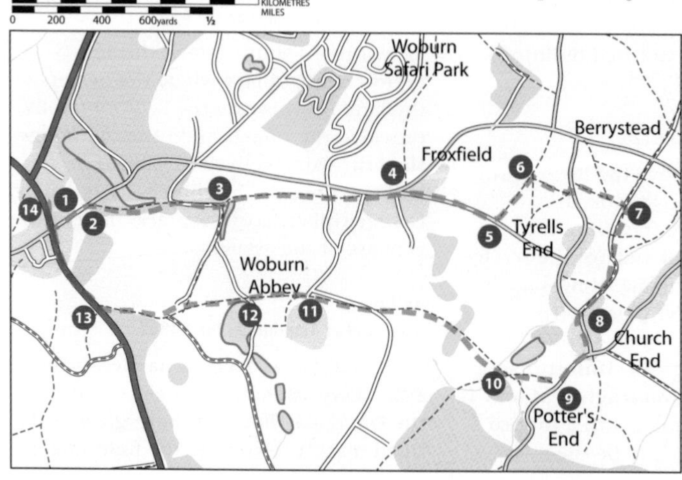

Walk Directions:

1 From Woburn Village car park opposite the Church of St Mary the Virgin, turn right down Park Street to reach cattle grid at lodge.

2 Take footpath signed right immediately after lodge, soon to pass lake on left. Continue as far as drive at Park Farm. Go up the drive and to left of further buildings, over staggered cross-paths, to reach long narrow strip of water.

3 Skirt the water to the left and proceed half-left across open parkland. Make for a lone tree near the top of a small rise, to meet the road at the vehicle entrance to Woburn Abbey at the crest of the rise. Continue downhill alongside the road to reach the estate gates before thebuildings at Froxfield.

4 The footpath signed to the left leads towards safari park. Our route lies to the right on the road leading to Milton Bryan, as far as cottages at Hills End and the footpath signed to the left.

5 Take the path and enter field by stile, then cross on the obvious path to reach the orange-topped waymark post. Keep ahead through scrub and at next such post turn to the right to reach a footbridge.

6 Cross footbridge and choose footpath leading straight ahead in next field. Enter via stile, gravel drive leading to lane. Here go left, past Helford House, to footpath off to right. Take footpath along left-hand edge of field and enter hedged path. Follow hedge boundary to right in next field. After next waymark post, path joins crossing track - Greensand Ridge Walk, which we follow back to Woburn.

7 Turn right along Greensand Ridge Walk, which emerges onto road at Church End, Eversholt.

8 Opposite church of St John the Baptist is Green Man public house, your handy halfway hostelry! Continue through village and at T-junction turn right on road. Just before bend, divert right through gate at Greensand Ridge Walk sign.

9 Follow path diagonally across field, cross stream at double stile and pass lake to right, to reach cross-paths and signpost.

10 Now keep ahead, shortly to re-cross stream twice more, to arrive at stile. Follow path across field and pass through narrow belt of trees, then proceed uphill through young plantation. Greensand Ridge Walk continues uphill and into deer park, then descends to path junction after car park and entrance to Abbey.

11 Keep ahead, soon to see large pond at left, with two smaller ponds on right.

12 At crossing track, look back for fine view of frontage of Woburn Abbey. Continue ahead to pass between ponds on narrow causeway and cross parkland on route delineated by occasional small posts. Leave deer park via gate at corner of woods to enter fenced path, leading to exit at A4012 road.

13 Now turn right to return to Woburn Village. At crossroads turn right into Park Street to finish walk at car park.

14 Alternatively, continue along main street to tourist information office housed in redundant church.

the Cistercian Abbey here in 1145. All but destroyed by fire in 1720, this pretty village has retained many of the pleasant Georgian houses that were built subsequently and the attractive shop fronts give the place a cheerful air. Situated at a major crossroads, between London and the north and Cambridge and Oxford, Woburn also saw prosperity during the stagecoach era and by 1851 there were 32 inns here.

Woburn Abbey (see panel below), ancestral home of the Dukes of Bedford, is renowned for its art treasures, its deer park and its antiques centre. The estate was given to the 1st Earl of Bedford in the will of Henry VIII but the original building was partially destroyed by fire and the present stately home dates mainly from the 1700s. Its extraordinary stock of treasures includes paintings by Van Dyck, Gainsborough, Reynolds and

Woburn Abbey

Woburn, Bedfordshire MK17 9WA
Tel: 01525 290666 Fax: 01525 290271
e-mail: enquiries@woburnabbey.co.uk
website: www.woburnabbey.co.uk

Built on the site of a Cistercian monastery founded in 1145 by Hugh de Bolebec, **Woburn Abbey** was given to the 1st Earl of Bedford in the will of Henry VIII and has been the home of the Dukes of Bedford for over 400 years. The original building was partially destroyed by fire and the present stately home dates mainly from the 18th century. Woburn Abbey houses one of the most impressive and important private art and furniture collections on view to the public.

Over 50 dealers are housed under one roof in a reconstruction of city streets in bygone days, with genuine 18th century shop façades that were rescued from demolition many years ago. Another attraction within the estate boundaries is the deer park, which, like the private gardens, was landscaped by Humphry Repton for the 6th Duke. Visitors to this marvellous place will also find gift shops, a pottery and a coffee shop. A mile from the Abbey is one of the country's leading animal attractions, Woburn Safari Park, among whose residents are lions, tigers, elephants, hippos, rhinos, eland, zebra and sea lions.

the famous Armada portrait of Elizabeth I by George Gower. The Venetian Room showcases 21 views of Venice by Canaletto while other rooms display outstanding collections of English and French furniture, porcelain and antique statuary. Another attraction on site is the Woburn Abbey Antiques Centre with more than 50 dealers housed in a reconstruction of city streets of bygone days that includes genuine 18th century shop facades rescued from demolition.

A short distance north of the Abbey is the **Wild Animal Kingdom and Leisure Park**, home to a vast range of animals including eland, zebra, hippos, rhinos, lions, tigers, elephants and sea lions.

There are fine views of Woburn Abbey and of Milton Keynes from **Aspley Woods**, one of the largest areas of woodland in Bedfordshire, set between Woburn and Woburn Sands. The woods offer peace, tranquillity and miles of tracks for walking.

Marston Moretaine

3 miles NW of Ampthill off the A421.

Forest Centre & Marston Vale Country Park is a new amenity that offers a splendid day out in the countryside for all the family. The wetland habitat is home to a wide variety of wildlife, and the park provides excellent walking and cycling; bikes can be hired from the Forest Centre, which also has an interactive 'Discover the Forest' exhibition, café bar, art gallery, gift shop, free parking and children's play area.

BIGGLESWADE

On the banks of the River Ivel, which was once navigable through to the sea, Biggleswade was an important stop on the Great North Road stage coach routes and several old inns have survived from that period. The town also has another link with transport as the home of Dan Albone (1860-1906), the inventor of the modern bicycle. He produced a number of variants, including a tandem and a ladies cycle with a low crossbar and a skirt guard, but is best known for his racing cycle, which in 1888 set speed and endurance records with the doughty CP Mills in the saddle. Dan Albone's inventiveness was not confined to bicycles, as he also developed the Ivel Agricultural Tractor, the forerunner of the modern tractor.

The Swiss Garden

Old Warden Park, Biggleswade, Bedfordshire SG18 9ER
Tel: 01767 627666
website: www.theswissgarden.co.uk

The **Swiss Garden** is set in 10 acres where visitors can wander among splendid shrubs and rare trees, at the centre of which is the Swiss Cottage. It brings together tiny follies, ornate bridges and winding ponds. Visitors can discover the breathtaking fernery and grotto, or lose themselves on the serpentine walks. In season the early bulbs and primroses, the rhododendrons and the old-fashioned roses make wonderful displays. Old Warden is a place of many other attractions, notably the Shuttleworth Collection. The Swiss Garden is licensed to hold civil wedding ceremonies. The Garden is open from 10am to 6pm on Sundays and from 1pm to 6pm every other day from March to September. Also open Sundays (and New Years Day) in January, February and October from 10am to 4pm. No dogs.

Sandy

3 miles N of Biggleswade on A1

The sandy soil that gave the town its name helped it rise to fame as a market gardening centre in the 16th century. The 14th century Church of St Swithun contains an interesting statue of Captain Sir William Peel, third son of Sir Robert Peel, famous Prime Minister and founder of the Police Force, who was awarded one of the first Victoria crosses for heroic action in the Crimean War.

Through the town runs the **Greensands Ridge Walk**, a long distance walk, which covers some 40 miles across the county. A little way southeast of the town, at **The Lodge**, are the headquarters of the Royal Society for the Protection of Birds and a nature reserve set in over 107 acres of open heath and woodland. As well as offering a great deal to those interested in birds, the formal gardens surrounding the mansion house were first created in the 1870s and were restored in the 1930s by Sir Malcolm Stewart and are well worth visiting in their own right. Also on the site is a newly developed wildlife garden.

Moggerhanger

5 miles N of Biggleswade off the A1

Grade I listed Moggerhanger Park was designed by Sir John Soane, architect of London's Bank of England, and is set among gardens and parkland designed by Humphry Repton. The house and grounds are currently undergoing major restoration but is scheduled to re-open to the public in September 2004.

Blunham

5 miles N of Biggleswade off the A1

This quiet rural village was the home of the poet John Donne while he was rector here from 1622 until his death in 1632, a post he held while also Dean of St Paul's in London. While he was convalescing here after a serious illness in 1523 he wrote *Devotions* which contains the immortal lines *No man is an island, entire of itself*, and *Never send to know for whom the bell tolls; it tolls for thee*. Donne divided his time between London and Blunham, where he stayed in the house opposite the parish church. He presented a chalice to the church in 1926 and inside can be seen some fine Norman work and interesting bosses.

Another building of interest is the Old Vicarage of 1874, constructed of startling yellow and orange bricks.

Old Warden

3 miles W of Biggleswade off B658

This charming village of thatched cottages along a single street has developed its unique character as a result of the influence of two local families. In the early 18th century, Sir Samuel Ongley, a London merchant, ship-owner, and former director of the South Sea Company, bought this country seat for himself and his family, who stayed here for over 200 years. In 1776 Robert Henley Ongley was awarded an Irish peerage for his services to Parliament, and it was his grandson, also called Robert, who created Old Warden as it is seen today. Taking the original estate cottages, and also building new ones, Sir Robert developed this rustic village and also embellished the 12th century church with some interesting Belgian woodwork.

However, Sir Robert's most famous piece of work is the **Swiss Garden** (see panel on page 46), laid out in the early 19th century. Within its 10 acres are ornate bridges, winding ponds, a breathtaking fernery and a number of tiny follies. In season, the early bulbs, primroses, rhododendrons and the old-fashioned roses make wonderful displays.

In 1872, his fortune depleted by the extensive building and remodelling programme, Sir Robert sold the estate to Joseph Shuttleworth. A partner in a firm of iron founders, it was Joseph who led the way to the development of the steam traction engine and also built the Jacobean-style mansion house that can still be seen today. A recently added attraction on the estate is the **English School of Falconry** at the **Bird of Prey & Conservation Centre**. 300 birds of various species are on public display and in addition to training and flying birds of prey from around the world, the centre is firmly committed to conservation and education, working with schools to create displays and informative workshops. Regular flying demonstration times are 11.30am for the 'Owl Experience', 1.30pm for 'Birds of the World' and 3pm for 'Out of Africa' featuring vultures, secretary birds, eagles, owls and falcons. The centre also features a children's adventure play ground, a picnic site, a restaurant and a gift shop.

Also at Old Warden is the famous **Shuttleworth Collection** of historic aircraft. In 1923, the 23-year-old Richard Ormande Shuttleworth, who had inherited the estate, bought his first aircraft, a de Havilland Moth. Over the years he added further planes to his collection. At the outbreak of World War II he naturally joined the RAF and was killed in a flying accident in 1940. After the war his mother put his collection on display and over the years other craft have been added. Housed in eight hangars, the collection now comprises some 40 airworthy craft, dating from 1909 to 1955. Throughout the year there are a number of flying days when these grand old planes take to the skies. Many of them have been featured in films such as *Reach for the Sky, The Battle of Britain* and *Pearl Harbour.* The planes are complemented by a number of vintage cars, motorcycles and bicycles.

A short drive north of Old Warden are two delightful villages, **Ickwell** and **Northill**. The former, which has a Maypole standing permanently on the green, is the birthplace of the great clock-maker Thomas Tompion. The 14th century Church of St Mary, which dominates the village of Northill, is noted for some fine 17th century glass and a one-handed clock built by

Tompion, who developed new techniques in the making of clocks and watches. Some of his clocks could run for a year without rewinding and he also made barometers and sundials, including pieces for King William III.

Houghton House

Stewartby

10 miles W of Biggleswade off the A421

Stewartby takes its name from Sir Malcolm Stewart, founder of the London Brick Company. He had the village built in 1926 to house employees at the nearby brickworks, which were thought to be the largest in the world and at their peak turned out 650 million bricks a year. The kiln took over a year to reheat after World War II.

Houghton Conquest

9 miles W of Biggleswade off the B530

That this village is home to Bedfordshire's largest parish church seems fitting, as Houghton Conquest also has links with the county's most famous son, John Bunyan. On a hilltop a little way south of the village stands **Houghton House**, reputedly the inspiration for the House Beautiful in *The Pilgrim's Progress*. Built in 1615 for Mary, Countess of Pembroke, the house was visited by Bunyan in his days as an itinerant tinker. The property later came into the hands of the Dukes of Bedford, one of whom had it partially demolished, and the ruins are now in the care of English Heritage.

Shefford

5 miles SW of Biggleswade on the A507

The small town of Shefford grew up, as the name suggests, around a sheep ford across the Rivers Hitt and Flitt and enjoyed a brief status as an inland port on the Ivel Navigation. This waterway was built primarily to bring coal from Kings Lynn by way of the River Ouse. In North Bridge Street a wall plaque marks the house of the pastoral poet Robert Bloomfield, a poor farm labourer and shoemaker who found fame when he published *The Farmer's Boy* in 1800. The poet, who died, as he had lived, in extreme poverty, is buried in the churchyard at nearby Campton.

In Hitchin Road is the **Hoo Hill Maze**, constructed with hedges more than 6ft high. It stands in an orchard with a picnic site and plenty of space for children to romp.

Shefford is also the starting point of the 21-mile-long cycle route, the **Jubilee Way**, a circular route that passes through undulating landscape and picturesque villages.

Lower Stondon

6 miles S of Biggleswade off the A600

Lower Stondon attracts visitors from near and far to its renowned **Transport Museum** (see panel on page 50) and garden centre. The museum contains a marvellous collection of more than 400 exhibits covering all forms of transport –

Stondon Transport Museum

Station Road, Lower Stondon, Henlow, Bedfordshire SG16 6JN
Tel: 01462 850339 Fax: 01462 850824
e-mail: info@transportmuseum.co.uk
website: www.transportmuseum.co.uk

Stondon Transport Museum invites visitors to take a trip down memory lane with its marvellous collection of over 400 exhibits. A hobby that got out of hand is how curator and director Maureen Hird describes the enterprise started by John Saunders and now one of the leading attractions in Bedfordshire. John is a former design engineer whose design work has included a one-man submarine and an amphibious caravan. Most of the exhibits are displayed under cover in a small area, thus keeping walking to a minimum and ensuring that the museum is accessible to all ages.

The exhibits cover all forms of transport, from motorcycles to helicopters, and spans the period from the beginning of the 20th century to the recent past. One of the greatest appeals of the collection is that it includes vehicles that are not usually museum pieces, among them a Bedford Dormobile open truck, a Jowett Javelin and a London bus. The centrepiece of the collection is a life-size replica of Captain Cook's bark *Endeavour*, in which he undertook one of his most important voyages of discovery, in 1768. The ship was constructed using the original plans. Regular guided tours of the ship take place each day, and the whole fascinating museum is open from 10am to 5pm seven days a week. A café on site sells refreshments and snacks throughout the day. The museum is located on the A600 next to Mount Pleasant golf course.

from motorcycles to helicopters, from a Jowett Javelin to a London bus – and covers the period from the early 1900s to the recent past. The centrepiece of the collection is a full size replica of Captain Cook's bark, *Endeavour*, in which he undertook one of his most important journeys in 1768. Guided tours of the museum are available and there's a café selling light refreshments.

BEDFORD

This lively cosmopolitan town owes its origins and development to the River Great Ouse which remains one of the most important and attractive features of the town. Bedford was already a thriving market place before the Norman Conquest and its market is still held on Wednesday and Saturday each week. There's also a farmer's market once a month and, in the summer months, a gourmet and speciality food market on Thursdays, a flower and garden market on Fridays, and an antiques and collectors market on Sundays.

The town's oldest visible structure is **Castle Mound**, all that remains of a fortress built here shortly after the battle of Hastings but destroyed in 1224. A regeneration project is currently under way to provide landscaped gardens here.

The **Church of St Peter de Merton**, Saxon in origin, boasts a fine Norman south doorway that was not actually intended for this building but was brought here from the Church of St Peter in Dunstable. St Peter's is not Bedford's main church: this is **St Paul's Church** in the centre of St Paul's Square, a mainly 14th and 15th century building, with some interesting monuments and brasses and a stone pulpit from which John Wesley preached in 1758. Outside the church is a statue of one of the best-known sons of Bedford, John Howard, an 18th century nonconformist landowner who denounced the appalling conditions in jails and prison ships. His name lives on in the Howard League for Penal Reform.

Bedford's most famous son, Bunyan was born just south of the town, in Elstow, but lived – and was twice imprisoned – in Bedford in the 1660s and 1670s. The son of a tinsmith, Bunyan followed the same trade as his father and so was able to travel the countryside more than most people of that time. In the 1650s, Bunyan met John Gifford, the then pastor of the Independent Congregation which held its meetings at St John's Church. It was their lengthy discussions that led to Bunyan's conversion and he was baptised shortly afterwards by Gifford in a backwater that leads off the Great Ouse. In 1660 Bunyan was arrested for preaching without a licence. He was to spend 12 years in goal, time he put to good use by writing *Grace Abounding*, his spiritual autobiography. But it was during a second imprisonment, in 1676, that he began writing his most famous work, *The Pilgrim's Progress*. This inspired allegory of the way to salvation still entrances even non-believers with the beauty and simplicity of its language. Following his release from prison in 1672, Bunyan was elected pastor of the Independent Congregation. The church seen today was constructed in 1849 and the magnificent bronze doors, with illustrations from *Pilgrim's Progress*, were given to the church by the Duke of Bedford in 1676. Within the church is also the **Bunyan Museum** (free) which tells graphically the story of the man as well as the times through which he lived. Among the many displays are the jug in which his daughter Mary brought him soup whilst in prison, his chair, his tinker's anvil, and the violin and flute which he made in prison. Another tribute to Bunyan in the town is **Bunyan's Statue**, which was presented to the town in 1874 by the Duke of Bedford. Made of bronze, the statue is the work of Sir JE Boehm; around the pedestal of the 9ft figure, which weighs more than three tons, are three bronze panels depicting scenes from *Pilgrim's Progress*.

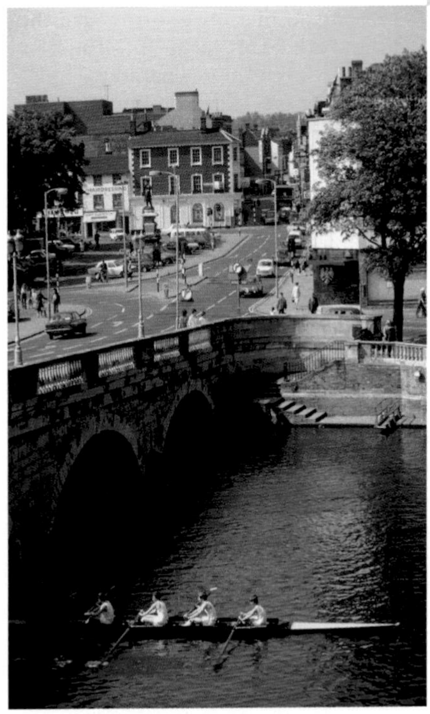

Bridge over the River Ouse, Bedford

Beside the river and running through the heart of the town are the **Bedford Embankment Gardens**, which provide a year-round display of plants. Close by is also the **Priory Country Park**, an area of 206 acres with a diverse habitat, which represents the flood meadows, reed beds and woodland that once surrounded the town. In Park Road North, Hill Rise Wildlife Area is a site for nature conservation specialising in butterflies, amphibians and small mammals.

For an insight into the history of the town and surrounding area the **Bedford Museum** is well worth a visit. Among the many interesting displays is a piece of wall which shows the construction of the wattle walls that were an essential building technique in the 14th century.

Housed within the unlikely combination of a Victorian mansion and an adjoining modern gallery, the **Cecil Higgins Art Gallery** was started in 1949 by a wealthy Bedford brewery family. It contains an internationally renowned collection of watercolours, prints, and drawings as well as some fine glass, ceramics, and furniture. The gallery hosts several important exhibitions each year. The permanent display includes works by Turner, Gainsborough, Picasso and Matisse and a needle panel entitled 'Bunyan's Dream'. This was designed by Edward Bawden in 1977 to commemorate the tercentenary of the publication of *Pilgrim's Progress*, the 350th anniversary of John Bunyan's birth and the Queen's Silver Jubilee. Other contemporary work can be seen at the **Bedford Creative Arts Gallery** which showcases the visual arts, including film, photography and animation.

A building with more modern connections is the **Corn Exchange** in St Paul's Square, from where Colonel Glenn Miller frequently broadcast during World War II. A bust of the bandleader who gave the world *In the Mood* and *Moonlight Serenade* stands outside the Exchange, and in 1994 a plaque was unveiled on the 50th anniversary of his mysterious disappearance over the English Channel.

AROUND BEDFORD

Elstow

1 mile S of Bedford off the A6

John Bunyan connections are everywhere in the picturesque village of Elstow. The cottage where he was born in 1628 no longer stands, but its site is marked by a stone erected in Festival of Britain Year, 1951. The **Abbey Church of St Helena and St Mary** has two renowned stained glass windows, one depicting scenes from *Pilgrim's Progress*, the other scenes from the Holy War. Here, too, are the font where Bunyan was christened in 1628 and the Communion Table used when he attended service. Bunyan's mother, father and sister are buried in the churchyard. The church also tells the story of the ill-fated R101 airship (see under Cardington), and there's a handsome memorial in the churchyard.

Elstow's notable buildings include a charming row of Tudor cottages and **Moot Hall** which was built in the 15th century. It served as a place for hearing disputes and as a store for equipment for the village fair. Restored by Bedfordshire County Council, it is now a museum depicting life in 17th century England with particular reference to Bunyan.

Cardington

1 mile E of Bedford off the A603

The Whitbread brewing family is closely connected with Cardington. The first Samuel Whitbread was born in the village in 1720, and it was another Whitbread, also Samuel, who restored the church and endowed the red-brick almshouses of 1787 overlooking the green.

But Cardington is best known for the two giant hangars that dominate the skyline. Built in 1917 and 1927 to construct and house the airships that were once thought to be the future of flying, they are best known as the birthplace of the R100 and the R101. The R101 first took off from Cardington in October 1929 with 52 people on board for a five-hour flight over the southeast. The passengers enjoyed a four-course lunch in the luxurious dining saloon and were amazed at the airship's quietness - they could hear the sounds of traffic and trains below. In July 1930 the R101 started her maiden flight across the Atlantic and tied up in Montreal after an uneventful flight of 77 hours. In October of that year the world's biggest airship left the hangars at Cardington for her first trip to India. Disaster struck not long into the journey when the R101 crashed into a hillside near Beauvais in France. Forty-four people, including the Air Secretary Lord Thomson of Cardington, died in the crash, which was believed to have been caused at least in part by lashing rain that caused the ship to dip suddenly. The Church of St Mary contains memorials to both Samuel Whitbreads, and in the churchyard extension is the tomb of those who perished in the R101 disaster.

Wilden

4 miles NE of Bedford off the A421

Bedford Butterfly Park has quickly become one of the county's leading family attractions. It stands in 10 acres of land untouched by modern farming practices and specially selected by its founder Andrew Green. Some 60 varieties of wildflowers flourish here, an irresistible attraction for 60 species of butterfly. The Wondrous World exhibit displays the variety of life found in rain forests and other attractions include an adventure playground, tea room and gift shop.

Stevington

4 miles NW of Bedford off A428

This is a typical English village with a church that was certainly here at the time of the Domesday survey, a village cross decorated with capitals and a large finial, and a holy well that attracted visitors in the Middle Ages. However, the most important building in the village is the **Post Mill**, the only one of the county's 12 remaining windmills that still retains its sails. Dating from the 1770s, the mill continued to operate commercially until 1936, having been rebuilt in 1921. Extensively restored in the 1950s, it is in full working order today. Though milling was an important part of village life here for many years, lace making too was a thriving industry and mat makers also settled here, taking advantage of the rushes growing on the banks of the nearby River Ouse.

Bromham

2 miles W of Bedford off A428

This quiet residential village has a splendid ancient bridge with no fewer than 26 arches. Close to the river is a watermill that dates back to the 17th century. Now fully restored and in working order, **Bromham Mill** is also home to displays of natural history, a gallery with regularly changing exhibitions of contemporary craftwork and fine art, and a tea room overlooking the river where, if you're lucky, you can watch kingfishers diving from the bank.

Charles I is known to have stayed at Bromham Hall, the home of Royalist Sir Lewis Dyve, who made his escape from the house during the Civil War by swimming the river.

Harrold

7 miles NW of Bedford off the A428

A typical country village with an old

bridge and causeway, an octagonal market house and an old circular lock-up that was last used in the 19th century. Close by is the **Harrold-Odell Country Park** (see panel below), which covers 144 acres of landscaped lakes, river banks and water meadows that are home to a wealth of plant, animal and bird life.

Hinwick

10 miles NW of Bedford off the A6

Built between 1709 and 1714, **Hinwick House** is a charming Queen Anne building that is still home to the descendants of the Orlebar family for whom it was constructed. Occasionally open to visitors, this delightful brownstone house with details picked out in lighter coloured stone has a particularly pleasing entrance hall and an interesting collection of furniture and paintings.

Yielden

10 miles N of Bedford off the A6

A village on the River Til, guarded by the earthworks of a long ruined castle. Mentioned in the Domesday Book, Yielden Castle, of which only an oblong motte, two large baileys and stone foundations can be seen, is reputed to have been built on the site of the battle between the Romans and the Iceni in which the warrior queen Boadicea (Boudicca) was killed. On one Christmas Day John Bunyan came to the village to preach in the church, as a result of which the incumbent vicar, William Bell, was removed from his post for allowing Bunyan this freedom.

BUCKINGHAMSHIRE

The south of the county, with the River Thames as its southern boundary, lies almost entirely within the chalk range of the Chiltern Hills, most of which is classed as an Area of Outstanding Natural Beauty. The county town since the 18th century has been Aylesbury, the market centre for the attractive Vale of Aylesbury, which runs from the Chilterns in the south to Buckingham in the north. Here, the visitor will discover a

Harrold-Odell Country Park

Carlton Road, Harrold, Bedfordshire MK43 7DS
Tel: 01234 720016 (Park) 01234 720002 (Café)

Set in the beautiful countryside of north Bedfordshire, **Harrold-Odell Country Park** is an ideal place to spend the day. Two lakes cover half the park's 144 acres and water meadows, riverside and woodland make up the rest. The variety of scenery and habitat provide a peaceful location for walking, picnicking, watching wildlife or just relaxing. A surfaced path around the main lake is suitable for all visitors and there are informal paths through the water meadows and nature sanctuary.

The park is a haven for wildlife, the lakes attracting both winter wildfowl and migrating summer birds. Wildflowers flourish in the water meadows and nature sanctuary through the spring and summer. The Visitor Centre is home to the Café in the Park, where visitors can enjoy delicious home-made treats including summer salads, winter soups and irresistible cakes, all made with as many organic and locally grown ingredients as possible. The Centre has an information room with displays about the park and the local area. The Centre has wheelchair access and baby changing facilities, and parking is free. Dogs are welcome in most areas, provided they are with a responsible owner. The park is signposted from Harrold and Carlton villages.

rural patchwork of secluded countryside, woodland and valleys, waterways, charming villages and busy market towns. A thousand miles of footpaths include the ancient Ridgeway, and the quiet country lanes and gentle undulations make cycling a real pleasure; the Vale is at the heart of the new National Cycle Network. The area around the former county town of Buckingham is perhaps the least discovered part of the county, still chiefly rural, with a wealth of attractive villages and a number of fine houses, including Ascott House, a former Rothschild residence; Claydon House, where Florence Nightingale was a frequent visitor; Winslow Hall, designed by Wren; and Stowe, where the deer park is being restored to its former glory. In this area are also two outstanding churches, the Saxon Church of All Saints at Wing and St Michael's Church at Stewkley, one of the finest Norman churches in the whole country. The northern region of the county is dominated by the new town of Milton Keynes, developed in the 1960s but incorporating many much older villages.

Milton's Cottage

CHALFONT ST GILES

Among the various ancient buildings of interest in this archetypal English village there is an Elizabethan mansion, The Vache, that was the home of friends of Captain Cook and, in the grounds is a monument to the famous seafarer. However, by far the most famous building in Chalfont St Giles, with an equally famous resident, is **Milton's Cottage**. John Milton moved to this 16th century cottage, found for him by his former pupil Thomas Ellwood, in 1665 to escape the plague in London. Though Milton moved back to London in 1666, he wrote *Paradise Lost* and began work on its sequel, *Paradise Regained*, while taking refuge in the village. The only house lived in by the poet to have survived, the cottage and its garden have been preserved as they were at the time Milton was resident. The building is now home to a museum which includes collections of important first editions of Milton's works and a portrait of the poet by Sir Godfrey Kneller.

Another fascinating and unusual place to visit in the village is the **Chiltern Open Air Museum**, which rescues buildings of historic or architectural importance due to be demolished from across the Chilterns region and re-erects them on its 45 acre site. The buildings rescued by the museum are used to house and display artefacts and implements that are appropriate to the building's original use and history. Also on the museum site is a series of fields farmed using medieval methods where, among the historic crops, organic woad is grown, from which indigo dye is extracted for use in dyeing demonstrations. Madame Tussaud, famous for her exhibitions in London, started her waxworks here in the village, and another well-known resident was Bertram Mills of circus fame. His tomb stands beside the war memorial in the churchyard of St Giles.

AROUND CHALFONT ST GILES

Jordans

1 mile S of Chalfont St Giles off the A40

This secluded village reached down a quiet country lane is famous as the burial place of William Penn, Quaker and founder of Pennsylvania. He and members of his family are buried in the graveyard outside the Quaker meeting house that is among the earliest to be found in the country. In the grounds of nearby Old Jordans Farm is the Mayflower Barn, said to have been constructed from the timbers of the ship that took the Pilgrim Fathers to America.

Chalfont St Peter

2 miles S of Chalfont St Giles on the A413

Now a commuter town, Chalfont St Peter dates back to the 7th century and, as its name means 'the spring where the calves come to drink', there is a long history here of raising cattle in the surrounding lush meadows. First mentioned in 1133, the parish Church of St Peter was all but destroyed when its steeple collapsed in 1708. The building seen today dates from that time as it was rebuilt immediately after the disaster.

Housed in a barn at Skippings Farm is the **Hawk and Owl Trust's National Education and Exhibition Centre**. Dedicated to conserving wild birds of prey in their natural habitats, the Trust concerns itself with practical research, creative conservation and imaginative educational programmes.

Stoke Poges

6 miles S of Chalfont St Giles off the A355

The ploughman homeward plods
his weary way
And leaves the world to
darkness and to me.

It was in the churchyard of this surprisingly still rural village that Thomas Gray was inspired to pen his *Elegy Written in a Country Churchyard*. He often visited Stoke Poges to see his mother and aunt who lived in a large late-Georgian house built for the grandson of the famous Quaker, William Penn. Gray lies buried with his mother in the church, and, to the east, is the imposing **Gray Monument**, designed by James Wyatt and erected in 1799. The Church of St Giles itself is very handsome and dates from the 13th century but perhaps its most interesting feature is the unusual medieval bicycle depicted in one of the stained glass windows. Behind the church is an Elizabethan manor house where Elizabeth I was entertained and Charles I imprisoned.

Beaconsfield

3 miles SW of Chalfont St Giles on the A40

This is very much a town in two parts: the old town, dating back to medieval times and, to the north, the new town which grew up following the construction of the Metropolitan line into central London and consisting chiefly of between the wars housing. The old town is best known for its wealth of literary connections. The poet and orator Edmund Waller was born in the nearby village of Coleshill in 1606 and had his family home just outside Beaconsfield. His best-known lines are perhaps the patriotic *Others may use the ocean as their road / Only the English make it their abode.* Waller's tomb in the churchyard of St

Mary and All Saints is marked by a very tall, sharply pointed obelisk with a tribute from fellow poet John Dryden. The church itself is one of the finest in the county and also contains the grave of the statesman and political theorist Edmund Burke (1729-1797). Beaconsfield was also the home of the writer of the *Father Brown* books GK Chesterton (his grave is in the nearby Catholic church), the poet Robert Frost and the much loved children's author Enid Blyton.

For a unique step back in time to the 1930s, or for anyone wanting to feel like Gulliver in Lilliput, a trip to the model village of **Bekonscot** is a must. The oldest model village in the world, Bekonscot was begun in the 1920s by Roland Callingham, a London accountant, who started by building models in his garden. As the number of buildings and models grew, Callingham purchased more land and, with the aid of a friend from Ascot who added a model railway, created the village seen today. When the model village first opened, people started throwing coins into buckets for charity and, even today, all surplus profits go to charity. Enid Blyton's house Green Hedges is depicted in Bekonscot, and she wrote a story about two children who visit the model village.

South of Beaconsfield, on the other side of the M40 at **Wooburn Common**, an entertaining day out is guaranteed at **Odds Farm Park**, home to many rare and interesting animals. The park was created particularly with children in mind and the regular events include pigs' tea time, pat-a-pet, bottle feeding lambs and goat milking. As one of 20 approved rare breed centres in the country, the farm combines the family attractions with the breeding and conservation of many of Britain's rarest farm animals.

Burnham Beeches

5 miles SW of Chalfont St Giles off the A355

A stretch of land bought in 1880 by the Corporation of the City of London for use in perpetuity by the public, and since then a favourite place for Londoners to relax. Burnham Beeches was designated a National Nature Reserve in 1993 and this extensive area of ancient woodland and heathland includes an important collection of old beeches and pollarded oaks.

Burnham Beeches in Autumn

Taplow

8 miles SW of Chalfont St Giles off the A4

The name is of Taplow is derived from Taeppa, a Saxon warrior whose grand burial site high above the Thames was excavated in 1883. Nothing is known of Taeppa himself, but the items discovered at the site are on display in the British Museum. To the north of the village lies the country house of **Cliveden**, once the home of Lady Nancy Astor, the first woman to take her seat as a Member of Parliament. The first house on the site was built in 1666 for the Duke of Buckingham, but the present magnificent mansion, most of which is now a hotel, dates from the 19th century. The splendid grounds include a great formal parterre with fountains, temples and statuary, a water garden and a wonderful rose garden. Some of the great names in architecture and garden design had a hand in the Cliveden of today: the house and terrace are the work of Sir Charles Barry, the rose garden was designed by Sir Geoffrey Jellicoe, and the renowned Italian country house architect Giacomo Leoni was responsible for the **Octagonal Temple**, now a chapel, where the American-born millionaire William Waldorf Astor, his son Waldorf and the ashes of Waldorf's wife Nancy are buried.

Penn

4 miles NW of Chalfont St Giles on the B474

A centre of the tiling industry after the Norman Conquest, Penn provided the flooring for Windsor Castle, the Palace of Westminster and many churches. But the village is best known as the ancestral home of William Penn, the Quaker and American pioneer, and in the village church are several memorials to the family. In the churchyard of Holy Trinity is the grave of the diplomat spy Donald Maclean, who died in Moscow in 1983. His ashes, contained in an urn decorated with a hammer and sickle, were brought back to England by his brother and buried in the family grave.

Amersham

3 miles N of Chalfont St Giles on the A413

Another town with a split personality. Top Amersham is a thriving commercial centre; Old Amersham is a popular tourist spot with a wide sweeping High Street, half-timbered buildings and picturesque period cottages. Set beside the River Misbourne, the Old Town boasts many fine old buildings, including Sir William Drake's Market Hall of 1682 and the Church of St Mary with some fine stained glass and monuments to the Drake family. The Old Town is well-known for its shopping – there's a wide selection of antique and craft shops, designer boutiques, and an impressive range of restaurants, snack bars and coaching inns.

The Romans were farming around Amersham in the 3rd and 4th centuries, the Saxons called it Agmodesham and to the Normans it was Elmondesham. So the town has plenty of history, much of which is told in the **Amersham Museum**.

The town was an important staging post in coaching days, and the Crown Hotel, one of the many coaching inns here, was featured in the film *Four Weddings and a Funeral*. Close to the town is Gore Hill, the site of a battle between the Danes and the Saxons in 921. It is recorded that in 1666 the Great Fire of London could be seen raging from the hill.

Chenies

3 miles E of Amersham off the A404

This picturesque village, with a pretty green surrounded by an old school, a chapel and a 15th century parish church, is also home to **Chenies Manor**, a fascinating 15th century manor house. Originally the home of the Earls (later Dukes) of Bedford, before they moved to Woburn, this attractive building has stepped gables and elaborately patterned high brick chimneys. Built by the architect who enlarged Hampton Court for Henry VIII, the house played host not only to the king but also to his daughter Elizabeth I, whose favourite oak tree still stands in the garden. Naturally, there is a ghost here, that of none other than Henry, whose footsteps can be heard as he drags his ulcerated leg around the manor house in an attempt to catch Catherine Howard in the act of adultery with one of his entourage, Tom Culpeper. The house has much to offer, not just from the exterior but also inside where there are tapestries, furniture and a collection of antique dolls, but the elaborate gardens should not be overlooked. Among the delights are a Tudor style sunken garden, some fine topiary, a turf maze, a kitchen garden and a physic garden with a variety of herbs that were used for both medicinal and culinary purposes.

HIGH WYCOMBE

The largest town in Buckinghamshire, High Wycombe is traditionally known for the manufacture of chairs and, in particular, the famous Windsor design. It is still a centre of furniture manufacture today as well as being a pleasant town in which to live for those commuting to London. Originally an old Chilterns gap market town, High Wycombe still has several old buildings of note. The **Little Market House** was designed by Robert Adams in 1761 and is of a rather curious octagonal shape, while the 18th century Guildhall is the annual venue for a traditional ceremony showing a healthy scepticism for politicians when the mayor and councillors are publicly weighed - to see if they have become fat at the expense of the citizens.

Located in an 18th century house with a flint facade, the **Wycombe Museum** has displays which give the visitor an excellent idea of the work and crafts of the local people over the years. There is, of course, a superb collection of chairs, including the famous Windsor chair. Several skills and several woods were involved in the making of this classic chair: bodgers used the ubiquitous beech for the legs; benders shaped ash for the bowed backs; and bottomers made use of the sturdy elm for the seats.

In the landscaped grounds of the museum is a medieval motte which would normally indicate that a castle once stood here but, in this case, the structure was probably little more than a wooden tower. The oldest standing building in the town is All Saints Church, a large, fine building dating from the 11th century.

AROUND HIGH WYCOMBE

Marlow

4 miles S of High Wycombe on the A4155

An attractive commuter town on the banks of the Thames, Marlow is famous for its suspension bridge built in 1832 to

The River Thames, Marlow

The Vanilla Pod

31 West Street, Marlow, Buckinghamshire SL7 2LS
Tel: 01628 898101 Fax: 01628 898108
e-mail: info@thevanillapod.co.uk
website: www.thevanillapod.co.uk

Located just off Marlow's High Street, **The Vanilla Pod** occupies a charming old house that was once the home of the poet TS Eliot. This outstanding restaurant owes its impressive reputation to the culinary skills of Aberdeen-born Michael Macdonald whose inspiration to become a chef was, he says, because "as a working family I used to be first home so one of my chores was to prepare dinner for the family". He went on to hone his skills at Keats Restaurant and Chez Nico then won a four-month scholarship in France. On his return he worked at La Tante Clare in London where Gordon Ramsey was, at the time, Sous Chef. Before becoming head chef at Danesfield House Hotel he also worked for Eric Chavot at The Interlude De Chavot.

His cuisine features modern English and French dishes – his own two favourites are roasted scallops on red onions braised in red wine, and vanilla poached pear with a vanilla gastric. He changes his menu every month to make the most of seasonal produce at its best and allows him to put different and exciting combinations together. The restaurant itself is an intimate, cosy beamed dining room where everything is beautifully presented and the dining experience made even more pleasurable by the team of French waiters who have been described as "charm personified".

the design of Tierney Clarke, who built a similar bridge linking Buda and Pest across the Danube. The High Street is lined with elegant houses, and Marlow has a good supply of riverside pubs; in one of them, the Two Brewers, Jerome K Jerome wrote his masterpiece *Three Men in a Boat*. Other literary connections abound: Mary Shelley completed *Frankenstein* while living here after her marriage to the poet Percy Bysshe Shelley and TS Eliot lived for a while in West Street, as did the author Thomas Love Peacock while writing *Nightmare Abbey*. Marlow hosts an annual regatta and is one of the places the Swan Uppers visit each year counting and marking the swans belonging to the Queen and to two London Livery Companies.

Bourne End

4 miles SE of High Wycombe on the A4155

A prosperous commuter town on the banks of the Thames; it began to expand in the late 19th century as the Victorians developed a passion for boating on the river. It was once the home of the writer Edgar Wallace, who died in Hollywood during work on the screenplay for *King Kong*. He is buried in the village cemetery at nearby Little Marlow.

Hambleden

6 miles SW of High Wycombe off the A4155

This much filmed village was given to the National Trust by the family of the bookseller WH Smith - who later became Viscount Hambleden. He lived close by at Greenlands, on the banks of the River

Thames and is buried in the village churchyard. The unusually large **Church of St Mary**, known as the cathedral of the Chilterns, dates from the 14th century and, though it has been altered over the years, it still dominates the area with its size and beauty. Inside the building's 18th century tower is a fascinating 16th century panel which is believed to have been the bedhead of Cardinal Wolsey - it certainly bears the cardinal's hat and the Wolsey arms.

15th Century Cottages in Church Street, West Wycombe

The village's other building of interest, Hambledon Mill, can be found by the River Thames and is reached by a road that was first used by the Romans.

West Wycombe

2 miles NW of High Wycombe on the A40

This charming estate village, where many of the houses are owned by the National Trust, has a main street displaying architecture from the 15th through to the 19th centuries. Close by is **West Wycombe Park** (National Trust), the home of local landowners the Dashwood family until the 1930s. Of the various members of the family, it was Sir Francis Dashwood who had most influence on both the house and the village. West Wycombe house was originally built in the early 1700s but Sir Francis boldly remodelled it several years later as well as having the grounds and park landscaped by Thomas Cook, a pupil of 'Capability' Brown. Very much a classical landscape, the grounds contain temples and an artificial lake shaped like a swan, and the house has a good collection of tapestries, furniture and paintings.

Hewn out of a nearby hillside are **West Wycombe Caves** which were created, possibly from some existing caverns, by Sir Francis as part of a programme of public works. After a series of failed harvests, which created great poverty and distress amongst the estate workers and tenant farmers, Sir Francis employed the men to extract chalk from the hillside to be used in the construction of the new road between the village and High Wycombe.

The village **Church of St Lawrence** is yet another example of Sir Francis' enthusiasm for remodelling old buildings. Situated within the remnants of an Iron Age fort, the church was originally constructed in the 13th century. Its isolated position, however, was not intentional as the church was originally the church of the village of Haveringdon, which has long since disappeared. Dashwood remodelled the interior in the 18th century in the style of an Egyptian hall and also heightened the tower, adding on the top a great golden ball where six people could meet in comfort and seclusion. The **Dashwood Mausoleum** near the church was built in 1765; a vast hexagonal building without a roof, it is the resting place of Sir Francis and other members of the Dashwood family. Sir Francis had a racier side to his character. As well as being remembered as a great traveller and a successful politician, he was the founder of the Hell-Fire Club. This group of rakes, who were also known as the Brotherhood of Sir Francis or Dashwood's Apostles, met a couple of times a years to engage in highly colourful activities. Though their exploits were legendary and probably loosely based on fact, they no doubt consumed large quantities of alcohol and enjoyed the company of women. Traditionally, the group meetings were held in the caves, or possibly the church tower, though between 1750 and 1774, their meeting place was nearby Medmenham Abbey.

Hughenden

2 miles N of High Wycombe off the A4128

This village is famous for being the home of the Queen Victoria's favourite Prime Minister Benjamin Disraeli; he lived here from 1848 until his death in 1881. He bought **Hughenden Manor** (National Trust) shortly after the publication of his novel *Tancred*. Though not a wealthy man, Disraeli felt that a leading Conservative politician should have a stately home of his own. In order to finance the purchase, his supporters lent him the money so that he could have this essential characteristic of an English gentleman. The interior is an excellent example of the Victorian Gothic style and contains an interesting collection of memorabilia of Disraeli's life as well as his library, pictures and much of his furniture. The garden is based on the designs of Disraeli's wife Mary Anne; the surrounding park and woodland offer some beautiful walks. Disraeli, who was MP for Buckinghamshire from 1847 to 1876 and Prime Minister in 1868 and from 1874 to 1880, is buried in the churchyard of St Michael. In the chancel of the church is a marble memorial erected in his memory by Queen Victoria. Disraeli was the son of a writer and literary critic, Isaac d'Israeli, who lived for a time in the village of Bradenham on the other side of High Wycombe. The Bradenham Estate, also owned by the National Trust, includes **Bradenham Woods**, an area of ancient beech that is among the finest in the whole Chilterns region. Although beech predominates, other trees, including oak, whitebeam, ash and wild cherry are being encouraged.

CHESHAM

A successful combination of a commuter town, industrial centre and country community, Chesham's growth from a sleepy market town was due mainly to its Metropolitan underground railway link with central London. Chesham was the birthplace of Arthur Liberty, the son of a haberdasher and draper, who went on to found the world famous Liberty's department store in London's Regent Street in 1875. Another resident of note was Roger Crabbe who, having suffered head injuries during the Civil War, was sentenced to death by Cromwell. After receiving a pardon, Crabbe opened a hat shop in the town where he is reputed to have worn sackcloth, eaten turnip tops and given his income to the poor. Perhaps not surprisingly, Crabbe was used by Lewis Carroll as the model for the Mad Hatter in *Alice in Wonderland*.

Great Missenden

3 miles W of Chesham off the A413

Home to the only other court house in the Chiltern Hundreds (the other is at Long Crendon), Great Missenden's **Old Court House** dates from the early 1400s. Also in this village is an attractive flint

Peterley Manor Farm

Peterley, Prestwood, Great Missenden,
Buckinghamshire HP16 0HH
Tel: 01494 863566 Fax: 01494 862959
website: peterleymanorfarm.co.uk

Peterley Manor Farm is a family-run business which has been steadily expanding since the Brills bought the property in 1982. Roger Brill is the fourth generation of the farming family of Brills in the business, and he now runs the farm with his wife Jane and other members of the family spanning three generations. It's a great place to come to take the country air, to Pick Your Own fruit and vegetables, visit the nursery and farm shop and to say 'hello!' to the friendly resident alpacas and Shetland ponies. The PYO season runs from mid-June to October with berries of all kinds - strawberries, raspberries, gooseberries,currants and blackberries. Plums, apples, beans, peas and other vegetables are all available in their season.

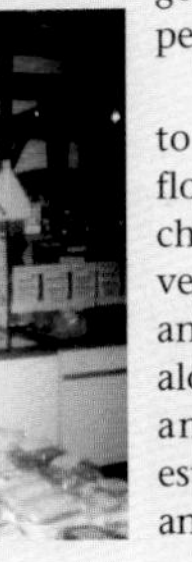

This produce is also on sale in the farm shop (open Tuesday to Sunday), along with home-produced apple juice, cut flowers, free range eggs, local honey, traditional preserves and chutneys, ice creams, cakes and self-service frozen fruit and vegetables. Herbaceous plants, fuchsias, geraniums, lobelia and petunias are amongst the extensive stock in the nursery, along with a huge selection of ready-planted hanging baskets and patio planters. Other offerings at this excellent establishment include home-grown pumpkins for Halloween and Christmas trees and festive gifts and produce in December.

and stone church and the site of Missenden Abbey, which was founded in 1133 by the Augustinian order. A daughter community of St Nicholas's Abbey in Normandy, the abbey has long since gone and in its place stands a fashionable Gothic mansion dating from 1810.

Great Missenden is probably best known as being the home of Roald Dahl, the internationally recognised author particularly loved for his children's books. He lived here for 30 years and is buried on the hillside opposite his home, Gipsy House, in the churchyard of St Peter and St Paul. His daughter Olivia, who died at the age of 7, is buried at Little Missenden in a plot that was intended for Dahl himself and his first wife, the actress Patricia Neal. But this plan was changed when Dahl and Neal were divorced in 1983, seven years before his death. The gardens of his home are open to the public once a year.

Lacey Green

8 miles W of Chesham off the A4010

Lacey Green is home to another of the county's preserved windmills, this one a

Smock Mill, Lacey Green

Cock and Rabbit Inn & Café Graziemille

The Lee, Nr. Great Missenden,
Buckinghamshire HP16 9LZ
Tel: 01494 837540
Fax: 01494 837512
e-mail: info@gianfranco.demon.co.uk
website: www.graziemille.co.uk

Hidden in the heart of the Chiltern Hills you can discover the delightful village of The Lee, familiar to many visitors as a filming location for a number of TV programmes, such as *'Midsommer Murders'*, *'Treasure Hunt'* and *'Pie in the Sky'*, to mention but a few. But who would have thought that in this quaint village, you would find a splendid Italian restaurant and pub? **The Cock & Rabbit Inn and Cafe Graziemille**, owned and run by Gianfranco Parola with his wife Victoria, is the perfect place for a relaxing lunch or elegant dinner. Surrounded by a lovely garden and sun terrace, this pub is an absolute delight. It has the appearance of a quintessential English country house, which of course it was when originally built, and Gianfranco arrived here in 1986 and renovated and restored it to what you see today.

Inside you will find two bar areas both with open fires, which add to the welcoming atmosphere and relaxed ambiance. The pub has become an ever more popular destination and stop off point for walkers, ramblers and tourists exploring the local countryside. Open at every lunchtime and evening, food is served at each session, with Gianfranco being responsible for the superb menu inspired by dishes from the Piedmont region of Italy where he was born. His specialities, many of which use the local wild garlic, include beef carpaccio, sautéed mushrooms and toasted goat's cheese to start, followed by Pasta Graziemille, Chicken Contessa Rosa or Salmon Graziemille in dill, cream and champagne sauce. To finish there is, of course, that most famous of Italian desserts, tiramisu, made to Gianfranco's family recipe. Meals can be enjoyed in the delightful Garden Restaurant or in the bars.

Cafe Graziemille is dedicated to catering for weddings and other functions and to providing a delightful location and intimate setting to dine with friends. Any event can be specially catered in a distinctive Italian style. Simply let Gianfranco, Victoria, and their friendly, efficient staff do all the hard work while you enjoy yourself.

Smock Mill, in which only the cap carrying the sails rotates to meet the wind. As a result, the body of the mill where the machinery is housed can be bigger, heavier and stronger. This example was built in the mid-1600s and moved from Chesham to this site in 1821. Lacey Green is the village where the young poet Rupert Brooke used to spend his weekends in the company of friends at a local pub. The son of a master at Rugby School and a student at Cambridge University, Brooke began writing poetry as a boy and travelled widely in the years leading up to World War I. Early on in the war his poetry showed a boyish patriotism, but his later works were full of bitter disillusion. He died in 1915 while on his way to the attempted landings at the Dardanelles in Turkey. Close to the village lies Speen Farm and the **Home of Rest for Horses**, whose most famous patient was Sefton, the cavalry horse injured in the Hyde Park bomb blast of the early 1980s.

Princes Risborough

9 miles W of Chesham on the A4010

A busy little town with many 16th century cottages, 17th and 18th century houses and, at its centre, a brick Market House of 1824. The ground floor is an empty space providing shelter for market stalls, while in the room above the Town Council meets.

The Prince in the name of this Chilterns Gap market town is the Black Prince, the eldest son of Edward III, who held land and had a palace here. The town stands on the Icknield Way and during the stage coach era was a major stopping place. It is said that the last regular stage-coach service to run in England ended its journey from London here in 1898.

Off the market square, opposite the church, the **Princes Risborough Manor House** (National Trust) is a 17th century redbrick house with a handsome Jacobean staircase.

Wendover

6 miles NW of Chesham on the A413

This delightful old market town, situated in a gap in the Chiltern Hills, has an attractive main street of half-timbered, thatched houses and cottages of which the best examples are **Anne Boleyn's Cottages**. A picturesque place, often seen as the gateway to the Chilterns, Wendover has a fine selection of antique and craft shops, tea rooms and bookshops.

The town also offers visitors an opportunity of seeing the glorious countryside through the medium of **Wendover Woods**. Created for recreational pursuits - there's a mountain bike course at Aston Hill - as well as for conservation and timber production, these Forestry Commission woods offer visitors numerous trails through the coniferous and broadleaved woodland. It is one of the best sites in the country to spot the tiny firecrest, a bird that is becoming increasingly rare.

Off the B4010 a short drive west of Wendover, **Coombe Hill** is the highest point in the Chilterns and affords superb views across the Vale of Aylesbury, the Berkshire Downs and the Cotswolds. On the summit is a monument dedicated to the men who died in the Boer War. The National Trust has introduced a flock of sheep on to the hill to control the invasion of scrub and to encourage the grass.

Rumsey's Handmade Chocolates

The Old Bank, 26 High Street, Wendover, Bucks
Tel: 01296 625060

Opened on Valentine's Day, 2004 **Rumsey's Handmade Chocolates** is a chocoholic's paradise. For ten years before that opening, Nigel Rumsey had been producing his exquisite chocolates from home. It was when his wife Mary gave up work that they decided to open the shop – "We didn't want to go down the mass production route," says Mary, "as that would mean sacrificing quality." They acquired premises in the heart of Wendover that had housed the NatWest bank, modelled the interior on the shop in the hit film *Chocolat*, and installed a glass wall between the shop and the kitchen so that customers can see former pastry chef Nigel handcrafting his wonderful treats.

There's no doubting the quality of his chocolates – over the last two years Nigel has received no fewer than eight awards at the Fine Foods Fayre at London's Olympia, including a Gold for his Orange Cointreau Truffles. With more than 40 different chocolates to choose from, and new flavours being added all the time, chocolate lovers are really spoiled for choice. While Nigel is creating these enticing confections, Mary is serving chocolates and a range of hot drinks, including freshly roasted coffee and, naturally, hot chocolate, as well as light savoury meals.

Field Cottage

St Leonards, Nr Tring, Hertfordshire HP23 6NS
Tel: 01494 837602 Fax: 01494 837137
e-mail: michael.jepson@lineone.net
website:
www.smoothhound.co.uk/hotels/field.html

Tucked away in the heart of the Chilterns on the Bucks/Herts borders, **Field Cottage** – as the name suggests – stands on the very edge of open fields with easy access to public footpaths and the Ridgeway. This charming cottage which is convenient for Amersham, Chesham, Wendover and Tring is the home of Mike and Sue Jepson, who welcome bed & breakfast guests to their peaceful retreat. The accommodation, which boasts a 4-Diamond and Silver Award from the English Tourism Council, comprises one double room en suite, one twin and one single, each with own private shower or bathroom.

All the rooms are attractively furnished and decorated, and provided with colour TV, hospitality tray and many other extras. There is a large sitting room which has access to the pretty cottage garden. A full English breakfast is served in the flower filled conservatory which enjoys panoramic views over the adjoining fields and woodland. There are numerous pubs in the area for eating out, and many places of interest. Field Cottage is a non-smoking house; children over 12 welcome; but pets are not allowed in the house.

AYLESBURY

Founded in Saxon times and the county town since the reign of Henry VIII, Aylesbury lies in rich pastureland in the shelter of the Chilterns. Postwar development took away much of the town's character, but some parts, particularly around the market square, are protected by a conservation order. At various times in the Civil War, Aylesbury was a base for both Cromwell and the King, and this period of history is covered in the splendidly refurbished **County Museum & Art Gallery**. The museum, housed in a splendid Georgian building, also has an exhibit on Louis XVIII of France, who lived in exile at nearby Hartwell House. Also within the museum is the award-winning **Roald**

Hunter's Farm & Country Shop

Fleet Marston Farm, Aylesbury, Buckinghamshire HP18 0PZ
Tel: 01296 651314 Fax: 01296 655855

A converted tithe barn and stables now house **Hunter's Farm & Country Shop** which offers a huge range of quality products. Edibles include a tempting variety of casseroles, cakes and desserts – all made locally – an extensive choice of jams, curds and chutneys, free range eggs, local honey, potatoes and a wide range of English wines. There are toys and games for both children and adults; quality clothing from producers such as Slimma, Double Two and Alice Collins; wonderful textiles, mugs and trays; exquisite jewellery from Kit Heath and unique gifts and cards. The shop is open from 9am to 5.30pm, Monday to Saturday; 10am to 4pm on Sundays.

Hartwell House Hotel

Restaurant & Spa, Oxford Road, nr Aylesbury, Buckinghamshire HP17 8NL
Tel: 01296 747444 Fax: 01296 747450
e-mail: info@hartwell-house.com
website: www.historichousehotels.com

Just one hour from London by road or rail, and 45 minutes from London Heathrow, **Hartwell House Hotel**, Restaurant & Spa has provided hospitality for many eminent guests and was the private house of the exiled King of France, Louis XVIII, for five years from 1809. More recently the house has been sympathetically restored by Historic House Hotels Limited and stands in 90 acres of parkland with a lake spanned by a stone bridge, a ruined church and many 18th century statues, follies and garden buildings. Inside, there's a dramatic Gothic hall with a staircase studded with Jacobean carved figures that lead to 30 superbly appointed individual bedrooms, some named after members of Louis XVIII's court.

On approaching the main house you have additional accommodation in the Hartwell Court, a converted 18th century coach house and stables, offering a further 16 bedrooms, 10 of which are suites, all decorated to the same standard as the house. Some have garden views and are ideal for guests seeking seclusion and privacy. Adjacent to the Hartwell Court is the Spa, housed in a splendid building modelled on an orangery which offers a heated indoor pool, whirlpool bath, steam room, sauna, well equipped gymnasium and four health and beauty treatments rooms.

Dahl Children's Gallery, an exciting hands-on gallery for children that uses Dahl's characters to introduce and explain the museum's treasures.

AROUND AYLESBURY

Mentmore

6 miles NE of Aylesbury off the B488

The village is home to the first of the Rothschild mansions, **Mentmore Towers**, which was built for Baron Meyer Amschel de Rothschild between 1852 and 1855. A splendid building in the Elizabethan style it was designed by Sir Joseph Paxton, the designer of Crystal Palace, and is a superb example of grandiose Victorian extravagance. However, the lavish decoration hides several technologically advanced details for those times, such as central heating, and, as might be expected from Paxton, there are large sheets of glass and a glass roof in the design. In the late 19th century the house became the home of Lord Rosebery and the magnificent turreted building was the scene of many glittering parties and gatherings of the most wealthy and influential people in the country. However, in the 1970s the house was put up for auction and, while the furniture and works of art were sold to the four corners of the world, the building was bought by the Maharishi Mahesh Yogi and it is now the headquarters of his University of Natural Law. Mentmore Towers is occasionally open to the public.

Ivinghoe

7 miles E of Aylesbury on the B488

As the large village church would suggest, Ivinghoe was once a market town of some importance in the surrounding area. In this now quiet village can be found **Ford End Watermill**, a listed building that, though probably much older, was first recorded in 1767. The only working watermill, with its original machinery, left in Buckinghamshire, the farm in which it is set has also managed to retain the atmosphere of an 18th century farm.

To the east lies the National Trust's **Ivinghoe Beacon**, a wonderful viewpoint on the edge of the Chiltern Hills. The site of an Iron Age hill fort, the beacon was also the inspiration for Sir Walter Scott's *Ivanhoe*. The Beacon is at one end of Britain's oldest road, the **Ridgeway National Trail**. The other end is the World Heritage Site of Avebury in Wiltshire, and the 85-mile length of the Ridgeway still follows the same route over the high ground used since prehistoric times. Walkers can use the whole length of the trail (April to November is the best time) and horseriders and cyclists can ride on much of the western part.

Pitstone

7 miles E of Aylesbury off the B489

Though the exact age of **Pitstone Windmill** (National Trust) is not known, it is certainly one of the oldest post mills in Britain. The earliest documentary reference to its existence was made in 1624. It is open to the public on a limited basis. Also in the village is a **Farm Museum**, where all manner of farm and barn machinery, along with domestic bygones, are on display. A delightful hour or two can be spent cruising from Pitstone Wharf along a lovely stretch of the Grand Union Canal.

Stoke Mandeville

2 miles S of Aylesbury on the A4010

The village is best known for its hospital, which specialises in the treatment of spinal injuries and burns. Just south of Stoke, on Old Risborough Road, **Bucks Goat Centre** has the most comprehensive collection of goat breeds in the country. Visitors can groom, cuddle and feed them with vegetables from the Farm Shop. Also here are the famous Aylesbury ducks and other poultry, pigs, small pet animals and donkeys, facilities for children, shops and a café.

Great Kimble

5 miles S of Aylesbury on the A4010

Though the village is home to a church with an interesting series of 14th century wall paintings, its real claim to fame is the nearby 16th century mansion, **Chequers**, the country residence of the British Prime Minister. Originally built by William Hawtrey in 1565, but much altered and enlarged in the 18th and 19th centuries, the house was restored to its original form by Arthur Lee in 1912. Later, in 1920, as Lord Lee of Fareham, he gave the house and estate to the nation to be used as the prime minister's country home. The first Prime Minister to make use of Chequers was Lloyd George, and many who came to know the house later moved to the area: Ramsay MacDonald's daughter lived at nearby Speen; Harold Wilson bought a house in Great Missenden; and Nye Bevan owned a farm in the Chilterns.

Wotton Underwood

8 miles W of Aylesbury off the A41

In this secluded village stands the privately owned **Wotton House**, a charming early-18th century building said to be practically identical to the original Buckingham Palace. The gardens, which feature more than a dozen follies, were laid out between 1757 and 1760 by Capability Brown.

WALK NUMBER 3

Ludgershall

Distance:	5.2 miles (8.3 kilometres)
Typical time:	180 mins
Height gain:	85 metres
Map:	Explorer 180
Walk:	www.walkingworld.com ID:1234
Contributor:	Ron and Jenny Glynn

Access Information:

Take the A4100 between Bicester and Aylesbury, turning right at sign for Ludgershall. There is ample parking on roadside in village.

Description:

This walk in Buckinghamshire is a mixture of footpaths, bridleways and quiet country roads. It starts from near the church in the attractive village of Ludgershall and takes a minor road to another part of the parish, before leaving it on footpaths in lovely countryside.

The small setting of Wotton Underwood is approached on a hard-laid path which passes the magnificent Wotton House in its wonderful surroundings. The estate is quite extensive and includes a cluster of charming cottages and a large area of beautiful parkland. There follows a lengthy stretch on a country road that runs between dense and peaceful woodland and eventually returns to Ludgershall.

The architecture in these parts is of red brick, very appealing and individual. There are no great heights to contend with, just a gradual incline on Windmill Hill, just before Wotton, so this walk is suitable for those not wanting too strenuous an exercise in the great outdoors.

Features:

Lake/Loch, Church, Stately Home, Wildlife, Birds, Flowers, Great Views, Butterflies, Woodland

Walk Directions:

1 Take the minor road signed to Wotton, just before the church at Peartree Farm, to walk along to junction.

2 Walk over to narrow path at Wotton End and follow hedge-line to cross a brook. Take the right-hand fork over common ground across to an opening.

3 Walk on, past stile on left where a network of paths lead off and continue with hedge on left, in ridge and furrow meadowland. Climb stile and continue over middle of next field and then another, in same direction and with Tittershall Wood over to the left.

4 Take double stile and footbridge to turn right on bridleway, with hedge on right. Enter walkers' gate ahead and continue through another gate, to cross road to another stile. Walk on over large field, with farm buildings on right, gradually climbing uphill.

5 Head slightly right over two stiles, aiming for the right of Middle Farm ahead. Take stile in corner of field onto hard track.

6 Walk over to white gate of farmhouse and take stile on the left of it; follow edge of small field to metal kissing-gate.

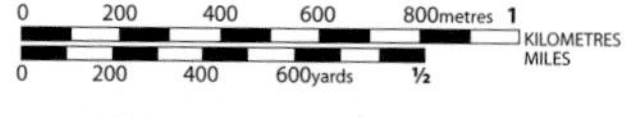

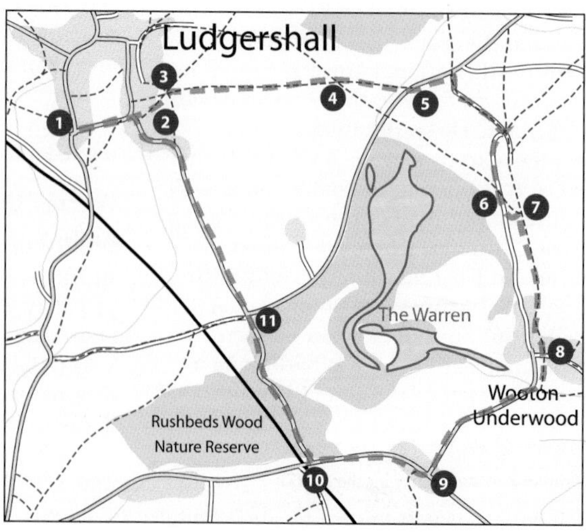

7 Turn right through wooden gate and pass back of farmhouse, to walk on a hard-laid path passing through a wildflower meadow. Cross over a miniature railway track, where you might be lucky enough to see a small-gauge locomotive being driven along. Pass a beautifully styled redbrick house, then turn right through gate to walk by Wotton House, a very large and imposing setting of three huge buildings standing behind high wrought-iron gates. The path runs downhill with the copper spire of Wotton Church in view.

8 Walk ahead over large green to join road and follow it along between trees and hedgerows. Pass pretty half-timbered estate cottages and notice a large reared deer herd on the right, on the way to junction.

9 Turn right to pass Lower Lawn Farm and cottages, with undulating countryside ahead.

10 Turn right towards Ludgershall and Kingswood on narrow road running through woodland. A glimpse of the rear of Wotton House can be seen across parkland where there is a clearing. Continue again through woodland to meet junction.

11 Walk on towards Ludgershall on a quiet country lane, hedged and tree-lined. Pass a row of houses on the edge of village and Brooklands Farm a bit further on. The road bends and passes other individually styled and interesting dwellings. Turn left into Church Lane and retrace steps to start, getting a better view from this direction of St Mary the Virgin Church, with its squat tower.

Boarstall

12 miles W of Aylesbury off the B4011

A curious feature here is the 17th century **Duck Decoy** set on the edge of a lake to catch birds for the table. The site, run by the National Trust, contains a nature trail and exhibition hall. The National Trust is also responsible for **Boarstall Tower**, the 14th century stone gatehouse of a long demolished fortified house.

Waddesdon

4 miles NW of Aylesbury on the A41

The village is home to another of the county's magnificent country houses, in this case **Waddesdon Manor** (National Trust). Built between 1874 and 1889 for Baron Ferdinand de Rothschild, in the style of a French Renaissance château, the house is set in rolling English countryside and borrows elements from several different French châteaux, surrounded by formal gardens and landscaped grounds. These contain, among many treasures, a French-style aviary in a part of the gardens designed by the popular 20th century American landscape artist Lanning Roper, hundreds of trees both native and foreign, a fabulous parterre, Italian, French and Dutch statuary, and a huge pheasant named Ferdinand made from 15,000 bedding plants on a steel frame. The French influence even extended to the carthorses used on the site - powerful Percheron mares that were imported from Normandy. The house contains one of the best collections of 18th century French decorative arts in the world, including Sèvres porcelain, Beauvais tapestries and

Waddesdon Manor

My Favourite Things

The Key Barn, Westcott Farm House, Ashendon Road,
Westcott, Buckinghamshire HP18 0NX
Tel: 01296 655252 Fax: 01296 655667
e-mail: beawork@aol.com
website: www.myfavouritethingsonline.com

Part of the success of **My Favourite Things** is that it is run by three professional interior designers each of whom naturally has a slightly different approach which enables them to offer customers both variety and originality. One of the first things you notice when you enter the showroom is how comfortably the mixture of contemporary furniture – such as chocolate leather chairs and glass tables – sits with the eclectic collection of antique pieces. All the items on display have been chosen for their individual aesthetics but also on the basis of quality of design, materials and craftsmanship. Many pieces are sourced locally; others may have been designed in Italy or manufactured in Germany but the principle remains the same – only the best will do.

The owners of My Favourite Things admit to having a real passion for fabrics – and it shows! There are countless samples of sumptuous materials, beautiful designs and a rainbow palette of colour schemes to choose from. Once you have selected your fabric, you can if you wish have items made up to your own requirements – whether it's curtains, upholstery, cushion covers or details like tie-backs and tassles, the professional staff make sure that they are precisely as specified and perfectly finished.

My Favourite Things also stocks a wide range of "accessories for the well-dressed home". Whatever your taste – modern or period, simple or exotic – you will surely find something here to fall in love with. Lighting to create different moods, from subtle to dramatic; unusual limited edition prints and interesting paintings (often by local artists); ranges of beautiful glassware, crystal and china; natural oil handmade candles and more – all of which also make superb gifts. A complimentary gift wrapping service is available.

If your home is in need of a makeover, the designers at My Favourite Things can advise on where improvements can be made, on layout, colour schemes, soft furnishings and all the final touches that "dress a room to perfection". Irrespective of the scale of the project – from transforming an empty shell to sourcing the perfect curtain for a cloakroom – they will go to any lengths to create the right look.

As well as this showroom in Westcott, My Favourite things also has a sister establishment at 12a High Street, Thame, which stocks an equally enticing range of covetable items.

fine furniture. There are also paintings by Gainsborough, Reynolds and 17th century Dutch and Flemish masters.

Quainton

5 miles NW of Aylesbury off the A41

A pleasant village with the remains of an ancient cross on the green, a number of fine Georgian houses and a row of almshouses built in 1687. Here, too, is another of the county's windmills, **Quainton Tower Mill**, built in the 1830s and 100ft high. Quite early in its life it was fitted with a steam engine, but despite this innovation the mill's working life extended barely 50 years. Just south of the village, at Quainton Railway Station, is the **Buckinghamshire Railway Centre** (see panel below), a working steam museum where visitors can relive the golden age of steam. The centre boasts one of the largest collections of preserved steam and diesel locomotives in the country, including engines from South Africa, the USA and Egypt as well as from Britain. Visitors can ride behind full-sized steam locos and on the extensive miniature railway. The beautifully restored Rowley Road Station (1851), moved here from Oxford, also serves as the main visitor centre.

BUCKINGHAM

This pleasant town, the centre of which is contained in a loop of the River Ouse, dates back to Saxon times and was granted a charter by Alfred the Great. Although it became the county town in AD 888, when Alfred divided the shires, from an early date many of the functions of a county town were performed by the more centrally located Aylesbury.

Thanks to a disastrous fire in 1725, this lively little market town is characterised by a fine array of Georgian buildings, including Castle House in West Street, the impressive Old Gaol, one of the first purpose-built county gaols in England, and the Town Hall, located at either end of the Market Square. The **Old Gaol Museum** not only illustrates the building's history but also has displays on the town's past and the county's military exploits. A high-tech glass roof was added in 2000, spanning the original prisoners' exercise yard to create a new light-filled area for special exhibits and an educational resource centre. One building that did survive the devastating fire of 1725 is the **Buckingham Chantry Chapel** (National Trust). The chapel was constructed in 1475 on the site of a

Buckinghamshire Railway Centre

Quainton Road Station, Quainton, Aylesbury,
Buckinghamshire HP22 4BY
Tel: 01296 655450
website: www.bucksrailcentre.org.uk

A working steam museum set in a 25-acre site, the **Buckinghamshire Railway Centre** was established in 1968 and boasts one of the largest collections of preserved steam and diesel locomotives in the country, including items from South Africa, the USA and Egypt as well as from Britain. Visitors can ride behind full-sized stream locomotives and on the extensive miniature railway. The Railway Centre is also home to the beautifully restored Rewley Road Station, which dates from 1851 and was moved here from Oxford, and is now the main visitor centre. Open Wednesdays to Sundays from March to the end of October, the steam trains operated on Sundays and on Wednesdays in the school holidays.

Norman building whose doorway has been retained. Well worth a visit, the chapel was restored by George Gilbert Scott in 1875.

A much more recent addition to this delightful country market town is the **University of Buckingham**, which was granted its charter in 1983.

AROUND BUCKINGHAM

Winslow

5 miles SE of Buckingham on the A413

A small country town of ancient origin, where Offa, the King of Mercia, stayed in AD752. The village's most prominent building is **Winslow Hall**, a delightful Wren house set in beautiful gardens. House and gardens are open for visits by appointment only.

Stewkley

10 miles SE of Buckingham on the B4032

Stewkley, renowned as being the longest village in England, is even better known for its wonderful **Church of St Michael**, one of the finest Norman churches in the land, with spectacular zigzag patterns and a massive tower. Built between 1150-1180, this mighty building has remained virtually unaltered.

Wing

12 miles SE of Buckingham on the A418

Another village famous for its church. **All Saints Church**, standing on a rise above the Vale of Aylesbury, retains most of its original Saxon features, including the nave, aisles, west wall, crypt and apse. The roof is covered in medieval figures, many of them playing musical instruments. This remarkable church also

The Crown

Gawcott, nr Buckingham MK18 4JF
Tel: 01280 816267
e-mail: lesley.a.Stafford@btinternet.com

Dating back to the early 1800s, **The Crown** is as traditional an English hostelry as you could hope to find. Colourful outside with hanging baskets and window boxes, its interior is a delight with lots of old beams bedecked with dried hops and gleaming brasses. A large inglenook, a small snug, an open fire and a wood-burning stove, a piano and pine pews all add to the charm. Outside there's a large secluded garden with picnic tables and a children's play area. The Crown is well-known for its excellent food. Mine host, Lesley Anne Stafford, offers a regular menu that includes traditional bar snacks such as ham, egg and chips.

The evening menu includes starters such as Dublin Bay prawns and main courses like herb-crusted pork chump chop and Mediterranean vegetable frittata. Lunch is served from noon until 3pm (Monday to Friday); to 4pm on Saturday and to 3pm or later on Sunday. After lunch has finished on Sundays, the restaurant becomes a Victorian tea room serving traditional teas and cakes. The restaurant is open for dinner from 7pm to 9.45pm. Gawcott village itself boasts a famous son in the Victorian architect Sir Gilbert Scott whose father was Vicar here. Scott's autobiography fondly recalls his childhood here.

contains numerous brasses and monuments, notably to the Dormer family who came to Ascott Hall in the 1520s. Just east of the village, **Ascott** was bought in 1874 by Leopold Rothschild who virtually rebuilt the original farmhouse round its timber-framed core. Now in the care of the National Trust, the house contains a superb collection of fine paintings, Oriental porcelain and English and French furniture. The grounds are magnificent, too, with specimen trees and shrubs, a herbaceous walk, lily pond, Dutch garden, an evergreen topiary sundial and two fountains, one in bronze, the other in marble, sculpted by the American artist Thomas Waldo Story.

Ascott House, Wing

Middle Claydon

5 miles S of Buckingham off the A413

The village is home to **Claydon House** (National Trust), a Jacobean manor house that was remodelled in the 1750s at a time of great enthusiasm for all things Oriental. The home of the Verney family for over 350 years, the house contains a number of state rooms with magnificent carved wood and plaster decorations on an Oriental theme. What makes the house particularly interesting is its associations with Florence Nightingale. Florence's sister married into the Verney family and the pioneer of modern hospital care spent long periods at the house, especially during her old age. Her bedroom in the house and a museum of her life and experiences during the Crimean War can be seen here. Florence died in 1910 after a long career which embraced concerns of public health as well as the training of nurses; she was the first woman to be awarded the Order of Merit.

Claydon House, Middle Claydon

Thornborough

3 miles E of Buckingham off the A422

This lively and attractive village is home to Buckinghamshire's only surviving medieval bridge. Built in the 14th century, the six-arched structure spans Claydon Brook. Close by are two large mounds which were opened in 1839 and revealed a wealth of Roman objects many of which are on display at th Old Gaol Musuem. Though it was known that there was a Roman temple here its location has not been found.

Dadford

3 miles N of Buckingham off the A422

Just to the south of the village lies **Stowe School**, a leading public school which occupies an 18th century mansion that was once the home of the Dukes of Buckingham. Worked upon by two wealthy owners who both had a great sense of vision, the magnificent mansion house, which was finally completed in 1774, is open to the public during school holidays. Between 1715 and 1749, the owner, Viscount Cobham, hired various well known landscape designers to lay out the fantastic **Stowe Landscape Gardens** (National Trust) gardens that can still be seen around the house. Taking over the house in 1750, Earl Temple, along with his nephew, expanded the grounds and today they remain one of the most original and finest landscape gardens in Europe. Temples, alcoves and rotundas are scattered around the landscape, strategically placed to evoke in the onlooker a romantic and poetic frame of mind. It is one of the more intriguing quirks of fate that Lancelot Brown, always known as 'Capability' Brown because he told his clients that their parks had capabilities, was head gardener at Stowe for 10 years. He arrived here in 1741 and began to work out his own style, a more natural style of landscape gardening which was to take over where gardens like the ones at Stowe left off.

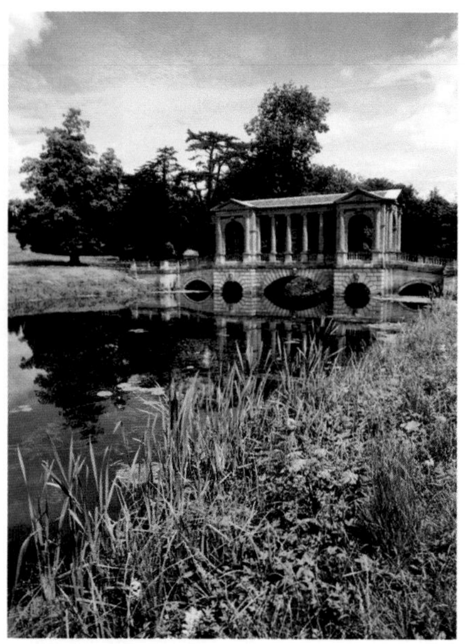

Stowe Landscape Gardens

Silverstone

5 miles N of Buckingham off the A43

The home of British motor racing,

Silverstone is best known as the venue for the British Formula I Grand Prix. But it hosts many varied motorsport events throughout the year, including the Silverstone Historic Festival, British F3, GT, Touring Car and Superbike championships. It is also the place of dreams for boy racers, who can try their hand at driving a wide range of cars round the circuit, including single-seaters, rally cars, 4X4s, E-type Jaguars, Lotus Elises and Porsche 911 Carrera Supercars.

Norfolk House, Milton Keynes

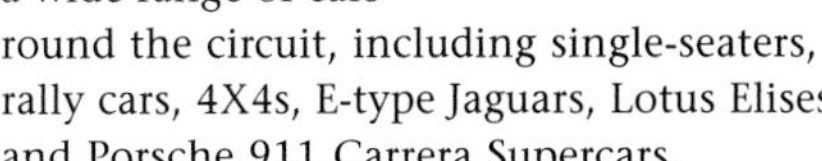

MILTON KEYNES

Most people's perception of this modern town is of a concrete jungle but the reality of Milton Keynes could not be more different. The development corporation that was charged, in 1967, with organising the new town has provided a place of tree-lined boulevards, uncongested roads, spacious surroundings, and acres of parkland. It is too, of course, a modern town, with new housing, high-tech industries, modern leisure facilities, and a large covered shopping centre. One of the town's most notable buildings is **Christ Church**, built in the style of Christopher Wren; the first purpose-built ecumenical city church in Britain, it was opened in March 1992 by the Queen. While Milton Keynes is certainly a place of the late 20th century, it has not altogether forgotten the rural past of the villages, which are now incorporated into the suburbs of the town. **Milton Keynes Museum**, run by a large and active group of volunteers, has a large collection of industrial, domestic and agricultural bygones that illustrates the lives of the people who lived in the area in the 200

The Country Collection

21-23 High Street, Woburn Sands, Buckinghamshire MK17 8RJ
Tel: 01908 588007 Fax: 01525 221749

With its huge range and variety of stock, **The Country Collection** provides a "one stop shop" for finding all your gifts and cards. Owned and run by Shirley and Stuart Fletcher, this Aladdin's Cave offers a wonderful choice of teddy bears, Jellycats and other soft toys, Bridgewater pottery and china mugs, Crabtree & Evelyn toiletries and perfumes, Isle of Wight Glass, Norfolk Lavender products, *Country Living* diaries and notelets, and an extensive selection of cards and gift paper. Look out for the locally made pottery and the delightful speciality cards hand-made by local craftspeople.

years leading up to the creation of the new town. A Victorian house features a working kitchen and laundry, and among other eye-catching exhibits are a local tramcar and an impressive collection of working telephones.

AROUND MILTON KEYNES

Bletchley

2 miles S of Milton Keynes on the A421

Now effectively a suburb of Milton Keynes, Bletchley is famous for **Bletchley Park** (see panel opposite), the Victorian mansion which housed the wartime codebreakers who beat odds of 150 million million million to 1 and cracked the Nazi Enigma cypher, the crucial key to German military and intelligence communications. Along with a display of military vehicles and a wealth of World War II memorabilia, there is a Cryptology Trail that allows visitors to follow the path of a coded message from its interception through decoding to interpretation. At the height of the war, more than 12,000 people worked at Bletchley Park.

Though Bletchley is now all but merged with its larger neighbour, it still retains a distinctive air. The original village here dates back to Roman times and was first recorded as a town in 1108.

Stony Stratford

3 miles NW of Milton Keynes off the A5

Often considered to be the jewel in the crown of the villages around Milton Keynes, Stony Stratford was a popular staging post on the old Roman road, Watling Street. Richard III, as the Duke of Gloucester, came in 1483 to detain the uncrowned Prince Edward before committing him to the Tower of

ChIna Seas

83 High Street, Stony Stratford, Milton Keynes, Buckinghamshire MK11 1AT
Tel: 01908 568666
e-mail: chinaseas@stonystratford.co.uk
website: www.stonystratford.co.uk/chinaseas.html

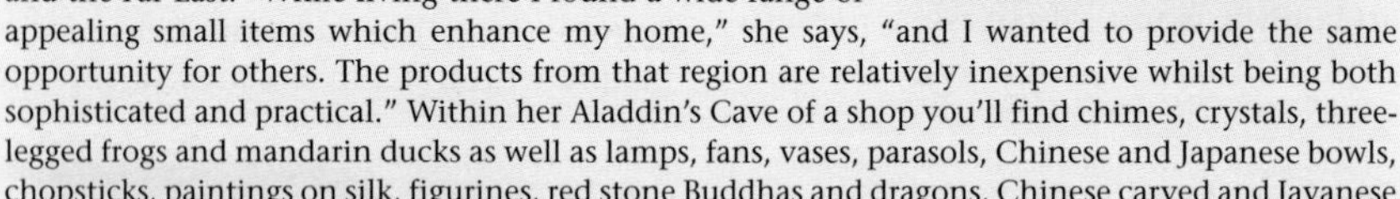

A fascinating gift and home furnishing store, **ChIna Seas** is the brain child of Linda Ruston who has worked in Hong Kong and the Far East. "While living there I found a wide range of appealing small items which enhance my home," she says, "and I wanted to provide the same opportunity for others. The products from that region are relatively inexpensive whilst being both sophisticated and practical." Within her Aladdin's Cave of a shop you'll find chimes, crystals, three-legged frogs and mandarin ducks as well as lamps, fans, vases, parasols, Chinese and Japanese bowls, chopsticks, paintings on silk, figurines, red stone Buddhas and dragons, Chinese carved and Javanese reclaimed teak furniture and much, much more. Some of the items come from Fair Trade sources.

Pieces like the three-legged frog, the money toads, ancient Chinese coins, the three gods of longevity and other items such as chimes which enhance the chi (positive energy) in the home or work place, are considered as 'cures' by Feng Shui practitioners. Linda regularly visits the Far East to find new pieces to add to the already extensive range on offer in ChIna Seas – a great place to browse for interior decoration and gift ideas. It's open from 9.30am to 5.30pm, Monday to Saturday. (Also 11am-4pm on Sundays before Christmas).

Bletchley Park

The Mansion, Bletchley Park, Milton Keynes, Buckinghamshire MK3 6EB
Tel: 01908 640404 Fax: 01908 274381
website: www.bletchleypark.org.uk

Bletchley Park, also known as 'Station X', was home to the famous code breakers of World War II and was the birthplace of modern computing communications. It is now a heritage site run by a charitable trust, with historic Victorian and wartime buildings, exhibitions and tours for visitors, community activities and non-residential conference facilities. Along with military vehicles and a mass of World War II memorabilia, there is the Cryptology Trail that allows visitors to follow the path of a coded message from its interception through decoding to interpretation. A truly fascinating place, Bletchley Park uncovers a side to wartime Britain that few people were aware of at the time. The park is open daily. There is an admission charge.

London, and other notable visitors include Charles Dickens, Samuel Johnson and John Wesley, who preached under the tree that still stands in the market place.

Gayhurst

4 miles N of Milton Keynes off the B526

Built during the reign of Elizabeth I, **Gayhurst House** was given to Sir Francis Drake in recognition of his circumnavigation of the world, though the building seen today was not the one that Drake lived in. It was later occupied by Sir Everard Digby, one of the conspirators behind the Gunpowder Plot of 1605.

Olney

8 miles N of Milton Keynes on the A509

Variety's the spice of life;
Monarch of all I survey;
God made the country and
man made the town...

All these familiar phrases are now embedded in the language but how many could name the writer? In fact, they all came from the pen of the 18th century poet William Cowper who spent the last 20 years of his life in the elegant market town of Olney.

He came to the town to be near his friend the Reverend John Newton, a former slave trader who had repented and become 'a man of gloomy piety'. The two men collaborated on a book of religious verse, the Olney Hymns, in which Cowper's contributions included such perennial favourites as

Oh! for a closer walk with God;
Hark, my soul! It is the Lord;
and *God moves in a mysterious way.*

The house in which Cowper lived from 1768 to 1786 is now the **Cowper and Newton Museum**, an interesting place that not only concentrates on Cowper's life and work but also has some exhibits and collections concerned with the times in which he lived and the life of Olney. Each of the rooms of the large early-18th century town house has been specially themed and there are numerous displays of Cowper's work, including the 'Olney Hymns'. Cowper was also a keen gardener and the summer house, where he wrote many of his poems, can still be seen out in the rear garden. Here he experimented with plants that were new to 18th century England. Also at the museum is the nationally important Lace Collection and items particular to the shoemaking industry which was another busy local trade in the 19th and early 20th century.

When Cowper died in 1800 he was buried at East Dereham in Norfolk but his associate, the reformed slave-trader, is interred in the churchyard of **St Peter and St Paul**, where he had been the curate. This church is a spacious building dating from the mid-14th century and its spire rises some 185 feet to dominate the skyline of Olney.

For more than 300 years Olney was a centre of lace-making by hand, using wooden or bone bobbins. When lace was at its most expensive, in the 1700s, only the well-to-do could afford to buy it, but the rise in machine-made lace from Nottingham saw a fall in prices and a sharp decline in Olney lace. A revival of the trade was tried by Harry Armstrong when he opened the Lace Factory in 1928 but, although handmade lace is still produced locally, the factory only lasted until Armstrong's death in 1943.

Amongst the town's present day claims to fame is the annual **Pancake Race** held every Shrove Tuesday. Legend has it that the first 'race' was run in the 15th century when a local housewife heard the Shriving Service bell ringing and ran to church complete with her frying pan and pancake. Today's re-enactment is open to any lady of Olney over 18 years of age; the rules state that she must wear a skirt, an apron and a scarf as well as carry a frying pan and pancake.

Nearby **Emberton Country Park**, located on the site of former gravel pits, is an ideal place to relax. Not only are

Longlands Farm

Warrington Road, Olney, Buckinghamshire MK46 4DU
Tel/Fax: 01234 712819

John Kitchener is the fourth generation of his family to run **Longlands Farm**, a 200-acre mixed farm just half a mile from Olney. Since 1994 he has been offering quality bed & breakfast accommodation in the 25-year-old bungalow set in farmland with lovely views over the Ouse Valley to Olney town with its soaring church spire. There are four guest bedrooms – one family en suite; one twin/ double, two singles – all tastefully decorated and equipped and provided with TV and hospitality tray. Breakfast is served in a conservatory that takes full advantage of those pastoral views.

A full English or vegetarian breakfast is served; dietary requirements can also be catered for. John's partner, Anne, hails from Paris but was educated in England and also speaks fluent German. Her English credentials are impeccable – she takes part in Olney's famous Pancake Race on Shrove Tuesday! Guests at Longlands Farm are welcome to make use of the picnic areas and before leaving would be well-advised to stock up at the Farm Shop with its wide range of fresh produce. Attractions within easy reach of the farm include Castle Ashby, Woburn Abbey, Gullivers Land and Althorp House.

there four lakes and a stretch of the River Ouse within the park's boundaries but facilities here include fishing, sailing, and nature trails.

Newport Pagnell

3 miles NE of Milton Keynes on the A422

Modern development hides a long history at Newport Pagnell, which local archaeological finds indicate was settled in the Iron Age and during the Roman occupation. It was an important administrative centre, and in the 10th century the Royal Mint was established here. Lacemaking was once an important industry, and the town is also associated with the car-maker Aston Martin which started life in the 1820s as a maker of coaches for the nobility.

In the distinctive red, white and black Victorian police station visitors are invited every Tuesday to look round the **Police Museum**, where the exhibits include more than 600 models of police cars, truncheons, handcuffs and a 1903 hand-drawn ambulance. *The Blue Lamp* and *Dixon of Dock Green* are remembered in the nostalgic Jack Warner Corner.

Chicheley

5 miles NE of Milton Keynes on the A422

This attractive village is home of **Chicheley Hall**, a beautiful baroque house that was built in the early 1700s for Sir John Chester and which remains today one of the finest such houses in the country. Down the years it was used by the military and as a school, but in 1952 it was bought by the 2nd Earl Beatty and restored to its former state of grace. The earl's father, the 1st Earl, was a particularly courageous naval commander and, as well as receiving the DSO at the age of just 25, he was also a commander in the decisive battle of Jutland in 1916.

Willen

1 mile NE of Milton Keynes on the A509

The village Church of St Mary Magdalene, built in the late 17th century, is an elegant building in the style of Sir Christopher Wren, but Willen is also home to another house of prayer, the **Peace Pagoda and Buddhist Temple**, opened in 1980. It was built by the monks and nuns of the Nipponsan Myohoji, and it was the first peace pagoda in the western hemisphere. In this place of great tranquillity and beauty, a thousand cherry trees and cedars, donated by the ancient Japanese town of Yoshino, have been planted on the hill surrounding the pagoda, in memory of the victims of all wars.

Great Linford

2 miles NE of Milton Keynes on the A422

Situated on the banks of the Grand Union Canal, this village, which is now more or less a suburb of Milton Keynes, has a 13th century church set in parkland, a 17th century manor house, and a **Stone Circle**, one of only a few such prehistoric monuments in the county. Despite the encroachment of its much larger neighbour, the village has retained a distinctive air that is all its own.

The central block of the present manor house was built in 1678 by Sir William Pritchard, Lord Mayor of London. As well as making Great Linford his country seat, Pritchard also provided a boys' school and almshouses for six unmarried poor of the parish. The manor house was extended in the 18th century by the Uthwatt family, relatives of the Lord Mayor, and they used various tricks to give an impressive and elegant appearance to the building. The Grand Union Canal cuts through the estate, whose grounds are now a public park.

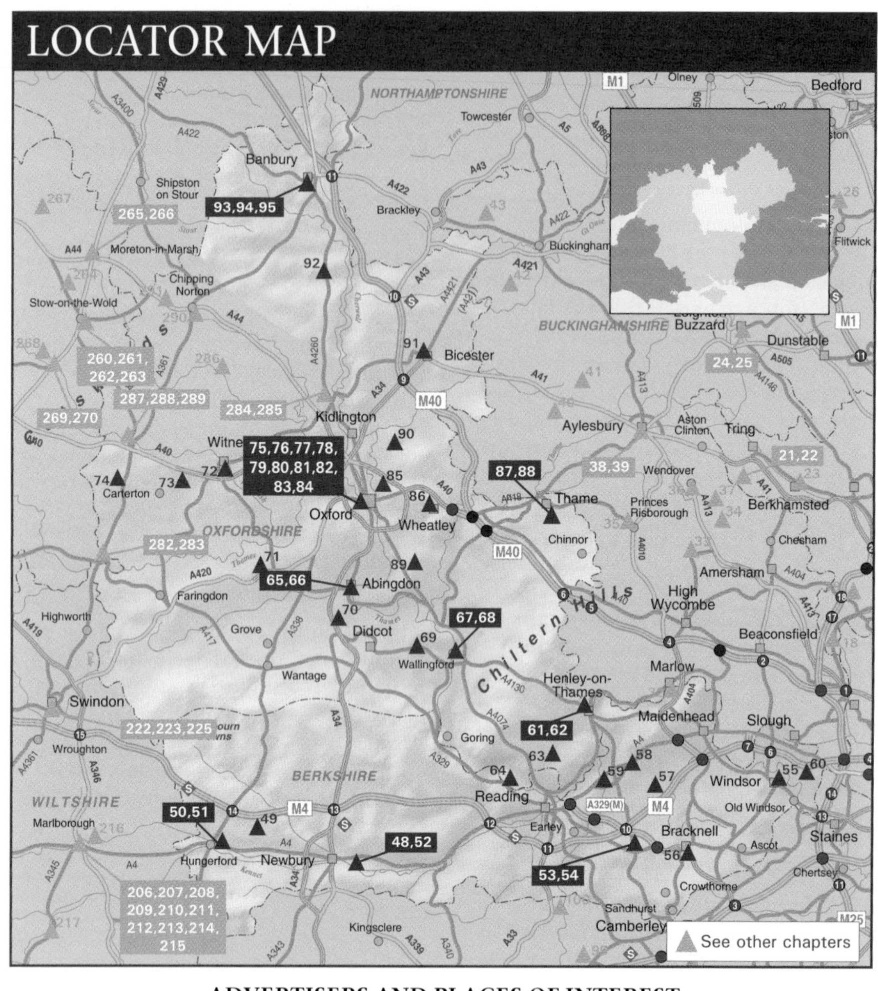

ADVERTISERS AND PLACES OF INTEREST

Accommodation, Food and Drink

Activities

Antiques and Restoration

Arts and Crafts

THE THAMES VALLEY 2

It rises in the Cotswolds and winds its way through the varied landscapes of several counties and on through London before entering the North Sea at Tilbury; the total length is some 210 miles and its tributaries include the Churn, Coln, Windrush, Evenlode, Cherwell, Kennet, Loddon, Wey and Mole. The Victorians and the Edwardians, with their passion for boating, were responsible for the development of many fashionable towns and villages along the Thames. One of the best known places on its banks is Henley-on-Thames, famous for the annual regatta that has attracted visitors and competitors for over 150 years. Villages and ancient crossing points are scattered along the river, and the banks and towpaths afford pleasant walks and delightful scenery. At various points along the river, visitors can watch the annual tradition of swan upping, an event that dates back to the 12th century.

Among the ancient towns, villages and landmarks are Wantage, the birthplace of Alfred the Great, and the region's most famous sight, the Uffington White Horse cut in chalk on a hillside. Oxford, the city of dreaming spires, began to develop from a small walled Saxon town with the influx of students and scholars in the 12th century. With more than 40 colleges making up the University, this seat of learning has influenced thinking throughout the world for centuries, but for the thousands of visitors who flock here each year the main attraction is the wealth of historic buildings.

West Berkshire Council manages a variety of sites for wildlife conservation and quiet recreation. Access is free and most sites have parking. For further information about these and other sites including Padworth Common and Hosehill Lake, and an extensive Rights of Way network of public footpaths, Tel: 01635 519858.

Thatcham Nature Discovery Centre

Thatcham Nature Discovery Centre is an exciting place to discover wetland wildlife. Visitors can enjoy a walk around Thatcham lake, visit the reedbed bird hide or let off steam in the adventure playgrounds. There are a wide range of hands-on exhibits in the Discovery Centre set against a dramatic backdrop of giant insect models and colourful wildlife banners. Refreshments are available from the Lakeside cafe.

Situated off the A4, Thatcham.

Muddy Lane, Lower Way,
Thatcham, Berkshire RG19 3FU
Tel: 01635 874381
Fax: 01635 866991

E-mail: naturecentre@westberks.gov.uk
Website: www.westberks.gov.uk

Greenham and Crookham Common

After many years as a military site, Greenham and Crookham Common has been restored and reopened to the public.

Paths and marked walk routes allow you to explore the heathland and woodland as well as taking you round old bombsites, taxi ways and the cruise missile silo enclosure. The area is a Site of Special Scientific Interest (SSSI) so it is important to stay on the paths to prevent damage to rare plant communities.

Car parks off Bury's Bank Road, Greenham.

Snelsmore Common Country Park

Snelsmore Common is a heathland site surrounded by woodland. It is an important area for ground nesting birds such as Nightjar and Woodlark and it is also a SSSI. There are many footpaths and tracks on the site as well as a bridleway and a right of way for horseriders and cyclists. An area is set aside for picnics and there are toilet facilities.

Car parks off Wantage Road (B4494), Newbury.

BERKSHIRE

The county of Berkshire extends over some 485 square miles in the valley of the middle Thames and is divided into six main districts. The western area of the county is important for racing and the training of racehorses, with a top-class course at Newbury and the training centres of Lambourn and East Ilsley.

Another feature of West Berkshire is the number of communication routes that flow across the region linking London with the West Country, dominated today by the M4 motorway. The ancient Ridgeway Path, England's oldest road, follows the county border with Oxfordshire, and the Kennet and Avon Canal, completed in 1810, crosses southern England from Bristol to join the River Thames at Reading. Entering the county at Hungerford, this major waterway passes through a charming rural landscape as it winds through villages and market towns. The canal prospered until the arrival of the Great Western Railway in 1841, after which it inevitably declined; by the 1950s it was largely unnavigable. After a full clearing and restoration programme the canal can now once again be travelled its full length, providing a wide variety of leisure activities for thousands of visitors each year.

The central region of Berkshire is dominated by Reading, a thriving commuter town with excellent links to both London and the West Country. Though seeming to be very much a product of the last two centuries, it has a long and interesting history.

The Thames, forming the northern county border with Oxfordshire, has, especially along its southern banks, many delightful villages which became fashionable thanks to the Victorian and Edwardian passion for boating and remain fashionable to this day. The most important landmark in the east of the county is the 900-year-old Windsor Castle, one of three official residences of the Queen and a major tourist attraction.

Across Windsor Great Park, the remains of a royal hunting forest, lies Ascot racecourse, founded in 1711 by Queen Anne. Five days in June see the worlds of fashion and horseracing meet at the highest level at the Royal Ascot meeting, but the course stages many meetings throughout the year.

LAMBOURN

Lying up on the Berkshire Downs, in the extreme west of the county, this village, which has the feel of a small town, is best known as a major centre for the training of racehorses. Over 1,200 horses are trained here, there are more than 100 miles of gallops, and the **Lambourn Trainers' Association** organise guided tours of the stables and trips to the gallops to view the horses going through their paces. Lambourn has been home to some of the greatest trainers in the history of the racing game, including Fred Winter and Fulke Walwyn over the jumps and Barry Hills and Peter Walwyn on the flat.

Lambourn's medieval **Church of St Michael** is one of the finest parish churches in Berkshire. Originally Norman and constructed on the cruciform plan, it has been greatly altered and extended, though the west end still has its Norman doorway, complete with zigzag ornamentation. The lychgate was dedicated to the memory of William Jousiffe, who brought horses from Newmarket to Lambourn in the 1870s and thus established a still-flourishing industry.

To the north of the village are **Lambourn Seven Barrows**, one of the most impressive Bronze Age burial sites in the country and actually comprising no fewer than 32 barrows.

AROUND LAMBOURN

East Ilsley

10 miles E of Lambourn off the A34

This attractive downland village has managed to retain several interesting features and in particular the winding mechanism of the now long disused village well by the pond. It was because of sheep that the village chiefly prospered – from the early 1600s East Ilsley held fortnightly sheep fairs that were second only in size to Smithfield, London. At their peak in the 19th century, permanent pens were erected in the main street to contain the animals and, on one day, it was recorded that 80,000 sheep were penned. During the 19th century the station in the nearby village of **Compton** became an important centre for the passage of sheep to and from the great East Ilsley sheep market, but the decline in the sheep trade resulted in the closure of the station. About a mile south of Compton lie the remains of an Iron Age fort, Perborough Castle, while to the northeast, just above the Ridgeway, is Lowbury Hill, where traces of a Roman temple and a Roman military outpost can be seen.

Today, along with its neighbour West Ilsley, the village is associated with racehorses which use the gallops on the downs as their training grounds.

NEWBURY

This crossroads town has, for many years, dominated the rural area of West Berkshire. Prospering during the Middle Ages, and afterwards, on the importance of the woollen industry, the town became famous as the Cloth Town. Among the various characters who made their money out of the weaving of the wool the best known is John Smallwood, always known as Jack of Newbury and the "richest clothier England ever beheld". Asked to raise two horsemen and two footmen for Henry VIII's campaign against the Scots, Jack raised 50 of each and led them himself. However, they only got as far as Stony Stratford in Buckinghamshire before news of the victory of Flodden reached them and they turned for home.

Evidence of the town's wealth can be seen in the splendid 'wool' **Church of St Nicholas**, which was constructed between 1500 and 1532. Built on the site of a Norman church, no expense was spared and Jack of Newbury gave the money for the magnificent five-bayed nave. The church has seen much restoration work, particularly during the Victorian age, but the fine pulpit and elaborately decorated nave roof have survived.

After the Civil War, the town's clothing industry declined. However, the 18th century saw the construction of turnpike roads and Newbury became a busy coaching stop on the road from London to Bath. The town further opened up to travellers and the needs of carriers with the completion of the **Kennet and Avon Canal** in 1810. **Newbury Lock**, built in 1796, was the first lock to be built along the canal and it is also the only one to have lever-operated ground paddles (the sluices that let in the water) which are known as 'Jack Cloughs'.

Back in the centre of the town, in the Market Square is the **Newbury Museum**, housed in the 17th century cloth hall and the adjacent 18th century granary, a store once used by traders travelling the canal. As well as the archaeological section, the history of the town is fully explained, including the two Battles of Newbury (1643 and 1644) during the Civil War.

Those arriving in Newbury from the south will pass the **Falkland Memorial**, which has nothing to do with the 1980s conflict in the South Atlantic. It is in fact a memorial to Lord Falkland, who was killed at the first battle of Newbury. To the east of the town lies **Newbury Racecourse**, which stages top-quality flat and National Hunt racing throughout the year.

AROUND NEWBURY

Hampstead Norreys

6 miles NE of Newbury on the B4009

Just to the north of the village lies **Wyld Court Rainforest**, an education and conservation charity devoted to the raising of awareness about the world's rain forests. Here, at the indoor rainforest, where the temperature never falls below 70°C, visitors can walk through the humid and shadowy jungles of the Lowland Tropical Forests, the cool, orchid-festooned and ferny Cloudforests, and the Amazon with its amazing flowers and wonderful bromeliads. There is also a unique collection of spectacular and rare plants, tranquil pools, the sounds of the tropics, and rainforest animals including a pair of Goeldi's monkeys, marmosets, tree frogs, iguanas, and Courtney the dwarf crocodile. Also on site are a shop selling plants and gifts, and a tea shop.

Donnington

1 mile N of Newbury on the B4494

Despite being so close to the town of Newbury, Donnington has managed to retain its village identity and atmosphere. To the west of the village, and visible from the road, is Donnington Grove House. Built in 1759 and designed by the architect John Chute, this was the home, in the late 18th century, of the Brummell family; Beau Brummell, the instigator of the Bath Society, lived here as a child. However, most visitors to the village come to see **Donnington Castle** (English Heritage), a late-14th century defence that was built by Sir Richard Abberbury. Once a magnificent structure, only the twin-towered gatehouse survives amidst the impressive earthworks. The castle had its most eventful period during the Civil War when it was the scene of one of the longest sieges of the conflict. Charles I's troops were held here for 20 months and it was during this period that most of the castle was destroyed.

Winterbourne

3 miles N of Newbury off the B4494

Just south of the village lies **Snelsmore Common Country Park**, one of the county's most important natural history sites. The common comprises several different habitats, including woodland, heathland and bog, and it supports a correspondingly wide variety of plant and animal life.

Wickham

6 miles NW of Newbury on the B4000

This ancient village with its typical Berkshire mix of brick and flint, thatch and tile is most notable for its **Church of**

Kennet Horse Boat Co Ltd

2 Rectory Cottage, Church Hill, Wickham, Newbury,
Berkshire RG20 8HD
Tel: 01488 658866
e-mail: kennethorseboat@btconnect.com

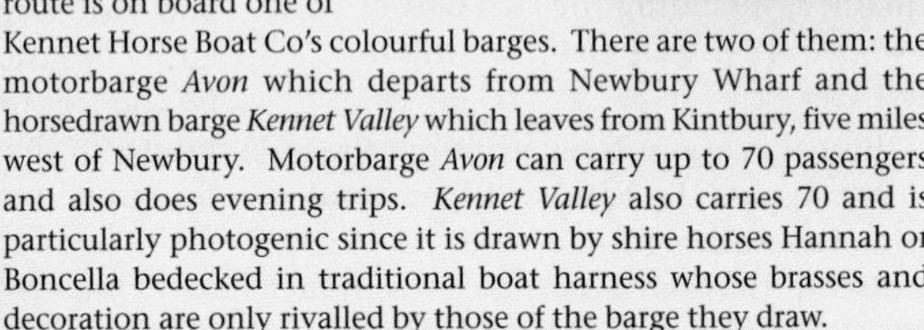

The stretch of the Kennet & Avon Canal between Newbury and Hungerford passes through some wonderfully peaceful and picturesque countryside. One of the best ways of enjoying this scenic route is on board one of Kennet Horse Boat Co's colourful barges. There are two of them: the motorbarge *Avon* which departs from Newbury Wharf and the horsedrawn barge *Kennet Valley* which leaves from Kintbury, five miles west of Newbury. Motorbarge *Avon* can carry up to 70 passengers and also does evening trips. *Kennet Valley* also carries 70 and is particularly photogenic since it is drawn by shire horses Hannah or Boncella bedecked in traditional boat harness whose brasses and decoration are only rivalled by those of the barge they draw.

From mid April to the end of September, both barges run day trips from 1½ to 4 hours duration. Departure times vary but a timetable is available on request. The barges are also available for private charter. Afternoon tea, lunch or supper can be arranged buffet style and there is a well stocked bar serving tea, coffee and alcoholic beverages. CD facilities are provided (motorbarge only) and a live jazz band or disco can be arranged at an extra cost.

The Gentleman's Shop

Charnham House, 29-30 Charnham Street,
Hungerford, Berkshire RG17 0EJ
Tel: 01488 684363/683536
e-mail: sales@gentlemans-shop.com
website: www.gentlemans-shop.com

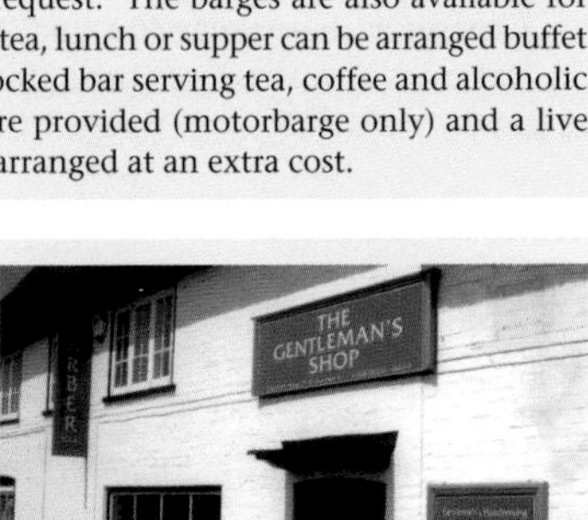

Housed in a Grade II listed, thatched building on the main A4 through Hungerford, **The Gentleman's Shop** is a unique combination of a Barber Shop and a Gift Shop devoted entirely to men.

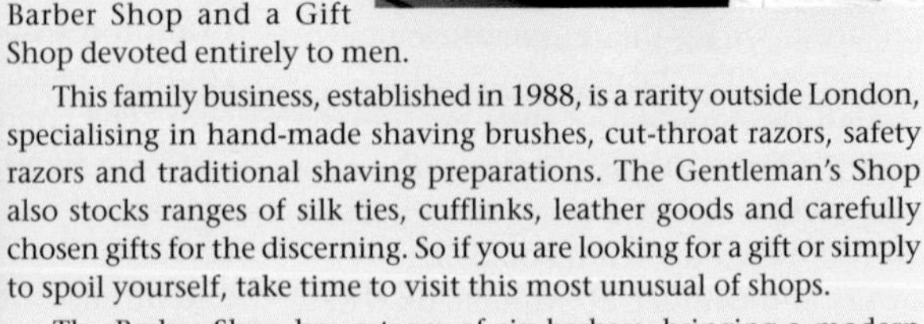

This family business, established in 1988, is a rarity outside London, specialising in hand-made shaving brushes, cut-throat razors, safety razors and traditional shaving preparations. The Gentleman's Shop also stocks ranges of silk ties, cufflinks, leather goods and carefully chosen gifts for the discerning. So if you are looking for a gift or simply to spoil yourself, take time to visit this most unusual of shops.

The Barber Shop has a team of six barbers, bringing a modern approach to the traditional skills of gentlemen's hairdressing. As well as a haircut, you can also indulge in a shave, complete with hot towels and shaving lessons are also available.

If you are unable to visit this time, gifts from The Gentleman's Shop can be sent worldwide by ordering from the website at www.gentlemans-shop.com.

St Swithin that stands atop a hill with grand views across the Kennet valley. It has a Saxon tower – unique in the county – but it is the interior that is truly remarkable because of its elephants. Made of papier-mâché and gilded they were purchased at the Paris Exhibition of 1862 and intended for the rectory. They were too large however so they now appear to support the spectacular wooden roof of the church.

Hungerford

9 miles W of Newbury on the A4

Although not mentioned in the Domesday Book, by the Middle Ages this old market town was well established, and the manor of Hungerford had some distinguished lords including Simon de Montfort and John of Gaunt. Hungerford's heyday came in the 18th century when the turnpike road from London to Bath was built, passing through the town. By 1840, the town had eight coaching inns serving the needs of travellers and the prosperity continued with the opening of the Kennet and Avon Canal. The building of the railway took much of that trade away and the town reverted to its early, gentle lifestyle. However, several of the old coaching inns have survived, notably **The Bear Hotel**. Although it has an impressive Georgian frontage, the building actually dates back to 1494, making it one of the oldest buildings in the town. It was here, in 1688, that a meeting took place between William of Orange and representatives of James II, which culminated in the end of the House of Stuart and the flight of James II to France.

As well as still holding a weekly market, the town also continues the ancient tradition known as the Hocktide Festival or **Tutti Day** (tutti meaning a

Ellie Dickins Shoes

97 High Street, Hungerford, Berkshire RG17 0NB
Tel: 01488 686480
e-mail: Elliedickins@ukonline.co.uk

"I love it when people exclaim, 'It's like having a new pair of feet'," says Ellie Dickins. "Some people want to kiss me, they are so overjoyed." Her High Street shop, Ellie Dickins Shoes, carries some £200,000 worth of stock at any one time with sizes ranging from 1 to 12 (including half-sizes) and widths from AA to EE – only ladies' shoes are stocked. Most of the shoes are imported from France, Spain and also Germany and are of the highest quality. Brands on offer include Gardenia, Amalfi, Carmen Poveda and Valentina Russo. "We don't sell cheap shoes," Ellie says, "but the shoes we do sell are an investment and they will last. In real terms they offer better value for money."

A qualified shoe fitter, Ellie believes that the personal service she and her staff offer has been the key to customer loyalty that sees regulars coming from as far away as Manchester. "It isn't just showing them one shoe and saying, 'That's all we've got.'" Ellie Dickins Shoes also has a thriving mail order business. A comprehensive catalogue is available and the service is of the same high standard as in the shop itself. "With customers we have seen in the shop, to get a better fit we often send two pairs of shoes in the same style for them to try and they will return one pair."

The Taste of England

Henwick Farm, Henwick Lane, Turnpike Road, Thatcham, Berkshire RG18 8AP
Tel: 01635 869760 (Pub), 07766201476 (Hotel Boats), 07900326732 (Hawking days)
website: www.stgeorgehotelboats.co.uk

The Taste of England offers an unusual combination of interests – falconry, narrowboat holidays and cruises, a farm shop, tea room and restaurant. The latter is located on the outskirts of Thatcham on the A4 and serves morning coffee, lunches, afternoon teas and evening meals. Licensed and with seating for 40, the restaurant offers an extensive menu with options ranging from fish to fowl, beef, lamb and curries. The Falconry is adjacent and offers exclusive days hunting with eagles. Short breaks on the Hotel Boats that include a day hunting with hawks, with meals included, are also available along with hands on hunting with hawks during the winter months.

Recently, owner Helen Tarry has extended the Taste of England Enterprise by establishing St George Hotel Boats. These are two full length (70ft) canal narrowboats, *Brackley* and *Ellesmere,* which work as a pair: *Brackley,* with her motor, leading the way; *Ellesmere,* the "butty", being silently towed behind. Starting life as a coal boat in 1870 and originally hauled by horse, *Ellesmere* is now retired and accommodates the galley and dining room as well as two en suite berthings. Total accommodation in the two boats comprises three single, two twin and one double cabin. All the twin and double cabins have their own en suite shower and flushing toilet. For daytime cruising there are open well decks with cushioned seats.

Various holiday options are available ranging from four to 10 days, and Helen is also happy to arrange themed holidays – for bird watchers, artists, anglers, cyclists, singles and over 60s for example.

The boats are owner-operated by Helen and Phil whose lives have revolved around the countryside. As a boy, Phil spent many an hour fishing from the riverbank or cruising the waterways on the family narrow boat, sea fishing and working on farms. He has a great love for animals, the countryside and the waterways. Helen was brought up on a farm and has spent the last 10 years running the farm shop and restaurant having gained an excellent reputation for her cooking.

Kennet & Avon Canal, Hungerford

bunch of flowers). Held every year on the second Tuesday after Easter, the festival was originally used as a means of collecting an early form of council tax. During the colourful event, two men carrying a six-foot pole decorated with ribbons and flowers go around each household collecting the tax. To ease the burden of their visit, the men share a drink with the man of the house, give him an orange, and kiss his wife before collecting their penny payment. Today, however, though the visits are still made, no money is collected but the kisses are still required.

Combe

7 miles SW of Newbury off the A338

The isolated hamlet of Combe is overlooked by **Walbury Hill**, which at 974 feet is the highest point in Berkshire and the highest chalk hill in England. A popular place for walking and hang-gliding, the hill offers terrific views and the bonus of an Iron Age fort on its summit. Close to the hill stands **Combe Gibbet**, one of the last public hanging places in the country. This gibbet was first used in 1676 to hang a pair of adulterous murderers, George Broomham and Dorothy Newman, and has a crossbar with a 'his' side and a 'hers' side.

Greenham

1½ miles SE of Newbury off the A34

Greenham Common and the adjacent **Crookham Common** make up the largest area of lowland heathland in Berkshire. In 1941 the common land was taken over by the Air Ministry and became an important military base, first for British squadrons and then for the US Air Force. In 1981 nuclear-armed Cruise missiles arrived at Greenham and the site became notorious for the anti-nuclear demonstrations. The airbase is gradually being returned to nature and the site is once again open to the public. Designated a Site of Special Scientific Interest (SSSI), it is home to many rare and endangered plants and animals.

Thatcham

3 miles E of Newbury on the A4

Believed to be the oldest village in Britain, it is hard to imagine that this now large suburb of Newbury was once a small place. **Thatcham Moor** is one of the largest areas of inland freshwater reed beds in the country and, as well as the reeds which can grow up to six feet in height, the area supports numerous species of marshland and aquatic plants. Birds also abound here and it is an important breeding ground for reed and sedge warblers.

Thatcham Nature Discovery Centre (free - see entry on page 84), situated close to the Thatcham Moors Local Nature Reserve, is a multi-activity based centre where visitors are encouraged to look, listen, touch and learn through an exciting range of interactive exhibits. In Discovery Hall they can find out what lives beneath the lake, get a birds-eye view of the world, or watch the wildlife

WALK NUMBER 4

Upper Woolhampton

Distance:	5.0 miles (8.0 kilometres)
Typical time:	140 mins
Height gain:	50 metres
Map:	Explorer 159
Walk:	www.walkingworld.com ID:683
Contributor:	Liz and David Fishlock

Access Information:

From M4 (Junction 12) take A4 towards Theale/Newbury and stay on this road for about six miles until you reach Woolhampton, where you should turn right just after the Falmouth Arms into Woolhampton Hill. The walk starts from the main entrance to Elstree School which you will see on your right. Park considerately along this road.

Description:

An undemanding ramble through typical Berkshire countyside which takes the walker along quiet country lanes, through woodland and across open farmland. However, if you are in need of a short break the Six Bells in the lovely village of Beenham is a little over halfway on this circular walk. The Elstree School from where the walk starts was founded over 150 years ago and moved to its present location from Elstree in 1939. The Benedictine Douai Abbey which can be seen in the distance at various points of the walk has a car park and is open to the public.

Features:

Pub, Play Area, Church, Birds, Flowers, Great Views, Butterflies, Food Shop, Woodland

Walk Directions:

1 Standing with your back to the main entrance of Elstree School, turn left along the road and after about 20 metres look out for and take signposted footpath on your right. The broad grassy track runs between fields and you will pass two ponds on your left. Go ahead over farm track to enter copse. Cross stile.

2 Leave copse and turn sharp right in the direction of the footpath sign, now to keep to right-hand field perimeter. Carry on ahead, passing footpath sign, until you reach further footpath sign where you should turn right to enter woodland. Follow clear path through woodland until you reach crossing track.

3 Turn right along broad track and shortly after bear right to enter field and then left, to follow left-hand field perimeter. At field corner turn right, still keeping field

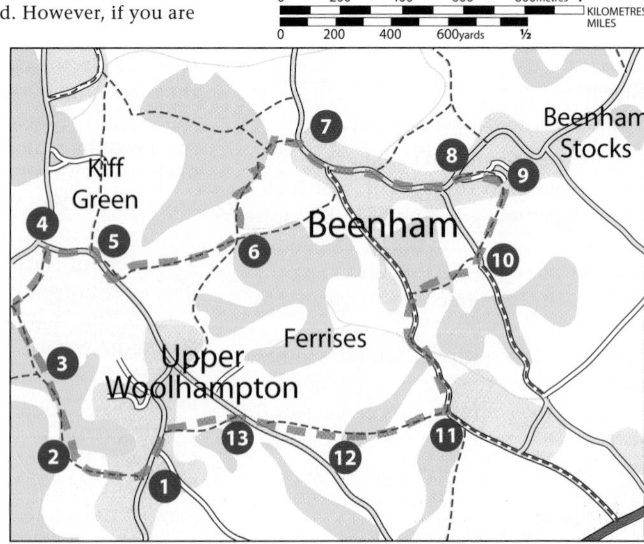

perimeter on your left. You will shortly be able to see Douai Abbey in the distance on your right. At field corner follow direction of footpath sign by turning left onto track to reach road.

4 Turn right along road. Where road bends right, ignore footpath off to your left to carry on for a further 75 metres to stile on your left.

5 Cross stile into field and keep close to right-hand field perimeter, until you reach footpath sign at field corner (at time of walking the field corner was somewhat overgrown). Turn left along broad track to enter field with field boundary on your left. At field corner continue ahead (field boundary will now be on your right).

6 At junction of paths in field corner turn left, keeping field boundary on your right and follow path as it bears sharp right before woodland. Stay on this path as it skirts the edge of the wood with fields on your right. At edge of Greyfield Wood ignore path off to left to carry on ahead, passing substation on your left. Stay on gravel track to reach road.

7 Turn right along road which you will follow for almost 1km through the lovely village of Beenham, passing the Six Bells public house and the children's playground until you reach the primary school on your left.

8 Walk past the school, cross the main road and pick up the footpath on the other side along Stoneyfield (small residential development). Turn right into Church View. Carry on ahead through metal barriers and along road until about 25 metres before road junction.

9 Turn sharp right into Wickens Corner and where the drive goes off to the left, carry on ahead along enclosed path which first descends and then rises. Follow path, eventually to reach the road.

10 Turn left along road and then enter churchyard on opposite side through lychgate. Follow path to the left of the church to exit across stile in corner. Keep to right-hand field fence to cross further stile and enter woodland. Follow clear path through woodland which initially descends steeply. Leave woodland across stile and turn left along gravel track. Stay on this track for about 600 metres and where it climbs you should look out for a large wooden building on your left.

11 Immediately after the wooden building, turn sharp right to enter field and keep close to new fence on your right. Where this goes off to the right carry on ahead to cross field, maintaining same direction and making for left-hand edge of wood ahead. At field corner cross into next field, keeping edge of wood on your right. There are far-reaching views to your left across the Kennet Valley (and Aldermaston). In field corner cross stile to enter wood. After 20 metres or so, where path forks, take left fork (following direction of faint arrow on tree ahead). The winding path through this narrow strip of woodland is fairly clear. However, to assist, it should take you no more than a minute or so to follow the path through the wood and exit it on your right to arrive at the next waymark.

12 At wood edge go over crossing track (permitted bridleway) to go through V-stile and cross field, making for V-stile in left-hand field boundary. Cross into next field and bear diagonally right to cut off field corner and go through V-stile onto driveway. Go through two more V-stiles, maintaining same direction (going under power lines) to reach field corner and stile to road.

13 Turn right along road for about 25 metres and then take path on your left through trees to cross private driveway and enter playing fields through gap between wooden fence and holly bushes. Initially keep to left-hand side of playing fields until Church spire comes into view and head towards it and gate into churchyard. Follow path through churchyard to main road. Turn left along road to return to start.

from the comfort of the lakeside observation area.

Woolhampton

6 miles E of Newbury on the A4

This tranquil village on the banks of the Kennet and Avon Canal had a watermill at the time of the Domesday Survey of 1086 and was mentioned again in 1351, when the manor and mill were owned by the Knights Hospitallers. The present mill, built in 1820 and extended in 1875, was powered by a brook which runs into the Kennet and was last used in 1930. It has since been turned into offices.

Beenham

7 miles E of Newbury off the A4

Set in 6,000 acres of beautiful woodlands, the **UK Wolf Conservation Trust** proves that wolves are not the big, bad, dangerous animal of nursery rhymes and legend. There are wolves here you can actually stroke and which are taken to schools, shows and seminars. The European wolves are the first to be successfully bred in England for 500 years and the Trust also cares for packs of North American wolves. The site is open all year round, by appointment.

READING

This thriving commuter town, which took its name from the Saxon chief Reada, is a delightful combination of over a thousand years of history and a vibrant and modern city. There are Victorian brick buildings nestling beside beautiful medieval churches, famous coaching inns opposite high tech offices and some of the best shopping in the area. However, Reading began as a Saxon settlement between the Rivers Thames and Kennet and as a defensible site was used by the Danes as a base for their attack on Wessex in the 9th century. The town grew up around its **Abbey**, which was founded in 1121 by Henry I, the youngest son of William the Conqueror, and it was consecrated by Thomas à Becket in 1164. The abbey went on to become one of the most important religious houses – its relics included a piece of Jesus' sandal, the tooth of St Luke, and a slice of Moses' rod. Henry, its great benefactor, was buried in front of the High Altar in 1136.

The atmospheric abbey ruins stand in **Forbury Gardens** on the banks of the River Kennet; these gardens are also home to the **Maiwand Lion**, a magnificent statue of a lion which commemorates the men of the Berkshire Regiment who died in the Afghan War of 1879.

Reading boasts several other pieces of distinguished public art, including the Robed Figure by Dame Elizabeth Frink and the Soane Obelisk designed by Sir John Soane, architect of the Bank of England. Adjacent to the abbey ruins is another of Reading's famous buildings – **Reading Gaol** where Oscar Wilde was imprisoned and where he wrote *De Profundis*. His confinement here also inspired the writer to compose the epic *Ballad of Reading Gaol* whilst staying in Paris in 1898.

Though the town developed during the Middle Ages as a result of a flourishing woollen industry, it was during the 18th century with the coming of both the turnpike roads and the opening of the **Kennet and Avon Canal** which saw the town boom. By the 19th century, Reading was known for its three Bs: beer, bulbs, and biscuits. As the trade of the canal and River Thames increased, the movement of corn and malt explains the growth of the brewing trade, and the leaders in the bulb trade were Sutton Seeds, founded here in 1806 but now just a memory. The world renowned biscuit-making firm of Huntley & Palmer began life here in 1826, when Joseph Huntley founded the firm, to be joined, in 1841, by George Palmer, inventor of the stamping machine.

The Story of Reading, a permanent exhibition at the **Museum of Reading**, is the ideal place to gain a full understanding of the history of the town, from the earliest times to the present day. Here, too, can be seen the world's only full size replica of the Bayeux Tapestry, made in the 19th century and featuring Edward the Confessor, once Lord of the Royal Manor in Reading, as a central figure. As a contrast to the museum's displays depicting the life of the town in the 20th century, The Silchester Gallery is devoted to the describing day to day life at Calleva Atrebatum, the Roman town of Silchester, using Roman artefacts unearthed there during early excavations. This museum, one of the most go-ahead in the country, has special events and changing exhibitions throughout the year, so every visit will reveal something new and exciting to see.

Situated on the banks of the River Kennet and housed in a range of canal buildings, **Blake's Lock Museum** describes the life of the town in the 19th and early 20th centuries. Originally part of a pumping station built at Blake's Weir in the 1870s, the buildings themselves are also of interest and are superb examples of Victorian industrial architecture combined with decorative Reading brickwork.

In 1925 Reading Extension College became a university in its own right. Lying to the south of the town centre at Whiteknights, the university campus is home to the **Rural History Centre**, the national centre for the history of food, farming and the countryside. The centre has one of the country's finest collections of artefacts relating to daily life and work in the countryside, an extensive library and archives and over 750,000 photographic images of rural life. Also in the university building are the Ure Museum of Greek Archaeology and the Cole Museum of Zoology.

AROUND READING

Sonning

3 miles NE of Reading off the A4

This pretty little village leading down to the Thames is a popular spot to visit, especially on summer weekends. In 1399, after he had been deposed, Richard II brought his young bride Isabella here to be looked after in the palace of the Bishops of Salisbury. Her ghost is said to appear on the paths beside the river. On Grove Street stands **Turpin's**, a house which belonged to the aunt of Dick Turpin and provided

Lock on the River Thames, Sonning

Holme Grange Craft Barn & Art Gallery

Holme Grange Craft Village, Heathlands Road,
Wokingham, Berkshire RG40 3AW
Tel: 0118 977 6753
website: www.holme–grange.co.uk

Holme Grange Craft Village, a varied complex of 19th and 20th Century farm buildings, is set in the heart of a rural farming area within easy reach of the M3/M4 motorways. The main buildings enclose a delightful courtyard, where snacks and light meals are served by the Tea Shoppe.

The spacious Craft Barn - once a milking barn - has retained its original wooden beams and cast-iron milking bays. It is an ideal setting in which to browse and admire the wide variety of work from around 90 local craftworkers.

The centrepiece of the Village is its Art Gallery, designed to reflect the wide range of artistic talent in the area. The work of over 60 local artists - painters, sculptors, workers in wood, decorative glass and other media - is on display for viewing and purchase. The Gallery also boasts an extensive range of hand-crafted greetings cards and a wide selection of high quality silk flowers. It holds special artists' exhibitions throughout the year, and supplies a range of quality artists' materials.

The Craft Barn and Art Gallery are open 7 days a week, throughout the year (closing only between Christmas and New Year). Their comprehensive web site carries all the information needed to get the most out of a visit to this artistic haven in the heart of Berkshire.

The Craft Shop

Ashridge Manor Garden Centre, Forest Road,
Wokingham, Berkshire RG40 5QY
Tel: 0118 977 0816
website: www.ashridgemanorgardencentre.com

Opened in 1991, **The Craft Shop** is the 'must visit' place for crafts and gifts. Owner Beryl Chapman is a self-confessed craft addict who attended craft classes and now encourages others by stocking a huge selection of materials and finished items. The latter range from ceramics to scented candles, hand-painted glass to pot pourri holders, silk flower arrangements to baskets and bins, and much, much more. Beryl's own expertise in needlework and embroidery is put to good use in personalising beautiful albums.

In the early days she stocked the shop virtually single-handed but today she has a wealth of local talent on which to draw with handicrafts inspired from American and Australia. It's safe to say that you'll certainly find something here that is completely different. Most of all, Beryl prides herself on personal, friendly service – new faces and old friends are greeted with a warm welcome and a smile. Visitors are welcome to browse at leisure or ask for help to find that perfect gift. Located within the Ashridge Manor Garden Centre, The Craft Shop is open from 10am to 4pm, Tuesday to Sunday.

occasional refuge for the notorious highwayman. Behind the wall of the old bishop's palace is Deanery Gardens, a house built in 1901 to the design of Sir Edwin Lutyens.

Woodley

3 miles E of Reading off the A329

At Woodley Airfield the **Museum of Berkshire Aviation** celebrates the contribution the county has made to the history of aviation. The exhibits include Spitfires and reconstructed Miles & Handley Page aircraft which are shown along with fascinating pictorial records and archives.

Hurst

4½ miles E of Reading off the A321

This attractive, scattered village is home to a Norman church, well endowed with monuments, and a row of fine 17th century almshouses. The village bowling green is said to have been made for Charles II.

Just to the south lies **Dinton Pastures Country Park**, a large area of lakes, rivers, hedgerows and meadows rich in wildlife. Until the 1970s, this area was excavated for sand and gravel, but the former pits are now attractive lakes and ponds; one of them has been stocked for coarse fishing and the largest is set aside for canoeing and windsurfing.

Wokingham

6 miles SE of Reading on the A329

This largely residential town has at its centre an old triangular market place with a matching triangular Town Hall built in 1860. In the mainly Victorian town centre is a sprinkling of attractive Georgian houses and shops, and the medieval parish church of All Saints. The most attractive building however is **Lucas Hospital**, built of mellow red brick and rather like a miniature Chelsea Hospital. It was originally built in 1666 as almshouses and a chapel, by Henry Lucas, a mathematician and MP for Cambridge University. Today, the hospital still cares for the elderly though now in the style of a retirement home. It can be visited by appointment with the resident matron.

Arborfield

4 miles S of Reading on the A327

Arborfield Garrison is the home base of REME, the Royal Electrical and Mechanical Engineers, and the site of their museum. To the south is **California Country Park**, a wooded beauty spot where the woods support 34 different species of tree and the bogland provides a range of habitats for the many animals, birds and plants that are found here.

Swallowfield

5 miles S of Reading off the A33

The manor house here, **Swallowfield Park**, has been associated with both royalty and other notables. The present house (unfortunately now but a shell) was built in 1678 by Wren's assistant William Talman for the 2nd Earl of Clarendon, who acquired the estate upon marrying the heiress. In 1719, the park was purchased by Thomas Pitt, a former Governor of Madras, who used the proceeds of the sale of a large diamond he bought while in India. The diamond can now be seen in the Louvre Museum, Paris. The story of Pitt and his diamond provided the inspiration for the novel, *The Moonstone*, by Wilkie Collins, who visited the house in 1860. The Italian Doorway, by Talman, is probably the house's most outstanding remaining feature and it marks the entrance to the walled garden. Here can be found a dog's graveyard where lies one of Charles Dickens' dogs. The novelist had bequeathed the pet to his friend and owner of the house, Sir Charles Russell.

Finchampstead

8 miles S of Reading off the A327

To the east of the village lie **Finchampstead Ridges**, a popular spot for walkers that offers wonderful views across the Blackwater Valley. Simon's Wood has a varied mixture of conifers and broad-leaved trees, and in the wood and on the heath are siskin and flycatchers, dragonflies, damselflies and a wide range of invertebrates and lichens.

Aldermaston

9 miles SW of Reading on the A340

It was in this tranquil village, in 1840, that the William pear was first propagated by John Staid, the then village schoolmaster. First known as the Aldermaston pear, a cutting of the plant is believed to have been taken to Australia where is it now called the Bartlett pear.

Still retaining much of its original 12th century structure and with a splendid Norman door, the lovely **St Mary's Church** provides the setting for the York Mystery Cycle, nativity plays dating from the 14th century, which are performed here each year. Using beautiful period costumes and contemporary music, including a piece written by William Byrd, the cycle lasts a week and the plays attract visitors from far and wide. Another old custom still continued in the village is the auctioning of the grazing rights of Church Acres every three years. Using the ancient method of a candle auction, a pin, in this case a horseshoe nail, is inserted into the tallow of a candle one inch from the wick. The candle is lit while bidding takes place and the grazing rights go to the highest bidder as the pin drops out of the candle.

Outside under a yew tree in the churchyard lies the grave of Maria Hale, formerly known as the Aldermaston witch. She was said to turn herself into a large brown hare and although the hare was never caught or killed, at one time a local keeper wounded it in the leg and from then on it was observed that Maria Hale had become lame.

Close to the village is a delightful walk along the Kennet & Avon Canal to **Aldermaston Wharf**. A Grade II-listed structure of beautifully restored 18th century scalloped brickwork, the wharf houses the **Kennet and Avon Canal Visitor Centre**, where the canal man's cottage contains an exhibition on the canal and information on its leisure facilities.

Pangbourne

6 miles NW of Reading on the A417

Situated at the confluence of the River Pang and the River Thames, the town grew up in the late 19th and early 20th centuries as a fashionable place to live. As a result there are several attractive Victorian and Edwardian villas to be seen including a row of ornate Victorian houses known as the Seven Deadly Sins. It was here that the author Kenneth Grahame retired, living at **Church Cottage** opposite the church. Grahame married late in life and it was whilst living here that he wrote for his son *The Wind in the Willows*.

Visitors to the town who cross the elegant iron bridge to neighbouring **Whitchurch** must still pay a toll, though now very small. The right to exact the toll has existed since 1792 and it is one of the very few surviving privately owned toll bridges. It was at **Whitchurch Lock** that the characters in Jerome K Jerome's *Three Men in a Boat* abandoned their craft, after a series of mishaps, and returned to London.

Basildon

8 miles NW of Reading on the A417

This small village is the last resting place of the inventor and agricultural engineer, Jethro Tull, and his grave can be seen in the churchyard. Outside the churchyard is a classic pavilion built in memory of his parents by the late Mr Childe-Beale which is, today, the focal point of **Beale Park**. Covering some 300 acres of ancient water meadow, the park is home to a wide range of birds and animals. There are small herds of unusual farm animals, including rare breeds of sheep and goats, Highland cattle, deer, and South American llama, more than 120 species of birds living in their natural habitat, and a pets' corner for smaller children. However, the park's work is not confined to the keeping of animals. As well as planting a **Community Woodland**, an ancient reed bed has been restored. The park's other main attraction housed in the pavilion is the **Model Boat Collection**, which is one of the finest of its kind.

However, the village's main feature is **Basildon Park** (National Trust), an elegant, classical house designed in the 18th century by Carr of York and undoubtedly Berkshire's foremost mansion. Built between 1776 and 1783 for Francis Sykes, an official of the East India Company, the house has the unusual addition of an Anglo-Indian room. The interior, finished by JB Papworth and restored to its original splendour after World War II, is rich in fine plaster work, pictures, and furniture and the rooms open to the public include the Octagon Room and a decorative Shell Room. If the name Basildon seems familiar it is probably as a result of the notepaper: the head of the papermaking firm of Dickinson visited the house and decided to use the name for the high quality paper.

Basildon Park

Aldworth

11 miles NW of Reading on the B4009

The parish Church of St Mary is famous for housing the **Aldworth Giants** - the larger than life effigies of the de la Beche family which date back to the 14th century. The head of the family, Sir Philip, who lies here with eight other members of his family, was the Sheriff of Berkshire and valet to Edward II. Though now somewhat defaced the effigies were so legendary that the church was visited by Elizabeth I. Outside, in the churchyard, are the remains of a once magnificent 1,000-year-old yew tree that was sadly damaged in a storm.

Nearby, at **Little Aldworth**, the grave of the poet Laurence Binyon, who wrote the famous lines '*At the going down of the sun and in the morning, we shall remember them*' can be seen in the churchyard. Opposite the

Bell Inn is one of the deepest wells in the country. Topped by great beams, heavy cogs, and wheels, it is some 327 feet deep.

WINDSOR

This old town grew up beneath the walls of the castle in a compact group of streets leading from the main entrance. Charming and full of character, this is a place of delightful timber-framed and Georgian houses and shop fronts, with riverside walks beside the Thames, and a wonderful racecourse. The elegant **Guildhall**, partly built by Wren in the 17th century, has an open ground floor for market stalls, while the council chambers are on the first floor. Concerned that they might fall through the floor onto the stalls below the council members requested that Wren put in supporting pillars in the middle of the market hall. As his reassurances that the building was sound fell on deaf ears, Wren complied with their wishes but the pillars he built did not quite meet the ceiling - thereby proving his point!

The grand central station, in the heart of the town, was built in 1897 to commemorate Queen Victoria's Diamond Jubilee and it is now home to a fascinating exhibition, **Royalty and Empire**, which charts the life and times of the country's longest reigning monarch. Close by, in the High Street, is another exhibition well worth visiting, **The Town and Crown Exhibition.** Here the development of the town and the influences of the Crown are explained in an imaginative and visual manner.

Meanwhile a trip to **The Dungeons of Windsor** provides a step back in time and an investigation of the town's history with a special regard for stories of crime and punishment from the early days of 13th century lawlessness through to the harsh Victorian era. The Household Cavalry also have their home in Windsor, at Combermere Barracks, and here is the superb **Household Cavalry Museum**, which displays collections of their uniforms, weapons, and armour from 1600 through to the present day.

In a pleasant setting close to the River Thames, **Royal Windsor Racecourse** is one of the most attractive in the country. Though less grand than neighbouring Ascot, its Monday evening meetings always bring a good crowd, but many regret the decision to give up the jumping fixtures.

The greatest attraction hereabouts is of course **Windsor Castle**, one of three official residences of the Queen (the others are Buckingham Palace and Holyrood House, in Edinburgh). The largest castle in the country and a royal residence for over 900 years, it was begun in the late 11th century by William the Conqueror as one in a chain of such defences which stood on the approaches to London. Over the years its role changed from a fortification to a royal palace; various monarchs added to the original typical Norman castle, the most notable additions being made by Henry VIII, Charles II and George IV. Various parts of the castle are open to the public, in particular the state apartments with their remarkable collection of furniture, porcelain and armour. Carvings by Grinling Gibbons are to be seen everywhere and the walls are adorned with a plethora of masterpieces, including paintings by Van Dyck and Rembrandt. The Gallery shows changing displays from the Royal Library, including works by Leonardo, Michelangelo and Holbein. On a somewhat smaller scale, but nonetheless impressive, is **Queen Mary's Dolls' House**. Designed by Sir Edwin Lutyens for Queen Mary, this is a perfect miniature palace, complete with working lifts and lights and running water. Built on a 1 to 12 scale, it took three years to complete, and 1,500 craftsmen were employed to ensure that every last detail was correct; the house was presented to the queen in 1924.

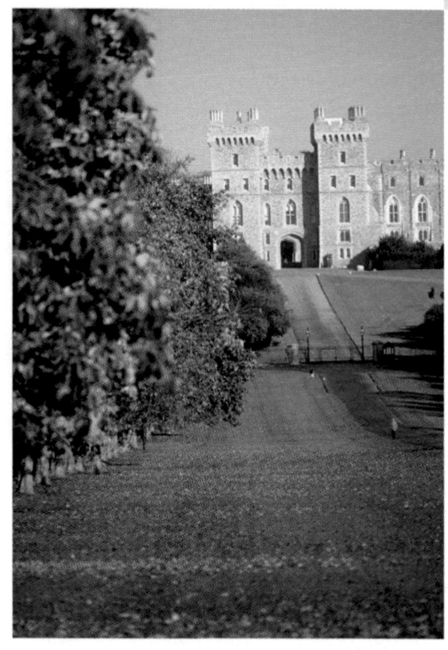

Windsor Castle

In November 1992, a massive fire swept through the northeast corner of the castle and no-one in the country at the time will forget the incredible pictures of the great tower alight. Following five years of restoration, the damaged areas were re-opened to the public.

Within the castle walls is the magnificent **St George's Chapel**. Started by Edward IV in 1478, and taking some 50 years to finish, the chapel is not only one of the country's greatest religious buildings but also a wonderful example of the Perpendicular Gothic style. It is the last resting place of 10 monarchs, from Edward IV himself to Henry VIII with his favourite wife Jane Seymour, Charles I, George V with Queen Mary, and George VI, beside whom the ashes of his beloved daughter Princess Margaret were laid in February 2002. It is also the Chapel of the Most Noble Order of the Garter, Britain's highest order of chivalry.

St. George's Chapel, Windsor

Frogmore House, a modest early-18th century manor house in Home Park, has over the years acted as a second, more relaxed royal residence than the nearby castle. It was bought in 1792 for Queen Charlotte, consort of George III, and later became a favourite retreat of Queen Victoria, who remarked that "all is peace and quiet and you only hear the hum of the bees, the singing of the birds". She and Prince Albert built a mausoleum in the grounds to house the remains of the Queen's mother, the Duchess of Kent, and their own - both Victoria and Albert are at rest here. The former library now contains furniture and paintings from the Royal Yacht *Britannia*. The house is surrounded by 30 acres of picturesque gardens containing masses of spring bulbs and some fine specimen trees.

To the south of the town lies the 4,800-acre **Windsor Great Park**, a remnant of the once extensive Royal Hunting Forest, and a unique area of open parkland, woodland, and impressive views. Within the park, at Englefield Green, is the **Savill Garden**, created by Sir Eric Savill when he was Deputy Ranger and one of the finest woodland gardens to be seen anywhere. A garden for all seasons, its attractions include colourful flower beds, secret glades, alpine meadows and a unique temperate house. The **Long Walk** stretches from the Castle to Snow Hill, some three miles away, on top of which stands a huge bronze of George III on horseback erected there in 1831. The three-mile ride to nearby Ascot racecourse was created by Queen Anne in the early 1700s. On the park's southern side lies **Smith's Lawn**, where polo matches are played most summer weekends. Windsor Great Park is also the setting for the Cartier International competition, polo's highlight event held every July, and the National Carriage Driving Championships.

To the southwest, set in 150 acres of parkland, is **Legoland Windsor**, where a whole range of amazing Lego models is on display, made from over 20 million bricks. Designed for children aged two to 12 – and their families – the site also offers more than 50 rides, shows and attractions including the Jungle Coaster with twists and turns at 60km.

AROUND WINDSOR

Ascot

6 miles SW of Windsor on the A329

A small village until 1711 when Queen Anne moved the Windsor race meeting to here and founded the world famous **Ascot Racecourse**. Its future was secured when the Duke of Cumberland established a stud at Windsor in the 1750s, and by the end of the century the meetings were being attended by royalty on a regular basis. Today, Royal Ascot, held every June, is an international occasion of fashion and style with pageantry and tradition and the very best flat racing spread over four days. To the west of the town lies **Englemere Pond**, a Site of Special Scientific Interest and also a local nature reserve. Once part of the royal hunting ground which surrounded Windsor Castle and still owned by the Crown Estate, the main feature is the shallow acidic lake which offers a wide range of habitats from open water to marsh, for the many species of plants, birds, and animals, and insects found here.

Horse Racing at Ascot

Bracknell

7 miles SW of Windsor on the A329

Designated a new town in 1948, Bracknell has developed quickly from a small village in poor sandy heathland, with some 3000 inhabitants, into a large modern town of around 60,000 residents. It boasts one of the first purpose built shopping centres in the country - opened in the 1960s. As well as being home to a number of high tech companies, Bracknell is also the home of the Meteorological Office.

Seen from many parts of the town and a very prominent landmark is the

Look Out Discovery Centre

Nine Mile Ride, Bracknell, Berkshire RG12 7QW
Tel: 01344 354400 Fax 01344 354422
e-mail: mark.croll@bracknell forest.govuk
website: www.bracknell-forest.gov.uk/lookout

The Look Out Discovery Centre in Bracknell is a great day out for all ages. The main attraction is an exciting hands on, interactive science and nature exhibition. Budding scientists will spend many hours exploring and discovering over 70 bright, fun filled exhibits within five themed zones.

In the exhibition there is The Look Out tower. Climb the 88 steps and see over the Centre towards Bracknell and beyond. In the surrounding 2,600 acres of Crown Estate woodland, visitors can enjoy nature walks, a picnic area, child's play area. In the Coffee Shop you can relax over a cup of tea or take a break and have a hot lunch. The Gift Shop offers a

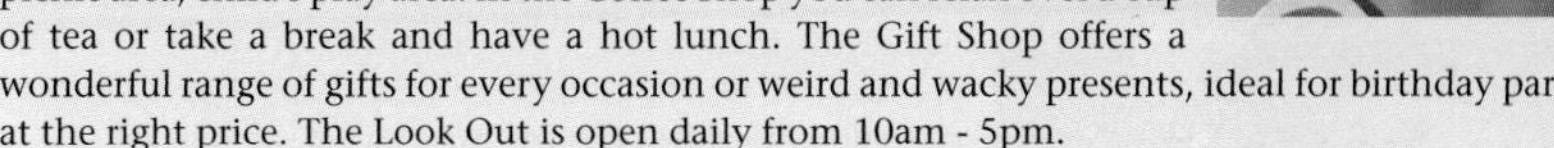

wonderful range of gifts for every occasion or weird and wacky presents, ideal for birthday party bags at the right price. The Look Out is open daily from 10am - 5pm.

The Royal Oak

Hungerford Lane, Shurlock Row, nr Twyford,
Berkshire RG10 0NY
Tel/Fax: 0118 934 5133

The attractive village of Shurlock Row is known for its noble and ancient royal oak that towers above the village inn called, what else, **The Royal Oak**. It's believed to be the only inn of that name that genuinely has its own royal oak. At the front of this appealing old hostelry are picnic tables; to the rear is the cricket ground of the neighbouring village, Waltham St Lawrence. You can tell that owner Paul Adams takes food very seriously – his pub sign blazons the name of the head chef, Scott Eyres. Scott trained at the Naval & Military Club in London and later worked as a chef at the Café Rouge.

His extensive menu specialises in classical English cuisine with a continental touch – starters such as Camembert stuffed with basil, garlic and onion compôte served with French bread, for example. Everything is freshly prepared and cooked to order and all the meat is supplied by local butcher, John King, who has been established in the village for more than 40 years. Food is served every lunchtime (noon until 2pm) and evening (6pm to 9.30pm), and to accompany your meal there's a good choice of wines from around the world, some of them available by the glass. In the bar, three real ales are on tap – Greene King, Abbot and IPA.

Sheeplands Farm Shop

Wyevale Garden Centre, Bath Road, Hare Hatch,
Twyford, Berkshire RG10 9SW
Tel: 0118 940 4399

A cow and her calf graze the forecourt of **Sheeplands Farm Shop** – well, actually they are models advertising the fresh milk available inside along with an extraordinary range of produce. Owner Andrew Cardy draws on more than 100 suppliers to stock the 3000sq ft shop. Sheeplands was established in 1981 by Andrew's family.

Cheese lovers will find a choice of more than 80 English and Continental varieties, and there's more continental flavour in the popular patisserie with its croissants, pain au chocolat, pain au raisin and other sweet treats. Frozen fruits, vegetables and bakery items are sold, along with a wide range of frozen ready meals supplied by Eazy Cuisine. These include the Petite Appetit range also available in one, two or four-portion sizes. Sheeplands also offers an extensive selection of free range and organic meats (frozen), vegetarian, gluten free or diabetic produce, and tasty ethic foods from Thai, Chinese and Indian cuisines. You can even bring your own fish here to have it smoked. The shop also has a baguette bar offering a huge variety of fillings in baguettes freshly baked in-store. Sheeplands also specialises in seasonal produce for Easter, Halloween and Christmas, including speciality free range Bronze Turkeys.

centrally located **Bill Hill**. At the top of the hill can be seen a circular mound of earth, hollowed out at the centre, which is all that remains of a Bronze Age round barrow. Used throughout that period, these burial mounds, which may cover either individuals or groups, are the most common prehistoric monuments in the country.

What remains of the great royal hunting ground, **Windsor Forest** (also called Bracknell Forest) lies to the south of the town and has over 30 parks and nature reserves and some 45 miles of footpaths and bridleways. Of particular interest in the area is The **Look Out Discovery Park** (see panel on page 103), an interactive science centre that brings to life the mysteries of both science and nature. In the surrounding 2,600 acres of Crown Estate woodland there are nature trails and walks to points of interest as well as the inappropriately named **Caesar's Camp**. Not a Roman fort, this camp is an Iron Age hill fort built over 2,000 years ago but, close by, lies the Roman link road between London and Silchester. Known locally as the **Devil's Highway**, it is said to have acquired the name because the local inhabitants thought that only the Devil could have undertaken such a prodigious feat of engineering.

Twyford

10 miles W of Windsor on the A4

At Twyford, the River Loddon divides into two separate streams from which the town takes its name – 'double ford'. With its watery location it's not surprising that there have been several mills here. A miller is mentioned in a document of 1163 although the first mill is dated 1363. There was a silk mill here until 1845 and a flour mill until 1976 when it was destroyed by fire. The

HodgePodge

19 Church Street, Twyford, Berkshire RG10 9DN
Tel: 0118 932 1441
e-mail: info@hodgepodge.uk.com
website: www.hodgepodge.uk.com

HodgePodge, is a place where children and adults can let their imagination run riot as they create their very own design on a piece of pottery. Painting your own pottery is great fun all year round so boredom will be a thing of the past.

Mark and Zahra Hodge, established HodgePodge in March 2004. They have more than 140 items to choose from - anything from a mug or a plate to a piggy bank or a egg cup. For a durable and food-safe finish, HodgePodge will fire your items in their on-site state of the art kiln which takes between five and seven days. "Don't worry if you are not artistic," says Zahra, "We have an extensive range of sponges, stamps, stencils and books to fill you with inspiration." On Thursday evenings there's a special session for adults who are welcome to bring along a bottle of wine and order a pizza if they wish.

During the day, HodgePodge offers its own tea, coffee and light refreshments. It also stocks an interesting range of hand-made gifts, including cards and wrapping paper. To avoid disappointment please phone to book a table on the above number or contact us via email.

replacement modern mill lacks the traditional appeal but it does continue the milling tradition in the town.

Binfield

8 miles SW of Windsor on the B3034

Binfield is famous as the boyhood home of the poet Alexander Pope. The family moved here after his father had amassed a fortune as a linen draper, and the boy Pope sang in the local choir and gained a local following for his poems about the Windsor Forest and the River Loddon. To the south of the village lies **Pope's Wood**, where the poet is said to have sought inspiration. Other connections include the artist John Constable, who sketched the parish church while here on his honeymoon, and Norah Wilmot, who was one of the first lady racehorse trainers to be allowed to hold a licence in her own name, having been forced to train for years in the name of her head lad. The Jockey Club abandoned this archaic ruling as recently as 1966.

Wargrave

10 miles W of Windsor on the A321

This charming village developed as a settlement in the 10th century at the confluence of the Rivers Thames and Loddon on an area of flat land in a wooded valley. The peace that generally prevails here was disturbed in 1914 when suffragettes burnt down the church in protest at the vicar's refusal to remove the word 'obey' from the marriage service. In the churchyard, undisturbed by the riot or anything since, stands the **Hannen Mausoleum**, a splendid monument that was designed for the Hannen family by Sir Edwin Lutyens in 1906.

Another interesting sight can be found on the outskirts of the village, at Park Place. In 1788 the estate was owned by General Henry Conway, Governor of Jersey. In recognition of his services, the people of the island gave the general a complete **Druids' Temple**. The massive stones were transported from St Helier to the estate and erected in a 25 foot circle in the gardens of his mansion. In 1870, Park Place was destroyed by fire and the estate broken up but today the temple stands in the garden of Temple Combe, close to a house designed by the famed American architect, Frank Lloyd Wright. The only house of his in this country, it was built in 1958 to an elaborate U-shaped design; its many unusual features include suede-panelled interior walls.

Sandhurst

11 miles SW of Windsor on the A3095

The town is famous as being the home of the **Royal Military Academy**, the training place for army officers since it was established in 1907. The academy's **Staff College Museum** tells the history of officer training from its inception to the present day. Close by is **Trilakes**, a picturesque country park set in 18 acres with, of course, some lakes. This is a wonderful place to visit with children as there are a wide assortment of pets and farm animals which they can get to know, including miniature horses, pygmy goats, donkeys, aviary birds, pot-bellied pigs and Soay sheep.

Dorney

2 miles NW of Windsor off the A308

One of the finest Tudor manor houses in England, **Dorney Court**, just a short walk from the River Thames, has been the home of the Palmer family since 1530. Built in about 1440, it is an enchanting building which also houses some real treasures, including early 15th and 16th century oak furniture, beautiful 17th century lacquer furniture, and 400 years of family portraits. It is here that the first pineapple in England was grown in 1665.

On **Dorney Common** is the village of **Boveney**, which served as a wharf in the 13th century when timber was being transported from Windsor Forest. The flint and clapboard church of St Mary Magdalene, down by the riverside, was the setting for several scenes in Kevin Costner's film *Robin Hood Prince of Thieves*.

Maidenhead

6 miles NW of Windsor on the A4130

Transport has played a major role down the years in the history of Maidenhead, first with Thames traffic, then as a stop on the London-Bath coaching route, and finally with the coming of the railway, which helped to turn the town into a fashionable Victorian resort. The **Maidenhead Rail Bridge** was built by Isambard Kingdom Brunel in 1839 to carry his Great Western Railway over the Thames. The bridge, which comprises the widest, flattest brick arches in the world, was hailed at the time as the pinnacle of engineering achievement and has been immortalised in Turner's incredibly exciting and atmospheric painting *Rain, Steam and Speed*.

Boulter's Lock, one of the biggest on the Thames, takes its name from an old word for a miller. A flour mill has stood on Boulter's Island since Roman times. The island was also the home of Richard Dimbleby, the eminent broadcaster and father of the famous broadcasters David and Jonathan. To the north and west of the town, **Maidenhead Commons** and **Cock Marsh** contain a variety of habitats, including woodland, scrub thickets, grassland, ponds and riverside. Both are popular with walkers and nature-lovers: Cock Marsh is an important site for breeding waders, and both sites are rich in flora and invertebrate fauna.

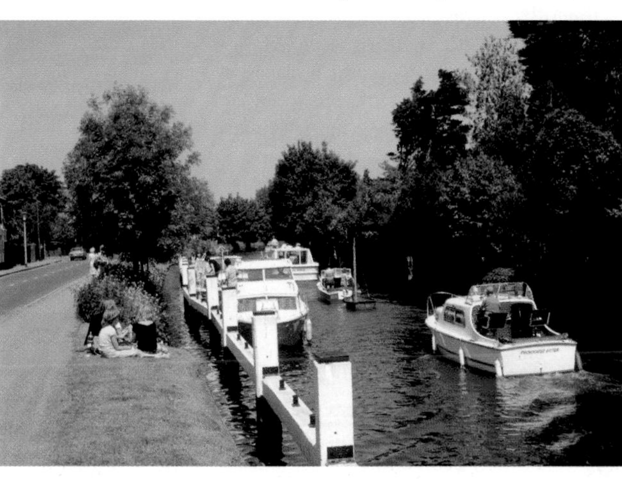

Boulters Lock on the River Thames, Maidenhead

Cookham

6 miles NW of Windsor on the A4094

This pretty, small town, on the banks of the River Thames, has been fortunate in being protected by **Cookham Woods** (National Trust) from becoming a suburb of Maidenhead and still has a distinctive character of its own. The town was made famous by the artist Sir Stanley Spencer, who used Cookham as the setting for many of his paintings. He was born here in 1891 and was buried here on his death in 1959. The town's tribute to its most renowned resident is the **Stanley Spencer Gallery**, a permanent exhibition of his work which is housed in the converted Victorian chapel Stanley visited as a child.

His painting, *Resurrection,* which depicts recognisable locals emerging from the graves in Cookham churchyard, caused some residents to protest when it was first exhibited in the 1930s.

Eton Schoolboys

Eton

1 mile N of Windsor on the A355

Just across the River Thames from Windsor, this town has grown up around **Eton College**, the famous public school that was founded in 1440 by Henry VI. Originally intended for 70 poor and worthy scholars and to educate students for the newly created King's College, at Cambridge University, the college has been added to greatly over the years. Of the original school buildings, only the College Hall and the kitchen have survived; the great gatehouse and Lupton's Tower were added in the 16th century and the Upper School dates from around 1690. However, the school has kept many ancient traditions over the years including the black tail mourning coats that were originally worn on the death of George III in 1820 and which are still worn today. For centuries the college has educated the great and the good, among them William Pitt the Elder, Harold Macmillan, Thomas Gray (author of *Elegy Written in a Country Churchyard*), Henry Fielding, Shelley, George Orwell and Ian Fleming. Eton has also been famous in the past for its strict discipline, personified in 1832 by a master who told the pupils when they rebelled: "Boys, you must be pure of heart, for if not, I will thrash you until you are."

Slough

3 miles N of Windsor on the A355

A small settlement until the creation of a trading estate in 1920, Slough then grew rapidly from around 7,000 to 100,000. The area does have a long history, however, and a visit to **Slough Museum** makes for an interesting hour or two delving into the past. Slough has a lovely surprise in the shape of one of the most splendid churches in the county. The **Church of St Mary** at Langley Marish is a real gem, notable particularly for the private family pew of the Kedermisters, totally screened from the main part of the church, and a library filled with painted panels.

Datchet

2 miles E of Windsor on the B470

Just across the river from Windsor Castle's Home Park, Datchet has a spacious green and some attractive riverside houses. The town featured in Shakespeare's *Merry Wives of Windsor* when Falstaff, concealed in a laundry basket, is brought here for his 'Datchet mead' – i.e. a ducking in the river.

Century Fine Art

The Shop on the Green, Datchet, nr Windsor,
Berkshire SL3 9JH
Tel: 01753 581284
e-mail: info@centuryfineart.co.uk
website: www.centuryfineart.co.uk

Established in the late 1980s, **Century Fine Art** occupies a prime position overlooking the green in the attractive Thames-side village of Datchet, just outside Windsor and only a mile from junction 5 of the M4. Over the last 15 years the gallery has earned a well-deserved reputation for providing a showcase for varied collections of work by leading contemporary British artists. Each month a new exhibition is staged in the main gallery and features group shows of work by prestigious artists, many of whom are members of leading national art societies such as the Royal Institute of Oil Painters, the Royal Watercolour Society and the Pastel Society.

Recent exhibitions, for example, have displayed work by artists such as Raymund M Rogers (seen painting in the BBC-TV series *A Coastal Parish*), Jenny Wheatley and Jeremy Barlow, as well as sculptures by Ron Cameron and Brendan Hesmondhalgh. The gallery also hosts solo shows and themed exhibitions while the second floor has a semi-permanent, but constantly updated, display of paintings. The gallery is open from 10am to 5pm, Tuesday to Saturday, and at other times by appointment.

OXFORDSHIRE

Oxfordshire is a county covering about 1,000 square miles, contained for the most part within the Thames Basin. Between Henley and Wallingford lie the beginnings of the Chiltern Hills, while in the north are the most easterly hills of the Cotswolds as well as rich farmland based on the clay soil that stretches up from Oxford to the Midlands. In the east, Henley is one of many attractive Thames-side settlements, towards the west are Faringdon and Witney, and in the north Bicester, Chipping Norton and Banbury. The county is of course dominated by its capital, Oxford, which from the 12th century grew from a small and little known market town into one of the major seats of learning in the world. It also prospered as a central point of communication, first as a stopping point on coaching routes and later with the coming of the canals and the railways. Industry grew, too, and in the suburb of Cowley Lord Nuffield's Morris car works were a major employer. Many palaeolithic, mesolithic and neolithic finds have been made in the county, but the most eyecatching early archaeological feature is the Uffington White Horse from the Iron Age. Dorchester and Alchester were the most important sites in Roman Oxfordshire, the Saxons built many settlements along the Thames, and the Danes overran the area in the 10th and 11th centuries. The county was heavily involved in the Civil War (1642-1651) and the towns of Oxford (for three years the Royalist headquarters), Banbury and Wallingford were all besieged by Parliamentary forces during the conflict. The northwest region of the county lies almost wholly in the Cotswolds and is included in Chapter seven.

HENLEY-ON-THAMES

Reputed to be the oldest settlement in Oxfordshire, this attractive riverside market town has over 300 listed buildings covering several periods. The Thames has always played an important role in its life; in 1829 the first varsity boat race, between Oxford and Cambridge, took place here on the river and, within a decade, the event was enjoying royal patronage. The **Henley Regatta**, held every year in the first week of July, is a marvellous and colourful event with teams competing on the mile long course from all over the world. Opened in 1998, the **River and Rowing Museum** is a fascinating place that traces the rowing heritage of Henley, the river's changing role in the town's history, and even provides the opportunity to 'walk' the length of the River Thames, from source to sea, taking in all the locks. Housed in spacious, purpose-built premises designed by the award-winning architect, David Chipperfield, its exhibits include the boat in which the British duo, Redgrave and Pinsent, won their gold medals at the 1996 Olympics.

Henley was the site of Rupert's Elm, where Prince Rupert is said to have hanged a Roundhead spy. A portion of the tree is preserved in this museum. Also situated on the riverbank, beside the town's famous 18th century bridge decorated with the faces of Father Thames and the goddess Isis, is the Leander Club, the headquarters of the famous rowing club.

Apart from the boating, which is available throughout the summer, and the pleasant walks along the riverbanks, there are lots of interesting shops, inns, and teashops in the town.

Just down river from the town centre lies **Fawley Court**, a wonderful private

Gabriel Machin Ltd

7 Market Place, Henley-on-Thames, Oxon RG9 2AA
Tel: 01491 574377 Fax: 01491 413530
e-mail: enquiries@gabrielmachin.co.uk
website: www.gabrielmachin.co.uk

What a pleasure to find an authentic traditional butcher's shop. Established in 1910, **Gabriel Machin Ltd** is proud of its reputation for supplying high quality food products to a discerning clientele that includes leading chefs such as Anthony Worrell-Thompson. The beef comes from selected farms in the Scottish Highlands and is hung for at least 10-14 days; in season a comprehensive range of game – including grouse, wild venison and boar – is available; and at Christmas-time you'll find a wide choice of geese, turkeys and other poultry. All year round the shop offers its own home-cured ham and bacon, smoked in the traditional fashion over a blend of English oak and beech wood.

The subtly cured then mildly smoked goose and duck breasts are especially popular – try them sliced thinly with a black cherry sauce or just horseradish. Gabriel Machin also sells a varied range of fresh and smoked fish including wild Scottish salmon, fresh rainbow trout, eel and haddock. Throughout the lengthy and intricate process of smoking, no colouring or artificial additives whatsoever are used. The flavours that result are an impressive reminder of the huge difference between these traditionally prepared products and standard supermarket fare. If you can't visit in person, Gabriel Machin offers a nationwide 'next day' mail order service.

Henley Royal Regatta

house that was designed by Christopher Wren and built in 1684 for a Colonel Freeman. Now owned by the Marian Fathers, the **Museum** it contains includes a library, documents relating to the Polish kings, and memorabilia of the Polish army. The house, gardens, and museum are open to the public from March to October.

To the northwest of Henley, at Rotherfield Greys, is another interesting house, **Greys Court** (National Trust), dating originally from the 14th century but much altered down the centuries; a beautiful courtyard and a tower survive from the earliest building. A Tudor wheelhouse is among the interesting outbuildings, and the gardens offer many delights, notably old-fashioned roses and wisterias, an ornamental vegetable garden, a ha-ha, an ice-house and the **Archbishop's Maze**, which was inspired, in 1980, by Archbishop Runcie's enthronement speech.

Gorvett & Stone

28 Duke Street, Henley-on-Thames, Oxon RG9 1UP
Tel: 01491 414485 Fax: 01491 411634
e-mail: gorvettandstone@btconnect.com
website: www.gorvettandstone.co.uk

A large sign in **Gorvett & Stone**'s chocolate heaven of a shop points out that chocolate is chemically very complex with up to 1,200 different compounds. "It's good for your general well-being and is an ***aphrodisiac!***" Chocoholics won't need any additional inducement to seek out this stylish town centre chocolaterie. Their favourite food is here in every shape, size, style and flavour imaginable. Many of them are hand-made on the premises but the husband and wife team, who opened their shop in the spring of 2004, also offer a wide choice of chocolate and other confectionery from around the world.

Amongst these delicacies are the Michel Cluizel range of chocolate bars from France, and the authentic Hazer Baba Turkish Delight from Istanbul. Also from France is the wonderful Bonnat drinking chocolate. Established in 1884 in Voiron, Bonnat is one of the few top chocolatiers who creates its chocolate from the cocoa bean itself. Real purists will want to sample the chocolate from the Gran Couva Domaine in Trinidad. Their chocolate comes from a single variety of bean, 'Trinitario', grown on a single estate and even from a single vintage.

WALK NUMBER 5

Henley-on-Thames

Distance:	6.0 miles (9.6 kilometres)
Typical time:	180 mins
Height gain:	90 metres
Map:	Chiltern Hills
Walk:	www.walkingworld.com ID:5
Contributor:	David and Chris Stewart

Access Information:

Easily reached by train on the Paddington line from London. The station is just a few yards from the walk start. Traffic and parking in Henley can be difficult. The Henley River and Rowing Museum has its own parking, inclusive in the entrance ticket price.

Additional Information:

The Henley River and Rowing Museum is new and well worth a visit. Henley-on-Thames is an affluent and attractive town, home of the well-known annual regatta, with galleries, old pubs, tea shops and more.

Description:

A short and pleasant walk taking in a famous stretch of the River Thames and the surrounding countryside, with a conveniently placed pub half way round.

Features:

River, Pub, Museum, Play Area, Great Views

Walk Directions:

1 Start by the Henley River and Rowing Museum and take the riverside path back towards the town centre

2 Cross the bridge to the south side of the river and turn left onto the tow path. The path starts by passing between some buildings but soon you are walking alongside the river. Continue along the path until you reach Hambledon lock.

3 At the lock you may want to take a detour to cross the river above the weir. Continue the walk from the end of the lock where you join a track. A short distance from the lock bear right on the track, away from the river.

4 Follow the track, ignoring the fork to the right, towards the Flowerpot Hotel. This is a great place to stop for lunch or a quick drink. From the Hotel turn right up Aston Lane.

5 Not far from the Hotel, turn left into a lane.

6 The lane turns into a path crossing a field. The recently renovated Culham Court is on your right. Pass in front of the house.

7 Crossing a field after Culham Court you come to a junction of paths. Take the path to the right, which switches back towards the lane leading to the House. At the entrance gate turn left up the lane (this is marked as a public footpath).

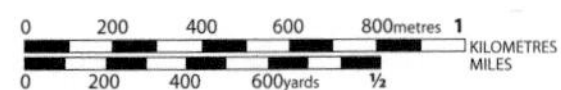

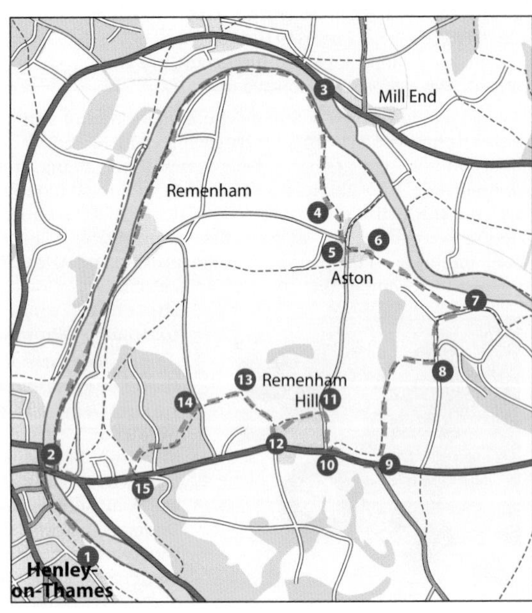

8 Turn right at this point to cross the field. At the woods, bear left. Ignore the path leading into the woods. At the corner of the woods, cross through the hedge and continue down the side of the hedge towards the houses.

9 Just before you reach the houses, turn right. The path passes along the end of the gardens. Finally you can bear left towards the junction of Aston Lane and the main road.

10 At the junction, turn right down Aston Lane.

11 After passing the last set of houses on the right, take the footpath on your left.

12 You come to a driveway. Take the path into the woods, to the left of the a white post.

13 Turn left to cross the field. You can see a stile in the middle of the field. Keep in the same direction until you reach the road.

14 Cross the road and take the path over the stile opposite. Follow the path down through the woods, following the white arrows on the trees.

15 At the main road, turn right and walk the short distance back to the bridge in Henley-on-Thames.

AROUND HENLEY-ON-THAMES

Sonning Common

3½ miles SW of Henley on the B481

Sonning Common was originally part of the manor of Sonning-on-Thames with the livestock driven up from the flooded riverside pastures to winter on the higher ground.

Widmore Pond, on the edge of the village, is rumoured to have been a Roman silver mine: according to a 17th century account, while the pond was emptied for cleaning out, upturned oak tree stumps were found in the bottom of the pond along with stag antlers and Roman coins.

Mapledurham

6½ miles SW of Henley off the A4074

A narrow winding lane leads to this famously picturesque village set beside the Thames. The cluster of brick and flint cottages and the church are overshadowed by the lovely Elizabethan mansion, **Mapledurham House.** It was built on the site of an older manor house by the Blount family and has remained with their descendants ever since. As well as viewing the great oak staircase and the fine collection of paintings housed here, visitors will find the house's literary connections are equally interesting: Alexander Pope was a frequent visitor in the 18th century; the final chapters of John Galsworthy's *The Forsyte Saga* were set here; and it was the fictional Toad Hall in *The Wind in the Willows*. The house has also featured in films such as *The Eagle has Landed* and the TV series *Inspector Morse*.

Another attraction on the estate is the old riverside **Watermill**, a handsome late-15th century construction, which stands on the site of an earlier building that was mentioned in the Domesday Book. The mill remained in operation until 1947 and it was then the longest surviving working mill on the river. Now fully restored, the traditional machinery can be seen in action grinding wholemeal flour, which is then sold through the mill shop.

The **Church of St Margaret** has a number of notable features. It provided a major location for the film *The Eagle has Landed* and is believed to be the only church in the country to have had a king's son as vicar – Lord Augustus FitzClarence, one of William IV's 10 illegitimate children by the actress Mrs Jordan, was appointed to the living in 1829. Another curiosity here is that the south aisle is owned outright by the Blount family and partitioned off from the rest of the church. Major restoration was carried out in 1863 by the architect William Butterfield who made great use of coloured brickwork and also refaced the tower with a bold chequered pattern using flint and brick.

Mapledurham Estate

Mapledurham, near Reading, Oxfordshire RG4 7TR
Tel: 01189 723350 Fax: 01189 794016
e-mail: Mtrust1997@aol.com
website: www.mapledurham.co.uk

Mapledurham House and Watermill nestle on the banks of the River Thames in the beautiful south Oxfordshire countryside. Visitors can watch the last working watermill in action – still producing flour – and tour the Elizabethan mansion. Cream teas are a speciality here and can be eaten in the Old Manor tearooms or on the lawns sloping down to the Thames. Arrival can also be by boat from nearby Caversham – a delightful way to start the afternoon. Open in the afternoons at weekends and Bank Holidays from Easter to the end of September.

Holiday cottages are also available for rent and the grounds of the house are the perfect venue for weddings, parties and a range of other outdoor events and activities.

Goring-on-Thames

9½ miles W of Henley on the B4009

This ancient small town lies across the River Thames from its equally ancient neighbour, Streatley, and, while today they are in different counties, they were once in different kingdoms. This is a particularly peaceful stretch of the river, with the bustle of Pangbourne and Henley-on-Thames lying downstream, and it is some distance to the towns of Abingdon and Oxford further upstream.

In the 19th century, after Isambard Kingdom Brunel had laid the tracks for the Great Western Railway through Goring Gap, the village began to grow as it was now accessible to the Thames-loving Victorians. Though there are many Victorian and Edwardian villas and houses here, the original older buildings have survived, adding an air of antiquity to this attractive place.

The Lock, Goring on Thames

Watlington

8 miles NW of Henley off the B480

There are superb views over the surrounding countryside from **Watlington Hill**, which rises 700ft above Watlington Park with its woods of beech and yew. Watlington Hill and its neighbour Pyrton Hill are designated a Site of Special Scientific Interest and are home to over 30 species of butterflies and a wide variety of chalk-loving plants.

Ewelme

9 miles NW of Henley off the B4009

At the centre of this pretty village is a magnificent group of medieval buildings, including the church, almshouses and school, which were all founded in the 1430s by Alice Chaucer, grand-daughter of the poet Geoffrey, and her husband, the Duke of Suffolk. There is a wonderfully elegant alabaster carving of Alice inside the church and under this effigy is another rather macabre carving of a shrivelled cadaver. In the churchyard is the grave of Jerome K Jerome, author of *Three Men in a Boat*, who moved to the village following the success of his book.

Chalgrove

10 miles NW of Henley on the B480

Chalgrove is the site of an English Heritage registered battlefield, where in 1643 Prince Rupert defeated John Hampden. An information board at the site gives details of the battle, and there is also a monument to John Hampden, a local squire and sometime MP for Buckinghamshire who refused to pay Ship Money to the king. He was taken to court in 1638 and incarcerated in the Tower of London. He was a cousin of

Added Ingredients

16 Stert Street, Abingdon, Oxon OX14 3JP
Tel/Fax: 01235 537405
e-mail: addedingredient@aol.com
website: www.addedingredients.co.uk

After many years working in consultancy, Jill Carver decided to change direction in 2001. She found an empty retail property in the heart of this attractive old town, named it **Added Ingredients** and proceeded to stock it, virtually from wall to ceiling, with an appetising range of food and drink sourced locally and from around the world, concentrating on quality food from small independent suppliers. Here you'll find breads by De Gustibus, the award-winning artisan baker; a wide range of British and Continental cheeses and meats; vegetarian pâtés, hummus and taramasalata; sun-blushed tomatoes, roasted onions, artichokes, cornichons and olives.

Then there are the oils and vinegars, flours, Minola smoked products and pastas; a wide variety of soft drinks and a range of spices and herbs as well as chutneys and preserves. Added Ingredients also stocks an extensive selection of local, European and New World wines and hosts wine tasting evenings. And if you are buying a gift for a favourite foodie friend, the shop offers a gift packaging service. There are also tables where customers can enjoy speciality coffees, teas, cakes and sample the deli delights in rolls, platters and salads. Samples of olive oils and vinegars before purchasing are always on offer. Added Ingredients is open from 9am to 6pm, Monday to Saturday.

The Finishing Touch

13 Stert Street, Abingdon, Oxon OX14 3JF
Tel: 01235 554533 Fax: 01235 554535

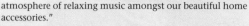

Run by the mother and daughter team of Esther and Layla Hurley, **The Finishing Touch** is an enticing shop where you can be sure of finding inspiration for your own home décor along with ideas for unusual and imaginative gifts. Esther, who previously managed the houseplant, gift and Christmas departments at Notcutts Garden Centre, says, "I wanted to create a haven from today's hustle and bustle, a place where customers could relax in an atmosphere of relaxing music amongst our beautiful home accessories."

The Finishing Touch's design team works closely with the 'Trend' analysts in mainland Europe who advise on the season's colours and textures based on their keeping a watchful eye on the catwalk and top designers. Esther's stock includes a wide variety of stylish glass ware, colourful ceramics, real plants, silk flowers, candles, pictures, water hyacinth woven trays and containers, and much, much more. Most of the alluring items on display are unique in the area so if you want to make your Christmas shopping for presents easy, come along to the Finishing Touch which stages special displays over the Christmas period.

Oliver Cromwell and in the Civil War became a leading opponent of the king.

Stonor

4 miles N of Henley on the B480

The village is the home of Lord and Lady Camoys and their house, **Stonor**, has been in the family for over 800 years. Set in the a wooded valley in the Chilterns and surrounded by a deer park, this idyllic house dates from the 12th century though the beautiful, uniform facade is Tudor and hides much of the earlier work. The interior of the house contains many rare items, including a mass of family portraits, and there is also a medieval Catholic Chapel here that was in continuous use right through the Reformation. In 1581, Edmund Campion sought refuge at the house and from a secret room in the roof supervised the printing of his book *Decem Rationes* – 'Ten Reasons for being a Catholic'. An exhibition features his life and work. The gardens too are well worth a visit with their lawns, orchard and lovely lavender hedges, and they offer splendid views over the rolling parkland.

ABINGDON

This is an attractive town and one of the country's oldest, as it grew up around a Benedictine **Abbey** that was founded in 675. Sacked twice by the Danes for its gold and silver, the abbey was practically derelict by the 10th century but, under the guidance of Abbot Ethelwold, the architect of the great Benedictine reform, it once again prospered and was, in its heyday, larger than Westminster Abbey. At one time the abbot here was the largest landowner in Berkshire after the Crown. Unfortunately little remains today of this great religious house, but the **Gatehouse**, built in the late 15th century, is a splendid reminder.

The largest town in the Vale of the White Horse, Abingdon was also the county town of Berkshire between 1556 and 1869. The prosperity this brought enabled the townspeople to build the impressive and outsize **County Hall** of 1678 that dominates the Market Place. This outstanding example of English Renaissance architecture was designed by a pupil of Sir Christopher Wren. In its former Assize court is the **Abingdon Museum** which provides interesting insights into the town's history.

Another of Abingdon's pleasing buildings, set close to the lovely bridge over the Thames, is the **Church of St Helen** whose 150ft-high steeple dominates the skyline here. Originally built in the 14th century, the church was remodelled in the 15th and 16th centuries, when the town prospered from

The River Thames, Abingdon

a thriving wool trade, to provide an altogether larger and more elaborate building. With its five aisles it is now broader than it is long. The main glory of the church, the painted ceiling of the Lady Chapel, has been retained from the 14th century. Beside the churchyard, which contains a curious small building that was the blowing chamber for the church organ, are three sets of almshouses. The oldest, Christ's Hospital, was founded in 1446 while the other two, Twitty's Almshouses and Brick Alley Almshouses, date from the early 1700s.

AROUND ABINGDON

Dorchester

5 miles SE of Abingdon off the A4074

This charming little town, situated on the River Thame just before it flows into the River Thames, has been described as "the most historic spot in Oxfordshire" since it was here that Christianity was established in the southwest of England by St Birinus. Known as the Apostle of the West Saxons, Birinus was consecrated in Genoa, landed in Wessex in 634, and converted the King Cynegils of Wessex in the following year. As a mark of his devotion to the church, Cynegils gave Dorchester to Birinus and the church he built here became the cathedral of Wessex.

The **Abbey Church of St Peter and St Paul** was built in 1170 on the site of that Saxon church and greatly extended during the next two centuries. Its chief glory is the 14th century choir and the huge Jesse window, showing the family tree of Jesus, which has retained its original stained glass. The story of the abbey, along with the history of settlement in the area going back to neolithic times, is told in the **Abbey Museum**, which is housed in a classroom of the former Grammar School, built in 1652.

The town itself has some attractive old houses with overhanging upper stories, a fine Georgian coaching inn, and there's a pleasant footpath that crosses fields to the bank of the Thames.

Little Wittenham

5 miles SE of Abingdon off the A4130

This village, which has a number of pretty cottages, lies beneath the **Wittenham Clumps**, which for centuries formed an important defensive position overlooking the Thames. In the village church of St Peter are effigies of Sir William Dunch, a former MP for Wallingford, and his wife, who was the aunt of Oliver Cromwell. A little way northwest, towards the village of Long Wittenham, is the unique **Pendon Museum**, whose main attraction is a model village built in tiny scale to resemble a typical 1930s village in the Vale of the White Horse. The model is the incredibly skilled and detailed work of Roye England, an Australian who came to this country in 1925 to study. The model incorporates a model railway (Roye England's first passion) and, as a tribute to the master, who died in 1995, there's a tiny model of himself in the 1:76 scale of the whole model.

Wallingford

8 miles SE of Abingdon on the A4130

A strategic crossing point of the Thames since ancient times. Alfred the Great first fortified the town, against the Danes, and the Saxon earth defences can still be seen. It was here that William the Conqueror crossed the river on his six-day march to London. Wallingford was also an important trading town; it received its charter in 1155 and for several centuries had its own mint. During the Civil War the town was a

The Gallery Coffee Shop in Pettits

46-50 St Mary's Street, Wallingford, Oxon OX10 0EY
Tel: 01491 835253 Fax: 01491 826009
e-mail: enquiries@pettitsofwallingford.co.uk

Located on the first floor of Pettits Department Store, **The Gallery Coffee Shop** is a bright and airy place, its walls adorned with attractive prints and owner Camille Scott's collection of unusual china teapots. Many of these have been donated by customers who use the Gallery as a favourite meeting place. Camille's family have a long history in the catering trade and everything on her menu is home-made and freshly prepared to order. It includes an All Day Breakfast, omelettes, salads (avocado & bacon, for example), home-made soup and quiche of the day, sandwiches and jacket potatoes.

Amongst the tea-time treats are home-made sponges, traybakes and some wonderful home-made cakes. Customers can see their fare being prepared in the spotless, open plan modern kitchen. The Gallery is open from 9.30am to 4.30pm, Monday to Saturday. Pettits Store is a fine old independent department store founded in 1856 and now owned and run as a family business. Managing Director Richard Rowse is proud of the fact that the store thrives on value for money and the quality of service – two members of staff recently completed 50 years of service each.

Pennifex

56 St Mary's Street, Wallingford, Oxon OX10 OEL
Tel: 01491 838150
e-mail: queries@pennifex.co.uk
website: www.pennifex.co.uk

Affordable art and unique gifts are the twin attractions at **Pennifex**, an alluringly stylish shop and gallery established by Deb Haire Mulley in 2003. Located close to the town centre, Pennifex specialises in the work of mainly local artists whose pictures in oils and other media are attractively displayed amidst the many other covetable items on show.

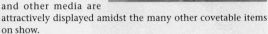

These include beaded jewellery from Christine Bloxham, contemporary furniture from Luke Mulley's 'Designs' company, textiles by Mollie Picken and collages by Mel Gannon. You'll also find a good range of pottery and soft furnishings. Ample car parking close by.

Royalist stronghold defending the southern approaches to Oxford, the site of the Royalist headquarters. It was besieged in 1646 by the Parliamentary forces under Sir Thomas Fairfax and its walls were breached after a 12-week siege; it was the last place to surrender to Parliament. The castle built by William the Conqueror was destroyed by Cromwell in 1652 but substantial earthworks can still be seen and the museum tells the story of the town from its earliest days.

River Thames, Wallingford

Blewbury

7 miles S of Abingdon on the A417

In the foothills of the Berkshire Downs, this pretty village was, and remains, a favoured spot for artists and writers. Among these was Kenneth Grahame, the author of *The Wind in the Willows*, who lived in a Tudor brick house in the village from 1910 to 1924. He wrote the book for his son, who tragically died while an undergraduate at Oxford. They

Root One Garden Centre

High Road, Brightwell-cum-Sotwell, Wallingford, Oxon OX10 0PT
Tel: 01491 836277 Fax: 01491 824151
e-mail: rootoneltd@aol.com
website: www.root-one.co.uk

Since he took over **Root One Garden Centre** in 2001, Jeremy Brudenell has revitalised this well-established garden centre, extending its range and improving the amenities. Gardeners will find a huge choice of plants, shrubs and trees, seeds, border plants and much more. The centre also stocks a vast selection of garden accessories – anything from pots and tubs to picnic tables, pergolas to fertilisers, tools to ornamental features.

Within the two-acre site, you'll find just about anything you might need for your garden all year round. Jeremy himself is an experienced plantsman and together with his knowledgeable staff is always happy to offer advice and information on horticultural matters. A recent addition to the amenities here is the smart new café with its blonde wood tables and chairs. The menu offers a good choice of beverages, afternoon teas, snacks and light lunches. The centre is also family friendly, with a children's play area at the rear accessed only through the main building, and there's plenty of parking space at the front.

are buried together in the churchyard of St Cross in Oxford. Mr Toad compares himself favourably with Oxford students in the book:

'The clever men at Oxford
Know all that there is to be knowed
But they none know one half as much
As intelligent Mr Toad.'

Sutton Courtenay

2 miles S of Abingdon on the B4016

A pretty village that was mentioned in the Domesday Book with an abbey that was founded in 1350. The village **Church of All Saints**, which dates back to Norman times, contains some fine stone carvings and woodwork but the real interest lies in the churchyard. Here can be found the chest tomb of Herbert Asquith, the last Liberal Prime Minister (from 1908 to 1916) and his wife; they lived by the Thames not far from the church. Also here is the grave of Eric Blair, better known as George Orwell, author of *1984* and *Animal Farm*; several yew trees are planted here in his memory.

Didcot

4½ miles S of Abingdon on the A4130

The giant cooling towers of Didcot's power station dominate the skyline for miles around and there is little left of the old town. But the saving grace is the **Didcot Railway Centre**, a shrine to the days of the steam engine and the Great Western Railway. Isambard Kingdom Brunel designed the Great Western Railway and its route through Didcot, from London to Bristol, was completed in 1841. Until 1892 its trains ran on their unique broad gauge tracks and the GWR retained its independence until the nationalisation of the railways in 1948. Based around the engine shed, where

Great Western Railway, Didcot

visitors can inspect the collection of steam locomotives, members of the Great Western Society have recreated the golden age of the railway at the centre which also includes a beautiful recreation of a country station, complete with level crossing. The locomotives on display include 4079 *Pendennis Castle*, repatriated from Australia in 2000, King class 6023 *King Edward II* and one of the streamlined and very distinctive Great Western diesel railcars, this one dating from 1940. The Firefly Trust has recently completed the building of a reproduction of the broad-gauge Firefly locomotive of 1839. Steam days are held throughout the year when locomotives once again take to the broad gauge track and visitors can also take in the Victorian signalling system and the centre's Relics Display.

WANTAGE

This thriving market town in the Vale of the White Horse was, in 849, the birthplace of Alfred the Great and remained a Royal Manor until the end of the 12th century. In the central market place, around which there are some fine Georgian and Victorian buildings, is a huge statue of the King of the West Saxons, who spent much of his life (he died in 899) defending his kingdom from the Danes in the north before becoming the overlord of England. An educated man (as a boy Alfred had visited Rome), he not only codified the laws of his kingdom but also revived the tradition of learning.

Unfortunately, only the **Church of St Peter and St Paul** has survived from medieval times and, though it was heavily restored in 1857 by GE Street, various features have survived from the original 13th century structure. There's also a brass commemorating the life of Sir Ivo Fitzwarren, the father of Dick Whittington's wife, Alice.

Opposite the church is the **Vale and Downland Museum Centre**, which is located in another of the town's old buildings - a house dating from the 16th century - and a reconstructed barn. Dedicated to the geology, history, and archaeology of Wantage and the Vale of the White Horse, the displays cover the centuries from prehistoric times to the present day.

Built as the home of the Wantage Sisterhood, an Anglican Order, in the 19th century, three architects were involved in the construction of **St Mary's Convent**: GE Street; William Butterfield, architect of Keble College, Oxford; and John Pearson, architect of Truro Cathedral. It was in Wantage that the first steam tramway operated, starting in 1873 and surviving until 1948.

Ardington

Chinese porcelain and hand-painted wallpaper. Within the mature parkland are many noble trees and a woodland garden – a detailed map is available giving the names and precise location of almost 300 plants. There's also a tea room and gift shop. Opening times are restricted: for details phone 01865 820259.

Steventon

5 miles NE of Wantage on the A4185

In Mill Street stand the National Trust's **Priory Cottages**, former monastic buildings now converted into two houses. South Cottage contains the priory's original Great Hall, which can be visited in the summer by written appointment.

Just to the east of the town lies **Ardington House**, a beautifully symmetrical, early-18th century building that is the home of the Baring family. Occasionally open to the public, the best feature here is the Imperial Staircase - where two flights come into one - of which this is a particularly fine example.

AROUND WANTAGE

Kingston Bagpuize

6 miles N of Wantage off the A420

The intriguing name of this straggling village goes back to Norman times when Ralf de Bachepuise, a contemporary of William the Conqueror, was given land in the area. The village grew to serve the needs of **Kingston Bagpuize House** (see panel on page 124), a fine mansion of 1660 with superb gardens. Notable features include a magnificent cantilevered staircase, panelled rooms with some good furniture and paintings,

Letcombe Bassett

2 miles S of Wantage off the B4001

This tiny village has a notable place in literary history: it is called Cresscombe in *Jude the Obscure*, which Thomas Hardy wrote while staying here. Earlier, Jonathan Swift spent the summer of 1714 at the village's rectory where he was visited by the poet Alexander Pope.

Just to the east of the village lies **Segsbury Camp**, which is sometimes also referred to as **Letcombe Castle**. Set on the edge of the Berkshire Downs, this massive Iron Age hill fort encloses some 26 acres of land.

Kingston Lisle

4½ miles W of Wantage off the B4507

Just to the southwest of the attractive Norman Church of St John lies the **Blowing Stone** (or Sarsen Stone), a piece of glacial debris that is perforated with holes. When blown, the stone emits a fog-horn like sound and tradition has it that the stone was blown by King Alfred.

Kingston Bagpuize House & Garden

Kingston Bagpuize, Nr Abingdon,
Oxfordshire OX13 5AX
Tel: 01865 820259 Fax: 01865 821659
website: www.kingstonbagpuizehouse.org.uk

The Bachepuis family leased the land of the local manor during the 11th and 12th centuries, during which time the name of the village was anglicised from Bachepuis to Kingston Bagpuize. The present **Kingston Bagpuize House**, the home of Francis and Virginia Grant and their children, was built in 1660 and numbers among its many treasures a superb cantilevered staircase and gallery dominating the entrance hall. Thought to date from 1720, the main flight of stairs and gallery have no supporting columns, the great weight being borne by the walls, which are three feet thick. Striking features here include hand-painted Chinese wallpaper and Chinese porcelain vases.

The elegant proportions and symmetry of the house are shown in the marvellous drawing room, with its twin fireplaces, fine French furniture from the 18th and 19th centuries, a pair of Queen Anne cabinets in laburnum and two Hepplewhite armchairs with tapestry seats in gros point and petit point worked by sometime owner Marlie Raphael. The pine-panelled library is balanced by the oak-panelled dining room, where the paintings include a portrait of Marlie aged three in 1907, and a Flemish painting showing scenes from the life of St Bernard. The house is truly magnificent, but it is the gardens which bring many visitors to Kingston Bagpuize. Showing traces of much earlier gardens, the grounds contain a large collection of trees, shrubs and perennials; some of the yews are over 300 years old, while the handsome Wellingtonias were planted in the 19th century.

The influence of Francis Grant's great aunt Marlie Raphael, who owned the house from 1939 to 1976, is particularly strong in the garden: in the 1950s and 1960s she planted extensively and created the lovely woodland garden to provide year-round colour and interest. She was advised in this work by Sir Harold Hillier, whose nurseries supplied most of her plants. The present owners are restoring the gardens and have planted many trees and shrubs to complement those already growing. One of their great achievements is a minutely detailed map of the garden showing the names and exact locations of almost 300 plants. On open days a selection of home-baking is served in the tearoom in the basement of the original kitchen; there's also a small gift shop and plants for sale.

House and garden are available for special events and group visits throughout the year by written appointment. Children under five are allowed in the garden but not in the house; no dogs. Open various dates from February to October - see the website or phone for details.

Uffington

5½ miles W of Wantage off the B4507

Uffington White Horse

This large village was, in 1822, the birthplace of Thomas Hughes, the son of the vicar. The author of *Tom Brown's Schooldays*, Hughes incorporates many local landmarks, including the White Horse and Uffington Castle, in his well-known work. The **Tom Brown's School Museum** tells the story of Hughes' life and works.

However, the village is perhaps best known for the **Uffington White Horse.** This mysteriously abstract and very beautiful figure of a horse, some 400 feet long, has been created by removing the turf on the hillside to expose the gleaming white chalk beneath. It is a startling sight which can be seen from far and wide, and many a tantalising glimpse of it has been caught through the window of a train travelling through the valley below. Popular tradition links it with the victory of King Alfred over the Danes at the battle of Ashdown, which was fought somewhere on these downs in 871, but modern thinking now considers that it dates from about 100 BC.

Above the White Horse is the Iron Age camp known as **Uffington Castle**, and to one side is a knoll known as **Dragon's Hill** where legend has it that St George killed the dragon.

Great Coxwell

8 miles NW of Wantage off the A420

This village is best known for the magnificent **Great Barn** of a monastic grange (farm) of the Cistercian Abbey at Beaulieu in Hampshire, dating back to around 1300 and its 12th century **Church of St Giles**. A simple and elegant building, the church is often overlooked in favour of the barn, originally staffed by lay brethren who took vows of obedience, poverty and chastity but never became monks or priests. An impressive building that is some 152ft long, with Cotswold stone walls more than four feet thick, this huge barn was used to store the tithe - or taxes - received from the tenants of the church land. At the Dissolution it passed into private ownership and is now owned by the National Trust.

Buscot

11 miles NW of Wantage on the A417

This small village, in the valley of the upper Thames, is home to two National Trust properties: **Buscot Old Parsonage** and **Buscot Park**. The parsonage is a lovely house with a small garden on the banks of the River Thames and was built of Cotswold stone in 1703. Buscot Park is a much grander affair, a classic example of a late Georgian house, built in 1780. It houses the magnificent Faringdon Art Collection which includes paintings by Rembrandt, Murillo and Reynolds; one room is decorated with a series of pictures painted by Edward Burne-Jones, the pre-Raphaelite artist who was a close friend of William Morris. Painted in 1890, they reflect Burne-Jones' interest in myths and legends and tell the story of the Sleeping Beauty. The grounds of Buscot Park were largely developed in the 20th century and include a canal garden by Harold Peto, a large kitchen garden and an Egyptian avenue created by Lord Faringdon in 1969 featuring sphinxes and statues based on originals in Hadrian's Villa outside Rome. Anyone interested in the work of Burne-Jones should also visit the village church where a stained glass window showing the Good Shepherd was designed by him in 1891, when he was working with William Morris's firm, Morris and Co. The church itself is very pleasantly situated by the river just outside the village.

WITNEY

Situated in rich sheep-farming land in the valley of the River Windrush, this old town's name is derived from Witta's Island and it was once of importance as the meeting place of the Wittan, the council of the Saxon kings.

From the Middle Ages onwards the town became much better known for its wool and even more so for its woollen blankets – the water of the River Windrush was said to contribute to their softness. The Witney Blanket Company was incorporated in 1710 but before that there were over 150 looms here working in the blanket trade employing more than 3000 people. The **Blanket Hall**, in the High Street, has on it the arms of the Witney Company of Weavers; it was built for the weighing and measuring of blankets in an age before rigid standardisation. Even though there has

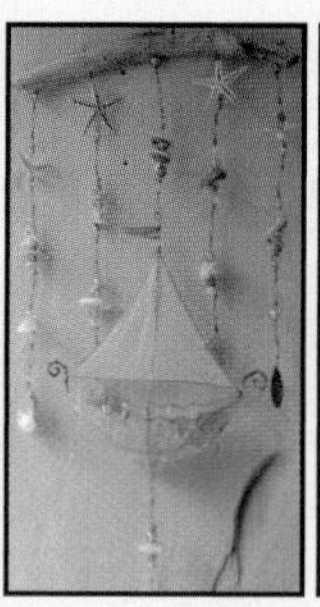

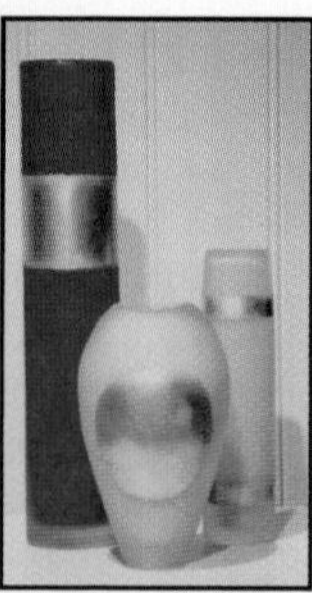

been a great decline in the industry since the 1930s, there are still a couple of blanket factories operating here. The story of the blanket trade and other local industries is recounted at the **Witney and District Museum**, located in a courtyard just off the High Street.

St Mary's Church is notable for its soaring spire which is all the more striking set amidst the surrounding level fields. Built on the scale of a mini-cathedral, the church and spire are 13th century; as Witney's wool trade prospered in the 14th and 15th centuries, chapels and aisles were added; but the interior is marred by over-enthusiastic restoration in Victorian times.

By 1278, Witney had a weekly market and two annual fairs and in the centre of the market place still stands the **Buttercross.** Originally a shrine, the cross has a steep roof with rustic-looking stone columns; it dates from about 1600.

Just outside the town is the **Cogges Manor Farm Museum**, which stands on the site of a now deserted medieval village of which only the church, priory, and manor house remain. The displays tell the story of the lives of those who worked the surrounding land down the centuries.

AROUND WITNEY

Brize Norton

3 miles SW of Witney off the A40

Best known for its RAF transport base, Brize Norton village lies to the north of the airfield. It's a long straggling village of old grey stone houses and a Norman church which is the only one in England dedicated to a little-known 5th century French bishop, St Brice.

Foxbury Farm Shop

Burford Road, Brize Norton, Oxon OX13 3NX
Tel: 01993 867385/844141
e-mail: shop@foxburyfarm.co.uk
website: www.foxburyfarm.co.uk

Conveniently located off the A40 near Burford, **Foxbury Farm** is an outstanding family-run business which was awarded the Best Meat Producer accolade in 2002 and has also won the National Small Food Producers Award. Featured in *Country Living* magazine, this 500-acre farm specialises in beef, lamb and pork, all of which is sold in the farm's own shop or at local farmers' markets. Owners Colin and Di Dawes take great pride in the quality of their meats: lambs are grazed on Cotswold grass, the Gloucester Old Spot pigs are allowed to grow at their own pace in open straw yards, beef is hung for a minimum of three weeks – all of which enhances the flavour of the meat.

Master butcher John Williams and his team in the butcher's shop will cut to any customer's requirements. All sausages and burgers in the shop are made using Foxbury meat, as are the Foxbury Fast Feast range of ready-made meals such as Steak & Kidney Pie and Vegetarian Curry. The shop also stocks a wide selection of other products, all of them British and as local as possible – cheeses, preserves, home-baked scones, pies and cakes, barbecue packs, and much more.

WALK NUMBER 6

North Leigh

Distance:	5.8 miles (9.3 kilometres)
Typical time:	180 mins
Height gain:	40 metres
Map:	Explorer 180
Walk:	www.walkingworld.com ID:2379
Contributor:	Ron and Jenny Glynn

Access Information:

North Leigh lies off the A4095 between Bicester and Witney. There is ample car parking by the village hall, opposite the church.

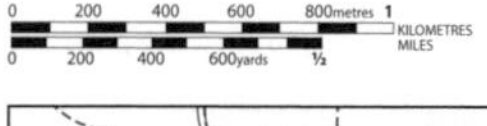

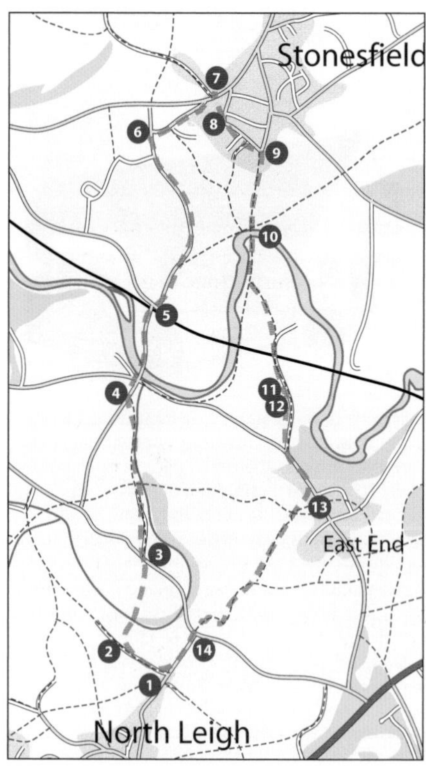

Description:

The beautiful west Oxfordshire village of North Leigh is the starting point for this super little walk to Stonesfield and East End. The Cotswold stone buildings and dry stone walling are attractive features of this area, combining with the splendour of green and glorious landscape that make up the wonderful scenes encountered. The Roman Villa of North Leigh is a tremendously interesting and exciting spectacle, a valuable relic of the distant past, giving us a little insight into life in ancient Britain. The paths and bridleways that we tread today link us to our ancestors who trod the very same ones, a fact that is brought sharply into focus on this historical route.

Features:

River, Pub, Church, Wildlife, Birds, Flowers, Great Views, Woodland, Ancient Monument

Walk Directions:

1 Starting from the church, turn left by The Old School and follow a hard track above open countryside.

2 A short distance on, turn right through a metal gate, and walk downhill in a meadow to cross a stream. Continue through a gate with fence on right, passing a large pond and newly planted trees.

3 Take metal gate and turn left on narrow road for few yards, then right on bridleway signed to Ashford Bridge. Pass Holly Farm in a lovely woodland setting, then stone barns and old stables before a cottage. Continue beside stream that runs below a high embankment, the path tree lined and partly enclosed.

4 Join a single track road and walk on over Ashford Bridge, crossing the River Evenlode, then uphill past Bridgefield Farm.

5 Go on to walk over the railway bridge and turn right with a spread of farmland and wooded areas in all directions. Pass a derelict barn and farm buildings and continue beside open fields for some distance.

6 Turn right beside Spratts Farm and walk downhill into Stonesfield. Turn right out of Witney Lane passing quaint and pretty stone cottages.

7 Turn right on the Oxfordshire Way on an uphill climb to reach the Wesleyan Chapel.

8 Turn right along Churchfields passing handsome residences.

9 Turn right into Brook Lane to leave village with lovely views over very picturesque landscape. Continue downhill to Stockey Bottom.

10 Cross River Evenlode on a superb wooden footbridge and continue over large meadow and through gateway to meet hedge on left. Arrive at large wooden gate and go through walker's gate beside it to join a track. Cross railway track on large brick built bridge.

11 Turn left to visit North Leigh Roman Villa remains, an English Heritage site. Much of it was excavated in 1815-16 by Henry Hakewell, and there is a wonderful mosaic floor housed in a little building for protection, at the side of the villa.

12 Take stile to walk beside the villa and follow a defined path towards woodland. Climb a stile onto woodland path, and follow it to turn right up the steep bank and onto a path above, following it to leave Sturt Wood. Turn left along road to pass the handsome Sturt House, then a mix of dwellings in East End.

13 Turn right over stile to walk between houses, then beside copse. Walk on between fields to another stile that is very walker friendly, and on past a new tree plantation. Go on between fields, then turn right on the Wychwood Way over a meadow, and onto a narrow path between hedgerows, then fencing.

14 Join road and walk the short distance to North Leigh, the village church in view.

Radcot

7 miles SW of Witney on the A4095

This tiny hamlet boasts the oldest bridge across the River Thames. Built in 1154, **Radcot Bridge** represents an important crossing place and, as a result, the hamlet has seen much conflict over the centuries. To the north of the bridge are the remains of a castle where, in 1141, King Stephen battled with the disenthroned Queen Matilda. In the following century King John fought his barons here before finally conceding and signing the Magna Carta.

Filkins

8 miles SW of Witney off the A361

This tiny Cotswold village is now the home of a flourishing community of craft workers and artists, many of whom work in restored 18th century barns. One of these groups operates the **Cotswold Woollen Weavers** (free), a working weaving museum with an exhibition gallery and a mill shop. In the same attractive village is the **Swinford Museum**, which concentrates on 19th century domestic and rural trade and craft tools.

Kelmscott

9 miles SW of Witney off the A4095

William Morris called the village of Kelmscott "a heaven on earth" and **Kelmscott Manor**, the exquisite Elizabethan manor house he leased jointly with Dante Gabriel Rosetti, "the loveliest haunt of ancient peace that can well be imagined". Located near the River Thames and dating from about 1570, the manor was his Morris's country home from 1871 until his death in 1896. He loved the house dearly and it is the scene of the end of his utopian novel *News from Nowhere*, in which he writes of a world where work has become a sought after pleasure. The house, which along with the beautiful garden is open to visitors during the summer, has examples of Morris's work; the four-poster in which he was born, and memorabilia of Dante Gabriel Rosetti. Rosetti is reputed to have found the village boring, so presumably the fact that he was in love with Morris' wife, Jane, drew him here. Rosetti's outstanding portrait of her, *The Blue Silk Dress*, hangs in the Panelled Room. Opening times at the manor are limited – more details on 01367 252486.

Morris is buried in the churchyard, under a tombstone designed by his associate Philip Webb on the lines of a Viking tomb house. The church itself is interesting, the oldest parts dating from the late 12th century, and the village includes some fine farmhouses from around the end of the 17th and beginning of the 18th centuries.

Bradwell Grove

7 miles W of Witney off the A361

The 160 acres of park and garden which make up **The Cotswold Wild Life Park** (see panel below) are home to a whole host of animals, many of whom roam free in the wooded estate. Rhinos, zebras, ostriches and tigers are just some of the animals in the spacious enclosures while tropical birds, monkeys, reptiles, and butterflies are all given the chance to enjoy the warmth of their natural habitat by staying indoors. With an adventure playground and a narrow-gauge railway, the park has something to offer all the family.

Stanton Harcourt

4 miles SE of Witney off the B4449

This beautiful village is noted for its historic manor house **Stanton Harcourt Manor**, which dates back to the 14th century. Famed for its well-preserved medieval kitchen, one of the most complete to survive in this country, the house is also renowned for its fine collection of antiques and the tranquil

Cotswold Wildlife Park & Gardens

Burford, Oxon OX18 4JW
Tel: 01993 823006 Fax: 01993 823807
website: www.cotswoldwildlifepark.co.uk

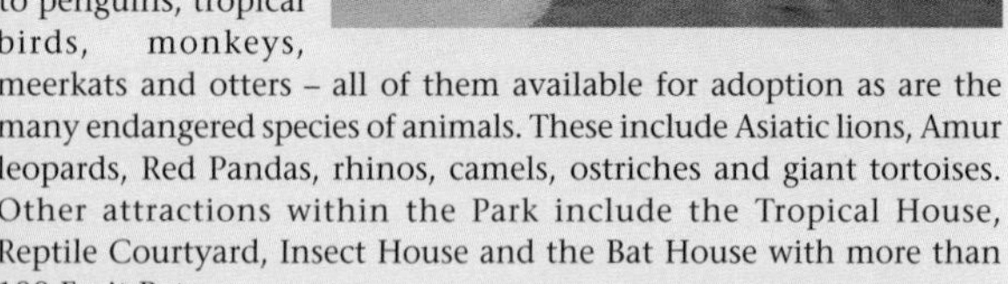

Cotswold Wildlife Park & Gardens is one of the leading attractions in the county and provides a perfect family day out. Children especially enjoy the Walled Garden which is home to penguins, tropical birds, monkeys, meerkats and otters – all of them available for adoption as are the many endangered species of animals. These include Asiatic lions, Amur leopards, Red Pandas, rhinos, camels, ostriches and giant tortoises. Other attractions within the Park include the Tropical House, Reptile Courtyard, Insect House and the Bat House with more than 100 Fruit Bats.

For gardeners there are formal plantings, the "Hot Bed", flamboyant borders, container planting and hanging baskets, while the 160 acres of beautiful parkland contain fine specimen trees including Giant redwood, Wellingtonia, cedars and a huge 600-year-old oak. Snacks and hot meals are served in the Oak Tree Restaurant and amenities for children include a farmyard, adventure playground, brass rubbing centre and a narrow gauge railway. The Park is open every day except Christmas Day from 10am; last admissions are at 4.30pm, March to September; 3pm, October to February. The Park is located on the A361, two miles south of its junction with the A40 at Burford.

gardens. It was while staying here, from 1717 to 1718, that Alexander Pope translated Homer's great work, the *Iliad*. He worked in the tower, part of the original manor house and now referred to as **Pope's Tower**. (The manor is currently – 2004 – closed and a re-opening date is not yet available).

While the manor house draws many people to the village, the splendid Norman **Church of St Michael** is also worthy of a visit. Naturally, the Harcourt chapel dominates but there are other features of interest, including an intricate 14th century shrine to St Edburg.

Standlake

5 miles SE of Witney on the A415

A little way south of the village is the three-arched **Newbridge**, built in the 13th century and now the second oldest bridge across the Thames. Newbridge saw conflict during the Civil War and the 'Rose Revived' pub was used by Cromwell as a refreshment stop.

OXFORD

The skyline of this wonderful city can be seen from many of the hilltops which surround it and the view is best described by the 19th century poet, Matthew Arnold:

'that sweet city with her dreaming spires'.

George Bernard Shaw was rather less effusive when he wrote:

'Very nice sort of place, Oxford, I should think, for people who like that sort of place'.

Oxford is not all beautiful ancient buildings but a town of commerce and industry and around the academic centre there are suburbs and factories. A city which has been the centre of the country's intellectual, political, religious and architectural life for over 800 years,

Sassi

55 High Street, Oxford OX1 4AS
Tel: 01865 205151
website: www.sassishoes.co.uk

After many years in the corporate world, Jayne Tidbury decided to devote her energies to the more feminine environment of selling womens shoes and in 2004 opened her stylish shop, **Sassi,** on Oxford's historic High Street, within close proximity to the main shopping area.

Jayne personally travels to the shoe fashion capital of Milan to select her exclusive ranges – "shoes to die for" as one customer put it. Her stock includes stunningly elegant shoes from designers such as Boccaccini, Barbara Bui, Kenzo, Eley Kishimoto, Luc Berjen, Jane Brown and United Nude and the range is constantly evolving. These covetable works of art are beautifully displayed on glass shelving, with mirrors and spot lighting setting them off to their best advantage.

Port Meadow Designs

104 Walton Street, Oxford OX2 6EB
Tel: 01865 311008

Walk into Port Meadow Designs and you meet glorious, gorgeous chaos. This shop defies category. It started as a wool shop but now carries anything from designer clothes to organic herbs and spices and includes possibly the best selection of jewellery in Oxford as well as soft furnishings, organic cotton baby clothes, ceramics, foot ware, lighting, hand knits, and much more. If you have visited *Country Living* Fair you'll find familiar names like Terry Macey, Inside Out and Shepard's Linen clothing; L'Occitane; English Stamp Company, and Jane Hogben Ceramics. It's a shop you could spend hours in.

it is still an academic stronghold, housing some of the finest minds in some of the finest buildings in the country. The best way to explore Oxford is on foot in the company of one of the official guides. Walking tours are offered daily (except 25th/26th December). Tickets are available from the Oxford Information Centre.

A walled town in Saxon times, Oxford grew on a ford where the River Thames meets the River Cherwell. The first students came here in the 12th century when they were forced out of Paris, at that time Europe's leading academic centre. Intellectual pursuits then were chiefly religious, and as the town already had an Augustinian Abbey it soon became the country's leading seat of theological thinking. However, there was considerable tension between the townsfolk and the intellectuals and in the 13th century, in a bid to protect their students, the university began to build colleges - enclosed quadrangles with large, sturdy front doors. The first colleges, University (1249), Balliol (1263) and Merton (1264) were soon joined by others which to this day maintain their own individual style while all coming under the administration of the university.

Merton College was founded by Walter de Merton, Lord Chancellor of England, as a small community of scholars. The present buildings mostly date from the 15th to 17th centuries, with Mob Quad as the university's oldest. The key feature of the college is its splendid medieval library where the ancient books are still chained to the desks. Once considered the poor relation to other, wealthier colleges, **Balliol College** was founded as an act of penance by John Balliol and for many years it was reserved for poor students only. Most of the college buildings now date from the 19th century when the

Uhuru Wholefoods

48 Cowley Road, Oxford OX4 1HZ
Tel: 01965 248249

Annette Mrigxitama was born in Kenya and came to England in 1969. She trained as a nurse but for the past 20 years has worked in **Uhuru Wholefoods**, a collective selling organic wholefoods. In Swahili *Uhuru* means 'freedom' and the shop stocks many Fair Trade items which give the local producers a fairer share of the profits from their commodities. The shop is organic registered with 90% of its products produced

organically.

The wholefood range includes vegetarian, vegan and macrobiotic produce as well as items catering for other dietary regimes. Also on sale are a range of aromatherapy products and Natural Bodycare Products. Organic chocolates, cordials, jams and preserves, rice and oat cakes, fresh fruits and vegetables – this is a great place to browse around in search of unusual products which are also environmentally friendly.

OxfordShortlets

Specialists in High Quality Short let Accommodation

1st Floor, Cranbrook House, 287/291 Banbury Road,
Oxford OX2 7AJ
Tel: 0870 160 2325 Fax: 0870 160 2327
e-mail: info@oxfordshortlets.co.uk
website: www.oxfordshortlets.co.uk

Specialising in high quality, short let accommodation, **OxfordShortlets** is a letting agency with a difference, providing visitors to the city with a cost-effective alternative to hotel accommodation or a six-month tenancy agreement. "Over the years," says owner and founder Emma Righton, "we have accommodated actors cast in local productions, people wanting to experience the city before they buy, visiting medics and academics, overseas visitors and many company-seconded employees." All the properties are located from within the city centre to just outside the ring road and range from studio apartments through town houses to country cottages.

They can accommodate from one up to seven guests and are available on contracts extending from one week up to five months. "The opportunity to live in Oxford and feel at home whilst you are away is the key to niche market," says Emma whose staff provide a personal tailored service to both owners and lessees. So, if you are visiting Oxford for a week or more and prefer the independence and privacy of your own property, somewhere in OxfordShortlets portfolio you will surely find an appropriate location.

Ducker & Son

6 Turl Street, Oxford OX1 3DQ
Tel: 01865 242461
e-mail: ducker.oxford@virgin.net
website: www.duckerandson.co.uk

Housed in traditional shop premises in the very heart of the city, the name of **Ducker & Son** has for more than a century been synonymous with the pinnacle of the art of bespoke shoemaking. The business has been run for some 40 years by brothers George and Stephen Purves. They learned their trade from their father who worked for Edward Ducker, the founder of the enterprise, and later took over his shop. When Mr Ducker arrived in Oxford with his boot-making tools in 1898 he joined at least 20 other shoemakers in the city – now there's just one and the company is one of very few traditional hand-sewn shoemakers outside the West End of London.

The shop window is filled with pairs of their highly desirable shoes whose prices range from around £250 for a machine-made pair from stock to £1,400 for a made-to-order hand-sewn pair, and £3,500 for a pair of hand-made riding boots. George and Stephen make weekly trips to Northampton – the country's traditional shoemaking centre – to buy leather for the uppers. The leather for the soles comes from America where some of the animals are bred purely for their hides. Among the celebrities shod by Ducker & Son are Evelyn Waugh, Chris Patten, Sir Robin Day and Jeremy Paxman.

college was instrumental in spearheading a move towards higher academic standards.

Thought by some to have been founded by Alfred the Great, **University College** was endowed in 1249 but the present college buildings are mostly 17th century. The poet Shelley was the college's most famous scholar though he was expelled in 1811 for writing a pamphlet on atheism. Shelley drowned at the age of 30 while in Italy, and his memorial can be seen in the Front Quad.

Magdalen Bridge, Oxford

One of the most beautiful colleges in the city, **Christ Church**, was founded in 1525 as Cardinal College by Thomas Wolsey and re-founded as Christ Church in 1546 by Henry VIII after Wolsey had fallen from royal favour. The visitor entrance is at the garden gate, through the Memorial Gardens, and leads through the bottom of Tom Tower (designed by Christopher Wren and home of the Great Tom bell) into Tom Quad, the largest of the city's quadrangles. From here there is access to the rest of the college and also to the college's chapel. Christ Church Cathedral is the only college chapel in the world to be designated a cathedral and was founded in 1546 on the remains of a 12th century building.

Another splendid college well worth a visit is **Magdalen College**, which has extensive grounds that include a riverside walk, a deer park, three quadrangles and a series of glorious well-manicured lawns. It was founded in 1458 by William Waynflete, Bishop of Winchester, and its bell tower is one of the city's most famous landmarks.

Oxford was closely involved in the Civil War and was for three years the King's headquarters. Several of the colleges were pressed into service as part of the headquarters by the Royalists: Wadham and New College were both used as stores for arms and gunpowder; Magdalen was Prince Rupert's headquarters and the tower was used as Charles' lookout when the Earl of Essex laid siege to the city. The damage caused by Cromwell's men is dramatically illustrated by bullet holes in the statue of the Virgin in the wonderful **Church of St Mary**. It was in this church that the trial of the Protestant martyrs Hugh Latimer, Nicholas Ridley and Thomas Cranmer was held. They were found guilty of heresy and burned to death in a ditch outside the city walls. The three are commemorated by the **Martyrs Memorial**, erected in 1841 in St Giles. If Oxford was the temporary home of countless luminaries (from Wolsey, Wesley and Wilde to 12 British Prime Ministers) it is also the permanent resting place of many others. In the churchyard of St Cross are buried Kenneth Grahame (*The Wind in the Willows*), Kenneth Tynan and the composer Sir John Stainer. William Laud,

Sarah Wiseman Gallery

40-41 South Parade, Summertown, Oxford OX2 7JL
Tel: 01865 515123
e-mail: sarahjane@wisegal.com
website: www.wisegal.com

The **Sarah Wiseman Gallery** opened in May 1998 (with an exhibition appropriately titled "Fresh Paint") and is now well-established as a premier showcase for contemporary artists such as Paul Kessling, Allyson Austin, Kathryn Thomas and the famous Icelandic painter Karulina Larudittir. Sarah, who studied Art History at Manchester University, recalls that when she set about opening the gallery, she had a very clear idea of what it should be – friendly and welcoming to customers and artists alike. "A place where people felt at ease to enjoy the paintings on display, which held regular exhibitions by interesting artists, and constantly worked towards helping artists to build their careers and giving customers excellent opportunities to buy art to build their personal collections."

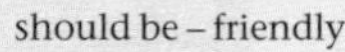

Early in 2004, Sarah carried out a major refurbishment which she believes has made the gallery space a very pleasant place to visit – "and to work in" she adds. There are three display areas but there is much more to see by each artist than the gallery has room for, so many more of their works are featured on the gallery's website.

Bridget Wheatley Contemporary Jewellery

38 Cowley Road, Oxford, Oxfordshire OX4 1HZ
Tel: 01865 722184 Fax: 01865 790858
website: www.bridgetwheatley.com

Bridget Wheatley Contemporary Jewellery is a haven of creativity and innovation. Bridget opened her shop in October 2000 with a degree from Birmingham School of Jewellery and many years' experience designing and making a wide range of jewellery. The essence of her work is simplicity allied to great attention to detail, and she takes her main inspiration from medieval and Celtic art. Bridget uses irregularly shaped freshwater pearls and richly coloured gemstones combined with gold and silver, and her work ranges from small items costing a few pounds to larger pieces such as necklaces.

The shop is bright, airy and chatty, and Bridget is happy to discuss customers' requirements, trying to find exactly the right piece for the right occasion, either from stock or as a specially made item. Alongside Bridget's own work, the shop is a showcase for an eclectic group of artists using diverse designs, materials and techniques to produce a stunning array of beautiful, totally individual pieces. The shop, which is located a leisurely 10-minute walk from the city centre, is open from 10am to 5.30pm Tuesday to Saturday.

17th century Archbishop of Canterbury, is buried in the chapel of St John's College; JRR Tolkien, Oxford professor and author of *The Lord of the Rings*, and the philosopher Sir Isiah Berlin lie in Wolvercote cemetery; and CS Lewis, critic and writer of the Nania series of books, is at rest in the churchyard of Holy Trinity, Headington.

Many of the colleges have lovely peaceful gardens, some of them open to the public at various times, and the **University Parks** are a perfect place for a stroll at any time. As well as the college buildings, Oxford has many interesting and magnificent places to explore. At the city's central crossroads, unusually named **Carfax** and probably derived from the Latin for four-forked, is a tower, **Carfax Tower**, which is all that remains of the 14th century Church of St Martin. A climb to the top of the tower offers magnificent views across the city. One of the most interesting buildings, the **Radcliffe Camera**, was built between 1737 and 1749 to a design by James Gibb. England's earliest example of a round reading room (camera means chamber, or room), this splendid domed building still serves this purpose for the **Bodleian Library**. Named after Sir Thomas Bodley, a diplomat and a fellow of Merton College, it contains over 5.5 million books and is one of the world's greatest libraries. The collection of early printed books and manuscripts is second only to the British Library in London and, though members of the University can request to see any book here, this is not a lending library and the books must be read and studied on the premises.

Close by is the **Clarendon Building**, the former home of the Oxford University Press and now part of the Bodleian, and also in this part of the city is the **Bridge of Sighs**, part of Hertford College and a 19th century copy of the original bridge in Venice. In Oxford the bridge crosses a street rather than a canal. The magnificent **Sheldonian Theatre** was designed and built in the style of a Roman theatre by Christopher Wren between 1664 and 1668 while he was Professor of Astronomy at the University. It is still used today for its intended purpose, as a place for University occasions including matriculation, degree ceremonies, and the annual Encaenia, when honorary degrees are conferred on distinguished people. As well as the superb wooden interior, the ceiling has 32 canvas panels, depicting Truth descending on the Arts, which are the work of Robert Streeter, court painter to Charles II.

Radcliffe Camera, Oxford

Naturally, the city has a wealth of museums and the best place to start is at the innovative **Oxford Story**, which presents a lively review of the last 800 years of university life, from the Middle Ages to the present day. The **Museum of Oxford**, with a different style, also covers the story of Oxford through a series of permanent displays showing various archaeological finds. First opened in 1683 and the oldest museum in the country, the **Ashmolean Museum** was originally established to house the collection of the John Tradescants, father and son. On display in this internationally renowned museum are archaeological collections from Britain, Europe, Egypt, and the Middle East; Italian, Dutch, Flemish, French, and English old masters; Far Eastern art, ceramics, and lacquer work and Chinese bronzes. The Ashmolean, named after the 17th century antiquary Elias Ashmole, also features many items from the Civil War, including Cromwell's death mask, his watch, King Charles' spurs and a collection of coins, among them the famous Oxford crown and a £3 coin minted by Charles. Here, too, is the **Museum of the History of Science**, a remarkable collection of early scientific instruments including Einstein's blackboard and a large silver microscope made for George III.

In a splendid high-Victorian building, near the University Science Area, is the **University Museum** where the remains of a dodo, extinct since around 1680, and a mass of fossilised dinosaur remains are on display. Also here is the **Pitt Rivers Museum**, with its interesting collection taken from all over the world. Musicians will enjoy the **Bate Collection of Historical Instruments**, while those captivated by old masters should take time to visit the **Christ Church Picture Gallery**, with its collection of works by Tintoretto, Van Dyck, Leonardo da Vinci and Michelangelo. Another place worthy of a visit and a particularly peaceful haven in the city is **Oxford Botanic Garden**, down by the river opposite Magdalen College. Founded in 1621, when plants were practically the only source of medicines, this was a teaching

Pine Castle Hotel

290-292 Iffley Road, Oxford, Oxfordshire OX 4 4AE
Tel: 01865 241497 Fax: 01865 727230
e-mail: stay@castle.co.uk
website: www.oxfordcity.co.uk/hotels/pinecastle

Adjacent redbrick town houses in typical Oxford style provide quiet, comfortable Bed & Breakfast accommodation on the southern side of the city close to the river. The eight well-appointed non-smoking bedrooms have en suite bath and shower, television, tea tray, hairdryer and direct dial telephone. Guests start the day with a good choice for breakfast. **The Pine Castle**, owned and run by Mrs Pavlovic and Mrs Trkulja, has a licensed bar in the lounge, pleasant gardens at the back and a car park.

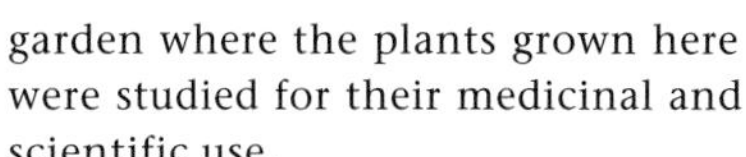

garden where the plants grown here were studied for their medicinal and scientific use.

Today the garden contains 8,000 species of plants in its 4.5 acres, including the National collection of euphorbias. Outside the entrance is a rose garden commemorating the work of Oxford's scientists in the discovery and use of penicillin. In the same ownership as the Botanic Garden is the **Harcourt Arboretum** at Nuneham Courtenay, six miles south of Oxford off the A4074. As well as a magnificent collection of trees, the site includes a bluebell wood and a 22-acre meadow.

Oxford is also the place where the River Thames changes its name to the poetic Isis and, at **Folly Bridge**, there are punts for hire and river trips can be taken, both up and down stream, throughout the day and evening.

The Painting Room

Tel: 01865 768854 Fax: 01865 872473
e-mail: carol@whetter2003.freeserve.co.uk

Carol Whetter has the distinction of being one of just a dozen artists in the country who specialise in hand-painted porcelain with exclusively Oriental motifs. She learnt her remarkable skills in oriental painting while living in Hong Kong and has spent many years perfecting her art. At her studio, The Painting Room (where visitors are welcome by appointment only), Carol creates a stunning range of pieces – plates, lamps, spice jars and more. All of them are exquisitely hand-painted with traditional oriental subjects such as dragons, butterflies and flowers.

Fish are a popular subject since they have a special significance for the Chinese. Carol uses French porcelain which is specially imported and 24-carat burnishing gold which means that the finished product is of a high standard. Much of her work is by commission from clients who require specific designs. Carol also teaches her art.

AROUND OXFORD

Headington

2 miles E of Oxford on the A40

Now a popular residential suburb of Oxford, Headington pre-dates the city by several centuries. It was the centre of an Anglo-Saxon royal domain with a palace where St Frideswide grew up and Henry I came to stay. From the nearby quarries came the stone for building many of the Oxford colleges. You can enjoy a grand view of them from **South Park** where Parliamentary troops camped during the Civil War.

Wheatley

4 miles E of Oxford on the A40

This former quarry village retains many old buildings, of which the most interesting is a curious conical lock-up. To the west, close to the M40 (junction 8), are the famous **Waterperry Gardens** of Waterperry House (the house is not open to the public). Established as a residential gardening school for women in the 1930s, Waterperry is now part pleasure garden and part commercial garden centre. The gardens are host each year to Art in Action, which brings together many of the world's finest craftspeople.

Garsington

4 miles SE of Oxford off the B480

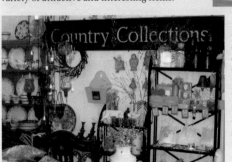

The most distinguished building hereabouts is **Garsington Manor**, built on a hilltop of mellow Cotswold stone in the 16th century. Between 1915 and 1927, this was the home of the socialite Lady Ottoline Morrell and her husband Philip who were hospitable to a whole generation of writers, artists, and intellectuals including Katherine

Mansfield, Lytton Strachey, Clive Bell, Siegfried Sassoon, DH Lawrence, TS Eliot, Rupert Brooke, Bertrand Russell and Aldous Huxley. Huxley based an account of a country house party in his novel *Crome Yellow* on his experiences at Garsington, thereby causing a rift with his hostess. She found his description all too recognisable and they were estranged for some time. It seems that Lady Ottoline was not very lucky in the artists on whom she lavished her attention and hospitality. DH Lawrence also quarrelled with her after drawing a less than flattering, but clearly recognisable, portrait of life at her house in *Women in Love*.

Garsington's other claim to literary fame is that Rider Haggard was sent to the school run by the Rev HJ Graham at the rectory in 1866. The present house is later, built in 1872, but across the road from the Church is a 16th century gateway from the rectory he would have known. While there Haggard became friendly with a local farmer named Quartermain whom he must have remembered with affection as he used the name for his hero, many years later, in his novel *King Solomon's Mines*.

The village **Church of St Mary** is a pleasant and cosy building with fine views to the south over the Chilterns from its hill top position, but it also looks over the industrial belt to the south of Oxford. Though the interior is chiefly Victorian, the church has retained its Norman tower and inside there is an elegant memorial to Lady Ottoline.

Thame

11 miles E of Oxford on the A418

Founded in 635 as an administrative centre for the Bishop of Dorchester, Thame first became a market town in the 13th century and its importance as a commercial centre is evident by the wide

Mi Casa

3 Upper High Street, Thame, Oxon OX9 3ER
Tel: 01844 218730 Fax: 01844 218983

Anyone in search of ideas to brighten up their home décor should make their way to **Mi Casa** in the centre of Thame. From the outside it looks quite small but the display areas extend right through to the back of the property and the many cabinets, gondolas and wall-mounted displays are stacked with a huge variety of items. The owner of Mi Casa, Adrian Mills, used to work in the information technology industry but left that business in 2000 for the more congenial lifestyle of developing this fascinating shop.

His selection includes Scandinavian tablewares, Polish glass, porcelain, pots, prints, artwork, jewellery, candleware and much, much more. Everything is contemporary and chosen for its elegant design and value for money. And if you want to add a distinctive touch to your house, there's a varied selection of house name and number plates. Mi Casa also stocks a wonderful choice of contemporary gifts, gift wraps and cards – a great place to visit in the run-up to Christmas.

main street it still has today. Lined with old inns and houses, some of which go back to the 15th century, this is a delightful place to visit.

The imposing **Church of St Mary**, tucked away at one end of the High Street, was built in the 13th century though the aisles were widened in the 14th century and the tower was heightened in the 15th century. In the centre of the chancel is a monument to Lord John Williams who was notorious for having helped burn Archbishop Thomas Cranmer in the 16th century. To the west of the church lies the **Prebendal House** which, in its oldest parts, dates from the 13th century. A prebend was an income granted to a priest by a cathedral or collegiate church. At Thame the prebend was established in around 1140 by Lincoln Cathedral. A special residence for the holders of the office was first mentioned in 1234.

The town also has a famous **Grammar School**, housed in a Tudor building in Church Lane. The schoolmaster's house faces the road and over the doorway are the arms of Lord Williams, who founded the school in 1558. John Hampden, one of the Parliamentary leaders during the Civil War, was at school here and he also died at Thame. When the Civil War broke out he raised a regiment of infantry for the Parliamentary Army and fought with great bravery at Edgehill and Reading. He was wounded at the battle of Chalgrove Field in June 1643 and was carried back to Thame where he died some days later in an inn which stood on the High Street. A plaque on a wall denotes the site.

Nuneham Courtenay

5 miles S of Oxford on the A4074

When the 1st Earl of Harcourt moved his family here from Stanton Harcourt in

The Old Bakery

Nuneham Courtenay, Oxon OX44 9NX
Tel: 01865 343585 Fax: 01865 341336
e-mail: addisonjill@hotmail.com
website: www.theoldbakery-oxford.com

The tall chimneys of **The Old Bakery** give some indication of its former function of providing the village with fresh bread. This charming 18th century listed building looks as if it had grown here but in fact it once stood at the other end of the village. The local squire, however, decided that the bakery and other buildings spoilt the view from the manor house so they were removed brick by brick and rebuilt out of his sight. Today the Old Bakery is the home of Jill Addison, a welcoming lady with interests in flower arranging, entering competitions – and providing wonderful food for her bed & breakfast guests.

A delicious breakfast is included in the tariff and Jill is happy to cook evening meals by arrangement. The accommodation here is equal to the English Tourism Board's 3-Crown standard and comprises three delightfully and decorated double rooms, all provided with TV and hospitality tray. One of the rooms is in the main house; and two are in the garden annexe. The garden itself is spacious and secluded with mature shrubs and trees, picnic tables and chairs. The Old Bakery is adjacent to an arboretum; there are pubs with good food locally; and the historic city of Oxford is just three miles away.

1756 he built the splendid **Nuneham Park**, one of the grandest mansions in Oxfordshire. The earl commissioned Capability Brown to landscape the grounds and observing the completed work deemed it *"as advantageous and delicious as can be desired, surrounded by hills that form an amphitheatre and, at the foot, the River Thames."* To achieve this idyllic result, the earl had the old village moved a mile away and out of sight. It's a charming model village of 18th century cottages facing each other in matched pairs on either side of the road. The mansion house is now a conference centre but its parkland forms the **Arboretum** of Oxford University and is open to the public. The 55 acres of woodland and meadow contain many rare species of trees and there are many pleasant walks.

Elsfield

2 miles N of Oxford off the A40

Elsfield was the home of the author and administrator John Buchan, 1st Baron Tweedsmuir, from 1919 until 1935 when he left to take up his appointment as Governor-General of Canada. During his time at Elsfield Manor House he wrote a number of books, including *Midwinter*, written in 1923 and partly set in the vicinity. His ashes are buried by the east wall of the churchyard of St Thomas of Canterbury. RD Blackmore, author of *Lorna Doone*, lived in Elsfield as a child while his father was the vicar.

Noke

5 miles NE of Oxford off the B4027

The tiny hamlet of Noke stands at the end of a winding lane that peters out at

Otmoor Holidays

Lower Farm, Noke, Oxford OX3 9TX
Tel: 01865 373766 Fax: 01865 371911
e-mail: info@oxfordholidays.co.uk
website: www.otmoorholidays.co.uk

The ancient village of Noke stands on the edge of Otmoor, an area of rare flora and fauna, part of it a sanctuary for breeding waders such as the lapwing and bittern. The last house in the village, at the end of a no through road, is Lower Farm, a working farm with 400 acres of arable and grassland. At its heart stands the farmhouse and a quadrangle of cottages which Emma and Austen Righton have converted to provide **Otmoor Holidays**. There are six properties altogether, sleeping between three and six people. All of them are furnished and decorated to the highest quality in pleasant natural shades.

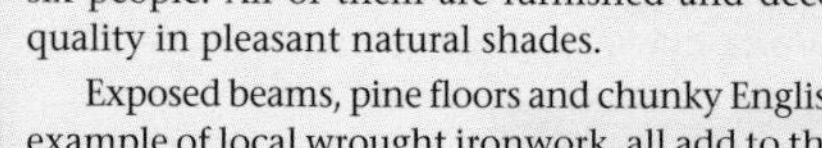

Exposed beams, pine floors and chunky English furniture, including example of local wrought ironwork, all add to the charm. The modern kitchens are comprehensively equipped; bedrooms have fitted carpets and double beds, or twin beds which can be converted to double beds; some bathrooms have a separate shower cubicle, others have a glazed cubicle integral with the bath. TV, video, CD/radio players and shelves of books are all provided, and there's a separate laundry/drying room with washing machine and token-operated tumble drier. There's a landscaped garden with rustic tables; a Wendy House and sand pit for children; and a sports area for basketball practice and badminton.

Peter Goss Butchers

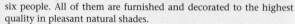

54 Bucknell Road, Bicester, Oxon OX26 8DW
Tel: 01869 243109 Fax: 01869 241879
website: www.petergossbutchers.co.uk

Traditional butcher's shops are few and far between these days so the people of Bicester are lucky to have **Peter Goss Butcher's** to supply their meat and poultry needs. Peter is a local man who has been in the butchery trade since 1954 when he started as a delivery boy for Waines butchers in Bicester. In 1967 he decided to start his own business and, he says "hasn't looked back since. I come from a farming back -ground which led me into farming myself where I breed sheep." Peter is also, incidentally, a keen cricketer who still plays for the Oxon/Berkshire Over 50s team and has travelled abroad to play. All this despite having a triple heart bypass a few years ago but, he says, he's now "fit as a flea".

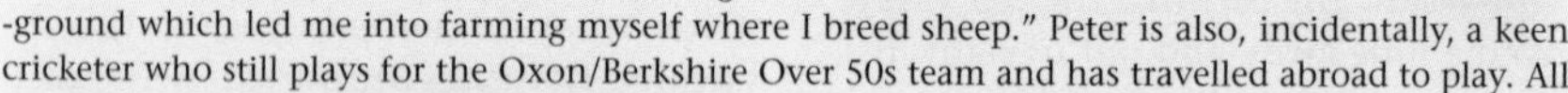

Peter insists on buying his meats from local sources, including his own farm and everything made here, such as the award-winning sausages and beefburgers, is prepared on the premises. He employs a staff of six, some of whom have been with him for 16 years or more. Amongst his regular customers is the National Trust property, Waddesdon Manor, which he has been supplying for many years.

the edge of Otmoor. It has a small medieval church with a notable Elizabethan brass that depicts Johan Bradshaw with her two husbands and eight children.

BICESTER

Though the name (which is pronounced Bister) suggests that this was a Roman settlement, the town was not, in fact, established until Saxon times and the Roman name comes as a result of the nearby and long since vanished Roman town of Alchester. By the time of the 12th century, the town was the home of both an Augustinian priory and a Benedictine nunnery. Growing up around these religious houses and its market, the town suffered a disastrous fire in the early 18th century and most of the buildings seen here today date from that time onwards. Hunting and horse-racing played as much a part in the prosperity of Bicester as agriculture though industrialisation has been sporadic.

AROUND BICESTER

Deddington

8 miles NW of Bicester off the A423

Visitors to this old market town might recognise it as the place that was demolished by a runaway crane in the television adaptation of Tom Sharpe's *Blott on the Landscape*. The damage was, of course, cleverly faked and Deddington, which hovers between a small town and a large village, still retains all its medieval character. Surveyed in the Domesday Book at twice the value of Banbury, the town never developed in the same way as Banbury and Bicester, but it remains a prosperous agricultural centre with a still bustling market place. Little can now be seen of the 12th century **Deddington**

Castle. This was destroyed in the 14th century and most of the building materials were put to good use in other areas of the town. However, excavations have revealed the remains of a curtain wall, a hall and a small rectangular keep.

Close by is **Castle House**, where Pier Gaveston, Edward II's favourite, was held before his execution in 1312. The house's two towers were added later, in the 1650s, when the house was in the ownership of Thomas Appletree. A supporter of Cromwell, Appletree was ordered to destroy the property of Royalists and it was material from two local houses that he used in his building work.

Lower Heyford

6 miles W of Bicester on the B4030

Situated at a ford across the River Cherwell, which was replaced in the late 13th century by a stone bridge, the village lies on the opposite bank from its other half - Upper Heyford. To the south of the village lies **Rousham House**, a fine mansion built in the mid-1600s for Sir Robert Dormer and set in magnificent gardens on the banks of the River Cherwell. The gardens as seen today were laid out by William Kent in 1738 and include many water features, sculptures and follies. Next to the house are very attractive pre-Kent walled gardens with a parterre, herbaceous borders, a rose garden and a vegetable garden. The garden is open to the public all year round; the house has limited opening times.

BANBURY

Famous for its cross, cakes, and the nursery rhyme, this historic and thriving market town has managed to hang on to many of its old buildings as well as become home to Europe's largest livestock market. The famous **Banbury Cross** can be found in Horsefair where it was erected, in 1859, replacing the previous one demolished by the Parliamentarians during the Civil War. It was built to commemorate the marriage of Queen Victoria's oldest daughter to the Prussian Crown Prince, and the figures around the bottom of the cross, of Queen Victoria, Edward VII, and George V, were added in 1914.

The town's other legendary claim to fame is its cakes, made of spicy fruit pastry, which can still be bought. Banbury was also, at one time, famous for its cheeses, which were only about an inch thick. This gave rise to the expression 'thin as a Banbury cheese'.

On the east side of the Horsefair stands **St Mary's Church**, a classical building of warm-coloured stone and hefty pillars which are pleasantly eccentric touches. The original architect was SP Cockerell, though the tower and portico were completed between 1818 and 1822 by his son, CR Cockerell. The style reflects the strong influence on English architecture of Piranesi's *Views of Rome*, using massive shapes and giving stone the deliberately roughened appearance which comes from the technique known as rustication.

In **Banbury Museum** can be found the story of the town's development, from the days when it came under the influence of the bishops of Lincoln, through the woollen trade of the 16th century, to the present day. Adjoining the museum is **Tooley's Boatyard** (see panel on page 148), a scheduled ancient monument that can be visited as part of a guided tour. Established in 1790 and in continuous use ever since, Tooley's is the oldest working dry dock in the country. It was designed to build and repair canal barges and narrowboats.

Cactus

20 Parsons Street, Banbury, Oxon OX16 5LY
Tel: 01295 262805

Originally a gallery owner and a set designer with the BBC, George Wisner established his **Cactus** ladies' clothing store to cater for the independently minded customer. To begin with he stocked many different labels but now selects five or six brands that work best and feels that this core range provides customers with the quality they are looking for. He stocks a wealth of styles from designers such as Ted Baker, Fenn Wright Mason, Jackpot and Nougat, and also offers a personal tailoring service – most designs can be altered to fit as Cactus stocks a variety of sizes in store, ranging from 10 to 20.

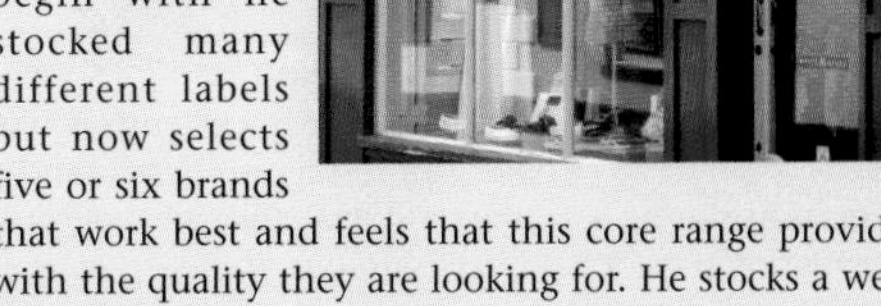

George doesn't rely solely on his own tastes – "I have two highly qualified fashion advisors in the shape of my daughters, Alice and Shelley. I believe that it's very important to get a woman's point of view on fashion." George also works closely with bespoke jewellery designer Tessa Tildsley who creates the accessories on sale in the shop. She works in silver and semi-precious stones to produce designs that harmonise with the clothes available at Cactus each season.

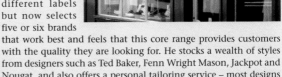

AROUND BANBURY

Broughton

2½ miles SW of Banbury on the B4035

Arthur Mee considered **Broughton Castle** *"One of the most fascinating buildings in the county"*. As you cross the ancient bridge over a moat and approach the sturdy 14th century gatehouse, it becomes clear that it is indeed something special, the perfect picture of a great Tudor mansion. The house has been owned by the Broughton family since 1451 – Nathaniel Fiennes, 21st Lord Saye & Sele is the present occupant. Over the years, there have been several royal visitors including Queen Anne of Denmark, wife of James I. Both James I and Edward VII used the aptly named King's Chamber, with its hand-painted Chinese wall paper. The house also played a part in the Civil War as it has a secret room where leaders of the Parliamentary forces laid their plans. Arms and armour from that period are displayed in the castle's grandest room, the Great Hall which is also notable for its dazzling plaster ceiling installed in 1599.

Bloxham

3½ miles SW of Banbury on the A361

Dominated by the 14th century St Mary's Church, whose spire is a highly visible local landmark and its Victorian public school, this large village is one of narrow lanes and fine gentlemen's houses. The old court house, to the south of the church, contains the **Bloxham Village Museum**, where there is a permanent collection of items on display which tell the life of the inhabitants of the village and surrounding area.

Rosamund the Fair

Tooleys Boatyard, Banbury Museum, Banbury, Oxon OX16 2PQ
Tel: 01295 278690 Mobile: 07831 616877
e-mail: info@tooleysboatyard.co.uk
website: www.rosamundthefair.co.uk

Rosamund the Fair is a delightful narrowboat which offers an opportunity to relax and enjoy exciting modern British cuisine freshly prepared on board and complemented by an excellent choice of wines. The restaurant is open on Saturday evenings and Sunday lunchtimes (advance booking essential), but can be hired any day of the week for private parties of up to 28 people. Full restaurant details and sample menus can be seen on the website; presentation dining vouchers are available on request. Rosamund is moored in Tooley's Boatyard, a fascinating part of Banbury Museum. It incorporates a dry dock, a chandlery with a full range of boating and repair requirements, and a forge which has remained virtually unchanged since it was built in 1790.

The museum holds Blacksmith courses in which students learn traditional techniques and can make their own poker in two hours! Guided tours of the boatyard are available, providing an interesting insight into the workings of a traditional boatyard and including a short trip on the *Henry II* day boat. Boat Handling courses are available. Also on site is the Café Quay, a calm and attractive waterside café/restaurant serving a variety of delicious home-made light refreshments throughout the day.

South Newington

6 miles SW of Banbury on the A361

This small village of ironstone dwellings is home to the **Church of St Peter and Vincula**, which contains the best medieval wall paintings in the county. Detail and colouring are both superb in the depictions, which include the murders of Thomas à Becket and Thomas of Lancaster (a rebel against Edward II), St Margaret slaying a dragon and a wonderful Virgin and Child.

Great Tew

7 miles SW of Banbury off the B4022

One of the most picturesque villages in the county, Great Tew, a planned estate village, had fallen into such disrepair by the 1970s that it was declared a conservation area in order to save it from complete dereliction. Today, the thatched cottages and houses from the 16th, 17th and 18th centuries nestle in a fold in the landscape of rolling countryside. The big house hereabouts is Great Tew Park, dating mainly from the 19th century. Only the garden walls remain of its 17th century predecessor, owned by Lucius Carey, Lord Falkland. It was a gathering place for some of the great writers and intellectuals of the day, including Edmund Waller and Ben Jonson. In the 17th century the 5th Viscount Falkland was Secretary to the Navy and gave his name to the Falkland Islands.

Hook Norton

7 miles SW of Banbury off the A361

This large village is best known for its brewery, which was set up by John Harris from his farmhouse in 1849. He started there as a maltster and after years of gaining expertise and learning from experiments he constructed a purpose-built brewery in 1872. The Brewery, which moved to its present premises in 1900, remains in the Harris family.

Swalcliffe

5 miles W of Banbury on the B4035

The village is dominated by the large **Church of St Peter and St Paul** which towers over all the other buildings here. Founded in Saxon times, the bulk of the building dates from the 12th, 13th and 14th centuries and it is the tracery in the east window which makes the church noteworthy. However, by far the most impressive building in Swalcliffe is the **Barn**, which has been acknowledged as one of the finest 15th century half-cruck barns in the country. Built as the manorial barn by New College, Oxford, in 1400-1409, it was used to store produce from the manor and never to store tithes. Today, it is home to a collection of agricultural and trade vehicles.

To the northeast of the village, on **Madmarston Hill**, are the remains of an Iron Age hill fort which was occupied from the 2nd century BC to the 1st century AD.

Wroxton

3 miles NW of Banbury on the A422

A charming village of brown stone cottages clustered round the village pond, from which a road leads to **Wroxton Abbey**. This impressive Jacobean mansion was built by Sir William Pope, Earl of Downe, and was the home of the North family for 300 years. The gardens and grounds of the Abbey, now restored as an 18th century park, are open to the public, but the house is not. All Saints Church contains several imposing monuments including those to Sir William and his wife, to Lord North who was Prime Minister from 1770 to 1782, and to the banker Thomas Coutts.

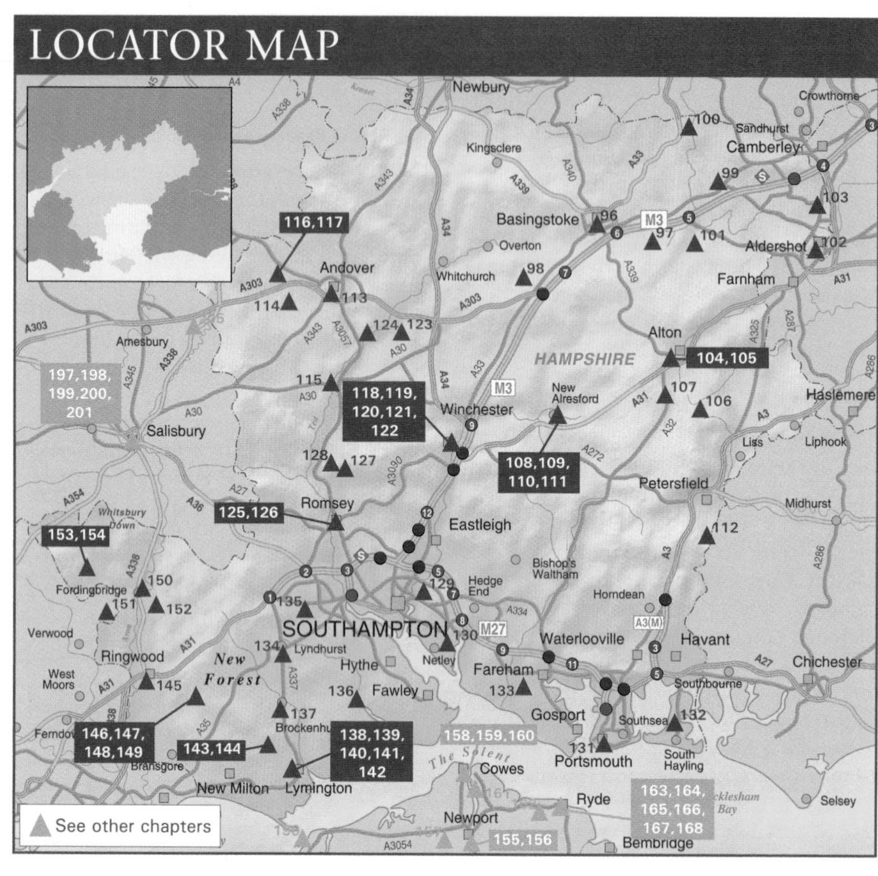

ADVERTISERS AND PLACES OF INTEREST

HAMPSHIRE AND THE NEW FOREST 3

The Mary Rose, Portsmouth

You only have to travel a dozen or so miles from the M25 near Staines before you cross the county boundary into Hampshire. So it's not surprising that this corner of the county is quite heavily populated, dotted with prosperous, sprawling towns such as Farnborough, Farnham and Basingstoke. What *is* surprising is that once you turn off the busy main roads, you can find yourself driving along narrow country lanes with very little traffic.

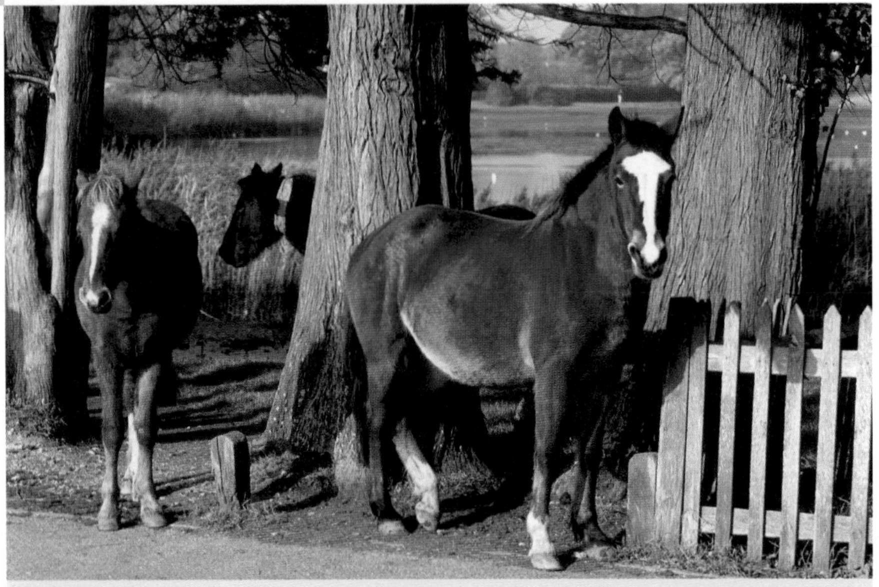

New Forest Ponies

This area forms part of the North Downs. Honouring the perverse tradition of English place-names, the Downs are actually uplands, softly rolling, wooded hills in whose folds lie scores of picturesque villages. As the crow flies, central London is little more than 30 miles away; for many of the north-eastern Hampshire villages, even today, the metropolis might just as well be 300 miles distant.

There are few grand houses in the area, although The Vyne near Basingstoke and the Duke of Wellington's home, Stratfield Saye House, are both very imposing. Two smaller dwellings, however, attract hundreds of thousands of visitors to this corner of the county: Jane Austen's House at Chawton, near Alton, and a few miles to the south in the village of Selborne, The Wakes, home of the celebrated naturalist, Gilbert White. Lovers of steam railways can combine a visit to these two houses with a ride on the Watercress Line which runs between Alton and Alresford.

The New Forest has been a Royal Forest for over 900 years. It aquired its name after William the Conqueror proclaimed it as his hunting ground and began a programme of planting thousands of trees. The area is famous for its wildlife, in particular the ponies, and is now a National Park, a status that will protect its 222 square miles from 'inappropriate development' in the future.

BASINGSTOKE

A vibrant, modern town whose name goes back to Saxon times when a farmer with a name something like Base, along with his extended family, or 'ing', established a 'stok', (stock or farmhouse) beside the River Lodden.

It comes as something of a surprise to discover that this busy, prosperous town with its soaring multi-storey buildings can boast no fewer than 25 parks and open spaces. A useful leaflet available from the Tourist Information Centre gives details of them all, ranging from the 16-hectare **War Memorial Park**, an 18th century park complete with bandstand, aviary and sports facilities, to **Southview Cemetery**, a site with a fascinating history. Some 800 years ago, during the reign of King John, England languished under an interdict pronounced by the Pope. Throughout the six years from 1208 to 1214, any baby christened, or dead person buried, lacked the official blessing of Mother Church. At Basingstoke during those years, the deceased were interred in a graveyard known as the Liten and when the interdict was finally lifted, the ground was consecrated and a chapel built, the **Chapel of the Holy Ghost.** Today, it's a striking ruin surrounded by a well-managed site which provides a peaceful refuge from the bustling town.

As befits such a thriving place, Basingstoke offers visitors a wide choice of attractions: theatre, cinema, a vast Leisure Park and, opened in 2002, **Festival Place** whose one million square feet of shopping and leisure contains some 165 shops, 26 bars, restaurants and cafés, and a 10-screen cinema.

The "Old Town" area offers a lively cosmopolitan mix of bars, theme pubs and restaurants. Here too, housed in the old Town Hall of 1832, is the excellent **Willis Museum** (free) which charts the town's history with lively displays featuring characters such as "Fred", a Roman skeleton, and "Pickaxe", a 19th century farm worker "forced to scrape a living from the streets of Basingstoke as a scavenger". The museum is named after George Willis, a local clockmaker and former mayor of Basingstoke who established the collection in 1931. Naturally, locally made grandfather clocks feature prominently in the displays.

A more recent attraction is **Milestones** (see panel below), a living history museum with reconstructed shops, factories, cobbled streets and staff in

MILESTONES

Leisure Park, Churchill Way West, Basingstoke, Hampshire RG21 6YR
Tel: 01256 477766 Fax: 01256 477784
website: milestones-museum.com

Opened in November 2000, this is Hampshire's living history museum, where the county's heritage comes to life in cobbled streets with shops, factories, interactive areas, staff in period costume and superb exhibits relating to industrial and everyday life. Among the many highlights are the Tasker and Thorneycroft collections of agricultural and commercial vehicles, and the renowned AA collection. Disabled access and audio guides are available and a gift shop sells souvenirs. A café serves teas, coffees and light snacks and there is a Victorian public house.

The Vyne, Sherbourne St. John

period costume. Highlights include the Tasker and Thorneycroft collections of agricultural and commercial vehicles and the fascinating AA collection. At the nearby **Viables Craft Centre**, visitors can watch craftspeople at work.

Just to the east of Basingstoke, **Basing House** was once one of the grandest residences in the realm. Built during the reign of Henry VIII, it rivalled even the king's extravagant mansions. Less than a hundred years later, during the Civil War, Cromwell's troops besieged the house for an incredible three years, one of them reporting that the mansion was "as large as the Tower of London". When Basing House was finally captured the victorious New Army burnt it to the ground, but a magnificent 16th century barn survived, its timber roof a marvel of the carpenter's craft.

The Vyne (National Trust), four miles north of Basingstoke, has enjoyed a much happier history. Built in the early 1500s for Lord Sandys, Lord

Chamberlain to Henry VIII, the house enjoys an idyllic setting with lawns sweeping down to a shimmering lake. A classical portico was added in 1654, the first of its kind in England. The Vyne's treasures include a fascinating Tudor chapel with Renaissance glass, a Palladian staircase, and a wealth of linenfold panelling and fine furniture.

AROUND BASINGSTOKE

Steventon

6 miles SW of Basingstoke, off the B3400

At Steventon Rectory on December 16th 1775, Cassandra Austen presented her husband, George, with their seventh child, Jane. George was the rector of Steventon and Jane was to spend the first 25 years of her short life in the village. There is now very little evidence of her time here. The rectory was later demolished but there are memorials to the Austen family in the church where George Austen served for 44 years. It was at Steventon that Jane wrote *Pride and Prejudice, Sense and Sensibility* and *Northanger Abbey*. When the Revd George retired in 1800, the family moved to Bath. After her father's death, five years later, Jane and her mother took the house in Chawton that is now the Jane Austen Museum.

Overton

8 miles W of Basingstoke, on the B3400

A large village near the source of the River Test, Overton has a broad main street lined with handsome houses. During the stage coach era, it was an important staging post on the London to Winchester route and the annual sheep fair was one of the largest in the county selling at its peak up to 150,000 lambs and sheep. The fair flourished for centuries only coming to an end in the early 1930s.

To the north of the village, set high on a ridge, is **Watership Down**, immortalised in Richard Adams' book of the same name. It is now a nature reserve. The down lies on the long distance footpath, the Wayfarer's Walk, which runs from Inkpen Beacon (just over the border in Berkshire) to Emsworth on the Hampshire coast.

Kingsclere

8 miles NW of Basingstoke, on the A339

Collectors of curiosities might like to make a short excursion to the little town of Kingsclere where the weather-vane on top of the parish church has baffled many visitors. With its six outstretched legs and squat body, the figure on the vane has been compared to a skate-boarding terrapin. Local historians, however, assert that it actually represents a bed bug and was placed here by the command of King John. The king had been hunting in the area when a thick fog descended and he was forced to spend the night at the Crown Hotel in Kingsclere. Apparently, he slept badly, his slumber continually disturbed by the attentions of a bed bug. The next morning, he ordered that the townspeople should forever be reminded of his restless night in Kingsclere by erecting this curious memorial to his tormentor.

Silchester

7 miles N of Basingstoke, off the A340

Excavation of the town which the Romans called **Calleva Atrebatum** took place at the turn of the 19th/20th centuries and revealed some remarkable treasures, most of which are now on display at Reading Museum. The dig also revealed the most complete plan of any Roman town in the country but, rather oddly, the site was 're-buried' and now only the 1.5 mile city wall is visible – the best-preserved Roman town wall in Britain. Also impressive is the recently restored 1st century amphitheatre which lay just beyond the town walls.

Tucked in next to part of the Roman wall is the pretty **Church of St Mary** which dates from the 1100s. It boasts a superb 16th century screen with a frieze of angels and some unusual bench-ends from 1909 executed in Art Nouveau style.

Pamber Heath

7 miles N of Basingstoke, on minor road off the A340

There are three 'Pambers' set in the countryside along the A340. At Pamber End stand the picturesque ruins of a once-magnificent 12th/13th century **Priory Church**, idyllically sited in sylvan surroundings. Set apart from the village, they invite repose and meditation. Pamber Green, as you might expect, is a leafy enclave; but for anyone in search of a good country pub, the Pamber to make for is Pamber Heath. Lots of pubs have a few pots scattered around, but the collection at The Pelican in Pamber Heath is something else. There are hundreds of them hanging from the ceiling beams, in every shape and colour you can imagine, some pewter and some ceramic.

Hartley Wintney

9 miles NE of Basingstoke, on the A30

Riding through Hartley Wintney in 1821, William Cobbett, the author of *Rural Rides* and a conservationist long before anyone had thought of such a creature, was delighted to see young oaks being planted on the large village green. They were the gift of Hartley Wintney's lady of the manor, Lady Mildmay, and were originally intended to provide timber for shipbuilding. Fortunately, by the time they matured they were no longer needed for that purpose and today the **Mildmay Oaks** provide the village centre with a uniquely sylvan setting of majestic oak trees.

Anyone with an interest in horticulture should also visit the magnificent gardens of **West Green House**, about a mile to the west of Hartley Wintney. Owned by the National Trust, this pretty early-18th century house is surrounded by lovely gardens planted with a dazzling variety of trees, shrubs and plants. One of its interesting features is a stone column surmounted by an elaborate finial which was erected in 1976. It bears a Latin inscription which declares that a large sum of money was needed to put the column in place, money "which would otherwise have fallen, sooner or later, into the

Hartley Upholstery & Antique Restorations

Unit 2, Priors Farm, West Green Road,
Mattingley, Hartley Wintney,
Hampshire RG27 8GU
Tel/Fax: 0118 9326567
e-mail: paul.bligh@btconnect.com
website: www.hartley-antiques.com

Paul Bligh, the owner of **Hartley Upholstery & Antique Restorations**, has more than 25 years experience in the furniture business, and in the 20 years since he set out on his own he has built up a loyal clientele who know that their treasured pieces are in the safest of hands. His expertise covers all aspects of manufacturing and restoring furniture, from reupholstery and French polishing to accepting commissions for new pieces.

Working to the individual requirements of the customer, he will design and make pieces of furniture using a variety of materials. Whatever the design, Paul's expertise and reliance on traditional skills will result in a beautifully crafted possession for life, a piece of which any owner (and there have been hundreds!) will be proud. His workshop, is located near the National Trust's West Green House on the edge of Mattingley.

hands of the Inland Revenue".

While you are in Hartley Wintney a visit to the **Old Church**, south of the village, is well worth while. Parts of the building date back to medieval times, but the fascination of old St Mary's lies in the fact that, after being completely renovated in 1834, it has remained almost totally unaltered ever since. High-sided box pews line the main aisle, there are elegant galleries for choir and congregation spanning the nave and both transepts, and colourful funeral hatchments add to St Mary's time-warp atmosphere.

Eversley

10 miles NE of Basingstoke, on the A327

Charles Kingsley, author of such immensely popular Victorian novels as *The Water Babies* and *Westward Ho!*, was Rector of the village for 33 years from 1842 until his death in 1875 and is buried in the churchyard here. The gates of the village school, erected in 1951 for the Festival of Britain, include a figure of a boy chimney-sweep, the main character of *The Water Babies*. Kingsley was an attractive character with a burning passion for social justice, but modern readers don't seem to share the Victorian enthusiasm for his works. It's a sad fate for a prolific man of letters, although perhaps not quite so dispiriting as that met by one of Kingsley's predecessors as preacher at Eversley. He was hanged as a highwayman.

About four miles west of Eversley, **Stratfield Saye House** was just one of many rewards a grateful nation showered on the Duke of Wellington after his decisive defeat of Napoleon at Waterloo. The Duke himself doesn't seem to have been reciprocally grateful: only lack of funds frustrated his plans to demolish the gracious 17th century house and

Wellington Country Park

Riseley, nr Reading, Berkshire RG7 1SP
Tel: 0118 9326444 Fax: 0118 9326445
e-mail: info@wellington-country-park.co.uk
website: www.wellington-country-park.co.uk

Just off the A33 between Reading and Basingstoke, **Wellington Country Park** is the perfect venue for a day out that's full of fun and interest. The Park, which is situated within the Duke of Wellington's Estate, is a wonderful place to visit at any time from spring to autumn, but it really comes into its own during the school summer holidays. There's no better place for parents with children, and the 350 acres of wooded parkland provide plenty of activities for all ages in a safe, natural environment. Children can let off steam in the adventure playground, romp in the sandpit, give Mum and Dad a lesson in crazy golf, meet the friendly animals in the children's animal farm or enjoy a ride on the miniature railway in a carriage pulled by the scarlet-painted locomotive Charlotte. There are four separate nature trails providing a chance to see a wide variety of bird, animal, insect and plant life. Easiest of the four is the Yellow Trail, which is suitable for buggies and small children. The Green Trail skirts the Lakes and is the best for birdwatching, with Egyptian and snow geese, great crested grebes, kingfishers, dippers and black swans among the many species to look out for. Rowing boats and pedaloes can be hired, and there's good fishing from the banks of the small lake for roach, tench, perch, bream, pike and chub. Snacks, soft drinks, Wellington ice cream and gifts are for sale in the Gift and Coffee Shop in the Visitor Reception, or visitors can bring their own food to cook at designated barbecue sites or to find a secluded place in the woods for a picnic. The camping and caravan site, set out in individual woodland glades, is an ideal base for touring the many places of interest in the vicinity, and guests using the site have free access to the Country Park during their stay.

The Park is open from 10am March to early November, closing at 4.30 in spring and early autumn and at 5.30 peak season (last admissions one hour before closing time). It is also open on certain winter weekends, and throughout the season there are special events, from half-term activities to kite festivals and music evenings. An attraction three miles away and very well worth seeing is the majestic Stratfield Saye House, given to the Duke of Wellington as a reward for his defeat of Napoleon at Waterloo.

replace it with an even more impressive mansion which he intended to call Waterloo Palace. Quite modest in scale, Stratfield Saye fascinates visitors with its collection of the Duke's own furniture and personal items such as his spectacles, handkerchiefs and carpet slippers. More questionable are the priceless books in the library, many of them looted from Napoleon's own bibliotheque. A good number of the fine Spanish and Portuguese paintings on display share an equally dubious provenance, "relieved" during the Duke's campaign in those countries as "spoils of war". That was accepted military practice at the time and, these quibbles apart, Stratfield Saye House is certainly one of the county's "must-see" attractions.

To the west of the estate is the **Wellington Country Park** (see panel opposite) where there are fine walks and numerous attractions.

Odiham

7 miles E of Basingstoke, on the A327

Odiham Castle must have a very good claim to being one of the least picturesque ruins in the country. It looks like something rescued from a giant dentist's tray, with gaping window holes and jagged, crumbling towers. Back in 1215, though, Odiham Castle was a state-of-the-art royal residence. Great pomp and circumstance attended King John's stay at the castle, then just seven years old, the night before he set off to an important meeting. The following day, in a meadow beside the River Thames called Runnymede, John reluctantly subscribed his name to a bill of rights. That document, known as Magna Carta, proved to be the embryo of democracy in western Europe.

Odiham itself is one of the most attractive villages in the county, with a

Grapevine Delicatessen

77 High Street, Odiham, Hampshire RG29 1LB
Tel: 01256 701900/704466
Open: Mon-Fri 9.00am-5.30pm, Sat 9.00am-3.30pm
e-mail: sales@grapevine-gourmet.co.uk
website: www.grapevine-gourmet.co.uk

The Grapevine Delicatessen, situated on Odiham's historic High Street is a gourmet's delight. The Deli, as it is known to locals, opened its doors in February 2000 in a timber-framed grade II listed building, bringing a world of wonderful food to the people of Odiham and the surrounding villages.

The Deli receives two daily deliveries of fresh bread, from local bakeries, daily fruit and vegetable deliveries from local suppliers and stocks a wide range of local, national and international produce. A

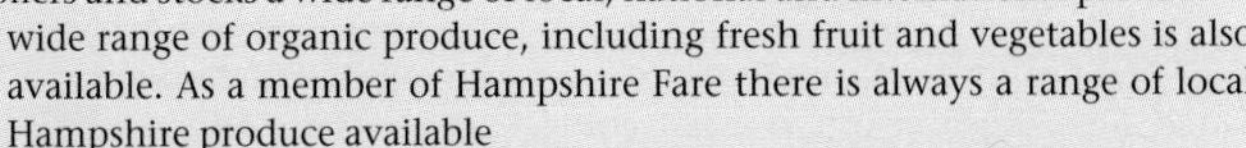

wide range of organic produce, including fresh fruit and vegetables is also available. As a member of Hampshire Fare there is always a range of local Hampshire produce available

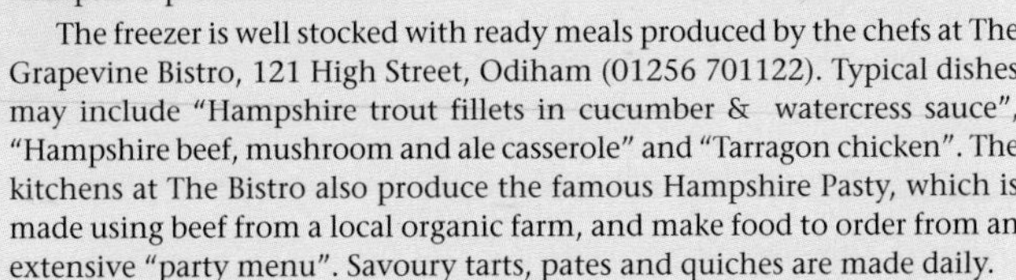

The freezer is well stocked with ready meals produced by the chefs at The Grapevine Bistro, 121 High Street, Odiham (01256 701122). Typical dishes may include "Hampshire trout fillets in cucumber & watercress sauce", "Hampshire beef, mushroom and ale casserole" and "Tarragon chicken". The kitchens at The Bistro also produce the famous Hampshire Pasty, which is made using beef from a local organic farm, and make food to order from an extensive "party menu". Savoury tarts, pates and quiches are made daily.

A mail order service is available, with Gourmet Gift Boxes a speciality. These make perfect presents for any occasion and are delivered tied with ribbon and personalised with a gift card.

handsome High Street and a 15th century church, the largest in Hampshire, in which collectors of curiosities will be pleased to find a rather rare item, a hudd. A portable wooden frame covered with cloth, the hudd provided Odiham's rector with graveside shelter when he was conducting burials in inclement weather. In a corner of the graveyard stands the **Pest House**, built around 1625 as an isolation ward for patients with infectious diseases. From 1780 until 1950, it served as an almshouse and is now open to visitors on most weekends.

Aldershot

14 miles E of Basingstoke on the A331

Back in 1854, Aldershot was a village of some 800 inhabitants. Then the Army decided to build a major camp here and the population has grown steadily ever since to its present tally of around 60,000. The story of how Aldershot became the home of the British Army is vividly recounted at the **Aldershot Military Museum** (see panel below) which stands in the middle of the camp and is a must for anyone with an interest in military history. Housed in the last two surviving Victorian barrack blocks, its tiny appearance from the outside belies the wealth of fascinating displays contained inside. For example, there's a detailed cutaway model of a cavalry barracks showing how the soldiers' rooms were placed above the stables, an economic form of central heating described as "warm, but aromatic".

It was the army at Aldershot who became the first military aviators in Britain, using Farnborough Common for flying and building their aircraft sheds where the Royal Aircraft Establishment stands today. **The Parachute Regiment and Airborne Forces Museum**, (moving to Duxford in Cambridgeshire in due course), has many interesting exhibits illustrating the part these pioneers played during the early days of the 20th century

Aldershot Military Museum

Queens Avenue, Aldershot, Hampshire GU11 2LG
Tel: 01252 314598
website: www.hants.gov.uk/museum/aldershot

The Museum covers the histories of Aldershot military town and the adjoining civil towns of Aldershot and Farnborough. The complex contains a rich mixture of buildings, objects, displays, vehicles and archives, and each of the several galleries has a different theme and character.

The John Reed Gallery covers the history of the Army in Aldershot from its arrival in 1854, and includes a rare example of a Victorian barrack room displayed in its original setting. Rushmoor Local History Gallery, which with the John Reed Gallery occupies a pair of unique barrack bungalows built in 1894, deals with the history of the civil towns of Aldershot and Farnborough. The Cody Gallery is named after an American, Samuel Franklin Cody, who made Britain's first powered flight at Farnborough in 1908. The Gallery includes a reconstruction of part of his workshop and many original objects, among them his flying helmet.

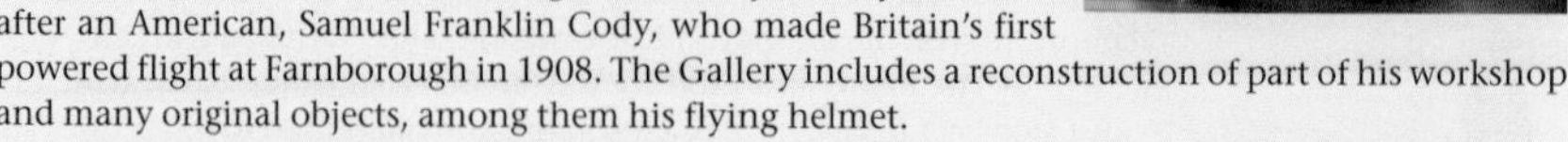

The Montgomery Gallery, which stood originally in the grounds of Monty's home at Isington near Alton, houses a collection of larger exhibits, including field guns and other vehicles. The museum's collection of vehicles, some here, some kept outside, ranges from the mass-produced Willys jeep of 1943 to the formidable 60-ton Chieftain tank; most are in full working order.

and during two World Wars. There are two further military museums to be found here: the **Army Medical Services Museum**, telling the story of medical services from 1660 to the present day, and the **Army Physical Training Corps Museum** where the Corps history is recounted with the help of numerous exhibits, pictorial records – and some Victorian gymnastic equipment.

In the town's Manor Park, the **Heroes Shrine** commemorates the dead of World War I, while a nearby walled and sunken garden, shaded by deodar trees, honours the fallen of World War II. Another celebrated military figure, the Duke of Wellington, is represented by an imposing bronze statue crowning Round Hill, just outside the town. The statue originally stood atop the Triumphal Arch at Hyde Park Corner in London but was moved to Aldershot in 1885.

Farnborough

14 miles E of Basingstoke on the A331

The town is best known for the **Farnborough Air Show** which is held every other year. The town's unique aviation heritage is explored at the **Farnborough Air Sciences Trust Museum** which holds an extensive collection of exhibits, records and artefacts.

Less well-known is **St Michael's Abbey,** now a Benedictine foundation but with a curious history. After the fall of Napoleon III, his wife the Empress Eugenie came to live at a large house called Farnborough Hill where she was later joined by her husband and her son, the Prince Imperial. Napoleon died at Chislehurst after an operation to remove bladder stones; her son was killed in the Zulu War. The heartbroken Empress commissioned the building of an ornate mausoleum for

Shuzu

23 Camp Road, North Camp, Farnborough,
Hampshire GU14 6EN
Tel: 01252 548585
e-mail: shuzu@btconnect.com
website: www.shuzu.co.uk

Just off the main A3011 on the southern edge of Farnborough, **Shuzu** is the place where parents come to guarantee that their children have the smartest and trendiest feet in town! The shoes in stock cover an impressive range, with tons of designs for all ages, from toddlers to teens, and in UK sizes S2 to L8.

The extensive range gives you no end of choice with designs from Start-rite, Ricosta, DKM, Piedro, Geox, Skechers and celebrities favourite Buckle My Shoe!

Friendly, fully trained staff provide an expert fitting service and are ready with advice on all aspects of shoe care. Shoes are just part of the stock at ShuZu, which also sell chic rainwear from Kidorable, umbrellas, hats, belts, bags and other great accessories. Trendy and fashionable clothes from No Added Sugar, Jakes & Eat Yer Greens complete the look.

Opening Times Monday to Saturday 9.00 – 5.30.

their tombs and a monastery in the flamboyant French style. The first monks arrived in 1895 from Solesmes Abbey, France, and they still continue their regime of liturgy, study and manual work. The abbey is open to the public and has a small farm and apiary that supplies not only the monks but also the abbey shop. Guided tours are available on Saturday and Bank Holiday afternoons.

Alton

10 miles SE of Basingstoke, off the A31

Surrounded by hop-fields and some of Hampshire's loveliest countryside, Alton is an appealing market town with a history stretching back far beyond Roman times. (The name actually means "Old Town"). Its market, held every Tuesday, has a history of more than 1,000 years and was the most valuable market recorded in the *Domesday Book*.

Alton boasts a large number of old coaching inns, and the impressive, partly-Norman **St. Lawrence's Church** which was the setting for a dramatic episode during the Civil War. A large force of Roundheads drove some 80 Royalists into the church where 60 of them were killed. The Royalist commander, Colonel Boles, made a last stand from the splendid Jacobean pulpit, firing repeatedly at his attackers before succumbing to their bullets. The church door and several of the Norman pillars are still pock-marked with bullet holes inflicted during this close-combat conflict. More cheerful are the comical carvings on these pillars of animals and birds, amongst them a wolf gnawing a bone and two donkeys kicking their heels in the air.

Nearby is the old cemetery and the well-tended **grave of Fanny Adams.** The

The Botanic Garden

11 Market Street, Alton, Hampshire GU34 1HA
Tel: 01420 544194

It was in 2000 that Melanie and Michael Jago started **The Botanic Garden** – 'a house and garden haven' that has gone from strength to strength, including winning an 'Alton in Bloom' prize for best retail frontage. Michael trained at the Royal Horticultural Society, Wisley and tends the huge range of plants, trees and shrubs on display. Melanie worked as an interior designer for some years and her informed taste is evident in the stylish French garden furniture and the Cath Kidston fabrics and accessories on sale here. The interior is "packed with colour" says Melanie, "to allure the senses" and always contains fresh country garden flowers.

West End Farm

Upper Froyle, Alton, Hampshire GU34 4JG
Tel: 01420 22130 e-mail: butlerfroyle@btopenworld.com
Fax: 01420 22930 website: www.hampshirebedandbreakfast.co.uk

Surrounded by open countryside, **West End Farm** offers quality bed & breakfast accommodation in a friendly and relaxing environment. The well-maintained gardens overlook a lake and lovely walks lead through farmland and woods. The host, Liz Butler, provides a choice of full English, vegetarian or continental breakfasts while for evening meals and drinks the Hen & Chicken public house is a pleasant five-minute walk away. Luxury twin and double-bedded rooms are available with en suite bathrooms and each is equipped with TV, alarm clock, hair dryer, hospitality tray and complimentary toiletries.

expression "Sweet Fanny Adams" arose from the revolting murder in 1867 of an eight-year-old girl in the town who was hacked into pieces by her assassin. With macabre humour, sailors used the phrase "Sweet Fanny Adams" to describe the recently-introduced tinned mutton for which they had a certain mistrust. Over the years, the saying became accepted as a contemptuous description for anything considered valueless. A poor memorial for an innocent girl.

There's a different sort of monument in Amery Street, a narrow lane leading off the market place. On a small brick house is a plaque commemorating the Elizabethan poet Edmund Spenser who came to Alton around 1590 to enjoy its "sweet delicate air".

Well worth a visit while you are in Alton is the **Allen Gallery** in Church Street (free), home to an outstanding collection of English, Continental and Far Eastern pottery, porcelain and tiles. Housed in a group of attractive 16th and 18th century buildings the gallery's other attractions include the unique Elizabethan Tichborne Spoons, delightful watercolours and oil paintings by local artist William Herbert Allen, and a comfortable coffee lounge. Across the road, the **Curtis Museum** (free) concentrates on exploring 100 million years of local history with displays devoted to the "shocking tale of Sweet Fanny Adams", other local celebrities such as Jane Austen, Lord Baden Powell, Montgomery of Alamein; and a colourful Gallery of Childhood with exhibits thoughtfully displayed in miniature cases at a suitable height for children.

On the western edge of the town lies **The Butts**, a pleasant open area of grassland that was once used for archery practice. Today it is the setting for events such as the annual Victorian Cricket Match.

A good time to visit the town is mid-July when the Alton Show takes place. Established in 1840, this is one of southern England's most important agricultural gatherings with a wide range of events featuring such attractions as heavy horses, llamas, beagles, gun dogs and birds of prey.

AROUND ALTON

Selborne

4 miles SE of Alton on the B3006

Like the neighbouring village of Chawton, Selborne also produced a great literary figure. **The Wakes** was the home of Gilbert White, a humble curate of the parish from 1784 until his death in 1793. He spent his spare hours meticulously recording observations on the weather, wildlife and geology of the area. Astonishingly, a percipient publisher to whom Gilbert submitted his notes recognised the appeal of his humdrum, day-to-day accounts of life in what was then a remote corner of England. *The Natural History and Antiquities of Selborne* was first published in 1788, has never been out of print, and still provides what is perhaps the most entertaining and direct access to late-18th century life, seen through the eyes of an intelligent, sceptical mind.

Visitors to The Wakes can see the original manuscript of his book along with other personal belongings, and the peaceful garden with its unusual old plant varieties.

The house also contains the **Oates Museum** which celebrates Francis Oates, the Victorian explorer, and his nephew Capt. Lawrence 'Titus' Oates who was with Capt. Scott on his doomed expedition to the South Pole. Titus' last words – "I am just going outside. I may

Town & Country Interiors

6 Hartley Business Park, Selborne,
Hampshire GU34 3HS
Tel: 01420 511711 Fax: 01420 511778
e-mail: penniknap@hotmail.com

Town & Country Interiors offers a dazzling range of ideas for interior decoration in a rural location far away from the hassle of High Street shopping. Owner Penny Knap, who has been trading since 1991, has gathered together a wonderful collection of furnishings and decorative items from a stellar group of designers and manufacturers.

The roll of honour includes names such as Colefax & Fowler, Zoffany, Osborne & Little, Nina Campbell and Nobilis. You'll also find pieces from the Designers' Guild, Andrew Martin, Jane Churchill, Manuel Canovas, Liberty, Cath Kidson, Lewis & Wood, Jean Munro, Mulberry, Coles and Fired Earth. Whether you are looking for something to add sparkle and distinction to your own décor, or seeking out a gift that's sure to please, you'll almost certainly find plenty to suit you here.

be some time" – are known around the world, as is Scott's diary entry describing Oates' selfless deed as "the act of a very gallant gentleman". The Wakes and the Oates Museum are open daily, and there's an excellent book and gift shop, and a tea-room specialising in 18th century fare.

Gilbert White is buried in the graveyard of the pretty **Church of St Mary**, his final resting place marked by a stone bearing the austere inscription *GW 26th June 1793*. A fine stained glass window depicts St Francis preaching to the birds described in Gilbert's book. Outside in the churchyard, is the stump of a yew tree which was some 1,400 years old when it succumbed to the great storm of January 1990.

From the village centre there are several walks, one which leads to the 'Zig-Zag' path constructed by Gilbert and

Boundary House

Gosport Road, Lower Farringdon, nr Alton, Hampshire GU34 3DH
Tel: 01420 587026 Fax: 01420 587047
e-mail: boundary@messages.co.uk web: www.boundaryhouse.co.uk

For many years Delia and Jim Gilchrist have been inviting Bed & Breakfast guests to share their immaculate bungalow. Three bedrooms under the eaves provide very comfortable accommodation, and the lovely landscaped grounds include a two-acre paddock that is home to sheep and chickens. Among the many local places of interest are Gilbert White's house in Selborne, Jane Austen's house in Chawton and the wonderful Watercress Railway Line. This is also great walking country, and a particularly pleasant summer walk takes in Chawton and both Lower and Upper Farringdon.

his brother in 1753. It winds its way up to the 'Hanger' (a wood on a steep hillside) that overlooks the village. The land at the summit is part of an area of meadow, woodland and common which is owned by the National Trust – the spot provides panoramic views across the South Downs.

Back in the village, the **Selborne Pottery** was established by Robert Goldsmith in 1985. Each piece of pottery made here is hand-thrown and turned, and the distinctive pots are not only functional but also decorative.

Chawton

2 miles SW of Alton, off the A31

From the outside, the home in which Jane Austen spent the last eight years of her life and where she wrote three of her most popular novels *(Mansfield Park, Emma* and *Persuasion)*, is a rather disappointingly dull, blank-faced building. Once you step inside, however, the mementoes on show are fascinating. In the parlour is the small round table where she wrote; in her bedroom the patchwork quilt she made with her mother and sister still lies on the bed; whilst in the old bake house is her donkey cart. Another room is dedicated to her brothers, Frank and Charles, who both had distinguished careers in the Royal Navy. Chawton village itself is a delightful spot with old cottages and houses leading up to the village green outside Jane's house.

Jane Austen's House, Chawton

Hinton Ampner

9 miles SW of Alton on the A272

The River Itchen, renowned for its trout and watercress beds, rises to the west of the village to begin its 25-mile journey to the sea at Southampton; the **Itchen Way** footpath follows the river throughout its course. Also to the west of the village are **Hinton Ampner Gardens** (National Trust), created by Ralph Dutton who inherited the house in 1936 and created a superb garden that combines formal and informal planting. The design produces some delightful walks with some unexpected vistas.

Alresford

10 miles SW of Alton, off the A31

Pronounced *Allsford*, Alresford was created around 1200 by a Bishop of Winchester, Geoffrey de Lucy, as part of his grand plan to build a waterway from Winchester to Southampton. Where the river Arle flows into the Itchen, he constructed a huge reservoir covering 200 acres, its waters controlled to keep the Itchen navigable at all seasons. The Bishop's reservoir is now reduced to some 60 acres but it's still home to countless wildfowl and many otters. Known today as **Old Alresford Pond**, it's one of the most charming features of this dignified

The Tapestry Centre

42 West Street, Alresford, Hamphire SO21 9AU
Tel: 01962 734944
e-mail: tapcent@ukonline.co.uk website: www.tapestrycentre.co.uk

Watercress and wool may have been what put the lovely old town of Alresford on the map and wool is still a factor for those with an interest in needlework. Over the past 20 years, Caroline Perry has developed the **Tapestry Centre** into one of the most delightful shops of its kind.

Behind the attractive frontage on West Street, there are two floors for the enthusiast or beginner. The Tapestry Centre website will tell you how to get there and you will find an unique collection of canvas work, cross stitch and crewel embroidery.

Names include Designers Forum, Coleshill, Stitchery, Jolly Red, Russell House, Lanarte, The Crewelwork Company and the accomplished designer Hervé Lelong. Also there are trammé canvases by Stitchery, Ivo and Beverley. Many wools and threads are stocked including Appleton, Paterna, Anchor, DMC and Medici. Services are professionally carried out for stretching, mounting, framing, cushion-making, upholstery and, exceptionally, tailor-made cording in up to four wools. Apart from a good in-house choice, furniture can be custom made to fit any finished needlework. Helpful, knowledgeable staff are always on hand to assist.

Hêtre

39 West Street, Alresford, Hampshire SO24 9AB
Tel: 01962 733312

Listed in *Vogue* magazine's "100 Best Shoe Shops" for the past three years, **Hêtre** was opened in 1998 by Carol Walton who is a self-confessed "enthusiastic, obsessive shoe-aholic" – so too are her staff. Over the years, Carol's collection has evolved to reflect current trends and what's new in fashion. It is always offering new labels and the shop stocks an enormous range of collections. Carol's selection of shoes includes designer names as well as quirky one-off pieces and is complemented by a fantastic selection of handbags and other accessories.

Hetre's dedicated staff will try and match outfits with shoes – and even telephone you with 'must-have' buys. The designer labels on offer include Paul Smith, Emma Hope, Anya Hindmarch, Lulu Guinness, Escada, Joseph Azagury and LK Bennett. Hetre occupies a beautifully renovated Georgian house near the centre of this attractive town, noted for its many Georgian houses. The shop is known for its incredible eye-catching window displays and the interior is equally striking with its contemporary décor of wood, etched glass and Andrew Martin furniture.

Georgian town. Alresford can also boast one of the county's most beautiful streets, historic Broad Street, lined with elegant, colour-washed Georgian houses interspersed with specialist shops and inviting hostelries.

Watercress Line, Alresford

Alresford's most famous son was Admiral Lord Rodney, a contemporary of Lord Nelson, who built the grand **Manor House** near the parish church, but the town can also boast two famous daughters. One was Mary Sumner, wife of the Rector of Alresford, who founded the Mother's Union here in 1876. The other was Mary Russell Mitford, author of the fascinating collection of sketches of 18th century life, *Our Village,* published in five volumes between 1824-1832. Mary's prolific literary output was partly spurred on by the need to repay the debts of her spendthrift father. Dr Mitford managed to dissipate his own inherited fortune of many thousands of pounds. His wife's lavish dowry, which

Moda Rosa

35 West Street, Alresford, Hampshire SO24 9AB
Tel: 01962 733277 Fax: 01962 735665
e-mail: moda_rosa@lineone.net

Opened in 1991, Moda Rosa is an inspiration to any style conscious woman requiring both day and evening wear - with two floors of contemporary and classic collections. The eclectic mix of designers include the unreserved Italian style of Giorgio Armani, Parisian chic by Paula Ka, sophisticated and relaxed casual wear by Ralph Lauren, exquisite fabrics by Caroline Charles, not forgetting Paddy Campbell who designs so cleverly with womens needs in mind. You are spoilt for choice with the classic sophistication of George Rech and the luxurious cashmere of Lamberto Losani, the contemporary style of Paul Smith and Matthew Williamson and the pretty dresses from Renato Nucci, Cacharel and Edina Ronay. The impressive selection of evening wear on the elegant first floor makes the visit even more worthwhile. There you find the most stunning evening dresses and party wear by red carpet designers such as Jenny Packham, Amanda Wakeley, Emmanuel Ungaro and Ben de Lisi. This amazing Boutique gives you the chance to be as understated or flamboyant as you wish- from size 8 to 16.

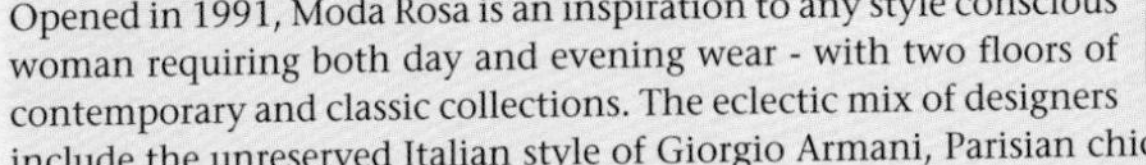

Moda Rosa is all about personal service. The knowledgeable staff are there to help and advise every customer, ensuring that they receive the individual attention necessary to find the perfect outfit for that special occasion. It is the personal touch that transforms an ordinary shopping trip into an experience to be relished. A professional alteration service is also available. Whatever the occasion Moda Rosa will endeavour to dress you with confidence from top to toe - with inspirational hats by Philip Treacy and divine shoes by Gina Couture.

almost doubled that income, disappeared equally quickly, and when Mary at the age of 10 won the huge sum of £20,000 in a lottery, the good doctor squandered that as well. Mary's classic book tells the story.

One of Alresford's attractions that should not be missed is the **Watercress Line**, Hampshire's only preserved steam railway, so named because it was once used to transport watercress from the beds around Alresford to London and beyond. The line runs through 10 miles of beautiful countryside to Alton where it links up with main line services to London. Vintage steam locomotives make the 35-minute journey up to eight times a day, and there are regular dining trains as well as frequent special events throughout the year. More details on 01962 733810.

Tichborne

12 miles SW of Alton off the A31

Two intriguing stories are associated with this lovely village of thatched and half-timbered cottages. The legend of the **Tichborne Dole** dates from the reign of Henry I. At that time the owner of Tichborne Park was the dastardly Sir Roger Tichborne. As his crippled wife, Mabella, lay dying her last wish was to provide food for the poor. Sir Roger agreed – but only from an area she could crawl around. The brave woman managed to encircle an area of more than 20 acres of arable land, carrying a flaming torch as she did so. Ever since then the Park's owners have provided bags of flour every year to the villages of Tichborne and Cheriton. The field is still known as 'The Crawls'.

Heronbrook House

New Farm Road, New Alresford, Hampshire SO24 9QH
Tel: 01962 738726 Fax: 01962 732602
e-mail: jane@heronbrookhouse.co.uk
website: www.heronbrookhouse.co.uk

Enjoying wonderful views of the Itchen Valley, **Heronbrook House** is a spacious family home located in the picturesque town of New Alresford. The house, which has been recently renovated, is well equipped and close to all local amenities with several pubs within walking distance as well as excellent local restaurants. Awarded a 4-Diamond Silver rating by the English Tourist Council, Heronbrook House has two attractively furnished and decorated guest bedrooms (one double; one twin/double), both en suite with bath and shower, and provided with TV, radio, hair dryer and hospitality tray. Bedrooms are reached through their own entrance which gives guests the privacy of self-catering accommodation as well the care and attention of a B&B.

Owner Jane Hankin provides a hearty breakfast which is served in the Bandstand room overlooking the garden and the Itchen Valley. During the summer months guests have the use of the swimming pool and will find plenty of other things to do and see in the area. New Alresford itself is a renowned centre of quality shopping for antique collectors and of course the famous steam railway, the Watercress Line has its main station in the town. Other places of interest within easy reach include the 13th century Bush Inn set beside the picturesque River Itchen at Ovington; the historic cathedral city of Winchester and prehistoric Stonehenge.

Equally notorious is the episode of the **Tichborne Claimant**. In 1871 a certain Arthur Orton, son of a Wapping butcher, returned from Wagga Wagga, Australia, claiming to be the heir to the estate. Although he bore no resemblance to the rightful heir who had disappeared while sailing round the world, Arthur was 'recognised' by the widow as her son and supported in his claim. She, apparently, detested her late husband's family. Arthur's claim was rejected in a trial that lasted 100 days and he was put on trial for perjury. After a further 188 days he was found guilty and sentenced to 14 days in prison.

Cheriton

13 miles SW of Alton on the B3046

The pretty village of Cheriton has a church which is believed to stand over a prehistoric burial ground. In 1644, the Battle of Cheriton, fought near Cheriton Wood, resulted in the deaths of 2,000 men as the Roundheads defeated the Royalists.

PETERSFIELD

An appealing market town, Petersfield is dominated by the bulk of **Butser Hill**, 900ft high and the highest point of the South Downs. It provides grand panoramic views over the town and even, on a clear day, to the spire of Salisbury Cathedral, some 40 miles distant. In the 1660s, Samuel Pepys noted his stay in Petersfield, at a hotel in which Charles II had slept before him. Another king is commemorated in The Square where William III sits on horseback, incongruously dressed in Roman costume. Unusually, the statue is made of lead.

Most of the elegant buildings around The Square are Georgian, but the

Church of St Peter is much older, dating back to Norman times and with a fine north aisle to prove it. Just off the Square, the **Flora Twort Gallery** was once the home and studio of the accomplished artist of that name who moved to Petersfield at the end of World War I. Her delightful paintings and drawings capture life in the town over some 40 years – "reminders of some of the things we have lost" as she put it shortly before her death at the age of 91 in 1985.

From the gallery, a short walk along Sheep Street, (which has some striking timber-framed 16th century houses and Georgian cottages), brings you to **The Spain**, a pleasant green surrounded by some of the town's oldest houses. It apparently acquired its rather unusual name because dealers in Spanish wool used to hold markets there.

Visitors with an interest in gardening will want to visit the **Physic Garden** in the centre of the town. Set in an ancient walled plot, the garden has been planted in a style and with plants that would have been familiar to the distinguished 17th century botanist, John Goodyer, who lived in Petersfield.

Other attractions include the Dragon Gallery, providing a showcase for contemporary artists; the Petersfield Museum, housed in the old Courthouse; and the Teddy Bear Museum, the first in the country to be dedicated to these cuddly comforters.

Just a short walk from the town centre is **Petersfield Heath**, an extensive recreational area with a cricket ground and a pond for boating and fishing. The town's annual Taro Fair is held here in October and the heath is also notable as the site of one of the most important groups of Bronze Age barrows, or burial mounds, in the country.

Steep

1 mile N of Petersfield, off the A3

Appropriately, the village is reached by way of a steep hill. The village is famous as the home of the writer and nature poet Edward Thomas who moved here with his family in 1907. It was while living at 2 Yew Tree Cottages that he wrote most of his poems. In 1909 he and his wife Helen moved to the Red House (private) where his daughter Myfanwy was born in 1913. Many years later, in 1985, she unveiled a plaque on the house. Her former home featured in two of her father's poems, *The New House* and *Wind and Mist*. Thomas was killed in action in World War I. His death is commemorated by two engraved lancet windows installed in 1978 in All Saints Church, and by a memorial stone on Shoulder of Mutton Hill above the village.

It was at Steep in 1898 that the educational pioneer John Badley established Bedales, the first boarding school for both sexes in the country. His "preposterous experiment" proved highly successful. Members of staff and pupils at Bedales call each other by their first names and there is no formal school uniform. There is an absence of petty rules and, says the school brochure, "because the pupils are listened to, they learn to listen to each other".

Buriton

2 miles S of Petersfield, on minor road off the A3

An old church surrounded by trees and overlooking a tree-lined duck pond is flanked by an appealing early-18th century Manor House (private) built by the father of Edward Gibbon, the celebrated historian. The younger Gibbon wrote much of his magnum opus *Decline and Fall of the Roman Empire* in his study here. He was critical of the house's position, "at the end of the village and the bottom of the hill", but was highly appreciative of the view over the Downs: "the long hanging woods in sight of the house could not perhaps have been improved by art or expense".

About five miles south-east of Buriton, **Uppark** (National Trust), is a handsome Wren-style mansion built around 1690 and most notable for its interior. Uppark was completely redecorated and refurnished in the 1750s by the Fetherstonhaugh family and that work has remained almost entirely unchanged – not only the furniture but even some of the fabrics and wallpapers remain in excellent condition. The servants' rooms are as they were in 1874 when the mother of HG Wells was housekeeper here – the boy's recollections of life at Uppark with his mother are fondly recorded in his autobiography.

Chalton

5 miles S of Petersfield off the A3

Situated on a slope of chalk down, Chalton is home to **Butser Ancient Farm**, a reconstruction of an Iron Age farm that has received worldwide acclaim for its research methodology and results. There's a magnificent great roundhouse, prehistoric and Roman crops are grown, ancient breeds of cattle roam the hillside, and metal is worked according to ancient techniques. The latest project here is the construction of a replica Roman villa, complete with hypocaust, using the same methods as the Romans did. A wonderful living laboratory, the farm is open one weekend each month when there are themed events.

Hambledon

8 miles SW of Petersfield, off the B2150

A village of red brick Georgian houses and well-known for its vineyard, Hambledon is most famous for its cricketing connections. It was at the Hambledon Cricket Club that the rules of the game were first formulated in 1774. The club's finest hour came in 1777 when the team, led by the landlord of the Bat and Ball Inn, beat an All England team by an innings and 168 runs! A granite monument stands on **Broadhalfpenny Down** where the early games were played.

The village itself featured in the *Domesday Book* and, in the 13th century, was granted a licence to hold a market. About this time, the church was extensively rebuilt around the original Saxon church. Many of the village houses have their 16th century origins concealed by the striking Georgian facades.

East Meon

5 miles W of Petersfield, on minor road off the A3 or A272

Tucked away in the lovely valley of the River Meon and surrounded by high downs, East Meon has been described as "the most unspoilt of Hampshire villages and the nicest". As if that weren't enough, the village also boasts one of the finest and most venerable churches in the county. The central tower, with walls four feet thick, dates back to the 12th century and is a stunning example of Norman architecture at its best. Inside, the church's greatest treasure is its remarkable 12th century **Tournai Font** of black marble, exquisitely carved with scenes depicting the Creation and the fall of Adam and Eve. Only seven of these wonderful fonts are known to exist in England (four of them in Hampshire) and East Meon's is generally regarded as the most magnificent of them.

In the churchyard are buried Thomas Lord, founder of the cricket ground in

WALK NUMBER 7

Hambledon

Distance:	6.3 miles (10.2 kilometres)
Typical time:	150 mins
Height gain:	189 metres
Map:	Explorer 119
Walk:	www.walkingworld.com ID:2139
Contributor:	Sylvia Saunders

Access Information:

Hambledon is to be found nine miles south west of Petersfield and 10 miles north of Portsmouth. From the Petersfield to Portsmouth A3(T)/A3(M) take the turn off signposted to Clanfield, Chalton and Hambledon. Hambledon is well signposted from here but be careful not to miss the turn off to the right when leaving Clanfield. Park in the main road near to The Vine.

There is a No. 45 bus service from Portsmouth city centre to Hambledon run by First. Check out their website www.firstgroup.com for more information.

Description:

This circular walk is a must for those who are interested in cricket, lovers of good food and beer in idyllic country pubs, or those who just like a cracking good walk in the beautiful, gentle Hampshire countryside. The walk starts from The Vine in Hambledon. The route takes you along Windmill Down with far reaching views over Hampshire countryside and then past the current cricket ground at Ridge-Meadow. Then walking through a mixture of woodland and fields you arrive at The Bat and Ball Inn which is known as the first headquarters of English cricket. The original Hambledon cricket ground is on Broadhalfpenny Down and opposite the pub.

The return route takes you along well defined tracks and through farmland with some super views as far as the Isle of Wight on a clear day. There is a steep descent down a quiet lane back to Hambledon's West Street and The Vine. Dog owners may find it useful to know that my dog, a slim, fit Labrador who cannot jump, managed to get through all the stiles and fences.

Features:

Hills or Fells, Pub, Wildlife, Birds, Flowers, Great Views, Butterflies, Public Transport, Restaurant, Tea Shop, Woodland

Walk Directions:

1 With The Vine on your left hand side walk along West Street until you reach a lane on the left marked "Unsuitable for HGVs". Turn left and walk up this lane. When the lane turns into a driveway, walk straight on and go over the stile into the field.

2 Walk straight ahead with the flint wall on your right hand side. At the end of the wall you will find a metal kissing gate. Pass through this gate and again walk with the wall on your right with a field fence on

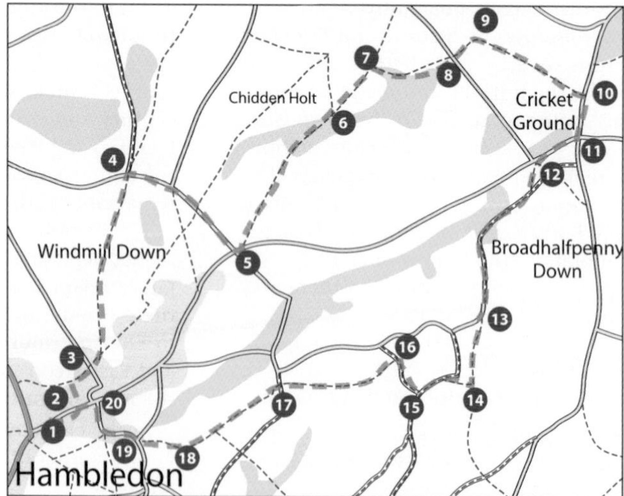

your left. This path brings you out at the churchyard. Walk straight ahead through the churchyard and you will shortly emerge out onto a lane. Turn left on this lane for a few metres and you will see the school entrance on your right hand side.

3 Turn right here and walk through the school entrance. When you reach the end of the buildings you are met with a choice of two footpaths. Turn left here and walk uphill past the back of the school building where you will see the entrance to a field on your right. Fork right across the field along the footpath. At the field corner walk straight across into the next field and continue uphill with the hedge on your right hand side. Enjoy the panoramic view as you descend until you reach a lane.

4 Turn right onto the lane. Ignore the left hand turn to Chidden, shortly after which you will pass Ridge - Meadow, the current home of Hambledon cricket club where they have played since 1782! Carry on along the road until you reach the crossroads.

5 Turn left here. After you have passed the big house on this corner (Park House) you will see a track marked with a fingerpost. Turn left onto this track. After a short distance you will see a metal gate ahead. Pass through the gap on the right hand side of this gate and walk along the track on the right hand side of the field. Follow the track as it leaves the field and enters woodland. You will arrive at a sign which says "Wildlife Conservation Area, do not enter". Turn left here along the footpath and follow it into the field. Here you will see two footpaths, both crossing the field.

6 Take the right hand path and walk across the field to the hedge and footpath post.

7 Turn right here and walk along the field edge with the hedge on your left hand side. Follow this route until you see a wooden post directing the footpath into woodland. This post is about halfway between the previous post and the field corner. Turn left here into the woodland. Walk the narrow, winding path. There are a few animal routes going off it which may confuse you. If in doubt, take a route to the left rather than to the right. The woodland doesn't last for long - you soon emerge into a field. Turn right here walking along the field edge with the hedge / trees on your right hand side. Follow the footpath out to the road.

8 Cross straight over to the metal gate opposite. There isn't a stile but you can open the gate by way of a chain on the right hand side. Follow the field edge on the left hand side to the stile ahead.

9 Cross over the stile and turn right, walking with the fence on your right hand side. Continue in the same direction crossing several stiles until you reach the road.

10 Cross the stile and turn right along the road. You will soon arrive at The Bat and Ball Inn with the original Broadhalfpenny cricket ground opposite. Here you will see the monument marking the birthplace of cricket. Pass the pub and arrive at the crossroads.

11 Turn right here along the road signposted to Hambledon, Fareham. Walk along the road until you see a road turning off to the right. Opposite this you will see a footpath and stile off to your left.

12 Climb over this stile and you will be met with a choice of two routes, neither of which is defined. Head for the stile which you can see up the hill and slightly to the right - at the end of the hedge line. Go over the stile and turn right along the track. But before you set off, pause to drink in the view. Continue along the track until you reach Scotland Cottage. Just past the cottage you will see a footpath off to the left.

13 Turn left along this footpath and walk until you emerge out onto a track.

14 Turn right along this track. In a short distance you will see a large tree ahead and a huge pile of manure. This manure heap has been here for years and I have every faith that it will have been renewed! Turn left here and you will soon arrive at a junction of tracks.

15 Turn right here and continue walking until you reach a rather smelly pond and some farm buildings.

16 Turn left here along the track just past the pond but before the buildings. When you reach the metal gate cross over the stile next to it. Follow the track up to another metal gate and stile, passing a barn on your left hand side. Go over this stile and continue walking straight ahead with the trees on your right hand side and you will arrive at another stile. Cross over and then follow the line of the telegraph poles until you reach another stile. Cross over this stile. This field was full of towering sweetcorn when I was last here and may well look entirely different now. Just follow the line of telegraph poles and you cannot go wrong. You will arrive at a stile. Go over this stile and cross straight over the track into the field.

17 Again, follow the line of the telegraph poles across this field and you will arrive at a stile. Cross over this stile into the narrow field still following the telegraph poles. Ignore the footpath off to the left as the field narrows further. Continue along in the same direction, finally losing the telegraph poles and you will arrive at a stile next to a metal gate.

18 Cross over this stile and walk straight ahead between the mobile home and the horseboxes. In a few metres you will arrive at a driveway. Turn left along this driveway and you will soon arrive at several metal gates. Turn right along the footpath between the two metal gates on your right hand side. This will bring you out upon a private driveway next to a house. Walk down the driveway and you will see two roads off to your right.

19 Take the 2nd right turn along the road walking down Speltham Hill until you arrive at the junction with West and East Street.

20 Turn left here and walk back to The Vine.

London, and the mother of the spy Guy Burgess. Her son's ashes were sprinkled on her grave in a suitably clandestine night-time ceremony.

Just across the road is the 15th century **Courthouse** which also has walls four feet thick. It's a lovely medieval manor house where for generations the Bishops of Winchester, as Lords of the Manor, held their courts. It would have been a familiar sight to the "compleat angler" Izaac Walton who spent many happy hours fishing in the River Meon nearby.

NORTHWEST HAMPSHIRE

Some of Hampshire's grandest scenery lies in this part of the county as the North Downs roll westwards towards Salisbury Plain. There's just one sizeable town, Andover, and one major city, Winchester: the rest of the region is quite sparsely populated (for southern England) with scattered villages bearing evocative names such as Hurstbourne Tarrant and Nether Wallop. Winchester is of course in a class of its own with its dazzling Cathedral, but there are many other attractions in this area, ranging in time from the Iron Age Danebury Hill Fort, through the Victorian extravaganza of Highclere Castle, to Stanley Spencer's extraordinary murals in the Sandham Memorial Chapel at Burghclere.

ANDOVER

Andover has expanded greatly since the 1960s when it was selected as a "spillover" town to relieve the pressure on London's crowded population. But the core of this ancient town, which was already important in Saxon times, retains much of interest. One outstanding landmark is **St Mary's Church**, completely rebuilt in the 1840s at the expense of a former headmaster of Winchester College. The interior is said to have been modelled on Salisbury Cathedral and if it doesn't quite match up to that sublime building, St Mary's is still well worth a visit.

Equally striking is the **Guildhall** of 1825, built in classical style, which stands alone in the Market Place where markets are still held every Tuesday and Saturday. Andover has also managed to retain half a dozen of the 16 coaching inns that serviced 18th century travellers at a time when the fastest stage coaches took a mere nine hours to travel here from London. As many as 50 coaches a day stopped at these inns to change horses and allow the passengers to take refreshments.

For a fascinating insight into the town's long history, do pay a visit to the **Andover Museum** (free) in Church Close. There are actually two museums here, both of them housed in buildings which began life as an elegant Georgian town house in 1750 and were later extended to serve as Andover's Grammar School from the 1840s to 1925. The Andover Museum traces the story of the town from Saxon times to the present day with a range of colourful exhibits which include a 19th century Period Room. There's also a fascinating display evoking Victorian Andover and a workhouse scandal of the time. The museum hosts an exciting programme of temporary exhibitions with subjects including art, craft, photography, history and much more. Former classrooms of the grammar school now house the **Museum of the Iron Age** (small charge) which tells the story of Danebury, an Iron Age hillfort that lies six miles southwest of Andover.

A good way of getting to know the town is to join one of the guided tours along the **Andover Heritage Trail**. Scheduled tours, lasting about 90 minutes, take place on Tuesday and Saturday afternoons but can also be arranged for groups at other times. More details on 01264 324068.

Two miles east of Andover, **Finkley Down Farm Park** (see panel opposite) provides a satisfying day out for families with young children. Youngsters can feed and handle the animals, groom a pony, ride on a mini-tractor, and expend any excess energy in the well-equipped playground. Romany caravans and farming bygones are on display and other attractions include a tea room, gift shop and picnic area with a sandpit.

Penton Mewsey

2 miles NW of Andover, on minor road off the A342 or A343

For those who enjoy deciphering the cryptic place-names of English villages, Penton Mewsey offers a satisfying challenge. The answer goes like this: Penton was a 'tun' (enclosure or farm) paying a 'pen' (penny) as annual rent. That's the Saxon part. Later, in the early

1200s, Penton was owned by Robert de Meisy so his surname provided the second part of the village's name.

The town of Andover has now expanded to Penton Mewsey's parish boundaries but the village itself remains more rural than urban, with a field at its centre.

Appleshaw

4 miles NW of Andover, off the A342

The houses in the village of Appleshaw sit comfortably along both sides of its broad, single street. Many of them are thatched and a useful, century-old clock in the middle of the street, placed here to celebrate Queen Victoria's Jubilee, adds to the time-defying atmosphere. The former Vicarage, built in Georgian times, is as gracious as you would expect of that era, and the neo-Gothic architecture of the parish church, rebuilt in 1830, is in entire harmony with its earlier neighbours.

Tangley

5 miles NW of Andover, on minor road off the A342 or A343

For the best views, approach Tangley from the east, along the country lane from Hurstbourne Tarrant. Its mostly Victorian church is notable for its rare font, one of only 38 in the whole country made of lead and the only one in Hampshire. Dating back to the early 1600s, it is decorated with Tudor roses, crowned thistles, and fleur-de-lys.

The old Roman road from Winchester to Cirencester, the **Icknield Way**, runs through the parish of Tangley. Most of this part of the county is designated an Area of Outstanding Natural Beauty and the scenery is enchanting.

Faccombe

12 miles N of Andover, on minor road off the A343

This appealing little village, which is owned by the Faccombe Estate, is tucked away in the Hampshire countryside close to the Berkshire border, set on chalk Downs some 750ft above sea level, with the highest points of the North Downs, Pilot Hill and Inkpen Beacon, both nearby. An extra attraction for walkers is the Test Way, a long-distance footpath which runs from Inkpen Beacon to the south coast following the track of the disused "Sprat & Winkle" railway.

About five miles west of Faccombe, **Highclere Castle** is a wondrous example of Victorian neo-Gothic architecture at its most exuberant. If the central tower reminds you of another well-known building, that may be because the castle was designed by Sir Charles Barry, architect of the Houses of Parliament. It stands on the site of a former palace of the Bishops of Winchester, overlooking an incomparably lovely park, one of Capability Brown's greatest

Highclere Castle

creations. The ornate architecture and furnishings of the castle interior delight many, others feel somewhat queasy at its unrelenting richness. Highclere is the family home of the 7th Earl and Countess of Carnavon. It was the present Earl's grandfather who in 1922 was with Howard Carter at the opening of Tutankhamun's tomb. A small museum in the basement of the castle recalls that breath-taking moment. Another display reflects the family's interest in horse racing. For more than a century, Earls of Carnavon have owned, bred and raced horses, and the present Earl is racing manager to the Queen. In addition to the superb parkland, there's also a Walled Garden, planted entirely with white blooms, a gift shop, restaurant and tea rooms.

Burghclere

11 miles NE of Andover, off the A34

A couple of miles northeast of Highclere Castle, at Burghclere, the **Sandham Memorial Chapel** (National Trust) is, from the outside, a rather unappealing construction, erected in 1926 by Mr and Mrs JL Behrend in memory of a relation, Lieutenant Sandham, who died in World War I. Their building may be uninspired but the Behrends can't be faulted on their choice of artist to cover the walls with a series of 19 murals. Stanley Spencer had served during the war as a hospital orderly and 18 of his murals represent the day-to-day life of a British Tommy in wartime. The 19th, covering the east wall of the Chapel, depicts the Day of Resurrection with the fallen men and their horses rising up. The foreground is dominated by a pile of white wooden crosses the soldiers have cast aside. The whole series is enormously moving, undoubtedly one of the masterpieces of 20th century British art.

Whitchurch

6 miles E of Andover on the B3400

This small market town was once an important coach stop on the London to Exeter route. The coaching inns have gone but the town still boasts a unique attraction – the **Whitchurch Silk Mill,** the last such working mill in the south of England. Located on Frog Island in the River Test, the mill's waterwheel has been fully restored although today's power is provided by electricity. The mill now functions as a museum making silks for interiors and costume dramas such as the BBC's acclaimed production of *Pride and Prejudice*. Visitors can see the working waterwheel, watch the late-19th century looms weave the silk, view the costume exhibition and enjoy the riverside garden. There's also a tea room and gift shop.

To the east of Whitchurch is **Bere Mill,** a weather-boarded construction where a French man, Henri Portal, set up a paper-making business in the early 18th century. By 1742 Portal's mill had won the contract to supply bank note paper to the Bank of England and he moved his operation upstream to Laverstoke. Now in Overton, the business continues to make paper for bank notes and supplies it to more than 100 countries.

Longparish

8 miles E of Andover, on the B3048

Living up to its name, Longparish village straggles alongside the River Test for more than two miles. This stretch of the river is famously full of trout but no one has yet beaten the record catch of Col. Peter Hawker who lived at Longparish House in the early 1800s. According to his diary for 1818, in that year this dedicated angler relieved the river of no less than one ton's weight of the succulent fish. A previous owner of the colonel's house had actually captured double that haul in one year, but the bounder had cheated by dragging the river.

Longparish Upper Mill, in a lovely location on the river, is a large flour mill with a working waterwheel. Visitors can see the restoration work in progress.

Stockbridge

7 miles S of Andover on the A3057/A30

The trout-rich River Test flows through, under and alongside Stockbridge's broad main street which reflects the street's earlier role as part of a drover's road. The town attracts many visitors for its famous antique shops, art galleries and charming tea rooms. Two exclusive clubs strictly control fishing on the River Test at this point but visitors may be lucky enough to catch glimpses of the fish from the bridge on the High Street.

Just to the south of Stockbridge are **Houghton Lodge Gardens**, the spacious gardens of an 18th century 'cottage orné' which have the tranquil beauty of the River Test as their border. Chalk cob walls shelter a kitchen garden with ancient espaliered fruit trees, glasshouses and herb garden, whilst in the Hydroponicum greenhouse plants are grown "without soil, toil or chemical pesticides".

Nether Wallop

8 miles SW of Andover, on minor road off the A343

The names of the three Wallops, (Over, Middle and Nether), have provided a good deal of amusement to visitors over the centuries, so it's slightly disappointing to discover that Wallop is just a corruption of the Old English word *waell-hop*, meaning a valley with a stream. At Nether Wallop the stream is picturesquely lined with willow trees, while the village itself is equally

The Owl & The Pussycat

High Street, Stockbridge, Hants.
Tel: 01264 811533

On the broad and handsome main street of Stockbridge, **The Owl & The Pussycat** is the perfect place to find a special gift. Small and quaint, it is filled with a constantly changing stock that ranges from casual clothes to cushions, from ceramics and glassware to artificial flowers and a cosseting range of oils and soaps. The lucky browsers and shoppers of the region now have a second equally delightful shop, also called The Owl & The Pussycat, and also in the main street.

This one is a children's shop, and the stock includes stylish children's clothes, nightwear and christening gowns, hand-knitted and hand-embroidered goods, baby shoes, magical nursery bedding and accessories, exquisite pampering toiletries, soft toys, and books and albums to treasure through childhood and beyond. Just as at Helen Jackson's first shop, customers are assured of ready advice and friendly, personal service, typified by a very special offering, a child's equivalent of a wedding list. People can go in, look around and make a list of things they like; their friends can choose something from the list to give as a present that will be both a surprise and a delight. This service is also ideal for celebrating a special event such as the birth of a child. Both shops offer gift wrapping and mail order services.

attractive with many thatched or timbered houses. The most notable building in Nether Wallop is **St Andrew's Church**, partly because of its Norman features and handsome West Tower of 1704, but also because of its striking medieval wall paintings which provide an interesting contrast with Stanley Spencer's at Burghclere. Some 500 years old, these lay hidden for generations under layers of plaster and were only rediscovered in the 1950s. The most impressive of them shows St George slaying the dragon. Outside St Andrew's stands an item of great interest for collectors of churchyard oddities. It's a dark grey stone pyramid, 15ft high, with red stone flames rising from its tip. This daunting monument was erected at his own expense and in memory of himself by Francis Douce, 'Doctor of Physick', who died in 1760. Dr Douce also left an endowment to build a village school on condition that the parishioners would properly maintain the pyramid.

Middle Wallop

7 miles SW of Andover on the A343

The village of Middle Wallop became famous during the Battle of Britain when the nearby airfield was the base for squadrons of Spitfires and Hurricanes. Many of the old buildings have been incorporated into the **Museum of Army Flying** which traces the development of Army Flying from the balloons and kites of pre-World War I years, through various imaginative dioramas, to a helicopter flight simulator in which visitors can test their own skills of 'hand and eye' co-ordination. Other attractions include a Museum Shop, licensed café & restaurant, and a grassed picnic area.

In the 1990s, Middle Wallop, with its picturesque timber-framed thatched buildings became familiar to television viewers when it provided the main location for the 'Miss Marple' mysteries.

Situated about a mile to the east of the village, **Danebury Vineyards** welcomes groups of visitors by arrangement for a guided tour of the six acres of vines and winery. Tastings and dinners can also be arranged. The vineyard was planted in 1988 on south facing slopes of free draining chalk, an excellent siting for the varieties of grape grown here. The British climate generally results in a late-ripening crop producing grapes which are most suitable for the white wines with which Danebury Vineyards has made its name.

About three miles east of Middle Wallop, **Danebury Ring** is Hampshire's largest Iron Age hill fort. Intensively occupied from about 550 BC until the arrival of the Romans, the site has been meticulously excavated over the last 30 years and the finds are now displayed at the Museum of the Iron Age in Andover. Visitors can wander the 13-acre site and with the help of explanatory boards reconstruct the once-bustling community with its clearly defined roads, shops, houses and what were probably temples.

Weyhill

3 miles W of Andover on the A342

In its day the October Weyhill Fair was an event of some importance. In Thomas Hardy's *Mayor of Casterbridge* it appears as the Weydon Priors Market where the future mayor sells his wife and child.

A good family day out can be enjoyed at **The Hawk Conservancy** where there are more than 200 birds of prey to see in 22 acres of grounds. The Hawk Conservancy is one of the largest collections of raptors in the world.

Cool Crimson

The Fairground, Weyhill, nr Andover, Hampshire SP11 0QN
Tel: 01264 772299

As a careers advisor, Sara Purkins used to urge her clients to "do something you love". In February 2004 Sara followed her own advice and established **Cool Crimson** where she now indulges her enthusiasm for paper craft and jewellery. In her converted rural building she offers an extensive range that includes hand-made cards using techniques such as iris folding, teabag folding, quilling, decoupage and collage; papier mâché pots, bowls and plates, along with a wide selection of stylish jewellery. Sara also runs workshops teaching the techniques where the emphasis is on "sharing ideas and having fun!"

JH Design

5 The Fairground Craft Centre, Weyhill, nr Andover, Hampshire SP11 0QN
Tel/Fax: 01264 773045
e-mail: info@fairgroundcraft.co.uk website: www.fairgroundcraft.co.uk

Made famous in Thomas Hardy's *Mayor of Casterbridge*, the fairground at Weyhill ('Weydon Priors' in the novel) is today home to the Fairground Craft & Design Centre – and to JH Design which specialises in all forms of decorative painting. Owner Julie Hayward sells unusual hand-made and painted gifts, furniture and accessories for the home, and she can restyle just about anything from furniture to walls. Julie also stocks blanks ready for painting, a range of liquid acrylic paints, light fittings, clock mechanisms and much more. Regular workshops are held on everything from folk art painting to marbling and faux finishes.

Flying demonstrations take place three times daily and include species such as owls, eagles, vultures and condors, falcons, kites, hawks and secretary birds. The grounds here are also home to Shire horses, Sika deer, Hampshire Down sheep and red squirrels that have been given their own aerial runway.

Thruxton

4 miles W of Andover off the A303

This large village with many thatched cottages is well known for its **Motor Racing Circuit** which is built on a World War II airfield. Its annual calendar of events takes in many aspects of sport including Formula Three, Touring Cars, British Super Bikes, Trucks and Karts.

WINCHESTER

One of the country's most historic cities, Winchester was adopted by King Alfred as the capital of his kingdom of Wessex, a realm which then included most of southern England. There had been a settlement here since the Iron Age and in Roman times, as Venta Belgarum, it became an important military base. **The Brooks Experience**, located within the modern Brooks Shopping Centre, has displays based on excavated Roman remains with its star exhibit a reconstructed room from an early-4th century town-house.

When the Imperial Legions returned to Rome, the town declined until it was refounded by Alfred in the late 800s. His street plan still provides the basic outline of the city centre. A Saxon cathedral had been built in the 7th century but the present magnificent **Cathedral**, easily the most imposing and interesting building in Hampshire, dates back to

1079. It's impossible in a few words to do justice to this glorious building and its countless treasures such as the famous Winchester Bible, a 12th century illuminated manuscript that took more than 15 years to complete using pure gold and lapis lazuli from Afghanistan. Winchester Cathedral boasts the longest nave in Europe, a dazzling 14th century masterpiece in the Perpendicular style, a wealth of fine wooden carvings, and gems within a gem such as the richly decorated Bishop Waynflete's Chantry of 1486. Sumptuous medieval monuments, like the effigy of William of Wykeham, founder of Winchester College, provide a striking contrast to the simple black stone floorslabs which separately mark the graves of Izaak Walton and Jane Austen. One of the memorials is to William Walker, a diver who spent seven years, from 1906, laboriously removing the logs that had supported the cathedral for 800 years and replacing those rotting foundations with cement.

Winchester Cathedral

The Hambledon

10 The Square, Winchester, Hampshire SO23 9ES
Tel: 01962 890055 Fax: 01962 890066
e-mail: shop@thehambledon.com
website: www.thehambledon.com

Occupying a lovely double-fronted Georgian building in Winchester's Cathedral Square, **The Hambledon** is a lifestyle store offering a fascinating mix of womenswear and accessories, children's clothing and toys, homeware, gifts and vintage pieces. As owner Victoria Suffield says, "We genuinely buy only what we love and are proud to sell. We're not interested in brands as such – the beauty of the object itself is paramount so the range is very eclectic and runs from handblown chandeliers from Syria to kitsch toys from Belgium, Cath Kidston retro to fine Cote Bastide toiletries, books on interior design to glittery glam French chocolates."

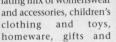

The Hambledon extends over two floors and 2,500 square feet with the ground floor divided roughly into separate areas for bed, bath, living, kids' clothes, toys and menswear, interspersed with an ever-changing selection of furniture both vintage and modern and including classic pieces from Eames and Panton. The first floor is dedicated to womenswear and accessories. Friendly, helpful staff are always at hand to advise and inform and if you are unable to visit this intriguing store in person, a mail order and online service are both available.

Cadogan & James

31a The Square, Winchester,
Hampshire SO23 9EZ
Tel: 01962 840805
Fax: 01962 850571
e-mail: cadoganandjames@ecosse.net

A sea-blue awning shades the pavement tables outside **Cadogan & James** and as you enter this outstanding delicatessen/ café you are engulfed with a medley of different aromas from the fresh bread, herbs and spices. Enjoying a picturesque setting in the city's famous Square, the shop is a veritable Aladdin's Cave for gourmets, selling a vast range of products from around the world.

The interior reflects a mixture of traditional Italian-inspired designs. The rustic *trompe l'oeil* ceiling is complemented by garlands of hops surmounting the shelves deeply filled with a huge variety of products from pastas to preserves, truffles to speciality teas, cheeses of every kind to freshly-made sandwiches and cakes.

Manager Gail Collier and her friendly staff are exceptionally helpful and with their vast knowledge and enthusiasm encourage customers to sample the exciting gourmet products on offer. This must be among the best delicatessens in the country – an absolute must for all food lovers.

Cadogan & James is also perfectly placed for tourist attractions, right next to Winchester Cathedral, close to the Guildhall, King Alfred's statue, the City Museum, Winchester College, the West Gate and the Great Hall where King Arthur's Round Table can be found.

Just south of the cathedral, on College Street, are two other buildings of outstanding interest. No. 8, College Street, a rather austere Georgian house with a first-floor bay window, is **Jane Austen's House** in which she spent the last six weeks of her life in 1817. The house is private but a slate plaque above the front door records her residence here. Right next door stands **Winchester College**, the oldest school in England, founded in 1382 by Bishop William of Wykeham to provide education for 70 'poor and needy scholars'. Substantial parts of the 14th century buildings still stand, including the beautiful Chapel. The Chapel is always open to visitors and there are guided tours around the other parts of the college from April to September. If you can time your visit during the school holidays, more of the college is available to view.

Two years after Jane Austen was buried in the cathedral, the poet John Keats stayed in Winchester and it was here that he wrote his timeless *Ode to Autumn – 'Season of mists and mellow fruitfulness'.* His inspiration was a daily walk past the cathedral and college and through the Water Meadows beside the River Itchen. A detailed step-by-step guide to **Keats' Walk** is available from the Tourist Information Centre.

The city's other attractions are so numerous one can only mention a few of the most important. **The Great Hall**, (free), off the High Street, is the only surviving part of the medieval castle rebuilt by Henry III between 1222 and 1236. Nikolaus Pevsner considered it "the finest medieval hall in England after Westminster Hall". Located within the castle grounds are no fewer than six military museums, including the Gurkha Museum, the King's Royal Hussars

Cadogan And Company

30-31 The Square, Winchester,
Hampshire SO23 9EZ
Tel: 01962 877399
website: www.cadoganandcompany.co.uk

In a superb city centre location, with parking adjacent, **Cadogan and Company** has built up an enviable reputation for style and quality in ladies' and gentlemen's fashion and accessories. Owner Alexander Edwards, who has spent all his working life in the retail trade, came to this address 10 years ago and turned what was effectively an empty shell into one of the city's leading private retailers.

Housed in a prestigious modern development, the shop is on three levels of open -plan display areas, all subtly lit and professionally laid out on stands and consoles, racks and shelves. Alexander travels the world seeking out what he knows will appeal to his discerning clientele, including elegant leather fashion garments and accessories from Italy.

Quality is the keynote throughout the range of goods on display, from indoor and outdoor fashion wear to boots and shoes, hats, nightwear, woollens, scarves and ties. Among the accessories are top-of-the-range suitcases, travel bags and accessories for the journey, umbrellas, the best leather briefcases and desk supplies, haberdashery, gold and silverware and a selection of lovely gifts, from glass and china ornaments to diaries, barometers and hip flasks.

Highly professional management and staff are on hand to attend to customers at this superb shop, which is open from 9.30am to 5.30pm Monday to Saturday. Within walking distance of the shop are most of the major places of interest in the city, including the wonderful Cathedral, the City Museum and the College, the oldest public school in England. Tradition and modern amenities stand side by side in Winchester, and Cadogan and Company fully deserves its place right in the heart of the city.

Museum whose displays include an exhibit on the famous Charge of the Light Brigade, and the Royal Green Jackets Museum which contains a superb diorama of the Battle of Waterloo.

Other buildings of interest include the early-14th century **Pilgrim Hall** (free), part of the Pilgrim School, and originally used as lodgings for pilgrims to the shrine of St Swithun, and **Wolvesey Castle** (English Heritage), the residence of the Bishops of Winchester since 963. The present palace is a gracious, classical building erected in the 1680s, flanked by the imposing ruins of its 14th century predecessor which was one of the grandest buildings in medieval England. It was here, in 1554, that Queen Mary first met Philip of Spain and where the wedding banquet was held the next day. Also well worth a visit is the 15th century **Hospital of St Cross**, England's oldest almshouse. Founded in 1132 by Henri du Blois, grandson of William the Conqueror, it was extended in 1446 by Cardinal Beaufort, son of John of Gaunt. It is still home to 25 Brothers and maintains its long tradition of hospitality by dispensing the traditional Wayfarer's Dole to any traveller who requests it.

About two miles east of the city, at Colden Common, **Marwell Zoological Park** is home to more than 200 species of animals, from meercats and red pandas to snow leopards and rhinos. Set in a 100-acre park, Marwell has the largest collection of hoofed animals in the UK, nine species of cat and many endangered species.

Just to the west of the city is a very modern attraction, **Intech**, which explores the technologies that shape our lives today – how light can be bent, for example, and how humans produce electricity. There are more than 100 exhibits, all of which have

The Clock-Work-Shop

6a Parchment Street, Winchester, Hampshire SO23 8AT
Tel: 01962 842331 Mobile: 07885 954302
website: www.clock-work-shop.co.uk

Everyone visiting the historic city of Winchester should take time to look in at the **Clock-Work-Shop**, which occupies two floors of an old building in a side street just off the main street. Owned by Peter Ponsford-Jones and run by him and his partners Kevin Hurd and Richard Scorey, the shop specialises in the sale, purchase, repair, restoration, after care and valuation of antique clocks, mostly English and mostly from the period from the 17th century to the First World War. Around 100 clocks are usually on display, including carriage clocks, wall clocks, mantel clocks and long case clocks, and the shop also deals in fine antique barometers and has a small stock of pocket watches.

The shop hours are 9am to 5pm Monday to Saturday, when all the clocks are available to view, but customers can visit the shop at any time of the day or night by accessing the splendid website, which includes comprehensive details, including photographs and prices, of the full stock. A typical entry from the long case clock catalogue: 'A very handsome eight day longcase of super quality. The silvered dial is particularly beautiful - a real work of the engraver's art! The oak case has excellent colour, finish and proportions. A most original clock. Circa 1780. Local delivery and set-up'. With notes as interesting and tempting as these, a browse through the website could easily result in a real-life visit to the shop. All sales and repairs carry a three-year guarantee.

Church Farm

Barton Stacey, Winchester, Hampshire SO21 3RR
Tel/Fax: 01962 760268

Set in beautiful countryside within easy reach of both Winchester and Salisbury, Oxford and Stonehenge, **Church Farm** was originally a 15th century tithe barn. It was extended in Georgian times but the Tudor Hall still has its original flagstone floor. James and Jean Talbot have lived in this lovely old property since 1934, its attractively furnished rooms full of much loved furniture, huge sofas and even a baby grand piano. Arriving guests are welcomed with tea and biscuits, cakes or a drink before being shown to one of the three immaculate rooms, each of which enjoys enchanting views. Guests have the use of a spacious sitting room with large latticed windows overlooking the beautifully maintained gardens where daffodils bloom in profusion in early spring.

Within the grounds there's also an unheated swimming pool, a croquet lawn, tennis court – and a secret tree house "for children and squirrels"! Evening meals are available on request and the price includes pre-dinner drinks and wine. In addition to the three rooms in the main house, accommodation is also available in the adjacent recently converted coach house which is particularly suitable for families. Smoking restrictions apply in both properties; Mastercard and Visa are accepted.

Neil Busby

Unit 12B, Stonefield Park, Chilbolton, Hampshire SO20 6BL
Tel/Fax: 01264 861279
e-mail: enquiries@neilbusby.co.uk
website: www.neilbusby.co.uk

In his workshop in Stonefield Park, located in a lovely countryside setting near the village of Chilbolton, **Neil Busby** continues a family tradition in woodworking that extends over three generations. His grandfather was a master craftsman who in 1977 won the Great Britain "Carpenter of the Year" award, and his father was also a carpenter who now runs his own building company. Before starting his own business, Neil worked as head restorer for Blanchard Antiques whose owner Stanley Blanchard praised Neil as "without doubt one of the finest antique restorers working today. Having been in the business for over 70 years myself, I have rarely worked with someone as talented and versatile as Neil". High praise, indeed.

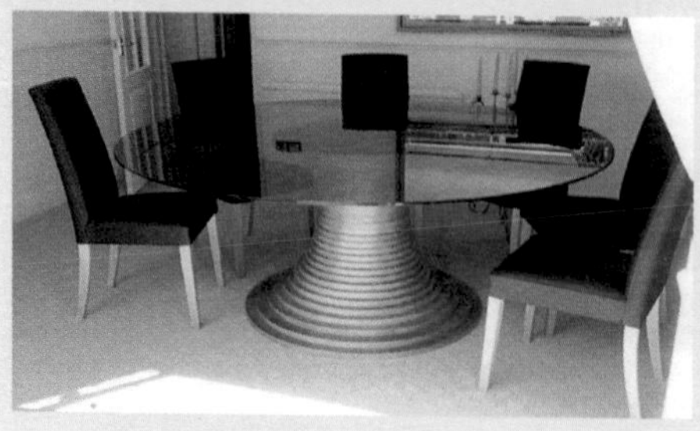

As well as restoring fine antiques to their former state of grace, Neil also offers a cabinet making service to make your ideal piece of furniture so that it fits just where you want it. His own designs are on display in the showroom – hand-made designer tables in square, twin pedestal, octagonal, rotating square and other shapes.

been designed to provide a genuine hands-on experience. Intech is open daily all year round.

Broadlands, Romsey

AROUND WINCHESTER

Crawley

5 miles NW of Winchester, on minor road off the B3049

Crawley is a possibly unique example of an early-20th century model village. The estate was bought in 1900 by the Philippi family who then enthusiastically set about adding to the village's store of genuine traditional cottages a number of faithful fakes built in the same style. (They also provided their tenants with a state-of-the-art bath house and a roller skating rink). Sensitive to tradition and history, they did nothing to blemish the partly Norman church, leaving its unusual interior intact. Instead of stone pillars, St Mary's has mighty wooden columns supporting its roof, still effective more than 500 years after they were first hoisted into place.

Sutton Scotney

6 miles N of Winchester, on the A34

Standing at a crossroads, Sutton Scotney was once a busy little place. Today, it is by-passed by the A34 so visitors can peacefully explore its picturesque side streets lined with thatched cottages and Georgian houses. Unusually, the village has no church but the clock tower of the Jubilee Hall, erected in 1897, has a distinctly ecclesiastical air about it.

Romsey

10 miles SE of Winchester, on the A27/A3090

"Music in stone", and "the second finest Norman building in England" are just two responses to **Romsey Abbey**, a majestic building containing some of the best 12th and 13th century architecture to have survived. Built between 1120 and 1230, the Abbey is remarkably complete. Unlike so many monastic buildings which were destroyed or fell into ruin after the Dissolution, the Abbey was fortunate in being bought by the town in 1544 for £100 – the bill of sale, signed and sealed by Henry VIII, is displayed in the south choir aisle. Subsequent generations of townspeople have carefully maintained their bargain purchase. The abbey's most spectacular feature is the soaring nave which rises more than 70ft and extends for more than 76ft. Amongst the abbey's many

Broadlands

Romsey, Hampshire SO51 9ZD
Tel: 01794 505010 Fax: 01794 505040
e-mail: admin@broadlands.net
website: www.broadlands.net

One of the finest stately homes in the country, this gracious Palladian mansion was built by Henry Holland for an ancestor of Lord Palmerston. It stands by the River Test in lovely grounds landscaped by Lancelot Capability Brown. The elegant interior houses important collections of furniture, porcelain, sculpture and paintings (including several Van Dycks) acquired by the Palmerstons. The house passed to the Mountbatten family and it was Lord Louis Mountbatten who first opened it to the public in 1979, shortly before his tragic death.

The present owner, Lord Romsey, carrying on the tradition started by his grandfather, established the Mountbatten Exhibition, which follows Lord Louis' remarkable career as sailor, commander, statesman, diplomat and sportsman. An audio-visual film is supported by a display of uniforms, decorations, trophies and mementoes. Visits are by guided tour only.

GJ Garner & Son (Wheelwrights)

Unit 4, Hawkes Farm, Dores Lane, Braishfield, Romsey, Hampshire SO51 0QJ
Tel/Fax: 01794 368151

For almost 30 years now the team, Graham, Annie and Daniel Garner have been wheelwrights, trading as **G.J. Garner & Son**. They make wooden wheels for every type of vehicle you can imagine and in a huge variety of sizes. They also carry out restoration of horse-drawn vehicles as well as authentic refurbishment of vintage cars and cannons. Another major aspect of the business is its Heritage Collection of elegant garden furniture hand-made by a small group of skilled craftsmen. They use a range of woods but most of the pieces are made using Iroko hardwood from Ghana.

With the environment in mind, the Garners insist that their supplies come from properly controlled sources with replanting policies. All the garden furniture is handcrafted using morticed and tenoned joints to achieve a rigid construction and the range includes chairs; benches; tables; troughs and gazebos which are delivered and erected free within a 50-mile radius. The Garners are always happy to make any of their products to suit individual requirements.

treasures is the 16th century **Romsey Rood** which shows Christ on the cross with the hand of God descending from the clouds.

Just across from the Abbey, in Church Court, stands the town's oldest dwelling, **King John's House**, built around 1240 for a merchant. It has served as a royal residence but not, curiously, for King John who died some 14 years before it was built. He may though have had a hunting lodge on the site. The house is now a museum and centre for cultural activities; the garden has been renovated and replanted with pre-18th century plants.

The **Moody Museum** occupies the Victorian home of the Moody family who were cutlers in Romsey from the 18th century up until the 1970s. Visitors are greeted by (models of) William Moody and his sister Mary in a reconstruction of the family parlour and the exhibits include fixtures and fittings from the family's gun shop.

Train enthusiasts will want to seek out the curious exhibit located behind the infants' school in Winchester Road. **Romsey Signal Box** is a preserved vintage signal box in working order, complete with signals, track and other artefacts.

Romsey's most famous son was undoubtedly the flamboyant politician Lord Palmerston, three times Prime Minister during the 1850s and 1860s. Palmerston lived at Broadlands, just south of the town, and is commemorated by a bronze statue in the town's small triangular Market Place.

Broadlands is a gracious Palladian mansion that was built by Lord Palmerston's father in the mid-1700s. The architect was Henry Holland, the landscape was modelled by the ubiquitous Capability Brown. The important collections of furniture, porcelain and sculpture were acquired by the 2nd Viscount Palmerston. The house passed to the Mountbatten family and it was Lord Louis Mountbatten who first opened Broadlands to the public shortly before he was killed in 1979. The present owner, Lord Romsey, has established the Mountbatten Exhibition in tribute to his grandfather's remarkable career as naval commander, diplomat, and last Viceroy of India. An audio-visual film provides an overall picture of the Earl's life and exhibits include his dazzling uniforms, the numerous decorations he was awarded, and an astonishing collection of the trophies, mementoes and gifts he received in his many roles.

Twyford

3 miles S of Winchester, on the B3335

Hampshire churchyards are celebrated for their ancient yew trees, but the one at Twyford is exceptional. A visitor in 1819 described the clipped tree as resembling "the top of a considerable green hillock, elevated on a stump". The grand old yew is still in apparently good health and provides a dark green foil to the trim Victorian church of striped brick and flint which was designed by Alfred Waterhouse, architect of the Natural History Museum in London.

Three well-known historical figures have strong associations with the village. Benjamin Franklin wrote much of his autobiography while staying at Twyford House; Alexander Pope attended school here until he was expelled for writing a lampoon on the Master; and it was at the old Brambridge House that Mrs Fitzherbert was secretly married to the Prince Regent, later George IV, in 1785.

An interesting example of our industrial heritage is the **Twyford Waterworks Museum.** It is housed in

Kimbridge on the Test Farm Shop & Annie's Restaurant

Kimbridge Lane, Kimbridge, nr Romsey, Hampshire SO51 0LE
Shop Tel: 01794 340777
Annies Tel: 01794 340556

Fine food abounds in the Test Valley, and for a true taste of the English countryside there's no finer place in the valley than **Kimbridge Farm Shop**. The whole place has an elegant country feel, and the reputation built up by Annie and David Powell brings lovers of the best of British food from many miles around. A beautiful covered bridge across a trout stream creates an entrance into the splendidly renovated oak beamed barn, the taste buds are tingled with a display of beautifully fresh fruit and vegetables that provides a foretaste of what is inside.

The spacious interior, with tiled floor and brick walls hung with framed pictures of proud cockerels, is filled with good things, including the pick of the produce of the local farms, freshly baked bread in a wooden crate, fine British cheeses, Annie's home-baked cakes, chutneys, pickles and preserves, fresh and smoked fish, freshly-laid eggs, fine wines, Kimbridge sherry and a range of exotic delicatessen products. There are oven-to-table cooking pots, greetings cards, fishing tackle and a selection of food-related gifts. Kimbridge is particularly noted for its trout, both fresh and smoked, and fish-feeding sessions take place daily at 11 and 3.

After stocking up at the farm shop, visitors can stroll across the bridge and look around the grounds, where ducks, chickens and guinea fowl roam freely. After that to Annie's Restaurant for morning coffee, lunch or afternoon tea. In the wooden-floored, raftered restaurant or out on the deck, the pick of the Kimbridge kitchens can be enjoyed, perhaps duck or trout pâté, then quiche, cottage pie or chicken with vegetables, peppers, baked potato and salad, with a slice of delicious lemon and lime cheesecake to finish. Please ring Kimbridge for opening hours; it lies three miles north of Romsey – turn off the A3057 Romsey-Stockbridge road opposite the Bear & Ragged Staff pub.

Twyford Waterworks which opened in 1898 to supply water to the surrounding rural area. Between 1903 and 1969 the water was also softened which explains the lime kilns found on the site. The present steam engine dates from 1914; the electric pumps were installed in 1951. Despite being scheduled as an Ancient Monument, the waterworks still extract more than five million gallons of water from the wells every day. The museum concentrates on the evolution of water supply during the 20th century and is open every Sunday between May and October, and every other Sunday during the rest of the year.

East Wellow

12 miles SW of Winchester, off the A27

The **Church of St Margaret** is the burial place of Florence Nightingale who lies beneath the family monument bearing the simple inscription: *FN 1820-1910*. The church itself has several interesting features, including 13th century wall paintings and Jacobean panelling.

Close to the village is Headlands Farm Fishery where there are two lakes available for fishing for carp, tench, perch, roach, pike and trout. Other facilities include rod hire, flies for sale and hot drinks.

Mottisfont

10 miles W of Winchester, off the A3057

Mottisfont's little Church of St Andrew boasts a wealth of 15th century stained glass, including a superb Crucifixion, and should not be overlooked on a visit to **Mottisfont Abbey** (National Trust). Built as an Augustinian priory in the 12th century, the abbey was converted into a country mansion after the Dissolution and was further modified in the 1700s. Some parts of the original priory have survived, amongst them the monks' cellarium – an undercroft with vast pillars – but the main attraction inside is the drawing room decorated with a Gothic trompe l'oeil fantasy by Rex Whistler. He was also commissioned to design the furniture but World War II intervened and he was killed in action.

The superb grounds contain the National Collection of old-fashioned roses, established in 1972, a lovely pollarded lime walk designed by Sir Geoffrey Jellicoe, and some superb trees, including what is thought to be the largest plane tree in England.

SOUTHEAST HAMPSHIRE

With a population of 1.2 million, Hampshire is the 5th most populous county in England. A goodly proportion of those 1.2 million people live along the coastal crescent that stretches from Southampton through Fareham and Portsmouth to Havant. Inland, though, there are parts of the South Downs as peaceful and scenic as anywhere in the county.

Southampton boasts one of the finest natural harbours in the world and has been the leading British deep-sea port since the days of the Norman Conquest. Portsmouth did not develop as a port until the 16th century but makes up for its shorter history by its romantic associations with such legendary ships as *HMS Victory*, the *Mary Rose*, and *HMS Warrior*. Portsmouth is also a popular seaside resort providing, together with its neighbour, Hayling Island, some seven miles of sandy beaches. Southsea Castle and massive Portchester Castle have interesting historical associations, and the ruins of Netley Abbey and the Bishop's Palace at Bishop's Waltham are both outstandingly picturesque.

Like most major ports, Southampton

and Portsmouth have something of a cosmopolitan air about them, providing an intriguing contrast with the rural charms of the inland villages.

SOUTHAMPTON

From this historic port, Henry V's army set sail for Agincourt in 1415, the Pilgrim Fathers embarked on their perilous journey to the New World in 1620, and, on April 10th, 1912, the *Titanic* set off on its maiden voyage, steaming majestically into the Solent. The city's sea-faring heritage is vividly recalled at the excellent **Maritime Museum** (free), housed in the 14th century Wool House. The museum tells the story of the port from the age of sail to the heyday of the great ocean liners.

As a major sea-port, Southampton was a prime target for air raids during World War II and suffered grievously. But the city can still boast a surprising number of ancient buildings. Substantial stretches of the medieval **Town Walls** have miraculously survived, its ramparts interspersed with fortifications such as the oddly-named 15th century **Catchcold Tower** and **God's House Gate and Tower,** which now houses the city's archaeological museum. Perhaps the most impressive feature of the walls is **Bargate**, one of the finest medieval city gates in the country. From its construction around 1200 until the 1930s, Bargate remained the principal entrance to the city. Its narrow archway is so low that Southampton Corporation's trams had to be specially modified for them to pass through. Inside the arch stands a statue of George III, cross-dressing as a Roman Emperor. Bargate now stands in its own pedestrianised area, its upper floor, the former **Guildhall**, now a museum of local history and folklore.

Another remarkable survivor is the **Medieval Merchant's House** (English Heritage) in French Street which has been expertly restored and authentically furnished, now appearing just as it was when it was built around 1290. One of the most popular visitor attractions in Southampton is the **Tudor House Museum & Garden**, a lovely 15th century house with an award-winning Tudor Garden complete with fountain, bee skeps (baskets) and 16th century herbs and flowers, (currently closed for restoration work).

Southampton City Art Gallery is a treasure house of works ranging over six centuries, while the John Hansard Gallery and the Mallais Gallery specialise in contemporary art. The painter Sir John Mallais was a native of Southampton as was Isaac Watts, the hymnologist whose many enduring hymns include *O God, Our Help In Ages Past*.

There's so much history to savour in the city, but Southampton has also proclaimed itself "A City for the New Millennium". Major

Ocean Village Marina, Southampton

Southampton Town Centre

developments include the flagship shopping area of WestQuay, the enhancement of the city's impressive central parks, the superbly appointed Leisure World; the state-of-the-art Swimming & Diving Complex which incorporates separate championship, diving and fun pools, and Ocean Village, an imaginatively conceived waterfront complex with its own 450-berth marina, undercover shopping, excellent restaurants and a multi-screen cinema.

As you'd expect in a city with such a glorious maritime heritage, there's a huge choice of boat excursions, whether along the River Hamble, around the Solent, or over to the Isle of Wight. Blue Funnel Cruises operate from Ocean Village; Solent Cruises from Town Quay.

The city also occupies an important place in aviation history. A short step from Ocean Village, at **Solent Sky** (formerly the Hall of Aviation),the story of aviation in the Solent is represented and incorporates the RJ Mitchell Memorial Museum. Mitchell lived and worked in Southampton in the 1930s and not only designed the Spitfire but also the S6 Seaplane which won the coveted Scheider Trophy. The centrepiece of the Hall of Aviation is the spectacular Sandringham Flying Boat which you can board and sample the luxury of air travel in the past – very different from the Cattle Class standards of today's mass travel.

AROUND SOUTHAMPTON

West End

2 miles NE of Southampton, on minor road off the A27

An ideal destination for a family outing is **Itchen Valley Country Park** on the outskirts of Southampton. Its 440 acres of water meadows, ancient woodland, conifer plantations and grazing pasture

Itchen Valley Country Park

High Wood Barn, Allington Lane, West End, Southampton, Hampshire SO30 3HQ
Tel/Fax: 023 8046 6091
e-mail: ivcp@eastleigh.gov.uk

A superb family day out is guaranteed at **Itchen Valley Country Park**, whose 440 acres of water meadows, ancient woodland, conifer plantations and grazing pasture span the River Itchen between Eastleigh and Southampton. The various areas support a great variety of bird life, insect and plant life and there are trails, cycle routes, picnic sites and a host of children's activities. The High Wood Barn Visitor Centre, built in 17th century style from timber recovered from the great storm of 1987, contains information, interactive exhibits, a café and a shop.

lie either side of the meandering River Itchen, famous for its clear waters and excellent fishing. The Park is managed by Eastleigh Borough Council's Countryside Service to provide informal recreation, enhance and conserve wildlife habitats and as an educational resource. The best place to begin your visit is the High Wood Barn Visitor Centre, an attractive timber structure built in the style of a 17th century Hampshire Aisle Barn. From the Visitor Centre, waymarked trails help you to discover the different areas of the Park and an informative leaflet reveals the history and wildlife of a landscape shaped by hundreds of years of traditional farming and woodland management. Children are well-provided for at the park. In High Hill Field there's an adventure play area for the under-12s that includes an aerial runway, and behind the Visitor Centre a play area for the under-5s has giant woodland animals designed by local school-children and built by sculptor Andy Frost.

Eastleigh

5 miles NE of Southampton on the A335

Eastleigh is first mentioned in a charter of 932AD but it wasn't until some 900 years later that it began to expand. That was when the Eastleigh Carriage and Engine Works was established in the town. At one time the works covered 60 acres and employed 3,600 people. The town's railway connection is commemorated by Jill Tweed's sculpture, The Railwayman, which stands in the town centre.

Nearby, in a former Salvation Army building, is the **Eastleigh Museum** whose exhibits concentrate on the town's railway heritage. Visiting heritage, art, craft and photography exhibitions are also held here. The **Point Dance and Arts Centre** stages a full programme of theatre, dance, cinema and music events, while the **Beatrice Royal Contemporary Art and Craft Gallery** offers exhibitions of art, sculpture, ceramics, jewellery and textiles.

Just outside the town is the **Lakeside Country Park**, home to a variety of wild life and also a place for model boating, windsurfing and fishing. Here too is the Eastleigh Lakeside Railway, a miniature steam railway that provides trips around the park.

To the south of Eastleigh lies Southampton International Airport, the home of **Carill Aviation** where you can take off for a scenic flight over the Solent or sign up for a trial flying lesson.

Bishop's Waltham

10 miles NE of Southampton, on the B2177/B3035

Bishop's Waltham is a charming and historic small town. It was the country residence of the Bishops of Winchester for centuries and through the portals of their sumptuous **Palace** have passed at least 12 reigning monarchs. Amongst them were Richard the Lionheart returning from the Crusades, Henry V mustering his army before setting off for Agincourt, and Henry VIII entertaining Charles V of Spain (then the most powerful monarch in Europe) to a lavish banquet. The palace's days of glory came to a violent end during the Civil War when Cromwell's troops battered most of it to the ground. The last resident bishop was forced to flee, concealing himself beneath a load of manure.

Set within beautiful moated grounds the ruins remain impressive, especially the Great Hall with its three-storey tower and soaring windows. Also here are the remains of the bakehouse, kitchen, chapel and lodgings for visitors. The Palace is now in the care of English Heritage and entrance is free.

The town itself offers visitors a good choice of traditional and specialist shops, amongst them a renowned fishmonger, butcher, baker – even a candle-maker. And just north of the town you can visit one of the country's leading vineyards. Visitors to **Northbrook Springs Vineyard** are offered a tour of the vineyard which explains the complex, labour-intensive process of planting, growing, pruning and harvesting the vines, and a free tasting in the Vineyard Shop (open Tuesday to Sunday) of a selection of crisp, clear, flavourful wines.

South of Bishop's Waltham, at Waltham Chase, **Jhansi Farm Rare Breed Centre** is dedicated to the conservation of rare breed farm animals, some of them critically endangered. The Farm has a pets' corner housing a large variety of pure bred rabbits, guinea pigs, chipmunks and birds, a souvenir and pet shop, tea room, picnic and play area, nursery and water gardens, with events such as sheep shearing and hand spinning taking place throughout the season.

Botley

7 miles E of Southampton on the A334

Set beside the River Hamble, Botley is an attractive village of red brick houses which remains as pleasant now as when William Cobbett, the 19th century writer and political commentator, described it as "the most delightful village in the world....it has everything in a village I love and none of the things I hate". The latter included a workhouse, attorneys, justices of the peace – and barbers. The author of *Rural Rides* lived a very comfortable life in Botley between 1804 and 1817 and he is honoured by a memorial in the Market Square.

Netley

5 miles SE of Southampton, off the A3025

A Victorian town on the shores of the Solent, Netley was brought into prominence when a vast military hospital was built here after the Crimean War. The foundation stone of **Netley Hospital** was laid by Queen Victoria in 1856 and the hospital remained in use until after World War II. A disastrous fire in the 1960s caused most of the buildings to be demolished but the hospital's Chapel, with its distinctive 100ft tower, did survive and now houses an exhibition about the hospital from the time of Florence Nightingale. The rest of the site has been developed as the **Royal Victoria Country Park** offering woodland and coastal walks, waymarked themed and nature trails, and trips around the park on a miniature steam railway.

Heritage of a different kind can be found at ruined **Netley Abbey** (English Heritage), a wonderfully serene spot surrounded by noble trees. "These are not the ruins of Netley," declared Horace Walpole in the mid-1700s, "but of Paradise." Jane Austen was equally entranced by the Abbey's romantic charm and she made many visits. Dating back to 1300, the extensive ruins provide a spectacular backdrop for open-air theatre performances during the summer.

Bursledon

6 miles SE of Southampton, off the A3024

Anyone interested in England's industrial heritage should pay a visit to Bursledon. Ships have been built here since medieval times, the most famous being the *Elephant*, Nelson's flagship at the Battle of Copenhagen. The yard where it was built, now renamed the Elephant Boatyard, is still in business. On a rise to the north of the village stands

Bursledon Windmill

Windmill Lane, Bursledon, Southampton, Hampshire SO31 8BG
Tel: 023 8040 4999
website: hants.gov.uk/museum/windmill

The last surviving working windmill in Hampshire was built by a Mrs Phoebe Langtry in 1814 at a cost of £800. Inactive from the time of the depression in the 1880s, the tower mill was restored to full working order between 1976 and 1991. Its sails - a fine sight on a hilltop setting - revolve whenever a good northerly or southerly wind blows, producing stoneground flour for sale.

Next to the mill is the Windmill Wood Nature Trail, a woodland habitat supporting a wide range of wildlife including woodpeckers.

Open all year - phone for admission times.

Bursledon Windmill, the only working windmill in Hampshire. Built in 1814 at a cost of £800, its vanes ground to a halt during the great agricultural depression of the 1880s. Happily, all the machinery remained intact and after a lengthy restoration between 1976 and 1991, the sails are revolving once again whenever a good northerly or southerly wind is blowing. The mill produces stoneground flour for sale and is open to visitors at weekends, or whenever the sails are turning!

The village can boast another unique industrial site. When **Bursledon Brickworks** was established in 1897 the machinery installed was at the very forefront of brick-making technology. The works closed in 1974 but a charitable trust has now restored its gargantuan machines, thus preserving the last surviving example of a steam-driven brickworks in the country. Special events are held here from time to time but the works are only open on a limited basis.

Hamble

7 miles SE of Southampton, on the B3397

Famous throughout the world as a yachting centre, Hamble takes its name from the river, a mere 10 miles long, that flows past the village into Southampton Water. Some 3,000 vessels have berths in the Hamble Estuary so there's an incredible variety of boats thronging the river during the season, anything from vintage barges to the sleekest of modern craft.

Park Gate

8 miles SE of Southampton, on the A27

Back in the days when strawberries still had real taste and texture, Park Gate was the main distribution centre for the produce of the extensive strawberry farms all around. During the season, scores of special trains were contracted to transport the succulent fruit to London, some 3,000 tons of it in 1913 alone. By the 1960s, housing had taken priority over fruit farms and today the M27 marks a very clear division between the built up areas to the south, and the unspoilt acres of countryside to the north.

PORTSMOUTH

Currently, any brochure promoting Portsmouth always adds the words "Flagship City". With good reason, since the port is home to the most famous flagship in British naval history, **HMS Victory.** From the outside it's a majestic, three-masted ship: inside it's creepily claustrophobic, except for the Admiral's and Captain's spacious, mahogany-panelled quarters. Visitors can pace the very same deck from which Nelson master-minded the decisive encounter with the French navy off Cape Trafalgar in 1805. Standing on this deck, ostentatiously arrayed in the gorgeous uniform of a British Admiral of the Fleet, Nelson presented a clear target to a sharp-sighted French sniper. The precise spot where Nelson fell and the place on the sheltered orlop (lowest) deck where he died are both marked by plaques.

City Museum & Art Gallery, Portsmouth

The death of Nelson was a tragedy softened by a halo of victory: the loss of the *Mary Rose,* some 260 years earlier was an unmitigated disaster. Henry VIII had ordered the ship, the second largest in his fleet, to be built. He was standing on Southsea Common above Portsmouth in 1545, watching the *Mary Rose* manoeuvre, when it suddenly heeled over and sank. All 700 men on board drowned. "And the King he screeched right out like any maid, 'Oh, my gentlemen! Oh, my gallant men!'" More than four centuries later, in 1982, the hulk of the *Mary Rose* was carefully raised from the seabed where it had lain for so long. The impressive remains are now housed in the timber-clad **Mary Rose Museum**.

Another ship you can see at Portsmouth doesn't possess the same historical glamour as the *Victory* or the *Mary Rose,* but **HMS Warrior** merits a visit because when this mighty craft was commissioned in 1860, she was the Navy's first ironclad warship. A great advance in technology, but the distinctions between the officers' and crew accommodation show little difference from those in Nelson's day.

Also within the dockyard area are the **Royal Naval Museum** which has a marvellous exhibition on the life and exploits of Nelson; and **The Dockyard Apprentice** where visitors can become a new apprentice for a day and learn the skills that helped construct the mighty Dreadnought battleships.

Like Southampton, Portsmouth suffered badly during World War II, losing most of its 17th and 18th century buildings. **St George's Church**, a handsome Georgian building of 1754 with large galleries, was damaged by a bomb but has been fully restored, and just to the north of the church, the barn-like **Beneficial Boy's School**, built in 1784, is another survivor.

One of the most interesting buildings is to be found in Southsea, the city's resort area. **Southsea Castle** was built in 1544 as one of Henry VIII's series of forts protecting the south coast from French attacks. It has been modified several times since then but the original Keep is

Flagship Portsmouth

Building 1/7, Porters Lodge, College Road,
HM Naval Base, Portsmouth, Hampshire PO1 3LJ
Tel: 023 9286 1533 Fax: 023 9229 5252
e-mail: mail@historicdockyard.co.uk
website: www.flagship.org.uk

Flagship Portsmouth, in the historic dockyard, is home port to three of the greatest ships ever built, but has many other attractions. The latest of these is the blockbusting Action Stations, where visitors can test their skills and abilities through a series of high-tech interactive displays and simulators.

The most famous of the ships is undoubtedly *HMS Victory*. From the outside it's a majestic three-master, but inside it's creepily claustrophobic except for the Admiral's and Captain's spacious, mahogany-panelled quarters. Visitors can pace the very same deck from which Nelson masterminded the decisive encounter with the French navy off Cape Trafalgar in 1805. Standing on the deck arrayed in his Admiral's finery, Nelson was an easy target for a keen-eyed French sniper; the precise spot where he fell and the place on the lower deck where he later died (knowing that the battle was won) are both marked by plaques.

The *Mary Rose*, the second largest ship in Henry VIII's fleet, was putting out to sea, watched proudly by the King from Southsea Common, when she suddenly heeled over and sank. All 700 men on board lost their lives. More than 400 years later, in 1982, the ship was raised in an amazingly delicate operation from the seabed. The impressively preserved remains of the ship are now housed in the timber-clad Mary Rose Museum. (One of the tombs in Portsmouth Cathedral is that of one of the Mary Rose's crew.) *HMS Warrior* was the Navy's first iron-clad warship and the most formidable fighting ship the world had seen in 1860: bigger, faster and more heavily armed than any warship afloat, built of iron and powered by both sail and steam. Her size and might proved to be a deterrent to potential enemies and she never actually had to go to war.

Boat trips round the harbour give a feel of the soul of the city that has been home to the Royal Navy for more than 800 years, and the most attractive part, picturesque Old Portsmouth, can be seen to advantage from the little ferry that plies the short route to Gosport.

The Royal Naval Museum is the most fascinating of its kind, with a marvellous exhibition of the life and deeds of Nelson, and the interactive Dockyard Apprentice Exhibition explains the skills and crafts of 1911 that went into the building of the world's finest fighting ships, the Dreadnoughts. A relatively new addition is Action Stations, an exciting insight into the modern high-tech Royal Navy of today. Five interective areas offer physical or electronic challenges and a ride on the 19 seat simulator is an experience not to be missed.

still intact and there are good views across the Solent from the gun platforms.

Portsmouth also offers visitors a wealth of varied museums, three of which deserve special mention: the **Royal Armouries**, housed in the huge Victorian Fort Nelson, claims to be 'Britain's Loudest Museum', with live firings every day; the **Charles Dickens Birthplace Museum** at 393 Old Commercial Road, has been restored and furnished to show how the house looked when the great novelist was born here in 1812; and the **D-Day Museum** in Southsea which commemorates the Allied invasion of Europe in 1944 and is most notable for the 83-metre-long Overlord Tapestry, a 20th century equivalent of the Bayeux Tapestry.

AROUND PORTSMOUTH

Hayling Island

4 miles E of Portsmouth on the A3023

A traditional family resort for more than a century, Hayling Island manages to provide all the usual seaside facilities without losing its rural character. Much of the foreshore is still open ground with wandering sand dunes stretching well back from the four-mile-long shingle beach. Bathing is safe here and West Beachlands even boasts a European Blue Flag which is only awarded to beaches meeting 26 environmental criteria. One of Hayling's more unusual beach facilities is the line of old-fashioned beach huts, all of which are available to rent.

A good way to explore the island is to follow the **Hayling Billy Leisure Trail**, once the Hayling Billy railway line, which provides a level footpath around most of the 14 miles of shoreline.

Hayling is something of a Mecca for board sailors. Not only does it provide the best sailing in the UK for beginners and experts alike, it is also the place where board-sailing was invented. Many places claim that honour but Peter Chilvers has a High Court ruling to prove it. In 1982 a judge decided that Mr Chilvers had indeed invented the sailboard at Hayling in 1958. As a boy of 10, he used a sheet of plywood, a tent fly-sheet, a pole and some curtain rings to sail up an island creek.

Gosport

2 miles W of Portsmouth on the A32

Gosport is home to another of Palmerston's forts – the circular **Fort Brockhurst** (English Heritage) which is in almost mint condition and open to visitors on Sundays from the end of March to the end of October. At the

Royal Navy Submarine Museum, located at HMS Dolphin, visitors can experience a century of submarines. Stories of undersea adventures and the heroism of the Royal Navy's submarine services are recounted and there are also guided tours around **HMS Alliance**, a late World War II submarine.

The town's connections with the Royal Navy are further explored at **Explosion! The Museum of Naval Firepower** which is dedicated to the people who prepared armaments used by the Navy from the Battle of Trafalgar to the Falklands War. As well as browsing through the unique collection of small arms, cannons, guns, mines and torpedoes, visitors can experience the pitch and roll of a moving gun-deck, help move barrels of gunpowder, and dodge mines on the seabed.

Away from the Navy's influence on the town, there is Gosport's splendid **Holy Trinity Church** which contains an organ that was played by George Frederick Handel when he was music master to the Duke of Chandos. The town bought the organ after the duke's death. Gosport also boasts one of the county's best local museums – **Gosport Museum & Gallery** – where the history of the area from prehistoric times is brought to life through a series of fascinating exhibits.

Portchester

3 miles NW of Portsmouth on the A27

Standing at the head of Portsmouth Harbour, **Portchester Castle** is not only the grandest medieval castle in the county but also stands within the best-preserved site of a Roman fort in northern Europe. Sometime around 280 AD, the Romans enclosed eight acres of this strategic headland and used it as a base for their ships clearing the Channel of pirates. The original walls of the fort were 20ft high and 10ft thick, their depth much reduced later by local people pillaging the stone for their own buildings.

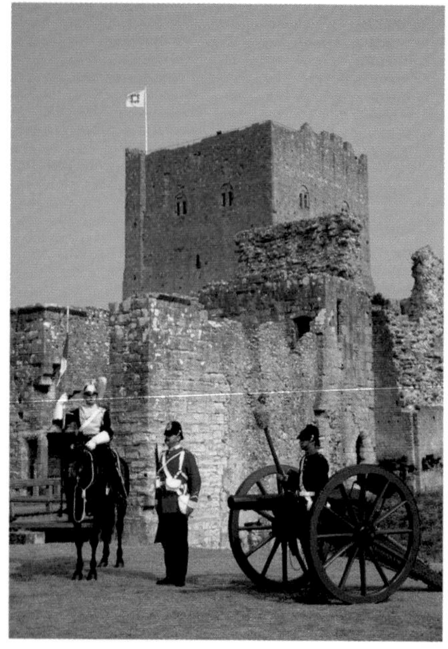

Portchester Castle

The medieval castle dates back to 1120 although the most substantial ruins are those of the royal palace built for Richard II between 1396 and 1399. Richard was murdered in 1399 and never saw his magnificent castle. Also within the walls of the Roman enclosure is **Portchester Church**, a superb Norman construction built between 1133 and 1150 as part of an Augustinian Priory. For some reason, the Priors moved inland to Southwick, and the church remained disused for more than five-and-a-half centuries until Queen Anne personally donated £400 for its restoration. Apart from the east end, the church is entirely Norman and, remarkably, its 12th century font of wondrously carved Caen stone has also survived the centuries.

Fareham

6 miles NW of Portsmouth on the A27

Fareham has expanded greatly since Thackeray described it as a "dear little Hampshire town". It still has considerable charm and the handsome houses on the High Street reflect its prosperous days as a ship-building centre. Many aspects of the town's history are featured in **Westbury Manor Museum** which occupies a large 17th century town house in the centre of Fareham. This old market town is also home to **The Royal Armouries at Fort Nelson** whose displays of artillery dating from the Middle Ages form one of the finest collections of its kind in the world. Among the 300 guns on show are a Roman catapult; a wrought-iron monster of 1450 that could fire a 60 kilogram granite ball almost a mile; Flemish guns captured at Waterloo, and parts of the notorious Iraqi 'Supergun'. Visitors can see some of the guns in action at daily firings and at special event days when the dramatic interpretations include accounts of the defence of Rorke's Drift, experiences under shellfire in the World War I trenches, and a Royalist account of the execution of Charles I.

Titchfield

7 miles NW of Portsmouth on the A27

Just to the north of the village are the ruins of the 13th century **Titchfield Abbey**, its presence reflecting the former prominence of Titchfield as an important market town and a thriving port on the River Meon. The parish church contains a notable treasure in the form of the **Wriothesley Monument** which was carved by a Flemish sculptor in the late 1500s. This remarkable and massive work is a triple tomb chest depicting Thomas Wriothesley, 1st Earl of Southampton, along with his wife and son. It was the 1st Earl who converted part of the now ruined abbey into a house and it was there that his grandson, the 3rd Earl, entertained William Shakespeare.

Wickham

8 miles NW of Portsmouth on the A334

This village was the home of William of Wykeham (1324-1404), Chancellor of England, Bishop of Winchester, founder of Winchester College and New College, Oxford.

The mill by the bridge over the River Meon will be of interest to American visitors since it contains beams from the American frigate, *Chesapeake*, which was captured in 1813 off Boston by the British frigate *Shannon*.

To the northwest of the village is **Wickham Vineyard** which was established in the 1980s and has expanded over the years. The vineyard and modern winery are open to visitors who can take advantage of an audio tour, sample the wines and browse through the gift shop.

THE NEW FOREST

The New Forest, as is the way with many English place-names, is neither New nor a Forest, although much of it is attractively wooded. Some historians believe that 'forest' is a corruption of an ancient British word, *gores* or *gorest,* meaning waste or open ground. 'gorse' comes from the same root word. The term New Forest came into use after William the Conqueror proclaimed the area a royal hunting ground, seized some 15,000 acres that Saxon farmers had laboriously reclaimed from the heathland, and began a programme of planting thousands of trees. To preserve wildlife for his sport, (the deer especially), William adopted all the rigorous venery laws of his Saxon royal predecessors and added some harsh measures of his own. Anyone who killed a deer would himself be killed. If he shot at the beast and missed, his hands were cut off. And, perhaps most ruthless of all, anyone who disturbed a deer during the breeding season had his eyes put out.

There are still plenty of wild deer roaming the 145 square miles of the Forest Park, confined within its boundaries by cattle grids, (known to Americans as Texas Gates). You are much more likely though to see the famous New Forest ponies, free-wandering creatures which nevertheless are all privately owned. They are also something of a hazard for drivers, so do take care, especially at night.

The Rufus Stone, New Forest

The largest wild area in lowland Britain, the Forest is ideal walking country with vast tracts virtually unpopulated but criss-crossed by a cat's cradle of footpaths and bridle-ways. The Forestry Commission has also established a network of waymarked cycle routes which make the most of the scenic attractions and are also designed to help protect the special nature of the Forest. A map detailing the cycle network is available, along with a vast amount of other information about the area, from the **New Forest Museum and Visitor Centre** in Lyndhurst. Visitors can watch an audio visual show, see life-sized models of Forest characters, make use of its Resource Centre and Library, and explore a gift shop specialising in locally made Forest crafts. The only town of any size within the New Forest, Lyndhurst is generally regarded as its 'capital', a good place then to begin a tour of the area.

Lyndhurst

8 miles SW of Southampton, on the A35/A337

The most striking building in this compact village is the **Church of St Michael**, rebuilt in mid-Victorian times in what John Betjeman described as "the most fanciful, fantastic Gothic style that I ever have seen". The rebuilding co-incided with the heyday of the Pre-Raphaelite movement so the church contains some fine stained glass by Burne-Jones, produced by the firm of William Morris, as well as a splendidly lush painting by Lord Leighton of *The Wise and Foolish Virgins.*

In St Michael's churchyard is the **Grave of Alice Liddell** who, as a young girl, was the inspiration for Lewis Carroll's *Alice in Wonderland.* As Mrs Reginald Hargreaves, Alice lived all her married life in Lyndhurst and was very active in local affairs.

Temple Lodge Guest House

2 Queen's Road, Lyndhurst,
Hampshire SO43 7BR
Tel: 023 8028 2392
Fax: 023 8028 4910
e-mail: templelodge@btinternet.com
website: www.templelodge-guesthouse.com

"**Temple Lodge Guest House** is where you arrive as a guest and depart as a friend". This is the motto adopted by Mike and Teresa Wrona who welcome guests personally into their charming guest house located in the heart of the New Forest.

They offer luxury en suite accommodation with colour TV, de luxe hospitality tray and hair dryers in all the rooms. Parking is available in the private car park. Temple Lodge enjoys a peaceful rural setting but is only minutes away from the village of Lyndhurst where you'll find pubs, restaurants and cafés to suit all tastes.

Next to the church is the **Queen's House** which rather confusingly is re-named the King's House whenever the reigning sovereign is male. Originally built as a royal hunting lodge, its medieval and Tudor elements are still visible. Many kings and queens have lodged here and the last monarch to stay, George III, graciously allowed loyal villagers to watch through the window as he ate dinner. The House is now the headquarters of the Forestry Commission and is also home to the **Verderer's Court**, an institution dating back to Norman times which still deals with matters concerning the forest's ancient commoning rights. The verderers (forest officials) still sit in public 10 times a year and work closely with the Commission in managing the forest. They also appoint agisters, or stockmen, who are responsible for the day-to-day supervision of the 5,000 ponies and cattle roaming the forest.

At the **New Forest Museum and Visitor Centre**, in the heart of the town, visitors can learn about the history and the wide variety of plants and animal life that the forest supports. There's also a display on the mysterious death in 1100 of William Rufus, son of William the Conqueror, who was killed by an arrow whilst out hunting. It was officially described as an accident but some believe that it was murder.

This little town is noted for its variety of small shops where you can find "anything from fresh food to Ferraris!" Many are located in the High Street, an attractive thoroughfare of mostly Edwardian buildings, which gently slopes down the hill to **Bolton's Bench**, a tree-crowned knoll where grazing ponies can usually be found. The spot enjoys excellent views over Lyndhurst and the surrounding forest. At the other end of the town, **Swan Green**, surrounded by picturesque thatched cottages, provides a much-photographed setting where cricket matches are held in summer.

AROUND LYNDHURST

MINSTEAD

2 miles NW of Lyndhurst off the A337

The village of Minstead offers two interesting attractions, one of which is the **Church of All Saints.** During the 18th century, the gentry and squirearchy of Minstead seem to have regarded church attendance as a necessary duty which, nevertheless, should be made as agreeable as possible. Three of the village's most affluent residents paid to have the church fabric altered so that they could each have their own entrance door leading to a private "parlour", complete with open fireplace and comfortable chairs. The squire of Minstead even installed a sofa on which he could doze during the sermon. It's easy to understand his concern since these sermons were normally expected to last for at least an hour; star preachers seem to have thought they were short-changing their flock if they didn't prate for at least twice that long. It was around this time that churches began introducing benches for the congregation.

Admirers of the creator of Sherlock Holmes, Sir Arthur Conan Doyle, will want to pay their respects at his grave in the churchyard here. A puzzle worthy of Sir Arthur's great detective is the idiosyncratic sign outside the Trusty Servant pub in the village. Instead of showing, as one might expect, a portrait of a dutiful domestic, the sign actually depicts a liveried figure with the feet of a stag and the face of a pig, its snout clamped by a padlock. A 10-line poem underneath this peculiar sign explains that the snout means the servant will eat any old scraps, the padlock that he will tell no tales about his master, and the stag's feet that he will be swift in carrying his master's messages.

Minstead's other main attraction is **Furzey Gardens**, eight acres of delightful, informal woodland gardens designed by Hew Dalrymple in the 1920s and enjoying extensive views over the New Forest towards the Isle of Wight. Beautiful banks of azaleas and rhododendrons, heathers and ferns surround an attractive water garden, and amongst the notable species growing here are incandescent Chilean Fire Trees and the strange 'Bottle Brush Tree'.

To the northwest of Minstead stands the **Rufus Stone** that is said to mark the spot where William Rufus was killed by an arrow while out hunting. William's body was carried on the cart of Purkis the charcoal burner to Winchester where William's brother had already arrived to proclaim himself king. William had not been a popular monarch and his funeral in the cathedral at Winchester was conducted with little ceremony and even less mourning.

Ashurst

2 miles NE of Lyndhurst on the A35

Just to the east of the village, in acres of ancient woodland, is the **New Forest Otter, Owl and Wildlife Conservation Park**. Conservation is the key word here. The park has an ongoing breeding programme for otters and barn owls, both of which are endangered species. Visitors can meander along woodland trails and encounter the otters and owls in their enclosures along with other native mammals such as deer, foxes and badgers.

Beaulieu National Motor Museum

Beaulieu, Brockenhurst, Hampshire SO42 7ZN
Tel: 01590 612345 Fax: 01590 612624
e-mail: info@beaulieu.co.uk
website: www.beaulieu.co.uk

The **National Motor Museum**, in the grounds of Lord Montagu's estate, houses over 300 vehicles covering all aspects of motoring. Among the exhibits - the oldest dates from 1896 - are world landspeed record-breakers *Bluebird* and *Golden Arrow*, Damon Hill's championship winning Formula 1 Williams Grand Prix car, an Outspan Orange car, Ariel and Vincent motorcycles and a large number of commercial vehicles.

Special attractions include a fabulous collection of over 2,000 toy vehicles in the Motoring Through Childhood Exhibition, and the exhibition of James Bond cars, including the Aston Martin from *Goldeneye* (the earlier ejector-seat Aston is in a museum in Amsterdam), the BMW 7 Series from *Tomorrow Never Dies* and Goldfinger's Rolls-Royce. The exhibition also includes examples of Q's gadgetry and some of the villains' trademarks, notably Jaws' steel teeth.

One of the many permanent displays is an accurate reconstruction of a 1938 garage complete with forecourt, servicing bay, machine shop and office.

Many Montagu family treasures are now on display in **Palace House**, formerly the Great Gatehouse of Beaulieu Abbey, where visitors can meet characters from Victorian days, among them the butler, housemaid and cook, who will talk about their lives. The old monks' refectory houses an exhibition of monastic life, and embroidered wall hangings designed and created by Belinda, Lady Montagu, depict the story of the Abbey from its earliest days. The glorious gardens are an attraction in their own right, and there are plenty of rides and drives for young and old alike - including a monorail that runs through the roof of the Museum in the course of its tour of the estate. Open every day 10am-5pm (6pm in summer)

Marchwood

5 miles E of Lyndhurst off the A326

The military port at Marchwood was built in 1943 for the construction of the Mulberry harbours deployed in Normandy after the D-Day landings. Today, the port provides a base for ships of the Royal Fleet auxiliary. Close by, at Cracknore Head, is the **British Military Powerboat Trust** where a number of historic military craft are on display. Visitors can wander around the craft in the static exhibition area and also take boat trips on certain days.

Hythe

8 miles SE of Lyndhurst off the A326

This is one of the very best places to watch the comings and goings of the big ships on Southampton Water, and no visit here is complete without taking a ride up the pier on the quaint little electric train, the oldest electric pier train in the world; from the end of the pier a ferry plies the short route across to Southampton. Hythe is the birthplace of the Hovercraft – its inventor Sir Christopher Cockerell lived in the village. In the 1930s Hythe was the home of the British Powerboat Company and of TE Lawrence (Lawrence of Arabia) while he was testing the RAF 200 series powerboats.

Beaulieu

7 miles SE of Lyndhurst, on the B3056

The ruins of a 13th century Cistercian Abbey, a stately home which grew up around the abbey's imposing gatehouse, and the **National Motor Museum** (see panel opposite) sited in its grounds are three good reasons why the village of Beaulieu has become one of the county's major visitor attractions. When Lord Montagu of Beaulieu first opened his family home to the public in the 1950s, he organised a display of a few vintage motor vehicles in homage to his father who had been a pioneer of motoring in Britain. That modest clutch of cars has now expanded to include some 250 of the oldest, newest, slowest and fastest motor-cars and bikes in British motoring history, plus some rare oddities. The motoring theme is continued in fun features such as Go Karts, Miniature Motors, and 'Fast Trax' which is promoted as the 'best in virtual racing simulators'.

Montagu family treasures are on display in **Palace House**, formerly the gatehouse of the Abbey, and visitors can meet characters from Victorian days who will talk about their lives in service.

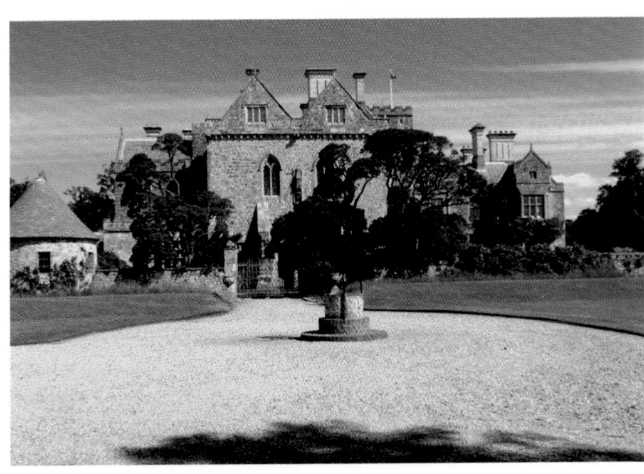

Beaulieu Palace House

It was an ancestor of Lord Montagu, the 2nd Duke of Montagu, who created the picturesque riverside village of **Buckler's Hard** in the early 1700s. It was designed as an inland port to receive and refine sugar from the Duke's

West Indian estates and His Grace planned his model village on a grand scale: the streets, for example, were to be 80ft wide. Unfortunately, the enterprise failed and only a single street was built. That 18th century street remains intact and unspoiled, and one of its buildings has been converted into a **Maritime Museum** reflecting the subsequent history of the village when it became a ship-building centre. More than 50 naval ships were built at Buckler's Hard, amongst them one of Nelson's favourite ships, the *Agamemnon*. Displays include models of ships, among them *Victory*, *Agamemnon* and the yacht *Bluebottle*, which Prince Philip raced with success. A special display recounts the exploits of Sir Francis Chichester, who sailed round the world in *Gypsy Moth* from his home port of Buckler's Hard.

A lovely riverside walk passes through **Bailey's Hard**, a former brickworks where the first naval vessel built on the river was completed in 1698. Henry Adams, the most distinguished of a family of shipbuilders, lived in the village in what is now the Master Builders Hotel. In the summer, half-hour cruises on *Swiftsure* depart from the pier at Buckler's Hard.

Fawley

5 miles E of Beaulieu on the A326

Oil is king here, and the terminals and refineries of what is probably the largest oil plant in Europe create a science fiction landscape; standing bravely apart is the village church, a link with earlier days, looking out over Southampton Water. Fawley is where some islanders from Tristan da Cunha settled after fleeing a volcano that threatened their island in 1961; a model of one of the boats they used for their escape can be seen in the chapel. Also of note in Fawley is **Cadland House**, whose eight-acre garden overlooking the Solent was designed for the banker Robert Drummond by Capability Brown. It houses the national collection of leptospermums and also features a splendid kitchen garden and a modern walled garden. Beyond the refineries a road leads off the B3053 Calshot road to **Ashlett Creek** and another world, the natural, unrefined world of creeks, mud flats and bird-haunted marshland.

Calshot

14 miles SE of Lyndhurst on the B3053

The RAF was based in both World Wars at Calshot, where seaplanes were prepared and tested for the Schneider Trophy races. The hangars once used by the RAF are now the Calshot Activity Centre, whose many activities include an artificial ski slope. At the very end of a shingle spit stands one of Henry VIII's coastal defence castles. This is **Calshot Castle**, which is now restored as a pre-World War I garrison. Visitors can admire the view from the roof of the keep, walk round the barrack room that looks as it did before World War I and see the exhibition of the Schneider air races. A little way to the west is **Lepe**, one of the major embarkation points for the 1944 D-Day invasion. The area at the top of the cliffs at Lepe is now a country park, and there's safe swimming off the beach.

Exbury

10 miles SE of Lyndhurst off the B3054

Created by Lionel de Rothschild in the 1920s and still run by members of the family, **Exbury Gardens** fully justify the reaction of one visitor, who described them as 'Heaven with the gates open'. 150 gardeners and workmen took 10 years to create the gardens, and Rothschild sent expeditions to the Himalayas to find the seeds he wanted. He himself bred hundreds of varieties of plants and the displays of rhododendrons, camellias and azaleas which he planted are renowned the world over. The 200-acre grounds are a delight to visit in spring, summer or autumn, with May perhaps the best time of all. A leisurely way of seeing the gardens is by taking a trip on the narrow-gauge Steam Railway. Many varieties of the Exbury specialities are on sale in the plant centre, where there's also a gift shop, tea room and restaurant – there is free entry to all of these.

Exbury's **Church of St Catherine** is best known for its moving, lifelike bronze memorial to two brothers who were killed in action in World War I. The work was commissioned by the brothers' parents and executed by Cecil Thomas, a gifted young sculptor who was a friend of the brothers. The area around Exbury and Lepe is featured in Nevil Shute's sad story *Requiem for a Wren*, which describes the preparations made in the New Forest for the D-Day landings. Shute himself was an aero-engineer as well as a writer, and for a time worked here on a top-secret pilotless plane.

Brockenhurst

3 miles S of Lyndhurst on the A337

A large village in a lovely setting in the heart of the New Forest. Forest ponies are frequent visitors to the main street and the village green (they naturally have right of way!). The **Church of St Nicholas** has a vast graveyard with a yew tree that is probably the oldest tree in the whole region. In the graveyard lie many soldiers, many of them from New Zealand, who had died of their injuries in a nearby military hospital. But the best known grave is that of Harry Mills, known as Brusher Mills, who brushed the New Forest cricket pitch and worked as a snake-catcher.

Thatched Cottage Hotel & Restaurant

16 Brookley Road, Brockenhurst,
Hampshire SO42 7RR
Tel: 01590 623090 Fax: 01590 623479
e-mail: sales@thatchedcottage.co.uk
website: www.thatchedcottage.co.uk

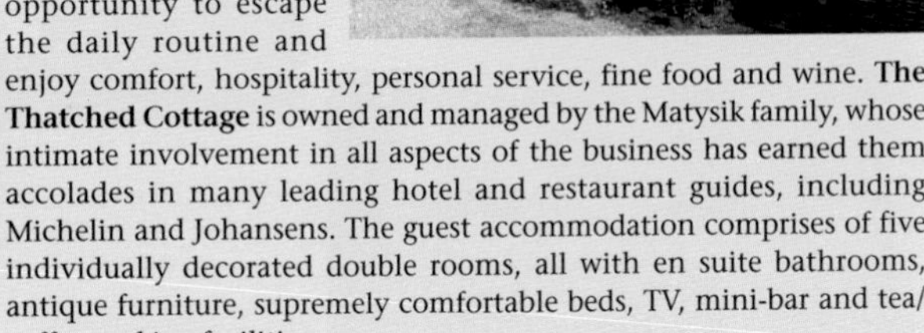

The 400-year-old Thatched Cottage is set in the attractive New Forest village of Brockenhurst. The hotel provides an ideal opportunity to escape the daily routine and enjoy comfort, hospitality, personal service, fine food and wine. **The Thatched Cottage** is owned and managed by the Matysik family, whose intimate involvement in all aspects of the business has earned them accolades in many leading hotel and restaurant guides, including Michelin and Johansens. The guest accommodation comprises of five individually decorated double rooms, all with en suite bathrooms, antique furniture, supremely comfortable beds, TV, mini-bar and tea/coffee-making facilities.

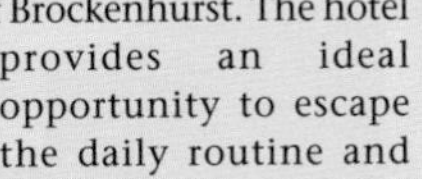

The small lounge is a cosy spot for a drink before or after dinner, which offers a wide choice of superb dishes on à la carte or set menus. The excellent food is accompanied by a list of fine wines. Other highlights at this outstanding place include speciality picnic hampers, international renowned cream teas and a delicatessen counter with an amazing array of farmhouse cheeses and other delicacies.

Cloud Cuckoo Land

6 St Thomas Street, Lymington, Hampshire
Tel: 01590 688840

Easily found next to Waitrose and by the town car park, **Cloud Cuckoo Land** is the place to find inspiration for your interior décor or gifts. The shop is owned and run by Claudia Jonkers, a welcoming lady with a larger than life personality and a flair for sourcing distinctive and unusual items.

There is a wonderful selection of lamps and shades, decorative candle sticks, beautiful wine glasses and decanters, fabulous fake fur throws, a vast collection of Limoges Pill Boxes, Pecksniffs Toiletries, Parks & Ken Turner Candles, Chelsea Textile Needlepoint and sumptious English Home velvet and cream damask cushions and throws. Wedding and baby gifts always available, not forgetting a brilliant range of hand-made cards. Finally, endless heaps of great jewellery spill out everywhere and in the run-up to Christmas, Claudia prides herself on being able to provide a one-stop shop and will often be found open late into the evening!

Style Angel

9a High Street, Lymington,
Hampshire SO41 9AA
Tel: 01590 689111

Located in a small close but signposted off the High Street, **Style Angel** is the creation of Ann Roper who worked for various designer shops before deciding to branch out on her own. It's well worth visiting because it's the only clothes shop of its kind in the town. Ann specialises in clothes and accessories for the 16- to 30-year-old group who will appreciate the style and quality of the wide range of clothing on sale here.

As well as a striking selection of dresses, blouses, t-shirts, trousers and so on, Style Angel also stocks a good choice of accessories such as handbags, purses and jewellery. Although the shop, with its elegant bow window, is quite small, everything is well-displayed and Ann makes the best use possible of the space available.

Truffles Of Lymington

97 High Street, Lymington, Hampshire SO41 9AP
Tel: 01590 673428
website: www.newforestonline.co.uk

In a 325-year-old building in the heart of the town, **Truffles of Lymington** is a paradise for chocolate lovers. Owned and run by Elisabeth Radcliffe, the shop is filled with the very finest chocolates and truffles from the Continent. The stock also includes sugar-free products, traditional English sweets of all kinds, the superb New Forest jams and chutneys, Moores famous Dorset biscuits and an impressive range of loose teas and coffees. The selection of greetings cards is unrivalled.

LYMINGTON

An ancient seaport and market town, Lymington was once a major manufacturer of salt, with hundreds of salt pans between the quay and the tip of the promontory at Hurst Castle. **St Barbe Museum**, in New Street, tells the story of the area between the New Forest and the Solent, with special reference to the salt industry (salt was made here beside the sea for hundreds of years), boatbuilding, smuggling and the area at war. There is also a changing exhibition of the work of artists both local and world-renowned – the gallery has in the past hosted works by artists as diverse as David Hockney and Goya. The broad High Street leading up from the quay is a hive of activity on Saturday, when the market established in the 13th century is held.

The Isle of Wight ferry runs from

Lymington Larder

7 St Thomas Street, Lymington, Hampshire SO41 9NA
Tel: 01590 676740
e-mail: eatlocal@uk2.net
website: www.lymington.larder.co.uk

St Thomas Street, where you will find many specialist shops full of appealing goodies, is home to **Lymington Larder.** "The Larder", as it is known to locals, is full of a fantastic selection of stock from mainly local suppliers and has a café at the rear which uses many of the same foods. In the Deli you will find cheeses's from all over the South of England, which Charles du Parc, the owner personally selects. He uses his knowledge and commitment to stock the deli with foods that are second to none. There are some continental specialities and Charles will spare no effort in obtaining items that are not stocked. You will also find bacon and air-dried ham from Denhay farm in Dorset, local free-range eggs and lots of olives and Mediterranean roasted vegetables. The Deli has a wide range of pies, pasties and home-made goodies from their own kitchen.

Charles and his staff are happy to make up hampers, while you wait and enjoy a coffee. You can even stay the night in their three cosy bed and breakfast rooms and wake up to a breakfast you won't forget in the café. Lymington Larder is open seven days a week from 8am (9am Sunday).

Jaeger

High Street, Lymington, Hampshire SO41 9AQ
Tel: 01590 678259 - 679913

Jaeger is known world-wide for its stylish clothing ranges for both men and women and you'll find all the latest fashions in their town centre store in Lymington. Drawing from their ancestry in the 19th century, Jaeger has sourced the finest natural fibres to create capsule wardrobes that epitomise the best in quality and craftsmanship. Classic and modern styling in coordinating tailoring from Couture Chic for Businesswear or simple and elegant pieces for Evening sophistication which then blend with sumptuous cashmere, silk/linen and cotton elements designed to offer their customers softer separates for the more relaxed lifestyle occasions. Finish the look with accessories such as scarves, gloves, handbags and jewellery designed exclusively for Jaeger. Definitely Collectors items! The staff in Jaeger Lymington is only too pleased to offer advice in how to create a new versatile wardrobe, or to add onto existing favourites as well as caring for your purchases. Enjoy the experience!

Claire Kitcher - Forest Images

Moulscombe Cottage, Church Lane, Sway, Hampshire SO41 6AD
Tel/Fax: 01590 683808
e-mail: enquiries@forestimages.co.uk
website: www.forestimages.co.uk

Artist **Claire Kitcher** lives in the village of Sway on the southern edge of the New Forest. In her garden studio she works in watercolours, pastels, graphite, and occasionally oils and is inspired by local scenes, wildlife and equestrian subjects. She exhibits annually at exhibitions in Sway and Burley and was recently featured in the Meridian TV series *The New Forest* which followed a horse portrait commission from start to finish. Claire's studio is also fully equipped for both printing and framing with the full range of her prints being available through her website www.ckart.co.uk.

The success of her prints inspired a new concept by her husband Steve – a new website "Images of the New Forest" – www.forestimages.co.uk. A number of popular local artists were invited to become involved in the project which has now grown into one of the biggest collections of prints available in the area, also taking in the coastal region, towns, villages and wildlife. High quality Giclée prints are produced to order only, keeping this an exclusive product. With a huge selection of frame mouldings available, customers can create a unique picture and have it delivered to their door. Print titles can be viewed easily, by artist or subject, and new artists and titles are regularly added. Prints are also available from local outlets – details on the website.

Walhampton, just outside Lymington, where a notable building is the Neale Obelisk, a memorial to Admiral Neale erected in 1840. At **Hordle**, just north of the A337 between Lymington and New Milton, **Apple Court** is a delightful garden with an important collection of hostas.

AROUND LYMINGTON

Boldre

2 miles N of Lymington, on the A337

"The village is here, there, and everywhere," wrote Arthur Mee in the 1930s, struggling to give some literary shape to an agglomeration of hamlets – Portmore, Pilley and Sandy Down, which together make up the parish of Boldre. Mee approved of the medieval church, with its squat square tower, standing isolated on a hill-top, and also paid due tribute to its 18th century rector, the Revd William Gilpin, whose books describing travels around Britain achieved cult status during his lifetime and even received a mention in Jane Austen's novel, *Sense and Sensibility.* Summing up his view of the village, Mee declared that "The quaint simplicity of Boldre is altogether charming". Some 70 years later, there's little reason to dispute his description.

In School Lane, **Spinners** is a charming, informal woodland garden with a national collection of trilliums.

Sway

3 miles N of Lymington off the A337

This rural village and the surrounding countryside were the setting for much of Captain Marryatt's *Children of the New Forest,* an exciting tale set in the time of the Civil War and written a year before Marryatt died in 1848. In Station Road,

WALK NUMBER 8

Keyhaven

Distance:	4.9 miles (7.8 kilometres)
Typical time:	165 mins
Height gain:	0 metres
Map:	Outdoor Leisure 29 & 22
Walk:	www.walkingworld.com ID:1327
Contributor:	Graham Hollier

Access Information:

Take the A337 New Milton/Lymington road and take the B3058 to Milford-On Sea. At junction turn left and left again, signed to Keyhaven (Hurst Castle) one mile. Continue along this road for just under a mile until you arrive at the Gun Inn on your right. Just past the Gun Inn, on your left, is the car park used for the start of the walk (toilets available).

Additional Information:

At the start or the end of the walk, an excursion can be made to Hurst Castle which you will see, together with a lighthouse at the end of a shingle spit. This castle, completed in 1544, was built by Henry VIII to defend the western approaches to Portsmouth. Charles 1st was imprisoned here in 1648 on his way to London and execution, from Carisbrooke Castle on the IoW. The castle was modernised during the Napoleonic Wars and modernised again in the 1860s when large armoured wings were built. It saw active service during WW2, being manned with searchlights and coastal guns to protect against invasion. It is well worth a visit and combined with the walk, makes an excellent day out.

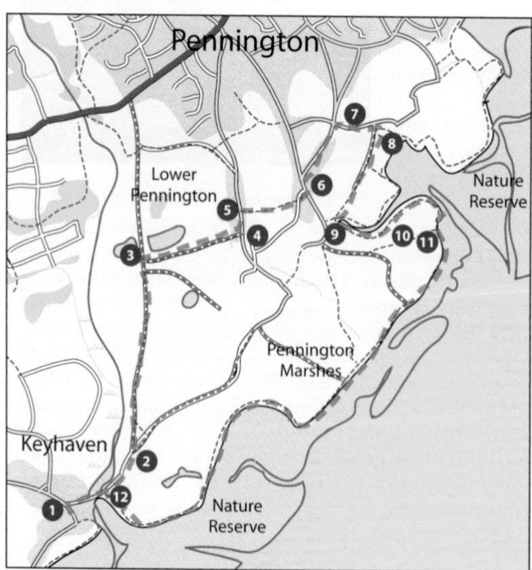

Description:

This is an easy-going short walk with plenty to see. If you are interested in birdlife, the sea, history, bracing air, then this walk is a must. Much of it is along the Solent Way. Pennington and Keyhaven Marshes were, from the middles ages until the mid-1800s, used for salt extraction. Before refrigeration, meat was salted as a preservative. One large consumer was the dockyard at Portsmouth, for naval ships. The name 'Keyhaven' is reputed to come from the Saxon word 'cy-haefenn' - roughly translated as meaning "the harbour where cows were shipped". If you have binoculars, do take them - they may be put to good use.

Features:

Lake/Loch, Pub, Toilets, Castle, Wildlife, Birds, Great Views, Butterflies, Mostly Flat, Ancient Monument

Walk Directions:

1 From car park, take a lane almost opposite the Gun Inn heading 080, keeping Keyhaven Harbour to the right. Continue on lane walking past a signpost, 'no vehicles beyond 200 yards ahead'. Walk on past a five-barred gate, small access to the left without having to climb over.

2 In about 100 yards is a large, rusty green gate. There is a broken stile to the left of this; go through on to pathway, Iley Lane. Continue on this

lane, keeping the quarry/landfill workings to your right. This can be a bit smelly but attracts a number of birds. The walk goes through this area for about a mile but it is well worth it for the coastal walk to which it leads. The Isle of Wight is visible on the right. Continue until you reach a council amenity tip which is 0.9 miles from the start of the walk.

3 Cross a stile in front of you, cross a roadway servicing the amenity tip and make for a track directly opposite, heading 082 and keeping the landfill workings to your left. After 1.1 miles of quarry/landfill workings you arrive at a six-barred metal gate. Go past the gate and walk on on a metalled roadway. Here you are surounded by pleasant fields and hedgerows. Continue to a green metal six-barred gate.

4 There is a small gap at the right of the gate; pass through on to a road and turn left.

5 In about 150 yards, there is a stile and a footpath leading through a hedge on your right (opposite some farm buildings on your left). Cross the stile, keeping the field edge on your right, until you arrive at a further stile. Cross this stile, making for some houses straight in front of you. About 150 yards before you reach the houses is a stile in the hedge on your right. Cross this stile and immediately turn left, making for a path which is situated to the left of the garden fence in front of you. Cross a stile and continue on to a further stile which is also crossed. Make for a metalled driveway , which shortly leads on to a road.

6 At the road, turn left, passing (or stopping!) at the Chequers public house on your left. Just past the Chequers the road forks. Take the right fork and walk along Platoff Road. This point is 1.5 miles from the start of the walk. In 300 yards is a bench on your right, with a road also leading off to your right. Take this road, signed 'Maiden Lane leading to Normandy Lane'.

7 In 180 yards, at a fork in the road turn right into Maiden Lane.

8 Follow road around to the right, through a yacht club yard and passing the clubhouse on the left. Continue on to join the Solent Way, where the walk now becomes an absolute delight. Continue on this path. Excellent views are available here of saltwater inlets, the IoW and an abundance of nature and wildlife. Take an unmade road to the left of the 'Salterns'. Path gives way to a delightful pathway, leading through a canopy of small trees and shrubs. Continue along this.

9 Continue on this track until you arrive at a clearing with a farm building on your left and a house on your right. Walk past the front of the house. Immediately past the house, turn left over a stile to walk along a pathway, keeping the waterway on the left. Keep on this pathway until you reach a stile; cross and make for a pair of lock gates which are easily visible from this point.

10 At the lock gates, continue along the sea defence wall (the sea is on the left all the way back to the start of the walk now) .

11 In the background is the sea with the Lymington/Yarmouth ferry just visible on the right. The foreground shows an area of marshland/old salt extraction workings, prevalent now to the end of the walk. Birdlife is prolific here throughout the year. The relatively rare little egret (a small version of a grey heron), white with black legs and yellow feet, is normally to be seen. Continue on the sea defence wall for a stunning two-mile walk; take your time, there is plenty to see.

12 If you have energy to spare, a trip can be taken to Hurst Castle. It can be reached by ferry which is just a short walk from the car park. Alternatively, you can walk/drive around to the start of the shingle spit and walk along this to the castle (hard work, walking on the shingle). Turn left when leaving the car park. If walking, go to sea wall and turn right until you reach the shingle spit. Alternatively if driving, turn left from the car park and follow the road for half a mile. Park on roadway in the spaces marked out, when you reach the shingle spit.

Artsway is a visual arts centre that was originally a coach house; the site contains a garden and a gallery. South of the village is a famous 220ft folly called **Peterson's Tower**. This curiosity was built by a retired judge, Andrew Peterson, in honour of his late wife and as proof of the efficacy of concrete. The tower was originally topped by a light that could be seen for many miles, but it was removed on the orders of Trinity House as a potential source of confusion to shipping. The judge's ashes were buried at the base of his folly but were later moved to be next to his wife in the churchyard at Sway.

Milford-on-Sea

5 miles SW of Lymington, on the B3058

This sizeable coastal village is most notable for its fine, remarkably well-preserved 13th century **Church of All Saints**; its grand views across the Solent to the Isle of Wight, and the odd-looking construction called **Hurst Castle.** At the centre of Hurst Castle is a squat fort built by Henry VIII to guard the Solent entrance against incursions by the French. Its tower is flanked by two long low wings added in the 1860s for gun emplacements, the square openings making them look rather like shopping arcades. The castle was used a garrison right up until World War II but is now in the care of English Heritage which has an on-site exhibition explaining its history.

Hurst Castle stands at the tip of a long gravel spit which stretches out across the Solent to within three quarters of a mile of the Isle of Wight coast. It can only be reached by a 1.5 mile walk along the shingle beach or, in the summer months, by ferries operating from Keyhaven Quay, one mile east of Milford-on-Sea. The excursion makes a pleasant day or half-day trip since in addition to the castle itself there's safe bathing north of the lighthouse, good fishing off the southern tip of the spit, and spectacular views of The Needles as well as of huge ships making their way up The Solent.

New Milton

4 miles W of Lymington on the A337

If you were allowed to see only one visitor attraction in New Milton, you would have a difficult choice. One option is the town's splendid **Water Tower** of 1900. Late-Victorian providers of water services seem to have enjoyed pretending that their storage towers and sewage treatment plants were really castles of the Middle Ages. They built these mock-medieval structures all around the country, but the one at New Milton is particularly striking. Three storeys high, with a castellated parapet, the octagonal building has tall, narrow windows.

Devotees of vintage motorcycles will make for a very different attraction. The **Sammy Miller Museum**, to the west of the town, is widely regarded as one of the best motorcycle museums in the world. Sammy Miller is a legend in his own lifetime, still winning competitions almost half a century after his first racing victory. More than 300 rare and exotic motorcycles are on display here. Also within the museum complex are a craft shop, tea rooms and a children's play area.

If you are more interested in the arts, you'll be pleased to hear about **Forest Arts** in New Milton. Music of all kinds is on offer, from jazz, salsa and blues, to traditional and classical matinée concerts. Performances are conveniently timed so that you can arrive after picking up the kids from school. Other daytime events include slide talks by experts on a wide range of topics. Forest Arts also hosts some of the best contemporary dance companies around, ensembles who have performed at The Place in London and indeed all over the world. And if you enjoy the buzz and excitement of seeing new, vibrant theatre, the type of theatre which is on offer at the Edinburgh Fringe Festival for example, Forest Arts provides that as well.

RINGWOOD

Wednesday morning is a good time to visit Ringwood since that is when its market square is filled with a notable variety of colourful stalls. The town has expanded greatly in recent years but its centre still boasts a large number of elegant Georgian houses, both large and small. **Ringwood Meeting House**, built in 1727 and now a museum, is an outstanding example of an early Nonconformist chapel, complete with the original, rather austere, fittings. **Monmouth House** is of about the same period and stands on the site of an earlier house in which the luckless Duke of Monmouth was confined after his unsuccessful uprising against James II. The duke had been discovered hiding in a ditch just outside the town and despite his abject pleas to the king to spare his life he was beheaded at Tower Hill a few days later.

Five miles west of the town stretch the great expanses of Ringwood Forest, which includes the **Moors Valley Country Park**. At the heart of the park stands an 18th century timber barn which is home to the Visitor Centre, where you will find a restaurant, a coffee shop, a gift shop and an exhibition area. A variety of other attractions including children's play areas, walks and cycle

Face the Music

7 The Mall, Ringwood Road, Burley, Hampshire BH24 4BS
Tel/Fax: 01425 403309
website: www.facethemusic-newforest.co.uk

Set in a delightful little square, **Face the Music** is a unique establishment dedicated to musical giftware of all kinds. Amanda Elliott who has created this fascinating shop has brought together thousands of different items all of which have some kind of musical theme. How about ear-rings with a ballerina *au pointe*? Or a bottle stopper with a tiny saxophone resting on the cork? Or, amongst a huge range of cuff-links, a pair in the shape of an acoustic guitar? Then there are the brooches, bracelets, pin badges and pendants; key-rings, clocks and socks; small-scale models of musical instruments; T-shirts; umbrellas and photo frames. For the kitchen, coasters and chopping boards; for the study, pens and stationery, cards with a humorous musical edge, gift wraps displaying musical scores.

Books on offer include *Getting a Handel on Messiah, The Musicians Joke Book* and *I Wanna be Sedated,* a study of pop music during the '70s. Children are also well-catered for: small instruments such as castanets, drums and harmonicas; music Snap cards and carrier bags with ballet position designs. Face the Music is a wonderful place to browse and a lifesaver if you have musical friends you struggle to find gifts for.

Holmans

Bisterne Close, Burley, Ringwood, Hampshire BH24 4AZ
Tel/Fax: 01425 402307

Standing on the edge of the picturesque village of Burley and enjoying wonderful open views across the New Forest, **Holmans** is a charming country house standing in four acres of its own grounds. This peaceful retreat is the home of Robin and Mary Ford, a welcoming and friendly couple who take very good care of their bed & breakfast guests. They have three attractively furnished and decorated guest bedrooms, (two doubles; one twin), all of which have en suite facilities.

The surrounding area is perfect for riding or carriage driving and guests are welcome to bring their own horses – Holmans has stabling for up to four horses or ponies. The house is ideally located for exploring the New Forest but it's also just a 15 minute drive to the nearest beach. There's a golf course nearby and the local pub is within easy walking distance. The manifold attractions of Bournemouth and Poole are both a short drive away, and if you feel like visiting the Isle of Wight, there's a regular ferry from Lymington.

routes, and an 18-hole golf course can also be found here. Particularly popular are the Tree Top Trail which offers the opportunity to walk on a wooden walkway through the tops of the trees, and the Play Trail with its wooden structures, including 'Giant Ants' Nest', 'Snakes and Ladders' and 'Spiders Web'.Another popular attractions here is the **Moors Valley Railway**, a delightful narrow gauge steam railway with rails just 7¼ inches apart. The railway has 11 locomotives, all in different liveries, and 33 passenger vehicles. The signal box at Kingsmere, the main station, was purpose-built but all the equipment inside comes from old redundant signal boxes – the main signal lever frame for example came from the Becton Gas Works in East London. At Kingsmere Station, in addition to the Ticket Office and the Engine and Carriage Sheds, there's also a Railway Shop, Buffet and Model Railway Shop.

AROUND RINGWOOD

Burley

4 miles SE of Ringwood, on minor road off the A31

At Burley, it's very clear that you are in the heart of the New Forest, with woodland running right through the village. A pleasant way to experience the peacefulness of the surrounding forest is to take a trip with **Burley Wagonette Rides** which run from the centre of the village. Rides in the open wagons last from 20 minutes to 1½ hours and are available from Easter to October. The village is also home to **New Forest Cider** where farmhouse cider is still made the old-fashioned way from local orchard

Bristow & Garland

45-47 Salisbury Street, Fordingbridge,
Hants, SP6 1AB
Tel: 01425 655520
website: www.bristowandgarland.co.uk

Bristow & Garland is a long-established business and their shop is to be found in an old slate-hung Grade II listed building. The shop has two very distinct sides. David Bristow is an experienced bookseller and visitors will find an eclectic selection of second-hand and antiquarian books to browse through. David specialises in autographs, manuscript diaries and historical documents all of which can be viewed and purchased on the website or by appointment at the premises.

David's wife Victoria, stocks an ever-changing selection of modern silver and gem-set jewellery together with other slightly more unusual contemporary pieces. Visitors will also find greeting cards, including hand-made, suitable for all occasions together with a small range of gifts which include items by English craftspeople.

Alderholt Mill

Sandleheath Road, Alderholt, Hampshire SP6 1PU
Tel: 01425 653130 Fax: 01425 652868
e-mail: alderholt-mill@zetnet.co.uk
website: www.alderholtmill.co.uk

Located in a delightfully pastoral setting on the Hampshire-Dorset borders, **Alderholt Mill** is one of the few working mills in the county still producing flour. Owners Sandra and Richard Harte use the freshly milled flour to make the bread that accompanies the full traditional English or Continental breakfast served to their bed & breakfast guests. They have four guest bedrooms (three doubles; one twin) all en suite with colour TV, radio alarm clock and hospitality tray. Guests have the use of a residents' lounge with a log burning stove, and a large garden.

The Hartes are also happy to provide evening meals – "bring your own tipple" – and on warm summer nights offer barbecues by the river. The Mill also has three self-catering flats, sleeping from two to six guests. These are all attractively furnished and decorated, comprehensively equipped and with garden access. The Mill is ideally located for exploring the New Forest and for visiting Salisbury Cathedral, Bournemouth, the Beaulieu Motor Museum, Broadlands, Poole Quay and the Isle of Wight. An additional attraction at the Mill for anglers is private fishing on the stretch of water surrounding the mill and there are also carp and trout lakes within a mile.

apples and cider fruit. Visitors can taste and buy draught cider from barrels stored in the former cowshed. The centre is open most times throughout the year although ideally you should time your visit to co-incide with pressing time when the grand old cider press is in operation.

Fordingbridge

7 miles N of Ringwood, on the A338

The painter Augustus John (1878-1961) loved Fordingbridge, a pleasant riverside town with a graceful medieval seven-arched bridge spanning the River Avon. He spent much of the last thirty years of his life at Fryern Court, a rather austere Georgian house just north of the town (not open to the public, but visible from the road). Scandalous stories of the Bohemian life-style he indulged in there circulated around the town but didn't deter the townspeople from erecting a strikingly vigorous statue to his memory in a park near the bridge.

Branksome China Works is well worth a visit. Visitors can see how the firm, established in 1945, makes its fine porcelain tableware and famous animal studies.

On the edge of the town, there's a special treat for anyone who savours daft public notices. As a prime example of useless information, it would be hard to beat the trim little 18th century milepost which informs the traveller: "Fordingbridge: 0".

Two miles west of Fordingbridge off the B3078 - follow the signposts - is **Alderholt Mill** (see panel opposite), a restored working water-powered corn mill standing on Ashford Water, a tributary of the Hampshire Avon. The site includes an arts and crafts shop and a place for the sale of refreshments and baking from the mill's own flour.

Breamore

3 miles N of Fordingbridge on the A338

Breamore is a lovely and largely unspoilt 17th century village with a very interesting little church with Saxon windows and other artefacts. Most notable, in the south porch, is a Saxon rood, or crucifixion scene. **Breamore House**, set above the village overlooking the Avon Valley, was built in 1583 and contains some fine paintings, including works of the 17th and 18th century Dutch School and a unique set of 14 Mexican ethnological paintings; superb period furniture in oak, walnut and mahogany; a very rare James I carpet and many other items of historical and

Thatched Cottage, Rockbourne

and a children's adventure play area. The Museum's Millennium project was the restoration of an extremely rare Bavarian four-train turret clock of the 16th century. On **Breamore Down** is one of those oddities whose origins and purpose remain something of a mystery: this is a mizmaze, a circular maze cut in the turf down as far as the chalk. Further north can be seen part of Grim's Ditch, built in late-Roman times as a defence against the Saxons.

family interest. The house has been the home of the Hulse family for well over 250 years, having been purchased in the early 18th century by Sir Edward Hulse, Physician in Ordinary at the Courts of Queen Anne, George I and George II. In the grounds of the house, the **Countryside Museum** is a reconstructed Tudor village with a wealth of rural implements and machinery, replicas of a farm worker's cottage, smithy, dairy, brewery, saddler's shop, cobbler's shop, general store, laundry and school. Amenities for visitors include a tea shop

Rockbourne

3 miles NW of Fordingbridge off the B3078

One of the prettiest villages in the region, Rockbourne lies by a gentle stream at the bottom of a valley. An attraction that brings in visitors by the thousand is **Rockbourne Roman Villa** (see panel below), the largest of its kind in the region. It was discovered in 1942 when oyster shells and tiles were found

Rockbourne Roman Villa

Rockbourne, Fordingbridge, Hampshire SP3 3PG
Tel: 01725 518541
website: www.hants.gov.uk/museum/rockbourne

Rockbourne Roman Villa, the largest of its kind in the region, was discovered in 1942 when oyster shells and tiles were found by a farmer in the course of digging out a ferret. A local chartered surveyor and noted antiquarian, the late AT Morley Hewitt, recognised the significance of the finds and devoted 30 years of his life to the villa. Excavations of the site, which is set in idyllic countryside, have revealed superb mosaics, part of the amazing underfloor heating system and the outline of the great villa's 40 rooms. Many of the hundreds of objects unearthed are on display in the site's museum, and souvenirs are for sale in the well-stocked museum shop.

Marsh Barn

Rockbourne, nr Fordingbridge,
Hampshire SP6 3NF
Tel: 01752 518768 Fax: 01752 518380

A superb 200-year-old mellow brick barn in a picture-postcard Hampshire village offers a particularly peaceful and civilised base for Bed & Breakfast guests. Tony and Lindy Ball's **Marsh Barn** has three letting bedrooms – a double room with en suite shower a twin room with private bath and, across the courtyard, a studio double with shower. All are beautifully appointed, with period furnishings and plenty of books for browsing, and throughout the barn seagrass matting, Moroccan rugs and antiques add to the unique atmosphere. A terrace overlooks the glorious garden, where one of the features is a pergola covered in wisteria, solanum, honeysuckle and roses.

The area around Marsh Barn offers splendid opportunities for walking, cycling, riding and fishing in and around the New Forest. Many of the region's best scenic, historic and sporting attractions, including Horse Racing at Salisbury, are also close at hand; closest of all is the renowned Rockbourne Roman Villa and an excellent pub.

by a farmer as he was digging out a ferret. Excavations of the site, which is set in idyllic surroundings, have revealed superb mosaics, part of the amazing underfloor heating system and the outline of the great villa's 40 rooms. Many of the hundreds of objects unearthed are on display in the site's museum and souvenirs are on sale in the well-stocked museum shop.

A mile or so beyond the Roman Villa, looking out on to the downs, is the little village of **Whitsbury**, a major centre for the breeding and training of racehorses.

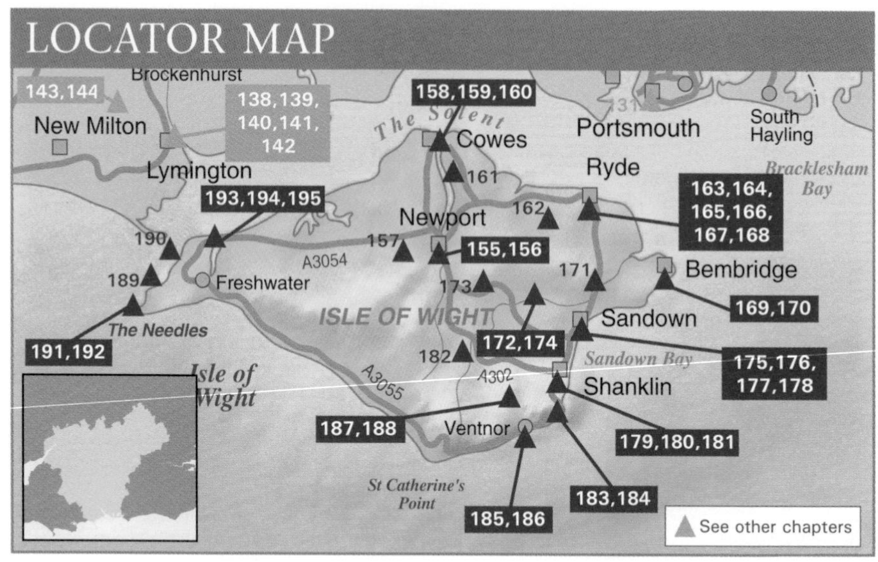

LOCATOR MAP

143,144	
New Milton	Brockenhurst
Lymington	138,139, 140,141, 142

Cowes — 158,159,160

Portsmouth

South Hayling

Ryde

Bracklesham Bay

163,164, 165,166, 167,168

Newport

Lymington — 193,194,195

190

189

Freshwater — A3054

162

Newport — 155,156

171

Bembridge

Sandown

169,170

The Needles

191,192

Isle of Wight

172,174

182

Sandown Bay

175,176, 177,178

Shanklin

187,188 — Ventnor

179,180,181

St Catherine's Point

185,186 — 183,184

▲ See other chapters

ISLE OF WIGHT

The Solent

173

157

161

A3055

A302

ADVERTISERS AND PLACES OF INTEREST

THE ISLE OF WIGHT 4

The Isle of Wight has adopted a motto which declares: "All this beauty is of God". It echoes the poet John Keats "A thing of beauty is a joy for ever", the first line of his poem *Endymion* which he wrote while staying on the island in the hope that its crisp country air would improve his health.

The Needles

Other distinguished visitors have described Wight as "The Garden Isle", and "England's Madeira" but it was quite late in the day before the island became popular as a resort. This was partly because for centuries, right up until the 1600s, the island was a first port of call for pestiferous French raiders who made the islanders' lives a misery with their constant incursions. These attacks ceased following the Napoleonic wars but the turning point came in the 1840s when Queen Victoria and Prince Albert bought an estate near East Cowes. They demolished the existing house and Albert designed and built an Italianate mansion he named Osborne House. A few years later, the Poet Laureate, Alfred, Lord Tennyson, bought Farringford on the eastern side of the island. Socially, the Isle of Wight had arrived.

Steam Engine, Havenstreet

Most of the island's 125,000 residents, (the mainland town of Peterborough outnumbers all of them by about 10,000), live in the northeast quadrant of the island, with its main resort towns of Sandown and Shanklin strung along the east coast. The rest of Wight is wonderfully peaceful with a quiet, unassertive charm all of its own.

We begin our tour of the island at its capital, Newport, and then make a clockwise circuit of the island starting at Cowes and ending up at Yarmouth.

NEWPORT

Set around the River Medina, Newport has a history going back to Roman times. Excavations in 1926 uncovered the well-preserved remains of a **Roman Villa**, a 3rd century farmhouse in which one side of the building was given over entirely to baths. Visitors can follow the bather's progress through changing room, cold room, warm and hot rooms with underfloor heating systems, and integral cold and hot plunge baths. A Roman style garden has been re-created in the grounds and provides an interesting insight into the wealth of new plants the Romans introduced into Britain.

Newport received its first charter back in 1190 but the growth of the small town received a severe setback in 1377 when it was completely burnt to the ground by the French. Recovery was slow and it wasn't until the 17th century that Newport really prospered again. Indirectly, the new prosperity was also due to the French since the island was heavily garrisoned during the Anglo-French wars of that period. Supplying the troops with provisions and goods brought great wealth to the town.

Some striking buildings have survived, amongst them **God's Providence House**, built in 1701 and now a tea room; John Nash's elegant **Town Hall** of 1816 which is now occupied by the Museum of Island History, a charming Tudor **Old Grammar School**, and the parish **Church of St Thomas** whose foundation stone was laid in 1854 by Queen Victoria's consort, Prince Albert. The church contains the tomb of the tragic Princess Elizabeth, daughter of Charles I, who died of a fever at the age of 14 while a prisoner at nearby Carisbrooke Castle.

There's also an 18th century brewer's

Miniature World

1 Grays Walk, Newport, Isle of Wight
Tel: 01983 822243
e-mail: web@miniature-world.co.uk
website: www.miniature-world.co.uk

A specialist shop for the discerning miniaturist, **Miniature World** stocks an extensive range of houses, cottages, shops, pubs, furniture and accessories in a scale of either 1:12 or 1:24. The shop was originally designed to enable customers to buy everything they needed for their miniature house in one place. When Dianne Nurse bought the business in April 2004 she began expanding the range of products on offer. Her future plans include demonstrations on all aspects of miniature house decoration.

The English-made dolls' houses are supplied either for self assembly or they can be built and decorated to customers' specifications. To decorate exteriors Dianne stocks a range of real brick and slate products – or you could even opt for realistic thatch. Wallpapers, carpets, wood flooring and lighting items are all available, along with furniture, conservatories, garden furniture and other garden accessories. For those who enjoy needlework, there are carpet, rug and embroidery kits available in wool or silk.

warehouse near the harbour which now houses the **Quay Arts Centre**, incorporating a theatre, two galleries, a craft shop, café and bar; another old warehouse is home to the **Classic Boat Museum**. Among the highlights here are a 1910 river launch and *Lady Penelope*, a fabulous speedboat once owned by the 1950s socialite Lady Docker. Other exhibits include beautifully restored sailing and power boats, along with engines, equipment and memorabilia.

Next door to the Boat Museum is the **Isle of Wight Bus Museum** which displays an impressive array of island buses and coaches and a former Ryde Pier tram. The buses include a 1920s Daimler and a Bristol Lodekka that completed a successful trip to Nepal.

Church Litten Park, on the site of an old churchyard whose Tudor gateway still remains, is a peaceful spot and

Carisbrooke Castle

Carisbrooke, Isle of Wight
Tel: 01983 522107

Dating from Saxon times, **Carisbrooke** is the Isle of Wight's foremost castle. Once prison to Charles I and home to Princess Beatrice, the castle is also famous for the donkeys that work in the well house. Throughout the summer costumed guides and colourful events bring the castle alive and its remarkable history is told in the museum and castle exhibitions. Open daily except 24-26 December and 1 January.

interesting for its memorial to Valentine Gray, a nine-year-old chimney sweep whose death in 1822 as a result of ill-usage by his master caused a national outcry.

To the northwest of Newport, **Parkhurst Forest** offers miles of woodland walks, while over to the northeast, at Wootton, **Butterfly World and Fountain World** is home to hundreds of exotic butterflies flying free inside a beautifully landscaped indoor garden with ponds, streams, fountains and waterfalls. Other attractions include an Italian water garden, a Japanese water garden with Koi Carp, a restaurant, garden centre and shop.

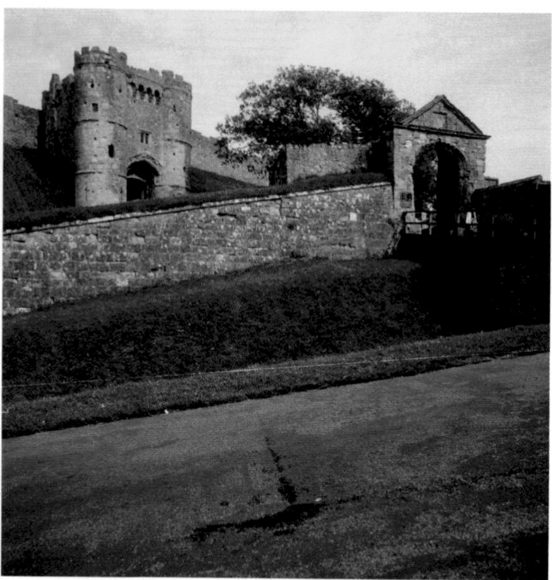

Carisbrooke Castle

Carisbrooke

1 mile SW of Newport, on the B3323/B3401

Another quote from John Keats: "I do not think I shall ever see a ruin to surpass **Carisbrooke Castle.**" The castle (see panel on page 227) is set dramatically on a sweeping ridge and it's quite a steep climb up from the picturesque village to the massive gatehouse. This was built in 1598 but the oldest parts of the castle date back to Norman times, most notably the mighty keep which, apart from Windsor Castle, is the most perfect specimen of Norman architecture in Britain. Archaeologists believe that the castle stands on the site a Roman fort built some thousand years earlier.

During the season costumed guides, or 'storytellers' as English Heritage prefers to call them, conduct visitors around the noble ruins. The most poignant of their stories concern Charles I and his youngest daughter, Elizabeth. Charles was imprisoned here in the months before his trial and the guides will point out the mullioned window through which he unsuccessfully attempted to escape. After the King's execution, Cromwell's Council of State ordered that his daughter Elizabeth, "for her own safety", should also be incarcerated at Carisbrooke. The 14-year-old implored them not to send her to her father's former prison, but they were adamant. Elizabeth was a sickly child and less than a week after her arrival at the Castle she "was stricken by fever and passed away, a broken-hearted child of fourteen". The story touched the heart of Queen Victoria who set up a monument in St Thomas' Church in Newport where the Princess was buried. The effigy, in pure white Carrara marble, bears an inscription stating that it had been erected "as a token of respect for her virtues, and of sympathy for her misfortunes by Victoria R 1856".

More cheerful aspects of a visit to the Castle include the Donkey Centre. Donkeys walking a treadmill were once used to turn the huge 16th century wheel in the wellhouse to draw water from a well 161ft deep. A light at the bottom of the well gives some idea of its depth. Before donkeys were trained to raise the water, the task was performed by prisoners and nowadays visitors are invited to have a go at walking the treadmill themselves.

Also within the Castle grounds are a Coach House Exhibition and Victorian Island Exhibition, the Isle of Wight Museum and a tea room.

Cowes

5 miles N of Newport, on the A3020

Cowes' origins as the most famous yachting resort in the world go back to the early 1800s. It was then a rather shabby port whose main business was shipbuilding. In 1811, the Duke of Gloucester came to stay and as part of the rather limited entertainment on offer watched sailing matches between local fishermen. The duke's patronage led to amateur gentlemen running their own race and founding a club. The Prince Regent joined in 1817 and on his accession as George IV it was first re-christened the Royal Yacht Club, and then the Royal Yacht Squadron with its headquarters in one of Henry VIII's castles. Nowadays, **Cowes Week** has become the premier yachting event of the year and also a fixture in the aristocratic social calendar.

Shipbuilding was for centuries the main industry of East Cowes, spanning ships for the Royal Navy, lifeboats, flying boats and seaplanes. Many of the seaplanes took part in the Schneider Trophy races, which brought great excitement to the Solent in the inter-war

Kathy's

13 York Avenue, East Cowes,
Isle of Wight PO32 6QY
Tel: 01983 297562
e-mail: ebbatson@messages.co.uk
website: www.kathysgiftshop.co.uk

Easily found in the middle of East Cowes, **Kathy's** is a delightful shop specialising in contemporary giftware and craftware. Behind the cheerful red-and-white double frontage adorned with flower troughs and hanging baskets, the open-plan interior is stocked with a wide variety of goods all given the seal of approval by long-standing owner Gail Ebbatson. She chooses the goods from near and far, as typified by glass from nearby Alum Bay, plates and pottery souvenirs of the Island and ceramic tiles from Canada.

There are classic canes and walking sticks, umbrellas, silver-plated photo frames, all sorts of animals in china and glass (Cats & Dogs, Broadway Birds, Cow Parade, Collage Safari Collection), Jellycat cuddly toys, crystal stemmed glassware, barometers and thermometers, pewter bath and basin plugs, herb and spice racks, fabric flowers and bonsai grow kits, and cards for all occasions. Kathy's is adjacent to the Red Funnel Ferries terminal, so visitors can look in twice – once when arriving and again just before they leave the Island!

years. Sir Donald Campbell's *Bluebird* was built here, and the hovercraft had its origins in what is now the home of Westland Aerospace. Westland's factory doors were painted with a giant Union Jack to mark the Queen's Jubilee in 1977 – a piece of patriotic paintwork that has been retained by popular demand. Two museums in Cowes have a nautical theme. The **Sir Max Aitken Museum** in an old sailmaker's loft in West Cowes High Street houses Sir Max's remarkable collection of nautical paintings, instruments and artefacts, while the **Cowes Maritime Museum** charts the island's maritime history and has a collection of racing yachts that includes the Uffa Fox pair *Avenger* and *Coweslip*. (Uffa Fox, perhaps the best known yachtsman of his day, is buried in the Church of St Mildred at Whippingham.) On the Parade, near the Royal Yacht

Phillips Fine Foods

339 Newport Road, Cowes, Isle of Wight PO31 8PG
Tel: 01983 282200 e-mail: enquiries@phillipsfinefoods.co.uk
Fax: 01983 281768 website: www.phillipsfinefoods.co.uk

Those who appreciate quality fish and seafood will be delighted with **Phillips Fine Foods** which recently expanded into bigger and better premises at Cowes. This is very much a family business with owners Jeff and Carole Dove supported by their daughters Jackie and Michelle. Their shop stocks an enormous choice of products – there are 14 different kinds of prawn, for example – and it has its own smoke room in which a wide variety of fish is cured over oak sawdust. Phillips also runs a mobile shop that makes home deliveries, and a mail order service with normal delivery by return of post.

The Red Duster Restaurant

High Street, West Cowes, Isle of Wight PO31 7RS
Tel: 01983 290311 Fax: 01983 296280
website: www.thereddusters-cowes.co.uk

One of the top restaurants on the Island, the **Red Duster** stands in a pedestrian precinct in the centre of West Cowes. In a 16th century building, with seats for about 70, it has two dining areas, one cheerfully contemporary, the other more traditional. Sailing pictures and prints reinforce the maritime connection (red duster is another name for the naval flag the red ensign), making an atmospheric setting for enjoying the top-notch cooking of owner John Bodley.

A chef with long international experience and a teacher and mentor of young chefs, John offers an excellent choice of dishes on à la carte and set-price menus, with daily specials extending the options even wider. Using local ingredients as much as possible, he takes his inspiration from near and far, with typical dishes including leek, gruyere and poppy seed tart; Malaysian-style poached salmon; Beaminster rack of lamb and chicken breast with tarragon and a truffle-oil mash. And with desserts like banana custard pancakes or gran's plum pudding, very few diners can resist the third course! Fine food deserves fine wine, and the Red Duster has a well-chosen international list.

Cowes Week

Squadron, the **Isle of Wight Model Railways Exhibition** has for almost 20 years been one of the most admired attractions of its kind in the country. The displays include models spanning the whole history of railways, from the *Rocket* to *Eurostar*. Some are set in a British landscape, others against a stunning Rocky Mountains backdrop, and there is even a low-level layout which small children can operate and see without being lifted.

Across the River Medina, linked by a chain ferry, East Cowes is most famous for **Osborne House**, a clean-cut, Italianate mansion designed and built by Prince Albert in 1846. Queen Victoria loved "dear beautiful Osborne" and so did her young children. They had their very own house in its grounds, a full-size Swiss Cottage, where they played at house-keeping, cooking meals for their parents, and tending its vegetable gardens using scaled-down gardening tools. In the main house itself, visitors can wander through both the State and private apartments which are crammed with paintings, furniture, ornaments, statuary and the random bric-à-brac that provided such an essential element in the decor of any upper-class Victorian home. Osborne House possessed a special place in the queen's affections. It had been built by the husband she adored

Barton Manor

Whippingham, East Cowes, Isle of Wight PO32 6LB
Tel: 01983 528989 Fax: 01983 528671

The estate of Barton is first mentioned in the Doomsday Book of 1086, and later an Augustinian oratory was founded. That fell into gradual decline, and from the 15th to the 19th centuries the estate was run as a farm. When Queen Victoria and Prince Albert bought Osborne House, **Barton Manor** and its estate became their home farm and the Prince has a new set of farm buildings erected. In 1902, after the Queen's death, King Edward VII made a gift of Osborne to the nation and kept Barton Manor for himself. It was eventually sold by the Crown in 1922 and has been in private hands ever since.

Today the property is owned by the film and stage entrepreneur Robert Stigwood, who is also a keen conservationist. The gardens are a real delight, with many treasures and surprises including the rhododendron walk, the splendid rose maze, a water garden, a secret garden and the national collections of Watsonia and red hot pokers. The estate is open on special days in the year in aid of the local Earl Mountbatten Hospice.

with an almost adolescent infatuation: together they had spent many happy family days here. After Albert's premature death from typhoid in 1861, she often returned to Osborne. Her staff had instructions to lay out the Prince's clothes in his dressing-room each night, and the queen herself retired to bed with his nightshirt clasped in her arms. In 1901 she returned to Osborne for the last time, dying here in her 83rd year, her death co-incidentally signalling the beginning of the slow decline of the British Empire over which she had presided as Queen-Empress.

Osborne House and its grounds featured prominently in the film *Mrs Brown* (2001) starring Judi Dench and Billy Connolly, which explored the controversial relationship between the queen and her Scottish ghillie, John Brown.

Whippingham

3 miles S of Cowes on the A3021

Queen Victoria also acquired **Barton Manor** (see panel on page 231) at nearby Whippingham, a peaceful retreat whose grounds are occasionally open to the public. Prince Albert had a hand in the design of the gardens and of the ornate Church of St Mildred, where the contractor and co-designer was AJ Humbert, who was also responsible for Sandringham. The royal family regularly worshipped at St Mildred's, which is predictably full of royal memorials, including a monument to Victoria's son-in-law Prince Henry of Battenberg, who succumbed to malaria in Africa at the age of 38. Alfred Gilbert's wonderful art nouveau screen in the chancel arcade is a unique work of art, and other notable pieces are a bronze angel and the font, both of them designed by Princess Louise, a daughter of the Queen, a memorial to Albert and a chair used by the Queen.

Wootton Creek

3 miles W of Ryde, off the A3054

Wootton is notable for its ancient bridge and mill-pond, and as the western terminus of the Isle of Wight Steam Railway, with an old wooden booking office and signal box moved from elsewhere on the island. It is also the home of **Butterfly World & Fountain World**. This complex comprises a sub-tropical indoor garden with hundreds of exotic butterflies flying free; a colourful Italian garden with computer-controlled fountains; a Japanese garden with Oriental buildings and a koi carp lake; and a five-acre garden centre.

Fishbourne

2 miles W of Ryde on the A3054

Fishbourne is the port where the car ferry from the mainland docks. Nearby **Quarr Abbey** is a handsome redbrick Benedictine monastery built around 1910 near the ruins of a 12th century Cistercian Abbey. The old abbey, founded by a certain Baldwin de Redvers, enjoyed 400 years of prestige and influence, owning much of the land and many of the grand houses, before its destruction in 1536.

The stone for the original Quarr Abbey at Fishbourne came from the quarries at nearby Binstead, where a major family draw is **Brickfields Horse Country**, a centre that is home to more than 100 animals, from magnificent shire horses to miniature ponies, farm animals and pets. Open daily throughout the year, the numerous attractions include racing pigs (the Lester Piglet Derby!), wagon rides, a parade of Cowboys and Indians, a blacksmith's forge and museums focusing on carriages, tractors and many aspects of farm life. The shire horses are the particular pride and joy of the centre's owner Phil Legge, whose

Montgomery and Prince won him top honours in an All-England ploughing match.

Havenstreet

3 miles SW of Ryde off the A3054

Headquarters and nerve centre of the **Isle of Wight Steam Railway,** Havenstreet has a small workshop and museum, gift shop and refreshment room. The locomotives working the line date back as far as 1876 and include a tiny A1 class engine acquired from the London, Brighton & South Coast Railway in 1913, and a W14, named *Calbourne*, which was built in 1891 and came to the island in 1925. The carriages and goods wagons are of a similar vintage.

The road south from Cowes to Newport (A3020) passes by the edge of **Parkwood Forest**, 1,000 acres of ancient royal hunting forest now managed by the Forestry Commission. From the car park and picnic area a waymarked trail leads through the forest, which is one of the few remaining 'safe houses' for the red squirrel.

Ryde

9 miles NE of Newport, on the A3054

Ryde is the largest town on the island and its attractions include a huge expanse of sandy beach and a half-mile long pier, one of the first to be built in Britain. Passenger ferries from Portsmouth dock here, the hovercraft service settles nearby, and the car ferry from the mainland disgorges its cargo a couple of miles to the west. The town is essentially Victorian, a popular resort in those days for affluent middle-class families. Then, as now, visitors enjoyed strolling along the elegant Esplanade with its sea views across Spithead Sound to Portsmouth.

Isle of Wight Steam Railway

The Railway Station, Havenstreet, Isle of Wight PO33 4DS
Tel: 01983 882204 e-mail: jimloe@iwsr.fsnet.co.uk
Fax: 01983 884515 website: www.iwsteamrailway.co.uk

The Isle of Wight once boasted 54 miles of railway, most of which was closed during the 1950s and 1960s. However, their atmosphere has been perfectly preserved by the largely volunteer run Isle of Wight Steam Railway. Carriages and locomotives, many dating back to Victorian times and possibly used by Queen Victoria herself, have been painstakingly restored to pristine condition, and are in almost daily use. This railway is a living, breathing museum - a real journey back in time. Trains and stations are clean and tidy, with flowers adding a blaze of colour during the season.

The railway is five miles in length, and extends from Wootton, via Havenstreet and Ashey to Smallbrook Junction. This is the interchange point with Island Line's electric trains that run from Shanklin to Ryde (for the Wightlink high-speed catamaran service to Portsmouth Harbour). The steam railway makes an ideal day trip from the mainland - the journey from Portsmouth Harbour to Smallbrook Junction only takes about 30 minutes. Through return tickets, which include the Wightlink Catamaran, Island Line Train, and unlimited travel on the steam railway are readily available from Wightlink at Portsmouth Harbour. Havenstreet is the railway's main station, with a cafeteria, railway shop, children's play area, woodland walk and museum. Numerous special events are held during the summer months. Trains operate selected days March to October (daily late May to mid September).

Ma Petite France Ltd

2 Pondwell Close, Ryde, Isle of Wight PO33 1QD
Tel/Fax: 01983 613999
e-mail: info@mapetitefrance.com
website: www.mapetitefrance.com

If you are looking for something that reminds you of your last holiday in France, or you ran out of space when packing the car and couldn't bring back all the lovely things you wanted – then welcome to **Ma Petite France Ltd.** Owned and run by Ron Boynton and his French-born wife Val, the company offers an enticing range of products from Provençal fabrics to traditional French linen with a selection of table cloths, table mats, napkins, linen bags and cushions. Dress your table with the fine French crockery, Provençal pottery and scented candles for a romantic evening.

Embellish your walls with some of the beautiful prints, landscapes, painting and metal posters. Accessorise and style your home with the range of small shelving and display units in wood and forged iron. Ma Petite France Ltd also offers a range of unique hand-blown glassware, scented oil lamps and, for the bathroom, fizzy bath pearls and essential oils body massage. "Innovation is our key to success," says Val, "so don't forget to visit us regularly to catch the special offers and new products. Look through our craft work selection and give your loved ones or friends a present they will cherish."

Fifty-One

51 Union Street, Ryde, Isle of Wight PO33 2LF
Tel/Fax: 01983 563666
website: www.fifty1.net

With a lifelong interest in all aspects of home furnishings and interior design, Barbara Hooper was fulfilling a long-held ambition when she opened **Fifty-One** on one of Ryde's main shopping streets. That was in the summer of 2001, and in its three years of trading this *Country Living*-style shop has established itself as the best of its kind on the Island.

Behind the large and alluring window displays, every inch of space is taken up with a vast range of things to enhance the home, from small decorative objects and gifts for all occasions to fabrics and soft furnishings, the very finest bed linen, quilts and throws and cushions, nightwear and children's wear, the cosseting range of Esteban toiletries – even some pretty pieces of country-style furniture from France. Fifty-One also offers a service for designing and making curtains and blinds.

Straw Bonnet

16 Union Street, Ryde, Isle of Wight PO33 1BX
Tel: 01983 812220 Mobile: 0788 783 7061

Lesley Evans, the owner of **Straw Bonnet**, declares that selling chocolate is the best job in the world – "everyone smiles when they see chocolates". Her shop offers the largest selection of loose chocolates to be found on the island with the range of English Creams proving to be the most popular choice. Lesley also stocks a beautiful selection of gift boxes and wrappings, along with gift cards and other, non-chocolatey gifts. Wedding favours are also available. Lesley is always happy to give advice on gifts for special occasions.

Reminders of the town's Georgian and Victorian heyday are still there in abundance, among them a fine arcade in Union Street opened in 1837, the year of Queen Victoria's accession. The town has some important churches including **All Saints**, which was designed by Sir George Gilbert Scott and the Roman Catholic church of **St Mary's** which boasts a Pugin chapel.

On the beach by Appley Park stands **Appley Tower**, built as a Victorian folly and now open to the public as a centre for fossils, crystals, natural gems, oracles and rune readings. Another public space is **Puckpool Park**, a leisure area behind the sea wall between Ryde and Seaview. It surrounds what was once a battery, built in the 19th century; its last gun was removed in 1927. At the Westridge Centre, just off the A3055 road to Brading, **Waltzing**

Sharon Orchard

Smallbrook Lane, Ashey, Ryde, Isle of Wight PO33 4BF
Tel: 01983 564595 Fax: 01983 884788
e-mail: sharonorchard@tesco.net
website: www.sharonorchard.com

Sharon Orchard was established in 1998 and over the subsequent two years owners Joe and Sharon McNally planted some 3,500 apple trees of 13 different varieties and 500 vines for vinegar. In 2000, 20 olive trees were added. The McNallys also built a pressing room to press the apples and bottle the juice. They produce six varieties of pure apple juice – there's absolutely no added water or sugar. The finished product is sold in 250ml and 735ml sizes.

Also produced on site is a wide variety of chutneys, pickles, relishes and mustards, as well as jams and marmalades. The orchard also has its own apiaries producing honey that is sold both creamed and clear. Other products include cider vinegar, white wine vinegar and, of course, apples in season. In 2003, the McNallys opened a shop on site which operates from Easter to the end of October. Each Friday they attend the farmer's market in Newport and also attend shows on the island and a few on the mainland. Their produce can now be found in farm shops, delicatessens, cafés and pubs right across the island and their apple juice is also sold on the Wightlink ferries.

Elizabeth Pack

29-30 Cross Street, Ryde,
Isle of Wight PO33 2AA
Tel: 01983 812252
Fax: 01983 613900

A family concern with a history going back to Victorian times, **Elizabeth Pack** is known throughout the Island and indeed way beyond it as the leading ladies fashion house on the Isle of Wight. Occupying a handsome three-storey building in a prime town-centre site, the business has been run for more than 30 years by a remarkable lady, Elizabeth Barrow, who has spent practically all her life in the worlds of drapery and fashion.

Elizabeth numbers local celebrities among her loyal clientele, who stay loyal in the certain knowledge that the lady and the shop will never let them down; nothing is too much trouble, no notice too short, and on more than one occasion her dresses have been sent across the world by special express courier. She knows all the leading manufacturers and has access to many of the major collections, enabling her to produce just the right garment or garments for any occasion, from a dinner dress to a complete wardrobe. The bridal service is something of a speciality, supplying everything from the bridal gown to top-to-toe outfitting for the bridesmaids and ushers. The shop has plenty of space to show off the clothes to the best advantage, and the stock includes a complete range of clothes, all accessories, shoes and jewellery.

Shoppers hesitating before making a final decision can relax with a cup of coffee and a snack in the Coffee Bean café on the first floor. Down the years the Elizabeth Pack trademarks of quality, style and professionalism have won both local and national recognition, and the business has rightly gained international standing. Ryde is a town of wide and varied appeal, with attractions as diverse as ex-London Underground trains and a George Gilbert Scott church, but there's only one Elizabeth Barrow and there's only one Elizabeth Pack.

Newnham Farm

Binstead, Ryde,
Isle of Wight PO33 4ED
Tel: 01983 882423
e-mail: newnhamfarm@talk21.com
website: www.newnhamfarm.co.uk

Newnham Farm is a perfect choice for a relaxing holiday in an outstanding setting, a haven of peace and tranquillity set in 400 acres of arable farmland just five minutes from the centre of Ryde and the Fishbourne car ferry terminal. The two sunny and spacious guest bedrooms (non-smoking) feature double-size shower cabinets and are equipped with an impressive array of extras, from television, radio, hairdryer and toiletries to typical thoughtful touches such as home-made shortbread, bottled water and fresh milk in the fridge. Breakfast, served by the fire in the cosy beamed dining room or out on the patio in the summer months, is a real feast offering delights such as home-baked bread, home-made jams and marmalade, and honey from the beehives on the farm.

Resident owner Diana Cleaver always puts her guests first, a policy that has earned her and the farm several awards, including Regional Winner in B&B of the Year 2003 from the Southern Tourist Board and finalist in the AA's Landlady of the Year 2002. And the farm has won the Isle of Wight Conservation Award three times, showing Diana's commitment to the care of the environment. The 17th-century farmhouse is surrounded by paddocks that insulate guests from the world around and provide excellent walking; ponies and horses graze, there are wild animals, red squirrels bound hither and thither, and there's a medieval carp pond at the bottom of the garden.

The farm is an excellent base for a walking or cycling holiday – the Havenstreet Trail passes the farm and gives access to the extensive network of footpaths and bridleways that run north to Quarr Abbey and south towards Havenstreet and Firestone Copse. Horse riding can be booked at nearby Brickfields Horse Country, and sailing, windsurfing and hang-gliding will attract the more adventurous. A rather more esoteric way of passing the time is joining in a Bat Detecting Session - sitting on the patio at the farmhouse and listening to the echolocation sounds of 5 different breeds of bat! The island has seven golf courses and dozens of sandy beaches, stately homes and many other attractions, all of which are easily reached from Newnham Farm.

Waters is an indoor water, light and music spectacular performed several times daily in a comfortable modern theatre.

Seaview

2 miles SE of Ryde, on the B3330/B3340

To the east of Ryde, the aptly named resort of Seaview has a good beach with clean firm sand, ideal for making sandcastles. There are little rock pools where small children can play in safety while trying to catch the abundant crabs and shrimps. Lines of clinker-built wooden dinghies bob about on the waves, and out to sea rise two of "Palmerston's Follies" – forts constructed in the 1850s as a warning signal to the French to keep away.

A short distance west of Seaview on the B3330 lies **Flamingo Park Waterfowl & Water Gardens**, whose colonies of flamingos, penguins, macaws and waterfowl are among the largest in the country. Visitors are encouraged to join in feeding the birds and also the giant carp and koi carp.

St Helens

4 miles SE of Ryde, on the B3330

Famed for its picturesque harbour and magnificent village green, St Helen's straggles down the hillside above the mouth of the River Yar, a quiet spot beloved by yachtsmen. It must be the only English village to be named after a Roman Emperor's wife – the Helen who was the wife of Constantine and in whose honour a church was erected here in 704.

Another "royal" figure, the Queen of Chantilly was actually born in the village, and if the name is unfamiliar to you, seek out **Sophie Dawes' Cottage** which bears a wall plaque stating that "Sophie Dawes, Madame de Fouchères, Daughter of Richard Dawes, Fisherman and Smuggler, known as the Queen of Chantilly, was born here in 1792". As a young girl, Sophie left St Helens to seek her fortune in London where she worked (non-professionally) in a Piccadilly brothel for a while before ensnaring the exiled Duc de Bourbon and becoming his mistress. The duke paid for her education and when he was able to return to France, took her with him, marrying her off to a compliant Baron. Eventually, she married her duke, now Prince de Condé and having made sure that his will was in order, contrived his murder. Although she was tried for the crime, political considerations led to the case being quietly dropped. Sophie returned to England with her ill-gotten gains but in her last years she seems to have been stricken with remorse and gave lavishly to charity.

Bembridge

5 miles SE of Ryde, on the B3350

The most easterly point of the island, this popular sailing centre was itself an island until the reclamation of the huge inland harbour of Brading Haven in the 1880s. The story of that major work is one of many aspects of the town's history featured in the **Shipwreck Centre & Maritime Museum** which also displays ship models, artefacts from shipwrecks, and diving equipment, as well as action videos of underwater footage and lifeboat rescues. A fascinating exhibition of life in Bembridge, past and present, is portrayed in photographs and artefacts at the **Bembridge Roy Baker Heritage Centre** in Church Road. Art lovers should find time to visit the **Ruskin Gallery**, where an impressive collection of paintings and manuscripts of the 19th century artist

Coastwatch Cottages

1 Norcott Drive, Bembridge, Isle of Wight, PO35 5TX
Tel: 01983 874403 e-mail: ssnharg@aol.com

Coastwatch Cottages offer self-catering accommodation in a choice of two former coastguard properties. Both have been comprehensively refurbished to a high standard, with all modern conveniences including fully equipped kitchens and central heating. They sleep four & six persons respectively in comfort and all linen etc. is provided. Both have private gardens, off street parking and are just 100yards from the sandy beach with its rock pools at low tide. The Isle of Wight coastal path passes close by and the mild climate makes the cottages an ideal base for walkers and explorers throughout the entire year.

Gowans Delicatessen

Lane End Road, Bembridge,
Isle of Wight PO35 5UE
Tel: 01983 873951
Fax: 01983 875949

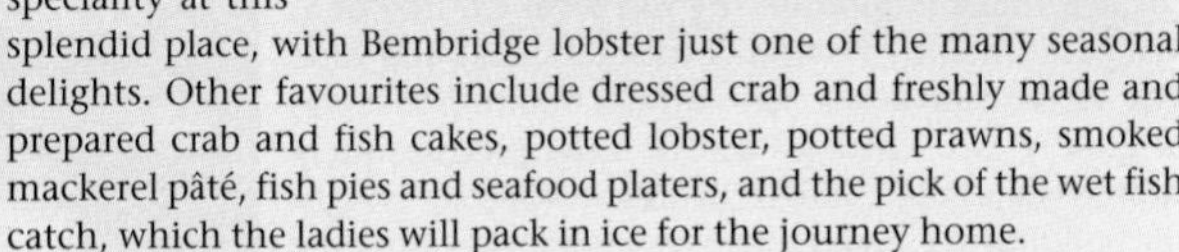

Elaine Smythe and Judy Sparkes have been running **Gowans Delicatessen** for the last eight years, putting contented smiles on the faces of food lovers throughout the Island and from further afield. Seafood is a speciality at this splendid place, with Bembridge lobster just one of the many seasonal delights. Other favourites include dressed crab and freshly made and prepared crab and fish cakes, potted lobster, potted prawns, smoked mackerel pâté, fish pies and seafood platers, and the pick of the wet fish catch, which the ladies will pack in ice for the journey home.

There's also a good selection of prepared-to-order sandwiches, fine cheeses, chutneys, preserves, pickles and sauces, herbs and spices and oils, mustards from the famous Island Mustard Company, lovely chocolate cakes and butter cream sponges, and the renowned Minghella ice cream. Elaine and Judy are always ready with advice on preparing fish and suggestions on what to serve with it.

are housed, and Bembridge Gallery in the High Street which features the work of island artists.

Also well worth a visit is the **Bembridge Windmill** (National Trust). Dating from around 1700, it is the only windmill to have survived on the island and much of its wooden machinery is still intact. There are spectacular views from the top floor.

Brading

2 miles N of Sandown on the A3055

For what is little more than a large village, Brading is remarkably well-stocked with visitor attractions. Amongst them are a diminutive **Town Hall** with whipping post and stocks outside, and a fine church housing some striking tombs of the Oglander family. The most ancient of the village's sights is the **Brading**

Roman Villa which in the 3rd century was the centre of a rich and prosperous farming estate. Discovered in 1880, the villa covers some 300 square feet and has fine mosaic floors with a representation of that master-musician, Orpheus, charming wild animals with his lyre.

The oldest surviving house on the island is now home to the **Brading Experience**, an all-weather family attraction displaying scenes and characters from island history. Naturally, there's a Chamber of Horrors, as well as a World of Nature Exhibition, Professor Copperthwaite's Extraordinary Exhibition of Oddities, some delightful gardens, and a shop. Close by, **The Lilliput Antique Doll & Toy Museum** exhibits more than 2000 dolls and toys, ranging across the centuries from around 2000 BC to 1945. The collection also includes dolls' houses, tinplate toys, trains, rocking horses, and many unusual and rare playthings.

On the edge of the village stands **Morton Manor**, a lovely old house, dating back to 1249, largely rebuilt in 1680, and now set amidst one of the finest gardens in England. The landscaped grounds feature rose and Elizabethan sunken gardens, ponds and cascades, and many mature specimen trees including the largest London Plane you're ever likely to see. Other attractions include the Stable Shop, licensed tearooms, a safe children's play area with a traditional Elizabethan turf maze, and even a vineyard. In fact,

The Wight House

44 High Street, Brading, Isle of Wight PO36 0DJ
Tel/Fax: 01983 400120
website: www.wight-house.co.uk

Located directly opposite the medieval Church of St Mary and the tiny town hall with its stocks and gaol, **The Wight House** is a 200-year-old building that was originally two cottages and is now picturesquely swathed in jasmine. When Nicola and Matthew bought the building to convert into a restaurant they carefully restored it, faithfully retaining its ancient beams, wooden floors, open fires and original brickwork. It's attractively decorated in gentle blues, cream and white which harmonises well with the blue Italian Spode china used. The restaurant has a wonderful atmosphere, whether you dine in the cosy open plan rooms and conservatory with their abundance of fresh flowers, or *al fresco* in the 100ft-long walled garden.

Matthew and Nicola insist on using local suppliers for their produce wherever possible – whether it's the locally caught fish, fresh fruit and vegetables, or meat from the local butcher. Even the wine is produced on the island. The regularly changing menus offer an excellent choice with the most popular regulars being the Lamb Poitevin (roast lamb slow roasted in cognac); the maple-glazed pork, and the duck confit cooked to a traditional French recipe. Vegetarians are also well-catered for with dishes such as the wild mushroom tagliatelli in a creamy Parmesan sauce.

Brading has two vineyards. The other is the well-known **Adgestone Vineyard**, planted in 1968 and the oldest on the island. Entry is free, as is the wine tasting, there are pony trap rides around the vineyard during the season, a gift shop and café.

A mile or so northwest of the village, **Nunwell House & Gardens** should definitely not be missed. The picturesque house has been a family home since 1522 and is of great historic and architectural interest. It was here that Sir John Oglander, an ancestor of the present owner, was host to Charles I on his last night of freedom and modern day visitors can still see the Parlour Chamber in which they met. The house is beautifully furnished, there are exhibits recalling the family's military connections, and Nunwell is surrounded by five acres of tranquil gardens enjoying views across the Solent.

Some of the grandest views on the island can be enjoyed from **Brading Down**, just west of the village on the minor road that leads to Downend.

Alverstone

2 miles NW of Sandown, off the A3055

A couple of miles west of Haseley Manor, the secluded and picturesque village of Alverstone sits beside the tiny River Yar. It has everything you expect of an English village – except for a pub. The deeds of the estate's owner, Lord Alverstone, specifically forbid the sale of intoxicating liquor within the village.

Newchurch

2 miles W of Sandown on the A3056

Amazon World is a popular family attraction that tells the story of the rain forest with the help of a large number of exotic animals and birds – conservation is the name of the game here. One of the

The Pottery At Little Mersley Barn

Mersley Farm, Newchurch, Isle of Wight PO36 0NR
Tel: 01983 731116/862028
website: www.axisartists.org.uk/all/ref1722.htm

The Pottery at Little Mersley Barn is the workplace of the renowned potter Molly Attrill, who works exclusively in earthenware making pots for the table and the kitchen. She also makes individually designed tiles and accepts commissions for larger tile panels. Born on the Island, she trained with Michael Leach in Devon and Henry Hammond at Farnham, then worked at studios in Canada and France before establishing her pottery in this lovely rural setting in 1982.

She uses two traditional methods, sgraffito and majolica, and many of her pieces feature beautiful representations of animals, birds, sea creatures and fruit. Her wheel is at the entrance to the barn, while upstairs is a gallery where her work is on display. Opening hours for visitors are 10.30 to 4 Monday to Saturday. Molly has recently been collaborating as mentor to a Benedictine monk at the nearly Quarr Abbey, helping him to develop his own distinctive style of pottery.

Arreton Manor

Main Road, Arreton, nr Newport, Isle of Wight PO30 3AA
Tel: 01983 528134
e-mail: Julia@arretonmanor.co.uk website: www.arretonmanor.co.uk

Undoubtedly one of the most historic houses on the island is **Arreton Manor**, a lovely Jacobean manor house that stands on the site of earlier dwellings going back to 872AD. The manor was once owned by Edward the Confessor, as noted in the Domesday Book, and it is specifically noted in his will by Alfred the Great in 885AD. Charles I stayed here before he was imprisoned at Carisbrooke Castle; Queen Victoria often visited and is reputed to have planted a conifer on the south lawn.

Today, it is the family home of Andy and Julia Gray-Ling who welcome guests to their charming, peaceful retreat. There are just two luxurious guest bedrooms, situated in the east wing and providing private first class accommodation. The Adrintone Bedchamber is accessed via its own landing to the north of the east wing. It has a four-poster bed and is furnished with antiques and rich fabrics of a Tudor style. There is a separate private bathroom.

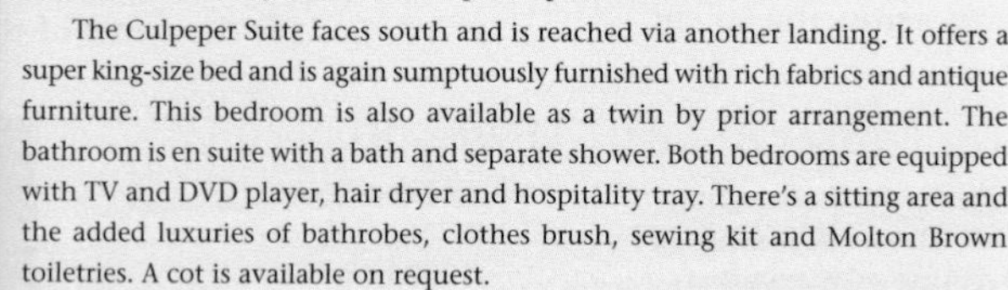

The Culpeper Suite faces south and is reached via another landing. It offers a super king-size bed and is again sumptuously furnished with rich fabrics and antique furniture. This bedroom is also available as a twin by prior arrangement. The bathroom is en suite with a bath and separate shower. Both bedrooms are equipped with TV and DVD player, hair dryer and hospitality tray. There's a sitting area and the added luxuries of bathrobes, clothes brush, sewing kit and Molton Brown toiletries. A cot is available on request.

The beautiful landscaped gardens and part of the house are open to the public for the peak summer months only. The owners offer a guided tour in some of the rooms including The Old Court Room and through a secret passageway to The Old Monks' Rooms. Arreton Manor was farmed by the Abbots of Quarr for over 400 years from 1156. With the ongoing development of the gardens including a Tudor style knot garden and parterre, Old Rose Garden, children's play area and The Manor Garden Room for light refreshments, Arreton Manor is a relaxing day out for everyone to enjoy. At certain times of the summer they hold special events like Plays on the Lawn and Living History visit every year, usually in August, to re-enact 17th Century life at the Manor.

The Garlic Farm

Newchurch, Isle of Wight PO36 0NR
Tel: 01983 865378 Fax: 01983 862294
e-mail: colin@thegarlicfarm.co.uk
website: www.thegarlicfarm.co.uk

One of the Island's most renowned and exclusive products is its garlic. At **The Garlic Farm Shop** you can see how it is produced, purchase from a range of garlic products catering for all tastes from garlic icecream to massive elephant garlic bulbs to smoked garlic butter and taste

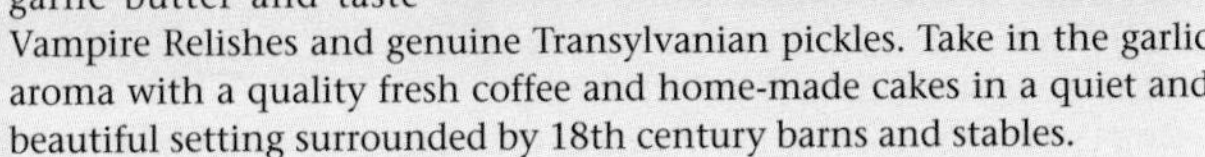

Vampire Relishes and genuine Transylvanian pickles. Take in the garlic aroma with a quality fresh coffee and home-made cakes in a quiet and beautiful setting surrounded by 18th century barns and stables.

Colin and Jenny Boswell have grown garlic for 30 years and are acknowledged specialists - they've even exported their product to France much to the acclaim of Punch magazine- "Gallic garlic freaks at dinner are now often heard to say Merde! this is our native product, what we want is ail anglais"

If you want to grow your own garlic, planting packs are available with a range of garlic types. In spring the shop and courtyard is filled with beautiful flowering alliums. In August visit the Garlic Festival of which the farm is a major sponsor, attracting 25,000 visitors and now in its 21st year. A full day of garlic food and drink and quality family entertainment.

highlights in Newchurch is the annual Garlic Festival, held on a weekend in August. The village church and its steeple are clad in wood.

Arreton

3 miles SE of Newport on the A3056

From Downend, it's less than a mile to **Arreton Manor** (see panel opposite) which claims, with some justification, to be "the most beautiful and intriguing house on the Isle of Wight". There was a house on this site long before Alfred the Great mentioned Arreton in his will of 885 AD and the manor was owned by successive monarchs from Henry VIII to Charles I. The present house was built during the reigns of Elizabeth and James I and it's a superb example of the architecture of that period, with mellow stone walls and Jacobean panelling complemented by furniture from the same era. Perhaps the most appealing aspect of Arreton is that indefinable atmosphere of a house that has been lived in for centuries. Other attractions here include a Museum of Childhood, Lace Museum, National Wireless Museum, gift shop, tea-rooms and picnic area.

A mile or so southwest of Arreton Manor stands another grand old house, **Haseley Manor**. In the mid-1970s, it was a deserted and decaying shell but in a heroic work of restoration has been saved by Raymond and Krystyna Young. They have furnished and decorated the rooms in period, adding audio-visual tableaux explaining the different eras. Visitors can also watch a film showing how the mammoth task of restoration was carried out. Inside the house, there's an indoor play area for small children, a working pottery where children can try their hand at the slippery craft, a tea-room and gift shop. Outside, the attractions include magnificent herb, flower and water

Sandhill Hotel

6 Hill Street, Sandown,
Isle of Wight PO36 9DB
Tel: 01983 403635 Fax: 01983 403695
e-mail: sandhillhotel@btconnect.com
website: www.sandhill-hotel.com

Trevor and Jane Sawtell ran a Bed & Breakfast hotel in Oxford before moving to the Island, where they took over the **Sandhill Hotel** in 1990. After investing a great deal of money and effort, they completely transformed the place, earning it 4 Diamond status from 2 and providing visitors with a very smart, practical and convivial base for touring the sights of the Island.

The hotel has 16 bedrooms, all with en suite facilities and including some family rooms, and the tariff includes an excellent breakfast and the option of an evening meal. Trevor and Jane are very hands-on proprietors, playing a leading role in the kitchen and in the comfortable bar. Meals are served in a bright, spacious dining room, and the bar, with its conservatory extension, and a paved terrace are pleasant spots to enjoy a drink and a chat and to plan the next day's excursions.

Denewood Hotel

Victoria Road, Sandown, Isle of Wight PO36 8AL
Tel/Fax: 01983 402980
e-mail: holidays@denewoodhotel.co.uk
website: www.denewood-hotel.co.uk

A handsome double-fronted Victorian detached property, the **Denewood Hotel** is a friendly, family-run hotel whose owners, Rosemarie Husain and Christina Bartle, pride themselves on excellent standards of customer care, freshly prepared home-cooked meals and comfortable surroundings. The hotel stands in a quiet avenue just two minutes from Sandown's award-winning sandy beach and the town centre, and is within easy walking distance of the leisure centre, pier and other attractions. The Isle of Wight Tiger Sanctuary and Dinosaur Isle are both close by.

The Denewood enjoys a 4-Diamond rating from the English Tourism Council and a 4-Diamond Sparkling from the RAC. Its licensed lounge bar provides an ideal meeting place and is the venue for quizzes and game nights during the high season. It opens out onto a garden patio which leads to a heated indoor spa pool which is open to guests in summer. All the guest bedrooms are en suite and centrally heated with colour TV, clock radio, beverage facilities and a hair-dryer. Guests can stay on either a B&B or half board basis. Meals are served in the spacious dining room where you can enjoy a choice of delicious home-prepared and cooked dishes.

gardens; a Children's Farm and Adventure Playground, and a picnic area.

SANDOWN

"A village by a sandy shore" was how a guide-book described Sandown in the 1870s. Since then, its superb position on sweeping Sandown Bay has transformed that village into the island's premier resort. Now a lively town, Sandown offers its visitors every kind of seaside attraction. There are miles of flat, safe sands where a Kidzone safety scheme operates during the season; a traditional pier complete with theatre; colourful gardens; a Sunday market; abundant sporting facilities, and even pleasure flights from the nearby airfield. On the edge of the town, the **Isle of Wight Zoological Gardens** specialises in

Puddle Duck

13 High Street, Sandown, Isle of Wight PO36 8DA
Tel: 01983 407907

A charming name for a charming shop specialising in casual and leisure wear for ladies and gentlemen. **Puddle Duck** is owned and run by Felga Stinson, who moved to this prime high street location after running a shop elsewhere on the Island. She is very experienced in the fashion business, and the stock in her little shop caters for a wide range of ages and styles. She sources the clothes from all parts of the UK and from Europe, changing the fabrics and the styles with the seasons, and accessories include hats, shawls, scarves and jewellery (some of it handmade locally).

Royal Cliff Holiday Apartments

Beachfield Road, Sandown, Isle of Wight
PO36 8NA
Tel: 01983 402138 Fax: 01983 402368
website: www.royalcliff.co.uk

Guests staying at the **Royal Cliff Holiday Apartments** will find everything they need for a relaxing break in the Island's leading holiday resort. All the 7 bright, well-maintained comfortable apartments in a large Mediterranean-style house have central heating, television, well-equipped kitchens and comfortable living areas, and facilities include south-facing gardens, a heated outdoor swimming pool and a large private car park.

The views along the shore and out to sea are absolutely stunning, and though quiet and secluded, the apartments are close to all the amenities of Sandown; the cliff path down to the safe, sandy beach can be reached directly from the grounds, and the traditional pier, the leisure centre, the shops, the Dinosaur Museum and all the other family attractions are an easy walk away. Resident proprietors Peter and Nali Smith are on hand to make sure that guests at the Royal Cliff have a holiday to remember and treasure.

Orchardcroft Hotel

Victoria Avenue, Shanklin, Isle of Wight PO37 6LT
Tel/Fax: 01983 862133
website: www.orchardcroft.co.uk
e-mail: admin@orchardcroft.co.uk

Friendly, family-run, warm and comfortable, the most often used words to describe the small and friendly **Orchardcroft Hotel**, a delightful base for a relaxed holiday in very pleasant surroundings. The 16 guest bedrooms – doubles, twins, a honeymoon room and family rooms – are all en suite, with central heating, television and hospitality tray, and can be booked on bed & breakfast or half-board terms. Discounts are offered at certain times for senior citizens on half board. The facilities are quite outstanding for a small hotel, including an indoor heated pool, jacuzzi, sauna, solarium, fitness suite and games room, as well as elegant lounges and secluded gardens.

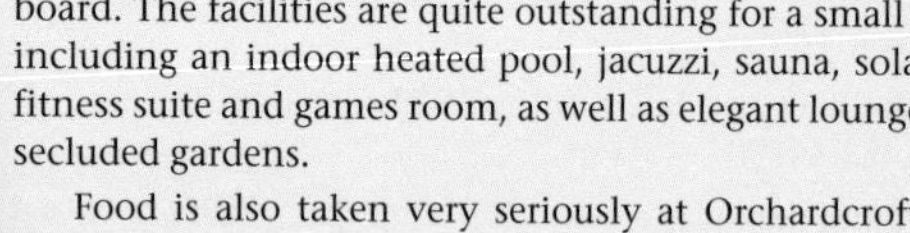

Food is also taken very seriously at Orchardcroft, and preparation, presentation and service are all important to the resident chef and the restaurant staff. Typical dishes on the regularly changing menu include tuna fish cocktail, lasagne, plaice meunière and roast beef, and the dessert trolley is definitely not to be missed. The hotel is well placed for a picturesque walk to the Old Village and Shanklin, and all the many attractions of the Island are within an easy drive.

Shanklin Chine

12 Pomona Road, Shanklin, Isle of Wight PO37 6PF
Tel: 01983 866432 Fax: 01983 866145
website: www.shanklinchine.co.uk

When the poet John Keats visited Shanklin in 1819, **Shanklin Chine** was already a major visitor attraction, noted for its natural beauty and its wealth of rare plants and wildlife. The word 'chine', now used only on the island and in Dorset, means a deep narrow ravine. At Shanklin this was created by water cutting through soft sandstone leading to the sea, a process extending over the last 10,000 years. In Victorian times, the Chine was on every visitor's itinerary and contemporary descriptions speak of it as "terrifically sublime" and "savagely grand".

Many years later the Chine was used for assault training by 40 Royal Marine Commando in preparation for the Dieppe Raid in 1942. Their Memorial is sited near the lower entrance. Also a section of PLUTO (Pipe Line Under The Ocean), which carried petrol to the Allied troops in Normandy, can still be seen in the Chine, together with pictures and an informative DVD in the PLUTO Room at the Heritage Centre. The current exhibition is "The Island Then and Now" with a special D-Day anniversary feature and in 2005 the display will be "Victory '45". At night during the summer months subtle lighting creates a place of magic and enchantment. Birds and chipmunks can be seen in the aviaries and there is a Victorian Tea Garden and Gift Shop. Open Easter (April) to end of October. Also pay a visit to Fisherman's Cottage at the foot of the Chine (family pub on the beach).

breeding severely endangered exotic species and is home to the UK's largest variety of Royal Bengal, Siberian and Chinese tigers. The zoo is also a World Health Organisation centre for venomous snakes, their venom extracted for use in antidotes for snake bites. You may well see TV "Snake Man" Jack Corney handling these lethal reptiles and children who are photographed with a small harmless snake are presented with a handling certificate to prove it! There are all-weather snake and parrot shows, a kiddies' play area and Pets' Corner, a seafront pub and café, the Zoofari Gift Shop, and a snack bar. A Road-Runner Train operates frequent services between the zoo and the town centre.

In Sandown's High Street, the **Museum of Isle of Wight Geology** is especially popular with children who love its life-sized dinosaurs – the Isle of Wight is renowned for the number and quality of the dinosaur remains that have been discovered here. The museum, "120 million years in the making", has excellent displays on all aspects of the island's geology. As part of its educational programme, museum staff will advise you on the best places to look for fossils and, when you return with your discoveries, will identify them for you.

Throughout the season, the Sandown Bay area hosts a wide range of special events – from the Regatta in August to Sunday markets, from the Isle of Wight Power Boat Festival in May to the National Strong Man finals in September.

Shanklin

2 miles SW of Sandown, on the A3055

Like Sandown, Shanklin was just a small village a century or so ago. The old village has survived intact, a charming little complex of thatched houses

Chestnut Mews

14 Vaughan Way, Old Village, Shanklin, Isle of Wight
PO37 6SD
Tel: 01983 861143
e-mail: chestnutmews@btinternet.com
website: www.chestnutmews.co.uk

Four superbly equipped modern holiday cottages in a secluded garden setting provide luxurious self-catering holiday accommodation. Tucked away from the main road, yet very easily accessed, **Chestnut Mews** comprises four cottages – Rose, Jasmine, Honeysuckle and Clematis, each with decor inspired by their names and all equipped to an impressively high standard. Three cottages sleep six in three bedrooms: the master double with an en suite shower and balcony, a twin bedded room and a single with a 3' bed and a roll-out under bed. There is a bathroom and a downstairs cloakroom. Rose Cottage has an extra single bedroom downstairs with a wash basin, ideal for a disabled or elderly guest. Downstairs is open-plan, with a spacious, fully equipped kitchen/diner and lounge, and French doors leading onto a patio overlooking the spacious gardens. Outside are an enclosed swimming pool and a safe children's play area. Each cottage has adjacent parking space, and all have wheelchair access.

Chestnut Mews is ideal for exploring the many delights of the coast and countryside, and some lovely walks begin at the end of the driveway. The Old Village is a short stroll away, and a cliff path and steps lead to the lovely sandy Appley Beach.

standing at the head of the **Shanklin Chine** (see panel on page 246). The famous Chine is a spectacular ravine some 300ft deep, 180ft wide, noted for its waterfalls and rare flora. There's a Nature Trail to follow or you can join a guided tour. The **Heritage Centre** contains an interesting exhibit on PLUTO (the PipeLine Under The Ocean) secretively constructed during World War II to transport fuel from the island to the Continent during the D-Day landings. There's also a memorial to the soldiers of 40 Commando who trained in this area for the disastrous assault on Dieppe in 1942.

Shanklin Pier

The old village stands on a 150ft-high cliff from which the ground slopes gently down to the safe, sheltered beach, with its long, seafront esplanade. With its scenic setting, many public gardens, and healthy climate, Shanklin has appealed to many celebrities. Charles Darwin was particularly fond of the town, the American poet Longfellow fell in love with it, and John Keats was a familiar figure in Sandown throughout the summer of 1818. The grassy open space known as **Keats Green** commemorates his stay here during which he wrote some of his best-known poems.

Godshill

4 miles W of Shanklin on the A3020

A short drive inland from Shanklin leads to the charming village of Godshill, which with its stone-built thatched cottages and its medieval **Church of All Saints** is one of the most popular stops on the tourist trail. The double-naved church, whose 15th century pinnacled

The Model Village

High Street, Godshill, Isle of Wight PO38 3HH
Tel/Fax: 01983 840270
e-mail: isleofwight.com/model village

Island life in miniature is portrayed in the magical **Model Village** at Godshill. The original owner built his model of Shanklin with the help of model-makers from Elstree film studios and local people, and opened it to the public in 1952. The present owners purchased the model village in 1969, by which time it was in a state of disrepair. Since then major repairs and rebuilding projects have filled the subsequent years, with all the work done in the workshop on site.

The 1/10 scale models are made of coloured cement and the detail is quite incredible. Real straw is prepared in the correct way for the thatching; the church on the hill took 600 hours of work and each house has its own tiny garden with miniature trees and shrubs. The airfield has 1920s style landing strips and the little railway is modelled on the older Island systems. Cricket, football, croquet and show-jumping are among the sports taking place on the beautifully tended lawns, and the sea is represented by a delightful pond complete with beach huts and fishermen's cottages. Open daily from March to October.

tower dominates the village, contains some notable treasures, including a 15th century wall painting of Christ crucified on a triple-branched lily, a painting of Daniel in the Lions' Den and many monuments to the Worsleys and the Leighs, two of the leading island families.

Godshill has much to entertain visitors, including the magical **Model Village** with its 1/10th scale stone houses, trains and boats, even a football match taking place on the green, and the **Natural History Centre** with its famed shell collection, minerals and aquarium. The miniature village was built with the help of model-makers from Elstree film studio and after two years' preparation was opened to the public in 1952. The models are made of coloured cement and the detail is quite incredible. Real straw was prepared in the traditional way for thatching; the church on the hill took 600 hours of work before being assembled in its position; each house has its own tiny garden with miniature trees and shrubs. The airfield is in the style of small landing strips of the 1920s and 1930s, and the little railway is modelled on the older Island systems. Things get even smaller in the model garden of the model Old Vicarage, where there is another (1/100 scale) model village with yet another Old Vicarage, and within its garden another (1/1000 scale) model village – a model of a model of a model!

Also in Godshill is the **Nostalgia Toy Museum**, where 2000 Dinky, Corgi and Matchbox toys and 1960s dolls bring back childhood memories.

Bonchurch

2 miles S of Shanklin on the A3055

The poet Algernon Swinburne spent some of his childhood in Bonchurch, and is buried in the churchyard of St

THE POND CAFÉ

Bonchurch Village Road, Bonchurch,
Isle of Wight PO38 1RG
Tel/Fax: 01983 855666
website: www.thepondcafe.com

Bonchurch is one of the most attractive and peaceful villages on the Island, admired by Charles Dickens, the poet Swinburne and thousands of visitors since. One of the very best reasons for a visit is to enjoy the relaxed atmosphere, the fine hospitality and excellent food at **The Pond Café**. It is set in a pretty little period house, with tables and chairs out at the front, and a garden at the back with a pond that gives the place its name. Inside, the tables are neatly set with white linen and sparkling crystal and cutlery, and subtle lighting is provided by little wall and ceiling lights. The Pond is open from 10 o'clock till late every day, and coffee and drinks are available throughout the day, along with sandwiches and snacks.

A full menu comes on stream at lunchtime, and in the evening a fine choice is offered on the fine dining menu. Chef-patron David Thomson sets great store by the finest and freshest local ingredients, and the creative menus change daily to take advantage of what's best in the markets; among his (and his customers') seasonal favourites are hand-picked scallops cooked simply to preserve their exquisite flavour, and sea bass, served perhaps with home-made chips and a lemon emulsion, or accompanied by a lobster ravioli. There's always a choice of vegetarian dishes, and special dietary requirements can be met with a little notice. The special four-course Sunday lunch is guaranteed to bring in the crowds, so booking is essential, as it is at main mealtimes in season and for the splendid gourmet evenings. These indulgent occasions bring a superb seven-course tasting menu that's a triumph form beginning to end, starting perhaps with foie gras and reaching a dazzling conclusion with a sparkling champagne and strawberry terrine. David and his team do a great job, and they are more than willing to pass on their secrets at the regular cookery classes, where they take small groups and teach them some classic techniques.

The Pond is child-friendly, and a high chair can be provided. Smoking is not allowed until late in the evening.

Boniface. Charles Dickens wrote part of *David Copperfield* while staying in Bonchurch. His first impressions of the place were very favourable – "I think it is the prettiest place I ever saw". He seemed likely to make it his permanent home, but he soon grew to dislike the weather and the place and returned to his familiar Broadstairs.

Ventnor

3 miles SW of Shanklin on the A3055

Along the south-eastern corner of the island stretches a six-mile length of ragged cliffs known as **Undercliffe**. Clinging to the slopes at its eastern end, Ventnor has been described as "an alpinist's town" and as "a steeply raked auditorium with the sea as the stage". Promoted as a spa town in the 1830s, its distinguished visitors have included a young Winston Churchill and an elderly Karl Marx.

Ventnor Heritage Museum houses a fascinating collection of old prints, photographs and working models relating to the town's history, while **Ventnor Botanical Gardens** shelters some 10,000 plants in 22 acres of grounds, amongst them many rare and exotic trees, shrubs, alpines, perennials, succulents and conifers. The gardens received a huge boost in the spring of 2000 with the opening of an exciting new **Visitor Centre** whose exhibits include an interactive display called The Green Planet – the Incredible Life of Plants. Many unusual varieties are for sale in the shop. There's a picnic area and children's playground, and during August the Gardens host open-air performances of Shakespearean plays. Also snuggling in the garden grounds is the **Smuggling Museum**, whose 300 exhibits illustrate 700 years of smuggling lore.

Ventnor

Back in town, the **Coastal Visitor Centre** provides a fascinating and educational insight into the island's coastal and marine environment, with special features on animal and plant life, coastal defences and living with landslides a problem very familiar to the island as well as to many parts of England's south coast.

Above the town, **St Boniface Down** (National Trust), at 785ft the highest point on the island, provides some dizzying views across coast and countryside.

The Wellington Hotel

Belgrave Road, Ventnor, Isle of Wight PO38 1JH
Tel: 01983 856600 Fax: 01983 856611
e-mail: reservations@thewellingtonhotel.net
website: www.thewellingtonhotel.net

"Arrive, breathe, unwind" is the message from **The Wellington Hotel** which enjoys an unrivalled position in this elegant coastal resort. Facing due south, the hotel commands breathtaking views over Ventnor Bay and the beach is accessible through the lovely terraced gardens, making it possible for guests to bathe straight from the hotel. The Wellington is also conveniently at town level for shops, buses and entertainment. Built in Victorian times, this beautiful old building has been lovingly restored to its original condition and furnished to a very high modern standard to create an idyllic retreat. All the bedrooms have en suite facilities and panoramic views; the Super De Luxe rooms have their own private balconies.

The Wellington Restaurant offers a varied and attractive selection of cross-continental dishes – including lobster fresh from the sea and sumptuous desserts – complemented by an extensive wine list which may be enjoyed in the dining room or on the decked terraces.

There are discounts for stays of three nights or more, and ferry crossings can be arranged through the hotel at all-inclusive rates. All major credit cards are accepted.

The Spyglass Inn

The Esplanade, Ventnor, Isle of Wight PO38 1JX
Tel: 01983 855338 Fax: 01983 855220

Enjoying superb locations on Ventnor's elegant Esplanade are two outstanding hostelries and a wonderful traditional chandler's shop. The famous **Spyglass Inn**, built around 1830, stands at the western end of the Esplanade, close to what was once a favourite haunt of smugglers. The inn boasts a massive collection of seafaring memorabilia and is renowned for its excellent Ventnor Bay lobsters and crabs, along with many other superb dishes. The well-stocked bar hosts nightly entertainment to suit all tastes – whether country, folk, jazz or other.

The Spyglass also offers quality bed & breakfast accommodation in self-contained suites, each with an en suite bathroom and a lounge with a balcony overlooking the sea. All suites are tastefully decorated and equipped with colour TV.

The Spyglass's sister pub, of roughly the same vintage, is the **Mill Bay Inn** at the eastern end of the Esplanade. It occupies one of the most enviable positions on the island's south coast, with a sea view from virtually every seat. The outside terraces with their palm trees create a Mediterranean atmosphere, ideal for enjoying the fresh, locally caught seafood. Also on offer is a wide variety of traditional and exotic pub food – anything from a ploughman's to a prosciutto salad, from home-made curry to a Glamorgan vegetarian sausage filled with leek, potato, Caerphilly and Cheddar cheese, and coated in light bread crumbs. The excellent fare is complemented by local real ales; service is truly friendly and there's regular live entertainment.

As you stroll along the Esplanade look out for **Josiah Tempest**'s chandlery with its ship's lantern and anchor flanking the old-fashioned sign that advertises its business as "Purveyor of Fine Nautical Instruments, Lamps & Cordage". Inside you'll find a fascinating array of binoculars, telescopes and marine artefacts old and new.

WALK NUMBER 9

Blackgang

Distance:	5.0 miles (8.0 kilometres)
Typical time:	140 mins
Height gain:	165 metres
Map:	Outdoor Leisure 29
Walk:	www.walkingworld.com ID:1059
Contributor:	David L White

Access Information:

Large Car Park, nearest bus stop 'Blackgang'. If travelling from the mainland best crossings: Ryde/Portsmouth - Catamaran; Ryde/Southsea - Hovercraft; Fishbourn/Portsmouth - Car ferry

Additional Information:

Seafaring history is very evident as may be seen in the form of its three lighthouses all built at different periods in history. The area of Blackgang and Niton featured strongly in the business of smuggling in earlier days. During the warmer weather an abundance of wildlife, and flowering plants are evident. Should you wish to take a short diversion from the Niton parish church further into the village, shops and a local pub may be found (the pub serves food). Opposite the church are the public toilets.

Description:

A walk with fabulous views over the Isle of Wight and English Channel taking in some of the local history and landmarks.

Features:

Hills or Fells, Sea, Pub, Toilets, Church, Wildlife, Birds, Flowers, Great Views

Walk Directions:

1 A Heritage Coast information board in the car park will tell you about the coastal area. Climb steps on seaward side of car park - follow path to cliff top. Turn left along cliff top towards Niton. Follow path past radio mast station on your left. After second stile beyond radio station turn immediately left over another stile heading inland.

2 From this high vantage point looking slightly South East St. Catherine's lighthouse may be seen. It was built in 1840 to replace the earlier lighthouses that were further inland. This coastline was famous for its many wrecks, one night it is said that there were as many as fourteen.

3 Keeping fence on your right walk across to far end of field to stile. Head across small meadow slightly to your left to stile, cross and walk through a coppice path until you reach the main road. Follow road to right - until it bears left (marked through traffic) to church. At lych gate turn left and go up Pan Lane, which eventually turns into a bridle path. Follow path eventually turning left and you soon reach a metal gate. Follow blue arrow sign straight ahead.

4 After passing through gate follow track indicated by blue waymark arrow, upon reaching metal gate at other end of the field (keeping radio mast on your left). After passing through this gate turn immediately

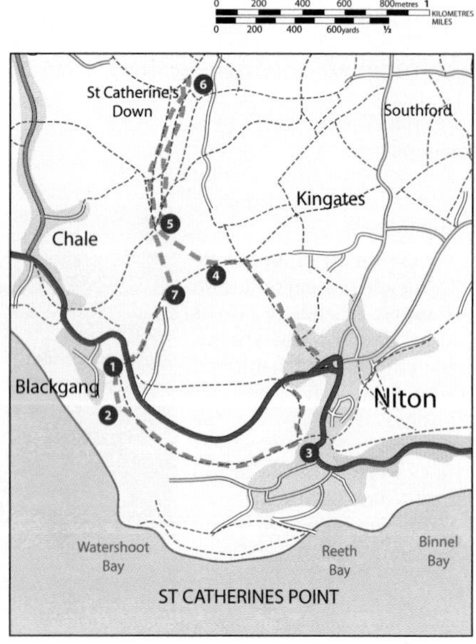

left and climb to summit of the hill where the 'Old Oratory' stands. Here you will see fantastic views. If you do not wish to visit Hoy's Monument ignore waymarks 5 and 6, proceed to waymark 7.

5 To visit Hoy's Monument, instead of turning left walk across the field bearing slightly to your right towards a visible signpost follow bridleway C6 to Hoy's monument.

6 Hoy's Monument - top right corner of photo. Viewed from the Old Oratory (waymark 6). Return to waymark 5 by same path.

7 The Oratory, known to locals as the 'Pepper Pot'. One of the original lighthouses built in 1314 and manned by a local duty monk. Also visible to the east from here is the 'Salt Pot', built later in history but before completion it was decided that due to mist and fog on the hills often obscuring the glow of the light the project would be abandoned in favour of a building closer to the coast and lower down (the present St. Catherine's). From Oratory, cross field heading towards the sea where you will see a stile. Standing on the stile and looking down slightly to your left you will see your starting point car park.

St Lawrence

1 mile W of Ventnor on the A3055

Nestling in the heart of the Undercliff, the ancient village of St Lawrence has a 13th century church that once laid claim to being the smallest in Britain. It was extended in 1842 but remains diminutive, measuring just 20 feet by 12 feet.

Not far away, old farm buildings were converted into **Isle of Wight Studio Glass**, where skills old and new produce glass of the highest quality. Lord Jellicoe, hero of Jutland, lived for some years in St Lawrence and often swam in Orchard's Bay, a small cove where Turner sketched.

The coast road continues through the village of Niton to **St Catherine's Point**, the most southerly and the wildest part of the island, in an area of Special Scientific Interest. Steps lead down to St Catherine's lighthouse and a path leads up to the summit of St Catherine's Hill, where the remains of a much older lighthouse, known as the Pepperpot, can be seen. Close by is the Hoy Monument erected in honour of a visit by Tsar Nicholas I.

Blackgang Chine, at the most southerly tip of the island, has been developed from an early Victorian scenic park into a modern fantasy park with dozens of attractions for children. Also inside the park are two heritage exhibitions centred on a water-powered sawmill and a quayside, with displays ranging from cooper's and wheelwright's workshops to a shipwreck collection, a huge whale skeleton and a 19th century beach scene complete with a bathing machine. The coastline here is somewhat fragile, and a large slice of cliff has been lost to storms and gales in recent years.

Wroxall

2 miles N of Ventnor on the B3327

Owls, falcons, vultures and donkeys all call Wroxall their home! **Appuldurcombe House** (see panel on page 257), once the grandest mansion on the whole island with gardens laid out by Capability Brown, was badly bombed in 1943 and has never been lived in since. The building has been partly restored and visitors can stroll in the 11 acres of ornamental grounds landscaped by Capability Brown which provide an enchanting setting for picnics. The **Owl & Falconry Centre**, in what used to be the laundry and brewhouse, stages daily flying displays with birds of prey from around the world and holds courses in the centuries-old art of falconry.

Heaven for 200 donkeys and many other animals is the **Isle of Wight**

Little Span Farm

Rew Lane, Wroxall, Ventnor, Isle of Wight PO38 3AU
Tel/Fax: 01983 852419
e-mail: info@spanfarm.co.uk
website: www.spanfarm.co.uk

Set within an Area of Outstanding Natural Beauty, **Little Span Farm** is a mixed arable and stock farm of 180 acres with woodland that was once part of the parkland designed by 'Capability' Brown for Appuldurcombe House. The farm is home to Felicity Coory who offers visitors to this lovely part of the island the choice of either bed & breakfast or self-catering accommodation. B&B guests stay either in the 17th century stone farmhouse or in the recently converted Harvester's Cottage. The farmhouse has a separate guests' dining room and a lounge with log fires in winter. A full English breakfast is served and special diets can be catered for on request.

The garden is available for guests' use and there's private off-road parking close to the house. For those who prefer self-catering, the newly converted Stable Cottage offers spacious 'upside-down' accommodation. Once the home of the farm's cart horses, this 18th century stone barn has a first floor sun deck and its own small enclosed garden to the rear. There's one double bedroom en suite; one twin and a children's room with 3ft bunk beds; a comprehensively equipped kitchen and an open plan beamed living/dining area.

Donkey Sanctuary at Lower Winstone Farm. The rescue centre is a registered charity relying entirely on donations, and visitors have several ways of helping, including the Adopt a Donkey scheme.

Shorwell

7 miles SW of Newport, on the B3323

Pronounced 'Shorell' by Caulkheads, as Isle of Wight natives are known, this village of thatched stone cottages has no fewer than three venerable manor houses within its boundaries. West Court, Wolverton, and North Court were built respectively during the reigns of Henry VIII, Elizabeth I, and James I. They possess all the charm you would expect from that glorious age of English architecture but sadly none of them is open to the public. However, you can visit **St Peter's Church** to gaze on its mesmerisingly beautiful 15th century wall-painting and admire its 500-year-old stone pulpit covered by an elaborate wooden canopy of 1620. The church also has a real oddity in a painting on wood of the Last Supper, brought from Iceland in 1898.

This small village boasts another attraction. **Yafford Mill** is an 18th century water mill in full working order. It's surrounded by ponds and streams where you'll find Sophie, the resident seal, and within the grounds there are paddocks which are home to rare cattle, sheep and pigs, a collection of antique farm machinery, a steam engine and narrow-gauge railway. There are also waymarked nature walks, a playground, picnic area, gift shop, tea gardens and a licensed bar.

Brighstone

8 miles S of Newport on the B3399

One of the prettiest villages on the island, Brighstone was once notorious as

Appuldurcombe House

Wroxall, Nr. Ventnor, Isle of Wight PO38 3EW
Tel: 01983 852484 Fax: 01983 840188
e-mail: enquiries@appuldurcombe.co.uk
website: www.appuldurcombe.co.uk

Appuldurcombe House was once the grandest and most striking house on the Island, and its 18th century baroque elegance is notable still in the partly restored building (it suffered bomb damage in 1943 and has not been lived in since). Visitors can stroll in the 11 acres of grounds designed by Capability Brown and maybe enjoy a picnic. The Owl & Falconry Centre is set up in the imaginatively restored servants' quarters and brewhouse. It puts on daily flying displays, featuring owls and other birds of prey from around the world. There is an excellent shop, a café for light refreshments, a photographic exhibition of the history of the house and a newly restored barn for indoor flying displays in poor weather. Open daily.

the home of smugglers and wreckers. Today, the National Trust runs a shop in a picturesque row of thatched cottages, and there's a little museum depicting village life down the years.

The island has long been known for its fossil finds, especially relating to dinosaurs. On a clifftop near the village the bones of a completely new species of predatory dinosaur were unearthed. The 15ft carnivore, which lived in the cretaceous period about 120 million to 150 million years ago, has been named *cotyrannus lengi* after Gavin Leng, a local collector who found the first bone. On Military Road (A3055) near Brighstone, the **Dinosaur Farm Museum** came into being following the unearthing in 1992 of the skeleton of a brachiosaurus, at that time the island's largest and most spectacular dinosaur discovery. This unique attraction follows the tale of this and other finds. Visitors are invited to bring their own fossils for identification, and the farm also organises guided fossil tours at various locations on the Island.

A mile or so west of Brighstone, the National Trust is also responsible for **Mottistone Manor Garden**, a charming hillside garden alongside an Elizabethan manor house. The garden is particularly known for its herbaceous borders and terraces planted with fruit trees. The Mottistone Estate extends from Mottistone Down in the north to the coast at Sudmoor. On **Mottistone Common**, where New Forest ponies graze, are the remains of a neolithic long barrow known as the Longstone.

Freshwater

11 miles W of Newport, on the A3055

Freshwater and the surrounding area are inextricably linked with the memory of Alfred, Lord Tennyson. In 1850, he succeeded Wordsworth as Poet Laureate, married Emily Sellwood, and shortly afterwards moved to **Farringford**, just outside Freshwater. The house, set in 33 acres of parkland, is now a hotel where visitors can relax in the luxuriously appointed drawing room with its delightful terrace and views across the downs. Tennyson was an indefatigable walker and however foul the weather would pace along nearby High Down dramatically arrayed in a billowing cloak and a black, broad-brimmed sombrero. After his death, the area was re-named **Tennyson Down** and a cross erected high on the cliffs in his memory.

There are more remembrances of the

great poet in the **Church of All Saints** in Freshwater town where Lady Tennyson is buried in the churchyard and a touching memorial inside commemorates their son Lionel, "an affectionate boy", who died at the age of 32 while returning from India. As Tennyson grew older, he became increasingly impatient with sightseers flocking to Farringford hoping to catch sight of the now-legendary figure. He moved to his other home at Blackdown in Sussex where he died in 1892.

Freshwater Bay

About a mile south of the town, **Freshwater Bay** was once an inaccessible inlet, much favoured by smugglers. Today, the bay is the start point of the 15-mile Tennyson Trail, which ends at Carisbrooke and its scenic beauty attracts thousands of visitors every year. They also flock in their thousands to **Dimbola**

Judy 'F' Designs

Small Horse Farm, Madeira Lane, Colwell Bay, Isle of Wight PO40 9SP
Tel/Fax: 01983 753262
website: www.rockinghorses-judyfdesigns.co.uk

Judy 'F' Designs is the name under which for many years Judy Fergusson has been designing and making exquisite laminated rocking horses to delight, inspire and capture the imagination of children of all ages. Many of her exclusive designs depict horses in action, including a showjumping pony and the superb dressage horse. The latter is a limited edition and can be ordered on rockers with full saddlery or on a decorative pedestal as a sculptural piece. Judy also runs courses for small groups in the art of making their own rocking horse, and sells plans of some of her designs.

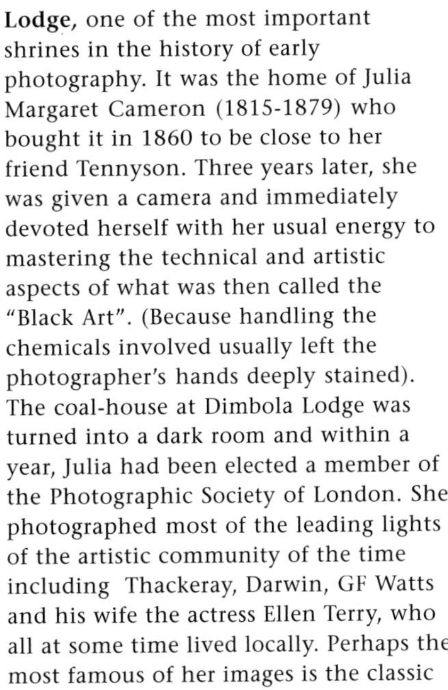

Lodge, one of the most important shrines in the history of early photography. It was the home of Julia Margaret Cameron (1815-1879) who bought it in 1860 to be close to her friend Tennyson. Three years later, she was given a camera and immediately devoted herself with her usual energy to mastering the technical and artistic aspects of what was then called the "Black Art". (Because handling the chemicals involved usually left the photographer's hands deeply stained). The coal-house at Dimbola Lodge was turned into a dark room and within a year, Julia had been elected a member of the Photographic Society of London. She photographed most of the leading lights of the artistic community of the time including Thackeray, Darwin, GF Watts and his wife the actress Ellen Terry, who all at some time lived locally. Perhaps the most famous of her images is the classic portrait of Tennyson himself, a craggy, bearded figure with a visionary gaze. Dimbola Lodge was acquired by the Julia Margaret Cameron Trust in 1993 and it has been converted into a museum and galleries devoted to her photography. There's also a gift shop, antiquarian bookshop, and vegetarian restaurant.

From the bay itself, there are regular cruises around the island's most spectacular natural feature, the dreaded **Needles**. The boat trip takes you through the swirling waters around the lighthouse, and past the line of jagged slabs of gleaming chalk towering some 200ft high. The sea has gouged deep caves out of the cliffs. Two of them are known as Lord Holmes' Parlour and Kitchen, named after a 17th century Governor of the Island who once entertained his guests in the 'Parlour' and kept his wines cool in the 'Kitchen'.

The Needles are undoubtedly at their

The Needles Park

Alum Bay, Isle of Wight PO39 0JD
Tel: 0870 458 0022
website: www.theneedles.co.uk

Set above the world-famous sand cliffs, overlooking The Needles Rocks and Lighthouse, the Park offers a range of attractions for all the family including Alum Bay Glass Studio, Isle of Wight Sweet Manufactory and the popular chairlift to the beach to view the Island's most dramatic landmark. A variety of gift shops and places to eat, as well as childrens attractions, can also be enjoyed here.

Special events include 'Magic in the Skies' fireworks finale very Thursday throughout August.

Frenchman's Cove

WEBSITE: WWW.FRENCHMANSCOVE.CO.UK

Alum Bay Old Road, Alum Bay, Isle of Wight PO39 0HZ
Tel: 01983 752227 Fax: 01983 755125
e-mail: boatfield@frenchmanscove.co.uk

The most westerly guest house on the Isle of Wight and the nearest to the Needles, **Frenchman's Cove** nestles beneath Tennyson Down in a peaceful rural location. The surrounding countryside is ideal walking country with many well-signed footpaths with both countryside and sea views. There are many cycle routes on the island and it is a perfect place to enjoy water sports, hang-gliding, horse riding and much more. Frenchman's Cove is the home of Sue and Chris Boatfield who spare no effort to make sure their guests feel at home. There's a lounge with TV, library, board games and jigsaw puzzles, and a bar with shove-halfpenny boards, chess, solitaire and other games.

View of the Solent from bedrooms

Outside, guests can enjoy the garden with its summerhouse, net for volleyball or badminton, and other outdoor games. The restaurant offers a choice of menu for both breakfast and evening meals. Accommodation comprises a mix of family and double rooms, all with en suite facilities, colour TV and hospitality tray; four of the rooms are on the ground floor. Two double bedrooms have large bay windows and along with the two family apartments enjoy magnificent views over the Solent. Also available is a self-contained apartment for two, The Coach House, where guests can enjoy the freedom of a self-catering holiday while taking advantage of the guest house facilities.

Blue

The Square, Yarmouth, Isle of Wight PO41 0NS
Tel: 01983 760362 Fax: 01983 761516

The little town of Yarmouth has plenty for the visitor to see, including narrow streets, picturesque quays, some fine old houses – even a castle, tucked away down by the ferry. It also has a number of delightful shops, none more delightful than **Blue**. In an old building fronting the main square, this ladies fashion shop was opened by owner-managers Kathy and Alison in 1998, having previously been an antiques shop.

Behind the neat double frontage topped by a cheerful blue blind, the regularly changing stock includes clothes from a variety of designers, some relatively small, others famous names such as Linen Press, Hobbs, Kew and Lysgaard. In addition to the clothes they stock a range of accessories including shoes, bags and jewellery which could come from as near as the Island or as far as Mexico. The friendly welcome and helpful, personal service has won Blue many loyal customers, both in the Island and among visitors who take the opportunity to look for something they might not find in their local shops at home.

most impressive when viewed from the sea, but they are still a grand sight from the land. There are some particularly striking vistas from the **Needles Old Battery** (National Trust), a Victorian coastal fort standing 250ft above the sea. Visitors pass through a 200ft long tunnel and emerge onto a platform with panoramic views.

Alternatively, **The Needles Pleasure Park** (see panel on page 259) at Alum Bay also has good views and offers a wide range of family entertainments, a chairlift from the clifftop to the beach, boat trips to the lighthouse, a glass-making studio and many other attractions. . In the car park at Alum Bay is a monument to Marconi, who sent messages to a tug in Alum Bay and set up the first wireless station here in 1897. The first paid Marconigram was sent in the following year by Lord Kelvin.

Yarmouth

10 miles W of Newport, on the A3054

A regular ferry links this picturesque little port to Lymington on the mainland. Yarmouth was once the principal port on the island which was why Henry VIII ordered the building of **Yarmouth Castle** (English Heritage) in the 1540s. It was garrisoned until 1885 but is now disused, though much remains. The town also boasts a quaint old **Town Hall**, a working pier, and a 13th century church rather unhappily restored in 1831. It's worth going inside to see the incongruous statue on the tomb of Sir Robert Holmes, Governor of the Island in the mid-17th century. During one of the endless conflicts with the French, Sir Robert had captured a ship on board which was a French sculptor with an unfinished statue of Louis XIV. He was travelling to Versailles

Angela's Delicatessen

The Square, Yarmouth, Isle of Wight PO41 0NS
Tel/Fax: 01983 761196

Next to the Town Hall in Yarmouth's main square, **Angela's Delicatessen** is owned and run by foodies Angela and Don Hollist, who enjoy searching on their travels for new products, particularly from small producers. Two large windows crammed with goodies tempt visitors inside, where they can browse to their heart's content among the stock assembled by people with a genuine passion for good food. Traditional cheeses, many unpasteurised and some excellent blues; home-cooked hams, other meats and speciality sausages; savoury pies and pastries cooked fresh throughout the day; oak-smoked kippers from Craster; Morecambe Bay potted shrimps; excellent pâté maison and smoked salmon pâté; interesting wines; ingredients from all over the world, especially China and Thailand - all this and much more makes Angela's Delicatessen a must for people who love their food. Trying to find new and interesting foods keeps Angela and Don very busy, but as they love their food so much they regard it as a labour of love. They also offer an outside catering service and, with so many yachtsmen dropping anchor in town, they sell a lot of frozen meals 'to go'. Usual opening hours are 8am to 5pm every day.

Fort Victoria Model Railway Ltd

Westhill Lane, Yarmouth,
Isle of Wight PO41 0RR
Tel: 01983-761553

Fort Victoria Model Railway is the largest and most sophisticated in Britain. It combines very detailed German digital trains with complex computer programs to give a huge repertoire of routes and manoeuvres. It breaks away completely from the normal format of trains running round in circles. The trains themselves, their lights, whistles, and couplings, the points, signals and even a level crossing are all controlled by computers.

But FVMR is much more than a model railway. It is a complete miniature Germany with over 400 buildings, 600 trees and a population of over 800 tiny people. It also has 30 additional working models, such as the popular burning tax office and an extensive fairground. Since 1995 it has fascinated thousands of families, not just model railway fans. It has appeared on national TV and four times on local TV.

It is located at Fort Victoria Country Park, less than one mile from Yarmouth ferry terminal and shares that campus with an aquarium, planetarium and sunken history museum.

to model the King's head from life. Sir Robert decided that the elaborate statue of the King (in full French armour) would do nicely for his own tomb. The sculptor was ordered to replace the Royal head with Sir Robert's. No doubt deliberately, the artist made a poor fist of the job and the head is decidedly inferior to the rest of the statue.

One mile west of this appealing little town, **Fort Victoria Country Park**, owned by the Isle of Wight Council, is one of the major leisure complexes on the island and uses the area around one of Palmerston's forts. Set on the Solent coastline, the park offers an enormous range of attractions. There are unspoilt sandy beaches, woodland walks, and Ranger-guided tours around the park highlighting the local and natural history of the area. (These must be booked ahead). Within the park you'll also find the largest model railway in Britain, a state-of-the-art Planetarium, a Marine Aquarium with some 80 different species of local and tropical fish, and a

Maritime Heritage Exhibition. Speedboat trips are also available from the slipway next to the Boathouse Lunch & Tea Gardens.

Newtown

5 miles E of Yarmouth off the A3054

Founded in the 13th century by a Bishop of Winchester, Newtown once had a large, busy harbour, but silting led to its decline as a maritime centre and the harbour is now a nature reserve. At its height, the town was the most important on the island and regularly sent two MPs to Westminster; among them were John Churchill, later the 1st Duke of Marlborough, and Prime Minister George Canning. The town's most notable building is the **Old Town Hall**, erected in 1699 and now owned by the National Trust. A small, unassuming building of brick and stone, it contains many interesting documents and memorabilia. The records include the exploits of Ferguson's Gang, an anonymous group of benefactors who gave donations to save selected properties. It is not recorded why this building was chosen, but in 1934 one of the gang went into the National Trust offices and discreetly dropped £500 on the secretary's desk to save the town hall.

At Porchfield, two miles east of Newtown, fun in the country for the whole family is promised at **Colemans Animal Farm**, where visitors are encouraged to stroke and feed the animals. Children will also love the huge wooden play area, the sandpit, the straw maze and the mini-farm with pedal tractors.

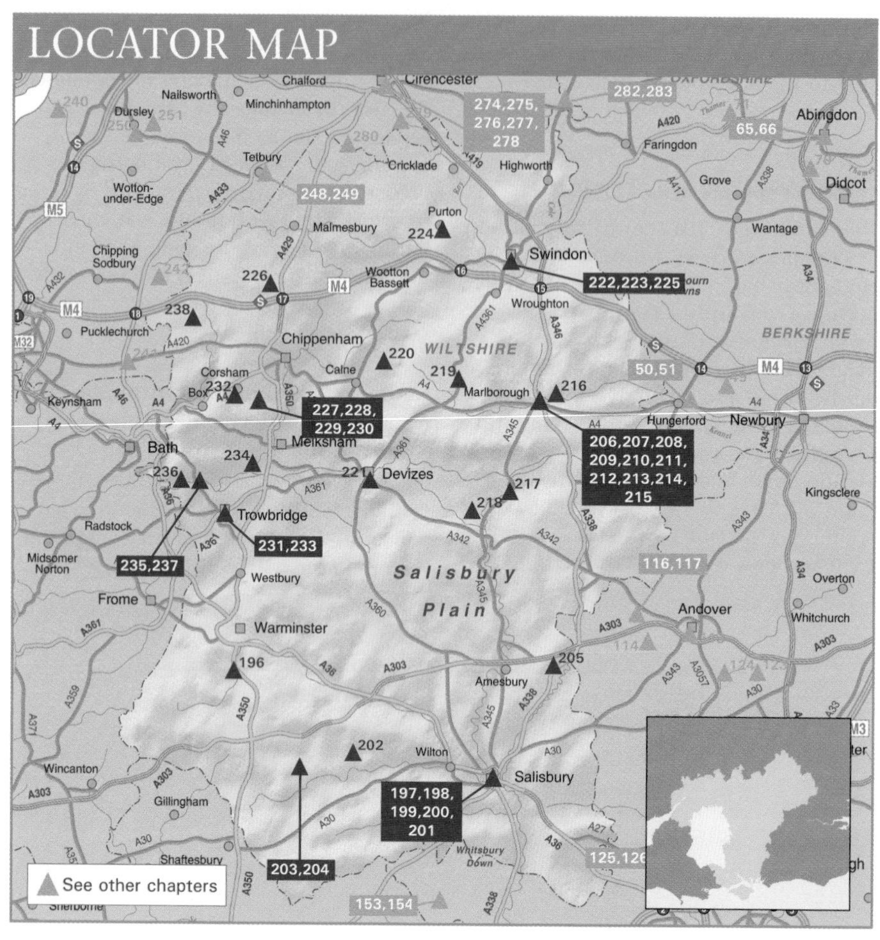

ADVERTISERS AND PLACES OF INTEREST

Accommodation, Food and Drink

198 The Polly Tea Rooms, Salisbury page 273
202 Howard's House Hotel, Teffont Evias page 278
208 Marlborough Art & Craft Centre and Coffee Shop, Marlborough page 282
214 The Polly Tea Rooms, Marlborough page 285
216 Fisherman's House, Mildenhall page 286
220 White Horse Inn, Compton Bassett page 292
221 The Bear Hotel, Devizes page 293
224 The Pear Tree at Purton, Purton page 297
226 Stanton Manor Hotel, Stanton St Quintin, Chippenham page 300
227 King John's Hunting Lodge, Lacock page 302
229 Lacock Pottery and B&B, Lacock page 304
230 Woodmans Cottage B&B Holistic Therapy, Lacock, Chippenham page 304
231 Hilbury Court Hotel, Trowbridge page 305
232 Wadswick Country Store, Corsham page 306
234 Church Farm Holiday Cottages & Farm Shop, Broughton Gifford page 309
236 Church Farm Cottages, Winsley page 310
237 Mr Salvats Coffee Room, Bradford-on-Avon page 311

Activities

230 Woodmans Cottage B&B Holistic Therapy, Lacock, Chippenham page 304

WILTSHIRE & SALISBURY PLAIN 5

Stonehenge

Wiltshire is a county that is rich in the monuments of prehistoric man; it also boasts one of the highest concentrations of historic houses and gardens in the country. This makes it a great place for the tourist, and it's also a perfect choice for walkers, cyclists and lovers of nature, with wide open spaces, woodland and downland and a number of chalk streams that are home to a huge variety of wetland wildlife.

The industrial heritage is also strong, taking in Brunel's Great Western Railway and the railway town of Swindon, brewing at Devizes and carpet-making at Wilton. And the county has many surprises, from the white horses carved in hillsides and the mysterious crop circles to the ancient hill forts and the greatest mystery of them all, the stone circles of Stonehenge - how *did* those stones get from the Marlborough Downs and the mountains of Pembrokeshire and what *was* their use? Pepys didn't have the answer when writing in his Diary in June 1668: *'.....to Stonage, over the plain and some great hills, even to fright us. Come thither, and find them as prodigious as any tales I ever heard of them, and worth going this journey to see. God knows what their use was! They are hard to tell, but yet may be told.'* ....and we don't have the full answer yet.

The jewel in the crown of Wiltshire is the city of Salisbury, at the confluence of the rivers Avon, Wylye, Bourne and Nadder, with its glorious cathedral, a masterpiece of the Early English style, and many other fine buildings. The cathedral for the episcopal see stood originally at nearby Old Sarum, a flourishing town in medieval days that lost its status when a 12th century bishop moved flock, stock and barrel down the hill to the more amenable surroundings of Salisbury and began to build a new cathedral. Atmospheric ruins are all that remain of Old Sarum.

Market Day, Marlborough

Westbury, at the western edge of the chalk downlands of Salisbury Plain, was an important centre of the medieval cloth and wool trades and still boasts some handsome buildings from its days of great prosperity. Like Old Sarum, Westbury was formerly a 'rotten borough', returning two MPs until the 1832 Reform Act stopped the cheating (Old Sarum was the more notorious, having two MPs at a time when it had no voters!). Stourhead, a beautiful Palladian mansion full of treasures, stands in magnificent grounds laid out by Henry Hoare, and another house filled with wonderful things is Longleat, whose grounds contain the famous safari park.

The National Trust village of Lacock, the market town of Devizes with its extraordinary flight of locks on the Kennet and Avon Canal, the historic abbey town of Malmesbury, the lovely Vale of Pewsey and the ancient 4,500-acre Savernake Forest, designated a Site of Special Scientific Interest, are other attractions that no visitor to this wonderful county should miss.

WESTBURY

Westbury, at the western edge of the chalk downlands of **Salisbury Plain**, was a major player in the medieval cloth and wool trades, and still retains many fine buildings from the days of great prosperity, including some cloth works and mills, Westbury was formerly a 'rotten borough' and returned two MPs until 1832, when the Reform Bill put an end to the cheating. Scandal and corruption were rife, and the **Old Town Hall** in the market place is evidence of such goings-on, a gift from a grateful victorious candidate in 1815. This was Sir Manasseh Massey Lopes, a Portuguese financier and slave-trader who 'bought' the borough to advance his political career.

All Saints Church, a 14th century building on much earlier foundations, has many unusual and interesting features, including a stone reredos, a copy of the Erasmus Bible and a clock with no face made by a local blacksmith in 1604. It also boasts the third heaviest peal of bells in the world.

On the southern edge of town is another church well worth a visit. Behind the simple, rustic exterior of St Mary's, Old Dilton, are a three-decker pulpit and panelled pew boxes with original fittings and individual fireplaces.

To the west of the town, at Brokerswood, is **Woodland Park and Heritage Centre**, 80 acres of ancient broadleaf woodland with a wide range of trees, plants and animals, nature trails, a lake with fishing, a picnic and barbecue area, a tea room and gift shop, a museum, a play area and a narrow-gauge railway.

By far the best-known Westbury feature is the famous **Westbury White Horse**, a chalk carving measuring 182 feet in length and 108 feet in height. The present steed dates from 1778, replacing an earlier one carved to celebrate King Alfred's victory over the Danes at nearby Ethandun (Edington) in 878. The white horse is well looked after, the last major grooming carried out in 1996. Above the horse's head are the ruins of Bratton Castle, an Iron Age hill fort covering 25 acres.

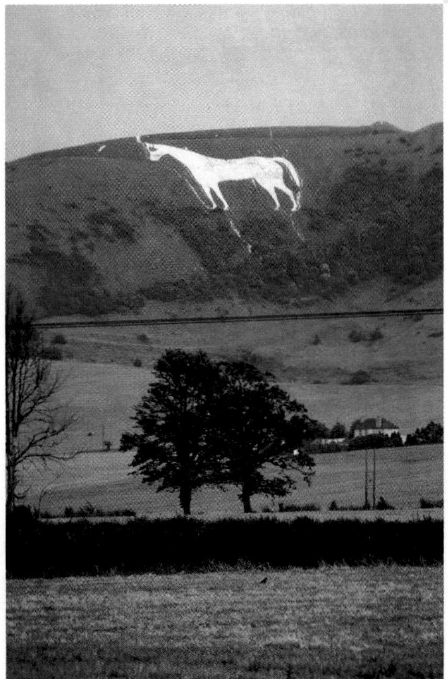

Westbury White Horse

AROUND WESTBURY

WARMINSTER

4 miles S of Westbury on the A350

Warminster is an historic wool, corn-trading and coaching town with many distinguished buildings, including a

Purely Organic Trout Farm & Shop

Deverill's Trout Farm, Longbridge Deverill,
Warminster, Wiltshire BA12 7D2
Tel: 01985 841093
e-mail: trout@prelyorganic.co.uk
website: www.prelyorganic.co.uk

Tony and Eleanor Free, owners of the **Purely Organic Trout Farm & Shop,** must be feeling really pleased with themselves. Leading chef Rick Stein named them amongst his Superheroes of Food; food writer and farmer Hugh Fearnley-Whittenstall declared their trout "Better than any I have tasted"; the *Independent* newspaper placed them in the top 10 Best British Fish or Meat Producers; and in 2002 the farm won the National Small Food Producer of the Year award for its trout, smoked trout and pâté. It also received the accolade of the Gold Prize for services to the environment in the 1999 Green Apple Awards.

This outstanding farm is located in the village of Longbridge Deverill on the A350 Warminster to Blandford road and attracts health-conscious and environmentally aware visitors from near and far with its range of organic fair trade products. Naturally, the best known of these are the trout which are among the best and most natural in the country. The spring water used is drawn at a constant temperature from 35 metres down and flows first through organic watercress beds which enrich it with natural freshwater shrimps, minnows, sticklebacks and the like which provide an excellent, nourishing base for the diet of the trout.

The fish grow from natural exercise rather than from additives in their food, making them firm and fibrous and totally unlike river or lake trout which can often be both earthy and mushy. Purely Organic sells the trout fresh, smoked, in pâté or fish cakes.

Other produce on sale in the well-stocked shop includes soups (the watercress is wonderful), local honey, dairy products, meat, general groceries, hen and duck eggs, flour for bread, ice creams, soft drinks, sandwiches, organic plant seeds and the Green Things range of body products. The shop is open from 9am to 6pm, seven days a week.

famous school with a door designed by Wren. In addition to the 18th and 19th century buildings, Warminster has a number of interesting monuments: the Obelisk with its feeding troughs and pineapple top erected in 1783 to mark the enclosure of the parish; the Morgan Memorial Fountain in the Lake Pleasure Grounds; and *Beyond Harvest*, a statue in bronze by Colin Lambert of a girl sitting on sacks of corn. Warminster's finest building is the Church of St Denys, mainly 14th century but almost completely rebuilt in the 1880s to the design of Arthur Blomfield. The **Dewey Museum** (free), in the public library, displays a wide range of local history from Iron Age times to the present day, including the Victor Manley collection of geology. To the west of town is the 800ft **Cley Hill**, an Iron Age hill fort with two Bronze Age barrows. Formerly owned by the Marquess of Bath, the hill was given to the National Trust in the 1950s and is a renowned sighting place for UFOs. (The region is also noted for the appearance of crop circles and some have linked the two phenomena.)

On the northern edge of Warminster, **Arn Hill Nature Reserve** forms a circular walk of two miles along public footpaths through woodland and open downland.

Codford St Peter & Codford St Mary

8 miles SE of Westbury on the A36

Sister villages beneath the prehistoric remains of Codford Circle, an ancient hilltop meeting place which stands 617 feet up on Salisbury Plain. The church in Codford St Peter has one of Wiltshire's finest treasures in an exceptional 9th century Saxon stone carving of a man holding a branch and dancing. East of Malmpit Hill and visible from the A36 is a rising sun emblem carved by Australian soldiers during World War I. In the military cemetery at Codford St Mary are the graves of Anzac troops who were in camp here. Anzac graves may also be seen at Sutton Veny.

Wylye

10 miles SE of Westbury off the A36

Peace arrived in Wylye in 1977, when a bypass diverted traffic from the busy main roads. It had long been an important junction and staging post on the London-Exeter coaching route. A statue near the bridge over the River Wylye (from which the village, Wilton and indeed Wiltshire get their names) commemorates a brave postboy who drowned here after rescuing several passengers from a stagecoach which had overturned during a flood.

Above the village is the little-known **Yarnbury Castle**, an Iron Age hill fort surrounded by two banks and an outer bank. To the west is a triangular enclosure from Roman times which could have held cattle or sheep. From the 18th century to World War I Yarnbury was the venue of an annual sheep fair.

Imber

5 miles E of Westbury off the B3098

The part of Salisbury Plain containing the village of Imber was closed to the public in 1943 and has been used by the Army ever since for live firing. The evicted villagers were told that they could return to Imber after the war, but the promise was not kept and the village remains basically inaccessible. A well-marked 30-mile perimeter walk skirting the danger area takes in Warminster, Westbury, Tilshead in the east and Chitterne in the south.

Longleat

6 miles SW of Westbury off the A362

2004 saw the 55th anniversary of the opening of **Longleat House** to the

Longleat House

public. The magnificent home of the Marquess of Bath was built by an ancestor, Sir John Thynne, in a largely symmetrical style, in the 1570s. The inside is a treasure house of old masters, Flemish tapestries, beautiful furniture, rare books and Lord Bath's racy murals. The superb grounds of Longleat House were landscaped by Capability Brown and now contain one of the country's best known venues for a marvellous day out. In the famous **Safari Park** the Lions of Longleat, first introduced in 1966, have been followed by a veritable Noah's Ark of exotic creatures, including rhinos, zebras and white tigers. The park also features safari boat rides, a narrow-gauge railway, children's amusement area, garden centre and the largest hedge maze in the world.

Stourton

9 miles SW of Westbury off the B3092

The beautiful National Trust village of Stourton lies at the bottom of a steep wooded valley and is a particularly glorious sight in the daffodil season. The main attraction is, of course, **Stourhead**, one of the most famous examples of the early-18th century English landscape movement. The lakes, the trees, the temples, a grotto and a classical bridge make the grounds, laid out by Henry Hoare, a paradise in the finest 18th century tradition, and the gardens are renowned for their striking vistas and woodland walks as well as a stunning selection of rare trees and specimen shrubs, including tulip trees, azaleas and rhododendrons. The house itself, a classical masterpiece built in the 1720s in Palladian style for a Bristol banker, contains a wealth of Grand Tour paintings and works of art, including furniture by Chippendale the Younger and wood carvings by Grinling Gibbons. On the very edge of the estate, some three miles by road from the house, the imposing King Alfred's Tower stands

Gardens at Stourhead

at the top of the 790ft Kingsettle Hill. This 160ft triangular redbrick folly was built in 1772 to commemorate the king, who reputedly raised his standard here against the Danes in 878.

Mere

12 miles SW of Westbury off the A303

A small town nestling below the downs near the borders with Dorset and Somerset. The town is dominated by **Castle Hill**, on which Richard, Earl of Cornwall, son of King John, built a castle in 1253. Nothing of the castle remains, though many of the stones were used in building Mere's houses. The Church of St Michael the Archangel in High Gothic style features some fine medieval and Victorian stained glass, carved Jacobean pews, an unusual octagonal font and a 12th century statue of St Michael slaying a dragon. **Mere Museum**, in the public library in Barton Lane, is principally a local history collection with a good photographic archive. Displays are changed regularly but a permanent feature is a large, detailed map of Mere drawn in colour by a local artist. This is a great area for rambling, one of the best spots being the Whitesheet Hill Nature Trail with wonderful views and a wealth of plants and insects, including some rare chalk-loving butterflies.

East Knoyle

14 miles S of Westbury on the A350

Two items of interest here. A simple stone monument marks the birthplace, in 1632, of Sir Christopher Wren, son of the village rector of the time. East Knoyle Windmill is a tower mill on a circular base, without sails and unused for over a century. It offers good views over Blackmoor Vale and has a large grassy area for picnics.

Tollard Royal

6 miles SE of Shaftesbury on the B3081

Tollard Royal is a historic village atop **Zigzag Hill** in the heart of Cranborne Chase. King John had a small estate here which he used on his hunting trips. **King John's House** is a part-stone, part-timber residence whose fine condition is largely due to the efforts of General Pitt Rivers, an eminent Victorian archaeologist who inherited the estate and spent the last 20 years of his life unearthing Bronze Age remains. His collection is housed in the Salisbury and South Wiltshire Museum, where a gallery is named in his honour.

Ludwell

2 miles E of Shaftesbury on the A30

Near the village is the National Trust-owned **Win Green Hill**, the highest point in Wiltshire, crowned by a copse of beech trees set around an ancient bowl barrow. From the summit there are wonderful views as far as the Quantock Hills to the northwest and the Isle of Wight to the southeast.

SALISBURY

The glorious medieval city of Salisbury stands at the confluence of five rivers, the Avon, Wylye, Bourne, Ebble and Nadder. Originally called New Sarum, it grew around the present Cathedral, which was built between 1220 and 1258 in a sheltered position two miles south of the site of its windswept Norman predecessor at Old Sarum. Over the years the townspeople followed the clergy into the new settlement, creating a flourishing religious and market centre whose two main aspects flourish to this day.

One of the most beautiful buildings in the world, **Salisbury Cathedral** is the only medieval cathedral in England to be built throughout in the Early English

The Gallery at Fisherton Mill & Café

108 Fisherton Street, Salisbury, Wiltshire SP2 7QY
Tel/Fax: 01722 415121
e-mail: thegallery@fishertonmill.co.uk
website: www.fishertonmill.co.uk

Built in 1880 as a grain mill, **Fisherton Mill** is now the south of England's largest independent art gallery. Spread over three floors and a courtyard, the Gallery retains many of the Mill's original features, which makes for a very unique setting. The beamed ceilings, cast iron pillars and fine old pieces of machinery will add to your visit as you enjoy the wide range of art on display.

The Gallery continuously shows work in the exhibition spaces by leading artists, sculptors and furniture makers, whilst the Gallery shop stocks an array of accessories, both functional and decorative, including ceramics, textiles, glasswork, jewellery and unframed prints as well as cards and carefully selected gifts, which complement the art work.

The Gallery Café, situated within the ground floor Gallery, offers an atmospheric setting in which to enjoy a great selection of home-made cakes, freshly made smoothies and juices, teas and Fair Trade Organic coffee. Lunch is light and modern, using fresh produce prepared to order, and includes soups, salads, sandwiches and main dishes as well as healthy choices for children. (Lunch is from 12 - 2.30pm). The courtyard has seating for fine days.

The studio workshops around the courtyard show images by photographer Alan Hayward, work by sculptor Paul Wilson and Lindsay Keir's paintings.

Fisherton Mill is known locally as 'Salisbury's best kept secret', as it is tucked away behind the shops on Fisherton Street, which leads from Salisbury town centre to the Railway Station. Turn in under the archway where you see the banner.

style - apart from the spire, the tallest in England, which was added some years later and rises to an awesome 404 feet. The Chapter House opens out of the cloisters and contains, among other treasures, one of the four surviving originals of Magna Carta. Six hundred thousand visitors a year come to marvel at this and other priceless treasures, including a number of magnificent tombs. The oldest working clock in Britain and possibly in the world is situated in the fan-vaulted north transept; it was built in 1386 to strike the hour and has no clock face. The cathedral is said to contain a door for each month, a window for each day and a column for each hour of the year. A small statue inside the west door is of Salisbury's 17th century **Boy Bishop**. It was a custom for choristers to elect one of their number to be bishop for a period lasting from St Nicholas Day to Holy

Salisbury Cathedral

The Polly Tea Rooms

8 St Thomas's Square, Salisbury, Wiltshire SP1 1BA
Tel: 01722 336037

A sister establishment to Polly's Tea Rooms in Marlborough, **The Polly Tea Rooms** in Salisbury maintains the same high standards as its elder sibling. Known as Snell's Tea Rooms until purchased by Sir Brian Mussell, Polly's in Salisbury opened in December 2003. Just a five minute walk from the city centre and next door to St Thomas's Church, which was originally built as a place of worship for the builders working on the cathedral, it has quickly established itself as ***the*** place to take tea in the city.

A light and airy building, it provides a welcoming, relaxed environment in which to enjoy breakfast, morning coffee, lunch or afternoon tea. In addition to its extensive choice of tea-time treats, Polly's also boasts its own chocolate factory on the first floor which produces an enticing selection of exquisite home-made chocolates.

Innocents Day (6th-28th December). One year the boy bishop was apparently literally tickled to death by the other choristers; since he died in office, his statue shows him in full bishop's regalia.

The Close, the precinct of the ecclesiastical community serving the cathedral, is the largest in England and contains a number of museums and houses open to the public. **Salisbury and South Wiltshire Museum**, in the 17th century King's House, is the home of the Stonehenge Gallery and a designated archaeological collection of national importance. Displays include early South Wiltshire, the Giant and Hob Nob, Romans and Saxons, the Pitt Rivers collection (see page 271), Old Sarum,

H.R. TRIBBECK & SON

FAMILY JEWELLERS SINCE 1905

12 Bridge Street, Salisbury, Wiltshire SP1 2LX
Tel: 01722 324395 Fax: 01722 421120
e-mail: shop@tribbeckdirect.com

Approaching its centenary in 2005, **HR Tribbeck & Son** is well-established as one of the leading goldsmiths, silversmiths, clock and watch makers in the county. Its city centre showroom stocks fine quality jewellery in both traditional and contemporary designs, watches and clocks by leading manufacturers, a comprehensive selection of new and antique silver, and a range of top quality accessories for gentlemen. The highly qualified and experienced staff offer an individual service that covers repair, restoration and valuation on all categories of goods sold. The shop is open from 9.15am to 5pm, Monday to Saturday.

Salisbury Playhouse

Malthouse Lane, Salisbury, Wiltshire SP2 7RA
Tel: 01722 320333 Fax: 01722 421991
e-mail: marketing@salisburyplayhouse.com
website: www.salisburyplayhouse.com

"It's great to know there are some beacons like the Playhouse out there for us non-metropolitans," wrote the theatre critic of the *Independent*. He was referring to **Salisbury Playhouse** which, throughout the year, stages a high quality programme of plays by writers as diverse as Shakespeare, Noel Coward and David Hare in its main theatre, along with cutting edge performances in the intimate Salberg Studio. Naturally, around Christmas there's a good old-fashioned pantomime. The Playhouse also stages regular performances for children aged from three to 13 and hosts workshops for schools and colleges.

Another attraction at the Playhouse is the Gallery which puts on a wide variety of exhibitions which change every few weeks. The theatre has its own restaurant which is open from 9.30am to 4.30pm serving morning coffee, tasty lunches and afternoon teas. It re-opens at 6pm when two- or three-course meals are available. It is fully licensed so customers can wine and dine in style. The bar is open from 6pm to 11pm on performance nights and offers a range of bar snacks.

ceramics, costume, lace, embroidery and Turner watercolours.

A few doors away is **The Royal Gloucestershire, Berkshire and Wiltshire Museum** housed in a 13th century building called the Wardrobe because it was originally used to store the bishop's clothes and documents. The museum tells the story of the county regiments since 1743 and the exhibits include Bobbie the Dog, the hero of Maiwand, and many artefacts from foreign campaigns. The house has a tea room and a riverside garden with views of the famous water meadows. The historic **Medieval Hall** is the atmospheric setting for a 30-minute history of Salisbury in sound and pictures. **Mompesson House**, a National Trust property, is a perfect example of Queen Anne architecture notable for its plasterwork, an elegant carved oak staircase, fine period furniture and the important Turnbull collection of 18th century drinking glasses. In the Market Place is the **John Creasey Museum** and the **Creasey Collection of Contemporary Art**, a permanent collection of books, manuscripts, objects and art. Also in the Market Place, in the library, is the **Edwin Young Collection** of 19th and early 20th century watercolours, drawings and oil paintings of Salisbury and its surrounding landscape.

Salisbury racecourse, a short drive west of the city, stages flat racing during the summer months.

There are many other areas of Salisbury to explore on foot and a short drive takes visitors to the ruins of **Old Sarum** (see panel below), abandoned when the bishopric moved into the city. Traces of the original cathedral and palace are visible on the huge uninhabited mound, which dates back to the Iron Age. Old Sarum became the most notorious of the 'rotten boroughs', returning two Members of Parliament, despite having no voters, until the 1832 Reform Act stopped the practice. A plaque on the site commemorates Old Sarum's most illustrious MP, William Pitt the Elder.

AROUND SALISBURY

Britford

1 mile S of Salisbury on the A338

Lying within branches of the Wiltshire Avon, Britford has a moated country house and a fine Saxon church with some early stone carvings. An ornate

Old Sarum

Tel: 01722 335398
website: www.english-heritage.org.uk

Situated high above Salisbury Plain, **Old Sarum**, the site of the ancient city of Salisbury, was first settled in the Iron Age when a massive hill fort was created here. Later occupied by the Romans (several Roman roads converge here), the town grew in Saxon times within its prehistoric ramparts until, by the time of the Norman Conquest, there were two palaces here along with Salisbury's first great cathedral. People continued to live at Sarum until the 16th century, although a new town grew up around the 13th century cathedral, and in the 19th century Old Sarum was one of the country's most notorious 'rotten boroughs'. Today, the massive earth ditches and ramparts remain intact and there are spectacular views across Salisbury and the surrounding countryside.

tomb is thought to be that of the Duke of Buckingham, who was beheaded in Salisbury in 1483. Nearby **Longford Castle**, mainly 16th century, houses an interesting collection of paintings.

Downton

5 miles S of Salisbury off the A338

The Saxons established a meeting place, or moot, on an earlier earthwork fortification, and it was in commemoration of that ancient parliament that the present **Moot House** was built on the foundations of the old castle. The building and its garden stand opposite a small 18th century amphitheatre built to resemble the Saxon moot. In 1955, a Roman villa comprising seven rooms and a bath house was discovered nearby.

Lover

6 miles SE of Salisbury off the A338

In the vicinity of this charmingly named village is the National Trust's **Pepperbox Hill** topped by an early 17th century octagonal tower known as **Eyre's Folly**. Great walking, great views, and a great place for nature-lovers, with a variety of plant and bird life.

Wilton

3 miles W of Salisbury on the A30

The third oldest borough in England and once the capital of Saxon Wessex. It is best known for its carpets, and the **Wilton Carpet Factory** on the River Wylye continues to produce top-quality carpets, maintaining a worldwide reputation for quality that goes back 300 years. Wilton carpets as we know them today were created by a French carpet weaver who was brought to England by the Earl of Pembroke in the early 1700s to teach the local weavers his skills. In 1835 redundant handlooms were brought from the Axminster factory in Devon and set up in Wilton. Luxurious hand-knotted Axminsters, with each tuft individually tied by hand, were made alongside traditional Wiltons up to 1958. Visitors can tour the carpet-making exhibition in the historic courtyard then go into the modern factory to see the carpets made on up-to-date machinery using traditional skills and techniques. Alongside the factory is the Wilton Shopping Village offering high-quality factory shopping in a traditional rural setting.

Wilton House is the stately home of the Earls of Pembroke. When the original house was destroyed by fire in 1647, Inigo Jones was commissioned to build its replacement. He designed both the exterior and the interior, including the amazing Double Cube Room, and the house was further remodelled by James Wyatt. The art collection is one of the very finest, with works

House & Grounds, Wilton

by Rembrandt, Van Dyke, Rubens and Tintoretto; the furniture includes pieces by Chippendale and Kent. There's plenty to keep children busy and happy, including a treasure hunt quiz and a huge adventure playground. There's a Tudor kitchen, a Victorian laundry and 21 acres of landscaped grounds with parkland, cedar trees, water and rose gardens and an elegant Palladian bridge. It was used as an operations centre during World War II and is thought to be where the Normandy landings were planned.

The Church of St Mary and St Nicholas is a unique Italianate church built in the style of Lombardy by the Russian Countess of Pembroke in 1845. The interior is resplendent with marble, mosaics, richly carved woodwork and early French stained glass.

The Fovant Badges

Broad Chalke

7 miles W of Salisbury off the A354

A Saxon village where the 17th century diarist John Aubrey had a small estate. A warden of the parish church, he was also a keen angler and wrote of his beloved River Ebble: *'There are not better trouts in the Kingdom of England than here'*. The designer and photographer Cecil Beaton spent his final years in Broad Chalke and is buried in the churchyard of All Saints.

Fovant

8 miles W of Salisbury on the A30

The **Fovant Badges** are badges carved in the chalk hillside by troops during the First World War. They include the Australian Imperial Force, the Devonshire Regiment, 6th City of London Regiment, the London Rifle Brigade, the Post Office Rifles, the Royal Corps of Signals, the Royal Wiltshire Yeomanry, the Wiltshire Regiment and the YMCA. The badges can be seen from the A30.

Dinton

9 miles W of Salisbury off the A30

There are two National Trust properties to visit near this lovely hillside village. **Little Clarendon** is a small but perfectly formed Tudor manor house with three oak-furnished rooms open to visitors; **Philipps House** is a handsome white-fronted neo-Grecian house with a great Ionic portico. Built by the early 19th century architect Jeffrey Wyattville for William Wyndham, it stands in the beautiful landscaped grounds of Dinton Park.

Teffont Evias

9 miles W of Salisbury off the B3089

Teffont Evias is a quiet little village with some handsome houses built with stone from the local Chilmark quarries.

Howard's House Hotel

Teffont Evias, nr Salisbury, Wiltshire SP3 5RJ
Tel: 01726 716392 Fax: 01722 716820
e-mail: enq@howardshousehotel.com
website: www.howardshousehotel.com

Built as a farmhouse in 1623 and restored in 1989, **Howard's House Hotel** stands in a quintessential English garden of rolling lawns, ancient box hedges, a pond with a fountain and secret corners for daydreaming and quiet contemplation. In this most civilised of settings, nine luxurious bedrooms were created, each with its own bathroom, bathrobes, telephone, TV and hairdryer. Floral prints and pastel shades combine to enhance the feeling of informality and relaxation, and the sitting room offers abundant comfort and calm, with French windows open to the garden in summer and a log fire glowing warmly in winter.

In the beautifully appointed, non-smoking dining room tip-top produce is handled with skill and flair on outstanding table d'hôte and à la carte dinner and Sunday lunch menus. Typical choices might include pan-seared king scallops with oven-baked tomatoes and a saffron vinaigrette, Gressingham duck breast with wild muchroom risotto, roast root vegetables and a beetroot jus, and char-sealed fillet of Scotch beef with a rosemary galette, garlic confit, green beans and Madeira. Howard's House is a real gem of a hotel and an ideal place for a relaxing break, for country walks or for visiting the many places of historic interest in the area.

Heaton's Antiques

2-3 High Street, Tisbury, Wiltshire SP3 8PS
Tel: 01747 873025 evenings 01747 870048
website: www.heatons-of-tisbury.co.uk

An enthusiastic connoisseur of arts and crafts since her schooldays, Ros King has for the past three years owned and run one of the most interesting arts, crafts and antiques centres in the region. On the main street of the pretty little town of Tisbury, **Heaton's Antiques** specialises in topographical and antiquarian prints and etchings.

The stock includes over 3,000 maps of regions and towns in the United Kingdom, some displayed framed on the walls, most carefully catalogued in boxes and drawers. They date mainly from between 1600 and 1830, and in addition to the maps Heaton's keeps an intriguing selection of original prints and engravings with sporting, hunting and animal themes, and, most notably, second strikes by the caricaturist Gillray and some early Hogarths. Among the general stock are period posters and postcards, decorative glass and chinaware, and a section devoted to local crafts including pottery, hats, scarves and small items of furniture. Heaton's Antiques is open from 10 to 4 Monday, Friday and Saturday, or by appointment.

Close by, on the road that connects with the A303, is **Farmer Giles Farmstead**, a 175-acre working farm where a wide variety of farm animals can be seen at close quarters.

Tisbury

12 miles W of Salisbury off the A30

Tisbury is the most prominent of the villages strung along the River Nadder. It has a fine parish church that has a 15th century clerestory and used to have a lofty spire. This was hit by lightning in 1742, rebuilt, and then struck by lightning again 20 years later. At this point the parishioners gave up.

To the east of the village stands the magnificent gateway of Place Farm. It was built for the abbesses of Shaftesbury in the late-14th and early-15th centuries and gives a clear idea of the splendour of the farm at that time. The only building that remains is the huge **Tithe Barn**, believed to be the largest in England. Built of local stone, it has a thatched roof that was originally covered by stone tiles.

Notable sons of the village include Thomas Mayhew, a prosperous mercer in the early 1600s who emigrated to New England where he acquired the off-shore islands of Martha's Vineyard and Nantucket. He and his family also helped establish the township of Tisbury.

In the churchyard of the Wiltshire Tisbury are buried John Lockwood and Alice Kipling, the parents of the author Rudyard Kipling. He often visited them at their home, The Gables in Hindon Lane, and wrote much of his novel *Kim* while staying in Tisbury.

Woodford Valley

6 miles N of Salisbury off the A345

A seven-mile stretch between Salisbury and Amesbury contains some of the prettiest and most peaceful villages in the county, among them **Great Durnford** with its Norman church and restored mill, **Lake**, with an imposing Tudor mansion, and **Middle Woodford**, where the internationally renowned **Heale Garden and Plant Centre** lies within the grounds of 16th century Heale House in an idyllic setting by a tributary of the Avon. Much of the garden was designed by Harold Peto (1854-1933), whose own garden at Iford Manor (see page 308) is in the Italianate style that he so favoured. Highlights at Heale include a superb collection of plants, shrubs and roses, a water garden and a Japanese bridge and teahouse made in 1910 with the help of four Japanese gardeners.

Amesbury

8 miles N of Salisbury on the A345

Stonehenge at Sunset

Queen Elfrida founded an abbey here in 979 in atonement for her part in the murder of her son-in-law, Edward the Martyr, at Corfe Castle. Henry II rebuilt the abbey's great Church of St Mary and St Melor, whose tall central tower is the only structure to survive from the pre-Norman monastery. A mile to the north of Amesbury, the A345 passes along the eastern side of **Woodhenge**, a ceremonial monument even older than Stonehenge. It was the first major prehistoric site to be discovered by aerial photography, its six concentric rings of post holes having been spotted as crop marks by Squadron Leader Insall in 1925. Like Stonehenge, it seems to have been used as an astronomical calendar. When major excavation was carried out in the

Cholderton Rare Breed Farm Park

Amesbury Road, Cholderton,
Salisbury, Wiltshire SP4 0EW
Tel: 01980 629438
website: www.rabbitworld.co.uk

Cholderton Farm Park, set in beautiful countryside just off the A303, first opened its gates in 1987, since when it has developed into one of the most popular family attractions in the county, and the winner of several awards from the tourist industry. Owned and run by Pamela and Jeremy McConnell and their family, the park is home to a large number of rare breeds. Rabbit World is just one small part, with over 50 breeds on show in spacious pens, often in family units. The under-cover unit also displays information on rabbit life and history and has a pen where children can sit and stroke some of the younger rabbits.

Also under cover are a poultry unit with 18 breeds and a sheep unit (see the seaweed-eating sheep!), while outdoor attractions include a waterfowl pond, water gardens, a nature trail, a woodland adventure playground and a separate area for very young visitors. There are picnic areas both in and out of doors, and a cafeteria in the farmhouse serves lunches, snacks and speciality cream teas. During peak times of year additional attractions are added, including tractor and trailer rides and the famous Cholderton 'Pork Stakes' pig races. The farm also has a formal educational side, with lectures, videos and a comprehensive teachers pack for visiting school groups. The farm is open every day from the end of March to the end of October; also open out of season at weekends (10.30am-4pm) for parties and educational visits by arrangement.The majority of the park is accessible by wheelchair.

1920s, a number of neolithic tools and other artefacts were found, along with the skeleton of a three-year-old child whose fractured skull suggested some kind of ritual sacrifice.

Two miles west of Amesbury at the junction of the A303 and A344/A360 stands **Stonehenge** itself, perhaps the greatest mystery of the prehistoric world, one of the wonders of the world, and a monument of unique importance. The World Heritage Site is surrounded by the remains of ceremonial and domestic structures, many of them accessible by road or public footpath. The great stone blocks of the main ring are truly massive, and it seems certain that the stones in the outer rings - rare bluestones from the Preseli Hills of west Wales - had to be transported over 200 miles. Stonehenge's orientation on the rising and setting sun has always been one of its most remarkable features, leading to theories that the builders were from a sun-worshipping culture or that the whole structure is part of a huge astronomical calendar ...or both. The mystery remains, and will probably remain for ever.

Stratford-sub-Castle

2 miles NE of Salisbury off the A343

Old Sarum is not the only impressive mound hereabouts, as three miles to the east is the Iron Age hill fort of **Figbury Rings**. Above it, the bleak expanse of Porton Down is a largely undisturbed conservation area where the great bustard has been making a comeback. This large, long-legged bird was once a common sight on Salisbury Plain and is incorporated in Wiltshire's coat of arms.

Newton Toney

8 miles NE of Salisbury on the A338

Close to this pleasant village is **Cholderton Rare Breeds Farm Park** (see panel opposite) set in beautiful countryside and a major family attraction since opening to the public in 1987. Highlights include Rabbit World, tractor and trailer rides, pig racing, a woodland adventure playground, nature trail and a cafeteria serving excellent clotted cream teas. The park is also home to many endangered farm animals.

MARLBOROUGH

Famous for its public school and its wide high street – where markets are held every Wednesday and Saturday, Marlborough is situated in the rural eastern part of Wiltshire in the upland valley of the Kennet, which flows through the town. It was once an important staging post on the coaching run from London to Bath and Bristol, and the presence of the A4 means that it

Wild Thymes

2 Old Hughenden Yard, High Street, Marlborough, Wiltshire SN8 1LT
Tel: 01672 516373

Old Hughenden Yard is a charming traffic free precinct off Marlborough's busy High Street and it's here you'll find Christopher Markham's intriguing organic food store, **Wild Thymes.** His stock contains a comprehensive range of organic products – grains, lentils, herbal teas, dried fruits, wheat and gluten free products and much, much more. The shop also offers natural beauty products, homoepathic remedies, flower essences, vitamins and supplements including Bioforce and Nature's Own brand ranges. Helpful and knowledgeable staff are at hand to give advice and the shop is open from 9am to 6pm, Monday to Saturday.

Brissi

106 High Street, Marlborough, Wiltshire SN8 1LT
Tel: 01672 515154

The enticing window displays at **Brissi** give a foretaste of the elegant and stylish items to be found inside. The shop was established in 2001 by Arianna Brissi who is a native of Verona in northern Italy but has lived for some 20 years in England. Arianna travels around the world to find distinctive and unusual products for the shop. You'll find Limoges china and the full range of Burleigh china; Italian pashminas and blankets; rare French toiletries and home-wares; Miller Harris perfumes; wall lights, mirrors and sconces from France; Damask cottons and nightwear, handbags and accessories, and the range of decorative products featured when Arianna was the subject of an article in *Homes and Gardens* magazine in December 2003.

Everything is displayed with flair using sitting room, dining room, kitchen and bedroom settings. Whether you are looking for something to enhance your own interior décor or seeking out something elegant and distinctive as a gift, you will find a wealth of ideas at Brissi – and all at very reasonable prices.

Marlborough Art & Craft Centre and Coffee Shop

St Peter's Church, High Street, Marlborough, Wiltshire SN8 1HQ
Tel: 01672 511453

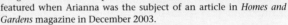

Marlborough Art & Craft Centre and Coffee Shop enjoy a very impressive location within St Peter's Church, a fine 15th Century building with a lofty tower, recently exposed Victorian tile work, and striking stained glass windows. Sadly, the church was made redundant in 1974 and remained closed until 1978 when a Charitable Trust was established to restore and re-open the building for public use. The building now houses Marlborough Art & Craft, a year-round display of high quality hand-made goods created by local artists including paintings of local scenes, glass, ceramics, pottery, jewellery, woodcraft, mirrors, and much more – in all, some 70 different craftspeople have their work on display here.

Also within the building is St Peters Coffee Shop, which serves delicious home-made scones and cakes (a choice of between eight and 10 each day), freshly made sandwiches, home-made soup, hot meals and lunchtime specials. Both the Art & Craft Centre and the Coffee Shop are open from 10am to 5pm, Monday to Saturday, all year round and also on Sundays in the high season and if you are visiting here on a Saturday between Easter and mid-October, an additional attraction is a guided tour to the top of the tower which offers some grand views of the town and countryside.

still has easy links both east and west. Its main street, one of the finest in the country, is dignified by many Tudor houses and handsome Georgian colonnaded shops, behind which are back alleys waiting to be explored. St Mary's Church, austere behind a 15th century frontage, stands in **Patten Alley**, so named because pedestrians had to wear pattens (an overshoe with a metal sole) to negotiate the mud on rainy days. The porch of the church has a ledge where churchgoers would leave their pattens before entering. Other buildings of interest include those clustered round The Green (originally a Saxon village and the working-class quarter in the 18th and 19th centuries); the turn-of-the-century Town Hall looking down the broad High Street; and the ornate 17th century Merchant's House, now restored as a museum.

La Petite Fromagerie

6 Old Hughenden Yard, High Street, Marlborough, Wiltshire SN8 1LT
Tel: 01672 514321 Fax: 01672 516373

Christopher Markham, the owner of Wild Thymes (see page 281), also established **La Petite Fromagerie**, an enticing specialist cheese outlet and delicatessen. Within the dairy style shop with its slate floor you'll find an extensive range of English and European cheeses including sheep and goat varieties along with a selection of delicacies such as hams, pastas, olive oils, chutneys,olives, pâté/terrines, Tyrell's Herefordshire crisps and much more. Also on sale is Italian style fresh bread from a local bakery – but call in early for this since it has usually all gone by lunchtime.

The India Shop

3 Hillier's Yard, Marlborough, Wiltshire SN8 1NB
Tel: 01672 515585 Fax: 01672 851642
e-mail: enquiries@theindiashop.co.uk
website: www.theindiashop.co.uk

Occupying a delightful old property in the pedestrian precinct of Hillier's Yard, **The India Shop** offers a huge variety of crafts and antiques, all of them from the sub-continent. The business was started in 1987 by owner Ann Wiles who subscribes to the Fair Trade policy and makes two or three visits to India each year to buy the pieces herself. The range of items on display is enormous – beautifully crafted antique dressers, chest of drawers, wardrobes, tables and mirrors; brilliantly coloured inexpensive throws, cushions and curtains; gift boxes crafted by hand; candles and scents; jewellery and jewel boxes; semi-precious coloured stones; hard-wearing jute floor mats and rugs; children's toys; inexpensive gifts and a host of room decorations.

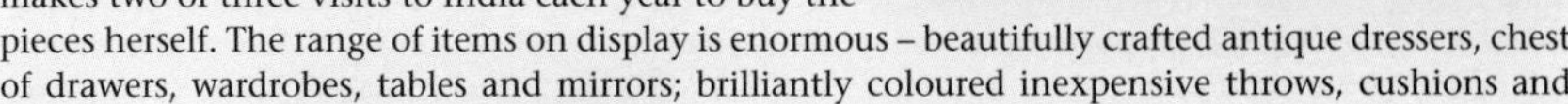

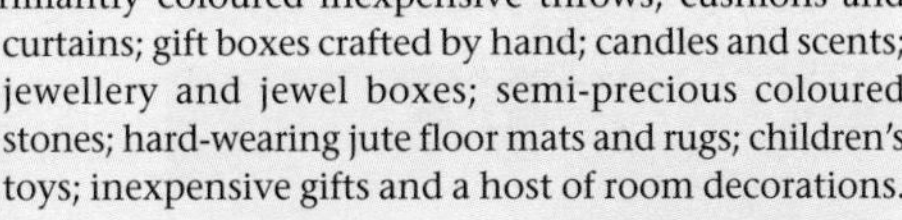

There are two floors of displays here but not enough room to display the full stock of antique furniture. Some 200 more pieces are stored in a warehouse nearby and can be visited by appointment. The India Shop is located in the town centre but there is ample parking in the Waitrose car park close by. And if you happen to be visiting Salisbury, there's another even larger India Shop there.

Marlborough Tiles

16 High Street, Marlborough, Wiltshire SN8 1AA
Tel/Fax: 01672 515287
e-mail: admin@marlboroughtiles.com
website: www.marlboroughtiles.com

One of the five main producers of decorative ceramic tiles in the UK, **Marlborough Tiles'** history goes back to the 1930s when two accomplished artists, Rosalind Ord and Sylvia Packard, joined forces with each putting up £50 to purchase their own kiln which they installed in a neighbour's outhouse. In 1936 they moved to Marlborough and although their trade at this time was mainly through friends and contacts they were already supplying tiles to Fortnum & Mason in London.

Making tiles with natural materials is a continuously evolving process that hovers tantalisingly between an art and a science. It is an individual skill too - no other company makes tiles quite like Marlborough. Their craftsmen use only the finest clay from Italy and then, in a carefully controlled production sequence, nurture it to create terracotta of peerless quality. Like the finest glass you can gauge that quality by ringing it – Marlborough's resounds with a crystal clear note. Their Lustre Range has won the *UK Tile Magazine's* award for "Wall Tile of the Year", so whether you're choosing between their own hand-made UK tiles or the stylish tiles they have scoured the world for, you'll surely find something to enhance your own interior décor. At the company's showrooms knowledgeable staff are at hand to offer practical advice and information on fitting and aftercare.

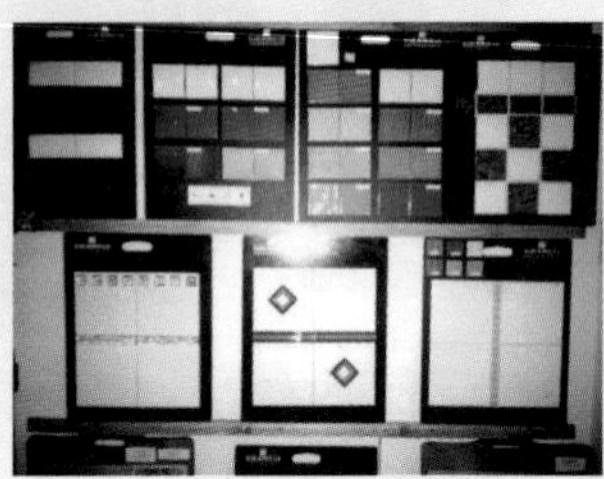

The Food Gallery - Delicatessen

42a High Street, Marlborough, Wiltshire SN8 1HQ
Tel: 01672 514069
website: www.thefoodgallery.co.uk

Located at the College end of Marlborough's High Street, Martin and Clare Earl's **The Food Gallery** is a gourmet's dream come true. Ever tried Can pujol spanish goat's cheese? Or Marlborough Downs honey? Or snail paste and sauce from the Dordogne? They're all on sale here along with produce from all around the world – exclusive Italian pastas, organic French soups, Pure Jersey Ice Creams and Welsh pâtés are just some of the global delicacies. English produce is also well represented with fresh fishcakes from Devon; Morecambe Bay potted shrimps and crayfish tails; Penrith Toffee Shop fudge; Tracklements sauces, vinaigrettes and chutneys from Wiltshire to name just a few.

There's a wonderful selection of British and European cheeses. Fresh produce from the deli counter is used for the gourmet sandwiches that you can enjoy at one of the cosy tables, either inside or outside, along with freshly ground coffee followed perhaps by one of Clare's marvellous brownies or other desserts. And if you would like a night off from cooking, there's a huge choice of made-to-order finger buffets, quiches, tarts, cakes, roulades, birthday cakes and other treats. A truly delightful shop combining delicious food with excellent gift ideas.

Marlborough College was founded in 1843 primarily for sons of the clergy. The Seymour family built a mansion near the site of the Norman castle. This mansion was replaced in the early-18th century by a building which became the Castle Inn and is now C House, the oldest part of the College. A mound in the private grounds of the school is linked with King Arthur's personal magician Merlin. It was said that he was buried under this

Market Day, Marlborough

Leathercraft of Marlborough

Old Hughenden Yard, High Street, Marlborough, Wiltshire SN8 1LT
Tel: 01672 512065 Fax: 01672 861656

If what you're looking for is made of leather, look no further than **Leathercraft of Marlborough**, located in a courtyard off the High Street. Here you'll find a huge and varied stock that includes fine quality handbags, briefcases and travel bags, belts and gloves, purses and wallets, toilet bags, Barbour country wear and even that essential accessory for every sportsman – a hip flask. The shop is run by Jean and Roger Upton. Their son Mark is a well known Sporting Artist. His Racing, Equestrian and other scenes are displayed around the shop and are for sale.

The Polly Tea Rooms

26-27 High Street, Marlborough, Wiltshire SN8 1LW
Tel: 01672 512146
e-mail: info@thepolly.com
website: www.thepolly.com

The Polly Tea Rooms has been hailed as "the finest tea room in England" and AA members also voted it amongst the Top 10 tea rooms in the country. Polly's was established way back in 1932 and after so many years no-one is quite sure where the name came from. Some cite the nursery rhyme *Polly, put the kettle on*, others claim that the two ladies who opened the tea room had a parrot of that name, but the most likely source is believed to be Polly Peacham, heroine of *The Beggar's Opera*. Whatever the origin of the name, this is an outstanding tea room and is today "a lovingly owned small group of tearooms" – a quote from the menu.

In addition to wonderful afternoon teas with home-made cakes, biscuits and breads, Polly's also offers an extensive breakfast and lunch menu with the not very often found Kedgeree amongst the former, and appetising dishes such as Polly's home-made fishcake on a leek and potato cream amongst the latter. There's a good selection of teas, coffees, soft drinks, beers and wine, a special children's menu, and a wide choice of speciality ice creams. And in the Polly Shop you'll find an enticing range of Polly's own hand-made chocolates, fudge, marzipan fruits, home-made jams and marmalade, and honey from Polly's own hives.

Made in Italy Boutique

123, High Street, Marlborough, Wiltshire SN8 1LZ
Tel/Fax: 01672 515636
e-mail: maura@made-italy.biz

Opened in December 2000, **Made in Italy Boutique** showcases a unique range of Italian fashion accessories, most of them only available here.

Every single item in the shop has been personally chosen during monthly trips to Italy where the owners get the most fashionable and exclusive pieces of jewellery, handbags and ladies accessories such as watches, silken scarves, gloves and purses.

There is a 'gent corner' as well, where you can find fine accessories suitable for gentlemen of any age.

Lots of object d'art typically Italian, like Murano glass and Venetian masks, hand-painted pottery, frames and lovely paintings, enhance the beauty of the shop. Everything is attractively gift-wrapped to make any customer even happier with his or her purchase.

Fisherman's House

Mildenhall, nr Marlborough, Wiltshire SN8 2LZ
Tel: 01672 315390 Fax: 01672 519009

Fisherman's House occupies a lovely setting with the River Kennet flowing past the foot of the garden with open countryside beyond. This charming period house is the home of Jeremy Coulter who has been welcoming bed & breakfast guests here since 1998. They have the use of a comfortable residents lounge, stocked with books on local history, and delightful conservatory overlooking the garden where a choice of English or Continental breakfast is served in the morning. There are four guest bedrooms with a 4-Diamonds rating, one en suite double, one twin and two singles, all with TV and hospitality tray.

mound and gave the town its name 'Merle Barrow' or Merlin's Tomb. Among the many notable pupils of the college were William Morris and John Betjeman.

AROUND MARLBOROUGH

Savernake Forest

2 miles E of Marlborough off the A346

The ancient woodland of **Savernake Forest** is a magnificent 4,500-acre expanse of unbroken woodland, open glades and bridle paths. King Henry VIII hunted wild deer here and married Jane Seymour, whose family home was nearby. Designated a Site of Special Scientific Interest, the forest is home to abundant wildlife, including a small herd of deer and 25 species of butterfly. One day each winter the Forest is closed to prevent rights of way being established.

Savernake Forest

Great Bedwyn

6 miles SE of Marlborough off the A4

In the chancel of the 11th century Church of St Mary the Virgin is the tomb of Sir John Seymour, the father of Henry VIII's third wife Jane. Nearby is **Lloyds Stone Museum**, a monument to the skills of the English stonemason. Among the items on display are an assortment of tombstones and a stone aeroplane with an 11ft wingspan.

Crofton

6 miles SE of Marlborough off the A338

The eastern end of the Vale of Pewsey carries the London-Penzance railway and the Kennet and Avon Canal, which reaches its highest point near Crofton. The site is marked by a handsome Georgian pumping station which houses the renowned **Crofton Beam Engines**. These engines - the 1812 Boulton & Watt and the 1845 Harvey of Hayle - have been superbly restored under the guidance of the Canal trust. The 1812 engine is the oldest working beam engine in the world, still in its original building and still doing its original job of pumping water to the summit level of the canal. Both engines are steamed from a hand-stoked, coal-fired Lancashire boiler. The brick chimney has also been restored, to its original height of 82 feet.

Wilton

8 miles SE of Marlborough off the A338

A footpath of about a mile links the Crofton Beam Engines with Wilton. This is the smaller of the two Wiltshire Wiltons and is the site of the **Wilton Windmill**. This traditional working mill, the only one operating in the county, was built in 1821 after the Canal Company has taken the water out of the River Bedwyn for their canal, thereby depriving the water mills of the power to drive their mills. The mill worked until 1920, when the availability of steam power and electricity literally took the wind out its sails. After standing derelict for 50 years the mill was restored at a cost of £25,000 and is now looked after by the Wilton Windmill Society. This superb old mill is floodlit from dusk until 10pm, making a wonderful sight on a chalk ridge 550 feet above sea level.

Clench Common

2 miles S of Marlborough on the A345

This is a lovely part of the world for walking or cycling. The Forestry Commission's West Woods, particularly notable for bluebells in May, has a picnic site, and nearby is Martinsell Hill topped by an ancient fort.

Wootton Rivers

4 miles S of Marlborough off the A345

An attractive village with a real curiosity

in its highly unusual church clock. The **Jack Sprat Clock** was built by a local man from an assortment of scrap metal, including old bicycles, prams and farm tools, to mark the coronation of King George V in 1911. It has 24 different chimes and its face has letters instead of numbers.

Pewsey

7 miles S of Marlborough on the A345

In the heart of the beautiful valley that bears its name, this is a charming village of half-timbered houses and thatched cottages. It was once the personal property of Alfred the Great, and a statue of the king stands at the crossroads in the centre. The parish church, built on a foundation of sarsen stones, has an unusual altar rail made from timbers taken from the *San Josef*, a ship captured by Nelson in 1797.

Attractions for the visitor include the old wharf area and the **Heritage Centre**, housed in an 1870 foundry building. It contains an interesting collection of old and unusual machine tools and farm machinery. The original **Pewsey White Horse**, south of the village on Pewsey Down, was cut in 1785, apparently including a rider, but was redesigned by a Mr George Marples and cut by the Pewsey Fire Brigade to celebrate the coronation of King George VI. **Pewsey Carnival** takes place each September, and the annual Devizes to Westminster canoe race passes through **Pewsey Wharf**.

A minor road runs past the White Horse across Pewsey Down to the isolated village of **Everleigh**, where the Church of St Peter is of unusual iron-framed construction. Rebuilt on a new site in 1813, it has a short chancel and narrow nave, an elegant west gallery and a neo-medieval hammerbeam roof.

Thomsons Wine Merchant & Delicatessen

18 River Street, Pewsey, Wiltshire SN9 5DH
Tel: 01672 563323 Fax: 01672 563530

An indication of how seriously Graham Thomson insists on top quality produce is the fact that he travels to France every other week to stock up on cheeses, vegetables, herbs, and fish and lobster from the port of Le Touquet. You'll find all these fresh delicacies on display at **Thomsons Wine Merchant and Delicatessen** in the picturesque village of Pewsey. Formerly a restauranteur and wine expert based in London's West End, Graham opened his shop in 2003 and it already attracts regular customers from miles around.

In addition to the extensive selection of wines from around the world (regular tastings are held), and the enticing array of healthy and appetising food, customers can also sample what have been described as the "best deli sandwiches in the country". Home-made foie gras, Dorset-made lavender fruit cakes and biscuits, soft drinks such as elderflower pressé, Kent fruit juices, local marmalades and relishes, and much more offer an enormous and varied choice. Currently, plans are under way to extend the choice even further with the provision of the deli's own ready meals. Thomsons is open from 9.30am to 6pm, Monday to Saturday.

Alton Barnes and Alton Priors

6 miles SW of Marlborough off the A345

The largest **White Horse** in Wiltshire can be seen on the hillside above Alton Barnes; cut in 1812, it is 54 metres high and 51 metres long and is visible from Old Sarum, 20 miles away. According to the local story the original contractor ran off with the £20 advance payment and the work was carried out by one Robert Pile, who owned the land. The runaway contractor was later arrested and hanged for a string of offences. Other notable Wiltshire White Horses in the locality are at Hackpen, just north of Marlborough (cut to commemorate Queen Victoria's coronation) and at Pewsey.

West Overton

3 miles W of Marlborough off the A4

The area between Marlborough and Avebury sees the biggest concentration of prehistoric remains in the country. The scattered community of West Overton stands at the foot of **Overton Hill**, the site of an early Bronze Age monument called **The Sanctuary**. These giant standing stones are at the southeastern end of West Kennet Avenue, an ancient pathway which once connected them to the main megalithic circles at Avebury (see page 291). Overton Hill is also the start point of the Ridgeway long-distance path, which runs for 80 miles to the Chilterns. Just off this path is **Fyfield Down**, now a nature reserve, where quarries once provided many of the great stones that are such a feature of the area. **Devil's Den** long barrow lies within the reserve. The local legend that Satan sometimes appears here at midnight attempting to pull down the stones with a team of white oxen has not in recent times been corroborated.

WALK NUMBER 10

Avebury

Distance:	5.3 miles (8.5 kilometres)
Typical time:	180 mins
Height gain:	60 metres
Map:	Explorer 157
Walk:	www.walkingworld.com ID:68
Contributor:	David and Chris Stewart

Access Information:

Buses are available from Devizes, Marlborough and Swindon (Wiltshire Bus Line 0345 090899). By car: Avebury is half way between Marlborough and Calne on the A4. The National Trust provide a free car park close by.

Additional Information:

This walk does involve crossing the busy A4 twice. The Avebury henge is part of the National Trust and a great deal of information is available from the Alexander Keiller Museum (01672 539 250).

Description:

Starting at the Avebury stone circle the walk takes you along the stone Avenue and up to the Ridgeway with spectacular Wiltshire views of "hedgehogs" and curious burial mounds.

The route then takes you to visit the Sanctuary, yet another ancient site, and then through lush farmland to see the famous West Kennet Long Barrow. You then return to Avebury via the amazing man-made Silbury Hill (carbon dating suggests that Silbury Hill was built around 2500 BC, making it an extraordinary feat for its time).

Features:

Pub, Museum, National Trust/ NTS, Great Views

Walk Directions:

1. Leave the car park and follow the signs to Avebury village. When you reach the road turn right before the Henge shop and the post office. You are now inside the ring. Follow it round to the left towards the main road.
2. Carefully cross the main road and go into the next part of the ring. Bear right and climb up onto the bank.
3. Go down the other side towards a gate. Cross the road and enter the field. This is the beginning of The Avenue. Walk down The Avenue between the stones.
4. When you reach the last stones of The Avenue you will find a gate. Cross the road and take the path on the opposite side. After a short distance you reach the one remaining stone of Falkner's Circle. Keeping on the same side of the hedge as the path you have just followed, cross into the next field. Follow the left hand edge of the field up a slight gradient to the next field boundary.
5. Turn right onto the track leading towards the clumps of trees on the horizon (these are known as 'hedgehogs').

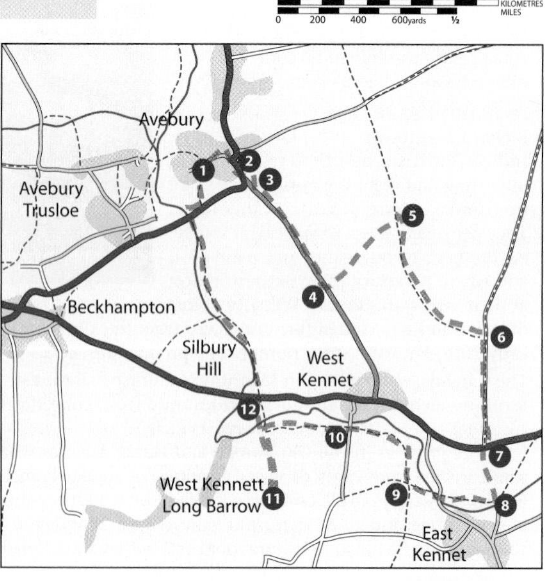

6 Just past the 'hedgehogs' the path bears left. Then you can turn right onto the very last section of the Ridgeway path. Follow the Ridgeway down to the main road.

7 Cross the road extremely carefully. Just on your right there is the Sanctuary, the site of an ancient wooden circle (later a stone one which was taken up in the 18th century). Having visited the Sanctuary, the path to take is the one signed 'Byway' directly opposite the end of the Ridgeway path. Follow this path down a gentle hill.

8 Just before the path turns to the left and crosses a bridge, take the path going right. Follow this path alongside the river until you reach a small road. Turn left and cross the bridge. Turn right onto the track.

9 This pathway is very easy to miss. It's just after where the track turns to the left. On the right there is a yellow sign which says 'Private Path' and an arrow to the left. Walk a few feet further on looking for a path on your right going down the middle of a hedgerow. There is a small arrow on a tree. Follow this path to a field and then keep along the lefthand edge of the field to reach a road.

10 Cross the road and continue on the track. When you reach the path leading up to West Kennet longbarrow, turn left and walk up a gentle slope to the barrow.

11 West Kennet longbarrow, where there is an informative sign about its origins and the opportunity to enter some of its chambers. After your visit retrace your steps down the path and continue straight on towards Silbury Hill.

12 Cross the main road again very carefully and take the path directly opposite. This follows a small stream and there are magnificent views of Silbury Hill on your left (it is no longer possible to climb the hill). Follow the path all the way back to Avebury - it brings you out at the main car park.

Avebury Stone Circles

Avebury, Wiltshire

A 28-acre World Heritage Site is the centre of the **Avebury Stone Circles**, the most remarkable ritual megalithic monuments in Europe. A massive bank and ditch enclose an outer circle and two inner circles of stones. The outer circle of almost 100 sarsen stones (sand and silica) enclose two rings with about 40 stones still standing. Archaeologists working on the site found the remains of a long-vanished avenue of stones leading south towards Beckhampton.

The **Avebury Stones** bear testimony to the enormous human effort that went into their construction: some of the individual stones weigh 40 tons and all had to dragged from Marlborough Downs. They are in two basic shapes, which have been equated with male and female and have led to the theory that the site was used for the observance of fertility rites.

Built by Celtic farmers and shepherds in around 1800 BC, the size of the monuments suggest that there was a well organized community here and one that was probably led by priests. In the Middle Ages, the Christian Church became concerned with the revival in pagan rites and, as Avebury certainly had such a meaning, the clergy gave orders for the stones to be buried. Excavations in the 1930s revealed the skeleton of a man, along with various coins and surgical tools, beneath one of the megaliths and, identified as a surgeon-barber who died in around 1320, it is thought that he was killed when the stone that he was helping to bury fell on him.

East and West Kennet

4 miles W of Marlborough on the A4

West Kennet Long Barrow, one of Britain's largest neolithic burial tombs, is situated a gentle stroll away from the twin villages. The tomb is of impressive proportions – 330ft long, 80ft wide and 10ft high - and is reached by squeezing past some massive stones in the semicircular forecourt.

Silbury Hill

5 miles W of Marlborough on the A4

The largest man-made prehistoric mound in Europe, built around 2800BC, standing 130ft high and covers five acres. Excavation in the late 1960s revealed some details of how it was constructed but shed little light on its purpose. Theories include a burial place for King Sil and his horse and a hiding place for a large gold statue built by the Devil on his way to Devizes. Scholarship generally favours the first.

Avebury

6 miles W of Marlborough on the A4361

A 28-acre World Heritage Site is the centre of the **Avebury Stone Circles** (see panel on page 291), the most remarkable ritual megalithic monuments in Europe. A massive bank and ditch enclose an outer circle and two inner circles of stones. The outer circle has almost 100 sarsen stones (made of sand and silica); the two inner rings have 40 stones still standing. Some of the individual stones weigh 40 tons and had to be dragged here from Marlborough Downs. They are in two basic shapes which have been equated with male and female, supporting the theory that the site was used in fertility rites. Archaeologists have also found the remains of a long-vanished avenue of stones leading south

The White Horse Inn

Compton Bassett, nr Avebury, Wiltshire SN11 8RJ
Tel: 01249 813118 Fax: 01249 811595
e-mail: dymaro@aol.com
website: www.comptonbassett/whitehorseinn.com

Set deep in the Wiltshire countryside just a few miles from prehistoric Avebury Stone Circle, Compton Bassett is a delightful village of stone-built whitewashed cottages and a fine traditional inn to match. **The White Horse Inn** dates back to the early 1700s but didn't become an inn until the 1860s when it also served as a bakery and grocer's shop. Today, it's a lively and welcoming place, just how you'd hope to find a traditional village hostelry, complete with low-beamed ceilings, mullioned windows, open log fireplace and, a popular amenity in this part of the country, a skittle alley.

Landlady Catherine Ritchie and chef Scott Hendry have also made the inn a popular venue for discriminating diners. Scott has been awarded the Gold Medal of the Jersey Salon Culinaire and his menu includes appetising dishes such as the smoked salmon & prawn timbale and a delicious crispy confit of duck with crispy leeks and beetroot jus. To accompany your meal there's a good choice of reasonably priced wines, three real ales and all the popular beverages. If you are planning to stay in this delightful corner of the county, the White Horse has seven guest bedrooms, some with balconies and all en suite with TV and hospitality tray.

Silbury Hill

towards Beckhampton, a discovery that vindicated the theory of the 18th century antiquary, William Stukeley, who made drawings of the stone circles with this avenue marked.

Many of the archaeological finds from the site are displayed in Avebury's **Alexander Keiller Museum**, which also describes the restoration of the site by Keiller in the 1930s.

Avebury has a gem from Elizabethan times in **Avebury Manor**, which stands on the site of a 12th century priory. The house and its four-acre walled garden, which features a wishing well, topiary, a rose garden and an Italian walk, are owned by the National Trust.

DEVIZES

The central market town of Wiltshire, Devizes boasts no fewer than 500 listed buildings within a quarter square mile. Many of the town's finest buildings are situated in and around the old market

Market Place, Devizes

place, including the Town Hall and the Corn Exchange. Also here is an unusual **Market Cross** inscribed with the story of Ruth Pierce, a market stall-holder who stood accused, on January 25th, 1753, of short-changing a customer. When an ugly crowd gathered round her, she stood and pleaded her innocence, adding, "May I be struck dead if I am lying". A rash move, as she fell to the ground and died forthwith. The missing money (three pence – 1.4p) was found clutched in her hand.

Devizes was founded in 1080 by Bishop Osmund, nephew of William the Conqueror. The bishop was responsible for building a timber castle between the lands of two powerful manors, and this act brought about the town's name, which is derived from the Latin ad divisas, or 'at the boundaries'. After the wooden structure burnt down, Roger, Bishop of Sarum, built a stone castle in 1138 that survived until the end of the Civil War, when it was demolished. Bishop Roger also built two fine churches in Devizes. Long Street is lined with elegant Georgian houses and also contains the **Wiltshire Heritage Museum** (free on Sunday, Monday), which has a splendid collection of artefacts from the area, and an art gallery with a John Piper window and regularly changing exhibitions. Here, amongst other local industries, you can learn about the Wadworth Brewery, founded in 1875 and still a family business. The brewery continues to use Shire horses for local deliveries and they have become a familiar and much-loved part of the local scene. Their stables can be visited by prior arrangement.

Devizes Visitor Centre offers a unique insight into the town. The Centre is based on a 12th century castle and takes visitors back to medieval times, when Devizes was home to the finest castle in Europe and the scene of anarchy and unrest during the struggles between Empress Matilda and King Stephen. An interactive exhibition shows how the town came to be at the centre of the 12th century Civil War and later thrived as a medieval town.

Devizes stands at a key point on the Kennet & Avon Canal, and the **Kennet and Avon Canal Museum** tells the complete story of the canal in fascinating detail. Many visitors combine a trip to the museum with a walk along the towpath, which is a public footpath. The route of the canal involved overcoming the rise of 237ft from the Avon Valley to Devizes. The engineer John Rennie devised the solution, which was to build one vast flight of locks, 29 in all of which 16 were set very close together down Caen Hill. The **Devizes Locks** Discovery Trail descends from Devizes Wharf, through the town and to the bottom of the flight at Lower Foxhangers, returning by way of open countryside and the village of Rowde. Each July the Canalfest, a weekend of family fun designed to raise funds for the upkeep of the canal, is held at the Wharf, which is also the start point of the annual Devizes-Westminster canoe race held every year on Good Friday.

AROUND DEVIZES

Bishops Cannings

4 miles NE of Devizes on the A361

The bishops of Salisbury once owned a manor here and built the very grand parish church before they started work on the Cathedral. This church, dedicated to St Mary, has often been likened to the Cathedral and does indeed bear some resemblance, notably in its tall, tapering spire. This is Moonraker country, and according to legend a group of 17th century smugglers from Bishops Canning fooled excisemen when caught recovering dumped brandy kegs from a pond known as the Crammer. The smugglers pretended to be mad and claimed that the moon's reflection on the pond was actually a cheese, which they were trying to rake in. The ruse worked, so who were the real fools? A hollow in the downs west of the village was the scene of a bloody Civil War battle in 1643, when the Royalist forces under Prince Rupert's brother Maurice defeated the Parliamentarian forces at Roundway Down. According to a local legend the cries of the dead can be heard coming from a burial ditch on the anniversary of the battle (July 13).

Market Lavington

5 miles S of Devizes on the B3098

The 'Village under the Plain' is home to a little museum in the former schoolmaster's cottage behind the old village school. Displays at **Market Lavington Museum** include a Victorian kitchen and archive photographs.

SWINDON

Think Swindon, think the Great Western Railway. Think GWR, think Isambard Kingdom Brunel. The largest town in Wiltshire, lying in the northeast corner between the Cotswolds and the Marlborough Downs, Swindon was an insignificant agricultural community before the railway line between London and Bristol was completed in 1835. Swindon Station opened in that year, but it was some time later, in 1843, that Brunel, the GWR's principal engineer, decided that Swindon was the place to build his locomotive works. Within a few years it had grown to be one of the largest in the world, with as many as 12,000 on a 320-acre site that incorporated the Railway Village; this was a model development of 300 workmen's houses built of limestone extracted from the construction of Box Tunnel. This unique example of early-Victorian town planning is open to the public as the **Railway Village Museum**, with a restored Victorian railway worker's cottage. Lit by gas, the cottage contains many original fittings such as the range and copper in the kitchen.

STEAM, the Museum of the Great Western Railway (see panel on 298) was voted Wiltshire Family Attraction of the Year, 2003, and provides both a great family day out and a tribute to one of the great railways of the world. The leading stars in its fascinating collection of locomotives are the *King George V*, heading 'The Bristolian' in the station platform, and the Castle class *Caerphilly Castle*. As well as displaying railway memorabilia such as engine nameplates,

The Croft Gallery

22 Devizes Road, Old Town, Swindon, Wiltshire SN1 4BH
Tel/Fax: 01793 615821
e-mail: info@thecroftgallery.co.uk
website: www.thecroftgallery.co.uk

Swindon's Old Town has become the fashionable part of town with up-market shops, good restaurants and an excellent art gallery in the form of **The Croft Gallery.** Opened in 2000, it is owned and run by Francesco Gregorace who is a keen artist himself. His tastes are catholic so he stocks a wide variety of traditional and contemporary art in oils, watercolours, acrylics and pastels. Alongside the 250 or so original works of art you'll also find a good selection of limited editions.

The subjects can range from Parisian street scenes or Hawaiian seascapes, to the Manhattan skyline or iconic portraits of starts such as Marilyn Monroe and Elvis Presley. Artists regularly featured include Carl Scanes, Mark Vidler, Steve Lynch, Ken White and local artist Judy Jones. The gallery also provides a showcase for ceramics by John Bean and a range of colourful toy boats made of wood. Gallery owner Francesco also offers a picture restoration service and the gallery's framing service enjoys a very good reputation for quality and professionalism.

Gallery 39

51 Godwin Court, Old Town, Swindon, Wiltshire SN1 4BA
Tel: 01793 433388 Fax: 01793 495293
e-mail: kevin@gallery39.com
website: www.gallery39.com

Opened in May 2004, **Gallery 39** has brought something different to Swindon's arts scene. The gallery is tucked away in the recently developed courtyard of Goodwin Court, just a short walk from the Old Town's Wood Street. Gallery director Kevin Money is a man with a passion for art and an avid collector himself. "We aim to offer out customers a unique selection of paintings, sculptures and ceramics," he says. "The sheer quality of composition, colour and feeling will make a stunning contribution to a home or business setting."

The gallery, with its clean, simple whitewashed walls, subtle but effective lighting, and well-thought out display space, provides a stylish showcase for works by artists that range from Royal Academicians such as John Wragg, Gillian Ayres, Sandra Blow and Sir Terry Frost to local artists and creatives. In addition to the paintings and original prints, Gallery 39 also displays sculptures, ceramics, studio glass and jewellery from Richard Brooks, Suzanne Emery, Colin and Louise Hawkins and others. At this friendly, sociable gallery there is no pressure to buy – and you can also enjoy a complimentary drink and a snack.

signalling equipment and an exhibition of the life and achievements of Brunel, the centre also focuses on the human aspects of the industry, telling the story of the men and women who built and repaired the locomotives and carriages of the GWR (God's Wonderful Railway) for seven generations. The last locomotive to be built at the works was 92220 *Evening Star*, a powerful 2-10-0 freight engine of a type that proved surprisingly versatile but was destined to have all too short a working life. Engineering work continued on the site until 1986, when the works finally closed. STEAM has a café and a shop with an impressive range of GWR and other railway gifts, books, souvenirs and pocket-money toys. It's family-friendly, and all areas are fully accessible to wheelchairs. The site now also contains the **National Monuments Record Centre** - the public archive of the Royal Commission on the Historical Monuments of England, with seven million photographs, documents and texts.

There's lots more to Swindon than the legacy of the GWR: it's a bustling and successful commercial town with excellent shopping and leisure facilities and plenty of open spaces. One such is **Coate Water Country Park** on the Marlborough road. In an elegant early-19th century house on the Bath Road, **Swindon Museum & Art Gallery** (free) contains a variety of displays on the history, archaeology and geology of the town and the surrounding area and also houses a fine collection of 20th century British art.

AROUND SWINDON

Cricklade

6 miles N of Swindon off the A419

The only Wiltshire town on the Thames was an important post on the Roman Ermine Street and had its own mint in

The Pear Tree at Purton

Church End, Purton, nr Swindon, Wiltshire SN5 4ED
Tel: 01793 772100 Fax: 01793 772369
e-mail: stay@peartreepurton.co.uk
website: www.peartreepurton.co.uk

A delightful building of mellow Cotswold stone, **The Pear Tree at Purton** was originally Purton Vicarage and stood in the churchyard next to the unique twin-towered Church of St Mary's, about 400 yards from its present position. The house was moved in 1911 because the churchyard was full – there were even graves right outside the front door. The vicarage remained in use until 1986. In the following year it was purchased by Anne and Francis Young and converted into a hotel and restaurant. Within two years, the *Egan Ronay Guide* awarded it the highest hotel rating in the Swindon area. A raft of other awards followed, including the RAC's highest award for excellence, the Blue Ribbon, which the hotel has won for the last 10 years in a row.

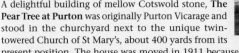

The Pear Tree has 17 individual en suite rooms and suites, each one named after a person associated with the village: the Anne Hyde Room, for example, is named after the wife of James II, Anne Hyde, who spent her childhood in the village. Dining at the Pear Tree provides a memorable experience – outstanding cuisine served in an elegant conservatory overlooking the extensive gardens and croquet lawn. This outstanding hotel specialises in celebrations of all kind – both the John Veysey suite with its high vaulted ceilings, and the Library are licensed for civil weddings.

STEAM - Museum Of The Great Western Railway

Kemble Drive, Swindon, Wiltshire SN2 2TA
Tel: 01793 466646 Fax: 01793 466615
website: www.steam-museum.org.uk

The award-winning **STEAM, the Museum of the Great Western Railway**, is located in a beautifully restored building at the heart of Swindon Railway Works, where for nearly 150 years thousands of men and women worked for the Great Western Railway. The main activity was the building of great steam locomotives, the last being 92220 *Evening Star*, one of a fleet of powerful 2-10-0 freight engines which were destined to have all too short a working life. The star of the show in the Museum is 6000 *King George V*, which stands in a platform at the head of the 'Bristolian' express. Visitors can climb aboard the footplate of this marvellous thoroughbred and relive the glory days of 'God's Wonderful Railway'. Another of the great GWR locomotives was the Castle class, and here visitors can actually walk underneath *Caerphilly Castle* as it stands in its inspection pit.

The sounds, sights and smells of the railway works live on in the workshops, where locomotives and carriages are restored, and one section of this fascinating place contains GWR accessories and road vehicles, including the famous Scammell 'mechanical horse', which could turn on a sixpence but sometimes had a mind of its own. The great figure of early railway days was the engineer Isambard Kingdom Brunel, whose story is told together with that of the thousands of less famous workers, from the navvies to drivers, signalmen and station masters, who built and operated the railway. There are many hands-on opportunities to relive the action, from building bridges to working the signals, shunting the wagons and driving the steam trains, and special events and family activities are held regularly throughout the year.

All areas of the museum are accessible to wheelchairs, and visitors who run out of steam can relax awhile in the stylish balcony café, open daily for drinks, cakes, pastries and light lunches. In the Steam Shop, an impressive range of GWR and railway gifts, books and souvenirs is for sale. A short walk from STEAM Museum is the Railway Village Museum, whose exhibits include a restored Victorian railway worker's cottage. STEAM Museum is open every day, the Railway Village Museum from Easter to the end of October. STEAM was funded by a partnership that brought together the Heritage Lottery Fund, Swindon Borough Council, Carillion Development Management and BAA McArthurGlen.

Saxon times. There are many buildings of interest, notably the Church of St Sampson, with its cathedral-like four-spired tower, where a festival of music takes place each September; the famous school founded by the London goldsmith Robert Jenner in 1651; and the fancy Victorian clock tower. **Cricklade Museum** contains displays on social history, Roman occupation, Rotten Borough elections and an archive of 2,000 photographs. Nearby **North Meadow** is a National Nature Reserve where the rare snakeshead fritillary grows.

Highworth

5 miles NE of Swindon on the A361

The name is appropriate, as the village stands at the top of a 400ft incline, and the view from **Highworth Hill** takes in the counties of Wiltshire, Gloucestershire and Oxfordshire. There are some very fine 17th and 18th century buildings round the old square, and the parish church is of interest: built in the 15th century, it was fortified during the Civil War and was attacked soon after by Parliamentarian forces under Fairfax. One of the cannonballs which struck it, is on display outside. The church contains a memorial to Lieutenant Warneford, who was awarded the VC for destroying the first enemy Zeppelin in 1915.

Wroughton

3 miles S of Swindon on the A4361

Wroughton Airfield, with its historic Second World War hangars, is home to the **National Museum of Science and Industry's** superb collections, including Air Transport and Aviation, Land Transport and Agriculture, Radar and Firefighting Equipment.

A popular attraction in Wroughton is **Butterfly World** at Studley Grange Garden & Leisure Park. Visitors can get close to some of the largest and most spectacular insects on the planet. They fly freely against a backdrop of tropical plants, skimming over fish-filled pools. The 'mini-beasts' house' home to a fascinating display of spiders, scorpions, mantis and other creepy crawlies.

Nearby **Clouts Wood Nature Reserve** is a lovely place for a ramble, and a short drive south, by the Ridgeway, is the site of **Barbury Castle**, one of the most spectacular Iron Age forts in southern England. The open hillside was the scene of a bloody battle between the Britons and the Saxons in the 6th century; the Britons lost and the Saxon kingdom of Wessex was established under King Cealwin. The area around the castle is a country park.

Broad Hinton

5 miles S of Swindon off the A4361

In the church at Broad Hinton is a memorial to local bigwig Sir Thomas Wroughton, who returned home from hunting to find his wife reading the Bible instead of making his tea. He seized the Bible and flung it into the fire; his wife retrieved it but in doing so severely burnt her hands. As punishment for his blasphemy Sir Thomas's hands and those of his four children withered away (very hard on the children, surely). The monument shows the whole handless family and a Bible with a corner burnt off.

Lydiard Tregoze

2 miles W of Swindon off the A3102

On the western outskirts of Swindon, **Lydiard Park** is the ancestral home of the Viscounts Bolingbroke. The park is a delightful place to explore, and the house, one of Wiltshire's smaller stately homes, is a real gem, described by Sir Hugh Casson as "a gentle Georgian house, sunning itself as serenely as an old grey cat". Chief attractions inside include the little blue Dressing Room devoted to the 18th century society artist Lady Diana Spencer who became the 2nd Viscountess Bolingbroke. St Mary's Church, next to the house, contains many monuments to the St John family, who lived here from Elizabethan times. The most striking is the **Golden Cavalier**, a life-size gilded effigy of Edward St John in full battledress (he was killed at the second Battle of Newbury in 1645).

Wootton Bassett

3 miles W of Swindon off the A3102

A small town with a big history. Records go back to the 7th century, and in 1219 Henry III granted a market charter (the market is still held every Wednesday). The town boasts some fine Georgian buildings, a good range of family-run businesses – including a butcher, baker, greengrocer and ironmonger – and some good eating places. You can eat al fresco across from the striking **Old Town Hall** which stands on a series of stone pillars, leaving an open-sided ground-floor area that once served as a covered market. The museum above, open on Saturday mornings, contains a rare ducking stool, silver maces and a mayoral sword of office.

A section of the **Wilts & Berks Canal** has been restored at **Templars Fir**. In May 1998 about 50 boats of all kinds were launched on the canal and a day of festivities was enjoyed by all. The railway station, alas, has not been revived after falling to the Beeching axe in 1966.

CHIPPENHAM

A dynamic town with a population of around 40,000 whose major employer today is the Westinghouse Brake & Signal Co. established here in 1920.

Stanton Manor Hotel

Stanton St Quintin, nr Chippenham, Wiltshire SN14 6DQ
Tel: 01666 837552 Fax: 01666 837022
e-mail: reception@stantonmanor.co.uk
website: www.stantonmanor.co.uk

Just a few minutes from junction 17 of the M4, **Stanton Manor Hotel** is an inviting country house hotel set in seven acres of Victorian landscaped gardens in the tranquil village of Stanton St Quintin. Within these grounds there's a croquet lawn and a nine hole pitch and putt golf course. The hotel itself has recently been completely refurbished and upgraded, its 23 guest bedrooms all individually designed with toning fabrics and furnishings. Some of the 5-star de luxe rooms have oak four-poster beds, antique brass beds or king size beds; some have whirlpool baths or a private patio terrace, all enjoy delightful views of the gardens.

The Gallery Restaurant is decorated with original works of art and offers a choice to suit every palate and pocket with dishes based on fresh local produce wherever possible. For special occasions, the Woodland Room & Lounge Suite is ideal, comfortably seating up to 60 guests. It's a room of real character with magnificent Tudor fireplaces, grand stone mullioned windows, crystal chandeliers and enjoying beautiful views over wooded countryside. Stanton Manor is a popular venue for weddings, its lovely grounds providing perfect photo opportunities, and for business meetings three conference rooms and one boardroom are available, even a helicopter pad.

Set on the banks of the Avon, Chippenham was founded around 600AD by the Saxon king Cyppa. It became an important administrative centre in King Alfred's time and later gained further prominence from the wool trade. It was a major stop on the London-Bristol coaching run and is served by the railway between the same two cities. Buildings of note include the Church of St Andrew (mainly 15th century) and the half-timbered Yelde Hall, once used by the burgesses and bailiffs of the Chippenham Hundred. This Grade I building has recently been restored and now houses the tourist information office.

The new **Chippenham Museum and Heritage Centre** (free) in the Market Place tells the story of the town from the Jurassic period onwards, and the displays focus on Saxon Chippenham, Alfred the Great, Brunel's railway, the celebrated cheese market, Victorian living conditions and Chippenham curiosities. At Hardenhuish Hall on the edge of town, John Wood the Younger of Bath fame built the Church of St Nicholas; completed in 1779, it is notable for its domed steeple and elegant Venetian windows.

Bowood House, Calne

In the flood plain to the east of Chippenham stands the 4.5 mile footpath known as **Maud Heath's Causeway**. This remarkable and ingenious walkway consisting of 64 brick and stone arches was built at the end of the 15th century at the bequest of Maud Heath, who spent most of her life as a market trader trudging her often muddy way between her village of Bremhill and Chippenham. She died a relatively wealthy woman, and the land and property she left in her will provided sufficient funds for the upkeep of the causeway, which is best seen near the hamlet of Kellaways. A statue of Maud, basket in hand, stands overlooking the flood plain at Wick Hill.

AROUND CHIPPENHAM

CALNE

5 miles E of Chippenham on the A4

A former weaving centre in the valley of the River Marden; the prominent wool church reflects the prosperity of earlier times. One of the memorials in the church is to Dr Ingenhousz, who is widely credited with creating a smallpox vaccination before Jenner. Another remembers the King of the Gypsies, who died of smallpox in 1774.

A short distance from Calne, to the west, stands **Bowood House**, built in 1625 and now a treasury of Shelborne family heirlooms, paintings, books and furniture. In the Bowood Laboratory Dr Joseph Priestley, tutor to the 1st Marquess of Lansdowne's son, conducted experiments that resulted in the

King John's Hunting Lodge

21 Church Street, Lacock, Chippenham,
Wiltshire SN15 2LB
Tel: 01249 730313 Fax: 01249 730725

Located in the idyllic National Trust village of Lacock, **King John's Hunting Lodge** is the oldest house here, with the main part of the lodge dating back to the 13th century. Much of its original cruck beam structure can be seen on the first floor; the rear of the building was added in Tudor times. King John (1167-1216) was Lord of the Manor of nearby Melksham and frequently indulged his passion for hunting in the adjoining forest. There being no manor house at Melksham, it is likely that the king made regular use of his hunting lodge at Lacock.

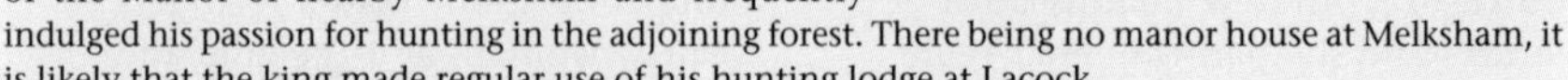

Eight centuries later, the tradition of hospitality is maintained by present-day proprietor Margaret Vaughan who had a colourful career as nurse, shepherdess and cook before opening her own tea room and restaurant. She has appeared on TV with Keith Floyd, presented her own TV series *Fruity Passions* and authored books such as *Tea with the Bennets* which features recipes that might have been used by the Bennet family of *Pride and Prejudice*. (Much of the acclaimed BBC-TV series of Jane Austen's novel was filmed in Lacock).

Margaret also offers comfortable bed & breakfast accommodation in the relaxed and friendly atmosphere of this delightful property. Providing a real sanctuary from the stresses and strains of modern life, the guest rooms are equipped with en suite bathrooms and hospitality tray, and a full English breakfast with home-made breads is served at a time to suit guests. Don't miss out on treating yourself to tea here – Margaret's tea room is renowned for its traditional English cream teas which are served in the delightful secluded garden in summer and in the Garden Tearoom, with its roaring log fire, in winter.

Wiltshire Crafts

Church Street, Lacock, Wiltshire SN15 2LB
Tel: 01249 730226

Also located within King John's Hunting Lodge (see above) **Wiltshire Crafts** offers an impressive range of individual hand-made gifts and keepsakes. Ken Giles started his business in 1985 in nearby Melksham and moved to this delightful location two years later. Almost everything in the extensive selection on display here has been made by local craftspeople. Ken himself creates wonderful pieces in wood. The corn dollies by Gill Henly, the superb children's clothes by Yvonne Heath and the wrought ironwork by Hazel Moore all come from Calne; Tony Smith's exquisite jewellery is made at Melksham; Rosemary Goff's soft toys come from Corsham as do the wooden toys and puzzles created by John Sawyer. Then there's the hand-painted silk by Maureen Hall of Kington Langley; pottery from Gordon Whittle of Chippenham; pressed flowers from Barbara Mayell and Shetland knitwear by Cynthia Rennie, both from Trowbridge; while the appliqué items by Paula Pawling are made in Radstock.

identification of oxygen. The house is set in lovely Capability Brown grounds with a lake and terraced garden. The mausoleum was commissioned in 1761 by the Dowager Countess of Shelborne as a memorial to her husband and was Robert Adam's first work for them. A separate woodland garden of 60 acres, with azaleas and rhododendrons, is open from late April to early June. Also within the grounds are an adventure playground for under-12s, a Soft Play Palace, a coffee shop and restaurant.

The **Atwell-Wilson Motor Museum**, on the A4 east of Calne, has a collection of over 125 vintage and classic cars and motorcycles from the years 1924 to the late 1980s. Most of them are still in running order.

Lackham

3 miles S of Chippenham on the A350

The **Lackham Museum of Agriculture & Rural Life** offers a variety of displays set within a wonderful complex of historic Wiltshire farm buildings. With 18th century Lackham House (private) as a backdrop, the extensive themed gardens contain a walled garden, a large ornamental pond, bog garden, sensory garden, wartime kitchen garden and Lackham's famous giant lemons. For children there's a willow house, a maze and Rupert the Bear's House. Souvenirs and Lackham-grown produce are on sale in the walled garden shop.

Lacock

4 miles S of Chippenham on the A350

The National Trust village of Lacock is one of the country's real treasures. The quadrangle of streets - East, High, West and Church - holds a delightful assortment of mellow stone buildings, and the period look (no intrusive power cables or other modern-day eyesores) keeps it in great demand as a film location. Every building is a well-restored, well-preserved gem, and overlooking everything is **Lacock Abbey**, founded in 1232 by Ela, Countess of Salisbury in memory of her husband William Longsword, stepbrother to Richard the Lionheart. In common with all monastic houses Lacock was dissolved by Henry VIII, but the original cloisters, chapter houses, sacristy and kitchens survive.

Much of the remainder of what we see today dates from the mid-16th century, when the abbey was acquired by Sir William Sharington. He added an impressive country house and the elegant octagonal tower that overlooks the Avon. The estate next passed into the hands of the Talbot family, who held it for 370 years before ceding it to the National Trust in 1944.

Lacock Village

The most distinguished member of the Talbot family was the pioneering photographer William Henry Fox Talbot, who carried out his experiments in the 1830s, mainly at the Abbey. The **Fox**

Lacock Pottery and B&B

1 The Tanyard, Lacock, nr Chippenham,
Wiltshire SN15 2LB
Tel: 01249 730266 Fax: 01249 730948
e-mail: simone@lacockbedandbreakfast.com
website: www.lacockbedandbreakfast.com

Owned and preserved by the National Trust, Lacock village is full of atmosphere, with traditional old English inns and a bakery, a 14th century Tithe Barn and a medieval Abbey set in beautiful grounds where you'll also find the Fox Talbot Museum of Photography. Lacock's half-timbered cottages, stone-roofed houses and fine Georgian buildings have made it popular with film and TV producers and it has appeared in films such as *Pride & Prejudice*. Located in a peaceful corner of the village is the **Lacock Pottery and B&B**.

Artist potter David McDowell has his workshop here and he is internationally known for his fine art ceramics. If you are planning to stay in this delightful village, David and his wife Simone offer accommodation in the old workhouse which has been imaginatively renovated to provide three guest bedrooms (two doubles, one twin). One of the double rooms is in the former Governor's house and has its own front door and walled garden. All the rooms enjoy charming views of the church and tanyard. Guests have the use of a spacious lounge furnished with antiques and, naturally, some interesting ceramics. Breakfast comes with free range eggs and home-made bread and jams, seasonal herbs, fruit and vegetables from the garden – and maybe even field fresh mushrooms.

Talbot Museum commemorates the life and achievements of a man who was not just a photographer but a mathematician, physicist, classicist, philologist and transcriber of Syrian and Chaldean cuneiform. In 1839 William Henry Fox Talbot presented to the Royal Society "an account of the art of photogenic drawing or the process by which natural objects may be made to delineate themselves without the aid of the artist's pencil" - photography, in short. Louis Daguerre was at the same time demonstrating a similar technique in France, and it is not certain which of the two pioneers should be called the father of photography. But it was indisputably true that Fox Talbot

Woodmans Cottage B&B Holistic Therapy

6 Bowden Hill, Lacock, nr Chippenham, Wiltshire SN15 2PW
Tel: 01249 730946 e-mail: debgoodfellow@yahoo.com
website: www.westcountrynow.com

Set in beautiful grounds and enjoying a superb view of the famous Lacock Abbey, **Woodmans Cottage** offers quality Bed & Breakfast accommodation, combined with the option of Aromatherapy, Reflexology, Massage and other treatments to provide total relaxation and rejuvenation. Owners Deborah and Mark Taylor, declare that their aim is to give guests the care and attention often overlooked in larger establishments. The attractively furnished and decorated bedrooms (2 doubles; 1 single) have a 4-Diamonds Silver Award rating and are equipped with TV, video, hairdryer and hospitality tray.

invented the positive/negative process that permitted multiple copies. The museum is located in an old barn at the entrance to the abbey and contains Fox Talbot memorabilia and a collection of early cameras. Fox Talbot also remodelled the south elevation of the abbey and added three new oriel windows. One of the world's earliest photographs shows a detail of a latticed oriel window of the abbey; the size of a postage stamp, it is the earliest known example of a photographic negative.

Melksham

Melksham

7 miles S of Chippenham on the A350

Once an important weaving centre, Melksham was also very briefly in vogue as a spa town. It didn't make much of a splash, being overshadowed by its near neighbour Bath, so it turned to manufacturing and was given a boost when the Wiltshire & Berkshire Canal was opened. The canal, built between 1795 and 1810, linked the Kennet and Avon Canal with Abingdon, on the Thames. The Wilts & Berks was abandoned in 1914, but much of its path still exists in the form of lock and bridge remains, towpaths and embankments. Not far from Melksham is Great Chalfield Manor, a beautiful moated manor house with a tiny parish church in the grounds. Owned by the National Trust, it is open between April and October for guided tours.

Trowbridge

13 miles S of Chippenham on the A350

The county town of Wiltshire, and another major weaving centre in its day. A large number of industrial buildings still stand, and the Town Council and Civic Society have devised an interesting walk that takes in many of them. The **Trowbridge Museum**, located in the town's last working woollen mill, has a variety of interesting displays, including a reconstructed medieval castle and tableaux of a weaver's cottage and Taylor's drapery shop. It also features some working textile looms. The chancel of the parish church of St James, crowned by one of the finest spires in the

Wadswick Country Store & Barn Cottages

Manor Farm, Corsham,
Wiltshire SN13 8JB
Tel: 01225 810733
Fax: 01225 810307
e-mail: shop@wadswick.com
website: www.wadswick.co.uk

A farm drive leads across fields from the B3109 Corsham-Bradford-on-Avon road to **Wadswick Country Store and Barn Cottages**. Carolyn Barton set up here in the late 1980s and has built up one of the largest retail equestrian country store in the west. Demand has never ceased to grow, and a new shop will double the sales area and add a coffee shop in 2005. In the bright, roomy wooden-floored showroom all equestrian needs are catered for, from saddles, bridles and other tack to riding, sports and country clothing. The clothing stock features all the top names, including Barbour, Musto fleeces and coats, Dubarry boots, Chatham sailing shoes and deck shirts and the Tagg range of jackets, shirts, tops, hats, bags and children's wear. Carolyn and her staff are always ready with help and advice, and Wadswick is a retail member of the British Equestrian Trade Association and the Society of Master Saddlers. Shoppers who live too far away can use the mail order facilities.

Alongside the farm is the second string to Wadswick's bow, a fine courtyard of old Cotswold-stone barns, once part of a 16th century farm and now sympathetically converted to offer superb self-catering holiday accommodation. Sleeping from 4 to 7, they all have great individual character, with many original features, and all are equipped with everything needed for a comfortable, go-as-you-please holiday. Each has its own garden area. Situated close to a designated Area of Outstanding Natural Beauty, the cottages are a perfect place to relax and an ideal base for a walking or cycling holiday, or for touring the many places of interest in the vicinity, including Corsham with its wealth of fine houses, Bradford-on-Avon, Lacock Abbey, picture-postcard-pretty Castle Combe and the historic city of Bath.

Valerie Anne Fashions

41 Stallard Street, Trowbridge, Wiltshire BA14 9AA
Tel: 01225 762840

This popular ladies clothes shop **Valerie Anne Fashions** is located a short walk from the centre of Trowbridge, close to the railway station. **Valerie Anne** has owned and run this shop for almost 30 years.

The wide selection of ever-changing stock offers value and style, from smart casual to formal wear, to suit all ages. Her regular customers know the helpful sales team are happy to advise on the latest fashions.

The shop is a leading stockist of the top Canadian designer, Joseph Ribkoff. Other featured designers are: John Charles, Gold, Personal Choice, Laura Lebek, Diane Freis, Doris Streich, Collection NP+, Pomodora and Slimma Fashions. Accessories include hats, scarves, wraps and jewellery.

county, contains the tomb of the poet and former rector George Crabbe, who wrote the work on which Benjamin Britten based his opera *Peter Grimes*. Trowbridge's most famous son was Isaac Pitman, the shorthand man, who was born in Nash Yard in 1813.

Corsham

3 miles SW of Chippenham off the A4

A town made prosperous by wool and the quarrying of local Bath stone. Pevsner was very much taken with Corsham, asserting that it had no match in Wiltshire "for wealth of good houses". The composer Sir Michael Tippett spent the 10 years between 1960 and 1970 living at Parkside on the High Street – he was attracted here by the peace of the town and its easy access to the countryside.

Corsham Court, based on an Elizabethan house of 1582, was bought by Paul Methuen in 1745 and later housed his inherited collection of paintings. The present house and grounds are chiefly the work of John

Corsham Court

Nash, Capability Brown, Thomas Bellamy and Humphry Repton, a top-pedigree setting for the treasures within, which include paintings by Caravaggio, Fra Filippo Lippi, Reynolds, Rubens and Van Dyck and furniture by Chippendale. The house has been used as the location for several films, including *Northanger Abbey* and *Remains of the Day*. Among other important buildings in Corsham are the magnificent Almshouses erected by Dame Margaret Hungerford in 1668 and still in use, the old market house (town hall) and a row of 16th century Flemish weavers' cottages. Mansion House, now a youth centre, was the home of Robert Neale, a leading clothier and sometime MP for Wootton Bassett. His firm produced the red coats worn by the Duke of Wellington's troops. The parish church, St Bartholomew's, contains tombs and memorials to some of Corsham's eminent clothiers, and also the famous flat-stone grave of Sarah Jarvis, who died in 1753 at the age of 107 having grown a third set of teeth!

Corsham Tourist Information Centre has an ongoing exhibition about the wool trade and about the mining of Bath stone. It includes items used in the old stone mine, which was also used as an ammunition depot during World War II, and relates the story of Bath stone from rock face to architectural heritage.

Box

6 miles SW of Chippenham on the A4

Bath stone is still quarried at this delightful spot, which is best known for one of the most remarkable engineering feats of its time, **Box Tunnel**. The 1.8 mile railway tunnel took five years to excavate and when completed in 1841 was the longest such tunnel in the world. According to local legend the sun shines through its entire length on only one occasion each year - sunrise on April 9th, the birthday of its genius creator, Isambard Kingdom Brunel. The tunnel is still in use; Box station, sadly, is not.

Holt

9 miles SW of Chippenham on the B3107

The village was once a small spa, and the old mineral well can still be seen in a factory in the village. Right at the heart of the village is **The Courts** (National Trust), an English country garden of mystery with unusual topiary, ponds, water gardens and an arboretum. The garden is mainly the work of Sir George Hastings and was created in the reign of Edward VII. The house is not open to the public.

Great Chalfield

9 miles SW of Chippenham off the B3107/3109

Great Chalfield Manor, completed in 1480, is a delightful moated manor house with an impressive great hall and a tiny parish church.

Bradford-on-Avon

13 miles SW of Chippenham on the A363

An historic market town at a bridging point on the Avon, which it spans with a superb nine-arched bridge with a lock-up at one end. The town's oldest building is the **Church of St Lawrence**, believed to have been founded by St Aldhelm around 700. It 'disappeared' for over 1,000 years, when it was used variously as a school, a charnel house for storing the bones of the dead, and a residential dwelling. It was re-discovered by a keen-eyed clergyman who looked down from a hill and noticed the cruciform shape of a church. The surrounding buildings were gradually removed to reveal the little masterpiece we see today. Bradford's Norman church, restored in the 19th century, has an interesting memorial to

Lieutenant-General Henry Shrapnel, the army officer who, in 1785, invented and gave his name to the shrapnel shell. Another of the town's outstanding buildings is the mighty **Tithe Barn**, once used to store the grain from local farms for Shaftesbury Abbey, now housing a collection of antique farm implements and agricultural machinery. The centrepiece of the museum in Bridge Street is a pharmacy which has stood in the town for 120 years before being removed lock, stock and medicine bottles to its new site.

Kennet & Avon Canal, Bradford-on-Avon

Off the A363, **Barton Farm Country Park** offers delightful walks in lovely countryside by the River Avon and the

Maples Delicatessen

4 The Shambles, Bradford-on-Avon, Wiltshire BA15 1JS
Tel: 01225 862203
website: www.maplesdeli.co.uk

Caroline Jones, the owner of **Maples Delicatessen**, has a passion for quality food, a passion she has been able to indulge to the full since opening her shop in 2001. It's tucked away in the pedestrianised Shambles and is well worth seeking out. The outstanding selection on display ranges from very local produce to Continental delicacies. Locally produced items include fresh bread from Hobs House Bakery at Chipping Sodbury, wonderful home-made cakes, muffins and tarts baked by Caroline and her mother, West Country ham, Hill Station ice cream from Calne, organic cream, honey, free range chicken, duck and quail eggs, smoked trout pâté from Mere, and Tracklements preserves.

From further afield come the Miniscoff range of proper, home-made food for children, Scottish wild salmon (from Inverawe), Scottish garlic, Italian pastas and olives, and the French Marche des Anges range of fruit and flower syrups for adding to champagne and puddings. A recently installed Italian machine provides aromatic espresso and cappuchino to take away, and there's an excellent choice of sandwiches. Friendly and knowledgeable staff are at hand to give helpful advice on all aspects of food preparation and presentation.

Church Farm Country Cottages

Church Farm, Winsley, Bradford-on-Avon,
Wiltshire BA15 2JH
Tel/Fax: 01225 722246
e-mail: stay@churchfarmcottages.com
website: www.churchfarmcottages.com

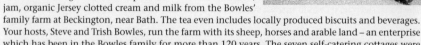

Guests arriving at **Church Farm Country Cottages** are greeted with a welcoming cream tea complete with home-made scones, jam, organic Jersey clotted cream and milk from the Bowles' family farm at Beckington, near Bath. The tea even includes locally produced biscuits and beverages. Your hosts, Steve and Trish Bowles, run the farm with its sheep, horses and arable land – an enterprise which has been in the Bowles family for more than 120 years. The seven self-catering cottages were originally traditional single storey cow byres but have been imaginatively renovated while preserving original features such as the natural stone walls, exposed beams, vaulted ceilings and stone pillars.

Each cottage has locally made natural wood kitchens, all well equipped and with many extras. Colour TV, video, CD/radio and cassette player are all provided along with hairdryers and alarm clock/radios in the bedrooms. Three of the cottages sleep two; the other four sleep four/five. All of them are non-smoking. A popular amenity on site is the indoor heated swimming pool, 12m by 5m, and there's also a set aside room with table tennis, table football and a pool table. If you get tired of cooking for yourself, the village pub, which was once owned by Steve's grandfather, is just a short stroll away and serves excellent food.

Mr Salvats Coffee Room

The Town House, St Margaret's Street,
Bradford-on-Avon, Wiltshire
Tel: 01225 867474

Mr Salvats Coffee Room occupies a building that was rebuilt about 1700, probably for a successful wool merchant. There's evidence of the earlier building in the Elizabethan fireplace in the cellar from where a spiral staircase rises to the top floor. Owner John Salvat describes himself as "originally a scientist from London, it is rumoured he was a contemporary of Sir Isaac Newton"! John has furnished his coffee shop in late-17th century style – the golden age of the coffee shop – with tables in booths with pew-style seating. In good weather, customers can enjoy their refreshments in the lovely garden to the rear which has won a Garden Award from Bradford's Town Council.

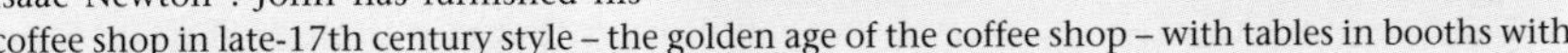

Along with coffee, tea and soft drinks, the menu offers some delicious home-made cakes baked by Kerry Edwards in her Bradford kitchen, along with freshly-made scones and other tea-time treats. There's also a choice of fresh soups as well as light meals such as vegetarian lasagne, live & bacon pâté, Cheddar ploughman's and jacket potatoes. Mr Salvat's is open from 10am to 5pm, every Saturday and Sunday, and four days during the week. Closing day varies so do phone ahead.

Kennet and Avon Canal. It was once a medieval farm serving Shaftesbury Abbey. Barton Bridge is the original packhorse bridge built to assist the transportation of grain from the farm to the tithe barn.

Half a mile south of town by the River Frome is the Italian-style **Peto Garden** at Iford Manor. Famous for its romantic, tranquil beauty, its steps and terraces, statues, colonnades and ponds, the garden was laid out by the architect and landscape gardener Harold Ainsworth Peto between 1899 and 1933. He was inspired by the works of Lutyens and Jekyll to turn a difficult hillside site into 'a haunt of ancient peace'.

Outside Bradford, off the A366, the charming 15th century **Westwood Manor** (National Trust) has many interesting features, including Jacobean and Gothic windows, ornate plasterwork and a topiary garden.

MALMESBURY

The 'Queen of Hilltop Towns' is England's oldest borough and one of its most attractive. The town is dominated by the impressive remains of the **Benedictine Malmesbury Abbey**, founded in the 7th century by St Aldhelm. In the 10th century, King Athelstan, Alfred's grandson and the first Saxon king to unite England, granted 500 acres of land to the townspeople in gratitude for their help in resisting a

Norse invasion. Those acres are still known as King's Heath and are owned by 200 residents who are descended from those far-off heroes. Athelstan made Malmesbury his capital and is buried in the abbey, where several centuries later a monument was put up in his honour.

Within the precincts of the abbey are **Abbey House Gardens**, an enchanting place with an abundance of flowers, around 2,000 medicinal herbs, woodland and laburnum walks, fish ponds and a waterfall.

The abbey tower was the scene of an early attempt at human-powered flight when in the early part of the 11th century Brother Elmer strapped a pair of wings to his arms, flew for about 200 yards and crashed to earth, breaking both legs and becoming a cripple for the rest of his long life. The flight of this intrepid cleric, who reputedly forecast the Norman invasion following a sighting of Halley's Comet, is commemorated in a stained glass window. Another window, by Burne-Jones, portrays Faith, Courage and Devotion.

The octagonal **Market Cross** in the town square is one of many interesting buildings that also include the Old Stone House with its colonnade and gargoyles, and the arched Tolsey Gate, whose two cells once served as the town jail.

Pound Hill Garden & Plant Centre

West Kington, nr Castle Combe, Wiltshire SN14 7JG
Tel: 01249 783880 Fax: 01249 782953
e-mail: info@poundhillplants.co.uk
website: www.poundhillplants.co.uk

A romantic walled garden, a plant centre stocked with unusual varieties, and an excellent tea room – three good reasons to seek out **Pound Hill Garden & Plant Centre**. From Bath or the M4 follow the A46, and turn onto the A420 towards Chippenham. Follow the brown signs to West Kington and just after entering the village you will find Pound Hill on the right. The garden is divided into several 'rooms'. The first, a Victorian kitchen garden, leads into an old-fashioned rose garden and then either to a Wisteria Walk or into a courtyard decorated with colourful containers. The main part of the garden has beautiful, deep herbaceous borders, a parterre planted with fragrant roses and a box garden. Then there's enchanting woodland with a wildlife pool that leads to a walkway through white-stemmed *Betula jacquemonti* into a grass walk with clipped sweet chestnuts and old shrub roses. The Garden is open daily 2-5pm March - October.

The Plant Centre was opened in 1992 to cater for the discerning gardener. Over the years it has become a Mecca for plant hunters and artistic gardeners alike as the centre specialises is perennials, old roses and topiary and has won several prestigious horticultural awards. The Plant Centre also contains the Barn Gift Shop, stocked with unusual gifts for gardeners, and the Pound Hill Pantry which serves delicious home-made light meals and refreshments, many of them produced from local and organic ingredients. The Plant Centre is open daily from 1st Feb to end December and also Bank Holiday Mondays.

In the **Malmesbury Athelstan Museum** (free) in the Town Hall are displays of lace-making, costume, rural life, coins, early bicycles and tricycles, a manually-operated fire engine, photographs and maps.

A more recent piece of history concerns the **Tamworth Two**, the pigs who made the headlines with their dash for freedom.

Castle Combe

AROUND MALMESBURY

Castle Combe

8 miles SW of Malmesbury on the B4039

The loveliest village in the region, and for some the loveliest in the country, Castle Combe was once a centre of the prosperous wool trade, famed for its red and white cloth. Many of the present-day buildings date from the 15th and 16th centuries, including the Perpendicular Church of St Andrew, the covered market cross and the manor house, which was built with stones from the Norman castle that gave the village its name. One of the Lords of the Manor in the 14th century was Sir John Fastolf, who was reputedly the inspiration for Shakespeare's Falstaff. A small museum dealing with the village's history is open on summer Sunday afternoons.

Easton Grey

3 miles W of Malmesbury on the B4040

Here the southern branch of the River Avon is spanned by a handsome 16th century bridge with five stone arches. A manor house has overlooked the village since the 13th century; the present house, with a classical facade and an elegant covered portico, dates from the 18th century. It was used as a summer retreat by Herbert Asquith, British Prime Minister from 1908 to 1916, and in 1923 the Prince of Wales was in residence during the Duke of Beaufort's hunting season at Badminton.

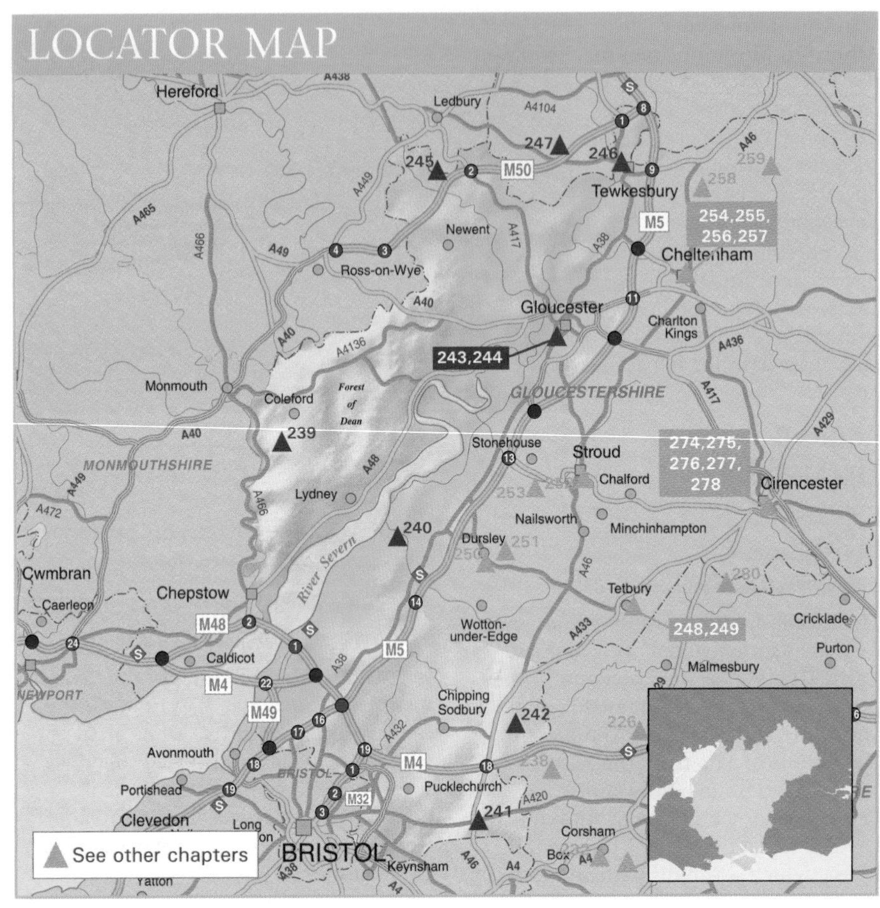

ADVERTISERS AND PLACES OF INTEREST

Accommodation, Food and Drink

Activities

Home and Garden

Places of Interest

ROYAL FOREST OF DEAN & WEST GLOUCESTERSHIRE 6

Wild woodland, royal hunting ground, naval timber reserve, important mining and industrial area. The Royal Forest of Dean, one of England's few remaining ancient forests, has been all these, and today its rich and varied landscape provides endless interest for walkers, historians and nature-lovers.

The forest covers an area of some 24,000 acres and lies in an area bordered by the Severn Estuary to the south and the Wye Valley to the west, effectively isolated from the rest of England and from Wales. As a result, 'this heart-shaped land' (Dennis Potter's description) has developed a character all its own.

Royal Forest of Dean

The forest has long been home to a variety of wildlife, and it was the presence of deer that led Edmund Ironside to designate it a royal hunting ground in the 11th century. Iron ore deposits were first discovered in the forest 2,500 years ago and were exploited by the Romans, but it was not until the 1600s that mineral began to be extracted on a large scale. The most ruinous development in the forest was the demand for timber for the process of iron smelting; at one time 72 furnaces were operating in the area, depleting the timber supplies to such an extent that a major replanting programme was initiated in the 1660s.

The Victorians exploited another of the forest's natural resources, coal, removing up to a million tons a year at the height of demand. This industry more or less came to an end in the 1930s, and the forest has gradually reclaimed most of the workings. In 1938 the forest was made into a Forest Park, the first to be created in England, balancing the needs of conservation and recreational use with commercial timber production.

In the northwest of the county the Leadon Valley, a peaceful and picturesque part of the world, has strong literary connections, including the influential Dymock poets, while in the Severn Vale lush meadows lie along the river, famous for its tidal bore and haven for thousands of wildfowl and wading birds. The Wildfowl and Wetlands Trust at Slimbridge, founded in 1946 by Peter Scott, and historic Berkeley Castle are among the diverse attractions here.

NEWENT

Capital of the area of northwest Gloucestershire known as the Ryelands, and the most important town in the Vale of Leadon, Newent stands in the broad triangle of land called Daffodil Crescent. The rich Leadon Valley soil was traditionally used for growing rye and raising the renowned Ryelands sheep, an ancient breed famed for the quality of its wool. The town was one of the county's principal wool-trading centres, and the wealth produced from that trade accounts for the large number of grand merchants' houses to be seen here. The most distinctive building in Newent is the splendid timber-framed **Market House**, built as a butter market in the middle of the 16th century, its upper floors supported on 16 oak pillars that form an open colonnade. The medieval **Church of St Mary** has many outstanding features, including the shaft of a 9th century Saxon cross, the 11th century 'Newent Stone' and the 17th century nave. Royalist troops had removed the lead from the roof to make bullets, an act which caused the roof to collapse during a snowstorm in 1674. A new nave was started after Charles II agreed to donate 60 tons of timber from the Forest of Dean. The 150ft spire is a landmark for miles around.

The Shambles Museum of Victorian Life is virtually a little Victorian town, a cleverly laid out jumble of cobbled streets, alleyways and squares, with shops and trades tucked away in all corners, and even a mission chapel and a Victorian conservatory.

There aren't too many windmills in Gloucestershire, but at **Castle Hill Farm** just outside town is a working wooden mill with great views from a balcony at the top.

AROUND NEWENT

A mile south of Newent is the **National Bird of Prey Centre** housing one of the largest and best collections of birds of prey in the world. Over 110 aviaries are home to eagles, falcons, owls, vultures, kites, hawks and buzzards. Between 20 and 40 birds are flown daily at the Centre, which is open every day from February to November.

On the road north towards Dymock, set in 65 acres of rolling countryside, the **Three Choirs Vineyard** is the country's largest wine producer.

DYMOCK

3 miles N of Newent on the B4216

Dymock boasts some fine old brick buildings, including the White House and the Old Rectory near the church, and outside the village, the Old Grange, which incorporates the remains of the Cistercian Flaxley Abbey.

At the heart of the village is the early Norman Church of St Mary, whose unusual features include a tympanum depicting the Tree of Life, a 13th century stone coffin lid, stained glass by Kempe – and the last ticket issued at Dymock station, in 1959. A corner of the church is dedicated to the memory of the **Dymock Poets**, a group who based themselves in Dymock from before World War I. The group, which comprised Lascelles Abercrombie (the first to arrive), Rupert Brooke, John Drinkwater, Wilfred Gibson, Edward Thomas and Robert Frost, sent out its *New Numbers* poetry magazine from Dymock's tiny post office; it was also from here that Brooke published his *War Sonnets*, including *The Soldier* (*'If I should die, think only this of me: That there's some corner of a foreign field that is forever England...'*). Brooke and Thomas died in the war, which led to the dissolution of the group. Two circular walks from Dymock take in places associated with the poets.

Many other literary figures are associated with the Forest. Dennis Potter, born at Coleford in 1935 the eldest son of a Forest coal-miner, is renowned for writing the screenplays for some of TV's most memorable programmes, including *Pennies From Heaven* and *The Singing Detective*. But he also wrote with passion about the Forest in *The Glittering Coffin* and *The Changing Forest: Life in the Forest of Dean Today*. Mary Howitt, born in Coleford in 1799, is known as a translator, poet and author of children's books. It was as a translator that she met a Danish story-teller called Hans Christian Andersen who asked Mary to translate his stories into English.

Upleadon

2 miles N of Newent off the B4215

The **Church of St Mary the Virgin** features some fine Norman and Tudor work but is best known for its unique tower, half-timbered from bottom to top; even the mullion windows are of wood. The church has a great treasure in its Bible, an early example of the Authorised Version printed by the King's printer Robert Barker. This was the unfortunate who later issued an edition with a small but rather important word missing. The so-called Wicked Bible of 1631 renders Exodus 20.14 as "Thou shalt commit adultery".

Kempley

3 miles NW of Newent on a minor road

A village famous for its cider and also for having two churches, of very different age and significance. The **Church of St Mary**, easily the most popular church in the area, dates from the end of the 11th century and would be a gem even without its greatest treasure. That treasure, in the chancel, is an almost complete set of 12th century frescoes, the most renowned in the region and among the finest in the land, protected by Reformation whitewash and Victorian varnish. Their subjects include St Peter and the Apostles, Christ with his feet resting on a globe, and the de Lacy family, local lords of the manor. The red sandstone Church of St Edward the Confessor was built in 1903 by the 7th Earl Beauchamp in the style of the Arts and Crafts Movement using exclusively local materials.

This is the area of **Dymock Woods**, an area of Forestry Commission woodland famous for its daffodils.

LONGHOPE

Another good starting point for a tour in and around the Forest of Dean is Longhope, a pleasant settlement south of the A40 Gloucester to Ross-on-Wye road.

Longhope is the location of the **Harts Barn Crafts Centre**, situated in a hunting lodge built by William Duke of Normandy and housing an array of working crafts including jewellery, pine furniture, art gallery, hand-made gifts, glassware, dried flowers and picture framing.

AROUND LONGHOPE

Mitcheldean

2 miles W of Longhope on the A4136

A peaceful community on the northern fringe of the forest. A mile or so south of the village is **St Anthony's Well**, one of many throughout the land said to have magical curative powers. The water at this well is invariably icy cold and bathing in it is said to provide a cure for skin disease (St Anthony's Fire was the medieval name for a rampant itching disease). The monks at nearby Flaxley Abbey swore by it.

Drybrook

5 miles SW of Longhope off the A4136

Hidden away at Hawthorns Cross on the edge of the Forest is the **Mechanical Organ Museum** with a vast collection of mechanical music spanning 150 years. The museum is open at Easter and on Tuesday and Thursday afternoons in April, May, July and August.

Ruardean

6 miles SW of Longhope on the A4136

A lovely old village whose **Church of St John the Baptist**, one of many on the fringe of the forest, has many interesting features. A tympanum depicting St George and the Dragon is a great rarity, and on a stone plaque in the nave is a curious carving of two fishes. These are thought to have been carved by craftsmen from the Herefordshire School of Norman Architecture during the Romanesque period around 1150. It is part of a frieze removed with rubble when the south porch was being built in the 13th century. The frieze was considered lost until 1985, when an inspection of a bread oven in a cottage at nearby Turner's Tump revealed the two fish set into its lining. They were rescued and returned to their rightful place in the church. Ruardean was the birthplace in the 1840s of James and William Horlick, later to be become famous with their Horlicks formula. Their patent for 'malted milk' was registered in 1883 and the granary where the original experiments were carried out still remains in the village.

Ruardean Hill is 951 feet above sea level and on a clear day Herefordshire, the Black Mountains and the Brecon Beacons can all be seen.

NEWNHAM-ON-SEVERN

One of the gateways to the Forest, and formerly a port, Newnham lies on a great bend in the river. Its heyday was at the beginning of the 19th century, when a quay was built and an old tramway tunnel converted into what was perhaps the world's first railway tunnel. The village has many interesting buildings which can be visited by following the Millennium Heritage Walk plaques installed by the parish council with funds provided by an open-air jazz concert.

AROUND NEWNHAM-ON-SEVERN

Westbury-on-Severn

3 miles NE of Newnham on the A48

The village, bounded on three sides by the river, is best known for the National Trust's **Westbury Court Garden**, a formal Dutch water garden laid out between 1696 and 1705. Historic varieties of apple, pear and plum, along with many other species introduced to England before 1700, make this a must for any enthusiastic gardener. The house was long ago demolished, and the only building to survive is an elegant two-storey redbrick pavilion with a tower and weather vane. Also worth a visit in Westbury is the Church of Saints Peter, Paul and Mary with its detached tower and wooden spire. Walmore Common is winter home to thousands of swans as well as many wading birds and unusual flora.

Westbury is an excellent spot to watch

the famous **Severn Bore**. This is a tidal wave that several times a month makes its way along the river. The bore travels at an average speed of about 10 miles an hour and has been known to reach a height of 6.5ft. The Severn Estuary experiences the second highest tide anywhere in the world, and the difference between the lowest and highest tide in any one day can be more than 14.5 metres. These high, or spring tides, occur on several days in each lunar cycle throughout the year.

Littledean

2 miles NW of Newnham off the A4151

Places of interest here include the 13th century church, the 18th century prison and, just south of the village, **Littledean Hall**, reputedly the oldest inhabited house in England. The house has Saxon and Celtic remains in the cellars and is thought to have originated in the 6th century; it became a Royalist garrison during the Civil War. Highlights in the grounds, from which balloon flights launch, include a Roman temple site, a Victorian walled garden and a number of ancient chestnut trees.

Cinderford

3 miles NW of Newnham on the A4151

A former coal-mining community with evidence of the mines visible among the trees.

At Camp Hill in the nearby hamlet of Soudley is the recently refurbished **Dean Heritage Centre**, where four galleries tell the story of the Forest and its people. It is a perfect setting for a family day out with woodland walks, café, adventure playground and children's activity room, museum and crafts shops, farm animals and woodland crafts, including charcoal burning and woodturning. A level trail runs round Soudley Ponds, a designated Site of Special Scientific Interest.

At nearby **Awre**, an ancient crossing place of the Severn, the Church of St Andrew has changed little in its 700 years. Its most notable possession is a massive mortuary chest carved from a single piece of wood and used as a laying out place for bodies recovered from the Severn. In the churchyard are examples of headstones featuring the local speciality - cherubs.

LYDNEY

The harbour and the canal at Lydney, once an important centre of the iron and coal industries and the largest settlement between Chepstow and Gloucester, are well worth exploring, and no visit to the town should end without a trip on the **Dean Forest Railway**. A regular service of steam and diesel trains operates between Lydney Junction, St Mary's Halt and Norchard. At **Norchard Railway Centre**, headquarters of the line, are a railway museum, souvenir shop and details of restoration projects, including the extension of the line to Parkend. Popular events throughout the year include Days Out with Thomas, Santa Specials and Steam Footplate Experience Courses.

A recently opened family tourist attraction is the **Forest Model Village & Gardens** which features more than 50 detailed miniatures of local landmarks and buildings in five landscaped garden zones.

One of the chief attractions in the vicinity is **Lydney Park Spring Gardens and Roman Temple Site**. The gardens, which lie beside the A48 on the western outskirts, are a riot of colour, particularly in May and June, and the grounds also contain the site of an Iron Age hill fort and the remains of a late-Roman temple excavated by Sir Mortimer Wheeler in the 1920s. The nearby museum houses a number of Roman artefacts from the site, including the famous 'Lydney Dog', and a number of interesting items brought back from New Zealand in the 1930s by the first Viscount Bledisloe after his term there as Governor General. Also in the park are traces of Roman iron-mine workings and Roman earth workings.

AROUND LYDNEY

Alvington

2 miles SW of Lydney on the A48

In the churchyard at Alvington are the graves of the illustrious Wintour family, leading figures in the defeat of the Spanish Armada. Half a century after that event came Sir John Wintour's remarkable escape from Cromwell's men at what is now known as **Wintour's Leap**. Sir John was an adventurer, Keeper of the Forest of Dean and sometime secretary to Queen Maria Henrietta of the Netherlands. In 1644 he was at the head of a Royalist force defeated at Blockley, near Chepstow, by Parliamentary troops. Wintour is said to have escaped from the battlefield by riding up by the Wye and hurling himself and his horse into the river from the cliffs.

COLEFORD

A former mining centre which received its royal charter from Charles I in the 17th century in recognition of its loyalty to the Crown. It was by then already an important iron processing centre, partly because of the availability of local ore deposits and partly because of the ready local supply of timber for converting into charcoal for use in the smelting process. It was in Coleford that the Mushet family helped to revolutionise the iron and steel industry. Robert Forester Mushet, a freeminer, discovered how spiegeleisen, an alloy of iron, manganese, silicon and carbon, could be used in the reprocessing of 'burnt iron' and went on to develop a system for turning molten pig iron directly into steel, a process which predated the more familiar one developed later by Bessemer.

Great Western Railway Museum, Coleford

Coleford, still regarded as the capital of the Royal Forest of Dean, is a busy commercial centre with an interesting church and a number of notable industrial relics. The Forestry Commission is housed at Bank House and has information on all aspects of the Forest. There are miles of way-marked walks and cycle trails in the forest, and the famous Sculpture Trail starts at Beechenhurst Lodge.

Coleford is also home to the **Great**

Western Railway Museum, housed in an 1883 GWR goods station next to the central car park. Another treat for railway fans is the **Perrygrove Railway**, where a narrow gauge steam train takes a 1.5 mile trip through farmland and woods. Nearby is another visitor attraction, also on the B4228 just south of town. This is **Puzzle Wood**, where 14 acres of open-cast ore mines have been redesigned as a family attraction, with paths forming an unusual maze, breathtaking scenery, wooden bridges, passageways through moss-covered rocks and lots of dead ends and circles.

AROUND COLEFORD

Staunton

3 miles NW of Coleford on the A4136

Lots to see here, including a Norman church with two stone fonts and an unusual corkscrew staircase leading up past the pulpit to the belfry door. Not far from the village are several enormous mystical stones, notably the **Buck Stone** and the **Suck Stone**. The former, looking like some great monster, used to buck, or rock, on its base but is now firmly fixed in place. The Suck Stone is a real giant, weighing in at many thousands of tons. There are several other stones in the vicinity, including the Near Harkening and Far Harkening down among the trees, and the Long Stone by the A4136 at Marion's Cross.

Cannop

4 miles E of Coleford on the B4226

Cannop Valley has many forest trails and picnic sites; one of the sites is at Cannop Ponds, picturesque ponds created in the 1820s to provide a regular supply of water for the local iron-smelting works. Nearby is **Hopewell Colliery**, a true Forest of Dean free mine where summer visitors can see old mine workings and some of the old tools of the trade, then relax with a snack from the café.

Parkend

3 miles SE of Coleford off the B4234

A community once based, like so many others in the area, on the extraction of minerals. In the early years of the 19th century, before steam engines arrived and horses did all the donkey work, Parkend became a tramroad centre and laden trams ran from coalpits, iron mines, quarries, furnaces and forges to river-borne outlets at Lydbrook and Lydney. New Fancy Colliery is now a delightful picnic area, with a nearby hill affording breathtaking views over the forestscape. Off the B4431, just west of Parkend, is the RSPB's **Nagshead Nature Reserve**, with hundreds of nest boxes in a woodland site with footpaths, way-marked trails and a summer information centre.

Clearwell

1.5 miles S of Coleford off the A466

Clearwell Caves (see panel on page 324) are part of the only remaining working iron mine in the Forest of Dean. This natural cave system became filled with iron ore around 180 million years ago and has been mined for at least 4,000 years. As a result, the cave complex now consists of many miles of passageways and hundreds of caverns. Visitors can take their own self-guided tour or take part in a more strenuous adventure caving trip. Other amenities on site include a gift shop and tea room. A memorable visit can be completed by wandering down to Clearwell village with its lovely French Gothic-style church and the pretty surrounding countryside.

WALK NUMBER 11

Clearwell

Distance:	5.0 miles (8.0 kilometres)
Typical time:	180 mins
Height gain:	280 metres
Map:	Explorer OL 14
Walk:	www.walkingworld.com ID:1729
Contributor:	Pat Roberts

Access Information:

Parking is at the car park for Clearwell Caves, signed from Clearwell which is near Newland.

Additional Information:

Anyone interested in caving, and the undreground passages should make inquiries at Clearwell caves, where trips are arranged. In the woodland are fine examples of scowles left by ancient iron miners as long ago as pre-Roman times. **Pingry Lane** Tradition says that at the time of the civil war this lane was running with blood and was known as "Bloody Lane". The red pigment was more likely to be red ochre from the iron ore.

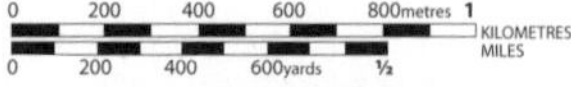

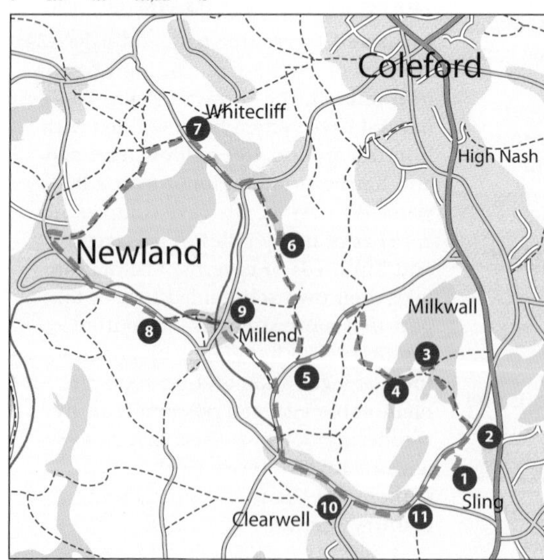

Description:

The area around here was once rich in iron mines, and the woods contain old workings, which are rich in ferns and other plant life, resulting in a fairy-glen appearance as you walk through. Lovely views over to the Welsh Mountains, and Newland Church, The Cathedral of the Forest, is well worth a visit.

Features:

Hills or Fells, Church, Wildlife, Birds, Flowers, Great Views, Cafe, Woodland

Walk Directions:

1 From the carpark, walk back down the approach track to the road, walk up to the right and pass the entrance to Clearwell farm on the left side of the road, and walk 20 metres further on.

2 20 metres past the entrance to the farm, cross the stile on the left side of the road and follow the fence on your left. After 50 metres there is a large tree with a fence round it on the left, below which see the entrance to a system of underground passages reaching to Coleford. Within 30 metres cross a stile leading further into the wood. The path keeps to a northwesterly direction, but divides in places, to emerge at the edge of a field near the buildings of Clearwell Farm.

3 Over the stile, walk diagonally across the field to a stile/gate on the edge of a small wood. Walk with the fence on your left and the trees on your right, to reach another stile.

4 The view here is outstanding, over to the Black Mountains and the Sugar Loaf. There are two yellow arrows, but we take the one to the right. Follow the hedge on the right down the field, enjoying the view. Over another stile in the bottom corner to follow the right hedge down to a stile in the corner.

(Can be very muddy at the bottom so plan your route!) Over the stile onto Pingry Lane where left. Walk as far as a wall on the left with a ruined barn behind it.

5 Go through this gate on the right. The sign points left, but walk to the left of the pond but ahead through a gap between the trees, then to the right BEHIND the trees and left up the field towards a gate with an arrow on it. The arrow points up the next field, but walk diagonally left across the field, below Breckness Court seen at the top of the field. Head for a point about 50 metres below the large house, and a gate in the hedge just below some trees. Once through the gate walk in a northerly direction the length of the field.

6 Over this stile into Galders Wood. Keep on the bottom of the wood to reach another stile into a field. Maintain direction to come down to a minor road by a house. Left past the house to a junction, here go straight ahead and pass under a bridge, and pass a ruin of a bridge which once carried the old mineral railway between Coleford and Newland. Ignore a turning off on the left into the wood to reach where the road bends right.

7 Here on the bend the sign says "Old Burial Route". This was used to carry the coffins from Coleford and the scowls to the church at Newland. Left here and arrive at a stile into a field. Good views ahead. DO NOT CROSS THE STILE, but bear left with the track and eventually reach a metal road down into Newland, next to the Ostrich Pub. Left through Newland, pass over Valley Brook and pass the entrance to Rookery Farm. Just after the road starts to gain height and bend right, look for a stile on the left.

8 The stile and footpath sign are in the hedge. Cross over. Walk in the direction of the arrow to another stile, then in the same direction head for Millend Farm. There left over a stile and a footbridge. At the end of the footbridge right with a fence on your left, cross the lawn to the drive where right and up to the road. Here turn left for 40 metres.

9 Take this bridle path up to the right. It is quite a pull in the beginning but soon levels out and drops down to Pingry Lane. This lane will bring you out to the main road through Clearwell, where left up through the village. Opposite the Post Office a small detour follows a stream to a spring inscribed "He sendeth the Springs into the Valleys which run among the Hills" Continue on up the road to a junction.

10 At this junction, with the monument in the centre, take the left road up and signed "Clearwell Caves". Good footpath on the right side of the road.

11 Where the pavement runs out, see a track up on the right bank. Follow this, pass the café and visitor centre for Clearwell Caves to return to the carpark.

St Briavels

5 miles S of Coleford on minor roads

On the edge of a limestone plateau high above the Wye Valley, this historic village is named after a 5th century Welsh bishop whose name appears in various forms throughout Celtic Wales, Cornwall and Brittany, but nowhere else in England. In the Middle Ages St Briavels was an important administrative centre for the royal hunting forest and also a leading manufacturer of armaments, supplying weapons and ammunition to the Crown.

The ample Church of St Mary the Virgin, Norman in origin, enlarged in the 12th and 13th centuries and remodelled by the Victorians, is the scene of a curious and very English annual custom, the St Briavels **Bread and Cheese Ceremony**. After evensong a local forester stands on the Pound Wall and throws small pieces of bread and cheese to the villagers, accompanied by the chant 'St Briavels water and Whyrl's wheat are the best bread and water King John can ever eat'. This ceremony is thought to have originated more than 700 years ago when the villagers successfully defended their rights of estover (collecting wood from common land) in nearby Hudnalls Wood. In gratitude each villager paid one penny to

Clearwell Caves

nr Coleford, Royal Forest of Dean, Gloucestershire GL16 8JR
Tel: 01594 832535
Fax: 01594 833362
e-mail: jw@clearwellcaves.com
website: www.clearwellcaves.com

Clearwell Caves are set in an Area of Special Landscape Value on the outskirts of the historic village of Clearwell. The caves are part of the last remaining working iron mine in the Forest of Dean and the last ochre mine in the UK. They are part of a natural cave system that became filled with iron ore around 180 million years ago.

Mining in the Forest of Dean is now believed to have begun over 7,000 years ago during the Mesolithic period (Middle Stone Age) as people migrated back into the area after the last Ice Age (10,000 years ago).

People were collecting ochre pigments, particularly red ochre which was very highly prized and had important decorative and ritual uses. Once the use of iron as a metal was established and certainly by the 1st century AD, there was a thriving iron industry here.

Large scale iron ore mining continued until 1945 and in its last year as a large scale mine it produced over 3,000 tons of ore. Today production of minerals rarely exceeds four tons per annum. Small scale ochre mining carries on, using traditional techniques which would be familiar to even the earliest miners.

Visitors to the caves are offered a wide range of activities, from a leisurely and fascinating self-guided underground walk, descending for more than 100ft, to a more strenuous adventure caving trip – or even a Natural Paint workshop. The cave shop is a treat in itself with unusual gift ideas, books, souvenirs and a wide range of spectacular minerals and crystals from around the world. And of course you can buy the ochre mined here.

Don't forget to pay a visit to the tearoom. Here you'll find a good selection of freshly prepared lunches and refreshments, along with some very interesting mining artefacts displayed around the ceiling and walls. An unusual day out for all ages and a great underground experience. Clearwell Caves are open from 10am to 5pm, daily, from 14th February until 31st October. Visitors are still welcome during November but the caves are then being prepared for the Christmas Fantasy (open 27th November – 24th December) so normal displays are interrupted.

the churchwarden to help feed the poor, and that act led to the founding of the ceremony. Small pieces of bread and cheese were considered to bring good luck, and the Dean Forest miners would keep the pieces in order to ward off harm.

St Briavels Castle, which stands in an almost impregnable position on a high promontory, was founded by Henry I and enlarged by King John, who used it as a hunting lodge. Two sturdy gatehouses are among the parts that survive and they, like some of the actual castle buildings, are now in use as a youth hostel.

Newland

1 mile SW of Coleford off the A466

Newland's Church of All Saints is often known as the **Cathedral of the Forest** because of its impressive size. Its aisle is almost as wide as its nave and its huge pinnacled tower is supported by flying buttresses. Like many churches in the county, it was built during the 13th and 14th centuries and remodelled by the Victorians. Inside, it has a number of interesting effigies, including an unusual brass relief of a medieval miner with a pick and hod in his hand and a candlestick in his mouth. Other effigies depict a forester in 15th century hunting gear with a hunting horn, a sword and knife; and, from the 17th century, an archer with wide-brimmed hat, bow, horn and dagger.

SOUTH GLOUCESTERSHIRE AND THE VALE OF BERKELEY

Frampton-on-Severn

8 miles SW of Gloucester off the A38

The 22-acre Rosamund Green, incorporating a cricket ground and three ponds, is one of the largest village greens in England, formed when the marshy ground outside the gates of **Frampton Court** was drained in the 18th century. The court is an outstanding example of a Georgian country house, built in the Palladian style in the 1730s and the seat of the Clifford family ever since. Fine porcelain, furniture and paintings grace the interior, and in the peacock-strutted grounds an ornamental canal reflects a superb Orangery in Dutch-influenced Strawberry Hill gothic. A unique octagonal tower was built in the 17th century as a dovecote.

On the other side of the green is **Frampton Manor**, the Clifford family's former home, built between the 12th and 16th centuries. This handsome timber-framed house is thought to be the birthplace of Jane Clifford, who was the mistress of Henry II and bore him two children. The manor, which has a lovely old walled garden with some rare plants, is open by written appointment. At the southern edge of the village stands the restored 14th century Church of St Mary with its rare Norman lead font. The church stands beside the **Sharpness Canal**, which was built to allow ships to travel up the Severn Valley as far as Gloucester without being at the mercy of the estuary tides. The canal has several swing bridges and at some of these, as at Splatt Bridge and Saul Bridge at Frampton, there are splendid little bridge-keeper's cottages with Doric columns.

To the west of Frampton, on a great bend in the river, is the Arlingham Peninsula, part of the Severn Way Shepperdine-Tewkesbury long-distance walk. The trail passes close to Wick Court, a 13th century moated manor house. The land on which the village of

Arlingham stands once belonged to the monks of St Augustine's Abbey in Bristol who believed it to be the point where St Augustine crossed the Severn on his way to converting the heathen Welsh tribes.

The Severn naturally dominated life hereabouts and at **Saul**, a small village on the peninsula, the inhabitants decorated their houses with carvings of sailors, some of which, in bright, cheerful colours, can be seen today. The village lies at the point where two canals cross. Two separate waterways, the Stroudwater Navigation and the Thames & Severn Canal, once linked the Severn and the Thames, a route of 37 miles. The canals, known collectively as the **Cotswold Canals**, were abandoned in respectively 1933 and 1954 but most of the route is intact and since 1972 the Cotswold Canals Trust has worked in partnership with local authorities on restoration work. Continuing round the bend in the river, **Epney** is the point from which thousands of baby eels are exported each year to the Netherlands and elsewhere to replenish their own stocks.

Slimbridge

4 miles S of Frampton on the A38

The **Wildfowl and Wetlands Centre** was founded as a trust on the banks of the Severn in 1946 by the distinguished naturalist, artist, sailor and broadcaster Peter (later Sir Peter) Scott. He believed in bringing wildlife and people together for the benefit of both, and the Trust's work continues with the same aims. Slimbridge has the world's largest collection of ducks, geese and swans, and spectacular flamingoes among the exotic wildfowl. Also at the centre are a tropical house, pond zone, children's play area, wildlife art gallery, restaurant and gift shop, and there are magnificent views from the observation tower. Sir Peter died in 1989 and his ashes were scattered at Slimbridge, where he had lived for many years. A memorial to him stands at the entrance to the Centre.

Berkeley

6 miles S of Frampton off the A38

The fertile strip that is the Vale of Berkeley, bounded on the north by the Severn and on the south by the M5, takes its name from the small town of Berkeley, whose largely Georgian centre is dominated by the Norman **Berkeley Castle**. Said to be the oldest inhabited castle in Britain, and home to 24 generations of the Berkeley family, this wonderful gem in pink sandstone was built between 1117 and 1153 on the site of a Saxon fort. It was here that the barons of the West met before making the journey to Runnymede to witness the signing of Magna Carta by King John in 1215. Edward II was imprisoned here for several months after losing his throne to his wife and her lover. He eventually met a gruesome death in the dungeons in the year 1327. Three centuries later the castle was besieged by Cromwell's troops and played an important part in the history of the Civil War. It stands very close to the Severn and once incorporated the waters of the river in its defences so that it could, in an emergency, flood its lands. Visitors passing into the castle by way of a bridge over a moat will find a wealth of treasures in the **Great Hall**, the circular keep, the state apartments with their fine tapestries and period furniture, the medieval kitchens and the dungeons.

The Berkeley family have filled the place with objects from around the world, including painted glassware from Damascus, ebony chairs from India and a cypress chest that reputedly belonged to Sir Francis Drake. Security was always

Berkeley Castle

extremely important, and two remarkable signs of this are a four-poster bed with a solid wooden top (no nasty surprises from above in the night) and a set of bells once worn by the castle's dray horses and now hanging in the dairy. The castle is surrounded by sweeping lawns and Elizabethan terraced gardens. Special features include a deer park, a medieval bowling alley, a beautiful lily pond and a butterfly farm with hundreds of exotic butterflies in free flight.

The parish church of St Mary, which contains several memorials to the Berkeley family, has a fine Norman doorway, a detached tower and a striking east window depicting Christ healing the sick. A curious piece of carving in the nave shows two old gossips with a giant toad sitting on their heads. Next to the castle and church is the **Jenner Museum** once the home of Edward Jenner, the doctor and immunologist who is best known as the man who discovered a vaccine against smallpox. The son of a local parson, Jenner was apprenticed to a surgeon in Chipping Sodbury in 1763 at the tender age of 14. His work over several decades led to the first vaccination against smallpox, a disease which had killed many thousands every year. His beautiful Georgian house in Church Lane has a state-of-the-art

The Jenner Museum

Church Lane, Berkeley, Gloucestershire BL13 9BH
Tel: 01453 810631 Fax: 01453 811690
e-mail: manager@jennermuseum.com
website: www.jennermuseum.com

Born in Berkeley in 1749, Edward Jenner returned here after completing his medical training and his house, The Chantry, is now home to the **Jenner Museum** where this pioneering doctor and immunologist's life and work is explored. Intrigued by the country lore that said that milkmaids who caught the mild cowpox could not catch smallpox, one of the most feared diseases of all time, Jenner set about developing a means of vaccinating against smallpox, which he successful did in 1798. In 1967, the World Health Organisation masterminded a final global plant to eradicate the disease and, in 1980, smallpox was declared dead.

Not only did Jenner develop the first vaccination but his discovery has now been developed into one of the most important parts of modern medicine – immunology. Along with his work on smallpox, Jenner also made several other important contributions to medicine: he was probably the first to link angina with hardening of the arteries, he described rheumatic heart disease and he purified important medicines. Both Jenner's medical work and also his work as a naturalist and geologist are described here through numerous displays and exhibits.

display showing the importance of the science of immunology. In the grounds of the house is a rustic thatched hut where Jenner used to vaccinate the poor free of charge and which he called the Temple of Vaccinia. The east window of the church is a memorial to Jenner, while in the churchyard is the grave of Dicky Pearce, one of the last court jesters, who died in 1728.

At **Sharpness**, a mile or so west of Berkeley, the world's first nuclear power station operated between 1962 and 1989. It marks the entrance to the **Gloucester & Sharpness Canal**, opened in 1827 to bypass the tricky waters of the lower Severn. Sixteen miles in length, it has a lock from the tidal River Severn at Sharpness and a lock back into the River Severn at the head of Gloucester Docks, from which the River Severn Navigation runs 43 miles north to Stourport. There are several interesting villages in the vicinity, including Breadstone, which has a church built entirely of tin.

THORNBURY

The woollen industry was important here in late medieval times, and the church, set away from the centre near the site of the old manor house, reflects the prosperity of those days. The side chapel is dedicated to the Stafford family, the local lords of the manor, whose emblem, the Staffordshire knot, is much in evidence. Edward Stafford, 3rd Duke of Buckingham, was responsible for starting work on **Thornbury Castle** in 1511 but did not live to see its completion. Charged with high treason by Henry VIII, he was beheaded on Tower Hill in London in 1522. The building was competed by Anthony Salvin in the 1850s.

AROUND THORNBURY

TORTWORTH

4 miles NE of Thornbury off the B4509

Overlooking the village green stands the Church of St Leonard, which contains some fine 15th century stained glass and a pair of canopied tombs of the Throckmorton family, former owners of the Tortworth Park estate. In a field over the church wall are several interesting trees, including an American hickory, a huge silver-leafed linden and two Locust trees. Nearby, and the most famous of all, is the famous **Tortworth Chestnut**, a massive Spanish chestnut which the diarist John Evelyn called 'the great chestnut of King Stephen's time'. Certainly it was well established by Stephen's time (the 1130s), and a fence was put up to protect it in 1800. At that time a brass plaque was put up with this inscription: *'May man still guard thy venerable form / From the rude blasts and tempestuous storms. / Still mayest thou flourish through succeeding time / And last long last the wonder of the clime.'* And last it has; its lower branches have bent to the ground and rooted in the soil, giving the impression of a small copse rather than a single tree.

ALMONDSBURY

6 miles S of Thornbury on the A38

The Church of St Mary has some fine windows, including a memorial to Charles Richardson, the 19th century engineer who designed the original Severn Tunnel. A curious event took place in 1817 at nearby Knole Park when a young woman arrived at the door of the local squire saying that she was an Oriental princess who had been kidnapped and taken on board a ship, from which she had escaped by jumping overboard. The squire believed the story and 'adopted' Princess Caraboo, who soon became the toast of Bath. Her fame spread far enough to come to the attention of her former Bristol landlady, who identified the fake princess as a certain Mary Baker, a penniless woman from Devon. The embarrassed squire raised the money to send the impostor to Philadelphia. She returned some years later to Bristol, where she died in 1865.

CHIPPING SODBURY

This pleasant market town was one of the earliest examples of post-Roman town planning, its settlement being arranged in strips on either side of the main street in the 12th century. The town once enjoyed prosperity as a market and weaving centre, and it was during that period that the large parish church was built.

A mile or so to the east, on a loop off the A432, is **Old Sodbury**, whose part-Norman church contains some exceptional tombs and monuments. One of these is a carved stone effigy of a 13th century knight whose shield is a very rare wooden carving of a knight. Also in the church is the tomb of David Harley, the Georgian diplomat who negotiated the treaty which ended the American War of Independence. A tower just to the east of the church marks a vertical shaft, one of a series sunk to ventilate the long tunnel that carried the London-South Wales railway through the Cotswold escarpment. Opened in 1903, the 2.5 mile tunnel required its own brickworks and took five years to complete.

A lane leads south from Old Sodbury to **Dodington House**, built between 1796 and 1816 where previously an Elizabethan house stood. It was designed in lavish neo-Roman style by the classical architect James Wyatt, who was killed in a carriage accident before seeing his work completed. The house, whose interior is even more ornate than the facade, is open daily in the summer. Connected to the house by an elegant conservatory is the private Church of St Mary, also designed by Wyatt, in the shape of a Greek cross.

AROUND CHIPPING SODBURY

BADMINTON

4 miles E of Chipping Sodbury off the B4040

The **Badminton Park** estate was founded by Edward Somerset, the son of the Marquis of Worcester, whose 25-foot monument stands in the little church

Bodkin House

Petty France, Badminton, Gloucestershire GL9 1AF
Tel: 01454 238310 Fax: 01454 238422
e-mail: info@bodkin-house-hotel.co.uk
website: www.bodkin-house-hotel.co.uk

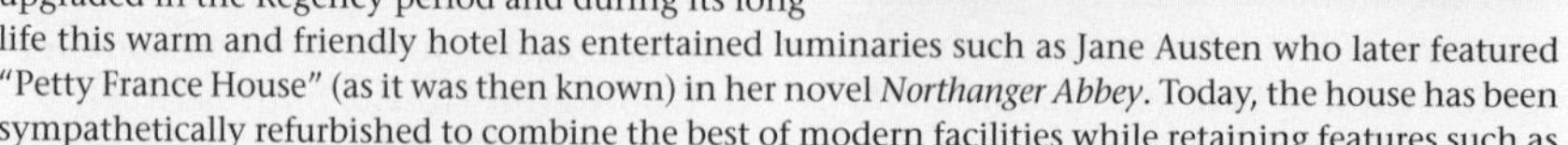

A picturesque 17th century former coaching inn, **Bodkin House** nestles in three acres of grounds next to the Badminton Estate. It was greatly extended and upgraded in the Regency period and during its long life this warm and friendly hotel has entertained luminaries such as Jane Austen who later featured "Petty France House" (as it was then known) in her novel *Northanger Abbey*. Today, the house has been sympathetically refurbished to combine the best of modern facilities while retaining features such as the flagstone floor, oak panelling, log fire and kitchen bygones in the delightful bar which was originally the kitchen.

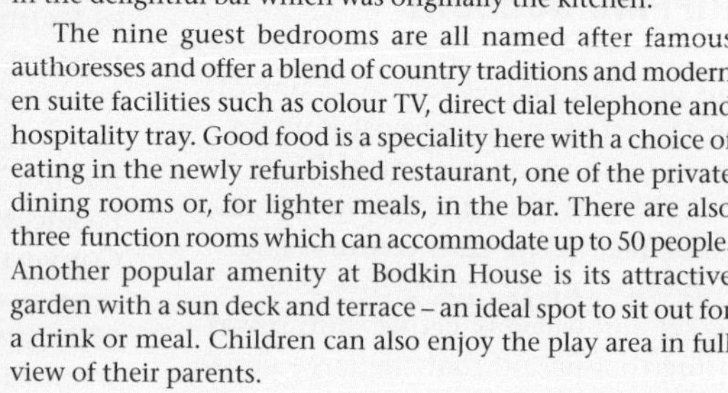

The nine guest bedrooms are all named after famous authoresses and offer a blend of country traditions and modern en suite facilities such as colour TV, direct dial telephone and hospitality tray. Good food is a speciality here with a choice of eating in the newly refurbished restaurant, one of the private dining rooms or, for lighter meals, in the bar. There are also three function rooms which can accommodate up to 50 people. Another popular amenity at Bodkin House is its attractive garden with a sun deck and terrace – an ideal spot to sit out for a drink or meal. Children can also enjoy the play area in full view of their parents.

next to the main house. The central section of the house dates from the 1680s and contains some marvellous carvings in lime wood by Grinling Gibbons. The rest of the house, along with the grounds and the many follies and gateways, is the work of the mid-18th century architect William Kent. The house contains an important collection of Italian, English and Dutch paintings. The game of badminton is said to have started here during a weekend party in the 1860s. The Duke of Beaufort and his guests wanted to play tennis in the entrance hall but were worried about damaging the paintings; someone came up with the bright idea of using a cork studded with feathers instead of a ball. In such a moment of inspiration was the game born, and it was one of the guests at that weekend bash who later took the game to Pakistan, where the first rules were formalised.

Many of the buildings on the estate, including the parish church and the estate villages of Great and Little Badminton, were designed in an ornate castellated style by Thomas Wright. The park is perhaps best known as the venue of the Badminton Horse Trials, which annually attract the best of the international riders, and spectators in their thousands.

Didmarton

8 miles NE of Chipping Sodbury on the A433

Plenty of interest here, notably the medieval Church of St Lawrence, left alone by the serial remodellers of Victorian times and retaining its original three-storey pulpit and antique box pews. Across the road a semicircle of stones marks the site of **St Lawrence's Well**, which the saint himself, after a personal visit, promised would never run dry. In the centre of the village,

Kingsmead House has two oddities in its garden: an octagonal gazebo from which the owner could get the first view of the stagecoaches arriving from Bath, and a Gothic hermit's house made of yew.

Horton

3 miles N of Chipping Sodbury off the A46

On high ground northeast of the long, narrow village stands the National Trust's **Horton Court**, a part-Norman manor house rebuilt for William Knight, the man given the task of presenting Henry VIII's case to the Pope when the King was trying to divorce Catherine of Aragon. Among the many interesting features is a covered walkway resembling a Roman cloister. The 12th century Great Hall survives from the earlier building.

Wickwar

5 miles N of Chipping Sodbury on the B4060

A market town of some importance in days gone by, Wickwar had its own mayor and corporation and two breweries; in the 1890s it became the first town in the west to install electric street lighting. Wickwar boasts a number of handsome Georgian buildings, notably the town hall with its distinctive bell tower and arches. A round tower close to the church marks a vertical shaft sunk in 1841 to ventilate the railway tunnel that runs below. To the east, across South Moon Ridings and up on to the ridge, stands the **Hawkesbury Monument**, designed in Chinese style and erected in 1846 as a memorial to Lord Robert Somerset of Badminton, a general at the Battle of Waterloo. It has 145 steps, and the reward for climbing to the top is great views along the Cotswold escarpment and across the Severn to the Welsh mountains.

GLOUCESTER

The capital city of Gloucestershire first gained prominence under the Romans, who in the 1st century AD established a fort to guard what was then the lowest crossing point on the Severn. A much larger fortress soon followed, and the settlement of Colonia Glevum became one of the most important military bases, crucial in confining the rowdy Celts to Wales. William the Conqueror held a Christmas parliament and commissioned the Domesday Book in Gloucester, and also ordered the rebuilding of the abbey, an undertaking which included the building of a magnificent church that was the forerunner of the superb Norman Cathedral. The elaborate carved tomb of Edward II, murdered at Berkeley Castle, is just one of many historic monuments in **Gloucester Cathedral**; another, the work

Gloucester Cathedral

of the Wedgwood designer John Flaxman, remembers one Sarah Morley, who died at sea in 1784. She is shown being delivered from the waves by angels. The ashes of the educationalist Dorothea Beale, who founded St Hilda's College, Oxford, are buried in a vault in the Lady Chapel.

The exquisite fan tracery in the cloisters is the earliest and among the finest in existence, and the great east window, 72ft by 38ft, is the largest surviving stained-glass window in the country. It was built to celebrate the English victory at the Battle of Crécy in 1346 and depicts the coronation of the Virgin surrounded by assorted kings, popes and saints. The young King Henry III was crowned here, with a bracelet on his little head rather than a crown.

The old area of the city around Gloucester Cross boasts some very fine early buildings, including St John's Church and the Church of St Mary de Crypt. Just behind the latter, near the house where Robert Raikes of Sunday School fame lived, stands an odd-looking tower built in the 1860s to honour Hannah, the wife of Thomas Fenn Addison, a successful solicitor. The tower was also a memorial to Raikes.

Three great inns were built in the 14th and 15th centuries to accommodate the scores of pilgrims who came to visit Edward II's tomb. Two of them survive. The galleried New Inn, founded by a monk around 1450, doubled as a theatre and still retains the cobbled courtyard. It was from this inn that Lady Jane Grey was proclaimed Queen. Equally old is the Fleece Hotel in Westgate Street, which has a 12th century stone-vaulted undercroft. In the same street is **Maverdine House**, a four-storey mansion reached by a very narrow passage. This was the residence and headquarters of Colonel Massey, Cromwell's commander, during the Civil War siege of 1643. Most of the region was in Royalist hands, but Massey survived a month-long assault by a force led by the king himself and thus turned the tide of war.

Gloucester Docks were once the gateway for waterborne traffic heading into the Midlands, and the handsome Victorian warehouses are always in demand as location sites for period films. The docks are now home to several award-winning museums. The **National Waterways Museum** (see panel opposite), occupying three floors of a beautiful warehouse, is entered by a lock chamber with running water and tells the fascinating story of Britain's canals with films, hands-on displays and floating historic boats. **Soldiers of Gloucestershire** uses archive film, photographs and life-size reconstructions to tell the history of the county's regiments.

Elsewhere in the city **Gloucester City Museum and Art Gallery** houses treasures from all over the county to reveal its history, from dinosaur bones and Roman remains to antique furniture and the decorative arts. Among the highlights are the amazing **Birdlip Mirror**, made in bronze for a Celtic chief just before the Roman conquest, two Roman tombstones and a section of the Roman city wall revealed under the cut-away gallery floor. English landscape painting is represented by Turner, Gainsborough and Richard Wilson.

Timber-framed Tudor buildings house **Gloucester Folk Museum**, where the exhibits include farming, fishing on the Severn, the port of Gloucester, the Civil War, a Victorian schoolroom, a dairy, an ironmongery and a wheelwright's workshop. **Gloucester Transport Museum** has a small collection of well-preserved vehicles and baby carriages housed in a 1913 former fire station. The **House of the Tailor of Gloucester**, in College Court, is the house sketched by Beatrix Potter in 1897 and used in her tale *The Tailor of Gloucester*. It now brings that story to life, complete with Simpkin the Cat and an army of helpful mice.

In the south-western suburbs of Gloucester are the ruins of **Llanthony Priory**. The explanation of its Welsh name is an interesting one. The priory of Llanthony was originally founded in the Black Mountains of Wales at the beginning of the 12th century, but the inmates were so frightened of the local Welsh that they begged the Bishop of

The National Waterways Museum

Llanthony Warehouse, Gloucester Docks, Gloucester, Gloucestershire GL1 2EH
Tel: 01452 318200 Fax: 01452 318202
website: www.nwm.org.uk

There's so much to see and do for all ages at the award-winning **National Waterways Museum** located in a splendid Victorian warehouse in historic Gloucester Docks. The Museum charts the fascinating 300-year story of Britain's inland waterways through interactive displays, touch-screen computers, working models and historic boats. Visitors can find out what made the waterways possible, from the business brains and design genius to the hard work and sweat of the navvies, and try their hand at designing and painting a narrow boat, building a canal and navigating a boat through a lock.

The Museum has a working blacksmith's forge, a floor of displays dedicated to waterway trade and cargoes, a marvellous interactive gallery and family room where weights and pulleys, water playareas, period costume, large jigsaw puzzles and brass rubbings bring history to life in a way that is both instructive and entertaining. The museum shop sells unusual gifts and souvenirs and refreshment is provided in the café. There are computerised information points throughout the Museum and visitors can even take to the water themselves on a 45-minute boat trip running along the adjacent Gloucester & Sharpness Canal between Easter and October. The National Waterways Museum is owned by the Waterways Trust, which preserves, protects and promotes our waterway heritage while giving new life to their future.

Hereford to find them a safer place. The Bishop passed their plea to Milo, Earl of Hereford, who granted this plot of land for a second priory bearing the same name as the first. Llanthony Secunda was consecrated in 1136. On a nearby hill the monks built St Ann's Well, whose water is believed to cure eye problems.

AROUND GLOUCESTER

Twigworth

2 miles N of Gloucester off the A38

Twigworth is the home of **Nature in Art**, a renowned museum of wildlife art housed in 18th century Wallsworth Hall.

Pauntley

8 miles N of Gloucester on the A417

The penniless orphan boy who in the pantomime fable was attracted by the gold-paved streets of London and who became its Lord Mayor was born at **Pauntley Court**. Richard Whittington, neither penniless nor an orphan, was born here about 1350, one of three sons of landowner Sir William de Whittington and Dame Joan. He became a mercer in London, then an important financier and was three times Mayor (not Lord Mayor - that title had not been invented). He married Alice Fitzwarren, the daughter of a wealthy landowner from Dorset. The origin of the cat connection is unclear, but an event which could have contributed to the

Lintridge Farm Riding Stables

Bromsberrow Heath, nr Ledbury,
Gloucestershire GL19 3JU
Tel: 01531 650690

When Heather Williams, the owner of **Lintridge Farm Riding Stables**, established the business in 1994 she started off with just four horses. Today, riders have the choice of 15 mounts. Heather has been around horses all her life and is qualified as a riding instructor by the BHS. The stables also has membership of the Association of British Riding Schools and maintains high standards in all aspects of the business. The farm is ideally situated for hacking – the farm itself extends over some 200 acres, there is woodland within easy reach and for longer hacks the Malvern Hills are easily accessible.

The Stables offer riding lessons for both adults and children over five years old and Heather is currently planning to also provide riding lessons for the disabled. In the summer months there are full day courses for children and Heather also intends to offer these for adults. Bromsberrow Heath is easily reached from junction 2 of the M50 and other attractions in the area include Eastnor Castle and the historic town of Ledbury.

myth was the discovery in 1862 of the carved figure of a boy holding a cat in the foundations of a house in Gloucester. The carving can be seen in Gloucester Museum.

Hartpury

5 miles NW of Gloucester on the A417

There are two very interesting listed buildings here: a rare medieval set of bee hives in a building known as a bee bole, and, in the churchyard, a Soper stone tomb with a shrouded body on top. At nearby **Ashleworth** is a magnificent 14th century tithe barn with a stone-tiled roof, projecting porches and elaborate interlocking roof timbers.

Redmarley d'Abitot

9 miles NW of Gloucester on the A417

This hilltop village, built on the red marle (clay) from which it takes its name and once the property of the French d'Abitot family, was for a time the home of the actress Lily Langtry, mistress of the Prince of Wales, later King Edward VII. The link with the actress is remembered in two streets in the village - Drury Lane and Hyde Park Corner.

TEWKESBURY

A town of historic and strategic importance close to the confluence of the Severn and Avon rivers. Those rivers also served to restrict the lateral expansion of the town, which accounts for the unusual number of tall buildings. Its early prosperity was based on the wool and mustard trades, and the movement of corn by river also contributed to its wealth. Tewkesbury's

Tewkesbury Abbey

main thoroughfares, High Street, Church Street and Barton Street, form a Y shape, and the area between is a marvellous maze of narrow alleyways and small courtyards hiding many grand old pubs and medieval cottages. At the centre of it all is **Tewkesbury Abbey**, the cathedral-sized parish church of St Mary. One of the largest and grandest parish churches in the country, it was founded in the 8th century and completely rebuilt in the 11th. It was once the church of the Benedictine Abbey and was among the last to be dissolved by Henry VIII. In 1540, it was saved from destruction by the townspeople, who raised £453 to buy it from the Crown. Many of its features are on a grand scale - the colossal double row of Norman pillars; the six-fold arch in the west front; and the vast main tower, 132ft in height and 46ft square, the tallest surviving Norman main tower in the world. The choir windows have stained glass dating from the 1300s, and the abbey has more medieval monuments than any besides Westminster. A chantry chapel was endowed by the Beauchamps, an influential family that married into another, that of Richard Neville, Warwick the Kingmaker.

Three museums tell the story of the town and its environs: the Little Museum, laid out like a typical old merchant's house; Tewkesbury Museum, with displays on the social history and archaeology of the area; and the **John Moore Countryside Museum**, a natural history collection displayed in a 15th century timber-framed house. The museum commemorates the work of John Moore, a well-known writer, broadcaster and naturalist, who was born in Tewkesbury in 1907.

The **Battle of Tewkesbury** was one of the fiercest in the Wars of the Roses. It took place in 1471 in a field south of the town which has ever since been known as Bloody Meadow. Following the Lancastrian defeat, those who had not been slaughtered in the battle fled to the Abbey, where the killing began again. Abbot Strensham intervened to stop the massacre, but the survivors, who included the Duke of Somerset, were handed over to King Edward IV and executed at Market Cross. The 17-year-old son of Henry VI, Edward Prince of Wales, was killed in the conflict and a plaque marking his final resting place can be seen in the Abbey. One of the victors of the battle was the Duke of Gloucester, later Richard III. Tewkesbury was again the scene of military action almost two centuries later during the Civil War. The town changed hands several times during this period and on one occasion Charles I began his siege of Gloucester by requisitioning every pick, mattock, spade and shovel in Tewkesbury.

AROUND TEWKESBURY

Bredon

4 miles NE of Tewkesbury on the B4080

Bredon Barn is a 14th century barn built of Cotswold stone, with a splendid aisled interior and unusual stone chimney cowling.

Deerhurst

3 miles S of Tewkesbury off the A38

On the eastern bank of the Severn, a village whose current size and status belies a distinguished past. The church, with a distinct Celtic feel, is one of the oldest in England, with parts dating back to the 7th century, and its treasures include a unique double east window, a 9th century carved font, a Saxon carving of the Virgin and Child and some fine brasses dating from the 14th and 15th centuries. One depicts the Cassey family, local landowners, and their dog Terri.

Another Saxon treasure, 200 yards from the church, is **Odda's Chapel**, dedicated in 1056 and lost for many centuries before being gradually rediscovered after 1885 under a half-timbered house. The connection was then made with a stone inscribed with the date of consecration discovered in 1675 and now on view in the Ashmolean in Oxford.

Forthampton

3 miles W of Tewkesbury off the A438

This unspoilt Severn Vale village is dominated by the ancient Church of St Mary and by **Forthampton Court**, sometime home to the abbots of Tewkesbury and still retaining its fine 14th century banqueting hall, chapel and a medieval wood-based picture of Edward the Confessor. Near the churchyard can be seen relics of harsher times - a set of stocks and a whipping post complete with manacles.

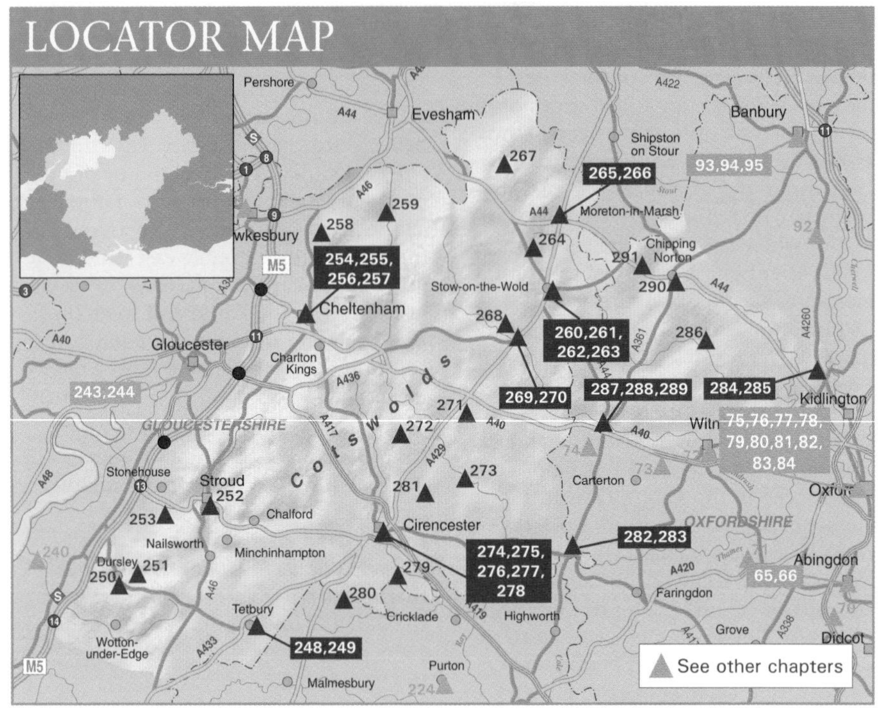

ADVERTISERS AND PLACES OF INTEREST

THE COTSWOLDS 7

City Centre, Cirencester

'The most English and the least spoiled of all our countrysides.' So wrote JB Priestley in 1933 in his *English Journey*, and 70 years on his verdict would surely have been the same. Part of the Jurassic uplands that cross the country from the southwest to the northeast, the Cotswold escarpment runs for 50 miles from Dyrham to Chipping Campden, mainly in Gloucestershire but also taking in part of north Oxfordshire. The general height is about 650 feet, but Cleeve Hill, the highest point, rises to over 900 feet. The Romans left their mark in roads and the remains of villas and camps, the best of the former

Lower Slaughter in Winter

being at Chedworth near Cheltenham. The oolitic limestone that makes up the Cotswolds produces fine building material, and the mellow stone buildings are one of the most characteristic features of the region. These range from pretty little cottages nestling in the valleys to sturdy barns and handsome churches, some modest, others built on the grand scale with wealth derived from the wool trade. The best of these are at Cirencester, Fairford, Chipping Campden and Northleach.

In the Middle Ages Gloucestershire was renowned throughout Europe as the source of prime wool: 'In Europe the best wool is English. In England the best wool is the Cotswold.' The Cotswolds were ideal grazing grounds and the abbeys and monasteries raised huge flocks. The Church and the merchants became rich, and reminders of those days are present in abundance in the churches, in the houses and in the mills, which at one time were numbered in their hundreds; many still survive, often restored to working order.

SOUTH GLOUCESTERSHIRE AND THE SOUTHERN COTSWOLDS

Dyrham

4 miles S of Chipping Sodbury on the A46

The National Trust-owned **Dyrham Park** stands on the slope of the Cotswold ridge, a little way south of the site of a famous 6th century battle between Britons and Saxons. This striking baroque mansion, used as a location for the filming of *Remains of the Day*, houses a wonderful collection of artefacts accumulated by the original owner William Blathwayt during diplomatic tours of duty in Holland and North America (he later became Secretary of State to William III). Among the most notable are several Dutch paintings and some magnificent Delft porcelain. The west front of the house looks out across a terrace to lawns laid out in formal Dutch style; much of the estate is a deer park, which perhaps it was originally, as the word Dyrham means 'deer enclosure' in Saxon. A charming little church in the grounds has a Norman font, a fine 15th century memorial brass and several memorials to the Winter and Blathwayt families.

Marshfield

8 miles SE of Chipping Sodbury on the A420

This old market town was once the fourth wealthiest town in Gloucestershire, after Bristol, Gloucester and Cirencester, its prosperity based on the malt and wool industries. Its long main street has many handsome buildings dating from the good old days of the 17th and 18th centuries, but not many of the coaching inns remain that were here in abundance when the town was an important stop on the London-Bristol run. Among the many notable buildings are the **Tolzey Market Hall** and the imposing Church of St Mary, which boasts a fine Jacobean pulpit and several impressive monuments from the 17th and 18th centuries. Each Boxing Day brings out the **Marshfield Mummers**, who take to the streets to perform a number of time-honoured set pieces wearing costumes made from newspapers and accompanied by a town crier. On the northern edge of town is a folk museum at Castle Farm.

A lane leads south through a pretty valley to the delightful hamlet of **St Catherine's**, whose church contains a splendid 15th century stained-glass window with four lights depicting the Virgin Mary, the Crucifixion, St John and St Peter.

Westonbirt

9 miles NE of Chipping Sodbury on the A433

Westonbirt - The National Arboretum, three miles south of Tetbury, contains one of the finest collections of temperate and shrubs in the world - 18,000 of them

Westonbirt Arboretum

spread over 600 acres of glorious Cotswold countryside. Wealthy landowner Robert Stayner Holford founded this tree wonderland by planting trees for his own interest and pleasure. His son, Sir George Holford, was equally enthusiastic about trees and continued his father's work until his death in 1926, when he was succeeded by his nephew, the 4th Earl of Morley. Opened to the public in 1956 and now managed by the Forestry Commission, the arboretum has something to offer all year round: a crisp white wonderland after winter snows, flowering shrubs and rhododendrons in spring, tranquil glades in summer, glorious reds and oranges and golds in the autumn. The grounds provide endless delightful walks, including 17 miles of footpaths, and there's a visitor centre, plant centre, café and picnic areas.

TETBURY

A really charming Elizabethan market town, another to have prospered from the wool trade. Its most famous building is the stone-pillared 17th century **Market House** in the heart of town, but a visit should also take in the ancient **Chipping Steps** connecting the market house to the old trading centre, and the Church of St Mary, an 18th century period piece with high-backed pews, huge windows made from recovered medieval glass and slender timber columns hiding sturdy iron uprights. **Tetbury Police Museum**, housed in the original cells of the old police station, has a fascinating collection of artefacts, memorabilia and uniforms from the Gloucestershire Constabulary.

Two miles northwest of Tetbury, west of the B4014, stands **Chavenage House**,

The Ormond's Head Hotel

23 Long Street, Tetbury, Gloucestershire GL8 8AP
Tel: 01666 505690 Fax: 01666 505956
e-mail: bookings@ormondshead.com
website: www.ormondshead.com

The oldest coaching inn in this delightful Cotswold market town, **The Ormond's Head Hotel** has been dispensing hospitality for more than 400 years. It started life as a town house some time in the 1400s and became an inn in the 1600s when it was known as the Lamb. It was re-named The Ormond's Head in the 1700s in honour of the second Duke of Ormond, a distinguished military figure of the time.

Today the inn is a bustling meeting place for locals and travellers who enjoy good ale and home cooked food. No frills value-for-money is the order of the day. The proprietors ensure that an informal atmosphere is maintained whilst retaining professional standards. The bar and restaurant offer traditional cask ales and home cooked food with a menu to suit every palate, while the courtyard, once alive with the bustle of coach and horses, is now a relaxed place in which to enjoy open air lunches and warm summer evenings. Free parking nearby adds to the convenience. And if you are planning to stay in this charming old town, the hotel has 20 guest bedrooms, each of which has en suite facilities and is equipped with colour TV, telephone and tea/coffee making facilities.

a beautiful Elizabethan mansion built of grey Cotswold stone on earlier monastic foundations in the characteristic E shape of the period. The elegant front aspect has remained virtually unchanged down the years, and the present owners, the Lowsley-Williams family, can trace their lineage back to the original owners. Two rooms are covered with rare 17th century tapestries, and the house contains many relics from the Cromwellian period. Cromwell is known to have stayed at the house, and during the Civil War he persuaded the owner, Colonel Nathaniel Stephens, a relative by marriage, to vote for the King's impeachment. According to the Legend of Chavenage the owner died after being cursed by his daughter and was taken away in a black coach driven by a headless horseman. The present owner, who conducts tours

Market Hall, Tetbury

round the property, welcomes visitors to 'Gloucestershire's second most haunted house' (Berkeley Castle is the most haunted!). In 1970 an astonishing find was made in the attic - a portfolio of watercolours by George IV of plans for the restoration of Windsor Castle.

Beverston

2 miles W of Tetbury on the A4135

The same Robert Stayner Holford who started the Westonbirt Arboretum built the model village of Beverston in conjunction with the architect Lewis Vulliamy. Their aim was to combine rural practicality with improved standards of accommodation, and the limestone terraces and model farms can be seen from the main road. The village also had a castle, once occupied by Earl Godwin, father of King Harold, and the earthworks are still visible.

Wotton-under-Edge

10 miles W of Tetbury on the B4508

A hillside former wool town with a number of interesting buildings: Berkeley House with its stone Jacobean front; the terraced house that was the family home of Isaac Pitman and where he devised his renowned method of shorthand; the Perry and Dawes almshouses; and the Church of St Mary with memorials to Lord Berkeley and his wife Margaret. The **Wotton-under-Edge Heritage Centre** (free), housed in a former fire station, provides an excellent introduction to the town and the surrounding area of outstanding natural beauty.

Ozleworth

11 miles W of Tetbury on minor roads

A secluded hamlet with a very unusual circular churchyard, one of only two in England. The church itself has a rare feature in a six-sided Norman tower. Also at Ozleworth is the National Trust's **Newark Park**, built as a hunting lodge by the Poyntz family in Elizabethan times. James Wyatt later converted it into a castellated country house. Open by appointment only.

This is great walking country, and one of the finest walks takes in the **Midger Wood Nature Reserve** on its way up to **Nan Tow's Tump**, a huge round barrow whose tomb is said to contain the remains of Nan Tow, a local witch.

DURSLEY

One of the most notable buildings in this former centre of the cloth-making trade is the 18th century market hall standing on 12 pillars at a busy town-centre junction. It has a bell turret on its roof and a statue of Queen Anne facing the fine parish church. William Shakespeare reputedly spent some time in Dursley after being spotted poaching, and there is a reference to a bailiff from the town in *Henry IV*. Cloth is still produced in the mill at Cam on the northern edge of Dursley, continuing a tradition started in the 16th century. Local legend is rich in stories about **Cam Long Down**, a small, isolated peak that is sometimes claimed as the scene of King Arthur's last battle. One story concerns the Devil, who decided one day to cart away the Cotswolds and dam the Severn. On setting out with his first cartload he met a cobbler and asked him how far it was to the river. The cobbler showed him one of the shoes he was taking home to mend and replied, 'Do you see this sole? Well, I've worn it out walking from the Severn.' This persuaded the Devil, who was obviously a lazy devil, to abandon his task; he tipped out his load, creating the hill that can be seen today.

Cotswold Collectables

35H Parsonage Street, Dursley, Gloucestershire GL11 4BP
Tel/Fax: 01453 546128
e-mail: sue@cotswold-collectables.fsnet.co.uk
website: www.cotswoldcollectables.com

Opened in October 2001 by Susan Oldfield, **Cotswold Collectables** is a wonderful place to browse with a huge stock of quality items selling at competitive prices. You'll find extensive range of gifts including a wide selection of Burleigh Blue and white china, Moorland sheep pottery from Devon, Tiffany lamps, collectable bears, wicker and seagrass baskets and many other interesting gifts and items for the home. The shop stocks a small range of pine and oak furniture, as well as providing an ordering service for the larger items of furniture. Cotswold Collectables also displays the local talents of the artists in the area – watercolours, decoupage, pastels to name but a few.

A popular line is the varied selection of hand-carved wooden animals, including elephants, giraffes, cats, dogs and various British birds. Or you might be more interested in the wide choice of photo frames, available in various sizes, colours and materials, including silver plate, pewter, glass and filigree. Then there are the baskets – everything from small wicker bread baskets to large seagrass log baskets, linen baskets, waste paper bins and storage baskets. The stock of Cotswold Collectables is always changing so you can count on finding something new on every visit.

Stinchcombe

3 miles W of Dursley off the A4135

Stancombe Park, on the southern edge of Stinchcombe, is a handsome country house built in 1880 on the site of a Roman villa, whose mosaic floor can be seen in Gloucester Museum. The gardens at Stancombe are occasionally open to the public.

North Nibley

2 miles SW of Dursley on the B4060

This village was the birthplace, around 1494, of William Tyndale, the first man to translate and print the Old and New Testaments. He used the original sources instead of the approved Latin, for which heresy he was burnt at the stake in Belgium in 1536. Three-and-a-half centuries later the imposing **Tyndale Monument**, paid for by public subscription, was erected on the ridge above the village to commemorate his life and work. Standing 111 feet high on the escarpment, it is one of the most prominent landmarks on the Cotswold Way and offers superb views. North Nibley is also the site of the last 'private' battle in England, which took place in 1471 between rival barons William Lord Berkeley and Viscount de Lisle.

Uley

11 miles NE of Chipping Sodbury on the B4066

Even in this part of the Cotswolds where almost every prospect pleases, Owlpen is uniquely lovely – "a breathtaking ensemble of truly English beauty" enthused one visitor; Prince Charles called it "the epitome of the English village". Manor house, church, mill and cottages of pearl-grey stone are framed by a natural amphitheatre of steep, wooded hills, a timeless setting for "the epitome of the English village".

The jewel in the crown of this enchanting village is **Owlpen Manor** (see panel below), a romantic Tudor building built between 1450 and 1616 and set in formal Queen Anne terraced yew gardens. Inside, contrasting with the ancient polished flagstones and the putty-coloured plaster, are fine pieces of William Morris-inspired Arts and Crafts furniture; there's also a rare beadwork collection and some unique 17th century wall hangings. Within the grounds are a Courthouse of 1620, an 18th century Mill and a licensed restaurant in a medieval Cyder House complete with a massive cider press.

The village lies in the shadow of **Uley Bury**, a massive Iron Age hill fort which has thrown up evidence of habitation by a prosperous community of warrior farmers during the 1st century BC. Another prehistoric site, a mile along the ridge, is Uley Long Barrow, known locally as **Hetty Pegler's Tump**. This chambered long barrow, 180 feet in length, takes its name from Hester Pegler, who came from a family of local landowners. Adventurous spirits can crawl into this Neolithic tomb on all fours, braving the dark and the dank smell to reach the burial chambers, where they will no longer be scared by the skeletons that terrified earlier visitors. The walls and ceilings of the chamber are made of huge stone slabs infilled with drystone material.

A little further north, at the popular picnic site of **Coaley Peak** with its adjoining National Trust nature reserve, is another spectacular chambered tomb, **Nympsfield Long Barrow**.

Owlpen Manor Cottages & Restaurant

STROUD

The capital of the Cotswold woollen industry, Stroud stands on the River Frome at a point where five valleys converge. The surrounding hill farms provided a constant supply of wool, and the Cotswold streams supplied the water-power. By the 1820s there were over 150 textile mills in the vicinity. Six survive, one of them specialising in green baize for snooker tables; another, Snow Mill, has cornered a niche market producing more than 160 types of snowflake for films and other entertainments. A stroll round the centre of town reveals some interesting buildings, notably the **Old Town Hall** dating from 1594 and the **Subscription Rooms** in neo-classical style. An easy walk from the centre is **Stratford Park**, a large park containing dozens of trees both ordinary and exotic, and with lots of ducks on the pond. The **Museum in the Park** (free) is a family-friendly place with innovative and colourful displays that include dinosaur remains, a Roman temple – and the world's first lawn-mower, invented by local entrepreneur Edwin Buddings.

AROUND STROUD

Bisley

4 miles E of Stroud on minor roads

Country roads lead across from Stroud or up from Oakridge Lynch to the delightful village of Bisley, which stands 780 feet above sea level and is known as 'Bisley-God-Help-Us' because of the winter winds which sweep across the hillside. Bisley's impressive **All Saints Church** dates from the 13th century and was restored in the early 19th by Thomas Keble, after whose poet and theologian brother John, Keble College in Oxford was named. The font has two carved fish inside the bowl and a shepherd and sheep on the base. In the churchyard is the Poor Souls' Light, a stone wellhead beneath a spire dating from the 13th century. It was used to hold candles lit for souls in purgatory. Below the church are the **Seven Wells of Bisley** (also restored by Thomas Keble), which are blessed and decorated with flowers each year on Ascension Day. At the top of the village is a double lock-up built in 1824, with two cells beneath an ogee gable.

The village's main claim to fame is the story of the Bisley Boy. When Bisley was a rich wool town it had a royal manor, Over Court, where the young Princess Elizabeth (later Queen Elizabeth I) often stayed. The story goes that during one of those visits the princess, then aged 10, caught a fever and died. Fearing the wrath of her father Henry VIII, her hosts looked for a substitute and found a local child with red hair and remarkably similar physical characteristics except for the rather important fact that the child was a boy called John Neville. Could this explain the Virgin Queen's reluctance to marry, her problem with hair loss and her 'heart that beats like a man's', or was the story made up to fit those facts?

Minchinhampton

4 miles SE of Stroud off the A419

A scattered community on a ridge between two picturesque valleys, Minchinhampton acquired its market charter as far back as 1213. The area is good for walking and exploring, with the old stone quarries at Ball's Green and the National Trust woodland and grassland at **Minchinhampton and Rodborough Commons**. The majority of the commons are open to walkers and riders, and nature-lovers might spot rare butterflies such as the Chalkhill Blue, the tiny Green Hairstreak and the Duke of Burgundy Fritillary. The Commons are also famous for their grassland species, including the lovely Pasque flower, whose resurgence has been assisted by the introduction of a small herd of Belted Galloways to help manage the rich grassland areas of the lower slopes.

Selsley

2 miles S of Stroud off the A46

All Saints Church, built in the 1860s by wealthy mill-owner Sir Samuel Marling, is notable chiefly for its exceptional stained glass. This was commissioned from William Morris and Company and features designs by many of the Morris partnership, including Philip Webb, Burne-Jones, Ford Madox Brown, Dante Gabriel Rossetti and Morris himself.

Woodchester

2 miles S of Stroud off the A46

Woodchester Park Mansion is one of Britain's most intriguing Victorian country houses. Building started in 1854 and was halted abruptly in 1868, three-quarters finished, with the scaffolding in place and the workmen's tools abandoned. What stands now, as in 1868, is a vast shell with gargoyles and flying buttresses on the Gothic facade, and all the props and stays and tools inside. The mansion is now used as a training ground for stonemasons.

Nailsworth

4 miles S of Stroud on the A46

This small residential and commercial town was once, like so many of its neighbours, a centre of the wool trade. Several of the old mills have been modernised, some playing new roles, others plying their original trades. **Ruskin Mill** is a thriving arts and crafts centre; **Stokescroft** an unusual 17th century building on Cossack Square. During restoration work in 1972 scribblings found on an attic wall suggested that soldiers had been billeted there in 1812 and 1815. Perhaps this is why it is known locally as 'the Barracks'. It is thought to have housed Russian prisoners during the Crimean War, which accounts for the name of the square.

About half a mile north of the town, the **Dunkirk Mill Centre** contains a fulling mill which lays on demonstrations of the finishing of fine woollen cloth.

Stonehouse

3 miles W of Stroud on the A419

The Domesday Book recorded a vineyard at Stonehouse in 1086; Elizabeth I spent a night here in what is now, appropriately, a luxury hotel.

Frocester

4 miles SW of Stroud off the A419

In the grounds of the village-centre chapel stands the wonderful **Frocester Tithe Barn** (free), a massive 186 feet in length and looking much as it did when built on the instructions of Abbot John de Gamages between 1284 and 1306.

VALE OF GLOUCESTER AND THE CENTRAL COTSWOLDS

Slad

2 miles N of Stroud on the B4070

Immortalised by Laurie Lee in his autobiographical *Cider With Rosie*, the sprawling village of Slad in the valley of the same name was for centuries a centre for milling and the production of fruit. Cider gave way to champagne on March 13th, 2002 after a Polish-bred horse called Galileo, trained by Tom George at Slad, was successful in one of the big novice hurdles at the Cheltenham Festival. A Roman villa was found in the Valley, and the votive tablets discovered at the site are now in Gloucester Museum.

Painswick

4 miles N of Stroud on the A46

This beautiful little town, known as the 'Queen of the Cotswolds', prospered with the wool trade, which had its peak in the second half of the 18th century. At that time 30 mills provided power within the parish, and the number of fine houses and farms in and around the town are witness to those days. Many of them are built of the pale grey limestone that was quarried at Painswick Hill.

Cottages at Painswick

St Mary's Church, which dates from around 1380, was the site of one of many local skirmishes in the Civil War when a party of Parliamentary soldiers came under cannon fire, which did considerable damage to the building. A later fire, a lightning strike, Victorian 'restoration' and more recent modernisation have left little of note inside the church apart from a fine 18th century reredos and some 300 modern kneelers depicting biblical scenes, views of the town, animals, birds and memorials to local people. The project involved around 60 people and took four years to complete.

But if St Mary's interior is generally disappointing, its churchyard is one of the must-see sights of the county. In the 1790s local people planted 99 yews – it was said that whenever a 100th was planted it would wither away - and these now stand sentinel over the graveyard's other extraordinary feature, the 33 richly carved table tombs all dating from the wool trade's boom years in the 17th and 18th centuries. The craftsman who created these striking rhapsodies in stone, John Bryan, is himself buried here beneath a pyramidal tomb.

Other buildings of interest include Court House, where King Charles I spent a night in 1643 before setting off for the siege of Gloucester, and the Post Office, dating back to the 1400s and the only surviving wooden-framed house in the town. In Bisley Street, the **Gloucestershire Guild of Craftsmen Gallery** (free) provides a showcase for pieces made by members of the guild which is one of the oldest in the country. This feast of creative design includes jewellery, glass, velvet and silk, turned woods, greeting cards and more.

In the grounds of early-18th century Painswick House, on the B4073 at the northern edge of town, **Painswick Rococo Garden**, hidden away in magnificent Cotswold countryside, is a unique restored 18th century garden with plants from around the world and a maze planted in 1999 with a path structure in the shape of '250' to commemorate the garden's 250th anniversary. Other attractions are carpets of snowdrops in early spring, a kitchen garden, a children's nature trail, a gift shop and a restaurant.

A little further north, at Cranham, **Prinknash Abbey Park** (pronounce it 'Prinnage') comprises an active monastery, chapel, replica of a Roman mosaic, gift shop and tearoom. The Benedictine monks of Caldey Island moved here in 1928 when the old house was made over to them by the 20th Earl of Rothes in accordance with the wishes of his grandfather. They no longer occupy the old house, having moved into the impressive new monastery in 1972. The abbey chapel is open daily for solitude and contemplation. Part of the abbey gardens are given over to the

Prinknash Bird & Deer Park, where visitors can feed and stroke the fallow deer and see the waterfowl, the peacocks and the African pygmy goats. By the lake is a charming two-storey Wendy House.

Edge

4 miles N of Stroud on the A473

Straddling a hilltop across the Spoonbed Valley, Edge has two delightful village greens and the mid-19th century Church of St John the Baptist with an ornate spire. To the west of the village lies **Scottsquarr Common**, an area of Special Scientific Interest with an abundance of wild flowers and butterflies and spectacular views.

Miserden

5 miles NE of Stroud off the B40470 or A417

Miserden Park Gardens, with views over the lovely Golden Valley, were created in the 17th century and are known for their spectacular spring bulbs, perennial borders, roses, topiary and an avenue of Turkish hazels.

CHELTENHAM

Smart, fashionable Cheltenham: a small, insignificant village until a mineral spring was accidentally discovered in 1716. According to tradition, the first medicinal waters were discovered when locals saw pigeons pecking at salty deposits which had formed around a spring. A local man, William Mason, built a pump room and began Cheltenham's transformation into one of Europe's leading Regency spa towns. Mason's son-in-law was the astute Captain Henry Skillicorne, who added a meeting room, a ballroom and a network of walks and carriageways, and called it a spa. A number of other springs were soon discovered, including one in the High

Lonsdale House

Montpellier Drive, Cheltenham, Gloucestershire GL50 1TX
Tel/Fax: 01242 232379 e-mail: lonsdalehouse@hotmail.com
website: www.theaa.com/hotels/46184.html

Lonsdale House is a handsome Georgian town house in a central but quiet part of the town where Chris and Liz Mallinson offer bed & breakfast accommodation in elegant and comfortable surroundings. They have a 3-Diamonds rating from both the AA and the English Tourism Council and the accommodation comprises nine spacious rooms – a mix of singles, twin, doubles and family rooms – all of them attractively furnished and decorated. Breakfast is served in the large dining room overlooking the pleasant garden and offers a choice of full English or vegetarian.

Seldom Seen Designs

22 St James Street, Cheltenham, Gloucestershire GL52 2SH
Tel: 01242 583562

Established in 1984, **Seldom Seen Designs** really lives up to its name, offering a striking range of diverse and distinctive works of art. The copious displays include representational and abstract paintings, prints, sculptures, ceramics and mirrors. The gallery is owned and run by David Atkinson who is a painter himself and also offers a quality framing service with both traditional and contemporary designs available. The gallery is open from 9am to 5.30pm, Tuesday to Friday; 9am to 1pm, Saturday.

Street around which the first Assembly Rooms were built. In 1788 the Royal seal of approval came in the shape of King George III, who spent five weeks taking the waters with his family and made Cheltenham a highly fashionable resort. An entirely new town was planned based on the best features of neoclassical Regency architecture, and as a result very few buildings of any antiquity still stand. One of these is the Church of St Mary, with parts going back to the 12th century and some very fine stained glass.

Skillicorne's walks and rides are now the tree-lined Promenade, one of the most beautiful boulevards in the

Cheltenham Art Gallery & Museum

Clarence Street, Cheltenham, Gloucestershire GL50 3JT
Tel: 01242 237431 Fax: 01242 262334
e-mail: artgallery@cheltenham.gov.uk
website: www.cheltenhammuseum.org.uk

Cheltenham Art Gallery & Museum is one of only 52 museums in the country officially designated as a museum with an outstanding collection. In this case it comprises furniture, silver, jewellery, ceramics, carvings and textiles, produced by the Arts & Crafts Movement, whose members were inspired by the ideology of William Morris. The Museum also has a fine collection of paintings from the 17th century onwards, and 20th century gems. Among other highlights are displays on the history and archaeology of the area and special events, talks and exhibitions take place throughout the year. There is also a café and gift shop.

Pump Room, Cheltenham

country, its crowning glory the wonderful Neptune's Fountain modelled on the Fontana di Trevi in Rome and erected in 1893. Housed in Pittville Park, overlooking picturesque gardens and ornamental lakes north of the town centre, is the magnificent **Pittville Pump Room**. Concerts and special exhibitions are held throughout the year. **Cheltenham Art Gallery and Museum** has an acclaimed collection of furniture and silver, much of it made by Cotswold craftsmen and inspired by William Morris's Arts and Crafts Movements, as well as some fine paintings, Oriental porcelain and English ceramics.

Gustav Holst was born in 1874 in a terraced Regency house in Clarence Road which is now the **Holst Birthplace Museum and Period House**. The original piano of the composer of *The Planets* is the centrepiece of the story of the man and his works, and there's a working kitchen, a Regency drawing room and a nursery.

Two remarkable modern pieces of public art take the eye in the centre of town. The **Wishing Fish Clock** in the Regent Arcade is a work in metal by the famous artist and craftsman Kit Williams: below the clock, from which a mouse pops out when disturbed by the arrival of an egg laid by a duck on high, is suspended a 12ft-long fish which celebrates the hour by swishing its tail and blowing bubbles, to the delight and fascination of shoppers below. The mechanical parts of the clock are the work of the renowned local clockmaker Michael Harding.

Off the High Street are the **Elephant Murals**, which portray an event that occurred in 1934 when three elephants from a travelling circus escaped and raided a provision shop stocked with corn - an incident which older locals with long memories still recall. **Cheltenham Racecourse**, two miles north of town, is the home of National Hunt Racing, staging numerous top-quality races highlighted by the March Festival when the Gold Cup and the Champion Hurdle find the year's best steeplechaser and best hurdler. Several other festivals have their home in Cheltenham, including the International Jazz Festival (April), the International Festival of Music (July), the International Festival of Literature (April) and the Cheltenham Festival of Science (June).

AROUND CHELTENHAM

Prestbury

1 mile NE of Cheltenham on the A46

Racing at Cheltenham started at Cleeve Hill but moved to land belonging to **Prestbury Park** in 1819, since when all the great names in steeplechasing and hurdling have graced the Prestbury turf. But Prestbury's greatest son was not a jump jockey but the amazing Fred Archer, undisputed champion of flat race jockeys, born in the village in 1857. In the King's Arms hangs a plaque with this inscription:

'At this Prestbury inn lived
FRED ARCHER the jockey
Who trained upon toast,
Cheltenham water & coffee.
The shoe of his pony
hangs in the bar
Where they drink to his prowess
from near and from far But the man in the street
passes by without knowledge
That 'twas here Archer
swallowed his earliest porridge.'

Cleeve Hill

3 miles NE of Cheltenham on the B4632

The Cotswolds rise to their highest point, over 1,000 feet above sea level, at **Cleeve Cloud** above Prestbury and a mile from the village of Cleeve Hill. The views from here are magnificent, and also worth the climb is a massive Neolithic long barrow known as **Belas Knap**, where excavations have revealed the bones of more than 30 people. It is very unusual in having a false entrance at the north end, apparently leading to no chambers.

Gotherington

5 miles NE of Cheltenham on the A435

This is the location of the famous **Prestbury Hillclimb**, scene of hillclimb championships and classic car meetings as well as the location of the **Bugatti Trust** (see panel below).

Winchcombe

6 miles NE of Cheltenham on the B4632

The Saxon capital of Mercia, where in medieval times the shrine of St Kenelm, martyred here by his jealous sister in the 8th century, was second only to that of Thomas à Becket as a destination for pilgrims. Winchcombe grew in importance into a walled town with an abbot who presided over a Saxon parliament. The abbey was destroyed in 1539 after the Dissolution of the Monasteries and all that remains today is a section of a gallery that is part of the George Inn. As well as pilgrims, the abbey gave rise to a flourishing trade in wool and sheep.

One of the most famous townsmen of the time was Jack Smallwood, the Jack o' Newbury who sponsored 300 men to fight at Flodden Field in 1513 and was a leading producer of woollen goods. Silk and paper were also produced, and for a

The Bugatti Trust

Prescott Hill, Gotherington, Nr Cheltenham,
Gloucestershire GL52 9RD
Tel: 01242 677201 e-mail: trust@bugatti.co.uk
Fax: 01242 674191 website: www.bugatti.co.uk/trust

Recommended to visitors with an interest in design, art in engineering as well as the history of the motor car.

Ettore Bugatti designed and built beautiful and world leading racing and sports cars in the 1920s and 1930s. There were numerous other sensational Bugatti products from the 'Royale' to world speed record trains and aricraft. The whole story of the Bugatti family from Carlo, Ettore's artist father, to the sad demise of the family control of the Molsheim factory in the 1950s, can be seen at the **Bugatti Trust**. The Trust is a Bugatti research centre and small museum, containing an amazing collection of drawings, documents, photographs, artefacts and a few cars. This history is an inspirational combination of art and engineering. Open Monday-Friday 10am-4.30pm. Free entry.

few decades tobacco was grown locally - a fact remembered in place names such as Tobacco Close and Tobacco Field. This activity ceased in 1670 when a law was passed banning home-produced tobacco in favour of imports from the struggling colony of Virginia.

The decline that followed had the effect of stopping the town's development, so many of the old buildings have survived largely unaltered. These include St Peter's Church, built in the 1460s and known particularly for its 40 grotesques and gargoyles, the so-called Winchcombe Worthies. **Winchcombe Folk and Police Museum**, in the Tudor-style Town Hall by the Tourist Information Centre, tells the history of the town from neolithic times to the present day and also keeps a collection of British and international police uniforms and equipment.

A narrow passageway by an ordinary-looking house leads to **Winchcombe Railway Museum and Garden**, a wonderland full of things to do: the railway museum contains one of the largest collections of railway equipment in the country, and visitors can work signals and clip tickets and generally get misty-eyed about the age of steam. The Cotswold garden is full of old and rare plants.

A mile or so north of Winchcombe stand the ruins of **Hailes Abbey**, founded in 1246 by Richard, Earl of Cornwall. Richard, caught in a storm at sea, vowed that he would found a religious house if he survived and in 1245 his brother Henry III gave him the manor at Hailes to do it. It was built on such an ambitious scale that the Cistercian monks were hard pressed to maintain it, but after Richard's son, Edmund, donated a phial said to contain the blood of Christ (later proved to be a fake) the abbey soon became an important place of pilgrimage and was even mentioned in Chaucer's *Canterbury Tales*. The closure of the abbey in 1539 brought great distress to the town: merchants lost the custom of the pilgrims and the poor no longer received their 'doles' from the monks.

The abbey fell into disrepair and today shattered walls and arches are all that remain of this mighty Cistercian foundation, yet the atmosphere of a 13th century monastery lingers most powerfully. Some of the many artefacts found at the site, including medieval sculptures and decorated floor tiles, are on display in the abbey's museum. Some of the medieval glass from the abbey is now in the church at Stanton.

One mile south of Winchcombe and set against the beautiful backdrop of the Cotswold Hills, is **Sudeley Castle** which has royal connections going back a thousand years. This magnificent palace was the last home of Catherine Parr, sixth and last wife of Henry VIII. King Charles I stayed at the castle, and his nephew, Prince Rupert, established his garrison headquarters here during the

Hailes Abbey

Civil War. The interior of the castle, restored by the owning Dent family in sumptuous Victorian style, is a treasure house of old masters (Turner, Rubens, Van Dyck), tapestries, period furniture, costumes and toys, and the beautiful grounds include a lake, formal gardens and a 15ft double yew hedge. Among the many other attractions are an exhibition on the evolution of the gardens, 'The Lace and Times of Emma Dent', a gift shop, plant centre, restaurant and adventure playground.

Sudeley Castle, Winchcombe

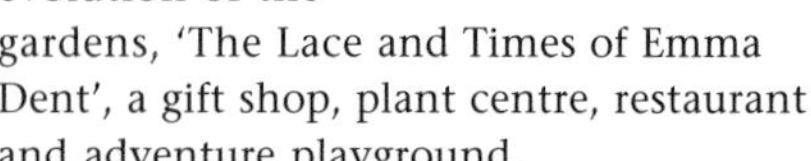

Toddington

8 miles NE of Cheltenham on the B4632/B4077

Toddington Station is the northern terminus of the restored **Gloucestershire Warwickshire Railway**, from where steam or diesel trains run a scenic round trip of 20 miles through delightful countryside by way of Winchcombe and Gotherington to Cheltenham racecourse. The line is open all year and there is a programme of special events and gala days.

Stanway

9 miles NE of Cheltenham on the B4077

A charming village clustered round Jacobean **Stanway House** which is surely one of the most perfect of Cotswold mansions. Built using the warm, honey-coloured local stone, surrounded by gardens and landscaped grounds, Stanway is a dwelling-place at peace with the world and with itself. Its towering bay window looks across a scene where for centuries the only changes have been those ordained by the passing of the seasons.

Nearby stands an immense Tithe Barn which was built in 1370 when the Manor

Toddington Garden Centre

Toddington, Winchcombe, Gloucestershire GL54 5DT
Tel: 01242 621314 Fax: 01242 620053

Located next door to the Gloucestershire-Warwickshire Steam Railway, **Toddington Garden Centre** was already well-established when Chris and Patricia Gregory took it over in 1984. Within the centre's 3.5 acres they now offer a huge variety of flourishing plants, shrubs and trees, all year round, along with every imaginable kind of garden tool or accessory. The emphasis at this family-run business is on personal customer service – whatever gardening requirement or advice you need, you'll find knowledgeable, friendly staff happy to assist.

of Stanway was a small satellite of Tewkesbury Abbey. Four monks dedicated themselves in prayer for the souls of the two Saxon nobles who had presented the land to the abbot in 715AD.

The present house was built in the 1580s with the Great Hall at its heart, a glorious room whose function changed by the hour – from business room to manorial court to dining room. The raised dais on which the Lord of the Manor and his family took their meals is still in place as is a 23-feet-long 16th century shuffleboard carved from a single piece of oak. The houses other treasures include fine paintings, two superb Broadwood pianos, and a Chippendale exercising chair on which keep-fit enthusiasts of the time would bounce for half an hour a day.

The grounds are equally interesting, with a water mill, ice house, brewery, dogs' cemetery and a pyramid erected in honour of John Tracy from the owning family. Another resident was Thomas Dover, the sea captain who rescued Alexander Selkirk from a desert island, an event which gave Daniel Defoe the inspiration for *Robinson Crusoe*. Also of note in Stanway is a thatched cricket pavilion resting on mushroom-shaped stones. The pavilion was a gift from JM Barrie, the author of *Peter Pan*, who was a regular visitor to the village.

Stanway's water gardens are regarded as the finest in England and their beauty has recently been enhanced with the installation of a 165ft high fountain – the tallest gravity fountain in the world.

Stanton

10 miles NE of Cheltenham on the B4632

One of the prettiest spots in the Cotswolds, an attractive village of steeply-gabled limestone cottages dating mainly from the 16th and 17th centuries. The whole village was restored by the architect Sir Philip Scott in the years before World War I; his home between 1906 and 1937 was **Stanton Court**, an elegant Jacobean residence built by Queen Elizabeth I's Chamberlain. The village church, dedicated to St Michael and All Angels, has many interesting features, including some stained glass from Hailes Abbey and a number of medieval pews with scarred ends caused perhaps by the leashes of dogs belonging to local shepherds. Most of the glass is the much more modern work of Sir Ninian Comper (1864-1960), the Aberdeen-born architect and prolific designer of church fittings and furnishings; stained glass was one of his specialities. John Wesley is said to have preached in the church. Beyond Stanton, on the road to Broadway, the National Trust-owned **Snowshill Manor** is an elegant manor house dating from Tudor times; once the home of Catherine Parr, it contains a fascinating collection of crafts and artefacts assembled by the last private owner, Charles Paget Wade.

Guiting Power

8 miles E of Cheltenham off the A436

A neat collection of Cotswold stone cottages round a triangular green. Noteworthy features include the part-Norman St Michael's Church and a World War I memorial cross. Close by is **Cotswold Farm Park** which was the first Rare Breeds Farm in England when it opened in 1971 and is now home to more than 50 flocks and herds of British farm animals. Using the hand-held audio guide, visitors can discover the animals' tales of survival. Among the many other attractions are shearing and spinning demonstrations, fleece sales, safari rides, an indoor tractor school, adventure playground, pets corner, woodland walk and a host of other activities guaranteed to keep children happy for hours.

Susan Megson Gallery

Digbeth Street, Stow-on-the-Wold, Gloucestershire GL54 1BN
Tel: 01451 870484 Fax: 01451 831051
e-mail: SueMegsonGallery@aol.com
website: www.susanmegsongallery.com

Susan Megson's interest in glass in all its forms led her to opening the **Susan Megson Gallery** in Stow-on-the-Wold, dedicated to original works of glass in a variety of styles and forms. The gallery was established in March 2000 and in November 2003 she opened another gallery in SoHo, New York, in partnership with her two sons.

The inherent qualities of hand-blown glass creates a unique piece of time. Each piece of glass is an original, each piece a creation which in its final form stands as a work of art.

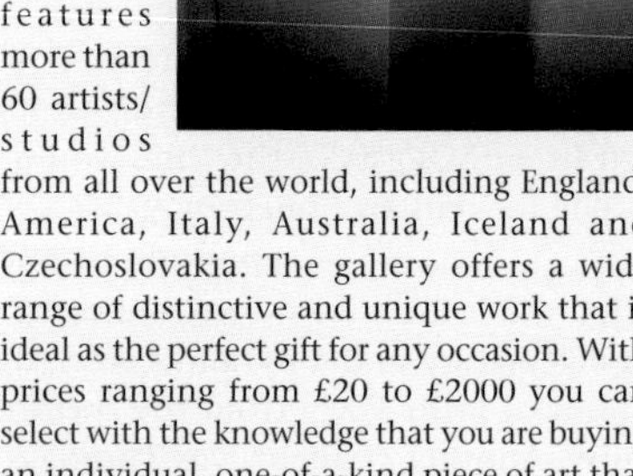

The gallery features more than 60 artists/ studios from all over the world, including England, America, Italy, Australia, Iceland and Czechoslovakia. The gallery offers a wide range of distinctive and unique work that is ideal as the perfect gift for any occasion. With prices ranging from £20 to £2000 you can select with the knowledge that you are buying an individual, one-of-a-kind piece of art that will provide years of enjoyment.

The profile of the artist or studio is a testament to the high quality of work that the Susan Megson Gallery is associated with.

STOW-ON-THE-WOLD

At 800ft above sea level, this is the highest town in the Cotswolds, and the winds sometimes prove it. The town's main source of wealth in earlier times was wool; twice-yearly sheep fairs were held on the Market Square, and at one such fair Daniel Defoe records that over 20,000 sheep were sold. Those days are remembered today in Sheep Street and Shepherds Way. The square holds another reminder of the past in the town stocks, used to punish minor offenders. The sheep fairs continued until they were replaced by an annual horse fair, which was held until 1985.

The Battle of Stow, in 1646, was the final conflict of the Civil War, and after it some of the defeated Royalist forces

Hamilton's Brasserie

Park Street, Stow-on-the-Wold, Gloucestershire GL54 1AQ
Tel: 01451 831700 Fax: 01451 831388
website: www.hamiltons.br.com

With its stylish contemporary décor and light and airy atmosphere, **Hamilton's Brasserie** is very inviting, especially in summer when customers can enjoy the excellent cuisine at pavement tables. The menu has a distinctly continental flavour with spicy butternut squash and parmesan ravioli with sage butter amongst the starters; sautéed garlic courgettes as a vegetable option, and Limoncello baba as a dessert. To accompany your meal there's an excellent selection of wines from around the world, some available by the glass. The Brasserie is open from 9am for breakfast, lunch is served until 2.30pm (3pm on Sunday); and dinner is served until last orders at 9.30pm, Monday to Saturday.

The Malthouse Antiques

The Malt House, Digbeth Street, Stow-on-the-Wold, Gloucestershire GL54 1BN
Tel/Fax: 01451 830592
e-mail: Malthousestow@aol.com
website: www.malthouseantiques.com

Dating back to at least the mid-1800s, the Malt House in Digbeth Street was formerly part of the Stow Brewery. Its louvred roof cowl helped to extract the moisture from the malted barley created by the kilning process. The brewery closed around 1914 and today the Malt House is home to **The Malthouse Antiques**, owned and run by the husband and wife team of Chris and Maryam Mortimer who have been antique collectors for more than 20 years.

Chris specialises in glass items, Sally (his sister) in boxes of all kinds, and their parents in ceramics, but their range extends much further into furniture from the 17th to 19th centuries; wine, medical and dental antiques; prints and paintings; interesting collectables and specialist books. This is a wonderful place to browse in and the Mortimers have made it even more so with the addition of Browsers Coffee Lounge where customers can consult the reference books on antiques while enjoying the freshly ground coffee and tasty fare on offer.

Roger Lamb Antiques

The Square, Stow-on-the-Wold, Gloucestershire GL54 1AB
Tel: 01451 831371 Fax: 01451 832485

Located in the attractive main square of this picturesque town, **Roger Lamb Antiques** has a frontage that dates back to around 1810 but the main part of the house is medieval in origin. Owner Roger Lamb has been here since the early 1990s and in the antiques business most of his working life. Specialising in 18th and early-19th century antique furniture and works of art, his pieces are selected for their quality and originality. The three showrooms contain an enviable selection of quality small furniture, lighting, decorative accessories and good oils and watercolours.

Roger also offers his customers a search service for particular needs and works extensively with interior designers to supply furniture for complete houses. As a member of both LAPADA and the Cotswold Antique Dealers' Association (CADA), if he doesn't have what you are looking for, he will know of – and guide you to - others who probably will. CADA members are also happy to give advice on where to stay in the area, and assistance with packing, shipping and insurance. Roger Lamb Antiques is open from 10am to 5pm, Monday to Saturday.

Longborough Farm Shop

Longborough, nr Stow-on-the-Wold,
Gloucestershire GL56 0QZ
Tel: 01451 830469 Fax: 01451 830413
e-mail: mail@longboroughfarmshop.com
website: www.longboroughfarmshop.com

Cotswold Life Winner Best Speciality Food Shop 2004
Runner-up NFU Southwest Region Best Farm Retailer 2003

On the A424 2 miles north of Stow-on-the-Wold, Katharine Assheton's multi-award winning **Longborough Farm Shop** is a foodie paradise, an absolute must for anyone driving or touring in the area. Under the beams of the stone-walled shop there's an amazing, mouthwatering display of specialist packaged foods along with bread, cakes baked by local ladies, cider, mead and fruit wines, and an assortment of food-related gifts, table accessories and paintings by local artists. From the fruit farm comes variety of soft fruits and orchard fruits, and asparagus in its short but sensational season. Most of the vegetables are from local producers, with the emphasis, as with everything here, on quality and seasonality. The cheeses, mostly British, are kept in superb condition, but perhaps pride of place goes to the superb meats, including local Dexter beef, Jacob lamb pork from Old Spot Gloucester pigs, Dorset bacon and sausages and seasonal game. This marvellous place is open every day, closed only on Sunday from January to Easter.

retreated to St Edward's Church, while others were cut down in the market square. The church, which suffered considerable damage at this time, has been restored many times down the centuries, not always to its advantage, but one undoubted treasure is a painting of the Crucifixion in the south aisle, thought to be the work of the 17th century Flemish artist Gaspard de Craeyer. The church is dedicated to King Edward the Martyr, who was murdered at Corfe Castle by his stepmother Elfrida. Other buildings of note in the town are the 15th century Crooked House and the 16th century Masonic Hall. On Digbeth Street stands the Royalist Hotel, said to be the oldest inn in England; an inn has certainly stood on the site since 947. In Park Street is the **Toy and Collectors Museum**, housing a charming display of toys, trains, teddy bears and dolls, games and books, along with textiles and lace, porcelain and pottery.

AROUND STOW-ON-THE-WOLD

Upper & Lower Swell

1 mile W of Stow on the B4077 & B4068

A couple of Swells, neighbouring villages on the banks of the River Dikler. Lower Swell's focal point is the triangular village green, while the large mill pond is one of Upper Swell's many delights. Nearby, in Condicote Lane, is **Donnington Trout Farm** with a hatchery, smokery, farm shop and a lake for fly fishing.

Moreton-in-Marsh

4 miles N of Stow on the A429

Moreton-in-the-Marsh is the scene, every Tuesday, of the biggest open-air street market in the Cotswolds. This attractive old town stands at the junction of the A44 and the A429 Fosse Way, and was once an important stop on the coaching route between London and the West Midlands. Its broad main street is lined with handsome 17th and 18th century buildings, while from earlier days are the old town gaol, the White Hart, where Charles I took refuge during the Civil War, and the Curfew Tower with its clock and bell dated 1633.

In Bourton Road, the **Wellington Aviation Museum** has a collection of World War II aircraft paintings, prints and models and a detailed history of the Wellington bomber.

One of the town's most popular amenities is **Batsford Park** which offers a variety of attractions. There's an arboretum set in 55 acres of typical Cotswold countryside and contains more than 1500 species and varieties of trees, shrubs, bamboos and wild flowers.

The Moreton Delicatessen

5a Oxford Street, Moreton-in-Marsh, Gloucestershire GL56 0LA
Tel: 01608 652115
e-mail: themoretondelicatessen@hotmail.com

Philip and Amy Carter have a great love and respect for good food, and for the past two years they have shared their enthusiasm with the lucky residents of Moreton-in-Marsh and the surrounding area. **The Moreton Delicatessen**, in an old Bath stone building just off the main street, is positively crammed with good things, from home-made pâtés, cooked and cured meats and smoked fish to breads and cheeses, oils and vinegars, preserves and pickles, chocolates and biscuits, local apple juices and fine wines. Sandwiches are made to order, and the Moreton Deli will put together lovely hampers for picnics, corporate events, special occasions and gifts.

Batsford Park: Arboretum, Garden Centre & Falconry Centre

Batsford Park, Moreton-in-Marsh, Gloucestershire GL56 9QB
Tel: 01386 701441 Fax: 01386 701829
e-mail: mail@batsarb.co.uk
website: www.batsarb.co.uk

Batsford Park is a place of several unique attractions, comprising an arboretum and wild garden, a garden centre and a falconry centre. The arboretum contains a rare and beautiful collection of over 1,500 species and varieties of trees, shrubs, bamboos and wild flowers set in 55 acres of typical Cotswold countryside. Visitors can wander along magical meandering paths and by the side of streams, discovering delights and surprises at very turn, including a Japanese Rest House, a hermit's cave and a number of magnificent bronze statues from the Far East, originally collected by Lord Redesdale. Each season brings its own special magic to this jewel in the Cotswold crown: in spring the snowdrops and daffodils; in early summer the magnolias and the Japanese cherry blossom; in autumn the reds and yellows and golds of the deciduous trees; and in winter the fairyland of frost and the waterfall of icicles suspended above the frozen lake.

The arboretum and gift shop are open daily from the beginning of February to mid-November, otherwise at weekends only. In the Apple Store Tea Room, teas, coffees and snacks can be enjoyed either inside or out on the terrace overlooking the garden. The Garden Centre at Batsford is a specialist plantsman's centre with many rare and unusual trees, shrubs, alpine plants, herbaceous and perennials, and a wide range of garden sundries, compost, mulches, terracotta and glazed pots, seeds and gifts. Advice is available on the stock of ferns, bamboos, Japanese maples and magnolias, many of which can be seen growing to maturity in the arboretum. Cotswold Falconry Centre is home to a large collection of falcons, hawks, owls, kites and vultures, which are flown at regular intervals throughout the day, enabling all visitors to see and admire their remarkable grace, speed and agility. The site has many breeding aviaries, including the owls in Owl Wood, and at various times of the year the birds are either nest building, sitting on eggs or feeding their young. In the Cotswold School of Falconry the Centre holds introductory courses, hunting days and a three-day hands-on falconry experience. Adoption schemes, whereby a bird can be adopted for a year, have proved very popular, especially as gifts. The Centre is open from mid-February to mid-November and has a picnic area, refreshments and gift shop.

Visitors can wander along meandering paths and discover surprises at every turn – a Japanese Rest House, a hermit's cave or a number of magnificent bronze statues from the far east. Also within the park is the **Cotswold Falconry Centre** which is home to a large collection of falcons, hawks, owls, kites and vultures which are flown at regular intervals during the day. Other attractions in the park include a gift shop, tea room and garden centre.

A mile east of town on the A44 stands the **Four Shires Stone** marking the original spot where the counties of Gloucestershire, Oxfordshire, Warwickshire and Worcestershire met.

Blockley

7 miles N of Stow off the A44/A429

Silk-spinning was the main industry here, and six mills created the main source of employment until the 1880s. As far back as the Domesday book water mills were recorded here, and the village also once boasted an iron foundry and factories making soap, collars and pianos. The mills have now been turned into private residences and Blockley is a quieter place. One of the chief attractions for visitors is **Mill Dene Garden**, set around a mill in a steep-sided valley. The garden has hidden paths winding up from the mill pool, and at the top there are lovely views over the Cotswolds. Also featured are a grotto, a potager, a trompe l'oeil and dye plants.

Chipping Campden

10 miles N of Stow on the B4081

The 'Jewel of the Cotswolds', full of beautifully restored buildings in golden Cotswold stone. It was a regional capital of the wool trade between the 13th and 16th centuries and many of the fine buildings date from that period of

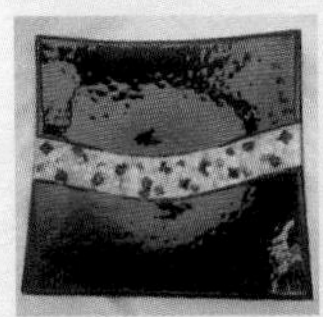

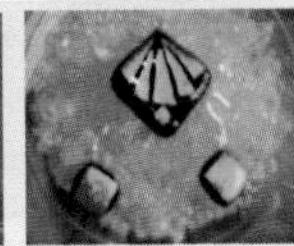

Jacobean Market Hall, Chipping Campden

prosperity. In the centre of town is the Jacobean **Market Hall**, built in 1627 and one of many buildings financed by the wealthy fabric merchant and financier Sir Baptist Hicks. He also endowed a group of almshouses and built Old Campden House, at the time the largest residence in the town; it was burnt down by Royalists to prevent it falling into the hands of the enemy, and all that survives are two gatehouses, the old stable block and the banqueting halls. The 15th century Church of St James was built on a grand scale and contains several impressive monumental brasses, the most impressive being one of William Grevel measuring a mighty eight feet by four feet.

Dover's Hill, a natural amphitheatre above the town, is the scene of the **Cotswold Olimpicks**, founded in the 17th century by Captain Robert Dover, who lived at Stanway House. The Games followed the traditions of ancient Greece and added some more down-to-earth activities such as shin-kicking and bare-knuckle boxing. The lawlessness and hooliganism that accompanied the games led to their being closed down in 1852 but they were revived in a modern form in 1951 and are still a popular annual attraction on the Friday following the spring bank holiday.

Broadway

10 miles NW of Stow on the A44

Just over the border into Worcestershire, where the Cotswolds join the Vale of Evesham, Broadway is one of the glories of the Cotswolds, a showpiece village with an abundance of scenic and historic attractions. The renowned Lygon Arms entertained both King Charles and Oliver Cromwell, and **Broadway Tower** at the top of Fish Hill affords spectacular views over the Severn Vale.

Broadway Tower, Broadway

A couple of miles southwest of Broadway, **Snowshill Manor Garden** (National Trust) is an Arts & Crafts garden designed to complement a handsome Cotswold manor house. Laid out by Charles Paget Wade as a series of outdoor 'rooms' with terraces and ponds, the garden is now run on organic principles.

Hidcote Bartrim

3 miles NE of Chipping Campden off the B4632

Hidcote Manor Garden is one of the most famous in the country, a masterpiece created in the first years of the 20th century by the eminent horticulturist Major Lawrence Johnston. A series of small gardens, each with a different character and appeal, Hidcote is renowned for its rare shrubs and trees, herbaceous borders and unusual plant species from all parts of the globe. Visitors can refresh themselves in the tea bar or licensed restaurant.

Upper and Lower Slaughter

2 miles SW of Stow off the A429/B4068

The Slaughters (the name means nothing more sinister than 'muddy place') are archetypal Cotswold villages set a mile apart on the little River Eye. Both are much visited by tourists, much explored and much photographed; they are also much as they have always been, since virtually no building work has been carried out since 1904. Francis Edward Witts, author of the *Diary of a Cotswold Parson*, was the rector here between 1808 and 1854.

At Lower Slaughter, the **Old Mill**, with its tall chimney and giant waterwheel, is

WALK NUMBER 12

The Slaughters

Distance:	5.5 miles (8.8 kilometres)
Typical time:	180 mins
Height gain:	65 metres
Map:	Outdoor Leisure 45
Walk:	www.walkingworld.com ID:1629
Contributor:	Ron and Jenny Glynn

Access Information:

On the A429 between Moreton in Marsh and Cirencester.

Additional Information:

Car park in Station Road. Charge is £3 for up to five hours. It is advisable to park here as the streets are narrow, often with double yellow lines.

Description:

Referred to as the Venice of the Cotswolds, Bourton-on-the-Water sits on the River Windrush, enhanced by its presence and character. Visitors to the village relax and take refreshment beside the waterside teashops, cafés and restaurants, and walk over the fine old stone footbridges that cross the river at various points. The village of Lower Slaughter is but a short distance, and although very small, presents a big impact to the sightseer, its beautiful character and Cotswold stone construction, unforgettable.

Upper Slaughter is another wonderful setting, with a cluster of stone dwellings and a pretty church that is open to visitors; a photographer's paradise. The countryside is marvellous, natural and unspoilt; a pleasure to behold. The bustling centre of Bourton-on-the Water is approached on the return journey along a lengthy street with attractive residences on one side, and the River Windrush on the other. The little shops and stores are delightfully varied, selling quality goods to tourists all the year round, one of the many attractions that draw visitors to this quiet, restful setting continually.

Features:

Hills or Fells, River, Pub, Toilets, Museum, Play Area, Church, Stately Home, Wildlife, Birds, Flowers, Great Views, Butterflies, Food Shop, Good for Kids, Tea Shop, Woodland

Walk Directions:

1 Leave car park from the main entrance and turn left onto Station Road. Walk past Moor Lane and a supermarket further on, then past The Cotswold School. Continue, to reach the main road.

2 Go right up the road for a short distance. Cross road and turn left on signed path just before Coach & Horses PH. Follow path through wide open meadows to reach a gate.

3 Continue on enclosed section to walk into Lower Slaughter.

4 Turn left on Wardens Way beside running water. Turn right past St Mary's Church and follow dry stone wall to pass a Gloucestershire Way marker, then walk on along village street.

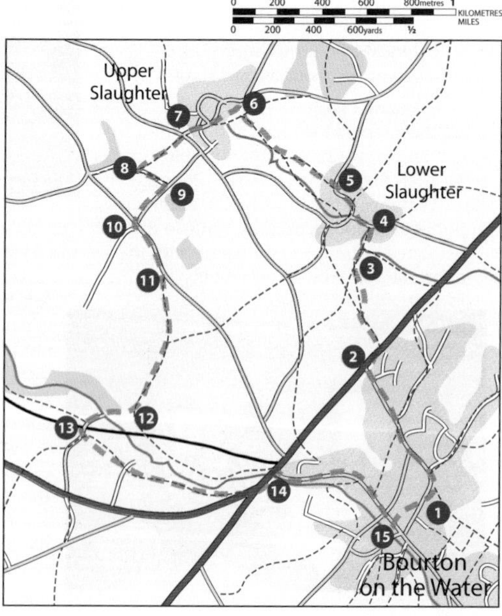

5 Turn left on footpath from bend in road and enter two gates to walk beside fencing and trees. Take kissing gate and large metal gate to walk over meadow to another small gate in view. Maintain direction on well trodden path in meadowland, trees all around. The next gate leads into sheep pastures with a lake below and the Manor House to the side of it. Cross River Eye on narrow stone bridge and continue on tree lined path to reach road.

6 Turn left and follow road past Lords Of The Manor Hotel & Restaurant in Upper Slaughter. Walk on to pass village hall and small enclosed green, and notice church on right. Carry on to leave the village.

7 Take gate ahead on footpath that runs uphill beside allotments, then between open fields. Look back on fabulous views over glorious Cotswold countryside. Take gate on right and turn left.

8 Take the gate immediately on left and walk downhill beside dry stone wall and hedges.

9 Turn right on narrow road, hedge and tree lined on an incline to reach another road.

10 Turn left towards Bourton on the Water, views on either side far and distant.

11 Take right fork onto bridleway track, taking two metal gates, then along beside fields, and on to another gate to walk beneath archway of trees on enclosed section.

12 Turn right past stables and follow track past a very handsome and large mill called Little Aston. Continue on track uphill then turn left opposite entrance to Aston Farm.

13 Take footpath on left and walk uphill to follow it along between fields. Leave hedge to walk on over large field area. Cross track and climb stile following stone wall then fenceline on right. At end of field go on below a bank, the River Windrush running below. Climb stile out into clearing and maintain direction in uneven meadowland between thick tree growth. Reach a gate and stile at far corner and continue on narrow enclosed path to reach main road. Cross over and turn left on pavement.

14 Turn right over river bridge on Lansdowne Road and walk beside River Windrush. Pass Mousetrap Inn and attractive stone dwellings on the way to centre of Bourton on the Water. St Lawrence Church stands on the left, plain and stark with a domed tower. The shops are all very individual and appealing, and the little riverside cafes are very popular with the many visitors.

15 Pass model railway exhibition and turn left by the Chestnut Gallery. Walk beside large hotel along a narrow alley alongside stone wall, turning left then right into carpark of start of walk.

a prominent feature by the river. This restored 19th century flour mill is open for visits and has a tearoom and organic ice cream parlour.

Upper Slaughter

Bourton-on-the-Water

4 miles S of Stow on the A429

Probably the most popular of all the Cotswold villages. The willow-fringed River Windrush flows through the centre, crossed by several delightful low-arched pedestrian bridges, two of which date from the late 18th century. The golden stone cottages are pretty as a picture, and among the notable larger buildings are St Lawrence's Church, with its 14th century chancel and rare domed Georgian tower, and a manor house with a 16th century dovecote. In the High Street, **Miniature World - The**

Museum of Miniatures is a unique exhibition of miniature scenes and models that took the country's leading master miniature makers three-and-a-half years to complete. It is accessible through another marvel of miniatures, the famous **Model Village**, complete with music in the church and the 'model of the model', and **Bourton Model Railway** with over 40 British and Continental trains running on three main displays in OO, HO and N gauge. The **Cotswold Motoring Museum and Toy Collection**, in an 18th century water mill, has a fascinating collection of antique toys, a display of historic advertising signs and 30 or so (full-size!) cars and motorcycles. Bourton has Europe's only **Perfumery Exhibition**, a permanent attraction where perfumes are manufactured on the

Motor Museum, Bourton-on-the-Water

THE DIAL HOUSE HOTEL

The Chestnuts, High Street, Bourton-on-the-Water, Gloucestershire GL54 2AN
Tel: 01451 822244
Fax: 01451 810126
e-mail: info@dialhousehotel.com
website: www.dialhousehotel.com

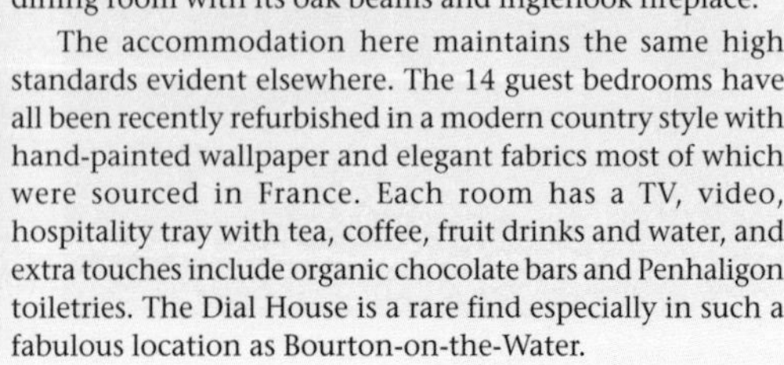

Adrian and Jane Campbell-Howard are your welcoming hosts at this 17th century country house standing in an acre-and-a-half of beautiful gardens in the middle of this picture postcard village. Awarded the accolade of Best Hotel in Gloucestershire 2002 and with two AA Rosettes,the **Dial House Hotel** is the perfect venue for a relaxing break and an ideal base for exploring the attractions in the area. The hotel is noted for the quality of its cuisine, with a team of four chefs led by Daniel Bunce producing superb home-made food. Meals are served in the delightful dining room with its oak beams and inglenook fireplace.

The accommodation here maintains the same high standards evident elsewhere. The 14 guest bedrooms have all been recently refurbished in a modern country style with hand-painted wallpaper and elegant fabrics most of which were sourced in France. Each room has a TV, video, hospitality tray with tea, coffee, fruit drinks and water, and extra touches include organic chocolate bars and Penhaligon toiletries. The Dial House is a rare find especially in such a fabulous location as Bourton-on-the-Water.

Wold Galleries

Halford House, Station Road, Bourton-on-the-Water,
Gloucestershire GL54 2AA
Tel/Fax: 01451 822092
e-mail: sales@woldgalleries.com website: www.woldgalleries.com

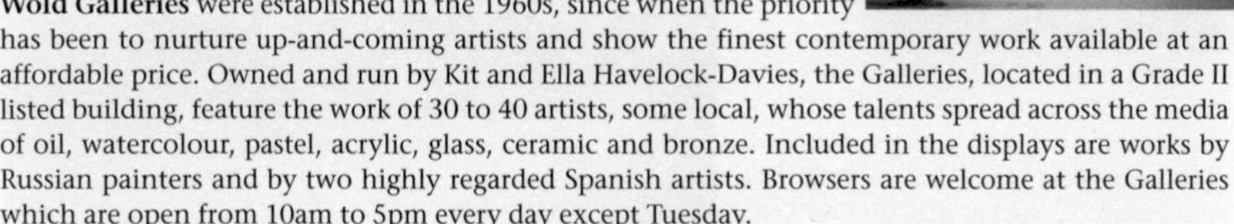

Wold Galleries were established in the 1960s, since when the priority has been to nurture up-and-coming artists and show the finest contemporary work available at an affordable price. Owned and run by Kit and Ella Havelock-Davies, the Galleries, located in a Grade II listed building, feature the work of 30 to 40 artists, some local, whose talents spread across the media of oil, watercolour, pastel, acrylic, glass, ceramic and bronze. Included in the displays are works by Russian painters and by two highly regarded Spanish artists. Browsers are welcome at the Galleries which are open from 10am to 5pm every day except Tuesday.

premises; the exhibition explores the origins of perfume and includes 'smelly-vision' in a specially constructed cinema, a perfume quiz and a beautiful perfume garden where all the plants have been selected for their aroma.

A five-minute walk from the town centre brings visitors to **Birdland Park & Gardens** set in seven acres of woodland, water and gardens. The natural setting is home to more than 500 birds, including flamingos, pelicans, cranes, storks and waterfowl; there are over 50 aviaries of parrots, falcons, pheasants, hornbills, toucans, touracos and many others, and tropical, temperate and desert houses are home to the more delicate species. Open all year, Birdland has a café and facilities for children, including a play area, pets' corner and penguin feeding time.

Keith Harding's World Of Mechanical Music

The Oak House, High Street, Northleach,
Gloucestershire GL54 3ET
Tel: 01451 860181
e-mail: keith@mechanicalmusic.co.uk
website: www.mechanicalmusic.co.uk

Keith Harding's love for mechanical music began 40 years ago in London, and since 1986 he has been based in a handsome period house in the main street of Northleach. Visitors of all ages will find plenty to amuse and delight them, as **Keith Harding's World of Mechanical Music** has the finest selection of musicals and automata, both antique and modern, to be found anywhere. The shop holds a large stock of musical boxes and clocks, puzzles, games and gifts of all kinds, videos and CDs and, for the collector, a large range of books on mechanical music, musical boxes and clocks. It is also a living museum of various kinds of self-playing musical instruments that were the proud possessions of former generations, from a tiny singing bird concealed in a snuff box to a mighty red Welte Steinway reproducing piano of 1907.

The instruments are introduced and played by the guides in the form of a live musical entertainment show, and the tours include demonstrations of restored barrel organs, barrel pianos, musical boxes, polyphons, automata, reproducing pianos, phonographs, gramophones and antique clocks, all in a period setting that enhances the enjoyment of a visit to this unique place. Keith Harding and his dedicated team are specialist craftsmen unrivalled in their field, and everything on show is maintained in perfect working order; customers' pieces can be restored and estimates are free. Opening times are 10am to 6pm daily.

The Seven Tuns

Queen Street, Chedworth,
nr Cheltenham,
Gloucestershire GL54 4AE
Tel: 01285 720242 Fax: 01285 720933
website: www.theseventuns.com

In a delightful village in the very heart of the Cotswolds, **The Seven Tuns** is a classic country pub where Alex and Fred Barrington have won many new friends since taking over the reins in 2003. It's a super place to visit at any time of year, with roaring log fires blazing a welcome when the weather's cool, and a spacious beer garden and patio to take advantage of the warmer months. The outside of the inn, which dates from the early 17th century, is partly covered in a luxuriant growth of creeper, while inside, in the cosy bar and the two dining areas, the look is splendidly traditional, with black slatted floorboards and a mixture of furniture. Young cask ales are kept in perfect condition on tap to quench country thirsts, while a choice of 15 malt whiskies will soon remove any winter chills.

Food is also taken seriously here, and chefs Al and Louis, assisted by Fred, produce a variety of well-prepared, unpretentious dishes with both classic English inspiration and some more contemporary touches. Filled baguettes and ploughman's platters are popular lunchtime choices, but for those with more time to spare the menu tempts with such dishes as tomato, basil and brie brochette; chicken, bacon and avocado salad; seafood chowder; home-made beefburger; traditional fish & chips; and sirloin steak served plain or with a thyme-infused red wine sauce. In the big beer garden, a revolving South African barbecue comes into its own on summer evenings. Families and dogs are welcome at the Seven Tuns, and the skittle alley above the bars is a popular spot for private functions, corporate events and special occasions. Plans for 2005 include an annexe of three rooms for Bed & Breakfast. The inn is a favourite venue for shoot lunches, and has two special cabinets for the safe keeping of guns. Chedworth, village of some 900 inhabitants that is said to be the longest village in England, is surrounded by excellent walking country. A mile away, in a beautiful wooded setting in the valley of the River Colne, stand the considerable ruins of Chedworth Roman Villa, whose 30 rooms and associated buildings feature some marvellous mosaics – well worth a visit, and a good way to build up a thirst and appetite that The Seven Tuns happy to deal with.

Two attractions outside the village are the Iron Age **Salmonsbury Camp** and **Cotswold Farm Park**, home of rare breed conservation. Voted Farm Park of the Year 2003, it is both interactive and educational, providing the opportunity to see unusual species of farm animals. Rabbit handling and bottle feeding of lambs and calves makes it ideal for children.

Northleach

10 miles S of Stow on the A429

A traditional market town with some truly magnificent buildings. It was once a major wool-trading centre that rivalled Cirencester in importance and as a consequence possesses what now seems a disproportionately large church. The **Church of St Peter and St Paul**, known as the 'Cathedral of the Cotswolds', is a fine example of Cotswold Perpendicular, built in the 15th century with pinnacled buttresses, high windows and a massive square castellated tower. Treasures inside include an ornately carved font and some rare monumental brasses of which rubbings can be made (permits obtainable from the Post Office).

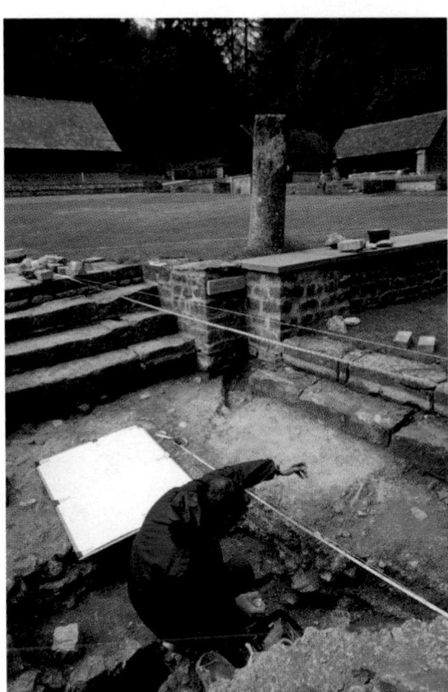

Chedworth Roman Villa & Museum

The town's most popular attraction is **Keith Harding's World of Mechanical Music** (see panel on page 369) which occupies a handsome period house in the main street. Keith's love of mechanical music goes back some 40 years and he has accumulated the finest collection of automata, both antique and modern, to be found anywhere. It includes a tiny singing bird concealed in a snuff box to a mighty Welte Steinway reproducing piano of 1907. The instruments are introduced and played by the guides in the form of a live musical entertainment show and the tours include demonstrations of restored barrel organs, barrel pianos, musical boxes, polyphons, gramophones and antique clocks.

Close to the pretty village of **Chedworth**, a couple of miles west of Northleach, is what must be the region's oldest stately home, the National Trust's **Chedworth Roman Villa**, a large, well-preserved Romano-British villa discovered by chance in 1864 and subsequently excavated to reveal more than 30 rooms and buildings, including a bath house and hypocaust. Some wonderful mosaics are on display, one depicting the four seasons, another showing nymphs and satyrs. The villa lies in a beautiful wooded combe overlooking the valley of the Colne. A natural spring rises at the head of the combe – probably the main reason for choosing this site.

Bibury

15 miles S of Stow on the B4425

William Morris, founder of the Arts & Crafts Movement, described Bibury as

Arlington Row, Bibury

"the most beautiful village in England" and, apart from the tourists, not a lot has changed since he made the claim. The Church of St Mary, with Saxon, Norman and medieval parts, is well worth a visit, but the most visited and most photographed buildings in Bibury are **Arlington Row**, a superb terrace of medieval stone cottages built as a wool store in the 14th century and converted three centuries later into weavers' cottages and workshops. Fabric produced here was supplied to nearby **Arlington Mill** for fulling, a process in which the material was cleaned in water and beaten with mechanically-operated hammers. Today the mill, which stands on the site of a corn mill mentioned in the Domesday Book, is a museum with a collection of industrial artefacts, crafts and furniture, including pieces made in the William Morris workshops.

Arlington Mill Museum & Restaurant

Bibury, Gloucestershire GL7 5NL
Tel: 01285 740368
e-mail: cateringatthemill@hotmail.com
website: www.arlingtonmill.co.uk

William Morris considered Bibury "the most beautiful village in England". Well over a century-and-a-half later, it remains almost completely unspoilt. One of the villages many attractions is **Arlington Mill Museum & Restaurant**. The mill itself is a 17th century building on the site of a much earlier one recorded in the Domesday Book in 1086. Production at Arlington stopped in 1913 and the building was allowed to fall into disrepair until 1965 when it was purchased by a local archaeological historian, David Verey. He renovated the building and replaced some of the missing mill machinery. Today, the three-storey mill contains a series of fascinating exhibits relating its history and that of Bibury village.

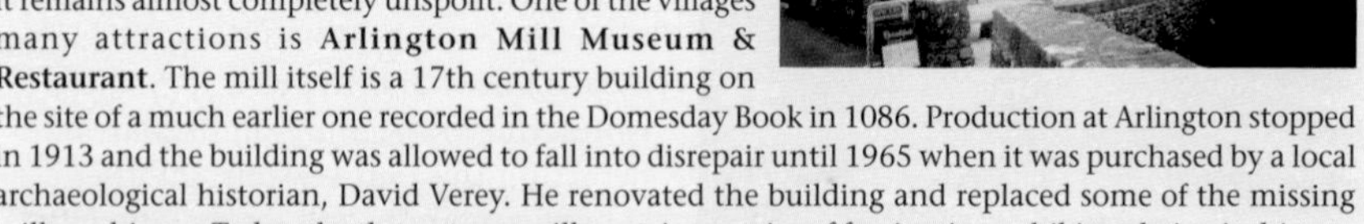

Also on site are a gift shop, crystal shop, art gallery and the excellent Arlington Mill Restaurant. It's open from 8am every day serving anything from a full English breakfast to grilled Bibury trout fresh from the adjacent trout farm. At teatime, enjoy a wonderful clotted cream & strawberry jam tea with scones served warm from the oven; in the evening, a four-course home-cooked dinner. In good weather, customers can enjoy their refreshments in the courtyard overlooking terraced gardens and lovely Cotswold countryside.

CIRENCESTER

The 'Capital of the Cotswolds', a lively market town with a long and fascinating history. As Corinium Dobonnorum it was the second largest Roman town in Britain (Londinium was the largest). Few signs remain of the Roman occupation, but the award-winning **Corinium Museum** features one of the finest collections of antiquities from Roman Britain, and reconstructions of a Roman kitchen, dining room and garden give a fascinating and instructive insight into life in Cirencester of almost 2000 years ago. The museum is currently closed for major refurbishment but is scheduled to re-open in September 2004.

The main legacy of the town's medieval wealth is the magnificent **Church of St John Baptist**, perhaps the grandest of all the Cotswold 'wool churches', its 120ft tower dominating the town. Its greatest treasure is the Anne Boleyn Cup, a silver and gilt cup made for Henry VIII's second wife in 1535, the year before she was executed for adultery. Her personal insignia - a rose tree and a falcon holding a sceptre - is on the lid of the cup, which was given to the church by Richard Master, physician to Queen Elizabeth I. The church has a unique three-storey porch which was used as the Town Hall until 1897.

Cirencester today has a thriving crafts scene, with workshops in the **Brewery Arts** House, a converted Victorian brewery. Sixteen resident craftworkers include a basket maker, jeweller, textile

Moonstruck

3 Silver Street, Cirencester, Gloucestershire GL7 2BJ
Tel: 01285 640444
e-mail: moonstruckhome@aol.com

"Beautiful objects for home and garden" is Sue Smart's description of the huge selection of varied items on display at **Moonstruck**. Her town centre shop, opened in 1997 and located close to the Corinium Museum, specialises in one-off items. You'll find well-made and original items, many of which are hand-made by artists and craftsmen from around the world and are exclusive to Moonstruck. There's a wide range of decorative pieces –glassware, dried flowers, prints, paintings and unusual items like the vintage French advertising posters.

Functional items include lamps and chandeliers, vases, kitchenware, magazine racks, toys, bird cages – even waste bins. The extensive selection of garden accessories offers distinctive garden furniture and functional objects such as patio heaters. Whether you are looking for something special for your own home, or a gift for someone else, you can be sure of finding something to inspire you at Moonstruck. The relaxed and friendly atmosphere here makes it a great place for leisurely browsing.

Parlour Farm

Unit 12, Wilkinson Road, Love Lane Industrial Estate,
Cirencester, Glos.
Tel: 01285 885 336
website:www.parlourfarm.com

Solid Pine Bespoke Kitchens and
Bespoke Reclaimed Kitchen Furniture

Located on the outskirts of Cirencester, Parlour Farm manufacture traditional bespoke kitchens at a very competitive price. A superb range of custom built reclaimed kitchen furniture and a stunning display of tables, chairs, free standing kitchen furniture and at least seven kitchens on display. Absolutely worth a visit. Give us a ring or visit our website. Open 7 days a week.

Also at 6 The Old George, Fountain Street, Nailsworth, Glos GL6 0BL

Polo Canteen

2a Sheep Street, Cirencester,
Gloucestershire GL7 1QW
Tel: 01285 650977
Fax: 01285 642777
website: www.polocanteen.co.uk

Polo Canteen, two minutes walk from the shops and spires of Cirencester town centre, is a stylish restaurant run by owner/ chef Paul Welch. One of the Cotswolds most highly regarded and most distinctive privately-run restaurants, it offers an outstanding selection of dishes making excellent use of the finest and freshest local produce, complemented by an alluring, well-chosen wine list. Everything from the bread to the desserts is made on the premises and, in addition to the full à la carte menu, there's a daily changing selection of chef's specials.

Typical dishes range from chicken and wild mushroom terrine, or dill and lime marinated salmon (as a starter or main course), to char-grilled tuna with potato and olive compote, breast of duck with herb mash and a rich roast gravy, and pepper-sauced sirloin steak.

There's always plenty of choice for vegetarians, and desserts such as pecan pie or baked apples in butterscotch round things off in style. The game of polo, played regularly at Cirencester Park, provides the inspiration for the colonial style décor. The restaurant is the perfect setting for intimate dining, family celebrations and – thanks to the famously large round tables – for small parties and wedding receptions.

The whole restaurant can be hired for private functions. Polo Canteen is open from noon until 2pm, and from 7pm to 10pm, Monday to Saturday.

Carriages At Three

3 The Woolmarket, Cirencester,
Gloucestershire GL7 2PR
Tel: 01285 651760
e-mail: rosemarie@carriagesatthree.co.uk
website: www.carriagesatthree.co.uk

In a courtyard setting close to the town centre and market square, **Carriages at Three** is a specialist in ladies' evening wear. One of the leading fashion retailers in the Cotswolds, Rosemary Watson's shop has two spectacular window displays that provide a beguiling sample of a vast choice that includes more than 1,500 dresses. Ball gowns, cocktail dresses, prom dresses, cruise wear, wedding wear and formal evening wear come in stunning variety, from a simple classic black dress to an eye-popping one-off creation to guarantee a grand and glamorous entrance.

Designers featured in the shop include Consortium, Frank Usher, Amanda Wakeley, John Charles, Joseph Ribkoff, Samuel Marks, Attire and Lulu Guinness. One room is especially for dresses for brides and bridesmaids. The dresses come in a wide range of sizes, and the shop also offers a made-to-measure service for 'plus' sizes and a bespoke alteration service.

A full range of accessories, from shoes and hats and shawls to costume jewellery, is available to complete the ensemble, and the staff at this unique place are among the best in the business: a chat with the customer will enable them to make sound suggestions on what will be most suitable for each individual. They are always ready with helpful advice on how best to store and look after the garments, even extending to recommending the best dry cleaners. Carriages at Three also includes a range of day wear, but first and foremost this is a place for the special occasion, and one that fully deserves the boast that this is 'where the best evenings begin.'

weaver, ceramicist and stained glass artist. A shop in the centre sells the best in British work, and there are galleries, a coffee house, arts and crafts classes and workshops.

Cirencester Open Air Swimming Pool, next to the park, was built in 1869 and is one of the oldest in the country. Both the main pool and the paddling pool use water from a private well. Other sites of interest include St Thomas' Hospital – 15th century almshouses for destitute weavers – the Barracks of 1857, and a Yew Hedge which was planted in 1720. It now stands 40ft high and is reputed to be the loftiest in Europe. It can be found in Cirencester Park, a 3,000-acre expanse which was designed by the poet Alexander Pope.

Cirencester certainly lives up to its reputation as a market town with street markets on Monday and Friday; a cattle market on Tuesday; a craft market in the Corn Hall on Saturdays, and regular antiques markets on Fridays.

AROUND CIRENCESTER

Shorncote

3 miles S of Cirencester off the A419

Two areas of flooded gravel workings form the **Cotswold Water Park**, an increasingly important wetland area with a greater expanse of water than the Norfolk Broads. The area, which includes **Keynes Country Park**, is a centre for water sports, fishing, bird watching, walking and cycling.

Kemble

4 miles SW of Cirencester on the A429

Located close to the source of the River Thames, Kemble is best known for the **Bristol Aero Collection** at Kemble

Manby's Farm Cottages & Riding Holidays

Oaksey, nr Cirencester, Gloucestershire SN16 9SA
Tel: 01666 577399
e-mail: enquiries@manbysfarm.com
website: www.manbysfarm.com

Located on a working farm in a peaceful corner of the Cotswolds and enjoying lovely pastoral views, **Manby's Farm Cottages & Riding Holidays** offer the perfect combination for lovers of equestrian activities. The farm is owned and run by Zoe and Alexander Maculan, a local couple who bought the 46-acre property in 2004. Zoe will be well-known to followers of competitive horse-riding as she has ridden for the British team in Portugal, Spain and India.

Accommodation at the farm comprises four self-catering cottages, with three more to be completed in 2005. The south-facing cottages sleep between two and four guests, and are all attractively furnished and comprehensively equipped to a 3-diamonds standard, with linen and towels provided. Guests also have the use of a smart indoor heated swimming pool. Dogs are welcome, so too are horses which can be accommodated in the brand new stables. Hunting can be arranged with the Beaufort and Vale of White Horse hunts, and there's also polo at nearby Cirencester.

Glebe Farm Holiday Cottages

Glebe Farm, Barnsley, nr Cirencester,
Gloucestershire GL7 5DY
Tel: 01285 659226 Fax: 01285 642622
e-mail: enquiries@glebefarmcottages.co.uk
website: www.glebefarmcottages.co.uk

Approached through a magnificent avenue of lime trees, **Glebe Farm Holiday Cottages** offer top quality self-catering accommodation with a 4-stars rating from the English Tourism Council. Located in the grounds of the owner, Polly Handover's house, the five spacious barn conversions are beautifully furnished with antiques and pine. The imaginative conversion makes the most of the fine roof structures, ancient beams and exposed stone walls. Sleeping between four and six guests, each of the properties is equipped to a very high standard, with colour TV, fridge, microwave and night storage heating. All electricity is included in the price and all linen and towels are provided.

Shared utilities are a washing machine, tumble dryer, freezer and a pay-phone; other facilities include a large patio, shared barbecue and ample parking. Baby-sitting and maid services are available. Dogs are welcome. There's plenty to see and do in the area. Historic Cirencester is just three miles away; the Cotswold Farm Park, Cotswold Wildlife Park, Slimbridge Wildfowl Trust, Blenheim Palace and Berkeley Castle are all within easy reach. Local activities include horse-riding, sailing, fishing, golf, racquets – and even dry slope skiing at Gloucester.

Airfield. The Bristol Company's most prestigious aircraft was Concorde – at Kemble visitors can walk through the furnished passenger cabin and look down on the droop nose and the powerful Olympus engine. Other exhibits include Bristol helicopters, the only Britannia in working condition, Bloodhound guided missiles, aero engines, a full scale Giotto satellite, scale models of various military aircraft – and a collection of Bristol buses.

Fairford

9 miles E of Cirencester on the A417

A welcoming little town in the valley of the River Coln, with many fine buildings of the 17th and 18th centuries and an abundance of inns as evidence that this was an important stop on the London-Gloucester coaching run. John and Edmund Tame, wealthy wool merchants, built the superb late-Perpendicular **Church of St Mary**, whose greatest glory is a set of 28 medieval stained glass windows depicting the Christian faith in picture-book style. John Tame's memorial stone, along with those of his wife and son, are set into the floor of the church.

In mid-July, nearby RAF Fairford hosts the annual **Royal International Air Tattoo**, the world's largest military air show which attracts thousands of visitors.

Lechlade-on-Thames

12 miles E of Cirencester on the A417

Now part of the Cotswold Water Park, Lechlade is the highest navigable point on the Thames and head of the Thames towpath walk. In and around the town visitors can hire rowing boats, go sailing or wind-surfing, and enjoy lake and river fishing.

A statue of Old Father Thames,

Lechlade & Bushyleaze Trout Fisheries

Burford Road, Lechlade, Gloucestershire GL7 3QQ
Tel: 01367 253266 Fax: 01367 252663
e-mail: trout@star.co.uk
website: www.lechladetrout.co.uk

Lechlade & Bushyleaze Trout Fisheries are the number one small stillwaters in the UK, offering outstanding facilities, superb countryside and great fishing. The fisheries lie near the headwaters of the River Thames, half a mile north of Lechlade, and are clearly signposted on the A361 Swindon to Burford road. Both fisheries are beautifully landscaped and offer a peaceful day's fishing in clear limestone water with an abundance of insect life. Lechlade Trout Fishery comprises a nine-acre lake and 250 yards of wild brown trout fishing on the River Leach. It is stocked as a 'Big Fish' water with an average of five-six pounds, big doubles and even 20-pounders introduced every week.

Bushyleaze fishery is a 22-acre water with a minimum stocking size of two pounds, along with five & six-pounders and a regular stocking of double-figure fish. Both waters are stocked with rainbow and brown trout. Day tickets and half-day tickets are available, with evening tickets on Bushyleaze also available. Boats can be hired and there are clubhouse facilities with food, drinks, tackle and lavatories. Both waters have disabled access and are open every day of the year from 8am to 45 minutes after sunset, or 10pm, whichever is the earlier. Corporate Hospitality a speciality.

Riverside Country Pub

Antiques Centre & Thamesside Homes,
Park End Wharf, Lechlade,
Gloucestershire GL7 3AQ
Tel: 01367 252229
website: www.riverside_lechlade.co.uk

There's something for everyone at **Riverside Country Pub, Antiques Centre & Thamesside Homes**, all of which enjoy lovely positions beside the River Thames. The pub is a charming old building of Cotswold stone with a terrace right beside the river and close to the old bridge. Food is served here from 9am to 9pm every day and the extensive menu includes an excellent choice of snacks, sandwiches, light meals and home-made specials such as steak & kidney pie and Bibury trout with a sherry and almond sauce. Other options include ploughmans, salads and vegetarian dishes. On Sundays a three-course lunch is served in the delightful oak-beamed restaurant overlooking the Thames – booking is essential.

Through the pub you can hire cycles, rowing boats, a cruiser or a canoe. From the nearby Marina, cruises to the start of the river (14 miles) or even to London (120 miles) can be arranged.

Lechlade has become something of a Mecca for bargain hunters and serious antiques collectors alike. At the entrance to the pub's car park you'll find Boat House Antiques, a shop brim full of antiques, including a large range of Tiffany lamps, brass and many unusual fireside accessories as well as collectables, quality gifts and bric à brac. On the outskirts of the complex is the Lechlade Antiques Arcade. This 17th century building is an Aladdin's Cave of 40 different booths filled by collectors and enthusiasts. It's open every day from 10am until 5pm.

Tim Lloyd, the owner of the Riverside Country Pub, is also the guiding spirit behind Thamesside Homes, 14 mews-style homes built in traditional local materials in 2003-4 and provided with landscaped Cotswold-walled gardens. Set just 50 yards from the river, these are available on long leases and plans are under way for more to be built in an area where the chandlery shops used to be – these have now moved to the Marina.

River Thames at Lechlade

originally created for the Great Exhibition of 1851, overlooks **St John's Lock**, where barges loaded with building stone bound for Oxford and London have given way to pleasure craft. This bustling market town surrounded by green meadows boasts a fine 15th century church with a slender spire and a structure that has remained unaltered since the early 1500s. In its lovely churchyard, in 1815, the poet Shelley was inspired to write his *Stanzas in a Summer Evening Churchyard*. The verses are inscribed on a stone at the churchyard entrance.

Another interesting building is the Halfpenny Bridge, built in 1792, which crosses the Thames in the town centre and has a tollhouse at its eastern end.

Inglesham

1 mile S of Lechlade off the A361

The splendidly unspoilt Church of St John the Baptist dates mainly from the 13th century, with some notable later additions. The chief features are important wall paintings, 15th century screens, 17th and 18th century pulpit and box pews and, perhaps its greatest treasure, a Saxon carving of the Virgin and Child blessed by the Hand of God. This is one of many churches in the care of the Churches Conservation Trust, formerly known as the Redundant Churches Fund. The trust was established to preserve churches which though no longer needed for regular worship are of historic or architectural importance.

Kelmscott

13 miles E of off the A4095

William Morris called the village of Kelmscott "a heaven on earth" and **Kelmscott Manor**, the exquisite Elizabethan manor house he leased jointly with Dante Gabriel Rosetti, "the loveliest haunt of ancient peace that can well be imagined". Located near the River Thames and dating from about 1570, the manor was Morris's country retreat from 1871 until his death in 1896. His wife, May, continued to live here until her death in 1938. The house's treasures include the early-17th century oak four-poster in which Morris was born at Walthamstow in 1834; Rosetti's ethereal portrait of Morris's wife, *The Blue Silk Dress*; and the 17th century tapestries that were already in place when Morris leased the house.

THE OXFORDSHIRE COTSWOLDS

Woodstock

8 miles NW of Oxford on the A44

Situated in the Glyme Valley, in an area of land that was originally part of the Wychwood Forest, the name of this elegant Georgian market town means a 'place in the woods'. To the north of the River Glyme is the old Saxon settlement, while on the opposite bank lies the town that was developed by Henry II in the 13th century to serve the Royal Park of Woodstock. There had been hunting lodges for the Kings of England here long before the Norman Invasion and it was Henry I who established the deer park around the manor of Woodstock. It was while at his palace here that Henry II first seduced Rosamund, whom he is said to have housed in a bower in the park. One story tells how Henry's wife, Queen Eleanor, managed to uncover the couple by following an unravelled ball of silk that had become attached to her husband's spur.

This long since disappeared medieval palace was also the birthplace of the Black Prince in 1330 and Princess Elizabeth was held prisoner here in 1558 during the reign of her sister, Queen Mary. On ascending the throne, a grateful Elizabeth I granted the town a second weekly market and two fairs for its loyalty. The palace was damaged during the Civil War, when it served as a Royalist garrison, and the last remains were demolished in 1710.

While the new town became an important coaching centre, many of the old inns survive to this day, and prospered as a result of the construction of the Oxford Canal and later the railway. The old town's trade was glove-making and traditionally a pair of new gloves are presented to a visiting monarch. Today's visitors can look round the showroom of **Woodstock Gloves**.

The town is also home to the **Oxfordshire County Museum** (free) which is housed in the wonderful and imposing 16th century Fletcher's House. As well as the permanent displays on the life of the county through the centuries, the museum hosts regular exhibitions and has a sculpture court and a peaceful garden at whose entrance stand the old town stocks.

It is the magnificent **Blenheim Palace**, one of only a handful of sites in the country to be included on the World Heritage List, which brings most people to Woodstock. The estate and the cost of building the palace was a gift from a grateful Queen Anne to the heroic John Churchill, 1st Duke of Marlborough, for his victory at the Battle of Blenheim during the Spanish War of Succession. However, the Queen's gratitude ran out before the building work was complete and the duke had to pay the remainder of the costs himself. As his architect, Marlborough chose Sir John Vanbrugh, whose life was even more colourful than that of his patron. He was at once both an architect (although at the time of his commission he was relatively unknown) and a playwright, and he also had the distinction of having been imprisoned in the Bastille in Paris. The result of his

Blenheim Palace

work was the Italianate palace (built between 1705 and 1722), which is now seen sitting in a very English park that was designed by Charles Bridgeman and Henry Wise and later landscaped by Capability Brown. Unfortunately, once completed, the new house did not meet with universal approval: it was ridiculed by Jonathan Swift and Alexander Pope, and Marlborough's wife, Sarah, who seems to have held the family purse strings, delayed paying Vanbrugh as long as possible.

Blenheim is a marvellous, grand place with a mass of splendid paintings, furniture, porcelain, and silver on show. Visitors will also be interested in the more intimate memorabilia of Sir Winston Churchill. Born here in 1874, Churchill was a cousin of the 9th Duke and the family name remains Churchill.

A recent addition to the palace's many attractions is the **Secret Garden** which was opened in 2004, the 300th anniversary of the Battle of Blenheim. The garden was originally planted in the 1950s by the 10th duke but after his death became overgrown and virtually inaccessible. Now restored, this 'Four Seasons' garden with its many unusual trees, shrubs and flowers offers an enchanting mix of winding paths, soothing water features, bridges, fountains, ponds and streams.

First grown by George Kempster, a tailor from Old Woodstock, the Blenheim Orange apple took its name from the palace. Though the exact date of the first apple is unknown, Kempster himself died in 1773 and the original tree blew down in 1853. So famous did the spot where the tree stood become that it is said that London-bound coaches and horses used to slow down so that passengers might gaze upon it.

Bladon

1.5 miles S of Woodstock on the A4095

The village lies on the southern edge of the Blenheim estate and it was in the churchyard here in 1965 that Sir Winston Churchill was laid to rest in a simple grave after a state funeral. Also interred here are his parents, his brother John, and his daughters. The ashes of his wife Clementine were buried in his grave in 1977.

Long Hanborough

2 miles S of Woodstock

Located next to Long Hanborough railway station, the **Oxford Bus Museum** has some 40 vehicles on display, all of which were used at one time for public transport in and around Oxford. They range from early 19th century horse-trams to buses from the 1980s. Also on show is the double-decker bus used in the Spice Girls movie. The museum is open at weekends and daily throughout August.

North Leigh

4.5 miles SW of Woodstock off the A4095

The Saxon-towered St Mary's Church is well worth a visit, and just to the north of the village lies the **Roman Villa** (English Heritage, free), one of several known to have existed in this area. Little remains apart from the foundations and some mosaic flooring, but this is enough to measure the scale of the place; it had over 60 rooms, two sets of baths and a sophisticated under-floor heating system, all built round a courtyard and clearly the home of a prosperous farming family.

Finstock

5 miles W of Woodstock on the B4022

A charming village with two notable literary associations. It was in 1927, at the 19th century Holy Trinity Church, that TS Eliot was baptised at the age of 38 following his controversial conversion to Catholicism. The novelist and churchwoman Barbara Pym lived in retirement with her sister in a cottage in the village; she died in 1980 and is buried in the churchyard. A lectern in the church is dedicated to her memory.

CHARLBURY

5 miles NW of Woodstock on the B4026

Now very much a dormitory town for Oxford, Charlbury was once famous for its glove-making as well as being a centre of the Quaker Movement - the simple Friends' Meeting House dates from 1779 and there is also a Friends' cemetery. **Charlbury Museum**, close to the Meeting House, has displays on the traditional crafts and industries of the town and the town's charters given by Henry III and King Stephen can also be seen. Well known for its olde-worlde **Railway Station**, built by Isambard Kingdom Brunel, complete with its fishpond and hanging baskets, the town also has two interesting great houses.

On the other bank of the River Evenlode is **Cornbury Park**, a large estate that was given to Robert Dudley by Elizabeth I. Although most of the house now dates from the 17th century, this was originally a hunting lodge in Wychwood Forest that had been used since the days of Henry I. Glimpses of the house can be seen from the walk around the estate.

Lying just to the west of the town is **Ditchley Park**, a restrained and classical house built in the 1720s by James Gibbs. The interiors are splendid, having been designed by William Kent and Henry Flitcroft, and Italian craftsmen worked on the stucco decorations of the great

BLUEBELLS FLORIST & GIFT SHOP

Sheep Street, Charlbury, Oxon OX7 3RR
Tel/Fax: 01608 811414
The Old Bakery, Market Place,
Deddington, OX16 0SE
Tel/Fax: 01869 338832
website: www.bluebellsflowershop.co.uk

Now established six years, business partners Catherine Young and Debra Harvey at **Bluebells Florist & Gift Shop**, offer a wide selection of the more unusual as well as the seasonal flowers. Both have trained in floristry, and their specialities range from country style weddings to the more exotic flowers for corporate events, as well as the daily bouquets and arrangements which are made up for customers.

The gifts at Bluebells offer the customers a variety of choice and are of high quality. Cath Kidston, Garden Trading and Bath House are featured, as well as colourful hand-made jewellery, design led cards and much more. Both shops are within 12 miles of each other, and deliver to all the surrounding villages and towns.

hall and the saloon; the first treated to give an impression of rich solemnity, the second with a rather more exuberant effect. The house has associations with Sir Winston Churchill, who used it as a weekend headquarters during World War II. Appropriately enough, given that Sir Winston had an American mother, Ditchley Park is now used as an Anglo-American conference centre.

BURFORD

Often referred to as The Gateway to the Cotswolds, Burford is an enchanting old market town of honey coloured Cotswold stone set on the banks of the River Windrush. It was the site of a battle between the armies of Wessex and Mercia in 752, and after the Norman Conquest the town was given to William I's brother, Bishop Odo of Bayeux. Lying on important trade routes, both north-south and east-west, the town prospered and its first market charter was granted in 1087. In the 16th century, the town was an important centre of the woollen trade and it was used as the setting for *The Woolpack*, in which the author Celia Harknett describes the medieval wool trade in Europe. After the decline in the wool trade, Burford became an important coaching centre and many of the old inns can still be seen today.

The **Church of St John the Baptist** was built on the wealth of the wool trade and this grand building has the atmosphere of a small cathedral. Originally Norman, the church has been added to over the centuries and there are several interesting monuments and plaques to be found. In the south wall of the tower stair is a carved panel, dated around 100 AD, which is thought to show the Celtic fertility goddess Epona,

The Cockatoo

39 High Street, Burford, Oxon OX18 4QA
Tel/Fax: 01993 822700
website: www.thecockatoo.co.uk

"Gifts of distinction for people with taste and humour" says the sign above **The Cockatoo's** front window, and customers soon realise that owner Suki Smith's description is fully justified. Her philosophy is that if she has to be surrounded all day by pieces she has chosen, she must enjoy each and every one herself. So, whether it's a bronze frog or an elegant wall clock, a snoozing hippopotamus or an exquisite dried flower arrangement, everything here has style and distinction. The wonderful frogs, come in every colour, shape and style, and since they are all individually sculpted each one is unique with a world wide limited edition.

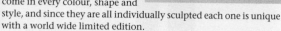

Other ranges include Tottering by Gently from Annie Tempest, tactile ceramic chickens by Catherine Hunter, and amazing silk roses with "built-in" fragrance by David Austin. There's an extensive range of prints with a very prominent country theme. Unusual men's gifts, leather accessories, stationary and gift wrap, children's presents, and much much more make The Cockatoo a delightful place to browse with everything displayed with great flair to its best advantage.

Terraced Cottages at Burford

with two male supporters and a horse. In the nave north aisle a monument erected to Edmund Harman, the barber-surgeon to Henry VIII, shows North American natives - possibly the first representation of native Americans in the country. In the south porch is a small plaque which commemorates three Leveller mutineers who were imprisoned in the church by Cromwell's men and shot in the churchyard in 1649.

The Levellers were troops from Cromwell's army who mutinied against what they saw as the drift towards the authoritarian rule they had been fighting against. While they were encamped at Burford, the Levellers were taken by surprise by Cromwell's forces. After a brief fight, some 340 prisoners were taken and placed under guard in the church. The next day a court martial was held and three of the rebels were shot as an example to the rest, who were made to watch the executions. They were spared similar punishment when their leader recanted in a sermon.

The town's old court house, built in the 16th century with an open ground floor and a half-timbered first floor, is now home to the **Tolsey Museum**. An interesting building in its own right, the collection on display here covers the history of the town and the surrounding area. Other buildings worth seeking out include the 16th century **Falkland Hall**, the home of a local wool and cloth merchant Edmund Sylvester, and **Symon Wysdom's Cottages**, which were built in 1572 by another of the town's important merchants.

Taynton

1.5 miles NW of Burford off the A424

Up until the end of the 19th century Taynton was a quarrying village, with the limestone taken from the quarries used in the construction of Blenheim Palace, Windsor Castle, St Paul's Cathedral as well as many Oxford colleges and local buildings.

Cornwell

9 miles N of Burford off the A436

This village had the distinction of being renovated in the 1930s by Clough Williams Ellis, best known for creating the remarkable Italianate Welsh holiday village of Portmeirion.

Chastleton

10 miles N of Burford off the A44

Chastleton is home to one of the best examples of Jacobean architecture in the country. In 1602, Robert Catesby, one of the Gunpowder Plot conspirators, sold his estate here to a prosperous wool merchant from Witney, Walter Jones. A couple of years later, Jones pulled the house down and built **Chastleton House**, a splendid Jacobean manor house with a dramatic five-gabled front and a garden where the original rules of croquet were established in 1865. Until it became a National Trust property, Chastleton had been inhabited by the same family for more than 400 years. One of the finest and most complete Jacobean houses in England, it is filled with a remarkable collection of furniture, textiles and items both rare and everyday. Visits by appointment only.

Over Norton

11 miles N of Burford off the A3400

To the northwest of Over Norton are the **Rollright Stones** - one of the most fascinating Bronze Age monuments in the country. These great gnarled slabs of stone stand on a ridge which offers fine views of the surrounding countryside. They all have nicknames: the **King's Men** form a circle; the **King Stone** is to the north of the circle; and, a quarter of a mile to the west, stand the **Whispering Knights**, which are, in fact, the remnants of a megalithic tomb. Naturally, there are many local legends connected with the stones and some say that they are the petrified figures of a forgotten king and his men that were turned to stone by a witch.

Shipton-under-Wychwood

4 miles NE of Burford on the A361

The suffix 'under-Wychwood' derives from the ancient royal hunting forest, **Wychwood Forest**, the remains of which lie to the east of the village. The name has nothing to do with witches - wych refers to the Hwicce, a Celtic tribe of whose territory the forest originally formed a part in the 7th century. Though cleared during the Middle Ages, it was still used as a royal hunting forest until the mid-1600s. By the late 1700s there was little good wood left and the clearing of the forest was rapid to provide arable land.

The forest was one of the alleged haunts of Matthew Arnold's scholar gypsy and in the poem, published in 1853, Arnold tells the legend of the brilliant but poor Oxford scholar who, despairing of ever making his way in the world, went to live with the gypsies to learn from their way of life.

The village itself is centred around its large green, which is dominated by the tall spire of 11th century **St Mary's Church**. Here, too, can be found **The Shaven Crown**, now a hotel, which was built in the 15th century as a guest house for visitors to the nearby (and now demolished) Bruern Abbey. Finally, there is the superb **Shipton Court**, built around 1603, which is one of the country's largest Jacobean houses.

Chipping Norton

10 miles NE of Burford on the A44

The highest town in Oxfordshire, at 650 feet above sea level, Chipping Norton was once an important centre of the wool trade and King John granted the town a charter to hold a fair to sell wool. Later changed to a **Mop Fair**, the tradition continues to this day when the fair is held every September.

The town's medieval prosperity can be seen in the fine and spacious **Church of St Mary** which was built in 1485 with money given by John Ashfield, a wool merchant. The splendid east window came from the Abbey of Bruern, a few miles to the southwest, which was demolished in 1535 following the Dissolution of the Monasteries. In 1549, the minister here, the Rev Henry Joyce, was charged with high treason and hanged from the then tower because he refused to use the new prayer book introduced by Edward VI.

As with many buildings in the town, there has been substantial 19th century remodelling and the present church tower dates from 1823.

Still very much a market town today - the market is held on Wednesdays - Chipping Norton has been little affected by the influx of visitors who come to see this charming place. The **Chipping Norton Museum** is an excellent place to

Create the Look

26 High Street, Chipping Norton, Oxon OX7 5AD
Tel/Fax: 01608 646556

Recently moved to new premises, **Create the Look** offers a huge range of stylish accessories for the home and is also a great place to visit if you are looking for gift ideas. The business is owned and run by Paula Thomas who has gathered together a wonderful collection of accessories from both the UK and the Far East. You'll find lots of elegant caneware, pots of every shape, size and colour, an extensive selection of ceramics, pictures, a wide range of glassware, candles, picture frames, bags and much, much more.

Paula regularly changes the eye-catching window display to attract passers-by. Chipping Norton itself, the highest town in the county and known as the Gateway to the Cotswolds, is a delightful place to explore with its fine medieval church, 17th century almshouses, a weekly market on Wednesdays and, just outside the town, the Bliss Tweed Mill with its strange tower that has been described as looking like a sink plunger.

Rectory Farm Sporting Breaks

Rectory Farm, Salford, Chipping Norton,
Oxon OX7 5YZ
Tel/Fax: 01608 643209
e-mail: colston@rectoryfarm75.freeserve.co.uk
website: www.rectoryfarm.info

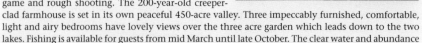

Set amongst the beautiful North Cotswold countryside **Rectory Farm** offers high quality bed & breakfast accommodation, fly fishing for trout and 'walked up' game and rough shooting. The 200-year-old creeper-clad farmhouse is set in its own peaceful 450-acre valley. Three impeccably furnished, comfortable, light and airy bedrooms have lovely views over the three acre garden which leads down to the two lakes. Fishing is available for guests from mid March until late October. The clear water and abundance of natural plant and fly life creates exciting dry fly fishing throughout the summer months.

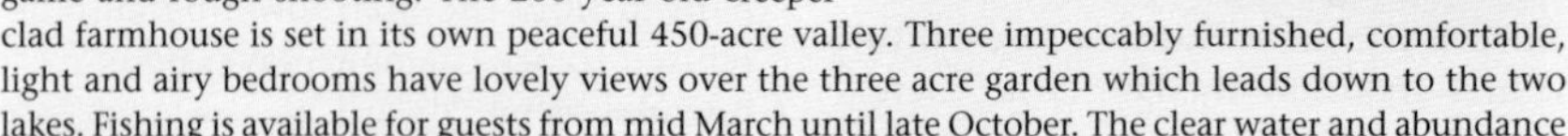

Throughout the winter months 'walked up' game and rough shooting (pheasant, partridge, duck and pigeon) are available to parties of three-six guests. Guests are invited to bring their own working gun dogs and walk the estate with the gamekeeper on organised small shoots. For the less energetic, time spent visiting the small Cotswold towns, fine gardens and historic houses in the area is always rewarding. Owners, Nigel and Elizabeth Colston who have lived here all their lives will ensure that your stay will be pleasurable.

start any exploration and the permanent displays here cover local history from prehistoric and Roman times through to the present day.

Found just to the west of the town centre is **Bliss Tweed Mill**, an extraordinary sight in this area as it was designed by a Lancashire architect, George Woodhouse, in 1872 in the Versailles style. With a decorated parapet and a tall chimney which acts as a local landmark, this very northern looking mill only ceased operation in the 1980s.

Minster Lovell

4.5 miles E of Burford off the B4047

One of the prettiest villages along the banks of the River Windrush, Minster Lovell is home to the ruins of a once impressive 15th century manor house. **Minster Lovell Hall** was built about 1431-42 and was, in its day, one of the great aristocratic houses of Oxfordshire, the home of the Lovell family. However, one of the family was a prominent Yorkist during the Wars of the Roses and, after the defeat of Richard III at Bosworth Field, he lost his lands to the Crown. The house was purchased by the Coke family in 1602, but around the middle of the 18th century the hall was dismantled by Thomas Coke, Earl of Leicester, and the ruins became lowly farm buildings. They were rescued from complete disintegration by the Ministry of Works in the 1930s and are now in the care of English Heritage. What is left of the house is extremely picturesque, and it is hard to imagine a better setting than here, beside the River Windrush. One fascinating feature of the manor house which has survived is the medieval dovecote, complete with nesting boxes, which provided pigeons for the table in a way reminiscent of modern battery hen houses.

Swinbrook

2 miles E of Burford off the A40

The Fettiplace family lived in a great manor house in this peaceful village in the valley of the Windrush. The manor has long gone, but the family is remembered in several impressive and highly distinctive monuments in the Church of St Mary. The family home of the Redesdales was also at Swinbrook, and in the churchyard are the graves of three of the six Mitford sisters, who were daughters of the 2nd Baron Redesdale. Nancy, Unity and Pamela are buried here.

TOURIST INFORMATION CENTRES

BEDFORDSHIRE

BEDFORD

St Pauls Square
Bedford
Bedfordshire
MK40 1SL
Tel: 01234 215226
Fax: 01234 217932
e-mail: TouristInfo@bedford.gov.uk

DUNSTABLE

The Library
Vernon Place
Dunstable
Bedfordshire
LU5 4HA
Tel: 01582 471012
Fax: 01582 666110
e-mail: dunstable-tic@bedfordshire.gov.uk

MID BEDFORDSHIRE

5 Shannon Court
High Street
Sandy
Bedfordshire
SG19 1AG
Tel: 01767 682 728
Fax: 01767 681 713
e-mail: tourist.information@midbeds.gov.uk

BERKSHIRE

BRACKNELL

The Look Out Discovery Centre
Nine Mile Ride
Bracknell
Berkshire
RG12 7QW
Tel: 01344 354409
Fax: 01344 354422
e-mail: TheLookOut@bracknell-forest.gov.uk

MAIDENHEAD

Maidenhead Library
St Ives Road
Maidenhead
Berkshire
SL6 1QU
Tel: 01628 796502
Fax: 01628 796971
e-mail: maidenhead.tic@rbwm.gov.uk

NEWBURY

The Wharf
Newbury
Berkshire
RG14 5AS
Tel: 01635 30267
Fax: 01635 519562
e-mail: tourism@westberks.gov.uk

READING

Church House
Chain Street
Reading
Berkshire
RG1 2HX
Tel: 0118 956 6226
Fax: 0118 939 9885
e-mail: touristinfo@reading.gov.uk

WINDSOR

24 High Street
Windsor
Berkshire
SL4 1LH
Tel: 01753 743900 or 01753 743901
Fax: 01753 743911 or 01753 743904
e-mail: windsor.tic@rbwm.gov.uk

BUCKINGHAMSHIRE

AYLESBURY

8 Bourbon Street
Aylesbury
Buckinghamshire
HP20 2RR
Tel: 01296 330559
Fax: 01296 330559
e-mail: info@aylesbury-tourist.org.uk

BUCKINGHAM

The Old Gaol Museum
Market Hill
Buckingham
Buckinghamshire
MK18 1JX
Tel: 01280 823020
Fax: 01280 823020
e-mail: buckingham.t.i.c@btconnect.com

HIGH WYCOMBE

Paul's Row
High Wycombe
Buckinghamshire
HP11 2HQ
Tel: 01494 421892
Fax: 01494 421893
e-mail: tourism_enquiries@wycombe.gov.uk

MARLOW

31 High Street
Marlow
Buckinghamshire
SL7 1AU
Tel: 01628 483597
Fax: 01628 471915
e-mail: tourism_enquiries@wycombe.gov.uk

WENDOVER

The Clock Tower
High Street
Wendover
Buckinghamshire
HP22 6DU
Tel: 01296 696759
Fax: 0871 2361551
e-mail: tourism@wendover-pc.gov.uk

GLOUCESTERSHIRE

BOURTON-ON-THE-WATER

Victoria Street
Bourton-on-the-Water
Gloucestershire
GL54 2BU
Tel: 01451 820211 or 01451 822583
Fax: 01451 821103
e-mail: bourtonvic@cotswold.gov.uk

CHELTENHAM

Municipal Offices
77 Promenade
Cheltenham
Gloucestershire
GL50 1PJ
Tel: 01242 522878 or 01242 517110
Fax: 01242 255848
e-mail: tic@cheltenham.gov.uk

CIRENCESTER

Corn Hall
Market Place
Cirencester
Gloucestershire
GL7 2NW
Tel: 01285 654180
Fax: 01285 641182
e-mail: cirencestervic@cotswold.gov.uk

COLEFORD

High Street
Coleford
Gloucestershire
GL16 8HG
Tel: 01594 812388
Fax: 01594 832889
e-mail: tourism@fdean.gov.uk

GLOUCESTER

28 Southgate Street
Gloucester
Gloucestershire
GL1 2DP
Tel: 01452 396572 or 01452 396576
Fax: 01452 504273 or 01452 309788
e-mail: tourism@gloucester.gov.uk

NEWENT

7 Church Street
Newent
Gloucestershire
GL18 1PU
Tel: 01531 822468
Fax: 01581 822468
e-mail: newent@fdean.gov.uk

STOW-ON-THE-WOLD

Hollis House
The Square
Stow-on-the-Wold
Gloucestershire
GL54 1AF
Tel: 01451 831082 or 01451 831971
Fax: 01451 870083
e-mail: stowvic@cotswold.gov.uk

STROUD

Subscription Rooms
George Street
Stroud
Gloucestershire
GL5 1AE
Tel: 01453 760960 or 01453 760900
Fax: 01453 760955
e-mail: tic@stroud.gov.uk

TETBURY

33 Church Street
Tetbury
Gloucestershire
GL8 8JG
Tel: 01666 503552
Fax: 01666 503552
e-mail: tourism@tetbury.com

TEWKESBURY

64 Barton Street
Tewkesbury
Gloucestershire
GL20 5PX
Tel: 01684 295027
Fax: 01684 292277
e-mail: tewkesburytic@tewkesburybc.gov.uk

WINCHCOMBE

Town Hall
High Street
Winchcombe
Gloucestershire
GL54 5LJ
Tel: 01242 602925

HAMPSHIRE

ALDERSHOT

39 High Street
Aldershot
Hampshire
GU11 1BH
Tel: 01252 320968 or 01252 311474
Fax: 01252 311479
e-mail: mail@rushmoorvic.com

ALTON

7 Cross and Pillory Lane
Alton
Hampshire
GU34 1HL
Tel: 01420 88448
Fax: 01420 543916
e-mail: altoninfo@btconnect.com

ANDOVER

Town Mill House
Bridge Street
Andover
Hampshire
SP10 1BL
Tel: 01264 324320
Fax: 01264 345650
e-mail: andovertic@testvalley.gov.uk

BASINGSTOKE

Willis Museum
Old Town Hall, Market Place
Basingstoke
Hampshire
RG21 7QD
Tel: 01256 817618
Fax: 01256 356231
e-mail: basingstoket.i.c@btconnect.com

FAREHAM

Westbury Manor
West Street
Fareham
Hampshire
PO16 0JJ
Tel: 01329 221342 or 01329 824896
Fax: 01329 282959
e-mail: touristinfo@fareham.gov.uk

FLEET

The Harlington Centre
236 Fleet Road
Fleet
Hampshire
GU13 8BY
Tel: 01252 811151
Fax: 01252 812191

FORDINGBRIDGE

Kings Yard
Salisbury Street
Fordingbridge
SP6 1AB
Tel: 01425 654560
Fax: 01425 654560
e-mail: fordingbridgetic@tourismse.com

GOSPORT

Gosport TIC
Bus Station Complex
South Street
Gosport
Hampshire
PO12 1EP
Tel: 023 9252 2944
Fax: 023 9251 1687
e-mail: tourism@gosport.gov.uk

HAVANT

1 Park Road South
Havant
Hampshire
PO9 1HA
Tel: 023 9248 0024
Fax: 023 9248 0024
e-mail: tourism@havant.gov.uk

HAYLING ISLAND

Central Beachlands
Seafront
Hayling Island
Hampshire
PO11 OAG
Tel: 023 9246 7111
Fax: 023 9246 5626
e-mail: tourism@havant.gov.uk

LYMINGTON

St Barb Museum & Visitor Centre
New Street
Lymington
Hampshire
SO41 9BH
Tel: 01590 689000
Fax: 01590 673990
e-mail: information@nfdc.gov.uk

LYNDHURST & NEW FOREST

New Forest Museum & Visitor Centre
Main Car Park
Lyndhurst
Hampshire
SO43 7NY
Tel: 023 8028 2269
Fax: 023 8028 4404
e-mail: information@nfdc.gov.uk

PETERSFIELD

County Library
27 The Square
Petersfield
Hampshire
GU32 3HH
Tel: 01730 268829
Fax: 01730 266679
e-mail: petersfieldinfo@btconnect.com

PORTSMOUTH (CLARENCE ESPLANADE)

Clarence Esplanade
Southsea
Portsmouth
Hampshire
PO5 3PB
Tel: 023 9282 6722
Fax: 023 9282 7519 or 023 9282 2693
e-mail: vis@portsmouthcc.gov.uk

PORTSMOUTH (THE HARD)

The Hard
Portsmouth
Hampshire
PO1 3QJ
Tel: 023 9282 6722
Fax: 023 9282 2693
e-mail: vis@portsmouthcc.gov.uk

RINGWOOD

The Furlong
Ringwood
Hampshire
BH24 1AZ
Tel: 01425 470896
Fax: 01425 461172
e-mail: information@nfdc.gov.uk

ROMSEY

Heritage & Visitor Centre
13 Church Street
Romsey
Hampshire
SO51 8BT
Tel: 01794 512987
Fax: 01794 512987
e-mail: romseytic@testvalley.gov.uk

SOUTHAMPTON

9 Civic Centre Road
Southampton
Hampshire
SO14 7FJ
Tel: 023 8083 3333
Fax: 023 8083 3381
e-mail:
tourist.information@southampton.gov.uk

WINCHESTER

Guildhall
Broadway
Winchester
Hampshire
SO23 9LJ
Tel: 01962 840500
Fax: 01962 850348
e-mail: tourism@winchester.gov.uk

HERTFORDSHIRE

BISHOP'S STORTFORD

The Old Monastery
Windhill
Bishop's Stortford
Hertfordshire
CM23 2ND
Tel: 01279 655831
Fax: 01279 653136
e-mail: tic@bishopsstortford.org

HEMEL HEMPSTEAD

Dacorum Information Centre
Marlowes
Hemel Hempstead
Hertfordshire
HP1 1DT
Tel: 01442 234222
Fax: 01442 230427
e-mail: stephanie.canadas@dacorum.gov.uk

HERTFORD

10 Market Place
Hertford
Hertfordshire
SG14 1DF
Tel: 01992 584322
Fax: 01992 534724
e-mail: hertford@eetb.info

LETCHWORTH GARDEN CITY

33-35 Station Road
Letchworth Garden City
Hertfordshire
SG6 3BB
Tel: 01462 487868
Fax: 01462 485332
e-mail: tic@letchworth.com

ST ALBANS

Town Hall
Market Place
St Albans
Hertfordshire
AL3 5DJ
Tel: 01727 864511
Fax: 01727 863533
e-mail: tic@stalbans.gov.uk

ISLE OF WIGHT

COWES

9 The Arcade
Cowes
Isle of Wight
PO31 7AR
Tel: 01983 813818
Fax: 01983 280078
e-mail: info@islandbreaks.co.uk

NEWPORT

The Guildhall
High Street
Newport
Isle of Wight
PO30 1TY
Tel: 01983 813818
Fax: 01983 823811
e-mail: info@islandbreaks.co.uk

RYDE

81-83 Union Street
Ryde
Isle of Wight
PO33 2LW
Tel: 01983 813818
Fax: 01983 567610
e-mail: info@islandbreaks.co.uk

SANDOWN

8 High Street
Sandown
Isle of Wight
PO36 8DG
Tel: 01983 813818
Fax: 01983 406482
e-mail: info@islandbreaks.co.uk

SHANKLIN

67 High Street
Shanklin
Isle of Wight
PO37 6JJ
Tel: 01983 813818
Fax: 01983 863047
e-mail: info@islandbreaks.co.uk

VENTNOR

IW Coastal Visitors Centre
Salisbury Gardens, Dudley Road
Ventnor
Isle of Wight
PO38 1EJ
Tel: 01983 813818
Fax: 01983 855859
e-mail: info@islandbreaks.co.uk

YARMOUTH

The Quay
Yarmouth
Isle of Wight
PO41 4PQ
Tel: 01983 813818
Fax: 01983 761047
e-mail: info@islandbreaks.co.uk

OXFORDSHIRE

ABINGDON

25 Bridge Street
Abingdon
Oxfordshire
OX14 3HN
Tel: 01235 522711 or 01235 535245
Fax: 01235 535245
e-mail: abingdontic@btconnect.com

BANBURY

Spiceball Park Road
Banbury
Oxfordshire
OX16 2PQ
Tel: 01295 259855
Fax: 01295 269469
e-mail: banbury.tic@cherwell-dc.gov.uk

BICESTER

Bicester Visitor Centre
Unit 86a, Bicester Village
Pingle Drive
Bicester
Oxfordshire
OX26 6WD
Tel: 01869 369055
Fax: 01869 369054
e-mail: bicester.vc@cherwell-dc.gov.uk

BURFORD

The Brewery
Sheep Street
Burford
Oxfordshire
OX18 4LP
Tel: 01993 823558
Fax: 01993 823590
e-mail: burford.vic@westoxon.gov.uk

CHIPPING NORTON

The Guildhall
Chipping Norton
Oxfordshire
OX7 5NJ
Tel: 01608 644379
Fax: 01608 644379
e-mail: chippingnortonvic@westoxon.gov.uk

DIDCOT

118 Broadway
Didcot
Oxfordshire
OX11 8AB
Tel: 01235 813243
Fax: 01235 813243
e-mail: didcottic@tourismse.com

FARINGDON

7a Market Place
Faringdon
Oxfordshire
SN7 7HL
Tel: 01367 242191
Fax: 01367 242191
e-mail: faringdontic@btconnect.com

HENLEY-ON-THAMES

King's Arms Barn
Kings Road
Henley on Thames
Oxfordshire
RG9 2DG
Tel: 01491 578034 or 01491 412703
Fax: 01491 411766
e-mail: henleytic@hotmail.com

OXFORD

Oxford Information Centre
15/16 Broad Street
Oxford
Oxfordshire
OX1 3AS
Tel: 01865 726871
Fax: 01865 240261
e-mail: tic@oxford.gov.uk

THAME

Market House
North Street
Thame
Oxfordshire
OX9 3HH
Tel: 01844 212834
Fax: 01844 212834
e-mail: thame.tic@btconnect.com

WALLINGFORD

Town Hall
Market Place
Wallingford
Oxfordshire
OX10 0EG
Tel: 01491 826972
Fax: 01491 832925
e-mail: ticwallingford@freenet.co.uk

WANTAGE

Vale and Downland Museum
19 Church Street
Wantage
Oxfordshire
OX12 8BL
Tel: 01235 760176
Fax: 01235 760176
e-mail: wantage_tic@btconnect.com

WITNEY

26A Market Square
Witney
Oxfordshire
OX28 6BB
Tel: 01993 775802
Fax: 01993 709261
e-mail: witney.vic@westoxon.gov.uk

WOODSTOCK

Oxfordshire Museum
Park Street
Woodstock
Oxfordshire
OX20 1SN
Tel: 01993 813276
Fax: 01993 813632
e-mail: woodstock.vic@westoxon.gov.uk

WILTSHIRE

AMESBURY

Amesbury Library
Smithfield Street
Amesbury
Wiltshire
SP4 7AL
Tel: 01980 622833 or 01980 623255
Fax: 01980 625541
e-mail: amesburytic@salisbury.gov.uk

AVEBURY

Avebury Chapel Centre
Green Street
Avebury
Wiltshire
SN8 1RE
Tel: 01672 539425
Fax: 01672 539296
e-mail: all.atic@kennet.gov.uk

BRADFORD ON AVON

The Greenhouse
50 St. Margaret's Street
Bradford on Avon
Wiltshire
BA15 1DE
Tel: 01225 865797 or 01225 868722
Fax: 01225 868722
e-mail: tic@bradfordonavon2000.fsnet.co.uk

CHIPPENHAM

Yelde Hall
Market Place
Chippenham
Wiltshire
SN15 3HL
Tel: 01249 706333
Fax: 01249 460776
e-mail: tourism@northwilts.gov.uk

CORSHAM

Arnold House
31 High Street
Corsham
Wiltshire
SN13 0EZ
Tel: 01249 714660
Fax: 01249 716164
e-mail: corshamheritage@northwilts.gov.uk

DEVIZES

Cromwell House
Market Place
Devizes
Wiltshire
SN10 1JG
Tel: 01380 729408
Fax: 01380 730319
e-mail: all.dtic@kennet.gov.uk

MALMESBURY

Town Hall
Market Lane
Malmesbury
Wiltshire
SN16 9BZ
Tel: 01666 823748
Fax: 01666 826166
e-mail: malmesburyip@northwilts.gov.uk

MARLBOROUGH

The Library
High Street
Marlborough
Wiltshire
SN8 1HD
Tel: 01672 513989
Fax: 01672 513989
e-mail: all.tics@kennet.gov.uk

MELKSHAM

Church Street
Melksham
Wiltshire
SN12 6LS
Tel: 01225 707424 or 01225 706068
Fax: 01225 707424
e-mail: visitmelksham@westwiltshire.gov.uk

MERE

The Library
Barton Lane
(between Castle St. & Church St.)
Mere, Warminster,
Wiltshire
BA12 6JA
Tel: 01747 861211 or 01747 860341
Fax: 01747 861127
e-mail: MereTIC@Salisbury.gov.uk

SALISBURY

Fish Row
Salisbury
Wiltshire
SP1 1EJ
Tel: 01722 334956
Fax: 01722 422059
e-mail: visitorinfo@salisbury.gov.uk

SWINDON

37 Regent Street
Swindon
Wiltshire
SN1 1JL
Tel: 01793 530328
Fax: 01793 434031
e-mail: infocentre@swindon.gov.uk

TROWBRIDGE

St Stephen's Place
Trowbridge
Wiltshire
BA14 8AH
Tel: 01225 777054
Fax: 01225 777054
e-mail: visittrowbridge@westwiltshire.gov.uk

WARMINSTER

Central Car Park
off Station Rd
Warminster
Wiltshire
BA12 9BT
Tel: 01985 218548
Fax: 01985 846154
e-mail:
visitwarminster@westwiltshire.gov.uk

WESTBURY

The Library
Edward Street
Westbury
Wiltshire
BA13 3BD
Tel: 01373 827158
Fax: 01373 827158
e-mail: visitwestbury@westwiltshire.gov.uk

INDEX OF ADVERTISERS

ACCOMMODATION, FOOD AND DRINK

ACTIVITIES

ANTIQUES AND RESTORATION

ARTS AND CRAFTS

FASHIONS

GIFTWARE

HOME AND GARDEN

JEWELLERY

PLACES OF INTEREST

SPECIALIST FOOD AND DRINK

INDEX OF WALKS

Looking for more walks?

The walks in this book have been gleaned from Britain's largest online walking guide, to be found at *www.walkingworld.com*.

The site contains 300 walks across eastern England, so there is plenty more choice in this region alone. If you are heading further afield there are walks of every length and type across England, Scotland and Wales – ideal if you are taking a short break as you can plan your walks in advance.

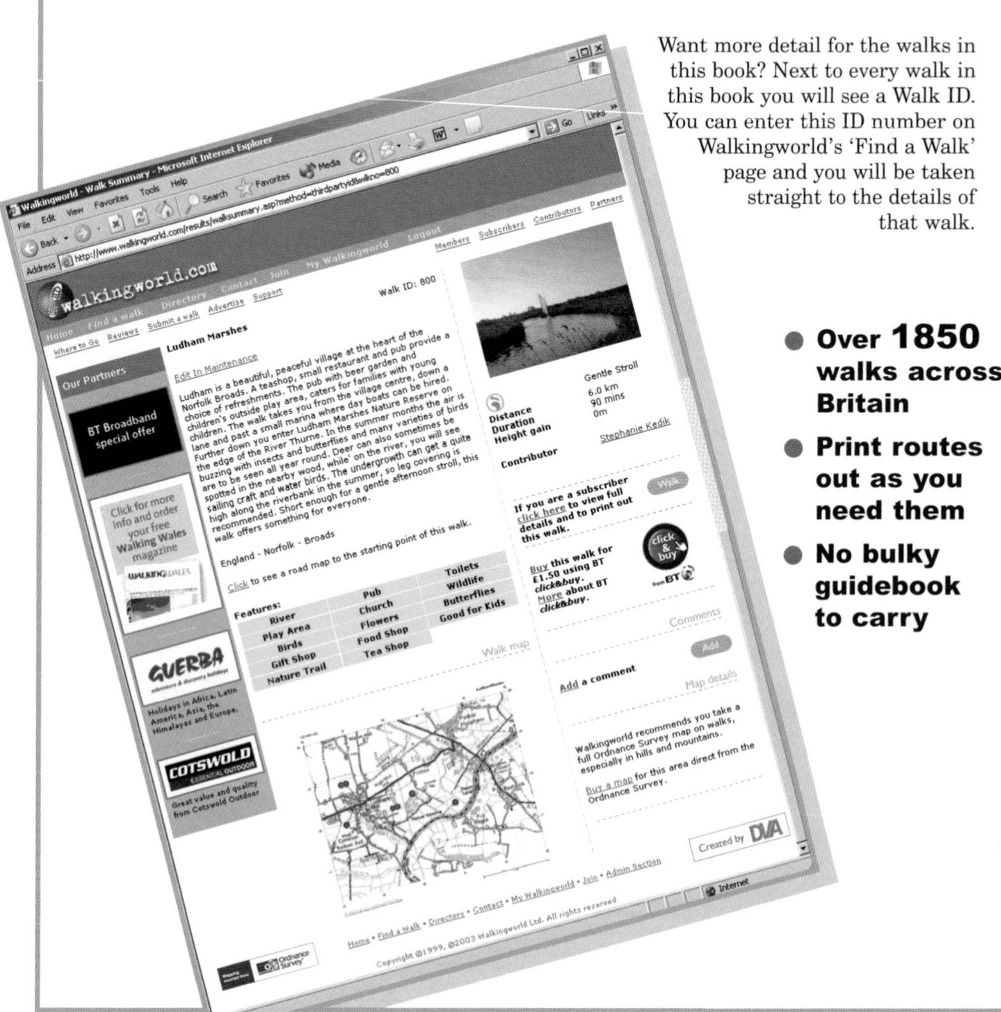

Want more detail for the walks in this book? Next to every walk in this book you will see a Walk ID. You can enter this ID number on Walkingworld's 'Find a Walk' page and you will be taken straight to the details of that walk.

- **Over 1850 walks across Britain**
- **Print routes out as you need them**
- **No bulky guidebook to carry**

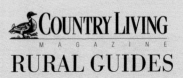

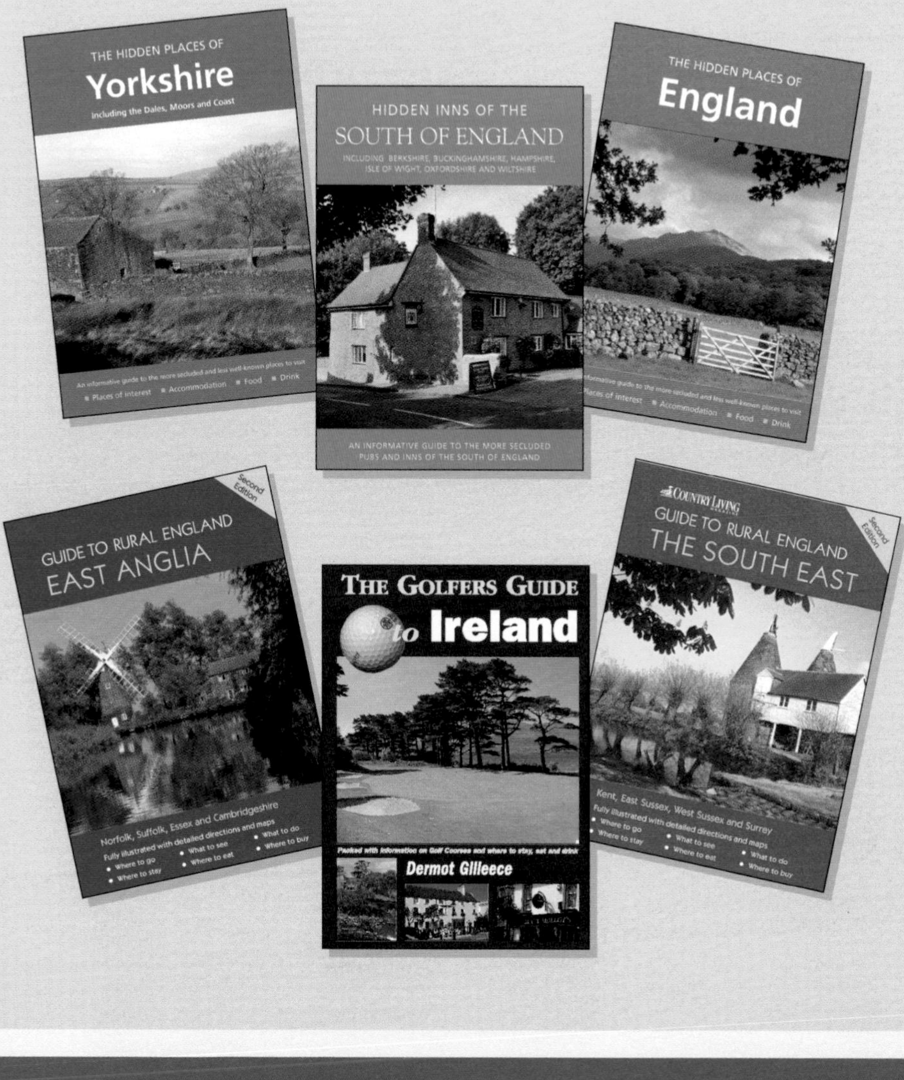

ORDER FORM

To order any of our publications just fill in the payment details below and complete the order form. For orders of less than 4 copies please add £1 per book for postage and packing. Orders over 4 copies are P & P free.

Please Complete Either:

I enclose a cheque for £ [ ] made payable to Travel Publishing Ltd

Or:

Card No: [ ] Expiry Date: [ ]

Signature: [ ]

NAME: [ ]

ADDRESS: [ ]

TEL NO: [ ]

Please either send, telephone, fax or e-mail your order to:

Travel Publishing Ltd, 7a Apollo House, Calleva Park, Aldermaston, Berkshire RG7 8TN
Tel: 0118 981 7777 Fax: 0118 982 0077 e-mail: info@travelpublishing.co.uk

Hidden Places Regional Titles	*Price*	*Quantity*
Cambs & Lincolnshire	£8.99	....
Chilterns	£8.99	....
Cornwall	£8.99	....
Derbyshire	£8.99	....
Devon	£8.99	....
Dorset, Hants & Isle of Wight	£8.99	....
East Anglia	£8.99	....
Gloucs, Wiltshire & Somerset	£8.99	....
Heart of England	£8.99	....
Hereford, Worcs & Shropshire	£8.99	....
Kent	£8.99	....
Lake District & Cumbria	£8.99	....
Lancashire & Cheshire	£8.99	....
Lincolnshire & Nottinghamshire	£8.99	....
Northumberland & Durham	£8.99	....
Sussex	£8.99	....
Yorkshire	£8.99	....
Hidden Places National Titles		
England	£11.99	....
Ireland	£11.99	....
Scotland	£11.99	....
Wales	£11.99	....

Hidden Inns Titles	*Price*	*Quantity*
East Anglia	£7.99	....
Heart of England	£7.99	....
Lancashire & Cheshire	£7.99	....
North of England	£7.99	....
South	£7.99	....
South East	£7.99	....
South and Central Scotland	£7.99	....
Wales	£7.99	....
Welsh Borders	£7.99	....
West Country	£7.99	....
Country Living Rural Guides		
East Anglia	£10.99	....
Heart of England	£10.99	....
Ireland	£11.99	....
North East of England	£10.99	....
North West of England	£10.99	....
Scotland	£11.99	....
South of England	£10.99	....
South East of England	£10.99	....
Wales	£11.99	....
West Country	£10.99	....

Total Quantity [ ]

Total Value [ ]

READER REACTION FORM

The *Travel Publishing* research team would like to receive readers' comments on any visitor attractions or places reviewed in the book and also recommendations for suitable entries to be included in the next edition. This will help ensure that the *Country Living series of Rural Guides* continues to provide its readers with useful information on the more interesting, unusual or unique features of each attraction or place ensuring that their visit to the local area is an enjoyable and stimulating experience. To provide your comments or recommendations would you please complete the forms below and overleaf as indicated and send to:

The Research Department, Travel Publishing Ltd,
7a Apollo House, Calleva Park, Aldermaston, Reading, RG7 8TN.

Your Name:

Your Address:

Your Telephone Number:

Please tick as appropriate: Comments ☐ Recommendation ☐

Name of Establishment:

Address:

Telephone Number:

Name of Contact:

READER REACTION FORM

Comment or Reason for Recommendation:

....

....

....

....

....

....

....

....

....

....

....

INDEX TO TOWNS & PLACES OF INTEREST

A

B

D

E

I

J

K

L

O

P

T

U

V

W

Y